PORTFOLIO MANAGEMENT PATHWAY

CFA® Program Curriculum
2026 • LEVEL III PORTFOLIO MANAGEMENT PATHWAY

WILEY

©2025 by CFA Institute. All rights reserved. This copyright covers material written expressly for this volume by the editor/s as well as the compilation itself. It does not cover the individual selections herein that first appeared elsewhere. Permission to reprint these has been obtained by CFA Institute for this edition only. Further reproductions by any means, electronic or mechanical, including photocopying and recording, or by any information storage or retrieval systems, must be arranged with the individual copyright holders noted.

CFA®, Chartered Financial Analyst®, AIMR-PPS®, and GIPS® are just a few of the trademarks owned by CFA Institute. To view a list of CFA Institute trademarks and the Guide for Use of CFA Institute Marks, please visit our website at www.cfainstitute.org.

This publication is designed to provide accurate and authoritative information in regard to the subject matter covered. It is sold with the understanding that the publisher is not engaged in rendering legal, accounting, or other professional service. If legal advice or other expert assistance is required, the services of a competent professional should be sought.

All trademarks, service marks, registered trademarks, and registered service marks are the property of their respective owners and are used herein for identification purposes only.

ISBN 978-1-39436-062-8

May 2025

Please visit our website at
www.WileyGlobalFinance.com.

SKY920D05E0-66C2-4CE0-9A02-4A49B664DB1E_022825

CONTENTS

How to Use the CFA Program Curriculum ix
 CFA Institute Learning Ecosystem (LES) ix
 Designing Your Personal Study Program ix
 Errata x
 Other Feedback x

Portfolio Management Pathway

Learning Module 1 **Index-Based Equity Strategies** 3
 Introduction 3
 Factor-Based Strategies 4
 Pooled Investments 7
 Pooled Investments 7
 Derivatives-Based Approaches and Index-Based Portfolios 11
 Separately Managed Equity Index-Based Portfolios 14
 Portfolio Construction 16
 Full Replication 16
 Stratified Sampling 18
 Optimization 19
 Blended Approach 20
 Tracking Error Management 20
 Tracking Error and Excess Return 21
 Potential Causes of Tracking Error and Excess Return 22
 Controlling Tracking Error 23
 Sources of Return and Risk in Index-Based Equity Strategies 24
 Attribution Analysis 24
 Securities Lending 26
 Investor Activism and Engagement by Index-Based Fund Managers 27
 Summary *29*
 References *30*
 Practice Problems *31*
 Solutions *36*

Learning Module 2 **Active Equity Investing: Strategies** 39
 Introduction 39
 Approaches to Active Management 40
 Differences in the Nature of the Information Used 42
 Differences in the Focus of the Analysis 43
 Difference in Orientation to the Data: Forecasting Fundamentals vs. Pattern Recognition 43
 Differences in Portfolio Construction: Judgment vs. Optimization 44
 Bottom-Up Strategies 46
 Bottom-Up Strategies 46
 Top-Down Strategies 53

	Country and Geographic Allocation to Equities	53
	Sector and Industry Rotation	53
	Volatility-Based Strategies	54
	Thematic Investment Strategies	54
Factor-Based Strategies: Overview		56
Factor-Based Strategies: Style Factors		60
	Value	60
	Price Momentum	61
	Growth	64
	Quality	64
Factor-Based Strategies: Unconventional Factors		66
Activist Strategies		69
	The Popularity of Shareholder Activism	70
	Tactics Used by Activist Investors	71
	Typical Activist Targets	72
Other Active Strategies		75
	Strategies Based on Statistical Arbitrage and Market Microstructure	75
	Event-Driven Strategies	78
Creating a Fundamental Active Investment Strategy		78
	The Fundamental Active Investment Process	79
	Pitfalls in Fundamental Investing	81
Creating a Quantitative Active Investment Strategy		85
	Creating a Quantitative Investment Process	85
	Pitfalls in Quantitative Investment Processes	88
Equity Investment Style Classification		92
	Different Approaches to Style Classification	92
	Strengths and Limitations of Style Analysis	100
Summary		*101*
References		*104*
Practice Problems		*105*
Solutions		*112*

Learning Module 3   **Active Equity Investing: Portfolio Construction**   **117**

Introduction		117
Building Blocks of Active Equity Portfolio Construction		118
	Fundamentals of Portfolio Construction	119
	Building Blocks Used in Portfolio Construction	121
Portfolio Construction Approaches		130
	The Implementation Process: The Choice of Portfolio Management Approaches	131
Measures of Benchmark-Relative Risk		134
Objectives and Constraints		141
Absolute vs. Relative Measures of Risk		147
	Absolute vs. Relative Measures of Risk	147
Determining the Appropriate Level of Risk		153
	Implementation Constraints	153
	Limited Diversification Opportunities	154
	Leverage and its Implications for Risk	154

Contents

Allocating the Risk Budget	155
Additional Risk Measures	160
Formal Constraints	161
The Risks of Being Wrong	163
Implicit Cost-Related Considerations	166
Implicit Costs—Market Impact and the Relevance of Position Size, Assets under Management, and Turnover	167
Estimating the Cost of Slippage	169
The Well-Constructed Portfolio	173
Long/Short, Long Extension, and Market-Neutral Portfolio Construction	178
The Merits of Long-Only Investing	179
Long/Short Portfolio Construction	181
Long Extension Portfolio Construction	182
Market-Neutral Portfolio Construction	183
Benefits and Drawbacks of Long/Short Strategies	184
Summary	*188*
References	*191*
Practice Problems	*192*
Solutions	*198*

Learning Module 4 **Liability-Driven and Index-Based Strategies** **203**

Introduction	203
Managing the Interest Rate Risk of a Single Liability	204
A Numerical Example of Immunization	205
Managing the Interest Rate Risk of Multiple Liabilities	217
Duration Matching	217
Derivatives Overlay	223
Contingent Immunization	226
Example: Defined Benefit Pension Plan	229
Model Assumptions	229
Model Inputs	230
Calculating Durations	231
Addressing the Duration Gap	232
Risks in Liability-Driven Investing	240
Model Risk in Liability-Driven Investing	240
Spread Risk in Liability-Driven Investing	241
Counterparty Credit Risk	242
Asset Liquidity Risk	242
Bond Indexes	244
Size and Breadth of the Fixed-Income Universe	246
Array of Characteristics	246
Unique Issuance and Trading Patterns	246
Primary Risk Factors	247
Alternative Methods for Establishing Passive Bond Market Exposure	250
Full Replication	251
Enhanced Indexing	251
Alternatives to Investing Directly in Fixed-Income Securities	254
Benchmark Selection	254

	Summary	*257*
	References	*261*
	Practice Problems	*262*
	Solutions	*272*
Learning Module 5	**Yield Curve Strategies**	**277**
	Introduction	277
	Key Yield Curve and Fixed-Income Concepts for Active Managers	278
	Yield Curve Dynamics	278
	Duration and Convexity	282
	Yield Curve Strategies	285
	Static Yield Curve	285
	Dynamic Yield Curve	291
	Key Rate Duration for a Portfolio	308
	Active Fixed-Income Management across Currencies	310
	A Framework for Evaluating Yield Curve Strategies	317
	Summary	*321*
	Practice Problems	*323*
	Solutions	*329*
Learning Module 6	**Fixed-Income Active Management: Credit Strategies**	**333**
	Introduction	334
	Key Credit and Spread Concepts for Active Management	334
	Credit Risk Considerations	335
	Credit Spread Measures	344
	Credit Strategies	359
	Bottom-Up Credit Strategies	359
	Top-Down Credit Strategies	367
	Factor-Based Credit Strategies	372
	Liquidity and Tail Risk	374
	Liquidity Risk	374
	Tail Risk	376
	Synthetic Credit Strategies	379
	Credit Spread Curve Strategies	385
	Static Credit Spread Curve Strategies	386
	Dynamic Credit Spread Curve Strategies	390
	Global Credit Strategies	396
	Structured Credit	400
	Fixed-Income Analytics	403
	Summary	*405*
	References	*407*
	Practice Problems	*408*
	Solutions	*417*
Learning Module 7	**Trade Strategy and Execution**	**421**
	Introduction	421
	Motivations to Trade	422
	Profit Seeking	422

Contents

Risk Management/Hedging Needs	424
Cash Flow Needs	425
Corporate Actions/Index Reconstitutions/Margin Calls	426
Trading Strategies and Strategy Selection	**428**
Trade Strategy Inputs	428
Reference Prices	**433**
Pre-Trade Benchmarks	433
Intraday Benchmarks	434
Post-Trade Benchmarks	435
Price Target Benchmarks	435
Trading Strategies	**436**
Short-Term Alpha Trade	437
Long-Term Alpha Trade	437
Risk Rebalance Trade	438
Client Redemption Trade	439
New Mandate Trade	440
Trade Execution	**441**
Trade Implementation Choices	442
Algorithmic Trading	444
Comparison of Markets	**449**
Equities	450
Fixed Income	450
Exchange-Traded Derivatives	451
Over-the-Counter Derivatives	451
Spot Foreign Exchange (Currency)	452
Trade Cost Measurement	**453**
Implementation Shortfall	454
Expanded Implementation Shortfall	455
Evaluating Trade Execution	**461**
Arrival Price	462
VWAP	462
TWAP	463
Market on Close	463
Market-Adjusted Cost	464
Added Value	466
Trade Governance	**467**
Meaning of Best Order Execution within the Relevant Regulatory Framework	468
Factors Used to Determine the Optimal Order Execution Approach	468
List of Eligible Brokers and Execution Venues	470
Process Used to Monitor Execution Arrangements	471
Summary	*473*
Practice Problems	*476*
Solutions	*486*

Learning Module 8	**Case Study in Portfolio Management: Institutional (Endowment)**	**495**
	Introduction	495
	Background: Liquidity Management	496

Liquidity Profiling and Time-to-Cash Tables	497
Rebalancing, Commitments	499
Stress Testing	500
Derivatives	501
Earning an Illiquidity Premium	501
Quadrivium University Investment Company Case: Background	502
Quadrivium University Investment Company	504
Investment Strategy: Background and Evolution	505
QUINCO Case: Strategic Asset Allocation	507
QUINCO Case: Liquidity Management	515
QUINCO Case: Asset Manager Selection	521
QUINCO Case: Tactical Asset Allocation	524
QUINCO Case: Asset Allocation Rebalancing	529
QUINCO Case: ESG Integration	532
Student Activity	533
QUINCO ESG Approach	533
QUINCO	534
Investment Response	534
Summary	*535*
References	*536*
Practice Problems	*537*
Solutions	*542*

Glossary G-1

How to Use the CFA Program Curriculum

The CFA® Program exams measure your mastery of the core knowledge, skills, and abilities required to succeed as an investment professional. These core competencies are the basis for the Candidate Body of Knowledge (CBOK™). The CBOK consists of four components:

> A broad outline that lists the major CFA Program topic areas (www.cfainstitute.org/programs/cfa/curriculum/cbok/cbok)

> Topic area weights that indicate the relative exam weightings of the top-level topic areas (www.cfainstitute.org/en/programs/cfa/curriculum)

> Learning outcome statements (LOS) that tell you the specific knowledge, skills, and abilities you should gain from each curriculum topic area. You will find these statements at the start of each learning module and lesson. We encourage you to review the information about the LOS on our website (www.cfainstitute.org/programs/cfa/curriculum/study-sessions), including the descriptions of LOS "command words" on the candidate resources page at www.cfainstitute.org/-/media/documents/support/programs/cfa-and-cipm-los-command-words.ashx.

> The CFA Program curriculum that candidates receive access to upon exam registration.

Therefore, the key to your success on the CFA exams is studying and understanding the CBOK. You can learn more about the CBOK on our website: www.cfainstitute.org/programs/cfa/curriculum/cbok.

The curriculum, including the practice questions, is the basis for all exam questions. The curriculum is selected/developed specifically to provide candidates with the knowledge, skills, and abilities reflected in the CBOK.

CFA INSTITUTE LEARNING ECOSYSTEM (LES)

Your exam registration fee includes access to the CFA Institute Learning Ecosystem (LES). This digital learning platform provides access to all the curriculum content and practice questions. The LES is organized as a series of learning modules consisting of short online lessons and associated practice questions. This tool is your source for all study materials, including practice questions and mock exams. The LES is the primary method by which CFA Institute delivers your curriculum experience. Here, you will find additional practice questions to test your knowledge, including some interactive questions.

DESIGNING YOUR PERSONAL STUDY PROGRAM

An orderly, systematic approach to exam preparation is critical. You should dedicate a consistent block of time every week to reading and studying. Review the LOS both before and after you study curriculum content to ensure you can demonstrate the knowledge, skills, and abilities described by the LOS and the assigned learning module. Use the LOS as a self-check to track your progress and highlight areas of weakness for later review.

Successful candidates report an average of more than 300 hours preparing for each exam. Your preparation time will vary based on your prior education and experience, and you will likely spend more time on some topics than on others.

ERRATA

The curriculum development process is rigorous and involves multiple rounds of reviews by content experts. Despite our efforts to produce a curriculum that is free of errors, we must make corrections in some instances. Curriculum errata are periodically updated and posted by exam level and test date on the Curriculum Errata webpage (www.cfainstitute.org/en/programs/submit-errata). If you believe you have found an error in the curriculum, you can submit your concerns through our curriculum errata reporting process found at the bottom of the Curriculum Errata webpage.

OTHER FEEDBACK

Please send any comments or suggestions to info@cfainstitute.org, and we will review your feedback thoughtfully.

Portfolio Management Pathway

LEARNING MODULE

1

Index-Based Equity Strategies

by David M. Smith, PhD, CFA, and Kevin K. Yousif, CFA.

David M. Smith, PhD, CFA, is at the University at Albany, New York (USA). Kevin K. Yousif, CFA, is at LSIA Wealth & Institutional (USA).

LEARNING OUTCOMES	
Mastery	The candidate should be able to:
☐	compare factor-based strategies to market-capitalization-weighted indexing
☐	compare different approaches to index-based equity strategies
☐	compare different approaches to index-based equity investing
☐	compare the full replication, stratified sampling, and optimization approaches for the construction of index-based equity portfolios
☐	discuss potential causes of tracking error and methods to control tracking error for index-based equity portfolios
☐	explain sources of return and risk to an index-based equity portfolio

INTRODUCTION

This learning module provides a broad overview of index-based equity investing, including index selection, portfolio management techniques, and the analysis of investment results.

Index-based strategies are rule-based, transparent strategies that do not involve identifying mispriced individual securities but instead seek to replicate the performance of an index. Indexes include broad market indexes, such as the S&P 500 Index, Nikkei 225, and FTSE 100, as well as those tailored more to a factor exposure, such as the Russell 1000 Growth and Russell 1000 Value Indexes. The main advantages of index-based investing are low costs, diversification, and tax efficiency.

In the next section, we will compare factor-based strategies to broad indexing strategies. Then, we will look at how to gain exposure to an index, whether through a pooled investment, a derivative-based approach, or a separately managed account. We will also cover portfolio construction techniques for index-based strategies and discuss how a portfolio manager can control tracking error against the benchmark, including the sources of tracking error. In addition, we will introduce methods a portfolio manager can use to attribute the sources of return in the portfolio, including country returns, currency returns, sector returns, and security returns. We will also describe the sources of portfolio risk. A summary of key points concludes the module.

2   FACTOR-BASED STRATEGIES

> compare factor-based strategies to market-capitalization-weighted indexing

Investors in index-based strategies may seek market return, otherwise known as beta exposure, and do not seek outperformance, known as alpha. A focus on beta is based on a single-factor model: the capital asset pricing model (CAPM). Index-based strategies based on more than a single factor (and a single factor other than beta) are becoming more popular as investors gain an understanding of what drives investment returns. These strategies maintain the low-cost advantage of index funds but provide an expected return based on exposure to various factors, such as the five discussed in Fama and French (2015) that explain US equity market returns: the market risk premium from the CAPM, size, book-to-market ratio (value or growth style classification), operating profitability, and investment intensity (total asset growth).

Although the concepts underlying factor investing, sometimes marketed as "smart beta," have been known for a long time, investors' use of the technique increased dramatically over time. There are many indexes and index-based investment vehicles that allow access to such factors as Value, Size, Momentum, Volatility, and Quality, which are described in Exhibit 1. Many investors apply factor tilts—intentionally overweighting and underweighting certain risk factors—to their portfolios based on their judgment of market conditions. Index-based factor strategies can be used in place of or to complement a more traditional market-cap-weighted indexed portfolio.

Exhibit 1: Common Equity Risk Factors

Factor	Description
Growth	Growth stocks are generally associated with companies with an above-average net income growth rate and high P/Es.
Value	Value stocks are generally associated with mature companies that have stable net incomes or are experiencing a cyclical downturn. Value stocks frequently have low price-to-book and price-to-earnings ratios as well as high dividend yields.
Size	A tilt toward smaller size involves buying stocks with low float-adjusted market capitalization.
Yield	Yield is identified as dividend yield relative to other stocks. High dividend-yielding stocks may provide excess returns in low interest rate environments.
Momentum	Momentum attempts to capture further returns from stocks that have experienced an above-average increase in price during the prior period.

Factor	Description
Quality	Quality stocks might include those with consistent earnings and dividend growth, high cash flow to earnings, and low debt-to-equity ratios.
Volatility	Low volatility is generally desired by investors seeking to lower their downside risk. Volatility is often measured as the standard deviation of stock returns.

While index-based factor strategies may labeled "passive," they frequently involve active decision making: Decisions on the timing and degree of factor exposure are being made. As Jacobs and Levy (2014) note, the difference between index-based factor investing and conventional active management is that with the former, active management takes place up front rather than continuously. Relative to broad-market-cap weighting, factor-based strategies tend to concentrate risk exposures, leaving investors exposed during periods when a chosen risk factor is out of favor. The observation that even strong risk factors experience periods of underperformance has led many investors toward multi-factor approaches. Index-based factor strategies tend to be transparent in terms of factor selection, weighting, and rebalancing. Possible risks include ease of replication by other investors, which can produce overcrowding and reduce the realized advantages of a strategy.

FUNDAMENTAL FACTOR INDEXING

Capitalization weighting of indexes and index-tracking portfolios involve treating each constituent stock as if investors were buying all the available shares. Arnott, Hsu, and Moore (2005) developed an alternative weighting method based on the notion that if stock market prices deviate from their intrinsic value, larger-cap stocks will exhibit this tendency more than smaller-cap stocks. Thus, traditional cap weighting is likely to overweight overpriced stocks and underweight underpriced stocks. The combination is intended to make cap-weighting inferior to a method that does not use market prices as a basis for weighting.

The idea advanced by Arnott, Hsu, and Moore is to use a cluster of company fundamentals—book value, cash flow, revenue, sales, dividends, and employee count—as a basis for weighting each company. A separate weighting is developed for each fundamental measure. In the case of a large company, its sales might be 1.3% of the total sales for all companies in the index, so its weight for this criterion would be 0.013. For each company, the weightings are averaged across all of the fundamental measures, and those average values represent the weight of each stock in a "composite fundamentals" index.

The authors show that over a 43-year period, a fundamental index would have outperformed a related cap-weighted index by an average of almost 200 basis points per year. They hasten to add that the result should not necessarily be considered alpha, because the fundamental portfolio provides heightened exposure to the Value and Size factors.

Since the time of the seminal article's publication, fundamental-weighted indexing strategies for country markets as well as market segments have gained in popularity and attracted a large amount of investor funds.

No matter the style of a factor-based strategy, its ultimate goal is to improve upon the risk or return performance of the market-cap-weighted strategy. Factor-based approaches gain exposure to many of the same risk factors that active managers seek to exploit. The strategies can be return oriented, risk oriented, or diversification oriented.

Return-oriented factor-based strategies include dividend yield strategies, momentum strategies, and fundamentally weighted strategies. Dividend yield strategies can include dividend growth as well as absolute dividend yield. The low interest rate environment, which followed the 2008–2009 global financial crisis, led to an increase in dividend yield strategies as investors sought reliable income streams. An example index is the S&P 1500 High Yield Dividend Aristocrats Index. This index selects securities within the S&P 1500 that increased dividends in each of the past 20 years and then weights those securities by their dividend yield, with the highest dividend-yielding stocks receiving the highest weight.

Another return-oriented strategy is momentum, which is generally defined by the amount of a stock's excess price return relative to the market over a specified time period. Momentum can be determined in various ways. One example is MSCI's Momentum Index family, in which a stock's most recent 12-month and 6-month price performance are determined and then used to weight the securities in the index.

Risk-oriented strategies take several forms, seeking to reduce downside volatility and overall portfolio risk. For example, risk-oriented factor strategies include volatility weighting, where all of an index's constituents are held and then weighted by the inverse of their relative price volatility. Price volatility is defined differently by each index provider, but two common methods include using standard deviation of price returns for the past 252 trading days (approximately one calendar year) or the weekly standard deviation of price returns for the past 156 weeks (approximately three calendar years).

Volatility weighting can take other forms as well. Minimum variance investing is another risk reducing strategy, and it requires access to a mean–variance optimizer. Minimum variance weights are those that minimize the volatility of the portfolio's returns based on historical price returns, subject to certain constraints on the index's construction. Constraints can include limitations on sector over/under weights, country selection limits, and limits on single stock concentration levels. Mean–variance optimizer programs can be accessed from such vendors as Axioma, BARRA, and Northfield.

Risk weighting has the advantages of being simple to understand and providing a way to reduce absolute volatility and downside returns. However, the development of these strategies is based on past return data, which may not reflect future returns. Thus, investors will not always achieve their objectives despite the strategy's stated goal.

Diversification-oriented strategies include equally weighted indexes and maximum-diversification strategies. Equal weighting is intuitive and has a low amount of single-stock risk. The low single-stock risk comes by way of the weighting structure of $1/n$, where n is equal to the number of securities held. Choueifaty and Coignard (2008) define maximum diversification by calculating a "diversification ratio" as the ratio of the weighted average volatilities divided by the portfolio volatility. Diversification strategies then can attempt to maximize future diversification by determining portfolio weights using past price return volatilities.

Portfolio managers who pursue factor-based strategies often use multiple benchmark indexes, including a factor-based index and a broad market-cap-weighted index. This can result in tracking error from the perspective of the end investor who has modeled a portfolio against a broad market-cap-weighted index. Tracking error indicates how closely the portfolio behaves like its benchmark and is measured as the standard deviation of the differences between a portfolio's returns and its benchmark returns. The concept of tracking error is discussed in detail later.

Finally, factor-based strategies can involve higher management fees and trading commissions than broad-market indexing. Factor-based index providers and managers demand a premium price for the creation and management of these strategies, and those fees decrease performance. Also, commission costs can be higher in factor-based strategies than they are in market-cap-weighted strategies. All else equal, higher costs will lead to lower net performance.

Factor-based approaches may offer an advantage for those investors who believe it is prudent to seek out groups of stocks that are poised to have desirable return patterns. Active managers also believe in seeking those stocks, but active management brings the burden of higher fees that can eat into any outperformance. Active managers may also own stocks that are outside the benchmark and are, thus, incompatible with the investment strategy. In contrast, factor-based strategies can provide nearly pure exposure to specific market segments, and there are numerous benchmarks against which to measure performance. Fees are generally modest because factor-based strategies are rules-based and thus do not require constant monitoring. An investor's process of changing exposures to specific risk factors as market conditions change is known as factor rotation. With factor rotation, investors can use index-based vehicles to make active bets on future market conditions.

POOLED INVESTMENTS

☐ compare different approaches to index-based equity strategies

Index-based equity investment strategies may be implemented using several approaches, from the do-it-yourself method of buying stocks to hiring a subadviser to create and maintain the investment strategy. Index-based investment strategies can be replicated by any internal or external portfolio manager who has the index data, trading tools, and necessary skills. In contrast, every actively managed fund, in theory, has a unique investment strategy developed by the active portfolio manager.

This section discusses different approaches to gain access to an investment strategy's desired performance stream: pooled investments (e.g., mutual funds and exchange-traded funds), derivatives-based portfolios (using options, futures, and swaps contracts), and direct investment in the stocks underlying the strategy.

Some index-based investments are managed to establish a target beta, and managers are judged on how closely they meet that target. Portfolio managers commonly use futures and open-end mutual funds to transform a position (in cash, for example) and obtain the desired equity exposure. This process is known as "equitizing." The choice of which method to use is largely determined by the financing costs of rolling the futures contracts over time.[1] With multinational indexes, it can be expedient to buy a set of complementary exchange-traded funds to replicate market returns for the various countries.

Pooled Investments

Pooled investments are the most convenient approach for the average investor because they are easy to purchase, hold, and sell. This section covers conventional open-end mutual funds and exchange-traded funds (ETFs).

---

[1] The indexes are rebalanced semi-annually. More information can be found at www.msci.com/eqb/methodology/meth_docs/MSCI_Momentum_Indices_Methodology.pdf.

The Qualidex Fund, started in 1970, was the first open-end index mutual fund available to retail investors. It was designed to track the Dow Jones Industrial Average. The Vanguard S&P 500 Index Fund, started in 1975, was the first retail fund to attract investors on a large scale. The primary advantage provided by a mutual fund purchase is its ease of investing and record keeping.

Investors who want to invest in an index-based mutual fund must take the same steps as those investing in actively managed ones. First, a needs analysis must be undertaken to decide on the investor's return and risk objectives as well as investment constraints, and then to find a corresponding strategy. For example, risk-averse equity investors may seek a low volatility strategy, while investors looking to match the broad market may prefer an all-cap market-cap-weighted strategy. Once the need has been identified, it is likely that a mutual fund can be found or built to match that need.

Traditional mutual fund shares can be purchased directly from the adviser who manages the fund, through a fund marketplace, or through an individual financial adviser. The process is the same for any mutual fund whether it is index based or actively managed. Investment companies generally have websites and call centers to help their prospective investors transact shares.

A fund marketplace is a brokerage company that offers funds from different providers. The advantage of buying a mutual fund from a fund marketplace is the ease of purchasing a mutual fund from different providers while maintaining a single account for streamlined record keeping.

A financial adviser can also help in purchasing a fund by offering the guidance needed to identify the strategy, providing the single account to house the fund shares, and gaining access to lower-cost share classes that may not be available to all investors.

No matter how mutual fund shares are purchased, the primary benefits of index-based mutual funds are low costs and the convenience of the fund structure. The investment manager handles all the needed rebalancing, reconstitution, and other changes that are required to keep the investment portfolio in line with the index. Index-based strategies require constant maintenance and care to reinvest cash from dividends and to execute the buys and sells required to match the additions and deletions of securities to the index. The portfolio manager of an index-based mutual fund also has most of the same responsibilities as a direct investor. These include trading securities, managing cash, deciding how to proceed with corporate actions, voting proxies, and reporting performance. Moreover, index-based mutual funds bear costs in such areas as registration, custodial, and audit, which are similar to those for actively managed mutual funds.

Record keeping functions for a mutual fund include maintaining a record of who owns the shares and when and at what price those shares were purchased. Record keepers work closely with both the custodian of the fund shares to ensure that the security is safely held in the name of the investor and the mutual fund sponsor who communicates those trades.

In the United States, mutual funds are governed by provisions of the Investment Company Act of 1940. In Europe, Undertakings for Collective Investment in Transferable Securities (UCITS) is an agreement among countries in the European Union that governs the management and sale of collective investment funds (mutual funds) across European borders.

ETFs are another form of pooled investment vehicle. The first ETF was launched in the Canadian market in 1990 to track the return of 35 large stocks listed on the Toronto Stock Exchange. ETFs were introduced in the US market in 1993. They are registered funds that can be bought and sold throughout the trading day and change hands like stocks. Advantages of the ETF structure include ease of trading, low management fees, and tax efficiency. Unlike with traditional open-end mutual funds, ETF shares can be bought by investors using margin borrowing; moreover, investors can take short positions in an ETF. ETFs offer flexibility in that they track a wide array of indexes.

ETFs have a unique structure that requires a fund manager as well as an authorized participant who can deliver the assets to the manager. The role of the authorized participant is to be the market maker for the ETF and the intermediary between investors and the ETF fund manager when shares are created or redeemed. To create shares of the ETF, the authorized participant delivers a basket of the underlying stocks to the fund manager and, in exchange, receives shares of the ETF that can be sold to the public. When an authorized participant needs to redeem shares, the process is reversed so that the authorized participant delivers shares of the ETF in exchange for a basket of the underlying stocks that can then be sold in the market.

The creation/redemption process is used when the authorized participant is either called upon to deliver new shares of the ETF to meet investor needs or when large redemptions are requested. The redemption process occurs when an authorized participant needs to reduce its exposure to the ETF holding and accepts shares of the underlying securities in exchange for shares of the ETF.

All else equal, for jurisdictions that require capital gains and losses to be passed through to investors like the US, an ETF has greater tax efficiency than a similarly managed mutual fund. Managers of mutual funds must sell their portfolio holdings to fulfill shareholder redemptions, creating a taxable event where gains and losses are realized. ETFs have the advantage of accommodating those redemptions through an in-kind delivery of stock, which is the redemption process. Capital gains are not recorded when a redemption is fulfilled through an in-kind delivery of securities, so the taxable gain/loss passed to the investor becomes smaller.

Disadvantages of the ETF structure include the need to buy at the offer and sell at the bid price, commission costs, and the risk of an illiquid market when the investor needs to buy or sell the actual ETF shares.

ETFs that track indexes are used to an increasing degree by financial advisers to provide targeted exposure to different sectors of the investable market. Large investors find it more cost effective to build their own portfolios through replication, stratified sampling, and optimization, concepts to be introduced later. Other investors find ETFs to be a relatively low-cost method of tracking major indexes. Importantly, like traditional open-end mutual funds, ETFs are an integrated approach in that portfolio management and accounting are conducted by the fund adviser itself. A limitation is that there are far more benchmark indexes than ETFs, so not all indexes have an exchange-traded security that tracks them, although new ETFs are constantly being created.

Exhibit 2 shows that factor-based ETFs have become a large segment of the market, accounting for 17% of the approximately $7 trillion in global equity ETF assets under management as of the fourth quarter 2022. Factor-based ETFs provide exposure to such single factors as Size, Value, Momentum, Quality, Volatility, and Yield. There are also multifactor ETFs, such as the iShares U.S. Equity Factor ETF, which emphasizes exposure to the Size, Value, Momentum, Quality, and Volatility factors. Meanwhile, the ETF attempts to maintain characteristics that are similar to the underlying STOXX U.S. Equity Factor Index, including sector exposures. As of 2023, the fund's expense ratio was 0.08%.

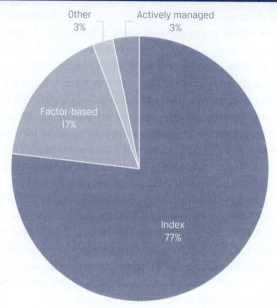

Exhibit 2: Globally Listed Equity ETFs by Investment Approach, Based on Assets under Management

Sources: ETFGI (December 2022); authors' analysis. https://etfgi.com/news/press-releases/2022/12/etfgi-reports-smart-beta-etfs-listed-globally-gathered-us755-billion.

Exhibit 3 shows that while they are large, assets under management in ETFs still represent only a small part of financial markets. ETFs represented just 9% of equity assets across the United States, Europe, and Asia Pacific at the end of 2022. Market share for fixed-income ETFs is much lower. These numbers reflect index ETFs as well as factor-based and other approaches.

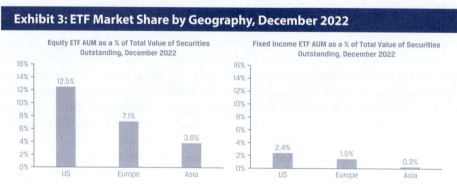

Exhibit 3: ETF Market Share by Geography, December 2022

Sources: Blackrock; authors' analysis.

The decision of whether to use a conventional open-end mutual fund versus an ETF often comes down to cost and flexibility. Investors who seek to mimic an index must identify a suitable tracking security. Long-term investors benefit from the slightly lower expense ratios of ETFs than otherwise equivalent conventional open-end mutual funds. However, the brokerage fees associated with frequent investor trades into ETF shares can negate the expense ratio advantage and thus make ETFs less economical.

DERIVATIVES-BASED APPROACHES AND INDEX-BASED PORTFOLIOS

☐ compare different approaches to index-based equity investing

Beyond purchasing a third-party-sponsored pooled investment and building it themselves, investors can access index performance through derivatives, such as options, swaps, or futures contracts. Derivative strategies are advantageous in that they can be low cost, easy to implement, and provide leverage. However, they also present a new set of risks, including counterparty default risk for derivatives that are not traded on exchanges or cleared through a clearing house. Derivatives can also be relatively difficult to access for individual investors.

Options, swaps, and futures contracts can be found on many of the major indexes, such as the MSCI EAFE Index and the S&P 500 Index. Options and futures are traded on exchanges and so are processed through a clearing house. This is important because a clearing house eliminates virtually all of the default risk present in having a contract with a single counterparty. Equity swaps, on the other hand, are generally executed with a single counterparty and so add the risk of default by that counterparty.

Derivatives allow for leverage through their notional value amounts. Notional value of the contracts can be many times greater than the initial cash outlay. However, derivatives expire, whereas stocks can be held indefinitely. The risk of an expiring options contract is a complete loss of the relatively small premium paid to acquire the exposure. Futures and swaps can be extended by "rolling" the contract forward, which means selling the expiring contract and buying a longer dated one.

Futures positions must be initiated with a futures commission merchant (FCM), a clearing house member assigned to trade on behalf of the investor. The FCM posts the initial margin required to open the position and then settles on a daily basis to comply with the maintenance margin required by the clearing house. The FCM also helps close the position upon expiration. However, futures accounts are not free of effort on the client's part. Having a futures account requires the management of daily cash flows, sometimes committing additional money and sometimes drawing it down.

It is uncommon for index-based portfolio managers to use derivatives in the long term to synthetically mimic the return from the underlying securities. Derivatives are typically used to adjust a pre-existing portfolio to move closer to meeting its objectives. These derivative positions are often referred to as an **overlay**. A **completion overlay** addresses an indexed portfolio that has diverged from its proper exposure. A common example is a portfolio that has built up a surplus of cash from investor flows or dividends, causing the portfolio's beta to be significantly less than that of the benchmark. Using derivatives can efficiently restore the overall portfolio beta to its target. A **rebalancing overlay** addresses a portfolio's need to sell certain constituent securities and buy others. Particularly in the context of a mixed stock and bond portfolio, using equity index derivatives to rebalance toward investment policy target weights can be efficient and cost-effective. A **currency overlay** assists a portfolio manager in hedging the returns of securities that are held in a foreign currency back to the home country's currency.

Equity index derivatives offer several advantages over cash-based portfolio construction approaches. A portfolio manager can increase or decrease exposure to the entire index portfolio in a single transaction. Managers who want to make tactical adjustments to portfolio exposure often find derivatives to be a more efficient tool than cash-market transactions for achieving their goals. Many derivatives contracts are highly liquid, sometimes more so than the underlying cash assets. Especially in this case, portfolio exposures can be tactically adjusted quickly and at low cost.

For the longer term, strategic changes to portfolios are usually best made using cash instruments, which have indefinite expirations and do not necessitate rolling over expiring positions. Futures markets, for example, can impose position limits on such instruments that constrain the scale of use. Derivatives usage is also sometimes restricted by regulatory bodies or investment policy statement stipulations, so in this case cash could be a preferred approach. Finally, depending on the index that is being tracked, a suitable exchange-traded futures contract may not be available.

In addition to options, which have nonlinear payoffs, the two primary types of equity index derivatives contracts are futures and swaps. Equity index futures provide exposure to a specific index. Unlike many commodity futures contracts, index futures are cash-settled, which means the counterparties exchange cash rather than the underlying shares.

The buyer of an equity index futures contract obtains the right to buy the underlying (in this case, an index) on the expiration date of the contract at the futures price prevailing at the time the derivative was purchased. For exchange-traded futures, the buyer is required to post margin (collateral) in the account to decrease the credit risk to the exchange, which is the effective counterparty. For S&P 500 Index futures contracts as traded on the Chicago Mercantile Exchange, every USD change in the futures price produces a USD250 change in the contract value (thus a "multiplier" of 250). For example, if the September S&P 500 futures contract settled at a price of 2,159.30 after settling at 2,157 the day before, then the change in contract value would be 250 × (USD2,159.30 − USD2,157) = USD575.

Equity index futures contracts for various global markets are shown in Exhibit 4.

Exhibit 4: Representative Equity Index Futures Contracts

Index Futures Contract	Market	Contract Currency and Multiplier
Americas		
Dow Jones mini	United States	USD 5
S&P 500	United States	USD 250
S&P 500 mini	United States	USD 50
NASDAQ 100 mini	United States	USD 20
Mexican IPC	Mexico	MXN 10
S&P/TSX Composite mini	Canada	CAD 5
S&P/TSX 60	Canada	CAD 200
Ibovespa	Brazil	BRL 1
Europe, Middle East, and Africa		
Euro STOXX 50	Europe	EUR 10
FTSE 100	United Kingdom	GBP 10
DAX 30	Germany	EUR 25
CAC 40	France	EUR 10
Swiss Market	Switzerland	CHF 10
IBEX 35	Spain	EUR 10

Europe, Middle East, and Africa		
WIG20	Poland	PLN 20
FTSE/JSE 40	South Africa	ZAR 10
Asia Pacific		
S&P/ASX 200	Australia	AUD 25
CSI 300	Chinese mainland	CNY 300
Hang Seng	Hong Kong SAR	HKD 50
H-Shares	Hong Kong SAR	HKD 50
Nifty 50	India	INR 50
Nikkei 225	Japan	JPY 1,000
Topix	Japan	JPY 10,000
KOSPI 200	Korea	KRW 500,000

Source: Please see www.investing.com/indices/indices-futures, October 2021.

Given that futures can be traded using only a small amount of margin, it is clear that futures provide a significant degree of potential leverage to a portfolio. Leverage can be considered either a positive or negative characteristic, depending on the manner with which the derivative instrument is used. Unlike some institutional investors' short-sale constraints on stock positions, many investors do not face constraints on opening a futures position with a sale of the contracts. Among other benefits of futures is the high degree of liquidity in the market, as evidenced by low bid–ask spreads. Both commission and execution costs also tend to be low relative to the exposure achieved. The low cost of transacting makes it easy for portfolio managers to use futures contracts to modify the equity risk exposure of their portfolios.

Equity index futures do come with some disadvantages. Futures are used by index fund managers because the instruments are expected to move in line with the underlying index. To the extent that the futures and spot prices do not move in concert, the portfolio may not track the benchmark perfectly. The extent to which futures prices do not move with spot prices is known as basis risk. Basis risk results from using a hedging instrument that is imperfectly matched to the investment being hedged. Basis risk can arise when the underlying securities pay dividends, while the futures contract tracks only the price of the underlying index. The difference can be partially mitigated when futures holders combine that position with interest-bearing securities.

As noted, futures account holders also must post margin. The margin amount varies by trading exchange. In the case of an ASX-200 futures contract, the initial margin required by the Sydney Futures Exchange for an overnight position is AUD 6,700. The minimum maintenance margin for one contract is AUD 5,300.

By way of example, assume an investor buys an ASX-200 futures contract priced at AUD 5,700, and the futures contract has a multiplier of 25. The investor controls AUD 142,500 [= 25 × AUD 5,700] in value. This currency amount is known as the contract unit value. With the initial margin of AUD 6,700 and a maintenance margin of AUD 5,300, a margin call will be triggered if the contract unit value decreases by more than AUD 1,400. A decrease of AUD 1,400 in the margin is associated with a contract unit value of AUD 142,500 − AUD 1,400 = AUD 141,100. This corresponds to an ASX-200 futures price of AUD 5,644 [= AUD 141,100/25]. Thus, a futures price decrease of 0.98% [= (AUD 5,644 − AUD 5,700)/AUD 5,700] is associated with a decrease in the margin account balance of 20%. This example demonstrates how even a small change in the index value can result in a margin call once the mark-to-market process occurs.

Another derivatives-based approach is the use of equity index swaps. Equity index swaps are negotiated arrangements in which two counterparties agree to exchange cash flows in the future. For example, consider an investor who has a EUR20 million notional amount and wants to be paid the return on her benchmark index, the Euro STOXX 50, during the coming year. In exchange, the investor agrees to pay a floating rate of return of Market Reference Rate (MRR) + 0.20% per year, with settlement occurring semi-annually. Assuming a six-month stock index return of 2.3% and annualized MRR of 0.18% per year, the first payment on the swap agreement would be calculated as follows. The investor would receive EUR20 million × 0.023 = EUR460,000. The investor would be liable to the counterparty for EUR20 million × (0.0018 + 0.0020) × (180/360) = EUR38,000; so, when the first settlement occurs the investor would receive EUR460,000 − EUR38,000 = EUR422,000. In this case, the payment received by the portfolio manager is from the first leg of the swap, and the payment made by that manager is from the second leg. MRR is used generically in this example, but the second leg can also involve the return on a different index, stock, or other asset, or even a fixed currency amount per period.

Disadvantages of swaps include counterparty, liquidity, interest rate, and tax policy risks. Relatively frequent settlement decreases counterparty risk and reduces the potential loss from a counterparty's failure to perform. Equity swaps tend to be non-marketable instruments, so once the agreement is made there is not a highly liquid market that allows them to be sold to another party (though it is usually possible to go back to the dealer and enter into an offsetting position). Although the equity index payment recipient is an equity investor, this investor must deliver an amount linked to MRR; the investor bears interest rate risk. One prime motivation for initiating equity swaps is to avoid paying high taxes on the full return amount from an equity investment. This advantage is dependent on tax laws remaining favorable, which means that equity swaps carry tax policy risk.

There are a number of advantages to using an equity swap to gain synthetic exposure to index returns. Exchange-traded futures contracts are available only on a limited number of equity indexes. Yet as long as there is a willing counterparty, a swap can be initiated on virtually any index. So swaps can be customized with respect to the underlying as well as to settlement frequency and maturity. Although most swap agreements are one year or shorter in maturity, they can be negotiated for as long a tenor as the counterparties are willing. If a swap is used, it is not necessary for an investor to pay transaction costs associated with buying all of the index constituents. Like futures, a swap can help a portfolio manager add leverage or hedge a portfolio, which is usually done on a tactical or short-term basis.

Separately Managed Equity Index-Based Portfolios

Building an index-based equity portfolio as a separately managed portfolio requires a certain set of capabilities and tools. An equity investor who builds an indexed portfolio will need to subscribe to certain data on the index and its constituents. The investor also requires a robust trading and accounting system to manage the portfolio, broker relationships to trade efficiently and cheaply, and compliance systems to meet applicable laws and regulations.

The data subscription can generally be acquired directly from the index provider and may be offered on a daily or less-frequent basis. Generally, the data are provided for analysis only and a separate license must be purchased for index replication strategies. The index subscription data should include company and security identifiers, weights, cash dividend, return, and corporate action information. Corporate actions can include stock dividends and splits, mergers and acquisitions, liquidations, and other reasons for index constituent inclusion and exclusion. These data are generally provided in electronic format and can be delivered via file downloads or fed through a portfolio manager's analytical systems, such as Bloomberg or FactSet. The data are then used as the basis for the indexed portfolio.

Certain trading systems, such as those provided by Charles River Investment Management Solution, SS&C Advent (through Moxy), and Eze Castle Integration, allow the manager to see her portfolio and compare it to the chosen benchmark. Common features of trading systems include electronic communication with multiple brokers and exchanges, an ability to record required information on holdings for taxable investors, and modeling tools so that a portfolio can be traded to match its benchmark.

Accounting systems should be able to report daily performance, record historical transactions, and produce statements. Portfolio managers rely heavily on their accounting systems and teams to help them understand the drivers of portfolio performance.

Broker relationships are an often-overlooked advantage of portfolio managers that can negotiate better commission rates. Commissions are a negative drag on a portfolio's returns. The commission rates quoted to a manager can differ on the basis of the type of securities being traded, the size of the trade, and the magnitude of the relationship between the manager and broker.

Finally, compliance tools and teams are necessary. Investors must adhere to a myriad of rules and regulations, which can come from client agreements and regulatory bodies. Sanctions for violating compliance-related rules can range from losing a client to losing the registration to participate in the investment industry; thus, a robust compliance system is essential to the success of an investment manager.

Compliance rules can be company-wide or specific to an investor's account. Company-wide rules take such forms as restricting trades in stocks of affiliated companies. Rules specific to an account involve such matters as dealing with a directed broker or steps to prevent cash overdrafts. Compliance rules should also be written to prohibit manager misconduct, such as front-running in a personal account prior to executing client trades.

To ensure that their portfolios closely match the return stream of the chosen index, indexed portfolio managers must review their holdings and their weightings versus the index each day. Although a perfect match is a near impossibility because of rounding errors and trading costs, the manager must always weigh the benefits and costs of maintaining a close match.

To establish the portfolio, the manager creates a trading file and transmits the file to an executing broker, who buys the securities using a program trade. **Program trading** is a strategy of buying or selling many stocks simultaneously. Index portfolio managers may trade thousands of positions in a single trade file and are required to deliver the orders and execute the trades quickly. The creation of trades may be done on something as rudimentary as an Excel spreadsheet, but it is more likely to be created on an order management system (OMS), such as Charles River.

Portfolio managers use their OMS to model their portfolios against the index, decide which trades to execute, and transmit the orders. Transmitting an order in the United States is generally done on a secure communication line, such as through FIX Protocol. FIX Protocol is an electronic communication protocol to transmit the orders from the portfolio manager to the broker or directly to the executing market place. The orders are first transmitted via FIX Protocol to a broker who executes the trade and then delivers back pricing and settlement instructions to the OMS. International trading is usually communicated using a similar protocol through SWIFT. SWIFT stands for "Society for Worldwide Interbank Financial Telecommunication," and is a service that is used to securely transmit trade instructions.

Index-based strategies seek to replicate an index that is priced at the close of business each day. Therefore, most index-based trade executions take place at the close of the business day using market-on-close (MOC) orders. Matching the trade execution to the benchmark price helps the manager more closely match the performance of the index.

Beyond the portfolio's initial construction, managers maintain the portfolio by trading any index changes, such as adds/deletes, rebalances, and reinvesting cash dividend payments. These responsibilities require the manager to commit time each day to oversee the portfolio and create the necessary trades. Best practice would be to review the portfolio's performance each day and its composition at least once a month.

Dividends paid over time can accumulate to significant amounts that must be reinvested into the securities in the index. Index fund managers must determine when the cash paid out by dividends should be reinvested and then create trades to purchase the required securities.

5. PORTFOLIO CONSTRUCTION

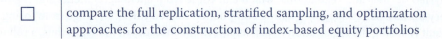

compare the full replication, stratified sampling, and optimization approaches for the construction of index-based equity portfolios

This section discusses the principal approaches that equity portfolio managers use when building an indexed portfolio by transacting in individual securities. The three approaches are full replication, stratified sampling, and optimization. According to Morningstar as of October 2021, among index-tracking equity ETF portfolios globally (the numbers do not sum to 100% because optimization techniques and over-the-counter derivatives can be used with either replication or sampling approaches):

- 74% of funds use full replication,
- 20% of funds use stratified sampling or optimization techniques, and
- 24% of funds use synthetic replication and/or over-the-counter derivatives.

Full Replication

Full replication in index investing occurs when a manager holds all securities represented by the index in weightings that closely match the actual index weightings. Advantages of full replication include the fact that it usually accomplishes the primary goal of matching the index performance and is easy to understand. Full replication, however, requires that the asset size of the mandate is sufficient, that there is sufficient liquidity, and that the index constituents are available for trading.

Not all indexes lend themselves to full replication. For example, the MSCI ACWI Investable Markets Index consists of over 8,000 constituents, but not all securities need be held to closely match the characteristics and performance of that index. Other indexes, such as the S&P 500, have constituents that are readily available for trading and can be applied to portfolios as small as USD10 million.

With respect to the choice between index replication versus sampling, as the number of securities held increases, tracking error decreases because the portfolio gets closer to replicating the index perfectly. Yet as the portfolio manager adds index constituent stocks that are smaller and more thinly traded than average, trading costs increase. The trading costs can take the form of brokerage fees and upward price pressure as a result of the portfolio's purchases. These transaction costs can depress performance and start to impose a small negative effect on tracking effectiveness. As the portfolio manager moves to the least liquid stocks in the index, transaction costs begin to dominate and tracking error increases again. Thus, for an index that

Portfolio Construction

has some constituent securities that are relatively illiquid, the conceptual relationship between tracking error and the number of securities held is U-shaped. The relation can be depicted as shown in Exhibit 5.

Exhibit 5: Relation Between Tracking Error and Transaction Costs versus Number of Benchmark Index Constituent Stocks Held

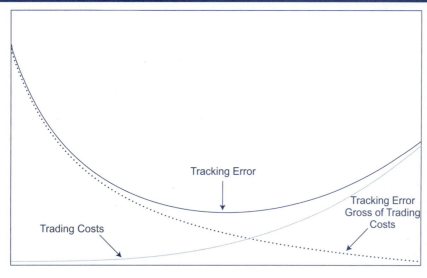

Source: Author team.

Many managers attempt to match an index's characteristics and performance through a full replication technique, but how does a manager create the portfolio? As mentioned in a prior section, the manager first obtains data from the index provider, including the constituent stocks, their relevant identifiers (ticker, CUSIP, SEDOL, or ISIN), shares outstanding, and price. Additional data, such as constituents' dividends paid and total return, facilitate management of the portfolio.

The manager then uses the index data to create the portfolio by replicating as closely as possible the index constituents and weights. The portfolio construction method may vary by investor, but the most common method is to import the provided data into a data compiler such as Charles River, Moxy, or some other external or internally created OMS. The imported data show the manager the trades that are needed to match the index. Exhibit 6 contains an example for a portfolio that has an initial investment of USD10 million.

Exhibit 6: Sample Index Portfolio Positions and Transactions

Identifier	Security Description	Price	Current Weight	Model Weight	Current Weight – Model Weight = Variance	Current Shares	New Shares	Shares to Trade
Cash	Cash	1	50%	0%	50%	5,000,000	0	−5,000,000
SECA	Security 1	100	50%	50%	0%	50,000	50,000	0
SECB	Security 2	50	0%	50%	−50%	0	100,000	100,000

Exhibit 6 shows a current portfolio made up of one security and a cash holding that needs to be traded to match a two-security index. The index becomes the model for the portfolio, and that model is used to match the portfolio. This type of modeling can easily and cheaply be conducted using spreadsheet and database programs, such as Excel and Access. However, the modeling is only a part of the portfolio management process.

The OMS should also be programmed to provide the investor with pre-trade compliance to check for client-specific restrictions, front-running issues, and other compliance rules. The OMS is also used to deliver the buy and sell orders for execution using FIX or SWIFT Protocol, as described previously.

After initial creation of the indexed portfolio, the manager must maintain the portfolio according to any changes in the index. The changes are announced publicly by the index provider. Index fund managers use those details to update their models in the OMS and to determine the number of shares to buy or sell. A fully replicated portfolio must make those changes in a timely manner to maintain its performance tracking with the index. Again, a perfectly replicated index portfolio must trade at the market-on-close price where available to match the price used by the index provider in calculating the index performance.

Stratified Sampling

Despite their preference to realize the benefits of pure replication of an index, portfolio managers often find it impractical to hold all the constituent securities. Some equity indexes have a large number of constituents, and not all constituents offer high trading liquidity. This can make trading expensive, especially if a portfolio manager needs to scale up the portfolio. Brokerage fees can also become excessive if the number of constituents is large.

Holding a limited sample of the index constituents can produce results that track the index return and risk characteristics closely. But such sampling is not done randomly. Rather, portfolio managers use stratified sampling. To stratify is to arrange a population into distinct strata or subgroupings. Arranged correctly, the various strata will be mutually exclusive and also exhaustive (a complete set), and they should closely match the characteristics and performance of the index. Common stratification approaches include using industry membership and equity style characteristics. Investors who use stratified sampling to track the S&P 500 commonly assign each stock to one of the eleven sectors designated by the Global Industry Classification Standard (GICS). For multinational indexes, stratification is often done first on the basis of country affiliation. Indexes can be stratified along multiple dimensions (e.g., country affiliation and then industry affiliation) within each country. An advantage of stratifying along multiple dimensions is closer index tracking.

Portfolio Construction

In equity indexing, stratified sampling is most frequently used when the portfolio manager wants to track indexes that have many constituents or when dealing with a relatively low level of assets under management. Indexes with many constituents are usually multi-country or multi-cap indexes, such as the S&P Global Broad Market Index that consists of more than 11,000 constituents. Most investors are reluctant to trade and maintain 11,000 securities when a significantly smaller number of constituents would achieve most portfolios' tracking objectives. Regardless of the stratified sampling approach used, index-based equity managers tend to weight portfolio holdings proportionately to each stratum's weight in the index.

> **KNOWLEDGE CHECK**
>
> ### Stratified Sampling
>
> 1. A portfolio manager responsible for accounts of high-net-worth individuals is asked to build an index portfolio that tracks the S&P 500 Value Index, which has more than 300 constituents. The manager and the client agree that the minimum account size will be USD750,000, but the manager explains to the client that full replication is not feasible at a reasonable cost because of the mandate size. How can the manager use stratified sampling to achieve her goal of tracking the S&P 500 Value Index?
>
> **Solution:**
>
> The manager recommends that the client set a maximum number of constituents (for example, 200) to limit the average lot size and to reduce commission costs. Next, the manager seeks to identify the constituents to hold based on their market capitalization. That is, the manager selects the 200 securities with the largest market capitalizations. Then the manager seeks to more closely match the performance of the index by matching the sector weightings of the sampled portfolio to the sector weightings of the index. After comparing sector weights, the manager reweights the sampled portfolio. Using this method of stratified sampling meets the manager's stated goal of closely tracking the performance of the index at a reasonable cost.

Optimization

Optimization approaches for index portfolio construction, such as full replication and stratified sampling, have index-tracking goals. Optimization typically involves maximizing a desirable characteristic or minimizing an undesirable characteristic, subject to one or more constraints. For an indexed portfolio, optimization could involve minimizing index tracking error, subject to the constraint that the portfolio holds 50 constituent securities or fewer. The desired output from the optimization process is identification of the 50 securities and their weights that results in the lowest possible tracking error. The number of security holdings is not the only possible constraint. Other common constraints include limiting portfolio membership to stocks that have a market capitalization above a certain specified level, style characteristics that mimic those of the benchmark, restricting trades to round lots, and using only stocks that will keep rebalancing costs low.

Roll (1992) and Jorion (2003) demonstrate that running an optimization to minimize tracking error can lead to portfolios that are mean–variance inefficient versus the benchmark. That is, the optimized portfolio may exhibit higher risk than the benchmark it is being optimized against. They show that a useful way to address this problem is to add a constraint on total portfolio volatility. Accordingly, the manager of an optimized index-based fund would aim to make its total volatility equal to that of the benchmark.

Fabozzi, Focardi, and Kolm (2010) note that in practice, index-based portfolio managers often conduct a mean–variance optimization using all the index constituents, the output from which shows highly diverse weightings for the stocks. Given that investing in the lowest-weight stocks may involve marginal transaction costs that exceed marginal diversification benefits, in a second, post-optimization stage, the managers may then delete the lowest-weighted stocks.

Optimization can be conducted in conjunction with stratified sampling or alone. Optimization programs, when run without constraints, do not consider country or industry affiliation but rather use security level data. Optimization requires an analyst who has a high level of technical sophistication, including familiarity with computerized optimization software or algorithms, and a good understanding of the output.

Advantages of optimization involve a lower amount of tracking error than stratified sampling. Also, the optimization process accounts explicitly for the covariances among the portfolio constituents. Although two securities from different industry sectors may be included in a portfolio under stratified sampling, if their returns move strongly together, one will likely be excluded from an optimized portfolio.

Usually the constituents and weights of an optimized portfolio are determined based on past market data; however, returns, variances, and correlations between securities tend to vary over time. Thus, the output from an optimization program may apply only to the period from which the data are drawn and not to a future period. Even if current results apply to the future, they might not be applicable for long. This means that optimization would need to be run frequently and adjustments made to the portfolio, which can be costly.

Blended Approach

For indexes that have few constituent securities, full replication is typically advisable. When the reverse is true, sampling or optimization are likely to be the preferred methods. But such indexes as the Russell 3000, the S&P 1500, and the Wilshire 5000 span the capitalization spectrum from large to small. For these indexes, the 1,000 or so largest constituents are quite liquid, which means that brokerage fees, bid–ask spreads, and trading costs are low. For the largest-cap portion of an indexed portfolio, full replication is a sensible and desirable approach. For the index constituents that have smaller market capitalizations or less liquidity, however, a stratified sampling or optimization approach can be useful for all the reasons mentioned previously in this section. Thus, an indexed portfolio can actually be managed using a blended approach consisting of full replication for more-liquid issues and one of the other methods for less-liquid issues.

6

TRACKING ERROR MANAGEMENT

☐ discuss potential causes of tracking error and methods to control tracking error for index-based equity portfolios

Tracking Error Management

As discussed previously, managers of index-based strategies use a variety of approaches to track indexes in cost-efficient ways. To the extent the portfolio manager's skills are ineffective, tracking error results. This section discusses the measurement and management of tracking error.

Tracking Error and Excess Return

Tracking error and excess return are two measures that enable investors to differentiate performance among index-based portfolio managers. Tracking error indicates how closely the portfolio behaves like its benchmark and measures a manager's ability to replicate the benchmark return. Tracking error is calculated as the standard deviation of the difference between the portfolio return and its benchmark index return. Excess return measures the difference between the portfolio returns and benchmark returns. Tracking error for portfolio p then can be expressed by Equation 1.

$$\text{Tracking error}_p = \sqrt{\text{Variance}_{(R_p - R_b)}}, \qquad (1)$$

where R_p is the return on the portfolio and R_b is the return on the benchmark index. Excess return for portfolio p is calculated as in Equation 2:

$$\text{Excess return}_p = R_p - R_b. \qquad (2)$$

Tracking error and excess return are distinct measures; the terms should not be used interchangeably. Tracking error measures the manager's ability to closely track the benchmark over time. In principle, a manager whose return is identical to that of the index could have arrived at that point by lagging and subsequently leading the index, producing a net difference of zero. But being a standard deviation, tracking error cannot be zero in cases such as the one described. Excess returns can be positive or negative and tell the investor how the manager performed relative to the benchmark. Tracking error, which is a standard deviation, is always presented as a non-negative number.

Index fund managers endeavor to have low tracking error and excess returns that are not negative. Low tracking error is important in measuring the skill of the index fund manager because the investor's goal is to mimic the return stream of the index. Avoiding negative excess returns versus the benchmark is also important because the manager will want to avoid underperforming the stated index.

Tracking error varies according to the manager's approach to tracking the index. An index that contains a large number of constituents will tend to create higher tracking error than those with fewer constituents. This is because a large number of constituents may prevent the manager from fully replicating the index.

For an index fund, the degree of tracking error fluctuates over time. Also, the value will differ depending on whether the data frequency is daily or less frequent.

KNOWLEDGE CHECK

Tracking Error and Excess Return

1. Exhibit 7 illustrates key portfolio metrics for three of the older and larger conventional open-end funds in the Australian and South Korean markets. Based on the levels of tracking error and excess return figures provided in the exhibit, explain whether the funds are likely replicating or sampling.

Exhibit 7: Major Conventional Index Mutual Funds in Australia and South Korea

Fund Name (Holdings)	Holdings	Annual Management Fee (bps)	3-Year Annualized Tracking Error	3-Year Annualized Excess Return
Australian market benchmark for the following funds is the S&P/ASX 300 Index. Number of securities in the index: 300.				
BlackRock Indexed Australian Equity Fund	296	20	0.0347%	−0.1684%
Macquarie True Index Australian Shares	259	0	0.0167%	0.0111%
Vanguard Australian Shares Index	293	18	0.1084%	−0.1814%
South Korean market benchmark for the funds below is the KRX KOSPI 200 Korea Index. Number of securities in the index: 200.				
KB Star Korea Index Equity CE	190	36	1.2671%	0.3356%
KIM Cruise Index F2.8 Equity-Deriv A	178	9	1.5019%	1.7381%
Samsung Index Premium Equity-Deriv A	204	40	1.3325%	1.1097%

Solution:

Based on the number of stocks in the fund compared to the index constituent number, it appears most funds are attempting to replicate. Two of the funds (Macquarie True Index and KIM Cruise Index) have 80% to 90% of the stocks in the index, which indicates they are more likely to be using sampling. One fund (Samsung Index Premium) actually holds more than the index, which can happen if buffering is used. No fund contains the same number of stocks as constituents in the index. Thus, it is not surprising that the funds failed to track their respective indexes perfectly. On an annualized basis, tracking error for the Australian funds is less than one-tenth the level of the Korean funds. However, the Korean funds' excess return—which is fund return less the benchmark index return—is positive in all three cases. The negative excess returns for two of the Australian funds are relatively close and possibly attributable to their management fees of 18–20 basis points.

Potential Causes of Tracking Error and Excess Return

Tracking error in an indexed equity fund can arise for several reasons. A major reason involves the fees charged. Although tracking error is expressed as an absolute value, fees are always negative because they represent a cost and drive down the excess return. Therefore, higher fees will contribute to lower excess returns and higher tracking error.

A second issue to consider is the number of securities held by the portfolio versus the benchmark index. Stock indexes that are liquid and investable may be fully replicated, while indexes with hard-to-find securities or a great number of securities are sampled. Sampled portfolios typically report greater tracking error than those that are fully replicated.

The intra-day trading of the constituent stocks of an indexed portfolio also presents an important issue to consider when attributing tracking error. The effect of intra-day trading can be positive or negative for a portfolio's returns compared to its benchmark index. The price levels used to report index returns are struck at the close of the trading day, so any securities that are bought or sold at a different price than that of the index will contribute to portfolio tracking error. Index fund managers can minimize this type of tracking error by transacting at the market-on-close price or as near to the closing time as feasible.

A secondary component of trading costs that contributes to tracking error is the trading commission paid to brokers. Commission costs make excess returns more negative and also affect tracking error. According to Perold and Salomon (1991), the trading cost for index-based portfolio managers is likely to be lower than the trading cost for active managers who are suspected by their counterparties to possess an information advantage.

Another issue to consider is the cash holding of the portfolio. Equity indexes do not have a cash allocation, so any cash balance creates tracking error for the index fund manager. Cash can be accumulated in the portfolio from a variety of sources, such as dividends received, sale proceeds, investor contributions, and other sources of income. Cash flows from investors and from the constituent companies may not be invested immediately, and investing them often entails a commission cost. Both may affect tracking error. The tracking error caused by temporarily uninvested cash is known **cash drag**. The effect of cash drag on portfolio value is negative when the market is rising and positive when it is falling.

Hill and Cheong (1996) discuss how to equitize a portfolio that would otherwise suffer from cash drag. One method is to use futures contracts. ETFs have been used widely for this purpose. Some portfolio managers establish a futures commission merchant relationship to offset their cash positions with a futures contract that represents the replicated index. When a manager does this, she will calculate the accrued dividends as well to hedge the dividend drag, which is cash drag attributable to accrued cash dividends paid to shareholders.

Controlling Tracking Error

The process of controlling tracking error involves trade-offs between the benefits and costs of maintaining complete faithfulness to the benchmark index, as illustrated in Exhibit 5. Portfolio managers who are unconstrained would keep the number of constituent securities and their weights as closely aligned to the benchmark index as possible. Even so, trading costs and other fees cause actual investment performance to deviate from index performance. Managers trade to accommodate inflows and outflows of cash from investors, to reinvest dividends, and to reflect changes in constituents of the underlying index.

Most index-based portfolio managers attempt to minimize cash held because a cash position generally creates undesirable tracking error. To keep tracking error low, portfolio managers need to invest cash flows received at the same valuations used by the benchmark index provider. Of course, because this is not always feasible, portfolio managers aim to maintain a beta of 1.0 relative to the benchmark index, while keeping other risk factor exposures similar to those of the index.

7 SOURCES OF RETURN AND RISK IN INDEX-BASED EQUITY STRATEGIES

 explain sources of return and risk to an index-based equity portfolio

Index-based portfolios began as a representation of market performance, and some investors accept the returns of the indexed portfolio without judgment. However, understanding both positive and negative sources of return through attribution analysis is an important step in the investment process.

Attribution Analysis

An investor has many choices across the investable spectrum of assets. An investor must first choose between stocks, bonds, and other asset classes and then partition each asset class by its sub-categories. In partitioning stocks, the process begins with choosing what countries to invest in, what market-cap sizes and investment style to use, and whether to weight the constituents using market cap or an alternative weighting method.

The return on an indexed portfolio can come from any of the aforementioned criteria. Return analyses are conducted ex-post, which means that the returns of the portfolio are studied after they have been experienced.

The sources of return for an equity index replication portfolio are the same as for any actively managed fund and include company-specific returns, sector returns, country returns, and currency returns. Beyond the traditional methods of grouping the risk and returns of the indexed portfolio, portfolio managers can group their indexed portfolios according to the stated portfolio objective. For example, a high dividend yield indexed portfolio may be grouped against the broad market benchmark by dividend yield. A low volatility portfolio could be grouped by volatility buckets to show how the lowest volatility stocks performed in the indexed portfolio as well as the broad market.

Most portfolio managers will rely on their portfolio attribution system to help them in understanding the sources of return. Index fund managers who track a broad market index need to understand what factors are driving the returns of that portfolio and its underlying index. Index fund managers of factor-based strategies should understand both the sources of return for their indexed portfolios and how those returns relate to the broad market index from which the constituents were chosen. In this way, factor-based strategies are similar to actively managed funds in the sense that they are actively chosen.

> **PORTFOLIO ATTRIBUTION ANALYSIS**
>
> Exhibit 8 shows an example of a portfolio attribution analysis using annual returns. Portfolio X is an index fund that seeks to replicate the performance of its benchmark. The manager of Portfolio X confirms that the portfolio, which has a return of 5.62%, is closely replicating the performance of the benchmark, which has a return of 5.65%.
>
> Using Exhibit 8, the manager analyzes the relative sector weights and sources of the three basis points of return difference. A portfolio that is within three basis points of its benchmark index is undoubtedly tracking the index closely. Beyond seeking the source of the tracking error, the portfolio manager will also seek to understand the source of the positive returns.

Sources of Return and Risk in Index-Based Equity Strategies

Exhibit 8: Example of Sector Attribution Analysis (all figures in %)

Sector	Sector Return (A)	Portfolio X Sector Weight (B)	Portfolio X Contribution to Return (C) = (A) × (B)	Benchmark Sector Weight (D)	Benchmark Contribution to Return (E) = (A) × (D)	Attribution Analysis Difference (F) = (C) − (E)
Total	5.62	100.00	5.62	100.00	5.65	−0.03
Telecom. Services	16.94	2.25	0.38	2.34	0.40	−0.02
Utilities	15.45	12.99	2.01	13.03	2.01	−0.01
Consumer Discretionary	12.09	3.89	0.47	3.90	0.47	0.00
Materials	9.61	2.08	0.20	2.08	0.20	0.00
Information Technology	7.03	2.82	0.20	2.85	0.20	0.00
Consumer Staples	6.82	15.07	1.03	15.09	1.03	0.00
Industrials	3.93	16.08	0.63	16.15	0.63	0.00
Financials	0.50	19.85	0.10	19.32	0.10	0.00
Health Care	0.31	12.70	0.04	12.77	0.04	0.00
Real Estate	0.80	5.04	0.04	5.23	0.04	0.00
Energy	7.21	7.23	0.52	7.24	0.52	0.00
[Cash]	0.00	0.00	0.00	0.00	0.00	0.00

Attribution analyses like the one in Exhibit 8 can be structured in many ways. This analysis is grouped by economic sector. Sector attribution can help an investor develop expectations about how a portfolio might perform in different market conditions. For example, during an era of low interest rates, high-dividend stocks such as utilities are likely to outperform while financial stocks such as banks are likely to underperform, other things held equal. To the extent the portfolio holds financial stocks in a lower concentration than the benchmark, the portfolio will likely outperform if interest rates stay low.

Column A in Exhibit 8 shows the total return for each sector. For example, the Telecommunications sector posted a return of 16.94% over this period.

Column B shows Portfolio's X's sector weight. The portfolio is heavily invested in Financials, because this is the largest sector in the benchmark index.

Column C shows each sector's contribution to the overall return of Portfolio X, obtained by multiplying each sector weight in Portfolio X by the sector's total return. The sum of the eleven sectors' contributions to return is equal to the total return of the portfolio.

Column D shows the benchmark's sector weights.

Column E shows the contribution to return of each sector held by the benchmark, obtained by multiplying each sector's weight in the benchmark by the sector's total return. The sum of the eleven sectors' contributions to return is equal to the total return of the benchmark.

Finally, column F shows the difference in contribution to returns between Portfolio X and the benchmark. Column F is the difference between columns C and E.

> Portfolio X has 15.07% invested in Consumer Staples, which compares to the benchmark index's 15.09% weight in that sector. The negligible underweighting combined with a sector return of 6.82% enabled the portfolio to closely match the contribution to return of the portfolio to that of the index.
>
> The Telecommunications and Utilities sectors were the best-performing sectors over the period. Telecommunications and Utilities holdings made up 15.24% of the portfolio's holdings and contributed 2.39 percentage points (or 239 basis points) of the 5.62% total return.
>
> Companies in the Telecommunications and Utilities sectors are high-dividend payers and are positively affected by falling interest rates. Given this information, the manager could then connect the positive performance of the sectors to the prevailing interest rate environment. The manager would also note in the attribution analysis that the same interest rate environment, in part, caused the Financials sector to underperform the market. These opposing forces act as a good hedge against interest rate movements in either direction and are part of a robust portfolio structure.
>
> The portfolio manager of the strategy may use the attribution analysis to determine the sources of tracking error. In this case, the analysis confirmed that the portfolio is meeting its goal of closely tracking the composition and performance of its benchmark. Further, the portfolio manager is able to determine the sources of return, which in this case are in large part from the high-dividend-yielding Telecommunications and Utilities sectors.

Securities Lending

Investors who hold long equity positions usually keep the shares in their brokerage accounts, so they are ready to sell when the time arises. But there is a demand for those shares from investors who want to sell short by borrowing the shares. The securities-lending income received by long portfolio managers can be a valuable addition to portfolio returns. At the very least, the proceeds can help offset the other costs of managing the portfolio. In the case of low-cost indexed portfolios, securities lending income can actually make net expenses negative, meaning that in addition to tracking the benchmark index, the portfolio earns a return in excess of the index.

An investor who wants to lend securities often uses a lending agent. In the case of institutional investors (e.g., mutual funds, pension funds, and hedge funds), the custodian (i.e., custody bank) is frequently used. Occasionally, the asset management firm will offer securities lending services. Two legal documents are usually put in place, including a securities lending authorization agreement between the lender and the agent and a master securities lending agreement between the agent and borrowers.

The lending agent identifies a borrower who posts collateral (typically 102–105% of the value of the securities). When the collateral is in securities rather than cash, the lending agent holds them as a guarantee. The lending agent evaluates the collateral daily to ensure that it is sufficient. When the collateral is in the form of cash, the lending agent invests it in money market instruments and receives interest income. In this case, the borrower sometimes receives a rebate that partially defrays its lost interest income. Regardless, the borrower pays a fee to the lender when borrowing the securities, and the lender typically splits part of this fee with the lending agent.

According to the International Securities Lending Association (2021), the 30 June 2021 global value of securities made available for lending by institutional investors was EUR28 trillion. Of this, EUR2.6 trillion in value was actually loaned. Collective investment vehicles and pension funds accounted for 59% of the total value of securities loaned. Collateral held with European triparty agents was in line with previous historical norms with equities and government bonds representing 45% and 44% of reported collateral, respectively.

Securities lending carries risks that can offset the benefits. The main risks are the credit quality of the borrower (credit risk) and the value of the posted collateral (market risk), although liquidity risk and operational risk are additional considerations. Lenders are permitted to sell loaned securities at any time under the normal course of the portfolio management mandate, and the borrowed shares must be returned in time for normal settlement of that sale. However, there is no guarantee that the borrower can deliver on a timely basis.

An additional risk is that lenders can invest cash held as collateral; and if a lender elects to invest the cash in long-term or risky securities, the collateral value is at risk of erosion. As long as the cash is invested in low-risk securities, risk is kept low. Typically, an agreed return on the invested cash is rebated by the lender to the borrower. Similarly, borrowers must pay cash to lenders in lieu of any cash dividends received because the dividends paid by the issuers of the shares will go to the holders. According to Duffie, Gârleanu, and Pedersen (2002), institutional investors such as index mutual funds and pension funds are viewed as preferred lenders because they are long-term holders of shares and unlikely to claim their shares back abruptly from borrowers.

The example of Sigma Finance Company illustrates collateral investment risk. Sigma Finance was a structured investment vehicle that primarily held long-term debt financed by short-term borrowings, and profit came from the interest differential. During the credit 2008–2009 global financial crisis, Sigma was downgraded by the rating agencies and lost its ability to borrow in the short-term markets, which led to default. Investors in Sigma's credit offerings, many of them security lenders, suffered substantial losses because of the default.

Borrowers take formal legal title to the securities, receive all cash flows and voting rights, and pay an annualized cost of borrowing (typically 2–10%). The borrowing cost depends on the borrower's credit quality and how difficult it is to borrow the security in question. Some securities are widely recognized as "easy to borrow" (ETB).

A popular exchange-traded fund (ETF) represents a good example of how securities lending revenue can provide a benefit to investment beneficiaries. As of 31 March 2021, the USD63.9 billion iShares Russell 2000 ETF (IWM) had lent USD5.97 billion in securities to various counterparties. This amount was 100% collateralized with cash. An affiliated party, BlackRock Institutional Trust Company, served as the securities lending agent in exchange for 4 basis points of collateral investment fees annually. IWM's net securities lending income for the year was slightly above USD63 million, which nearly offset the approximately USD90.7 million in investment advisory fees charged by the portfolio managers.

Investor Activism and Engagement by Index-Based Fund Managers

Institutional investors, especially index fund managers, are among the largest shareholders of many companies. The shares that they vote can have a large influence on corporate elections and outcomes of the proxy process. Their status as large shareholders often gives such investors access to private meetings with corporate management to discuss their concerns and preferences regarding corporate policies on board structure and composition, management compensation, operational risk management, the integrity of accounting statements, and other matters. Goldstein (2014) reports that in a survey, about two-thirds of public companies indicate investor engagement in 2014 was higher than it had been three years earlier. The typical points of contact were investor relations specialists, general counsel/corporate secretary, the board chair, and the CEO or CFO of the company. The respondents also reported that engagement is now covering more topics, but the subject matter is not principally financial. Governance policies, executive compensation, and social, environmental, and strategy issues are dominant.

Ferguson (2010) argues that institutional investors—who are themselves required to act in a fiduciary capacity—have a key responsibility to carry out their duties as voting shareholders. Lambiotte, Gibney, and Hartley (2014) assert that if done in an enlightened way, voting and engagement with company management by index-based investors can be a return-enhancing activity. Many hedge funds and other large investors even specialize in activism to align governance in their invested companies with shareholder interests.

Activist investors are usually associated with active portfolio management. If their activism efforts do not produce the desired result, they can express their dissatisfaction by selling their shares. In contrast, index-based investors do not have the same flexibility to sell. Yet both types of investors usually have the opportunity to vote their shares and participate in governance improvements.

Why should governance matter for index-based investors in broadly diversified portfolios? Across such portfolios, governance quality is broadly diversified; moreover, by definition, index-based investors do not try to select the best-performing companies or avoid the worst. However, corporate governance improvements are aimed at improving the effectiveness of the operations, management, and board oversight of the business. If the resulting efficiency improvements are evidenced in higher returns to index-constituent stocks, the index performance rises and so does the performance of an index-tracking portfolio. Thus, a goal of activism is to increase returns.

Index-based investors may even have a higher duty than more-transient active managers to use their influence to improve governance. As long as a stock has membership in the benchmark index, index-based managers can be considered permanent shareholders. Such investors might benefit from engaging with company management and boards, even outside the usual proxy season. Reinforcing the concept of permanence, some companies even give greater voting rights to long-term shareholders. Dallas and Barry (2016) examine 12 US companies with voting rights that increase to four, five, or even ten votes per share if the holding period is greater than three and sometimes four years.

Most index-based managers have a fiduciary duty to their clients that includes the obligation to vote proxy ballots on behalf of investors. Although shareholder return can be enhanced by engagement, the costs of these measures must also be considered. Among the more significant costs are staff resources required to become familiar with key issues and to engage management, regulators, and other investors. Researching and voting thousands of proxy ballots becomes problematic for many managers. They frequently hire a proxy voting service, such as Institutional Shareholder Services or Broadridge Financial Services, to achieve their goal of voting the proxy ballots in their clients' favor.

Although a strong argument can be made in favor of even index-based managers voting their shares in an informed way and pursuing governance changes when warranted, potential conflicts of interest may limit investors' propensity to challenge company management. Consider the hypothetical case of a large financial firm that earns substantial fees from its business of administering corporate retirement plans, including the pension plan of Millheim Corp. Let us say that the financial firm also manages index funds, and Millheim's stock is one of many index constituents. If Millheim becomes the target of shareholder activism, the financial firm's incentives are structured to support Millheim's management on any controversial issue.

Some may question the probable effectiveness of activist efforts by index-based investors. Management of the company targeted by activist investors is likely to see active portfolio managers as skillful and willing users of the proxy process to effect changes and accordingly will respond seriously. In contrast, index-based investors hold the company's shares to fulfill their tracking mandate (without the flexibility to sell or take a short position), so management may take these investors' activist activities less seriously.

SUMMARY

- Increasingly, investors use index-based strategies to gain exposure to a variety of risk factors beside the market factor. Examples include Capitalization, Style, Yield, Momentum, Volatility, and Quality.
- For index investors, portfolio tracking error is the standard deviation of the portfolio return net of the benchmark return.
- Indexing involves the goals of non-negative excess returns and minimizing tracking error subject to realistic portfolio constraints.
- Methods index-based investing include the use of such pooled investments as mutual funds and exchange-traded funds (ETFs), a do-it-yourself approach of building the portfolio stock by stock, and using derivatives to obtain exposure.
- Conventional open-end index mutual funds generally maintain low fees. Their expense ratios are slightly higher than for ETFs, but a brokerage fee is usually required for investor purchases and sales of ETF shares.
- Index exposure can also be obtained through the use of derivatives, such as futures and swaps.
- Building an index-based portfolio by full replication, meaning to hold all the index constituents, requires a large-scale portfolio and high-quality information about the constituent characteristics. Most equity index portfolios are managed using either a full replication strategy to keep tracking error low, are sampled to keep trading costs low, or use optimization techniques to match as closely as possible the characteristics and performance of the underlying index.
- The principal sources of index-based portfolio tracking error are fees, trading costs, and cash drag. Cash drag refers to the dilution of the return on the equity assets because of cash held. Cash drag can be exacerbated by the receipt of dividends from constituent stocks and the delay in getting them converted into shares.
- Portfolio managers control tracking error by minimizing trading costs, netting investor cash inflows and redemptions, and using equitization tools like derivatives to compensate for cash drag.
- Many index fund managers offer the constituent securities held in their portfolios for lending to short sellers and other market participants. The income earned from lending those securities helps offset portfolio management costs, often resulting in lower net fees to investors.
- Investor activism is engagement with portfolio companies and recognizing the primacy of end investors. Forms of activism can include expressing views to company boards or management on executive compensation, operational risk, board governance, and other value-relevant matters.
- Successful index-based equity investment requires an understanding of the investor's needs, benchmark index construction, and methods available to track the index.

REFERENCES

Arnott, Robert, Jason Hsu, and Philip Moore. 2005. "Fundamental Indexation." *Financial Analysts Journal* 61 (2): 83–99. 10.2469/faj.v61.n2.2718

Choueifaty, Yves and Yves Coignard. 2008. "Toward Maximum Diversification." *Journal of Portfolio Management* 35 (1): 40–51. 10.3905/JPM.2008.35.1.40

Dallas, Lynne and Jordan M. Barry. 2016. "Long-Term Shareholders and Time-Phased Voting." *Delaware Journal of Corporate Law* 40 (2): 541–646.

Duffie, Darrell, Nicolae Gârleanu, and Lasse Heje Pedersen. 2002. "Securities Lending, Shorting, and Pricing." *Journal of Financial Economics* 66 (2–3): 307–39. 10.1016/S0304-405X(02)00226-X

Fabozzi, Frank J., Sergio M. Focardi, and Petter N. Kolm. 2010. *Quantitative Equity Investing: Techniques and Strategies.* Hoboken, NJ: John Wiley & Sons.

Fama, Eugene F. and Kenneth R. French. 2015. "A Five-Factor Asset Pricing Model." *Journal of Financial Economics* 116 (1): 1–22. 10.1016/j.jfineco.2014.10.010

Ferguson, Roger W. 2010. "Riding Herd on Company Management." *Wall Street Journal* (27 April).

Goldstein, Marc. 2014. *Defining Engagement: An Update on the Evolving Relationship between Shareholders, Directors, and Executives.* Institutional Shareholder Services for the Investor Responsibility Research Center Institute.

Hill, Joanne M. and Rebecca K. Cheong. 1996. "*Minimizing Cash Drag with S&P 500 Index Tools.*" Working paper, Goldman Sachs New York.

International Securities Lending Association. 2021. "*Securities Lending Market Report*" (June). www.islaemea.org/assets/smart-pdfs/isla-securities-lending-market-report-june-2021/.

Jacobs, Bruce I. and Kenneth N. Levy. 2014. "Smart Beta versus Smart Alpha." *Journal of Portfolio Management* 40 (4): 4–7. 10.3905/jpm.2014.40.4.004

Jorion, Philippe. 2003. "Portfolio Optimization with Tracking-Error Constraints." *Financial Analysts Journal* 59 (5): 70–82. 10.2469/faj.v59.n5.2565

Lambiotte, Clay, Paul Gibney, and Joel Hartley. 2014. "*Activist Equity Investing: Unlocking Value by Acting as a Catalyst for Corporate Change.*" Lane, Clark, and Peacock LLP (August).

Perold, André and Robert S. Salomon. 1991. "The Right Amount of Assets under Management." *Financial Analysts Journal* 47 (3): 31–39. 10.2469/faj.v47.n3.31

Roll, Richard. 1992. "A Mean/Variance Analysis of Tracking Error." *Journal of Portfolio Management* 18 (4): 13–22. 10.3905/jpm.1992.701922

PRACTICE PROBLEMS

The following information relates to questions 1-8

Evan Winthrop, a senior officer of a US-based corporation, meets with Rebecca Tong, a portfolio manager at Cobalt Wealth Management. Winthrop recently moved his investments to Cobalt in response to his previous manager's benchmark-relative underperformance and high expenses.

Winthrop resides in Canada and plans to retire there. His annual salary covers his current spending needs, and his vested defined benefit pension plan is sufficient to meet retirement income goals. Winthrop prefers exposure to global equity markets with a focus on low management costs and minimal tracking error to any index benchmarks. The fixed-income portion of the portfolio may consist of laddered maturities with a home-country bias.

Tong proposes using an equity index as a basis for an investment strategy and reviews the most important requirements for an appropriate benchmark. With regard to investable indexes, Tong tells Winthrop the following:

Statement 1   A free-float adjustment to a market-capitalization weighted index lowers its liquidity.

Statement 2   An index provider that incorporates a buffering policy makes the index more investable.

Winthrop asks Tong to select a benchmark for the domestic stock allocation that holds all sectors of the Canadian equity market and to focus the portfolio on highly liquid, well-known companies. In addition, Winthrop specifies that any stock purchased should have a relatively low beta, a high dividend yield, a low P/E, and a low price-to-book ratio (P/B).

Winthrop and Tong agree that only the existing equity investments need to be liquidated. Tong suggests that, as an alternative to direct equity investments, the new equity portfolio be composed of the exchange-traded funds (ETFs) shown in Exhibit 1.

Exhibit 1: Available Equity ETFs

Equity Benchmark	ETF Ticker	Number of Constituents	P/B	P/E	Fund Expense Ratio
S&P/TSX 60	XIU	60	2.02	17.44	0.18%
S&P 500	SPY	506	1.88	15.65	0.10%
MSCI EAFE	EFA	933	2.13	18.12	0.33%

Winthrop asks Tong about the techniques wealth managers and fund companies use to create index-tracking equity portfolios that minimize tracking error and costs. In response, Tong outlines two frequently used methods:

Method 1   One process requires that all index constituents are available for trading and liquidity, but significant brokerage commissions can occur when the index is large.

Method 2   When tracking an index with a large number of constituents and/or managing a relatively low level of assets, a relatively straightforward and technically unsophisticated method can be used to build an index-based portfolio that requires fewer individual securities than the index and reduces brokerage commission costs.

Tong adds that portfolio stocks may be used to generate incremental revenue, thereby partially offsetting administrative costs but potentially creating undesirable counterparty and collateral risks.

After determining Winthrop's objectives and constraints, the CAD147 million portfolio's new strategic policy is to target long-term market returns while being fully invested at all times. Tong recommends quarterly rebalancing, currency hedging, and a composite benchmark composed of equity and fixed-income indexes. Currently the US dollar is worth CAD1.2930, and this exchange rate is expected to remain stable during the next month. Exhibit 2 presents the strategic asset allocation and benchmark weights.

Exhibit 2: Composite Benchmark and Policy Weights

Asset Class	Benchmark Index	Policy Weight
Canadian equity	S&P/TSX 60	40.0%
US equity	S&P 500	15.0%
International developed markets equity	MSCI EAFE	15.0%
Canadian bonds	DEX Universe	30.0%
Total portfolio		100.0%

In one month, Winthrop will receive a performance bonus of USD5,750,000. He believes that the US equity market is likely to increase during this timeframe. To take advantage of Winthrop's market outlook, he instructs Tong to immediately initiate an equity transaction using the S&P 500 futures contract with a current price of 2,464.29 while respecting the policy weights in Exhibit 2. The S&P 500 futures contract multiplier is 250, and the S&P 500 E-mini multiplier is 50.

Tong cautions Winthrop that there is a potential pitfall with the proposed request when it comes time to analyze performance. She discloses to Winthrop that equity index futures returns can differ from the underlying index, primarily because of corporate actions such as the declaration of dividends and stock splits.

1. Which of Tong's statements regarding equity index benchmarks is (are) correct?

    A. Only Statement 1

    B. Only Statement 2

    C. Both Statement 1 and Statement 2

2. To satisfy Winthrop's benchmark and security selection specifications, the Canadian equity index benchmark Tong selects should be:

    A. small capitalization with a core tilt.

    B. large capitalization with a value tilt.

Practice Problems

C. mid-capitalization with a growth tilt.

3. Based on Exhibit 1 and assuming a full-replication indexing approach, the tracking error is expected to be highest for:

    A. XIU.

    B. SPY.

    C. EFA.

4. Method 1's portfolio construction process is *most likely*:

    A. optimization.

    B. full replication.

    C. stratified sampling.

5. Method 2's portfolio construction process is *most likely*:

    A. optimization.

    B. full replication.

    C. stratified sampling.

6. The method that Tong suggests to add incremental revenue is:

    A. program trading.

    B. securities lending.

    C. attribution analysis.

7. In preparation for receipt of the performance bonus, Tong should immediately:

    A. buy two US E-mini equity futures contracts.

    B. sell nine US E-mini equity futures contracts.

    C. buy seven US E-mini equity futures contracts.

8. The risk that Tong discloses regarding the equity futures strategy is *most likely*:

    A. basis risk.

    B. currency risk.

    C. counterparty risk.

The following information relates to questions 9-14

The Mackenzie Education Foundation funds educational projects in a four-state region of the United States. Because of the investment portfolio's poor benchmark-relative returns, the foundation's board of directors hired a consultant, Stacy McMahon, to analyze performance and provide recommendations. McMahon meets with Autumn Laubach, the foundation's executive director, to review the existing asset allocation strategy. Laubach believes the portfolio's underperformance is attributable to the equity holdings, which are allocated 55% to a US large-capitalization index fund, 30% to an actively managed US small-cap fund, and 15% to an actively managed developed international fund.

Laubach states that that the board is interested in following an index-based approach for some or all of the equity allocation. In addition, the board is open to approaches that could generate returns in excess of the benchmark for part of the equity allocation. McMahon suggests that the board consider following a factor-based momentum strategy for the allocation to international stocks.

McMahon observes that the benchmark used for the US large-cap equity component is a price-weighted index containing 150 stocks. The benchmark's Herfindahl–Hirschman Index (HHI) is 0.0286.

McMahon performs a sector attribution analysis based on Exhibit 1 to explain the large-cap portfolio's underperformance relative to the benchmark.

Exhibit 1: Trailing 12-Month US Large-Cap Returns and Foundation/Benchmark Weights

Sector	Sector Returns	Foundation Sector Weights	Benchmark Sector Weights
Information technology	10.75%	18.71%	19.06%
Consumer staples	12.31%	16.52%	16.10%
Energy	8.63%	9.38%	9.53%
Utilities	−3.92%	8.76%	8.25%
Financials	7.05%	6.89%	6.62%

The board decides to consider adding a mid-cap manager. McMahon presents candidates for the mid-cap portfolio. Exhibit 2 provides fees and cash holdings for three portfolios and an index fund.

Exhibit 2: Characteristics of US Mid-Cap Portfolios and Index Fund

	Portfolio 1	Portfolio 2	Portfolio 3	Index Fund
Fees	0.10%	0.09%	0.07%	0.03%
Cash holdings	6.95%	3.42%	2.13%	0.51%

9. Compared with broad-market-cap weighting, the international equity strategy suggested by McMahon is *most likely* to:

    A. concentrate risk exposure.

    B. be based on the efficient market hypothesis.

    C. overweight stocks that recently experienced large price decreases.

10. The international strategy suggested by McMahon is *most likely* characterized as:

    A. risk based.

Practice Problems

    B. return oriented.

    C. diversification oriented.

11. The initial benchmark used for the US large-cap allocation:

    A. is unaffected by stocks splits.

    B. is essentially a liquidity-weighted index.

    C. holds the same number of shares in each component stock.

12. Based on its HHI, the initial US large-cap benchmark *most likely* has:

    A. a concentration level of 4.29.

    B. an effective number of stocks of approximately 35.

    C. individual stocks held in approximately equal weights.

13. Using a sector attribution analysis based on Exhibit 1, which US large-cap sector is the primary contributor to the portfolio's underperformance relative to the benchmark?

    A. Utilities

    B. Consumer staples

    C. Information technology

14. Based on Exhibit 2, which portfolio will *most likely* have the lowest tracking error?

    A. Portfolio 1

    B. Portfolio 2

    C. Portfolio 3

SOLUTIONS

1. B is correct. The three requirements for an index to become the basis for an equity investment strategy are that the index be (a) rule based, (b) transparent, and (c) investable. Buffering makes index benchmarks more investable (Statement 2) by making index transitions a more gradual and orderly process.

   A is incorrect because basing the index weight of an individual security solely on the total number of shares outstanding without using a free-float adjustment may make the index less investable. If a stock market cap excludes shares held by founders, governments, or other companies, then the remaining shares more accurately reflect the stock's true liquidity. Thus, a free-float adjustment (Statement 1) to a market index more accurately reflects its actual liquidity (it does not lower its liquidity). Many indexes require that individual stocks have float and average shares traded above a certain percentage of shares outstanding.

2. B is correct. To address Winthrop's concerns (sector diversification, liquidity, risk, dividend yield, P/E, and P/B), the Canadian equity index benchmark should consist of large-capitalization stocks with a value tilt. A large-capitalization index contains the largest-cap stocks, which tend to have the highest liquidity. Value stocks tend to exhibit high dividend yields and low P/Es and P/Bs.

   A is incorrect because small-capitalization stocks tend to be riskier than large-capitalization stocks. Winthrop has a preference for low-beta (low-risk) stocks.

   C is incorrect because a growth index will not address Winthrop's preference for a low P/E. Growth stocks exhibit such characteristics as high price momentum, high P/Es, and high EPS growth.

3. C is correct. An index that contains a large number of constituents will tend to create higher tracking error than one with fewer constituents. Based on the number of constituents in the three indexes (S&P/TSX 60 has 60, S&P 500 has 506, and MSCI EAFE has 933), EFA (the MSCI EAFE ETF) is expected to have the highest tracking error. Higher expense ratios (XIU: 0.18%; SPY: 0.10%; and EFA: 0.33%) also contribute to lower excess returns and higher tracking error, which implies that EFA has the highest expected tracking error.

4. B is correct. Full replication occurs when a manager holds all securities represented by the index in weightings that closely match the actual index weightings. Thus, it requires that all index constituents be liquid and available for trading, and the asset size of the mandate must also be sufficient. Significant brokerage commissions can occur, however, when the index is large.

5. C is correct. Stratified sampling methods are most frequently used when a portfolio manager is tracking an index that has a large number of constituents, or when managing a relatively low level of assets. Brokerage fees can become excessive when the number of constituents in the index is large.

   A is incorrect because optimization does not involve simple techniques. Optimization requires a high level of technical sophistication, including familiarity with computerized optimization software or algorithms, and a good understanding of the output.

   B is incorrect because full replication occurs when a manager holds all (not fewer) securities represented by the index in weightings that closely match actual index weightings. Full replication techniques require that the mandate's asset size be sufficient and that the index constituents be available for trading. Full replication can create significant brokerage commissions when the index is large.

Solutions

6. B is correct. Securities lending is typically used to offset the costs associated with portfolio management. By lending stocks, however, the investor is exposed to the credit quality of the stocks' borrower (counterparty or credit risk) and to risks involved with the posted collateral (market risk).

   A is incorrect because program trading is a strategy of buying or selling many stocks simultaneously. It is used primarily by institutional investors, typically for large-volume trades. Orders from the trader's computer are entered directly into the market's computer system and executed automatically.

   C is incorrect because attribution analysis is not a method of generating incremental revenue. Attribution analysis is a method that helps the manager understand the sources of return.

7. C is correct. The amount of the performance bonus that will be received in one month (USD5,750,000) needs to be invested passively based on the strategic allocation recommended by Tong. Using the strategic allocation of the portfolio, 15% (USD862,500.00) should be allocated to US equity exposure using the S&P 500 E-mini contract, which trades in US dollars. Because the futures price is 2,464.29 and the S&P 500 E-mini multiplier is 50, the contract unit value is USD123,214.50 (2,464.29 × 50).

   The correct number of futures contracts is (5,750,000.00 × 0.15)/123,214.50 = 7.00.

   Therefore, Tong will buy seven S&P 500 E-mini futures contracts.

8. A is correct. Basis risk results from using a hedging instrument that is imperfectly matched to the investment being hedged. Basis risk can arise when the underlying securities pay dividends, because the futures contract tracks only the price of the underlying index. Stock splits do not affect investment performance comparisons.

9. A is correct. Compared with broad-market-cap weighting, factor-based index strategies tend to concentrate risk exposure, leaving investors vulnerable during periods when the risk factor (e.g., momentum) is out of favor.

10. B is correct. McMahon suggests that the foundation follow a factor-based momentum strategy, which is generally defined by the amount of a stock's excess price return relative to the market during a specified period. Factor-based momentum strategies are classified as return oriented.

11. C is correct. The initial benchmark used for the US large-cap allocation is a price-weighted index. In a price-weighted index, the weight of each stock is its price per share divided by the sum of all the share prices in the index. As a result, a price-weighted index can be interpreted as a portfolio composed of one share of each constituent security.

12. B is correct. The HHI measures stock concentration risk in a portfolio, calculated as the sum of the constituent weightings squared:

    $$\text{HHI} = \sum_{i=1}^{n} w_i^2.$$

    Using the HHI, one can estimate the effective number of stocks, held in equal weights, that would mimic the concentration level of the respective index. The effective number of stocks for a portfolio is calculated as the reciprocal of the HHI. The HHI is 0.0286; the reciprocal (1/0.0286) is 34.97. Therefore, the effective number of stocks to mimic the US large-cap benchmark is approximately 35.

13. C is correct. The following is the attribution analysis for selected sectors of the

US large-cap portfolio.

		US Large-Cap Core Portfolio			Large-Cap Benchmark		Attribution Analysis
Sector	Sector Return (A)	Sector Weight (B)	Contribution to Return (C) = (A) × (B)		Sector Weight (D)	Contribution to Return (E) = (A) × (D)	Difference (F) = (C) − (E)
Information technology	10.75%	18.71%	2.01%		19.06%	2.05%	−0.04%
Consumer staples	12.31%	16.52%	2.03%		16.10%	1.98%	0.05%
Energy	8.63%	9.38%	0.81%		9.53%	0.82%	−0.01%
Utilities	−3.92%	8.76%	−0.34%		8.25%	−0.32%	−0.02%
Financials	7.05%	6.89%	0.49%		6.62%	0.47%	0.02%

Based on this analysis, the US large-cap portfolio's information technology sector is the primary contributor to the portfolio's disappointing equity returns because it provided the largest negative differential relative to the benchmark—a differential of −0.04%. Although the information technology sector had a positive return, this sector was underweighted relative to the benchmark, resulting in a negative contribution to the portfolio's returns.

14. C is correct. Of the three portfolios, Portfolio 3 has the lowest cash holding and the lowest fees. As a result, Portfolio 3 has the potential for the lowest tracking error compared with the other proposed portfolios.

# LEARNING MODULE 2

Active Equity Investing: Strategies

by Bing Li, PhD, CFA, Yin Luo, CPA, PStat, CFA, and Pranay Gupta, CFA.

Bing Li, PhD, CFA, is at Yuanyin Asset Management (Hong Kong SAR). Yin Luo, CPA, PStat, CFA, is at Wolfe Research LLC (USA). Pranay Gupta, CFA, is at Allocationmetrics Limited (USA).

LEARNING OUTCOMES	
Mastery	The candidate should be able to:
☐	compare fundamental and quantitative approaches to active management
☐	analyze bottom-up active strategies, including their rationale and associated processes
☐	analyze top-down active strategies, including their rationale and associated processes
☐	analyze factor-based active strategies, including their rationale and associated processes
☐	analyze activist strategies, including their rationale and associated processes
☐	describe active strategies based on statistical arbitrage and market microstructure
☐	describe how fundamental active investment strategies are created
☐	describe how quantitative active investment strategies are created
☐	discuss equity investment style classifications

INTRODUCTION

This reading provides an overview of active equity investing and the major types of active equity strategies. The reading is organized around a classification of active equity strategies into two broad approaches: fundamental and quantitative. Both approaches aim at outperforming a passive benchmark (for example, a broad equity market index), but they tend to make investment decisions differently. Fundamental approaches stress the use of human judgment in processing information and making investment decisions, whereas quantitative approaches tend to rely more heavily on rules-based quantitative models. As a result, some practitioners and academics refer to the fundamental, judgment-based approaches as "discretionary" and to the rules-based, quantitative approaches as "systematic."

This reading is organized as follows. Section 2 introduces fundamental and quantitative approaches to active management. Sections 3–9 discuss bottom-up, top-down, factor-based, and activist investing strategies. Section 10 describes the process of creating fundamental active investment strategies, including the parameters to consider as well as some of the pitfalls. Section 11 describes the steps required to create quantitative active investment strategies, as well as the pitfalls in a quantitative investment process. Section 12 discusses style classifications of active strategies and the uses and limitations of such classifications. A summary of key points completes the reading.

2. APPROACHES TO ACTIVE MANAGEMENT

> compare fundamental and quantitative approaches to active management

Active equity investing may reflect a variety of ideas about profitable investment opportunities. However, with regard to how these investment ideas are implemented—for example, how securities are selected—active strategies can be divided into two broad categories: fundamental and quantitative. Fundamental approaches are based on research into companies, sectors, or markets and involve the application of analyst discretion and judgment. In contrast, quantitative approaches are based on quantitative models of security returns that are applied systematically with limited involvement of human judgment or discretion. The labels *fundamental* and *quantitative* in this context are an imperfect shorthand that should not be misunderstood. The contrast with quantitative approaches does not mean that fundamental approaches do not use quantitative tools. Fundamental approaches often make use of valuation models (such as the free cash flow model), quantitative screening tools, and statistical techniques (e.g., regression analysis). Furthermore, quantitative approaches often make use of variables that relate to company fundamentals. Some investment disciplines may be viewed as hybrids in that they combine elements of both fundamental and quantitative disciplines. In the next sections, we examine these two approaches more closely.

Fundamental research forms the basis of the fundamental approach to investing. Although it can be organized in many ways, fundamental research consistently involves and often begins with the analysis of a company's financial statements. Through such an analysis, this approach seeks to obtain a detailed understanding of the company's current and past profitability, financial position, and cash flows. Along with insights into a company's business model, management team, product lines, and economic outlook, this analysis provides a view on the company's future business prospects and includes a valuation of its shares. Estimates are typically made of the stock's intrinsic value and/or its relative value compared to the shares of a peer group or the stock's own history of market valuations. Based on this valuation and other factors (including overall portfolio considerations), the portfolio manager may conclude that the stock should be bought (or a position increased) or sold (or a position reduced). The decision can also be stated in terms of overweighting, market weighting, or underweighting relative to the portfolio's benchmark.

In the search for investment opportunities, fundamental strategies may have various starting points. Some strategies start at a top or macro level—with analyses of markets, economies, or industries—to narrow the search for likely areas for profitable active investment. These are called top-down strategies. Other strategies, often referred to as bottom-up strategies, make little or no use of macro analysis and instead rely on individual stock analysis to identify areas of opportunity. Research distributed by investment banks and reports produced by internal analysts, organized by industry or economic sector, are also potential sources of investment ideas. The vetting of such ideas may be done by portfolio managers, who may themselves be involved in fundamental research, or by an investment committee.

Quantitative strategies, on the other hand, involve analyst judgment at the design stage, but they largely replace the ongoing reliance on human judgment and discretion with systematic processes that are often dependent on computer programming for execution. These systematic processes search for security and market characteristics and patterns ("factors") that have predictive power in order to identify securities or trades that will earn superior investment returns, in the sense of expected added value relative to risk or expected return relative to a benchmark—for example, an index benchmark or peer benchmark.

Factors that might be considered include valuation (e.g., earnings yield), size (e.g., market capitalization), profitability (e.g., return on equity), financial strength (e.g., debt-to-equity ratio), market sentiment (e.g., analyst consensus on companies' long-term earnings growth), industry membership (e.g., stocks' GICS classification), and price-related attributes (e.g., price momentum). While a wide range of security characteristics have been used to define "factors," some factors (e.g., the aforementioned size, valuation, momentum, and profitability) have been shown to be positively associated with a long-term return premium. We call these *rewarded* factors. Many other factors are used in portfolio construction but have not been empirically proven to offer a persistent return premium, and are thus called *unrewarded* factors.

Once a pattern or relationship between a given variable (or set of variables) and security prices has been established by analysis of past data, a quantitative model is used to predict future expected returns of securities or baskets of securities. Security selection then flows from expected returns, which reflect securities' exposures to the selected variables with predictive power. From a quantitative perspective, investment success depends not on individual company insights but on model quality.

Exhibit 1 presents typical differences between the main characteristics of fundamental and quantitative methodologies.

Exhibit 1: Differences between Fundamental and Quantitative Approaches

	Fundamental	Quantitative
Style	Subjective	Objective
Decision-making process	Discretionary	Systematic, non-discretionary
Primary resources	Human skill, experience, judgment	Expertise in statistical modeling
Information used	Research (company/industry/economy)	Data and statistics
Analysis focus	Conviction (high depth) in stock-, sector-, or region-based selection	A selection of variables, subsequently applied broadly over a large number of securities
Orientation to data	Forecast future corporate parameters and establish views on companies	Attempt to draw conclusions from a variety of historical data
Portfolio construction	Use judgment and conviction within permissible risk parameters	Use optimizers

In the following section, we take a closer look at some of the distinguishing characteristics listed in Exhibit 1 and how they are evolving with the advent of new technologies available to investors.

Differences in the Nature of the Information Used

To contrast the information used in fundamental and quantitative strategies, we can start by describing typical activities for fundamental investors with a bottom-up investment discipline. Bottom-up fundamental analysts research and analyze a company, using data from company financial statements and disclosures to assess attributes such as profitability, leverage, and absolute or peer-relative valuation. They typically also assess how those metrics compare to their historical values to identify trends and scrutinize such characteristics as the company's management competence, its future prospects, and the competitive position of its product lines. Such analysts usually focus on the more recent financial statements (which include current and previous years' accounting data), notes to the financial statements and assumptions in the accounts, and management discussion and analysis disclosures. Corporate governance is often taken into consideration as well as wider environmental, social, and governance (ESG) characteristics.

Top-down fundamental investors' research focuses first on region, country, or sector information (e.g., economic growth, money supply, and market valuations). Some of the data used by fundamental managers can be measured or expressed numerically and therefore "quantified." Other items, such as management quality and reputation, cannot.

Quantitative approaches often use large amounts of historical data from companies' financial reports (in addition to other information, such as return data) but process those data in a systematic rather than a judgmental way. Judgment is used in model building, particularly in deciding which variables and signals are relevant. Typically, quantitative approaches use historical stock data and statistical techniques to identify variables that may have a statistically significant relationship with stock returns; then these relationships are used to predict individual security returns. In contrast to the fundamental approach, the quantitative approach does not normally consider information or characteristics that cannot be quantified. In order to minimize survivorship and look-ahead biases, historical data used in quantitative research should include stocks that are no longer listed, and accounting data used should be the original, un-restated numbers that were available to the market at that point in time.

> **INVESTMENT PROCESS: FUNDAMENTAL VS. QUANTITATIVE**
>
> The goal of the investment process is to construct a portfolio that best reflects the stated investment objective and risk tolerance, with an optimal balance between expected return and risk exposure, subject to the constraints imposed by the investment policy. The investment processes under both fundamental and quantitative approaches involve a number of considerations, such as the methodology and valuation process, which are the subject of this reading. Other considerations, such as portfolio construction and risk management, trade execution, and ongoing performance monitoring, are the subjects of subsequent curriculum readings.

	Fundamental	**Quantitative**
Methodology	Determine methodology to evaluate stocks (bottom-up or top-down, value or growth, income or deep value, intrinsic or relative value, etc.)	Define model to estimate expected stock returns (choose time-series macro-level factors or cross-sectional stock-level factors, identify factors that have a stable positive information coefficient IC, use a factor combination algorithm, etc.)
Valuation process	<ul><li>Prescreen to identify potential investment candidates with stringent financial and market criteria</li><li>Perform in-depth analysis of companies to derive their intrinsic values</li><li>Determine buy or sell candidates trading at a discount or premium to their intrinsic values</li></ul>	<ul><li>Construct factor exposures across all shares in the same industry</li><li>Forecast IC and/or its volatility for each factor by using algorithms (such as artificial intelligence or time-series analysis) or fundamental research</li><li>Combine factor exposures to estimate expected returns</li></ul>
Portfolio construction and rebalancing	<ul><li>Allocate assets by determining industry and country/region exposures</li><li>Set limits on maximum sector, country, and individual stock positions</li><li>Determine buy-and-sell list</li><li>Monitor portfolio holdings continuously</li></ul>	<ul><li>Determine which factors to underweight or overweight</li><li>Use risk model to measure *ex ante* active risk</li><li>Run portfolio optimization with risk model, investment, and risk constraints, as well as the structure of transaction costs</li><li>Rebalance at regular intervals</li></ul>

Differences in the Focus of the Analysis

Fundamental investors usually focus their attention on a relatively small group of stocks and perform in-depth analysis on each one of them. This practice has characteristically given fundamental (or "discretionary") investors an edge of depth in understanding individual companies' businesses over quantitative (or "systematic") investors, who do not focus on individual stocks. Quantitative investors instead usually focus on factors across a potentially very large group of stocks. Therefore, fundamental investors tend to take larger positions in their selected stocks, while quantitative investors tend to focus their analysis on a selection of factors but spread their selected factor bets across a substantially larger group of holdings.[1]

Difference in Orientation to the Data: Forecasting Fundamentals vs. Pattern Recognition

Fundamental analysis places an emphasis on forecasting future prospects, including the future earnings and cash flows of a company. Fundamental investors use judgment and in-depth analysis to formulate a view of the company's outlook and to identify the catalysts that will generate future growth. They rely on knowledge, experience, and their ability to predict future conditions in a company to make investment decisions. Conceptually, the fundamental approach aims at forecasting forward parameters in order to make investment decisions. That said, many fundamental investors use a

---

[1] The implications for portfolio risk of using individual stocks or factors will be considered in the reading on portfolio construction.

quantitative component in their investment process, such as a quantitative screen or a commercial quantitative risk model such as those produced by Axioma, MSCI, Northfield, and Bloomberg.

In contrast, the quantitative approach aims to predict future returns using conclusions derived from analyzing historical data and patterns therein. Quantitative investors construct models by back-testing on historical data, using what is known about or has been reported by a company, including future earnings estimates that have been published by analysts, to search for the best company characteristics for purposes of stock selection. Once a model based on historical data has been finalized, it is applied to the latest available data to determine investment decisions. While the process is distinct from the fundamental approach, the active return and risk profiles of many fundamentals managers have been explained or replicated using well-known quantitative factors. See, for example, Ang, Goetzman, and Schaefer 2009 and Frazzini, Kabiller, and Pedersen 2013.

> **FORESTALLING LOOK-AHEAD BIAS (HISTORICAL EXAMPLE)**
>
> Satyam Computers was an India-based company that provided IT consulting and solutions to its global customers. In the eight years preceding 2009, Satyam overstated its revenues and profits and reported a cash holdings total of approximately $1.04 billion that did not exist. The falsification of the accounts came to light in early 2009, and Satyam was removed from the S&P CNX Nifty 50 index on 12 January.
>
> If a quantitative analyst ran a simulation benchmarked against the S&P CNX Nifty 50 index on 31 December 2008, he or she should have included the 50 stocks that were in the index on 31 December 2008 and use only the data for the included stocks that were available to investors as of that date. The analyst should therefore include Satyam as an index constituent and use the original accounting data that were published by the company at that time. While it was subsequently proved that these accounting data were fraudulent, this fact was not known to analysts and investors on 31 December 2008. As a result, it would not have been possible for any analyst to incorporate the true accounting data for Satyam on that date.

Differences in Portfolio Construction: Judgment vs. Optimization

Fundamental investors typically select stocks by performing extensive research on individual companies, which results in a list of high-conviction stocks. Thus, fundamental investors see risk at the company level. There is a risk that the assessment of the company's fair value is inaccurate, that the business's performance will differ from the analyst's expectations, or that the market will fail to recognize the identified reason for under- or overvaluation. Construction of a fundamental portfolio therefore often depends on judgment, whereby the absolute or index-relative sizes of positions in stocks, sectors, or countries are based on the manager's conviction of his or her forecasts. The portfolio must, of course, still comply with the risk parameters set out in the investment agreements with clients or in the fund prospectus.

In quantitative analysis, on the other hand, the risk is that factor returns will not perform as expected. Because the quantitative approach invests in baskets of stocks, the risks lie at the portfolio level rather than at the level of specific stocks. Construction of a quantitative portfolio is therefore generally done using a portfolio optimizer, which controls for risk at the portfolio level in arriving at individual stock weights.

The two approaches also differ in the way that portfolio changes or rebalancings are performed. Managers using a fundamental approach usually monitor the portfolio's holdings continuously and may increase, decrease, or eliminate positions at any time. Portfolios managed using a quantitative approach are usually rebalanced at regular intervals, such as monthly or quarterly. At each interval, the program or algorithm, using pre-determined rules, automatically selects positions to be sold, reduced, added, or increased.

> **EXAMPLE 1**
>
> ### Fundamental vs. Quantitative Approach
>
> Consider two equity portfolios with the same benchmark index, the AC MSCI Asia ex Japan Index. The index contains 1,210 stocks as of September 20211. One portfolio is managed using a fundamental approach, while the other is managed using a quantitative approach. The fundamental approach–based portfolio is made up of 50 individually selected stocks, which are reviewed for potential sale or trimming on an ongoing basis. In the fundamental approach, the investment universe is first pre-screened by valuation and by the fundamental metrics of earnings yield, dividend yield, earnings growth, and financial leverage. The quantitative approach–based portfolio makes active bets on 400 stocks with monthly rebalancing. The particular approach used is based on a five-factor model of equity returns.
>
> Contrast fundamental and quantitative investment processes with respect to the following:
>
> 1. Constructing the portfolio
>
> **Solution:**
>
> Fundamental: Construct the portfolio by overweighting stocks that are expected to outperform their peers or the market as a whole. Where necessary for risk reduction, underweight some benchmark stocks that are expected to underperform. The stocks that fell out in the pre-screening process do not have explicit forecasts and will not be included in the portfolio.
>
> Quantitative: Construct the portfolio by maximizing the objective function (such as portfolio alpha or information ratio) with risk models.
>
> 2. Rebalancing the portfolio
>
> **Solution:**
>
> Fundamental: The manager monitors each stock continuously and sells stocks when their market prices surpass the target prices (either through appreciation of the stock price or through reduction of the target price due to changes in expectations).
>
> Quantitative: Portfolios are usually rebalanced at regular intervals, such as monthly.

3. BOTTOM-UP STRATEGIES

☐ analyze bottom-up active strategies, including their rationale and associated processes

Equity investors have developed many different techniques for processing all the information necessary to arrive at an investment decision. Multiple approaches may be taken into account in formulating an overall opinion of a stock; however, each analyst will have his or her own set of favorite techniques based on his or her experience and judgment. Depending on the specifics of the investment discipline, most fundamental and quantitative strategies can be characterized as either bottom-up or top-down.

Bottom-Up Strategies

Bottom-up strategies begin the asset selection process with data at the individual asset and company level, such as price momentum and profitability. Bottom-up quantitative investors harness computer power to apply their models to this asset- and company-level information (with the added requirement that the information be quantifiable). The balance of this section illustrates the bottom-up process as used by fundamental investors. These investors typically begin their analysis at the company level before forming an opinion on the wider sector or market. The ability to identify companies with strong or weak fundamentals depends on the analyst's in-depth knowledge of each company's industry, product lines, business plan, management abilities, and financial strength. After identifying individual companies, the bottom-up approach uses economic and financial analysis to assess the intrinsic value of a company and compares that value with the current market price to determine which stocks are undervalued or overvalued. The analyst may also find companies operating efficiently with good prospects even though the industry they belong to is deteriorating. Similarly, companies with poor prospects may be found in otherwise healthy and prosperous industries.

Fundamental investors often focus on one or more of the following parameters for a company, either individually or in relation to its peers:

- business model and branding
- competitive advantages
- company management and corporate governance

Valuation is based on either a discounted cash flow model or a preferred market multiple, often earnings-related. We address each of these parameters and valuation approaches in turn.

Business Model and Branding.
The business model of a company refers to its overall strategy for running the business and generating profit. The business model details how a company converts its resources into products or services and how it delivers those products or services to customers. Companies with a superior business model compete successfully, have scalability, and generate significant earnings. Further, companies with a robust and adaptive business model tend to outperform their peers in terms of return on shareholder equity. The business model gives investors insight into a company's value proposition, its operational flow, the structure of its value chain, its branding strategy, its market segment,

and the resulting revenue generation and profit margins. This insight helps investors evaluate the sustainability of the company's competitive advantages and make informed investment decisions.

Corporate branding is a way of defining the company's business for the market in general and retail customers in particular and can be understood as the company's identity as well as its promise to its customers. Strong brand names convey product quality and can give the company an edge over its competitors in both market share and profit margin. It is widely recognized that brand equity plays an important role in the determination of product price, allowing companies to command price premiums after controlling for observed product differentiation. Apple in consumer technology and BMW in motor vehicles, for example, charge more for their products, but customers are willing to pay the premium because of brand loyalty.

Competitive Advantages.
A competitive advantage typically allows a company to outperform its peers in terms of the return it generates on its capital. There are many types of competitive advantage, such as access to natural resources, superior technology, innovation, skilled personnel, corporate reputation, brand strength, high entry barriers, exclusive distribution rights, and superior product or customer support.

For value investors, who search for companies that appear to be trading below their intrinsic value (often following earnings disappointments), it is important to understand the sustainability of the company's competitive position when assessing the prospects for recovery.

Company Management.
A good management team is crucial to a company's success. Management's role is to allocate resources and capital to maximize the growth of enterprise value for the company's shareholders. A management team that has a long-term rather than a short-term focus is more likely to add value to an enterprise over the long term.

To evaluate management effectiveness, one can begin with the financial statements. Return on assets, equity, or invested capital (compared either to industry peers or to historical rates achieved by the company) and earnings growth over a reasonable time period are examples of indicators used to gauge the value added by management.

Qualitative analysis of the company's management and governance structures requires attention to (1) the alignment of management's interests with those of shareholders to minimize agency problems; (2) the competence of management in achieving the company's objectives (as described in the mission statement) and long-term plans; (3) the stability of the management team and the company's ability to attract and retain high-performing executives; and (4) increasingly, risk considerations and opportunities related to a company's ESG attributes. Analysts also monitor management insider purchases and sales of the company's shares for potential indications of the confidence of management in the company's future.

The above qualitative considerations and financial statement analysis will help in making earnings estimates, cash flow estimates, and evaluations of risk, providing inputs to company valuation. Fundamental strategies within the bottom-up category may use a combination of approaches to stock valuation. Some investors rely on discounted cash flow or dividend models. Others focus on relative valuation, often based on earnings-related valuation metrics such as a P/E, price to book (P/B), and enterprise value (EV)/EBITDA. A conclusion that a security's intrinsic value is different from its current market price means the valuation is using estimates that are different from those reflected in current market prices. Conviction that the analyst's forecasts are, over a particular time period, more accurate than the market's is therefore important, as is the belief that the market will reflect the more accurate estimates within a time frame that is consistent with the strategy's investment horizon.

Bottom-up strategies are often broadly categorized as either value-based (or value-oriented) or growth-based (or growth-oriented), as the following section explains.

Value-Based Approaches

Benjamin Graham is regarded as the father of value investing. Along with David Dodd, he wrote the book *Security Analysis* (1934), which laid the basic framework for value investing. Graham posited that buying earnings and assets relatively inexpensively afforded a "margin of safety" necessary for prudent investing. Consistent with that idea, value-based approaches aim to buy stocks that are trading at a significant discount to their estimated intrinsic value. Value investors typically focus on companies with attractive valuation metrics, reflected in low earnings (or asset) multiples. In their view, investors' sometimes irrational behavior can make stocks trade below the intrinsic value based on company fundamentals. Such opportunities may arise due to a variety of behavioral biases and often reflect investors' overreaction to negative news. Various styles of value-based investing are sometimes distinguished; for example, "relative value" investors purchase stocks on valuation multiples that are high relative to historical levels but that compare favorably to those of the peer group.

Relative Value

Investors who pursue a relative value strategy evaluate companies by comparing their value indicators (e.g., P/E or P/B multiples) to the average valuation of companies in the same industry sector with the aim of identifying stocks that offer value relative to their sector peers. As different sectors face different market structures and different competitive and regulatory conditions, average sector multiples vary.

Exhibit 2 lists the key financial ratios for sectors in the Hang Seng Index on the last trading day of 2016. The average P/E for companies in the energy sector is almost five times the average P/E for those in real estate. A consumer staples company trading on a P/E of 12 would appear undervalued relative to its sector, while a real estate company trading on the same P/E multiple of 12 would appear overvalued relative to its sector.

Exhibit 2: Key Financial Ratios of Hang Seng Index (30 December 2016)

	Weight	Dividend Yield	Price-to-Earnings Ratio (P/E)	Price-to-Cash-Flow Ratio (P/CF)	Price-to-Book Ratio (P/B)	Total Debt to Common Equity (%)	Current Ratio
Hang Seng Index	100.0	3.5	12.2	6.1	1.1	128.4	1.3
Consumer discretionary	2.9	4.1	21.3	12.5	3.0	26.3	1.4
Consumer staples	1.6	2.6	16.8	14.3	3.3	62.1	1.4
Energy	7.0	2.6	39.5	3.7	0.9	38.5	1.0
Financials	47.5	4.3	10.1	5.0	1.1	199.8	1.1
Industrials	5.5	3.8	11.8	6.0	0.9	158.7	1.2
Information technology	11.4	0.6	32.7	19.9	8.2	60.2	1.0
Real estate	10.6	3.9	8.3	8.0	0.7	30.3	2.5
Telecommunication services	7.8	3.2	13.3	4.6	1.4	11.5	0.7
Utilities	5.6	3.7	14.2	10.8	1.7	47.0	1.3

Source: Bloomberg.

Investors usually recognize that in addition to the simple comparison of a company's multiple to that of the sector, one needs a good understanding of why the valuation is what it is. A premium or discount to the industry may well be justified by the company's fundamentals.

Contrarian Investing

Contrarian investors purchase and sell shares against prevailing market sentiment. Their investment strategy is to go against the crowd by buying poorly performing stocks at valuations they find attractive and then selling them at a later time, following what they expect to be a recovery in the share price. Companies in which contrarian managers invest are frequently depressed cyclical stocks with low or even negative earnings or low dividend payments. Contrarians expect these stocks to rebound once the company's earnings have turned around, resulting in substantial price appreciation.

Contrarian investors often point to research in behavioral finance suggesting that investors tend to overweight recent trends and to follow the crowd in making investment decisions. A contrarian investor attempts to determine whether the valuation of an individual company, industry, or entire market is irrational—that is, undervalued or overvalued at any time—and whether that irrationality represents an exploitable mispricing of shares. Accordingly, contrarian investors tend to go against the crowd.

Both contrarian investors and value investors who do not describe their style as contrarian aim to buy shares at a discount to their intrinsic value. The primary difference between the two is that non-contrarian value investors rely on fundamental metrics to make their assessments, while contrarian investors rely more on market sentiment and sharp price movements (such as 52-week high and low prices as sell and buy prices) to make their decisions.

High-Quality Value

Some value-based strategies give valuation close attention but place at least equal emphasis on financial strength and demonstrated profitability. For example, one such investment discipline requires a record of consistent earnings power, above-average return on equity, financial strength, and exemplary management. There is no widely accepted label for this value style, the refinement of which is often associated with investor Warren Buffett.[2]

Income Investing

The income investing approach focuses on shares that offer relatively high dividend yields and positive dividend growth rates. Several rationales for this approach have been offered. One argument is that a secure, high dividend yield tends to put a floor under the share price in the case of companies that are expected to maintain such a dividend. Another argument points to empirical studies that demonstrate the higher returns to equities with these characteristics and their greater ability to withstand market declines.

Deep-Value Investing

A value investor with a deep-value orientation focuses on undervalued companies that are available at extremely low valuation relative to their assets (e.g., low P/B). Such companies are often those in financial distress. The rationale is that market interest in such securities may be limited, increasing the chance of informational inefficiencies. The deep-value investor's special area of expertise may lie in reorganizations or related legislation, providing a better position from which to assess the likelihood of company recovery.

---

2 See Greenwald, Kahn, Sonkin, and Biema (2001).

Restructuring and Distressed Investing

While the restructuring and distressed investment strategies are more commonly observed in the distressed-debt space, some equity investors specialize in these disciplines. Opportunities in restructuring and distressed investing are generally counter cyclical relative to the overall economy or to the business cycle of a particular sector. A weak economy generates increased incidence of companies facing financial distress. When a company is having difficulty meeting its short-term liabilities, it will often propose to restructure its financial obligations or change its capital structure.

Restructuring investors seek to purchase the debt or equity of companies in distress. A distressed company that goes through restructuring may still have valuable assets, distribution channels, or patents that make it an attractive acquisition target. Restructuring investing is often done before an expected bankruptcy or during the bankruptcy process. The goal of restructuring investing is to gain control or substantial influence over a company in distress at a large discount and then restructure it to restore a large part of its intrinsic value.

Effective investment in a distressed company depends on skill and expertise in identifying companies whose situation is better than the market believes it to be. Distressed investors assume that either the company will survive or there will be sufficient assets remaining upon liquidation to generate an appropriate return on investment.

Special Situations

The "special situations" investment style focuses on the identification and exploitation of mispricings that may arise as a result of corporate events such as divestitures or spinoffs of assets or divisions or mergers with other entities. In the opinion of many investors such situations represent short-term opportunities to exploit mispricing that result from such special situations. According to Greenblatt (2010), investors often overlook companies that are in such special situations as restructuring (involving asset disposals or spinoffs) and mergers, which may create opportunities to add value through active investing. To take advantage of such opportunities, this type of investing requires specific knowledge of the industry and the company, as well as legal expertise.

Growth-Based Approaches

Growth-based investment approaches focus on companies that are expected to grow faster than their industry or faster than the overall market, as measured by revenues, earnings, or cash flow. Growth investors usually look for high-quality companies with consistent growth or companies with strong earnings momentum. Characteristics usually examined by growth investors include historical and estimated future growth of earnings or cash flows, underpinned by attributes such as a solid business model, cost control, and exemplary management able to execute long-term plans to achieve higher growth. Such companies typically feature above-average return on equity, a large part of which they retain and reinvest in funding future growth. Because growth companies may also have volatile earnings and cash flows going forward, the intrinsic values calculated by discounting expected future cash flows are subject to relatively high uncertainty. Compared to value-focused investors, growth-focused investors have a higher tolerance for above-average valuation multiples.

GARP (growth at a reasonable price) is a sub-discipline within growth investing. This approach is used by investors who seek out companies with above-average growth that trade at reasonable valuation multiples, and is often referred to as a hybrid of growth and value investing. Many investors who use GARP rely on the P/E-to-growth (PEG) ratio—calculated as the stock's P/E divided by the expected earnings growth rate (in percentage terms)—while also paying attention to variations in risk and duration of growth.

EXAMPLE 2

Characteristic Securities for Bottom-Up Investment Disciplines

1. The following table provides information on four stocks.

Company	Price	12-Month Forward EPS	3-Year EPS Growth Forecast	Dividend Yield	Industry Sector	Sector Average P/E
A	50	5	20%	1%	Industrial	10
B	56	2	2%	0%	Information technology	35
C	22	10	−5%	2%	Consumer staples	15
D	32	2	2%	8%	Utilities	16

Using only the information given in the table above, for each stock, determine which fundamental investment discipline would most likely select it.

Solution:

- Company A's forward P/E is 50/5 = 10, and its P/E-to-growth ratio (PEG) is 10/20 = 0.5, which is lower than the PEGs for the other companies (28/2 = 14 for Company B, negative for Company C, and 16/2 = 8 for Company D). Given the favorable valuation relative to growth, the company is a good candidate for investors who use GARP.

- Company B's forward P/E is 56/2 = 28, which is lower than the average P/E of 35 for its sector peers. The company is a good candidate for the relative value approach.

- Company C's forward P/E is 22/10 = 2.2, which is considered very low in both absolute and relative terms. Assuming the investor pays attention to company circumstances, the stock could be a good candidate for the deep-value approach.

- Company D's forward P/E is 32/2 = 16, which is the same as its industry average. Company D's earnings are growing slowly at 2%, but the dividend yield of 8% appears high. This combination makes the company a good candidate for income investing.

EXAMPLE 3

Growth vs. Value

Tencent Holdings Limited is a leading provider of value-added internet services in China. The company's services include social networks, web portals, e-commerce, and multiplayer online games.

Exhibit 3 shows an excerpt from an analyst report on Tencent published following the release of the company's Q4 2020 results on 2 November 2021.

Exhibit 3: Financial Summary and Valuation for Tencent Holdings Limited

Market Data: 2 November 2021			2017	2018	2019	2020	2018E
Closing price	464.0	Revenue (HKD millions)	274,158	370,372	427,814	541,692	276,538
	251.5	YOY (%)		35.1	15.5	26.6	30.15
	9,380	Net income (HKD millions)	82,457	93,239	105,806	179,619	68,994
	3,669	YOY (%)	53.49	13.1	13.5	69.8	22.04
52-Week high/low	412.20/775.50	EPS (HKD)	8.76	9.87	11.18	18.93	7.39
Market cap (HKD millions)	4,470,000	Diluted EPS (HKD)	8.65	9.74	11.02	18.57	7.31
		ROE (%)	29.09	23.84	26.11	26.18	24.71
Shares outstanding	33,006,000	Debt/Assets (%)	52.02	60.20	61.33	61.26	60.37
Exchange rate (RMB/HKD)	0.8197	Dividend yield (%)	0.20	0.20	0.28	0.38	0.46
		P/E	54.78	55.17	38.27	28.80	23.60
		P/B	22.31	19.35	13.39	9.99	7.54
		EV/EBITDA	40.79	35.88	28.06	20.09	15.39

Notes: Market data are quoted in HKD; the company's filing is in RMB. Diluted EPS is calculated as if all outstanding convertible securities (such as convertible preferred shares, convertible debentures, stock options, and warrants) were exercised. P/E is calculated as closing price divided by each year's EPS.

Source: Blomberg,

author's analysis

From the perspective of the date of Exhibit 3:

1. Which metrics would support a decision to invest by a growth investor?

Solution:

A growth investor would focus on the following:

- The year-over-year change in revenue, which exceeded 25% in 2020.
- The year-over-year change in net income, which was nearly 70% in 2020.

2. Which characteristics would a growth investor tend to weigh less heavily than a high-quality value investor?

Solution:

A growth investor would tend to be less concerned about the relatively high valuation levels (high P/E, P/B, and EV/EBITDA) and low dividend yield.

TOP-DOWN STRATEGIES

☐ analyze top-down active strategies, including their rationale and associated processes

As the name suggests, in contrast to bottom-up strategies, top-down strategies use an investment process that begins at a top or macro level. Instead of focusing on individual company- and asset-level variables in making investment decisions, top-down portfolio managers study variables affecting many companies, such as the macroeconomic environment, demographic trends, and government policies. These managers often use instruments such as futures contracts, ETFs, swaps, and custom baskets of individual stocks to capture macro dynamics and generate portfolio return. Some bottom-up stock pickers also incorporate top-down analysis as part of their process for arriving at investment decisions. A typical method of incorporating both top-down macroeconomic and bottom-up fundamental processes is to have the portfolio strategist set the target country and sector weights. Portfolio managers then construct stock portfolios that are consistent with these preset weights.

Country and Geographic Allocation to Equities

Investors using country allocation strategies form their portfolios by investing in different geographic regions depending on their assessment of the regions' prospects. For example, the manager may have a preference for a particular region and may establish a position in that region while limiting exposure to others. Managers of global equity funds may, for example, make a decision based on a tradeoff between the US equity market and the European equity market, or they may allocate among all investable country equity markets using futures or ETFs. Such strategies may also seek to track the overall supply and demand for equities in regions or countries by analyzing the aggregate volumes of share buybacks, investment fund flows, the volumes of initial public offerings, and secondary share issuance.

The country or geographic allocation decision itself can be based on both top-down macroeconomic and bottom-up fundamental analysis. For example, just as economic data for a given country are available, the market valuation of a country can be calculated by aggregating all company earnings and market capitalization.

Sector and Industry Rotation

Just as one can formulate a strategy that allocates to different countries or regions in an investment universe, one can also have a view on the expected returns of various sectors and industries across borders. Industries that are more integrated on a global basis—and therefore subject to global supply and demand dynamics—are more suitable to global sector allocation decisions. Examples of such industries include information technology and energy. On the other hand, sectors and industries that are more local in nature to individual countries are more suitable to sector allocation within a country. Examples of these industries are real estate and consumer staples. The availability of sector and industry ETFs greatly facilitates the implementation of sector and industry rotation strategies for those portfolio managers who cannot or do not wish to implement such strategies by investing in individual stocks.

As with country and geographic allocation, both top-down macroeconomic and bottom-up fundamental variables can be used to predict sector/industry returns. Many bottom-up portfolio managers also add a top-down sector overlay to their portfolios.

Volatility-Based Strategies

Another category of top-down equity strategies is based on investors' view on volatility and is usually implemented using derivative instruments. Those managers who believe they have the skill to predict future market volatility better than option-implied volatility (reflected, for example, in the VIX Index) can trade the VIX futures listed on the CBOE Futures Exchange (CFE), trade instruments such as index options, or enter into volatility swaps (or variance swaps).

Let's assume that an investor predicts a major market move, not anticipated by others, in the near term. The investor does not have an opinion on the direction of the move and only expects the index volatility to be high. The investor can use an index straddle strategy to capitalize on his or her view. Entering into an index straddle position involves the purchase of call and put options (on the same underlying index) with the same strike price and expiry date. The success of this long straddle strategy depends on whether or not volatility turns out to be higher than anticipated by the market; the strategy incurs losses when the market stays broadly flat. Exhibit 4 shows the payoff of such an index straddle strategy. The maximum loss of the long straddle is limited to the total call and put premiums paid.

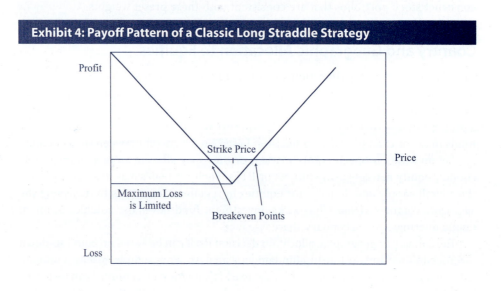

Exhibit 4: Payoff Pattern of a Classic Long Straddle Strategy

Thematic Investment Strategies

Thematic investing is another broad category of strategies. Thematic strategies can use broad macroeconomic, demographic, or political drivers, or bottom-up ideas on industries and sectors, to identify investment opportunities. Disruptive technologies, processes, and regulations; innovations; and economic cycles present investment opportunities and also pose challenges to existing companies. Investors constantly search for new and promising ideas or themes that will drive the market in the future.

It is also important to determine whether any new trend is structural (and hence long-term) or short-term in nature. Structural changes can have long-lasting impacts on the way people behave or a market operates. For example, the development of smartphones and tablets and the move towards cloud computing are probably structural changes. On the other hand, a manager might attempt to identify companies with significant sales exposure to foreign countries as a way to benefit from short-term views on currency movements. The success of a structural thematic investment depends equally on the ability to take advantage of future trends and the ability to avoid what will turn out to be merely fashionable for a limited time, unless the strategy specifically focuses on short-term trends. Further examples of thematic investment drivers include new technologies, mobile communication and computing devices, clean energy, fintech, and advances in medicine.

IMPLEMENTATION OF TOP-DOWN INVESTMENT STRATEGIES

A global equity portfolio manager with special insights into particular countries or regions can tactically choose to overweight or underweight those countries or regions on a short-term basis. Once the country or region weights are determined by a top-down process, the portfolio can be constructed by selecting stocks in the relevant countries or regions.

A portfolio manager with expertise in identifying drivers of sector or industry returns will establish a view on those drivers and will set weights for those sectors in a portfolio. For example, the performance of the energy sector is typically driven by the price of crude oil. The returns of the materials sector rest on forecasts for commodity prices. The consumer and industrials sectors require in-depth knowledge of the customer–supplier chains and a range of other dynamics. Once a view is established on the return and risk of each sector, a manager can then decide which industries to invest in and what weightings to assign to those industries relative to the benchmark.

The significant growth of passive factor investing—sometimes marketed as "smart beta" products—has given portfolio managers more tools and flexibility for investing in different equity styles. Smart beta investment portfolios offer the benefits of passive strategies combined with some of the advantages of active ones. One can exploit the fact, for example, that high-quality stocks tend to perform well in recessions, or that cyclical deep-value companies are more likely to deliver superior returns in a more "risk-on" environment, in which the market becomes less risk-averse. For example, where the investment mandate permits, top-down managers can choose among different equity style ETFs and structured products to obtain risk exposures that are consistent with their views on different stages of the economic cycle or their views on market sentiment.

PORTFOLIO OVERLAYS

Bottom-up fundamental strategies often lead to unintended macro (e.g., sector or country) risk exposures. However, bottom-up fundamental investors can incorporate some of the risk control benefits of top-down investment strategies via portfolio overlays. (A **portfolio overlay** is an array of derivative positions managed separately from the securities portfolio to achieve overall portfolio characteristics that are desired by the portfolio manager.) The fundamental investor's sector weights, for example, may vary from the benchmark's weights as a result of the stock selection process even though the investor did not intend to make sector bets. In that case, the investor may be able to adjust the sector weights to align with the benchmark's weights via long and short positions in derivatives. In this way, top-down strategies can be effective in controlling risk exposures. Overlays can also be used to attempt to add active returns that are not correlated with those generated by the underlying portfolio strategy.

5. FACTOR-BASED STRATEGIES: OVERVIEW

☐ analyze factor-based active strategies, including their rationale and associated processes

A factor is a variable or characteristic with which individual asset returns are correlated. It can be broadly defined as any variable that is believed to be valuable in ranking stocks for investment and in predicting future returns or risks. A wide range of security characteristics have been used to define "factors." Some factors (most commonly, size, value, momentum, and quality) have been shown to be positively associated with a long-term return premium and are often referred to as *rewarded* factors. In fact, hundreds of factors have been identified and used in portfolio construction, but a large number have not been empirically proven to offer a persistent return premium (some call these *unrewarded* factors).

Broadly defined, a factor-based strategy aims to identify significant factors that can predict future stock returns and to construct a portfolio that tilts towards such factors. Some strategies rely on a single factor, are transparent, and maintain a relatively stable exposure to that factor with regular rebalancing (as is explained in the curriculum reading on passive equity investing). Other strategies rely on a selection of factors. Yet other strategies may attempt to time the exposure to factors, recognizing that factor performance varies over time.

For new factor ideas, analysts and managers of portfolios that use factor strategies often rely on academic research, working papers, in-house research, and external research performed by entities such as investment banks. The following exhibits illustrate how some of the traditional style factors performed in recent decades, showing the varying nature of returns. Exhibit 5 shows the cumulative performance of large-cap versus small-cap US equities, using the S&P 500 and Russell 2000 total return indexes. Exhibit 6 presents the total returns of value (Russell 1000 Value Index) versus growth (Russell 1000 Growth Index) styles. Over the ten years ended 31 October 2021, growth significantly outperformed value in terms of both returns and risk-adjusted returns, measured by the Sharpe ratio (see Exhibit 7).

Equity style rotation strategies, a subcategory of factor investing, are based on the belief that different factors—such as size, value, momentum, and quality—work well during some time periods but less well during other time periods. These strategies use an investment process that allocates to stock baskets representing each of these styles when a particular style is expected to offer a positive excess return compared to the benchmark. While style rotation as a strategy can be used in both fundamental and quantitative investment processes, it is generally more in the domain of quantitative investing. Unlike sector or country allocation, discussed earlier, the classification of securities into style categories is less standardized.

Factor-Based Strategies: Overview

Exhibit 5: Large-Cap vs. Small-Cap Equities

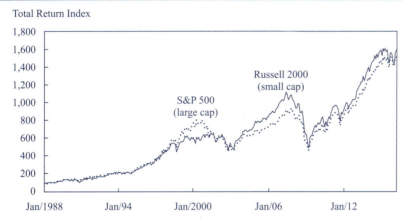

Source: Morningstar Direct, November 2021.

Exhibit 6: Value vs. Growth Equities

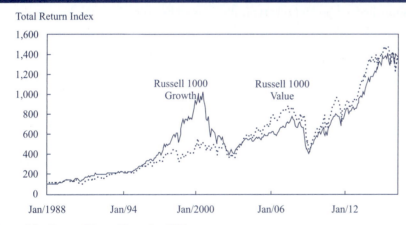

Source: Morningstar Direct, November 2021.

Exhibit 7: Summary Statistics (10 Years Ended 31 October 2021, Total Return Indices)

	S&P 500	Russell 2000	Russell 1000 Value	Russell 1000 Growth
Annual return (%)	16.21	16.47	13.90	29.41
Annual volatility (%)	13.03	24.74	19.98	19.52
Sharpe Ratio	1.18	0.77	0.791	1.30

Source: Morningstar.

The most important test, however, is whether the factor makes intuitive sense. A factor can often pass statistical backtesting, but if it does not make common sense—if justification for the factor's efficacy is lacking—then the manager may be data-mining. Investors should always remember that impressive performance in backtesting does not necessarily imply that the factor will continue to add value in the future.

> An important step is choosing the appropriate investment universe. Practitioners mostly define their investment universe in terms of well-known broad market indexes—for the United States, for example, the S&P 500, Russell 3000, and MSCI World Index. Using a well-defined index has several benefits: Such indexes are free from look-ahead and survivorship biases, the stocks in the indexes are investable with sufficient liquidity, and the indexes are also generally free from foreign ownership restrictions.

The most traditional and widely used method for implementing factor-based portfolios is the hedged portfolio approach, pioneered and formulated by Fama and French (1993). In this approach, after choosing the factor to be scrutinized and ranking the investable stock universe by that factor, investors divide the universe into groups referred to as *quantiles* (typically quintiles or deciles) to form quantile portfolios. Stocks are either equally weighted or capitalization weighted within each quantile. A long/short hedged portfolio is typically formed by going long the best quantile and shorting the worst quantile. The performance of the hedged long/short portfolio is then tracked over time.

There are a few drawbacks to this "hedged portfolio" approach. First, the information contained in the middle quantiles is not utilized, as only the top and bottom quantiles are used in forming the hedged portfolio. Second, it is implicitly assumed that the relationship between the factor and future stock returns is linear (or at least monotonic), which may not be the case.[3] Third, portfolios built using this approach tend to be concentrated, and if many managers use similar factors, the resulting portfolios will be concentrated in specific stocks. Fourth, the hedged portfolio requires managers to short stocks. Shorting may not be possible in some markets and may be overly expensive in others. Fifth, and most important, the hedged portfolio is not a "pure" factor portfolio because it has significant exposures to other risk factors.

Exhibit 8 shows the performance of a factor called "year-over-year change in debt outstanding." The factor is calculated by taking the year-over-year percentage change in the per share long-term debt outstanding on the balance sheet, using all stocks in the Russell 3000 universe. The portfolio is constructed by buying the top 10% of companies that reduce their debt and shorting the bottom 10% of companies that issue the most debt. Stocks in both the long and short portfolios are equally weighted.[4] The bars in the chart indicate the monthly portfolio returns. The average monthly return of the strategy is about 0.22% (or 2.7% per year), and the Sharpe ratio is 0.53 over the test period. All cumulative performance is computed on an initial investment in the factor of $100, with monthly rebalancing and excluding transaction costs.

---

[3] The payoff patterns between factor exposures and future stock returns are becoming increasingly non-linear, especially in the United States and Japan.
[4] Stocks can also be weighted based on their market capitalization.

Factor-Based Strategies: Overview

Exhibit 8: Hedged Portfolio Return, "Year-over-Year Change in Debt Outstanding" Strategy

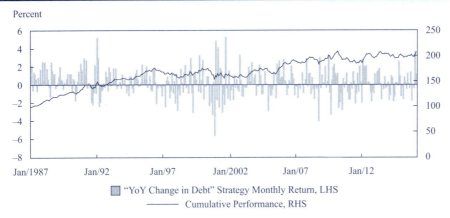

Sources: Compustat, FTSE Russell.

Exhibit 9 shows the average monthly returns of the 10 decile portfolios. It shows that companies with the highest year-over-year increase in debt financing (D10 category) marginally underperform companies with the lowest year-over-year increase in debt financing (average monthly return of 0.6% versus average monthly return of 0.8%). However, it can also be seen that the best-performing companies are the ones with reasonable financial leverage in Deciles 3 to 6. A long/short hedged portfolio approach based on the 1st and 10th deciles (as illustrated in Exhibit 9) would not take advantage of this information, as stocks in these deciles would not be used in such a portfolio. Portfolio managers observing this pattern concerning the different deciles could change the deciles used in the strategy if they believed the pattern would continue into the future.

Exhibit 9: Average Decile Portfolio Return Based on Year-over-Year Change in Debt Outstanding

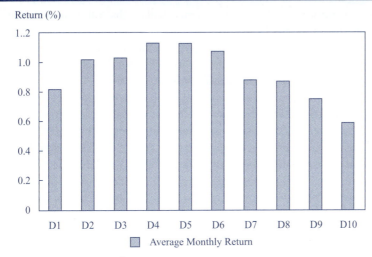

Sources: Compustat, FTSE Russell.

For investors who desire a long-only factor portfolio, a commonly used approach is to construct a factor-tilting portfolio, where a long-only portfolio with exposures to a given factor can be built with controlled tracking error. The factor-tilting portfolio tracks a benchmark index closely but also provides exposures to the chosen factor. In this way, it is similar to an enhanced indexing strategy.

A "factor-mimicking portfolio," or FMP, is a theoretical implementation of a pure factor portfolio. An FMP is a theoretical long/short portfolio that is dollar neutral with a unit exposure to a chosen factor and no exposure to other factors. Because FMPs invest in almost every single stock, entering into long or short positions without taking into account short availability issues or transaction costs, they are very expensive to trade. Managers typically construct the pure factor portfolio by following the FMP theory but adding trading liquidity and short availability constraints.

6. FACTOR-BASED STRATEGIES: STYLE FACTORS

☐ analyze factor-based active strategies, including their rationale and associated processes

Factors are the raw ingredients of quantitative investing and are often referred to as signals. Quantitative managers spend a large amount of time studying factors. Traditionally, factors have been based on fundamental characteristics of underlying companies. However, many investors have recently shifted their attention to unconventional and unstructured data sources in an effort to gain an edge in creating strategies.

Value

Value is based on Graham and Dodd's (1934) concept and can be measured in a number of ways. The academic literature has a long history of documenting the value phenomenon. Basu (1977) found that stocks with low P/E or high earnings yield tend to provide higher returns. Fama and French (1993) formally outlined value investing by proposing the book-to-market ratio as a way to measure value and growth.

Although many academics and practitioners believe that value stocks tend to deliver superior returns, there has been considerable disagreement over the explanation of this effect. Fama and French (1992, 1993, 1996) suggested that the value premium exists to compensate investors for the greater likelihood that these companies will experience financial distress. Lakonishok, Shleifer, and Vishny (1994) cited behavioral arguments, suggesting that the effect is a result of behavioral biases on the part of the typical investor rather than compensation for higher risk.

Value factors can also be based on other fundamental performance metrics of a company, such as dividends, earnings, cash flow, EBIT, EBITDA, and sales. Investors often add two more variations on most value factors by adjusting for industry (and/or country) and historical differences. Most valuation ratios can be computed using either historical (also called *trailing*) or forward metrics. Exhibit 10 shows the performance of the price-to-earnings multiple factor implemented as a long/short decile portfolio.

Exhibit 10: Performance of the P/E Factor (Long/Short Decile Portfolio)

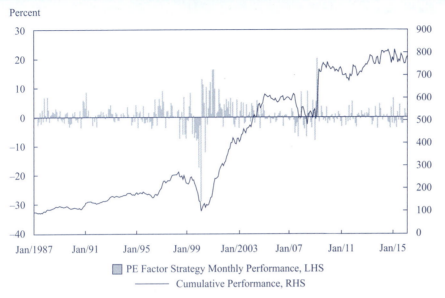

Sources: Compustat, FTSE Russell.

Price Momentum

Researchers have also found a strong price momentum effect in almost all asset classes in most countries. In fact, value and price momentum have long been the two cornerstones of quantitative investing.

Jegadeesh and Titman (1993) first documented that stocks that are "winners" over the previous 12 months tend to outperform past "losers" (those that have done poorly over the previous 12 months) and that such outperformance persists over the following 2 to 12 months. The study focused on the US market during the 1965–1989 period. The authors also found a short-term reversal effect, whereby stocks that have high price momentum in the previous month tend to underperform over the next 2 to 12 months. This price momentum anomaly is commonly attributed to behavioral biases, such as overreaction to information.[5] It is interesting to note that since the academic publication of these findings, the performance of the price momentum factor has become much more volatile (see Exhibit 11). Price momentum is, however, subject to extreme tail risk. Over the three-month March–May 2009 time period, the simple price momentum strategy (as measured by the long/short decile portfolio) lost 56%. For this data period, some reduction in downside risk can be achieved by removing the effect of sector exposure from momentum factor returns: We will call this modified version the "sector-neutralized price momentum factor."[6] The results are shown in Exhibit 12 and Exhibit 13 for US, European, and Japanese markets.

---

5 Behavioral biases are covered in the Level III readings on behavioral finance.
6 The methods for removing sector exposure are beyond the scope of this reading.

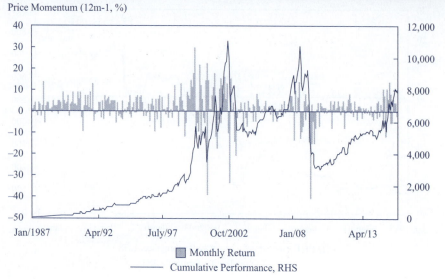

Exhibit 11: Performance of the Price Momentum Factor (Long/Short Decile Portfolio)

Sources: Compustat, FTSE Russell.

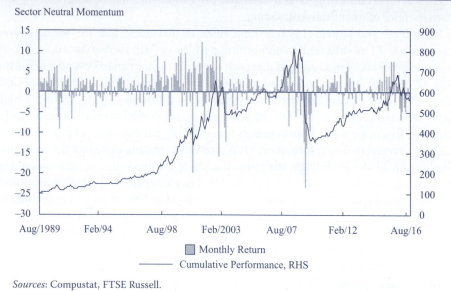

Exhibit 12: Performance of the Sector-Neutralized Price Momentum Factor (Long/Short Decile Portfolio)

Sources: Compustat, FTSE Russell.

Exhibit 13 extends the analysis to include European and Japanese markets, where a similar effect on downside risk can be shown to have been operative over the period.

Factor-Based Strategies: Style Factors

Exhibit 13: Performance of the Sector-Neutralized Price Momentum Factor in US, European, and Japanese Markets (Long/Short Decile Portfolio)

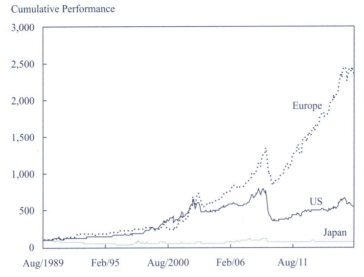

Sources: Compustat, FTSE Russell.

EXAMPLE 4

Factor Investing

A quantitative manager wants to expand his current strategy from US equities into international equity markets. His current strategy uses a price momentum factor. Based on Exhibit 13:

1. State whether momentum has been a factor in European and Japanese equity returns overall in the time period examined.

Solution:

As shown in Exhibit 13, price momentum has performed substantially better in Europe than in the United States. On the other hand, there does not appear to be any meaningful pattern of price momentum in Japan. Exhibit 13 suggests that the price momentum factor could be used for a European portfolio but not for a Japanese portfolio. However, managers need to perform rigorous backtesting before they can confidently implement a factor model in a market that they are not familiar with. Managers should be aware that what appears to be impressive performance in backtests does not necessarily imply that the factor will continue to add value in the future.

2. Discuss the potential reasons why neutralizing sectors reduces downside risk.

Solution:

Using the simple price momentum factor means that a portfolio buys past winners and shorts past losers. The resulting portfolio could have exposure to potentially significant industry bets. Sector-neutral price momentum focuses on stock selection without such risk exposures and thus tends to reduce downside risk.

Growth

Growth is another investment approach used by some style investors. Growth factors aim to measure a company's growth potential and can be calculated using the company's historical growth rates or projected forward growth rates. Growth factors can also be classified as short-term growth (last quarter's, last year's, next quarter's, or next year's growth) and long-term growth (last five years' or next five years' growth). While higher-than-market or higher-than-sector growth is generally considered to be a possible indicator for strong future stock price performance, the growth of some metrics, such as assets, results in weaker future stock price performance.

Exhibit 14 shows the performance of the year-over-year earnings growth factor. The exhibit is based on a strategy that invests in the top 10% of companies with the highest year-over-year growth in earnings per share and shorts all the stocks in the bottom 10%.

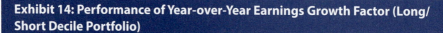
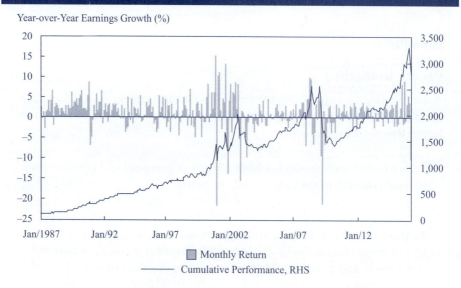

Exhibit 14: Performance of Year-over-Year Earnings Growth Factor (Long/Short Decile Portfolio)

Sources: Compustat, FTSE Russell.

Quality

In addition to using accounting ratios and share price data as fundamental style factors, investors have continued to create more complex factors based on the variety of accounting information available for companies. One of the best-known examples of how in-depth accounting knowledge can impact investment performance is Richard Sloan's (1996) seminal paper on earnings quality, with its proposition of the accruals

Factor-Based Strategies: Style Factors

factor. Sloan suggests that stock prices fail to reflect fully the information contained in the accrual and cash flow components of current earnings.[7] The performance of the accruals anomaly factor, however, appears to be quite cyclical.

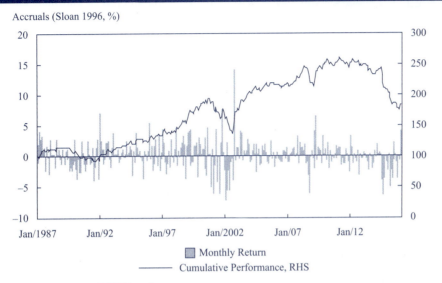

Exhibit 15: Performance of Earnings Quality Factor

Sources: Compustat, FTSE Russell.

In addition to the accruals anomaly, there are many other potential factors based on a company's fundamental data, such as profitability, balance sheet and solvency risk, earnings quality, stability, sustainability of dividend payout, capital utilization, and management efficiency measures. Yet another, analyst sentiment, refers to the phenomenon of sell-side analysts revising their forecasts of corporate earnings estimates, which is called *earnings revision*. More recently, with the availability of more data, analysts have started to include cash flow revisions, sales revisions, ROE revisions, sell-side analyst stock recommendations, and target price changes as variables in the "analyst sentiment" category.

A new and exciting area of research involves news sentiment. Rather than just relying on the output of sell-side analysts, investors could use natural language processing (NLP) algorithms to analyze the large volume of news stories and quantify the news sentiment on stocks.

---

[7] Sloan (1996) argues that in the long term, cash flows from operations and net income (under accruals-based accounting) should converge and be consistent. In the short term, they could diverge. Management has more discretion in accruals-based accounting; therefore, the temporary divergence between cash flows and net income reflects how conservative a company chooses to be in reporting its net income.

7 FACTOR-BASED STRATEGIES: UNCONVENTIONAL FACTORS

> analyze factor-based active strategies, including their rationale and associated processes

With the rapid growth in technology and computational algorithms, investors have been embracing big data. "Big data" is a broad term referring to extremely large datasets that may include structured data—such as traditional financial statements and market data—as well as unstructured or "alternative" data that has previously not been widely used in the investment industry because it lacks recognizable structure. Examples of such alternative data include satellite images, textual information, credit card payment information, and the number of online mentions of a particular product or brand.

EXAMPLE 5

Researching Factor Timing

An analyst is exploring the relationship between interest rates and style factor returns for the purpose of developing equity style rotation strategies for the US equity market. The analysis takes place in early 2017. The first problem the analyst addresses is how to model the interest rate variable. The data in Exhibit 16 show an apparent trend of declining US government bond yields over the last 30 years. Trends may or may not continue into the future. The analyst decides to normalize the yield data so that they do not incorporate a prediction on continuation of the trend and makes a simple transformation by subtracting the yield's own 12-month moving average:

$$\text{Normalized yield}_t = \text{Nominal yield}_t - \frac{1}{12}\sum_{\tau=1}^{12}\text{Nominal yield}_{t-\tau+1}$$

The normalized yield data are shown in Exhibit 17. Yields calculated are as of the beginning of the month. Do the fluctuations in yield have any relationship with style factor returns? The analyst explores possible contemporaneous (current) and lagged relationships by performing two regressions (using the current month's and the next month's factor returns, respectively) against the normalized long-term bond yield:

$$f_{i,t} = \beta_{i,0} + \beta_{i,1}\text{Normalized yield}_t + \varepsilon_{i,t}$$

and

$$f_{i,t+1} = \beta_{i,0} + \beta_{i,1}\text{Normalized yield}_t + \varepsilon_{i,t}$$

where $f_{i,t}$ is the return of style factor i at time t and $f_{i,t+1}$ is the subsequent (next) month's return to style factor i. The first regression reveals the contemporaneous relationship between interest rate and factor performance—that is, how well the current interest rate relates to the current factor performance. The second equation states whether the current interest rate can predict the next month's factor return. Exhibit 18 shows the findings.

Factor-Based Strategies: Unconventional Factors

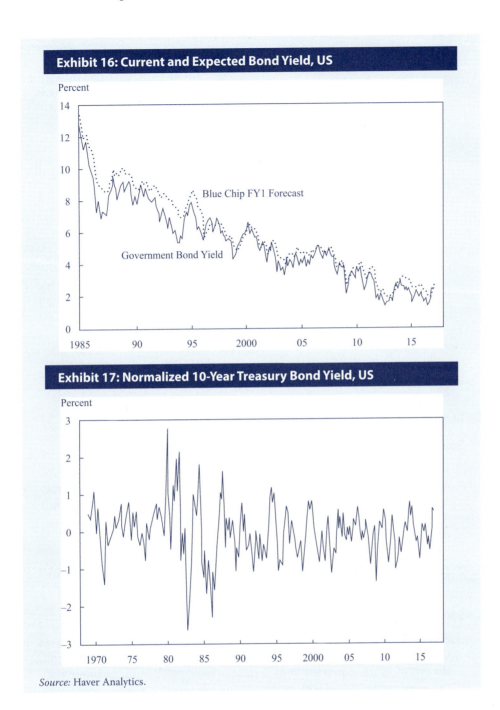

Exhibit 16: Current and Expected Bond Yield, US

Exhibit 17: Normalized 10-Year Treasury Bond Yield, US

Source: Haver Analytics.

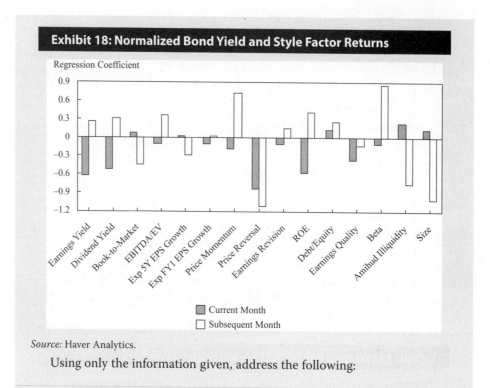

Source: Haver Analytics.

Using only the information given, address the following:

1. Interpret Exhibit 18.

Solution:

Exhibit 18 suggests an inverse relationship between concurrent bond yields and returns to the dividend yield, price reversal, and ROE factors. For some factors (such as earnings quality), the relationship between bond yields and forward (next month's) factor returns is in the same direction as the contemporaneous relationship.

2. Discuss the relevance of contemporaneous and forward relationships in an equity factor rotation strategy.

Solution:

Attention needs to be given to the timing relationship of variables to address this question. A contemporaneous style factor return becomes known as of the end of the month. If the known value of bond yields at the beginning of the month is correlated with factor returns, the investor may be able to gain some edge relative to investors who do not use that information. The same conclusion holds concerning the forward relationship. If the contemporaneous variable were defined so that it is realized at the same time as the variable we want to predict, the forward but not the contemporaneous variable would be relevant.

3. What concerns could the analyst have in relation to an equity factor rotation strategy, and what possible next steps could the analyst take to address those concerns?

Solution:

The major concern is the validity of the relationships between normalized interest rates and the style variables. Among the steps the analyst can take to increase his or her conviction in the relationships' validity are the following:

- Establish whether the relationships have predictive value out of sample (that is, based on data not used to model the relationship).
- Investigate whether or not there are economic rationales for the relationships such that those relationships could be expected to persist into the future.

Exhibit 18 shows both weak relationships (e.g., for earnings revision) and strong relationships (e.g., for size and beta) in relation to the subsequent month's returns. This fact suggests some priorities in examining this question.

ACTIVIST STRATEGIES

analyze activist strategies, including their rationale and associated processes

Activist investors specialize in taking stakes in listed companies and advocating changes for the purpose of producing a gain on the investment. The investor may wish to obtain representation on the company's board of directors or use other measures in an effort to initiate strategic, operational, or financial structure changes. In some cases, activist investors may support activities such as asset sales, cost-cutting measures, changes to management, changes to the capital structure, dividend increases, or share buybacks. Activists—including hedge funds, public pension funds, private investors, and others—vary greatly in their approaches, expertise, and investment horizons. They may also seek different outcomes. What they have in common is that they advocate for change in their target companies.

Shareholder activism typically follows a period of screening and analysis of opportunities in the market. The investor usually reviews a number of companies based on a range of parameters and carries out in-depth analysis of the business and the opportunities for unlocking value. Activism itself starts when an investor buys an equity stake in the company and starts advocating for change (i.e., pursuing an activist campaign). These equity stakes are generally made public. Stakes above a certain threshold must be made public in most jurisdictions. Exhibit 19 shows a typical activist investing process. The goal of activist investing could be either financial gain (increased shareholder value) or a non-financial cause (e.g., environmental, social, and governance issues). Rather than pursuing a full takeover bid, activist investors aim to achieve their goals with smaller stakes, typically of less than 10%. Activist investors' time horizon is often shorter than that of buy-and-hold investors, but the whole process can last for a number of years.

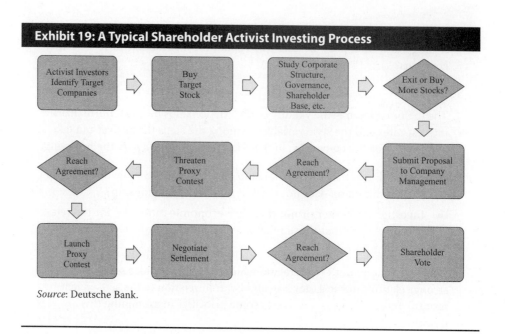

The Popularity of Shareholder Activism

Shareholder (or investor) activism is by no means a new investment strategy. Its foundations go back to the 1970s and 1980s, when investors known as corporate raiders took substantial stakes in companies in order to influence their operations, unlock value in the target companies, and thereby raise the value of their shares. Proponents of activism argue that it is an important and necessary activity that helps monitor and discipline corporate management to the benefit of all shareholders. Opponents argue that such interventionist tactics can cause distraction and negatively impact management performance.

Activist hedge funds—among the most prominent activist investors—saw growing popularity for a number of years, with assets under management (AUM) reaching $50 billion in 2007[8] before falling sharply during the global financial crisis. Activist hedge fund investing has since strongly recovered, with AUM close to $46 billion in 2018.[9] The activity of such investors can be tracked by following the activists' announcements that they are launching a campaign seeking to influence companies. Exhibit 20 shows various activist events reported by the industry. Hedge funds that specialize in activism benefit from lighter regulation than other types of funds, and their fee structure, offering greater rewards, justifies concerted campaigns for change at the companies they hold. The popularity and viability of investor activism are influenced by the legal frameworks in different jurisdictions, shareholder structures, and cultural considerations. The United States has seen the greatest amount of activist activity initiated by hedge funds, individuals, and pension funds, but there have been a number of activist events in Europe too. Other regions have so far seen more limited activity on the part of activist investors. Cultural reasons and more concentrated shareholder ownership of companies are two frequently cited explanations.

---

8 Hedge Fund Research.
9 See "Activist Funds: An Investor Calls," *Economist* (7 February 2015).

Activist Strategies

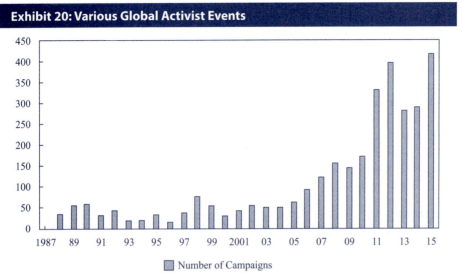

Exhibit 20: Various Global Activist Events

Source: Thomson Reuters Activism database.

Tactics Used by Activist Investors

Activists use a range of tactics on target companies in order to boost shareholder value. These tactics include the following:

- Seeking board representation and nominations
- Engaging with management by writing letters to management calling for and explaining suggested changes, participating in management discussions with analysts or meeting the management team privately, or launching proxy contests whereby activists encourage other shareholders to use their proxy votes to effect change in the organization
- Proposing significant corporate changes during the annual general meeting (AGM)
- Proposing restructuring of the balance sheet to better utilize capital and potentially initiate share buybacks or increase dividends
- Reducing management compensation or realigning management compensation with share price performance
- Launching legal proceedings against existing management for breach of fiduciary duties
- Reaching out to other shareholders of the company to coordinate action
- Launching a media campaign against existing management practices
- Breaking up a large conglomerate to unlock value

The effectiveness of shareholder activism depends on the response of the existing management team and the tools at that team's disposal. In many countries, defense mechanisms can be employed by management or a dominant shareholder to hinder activist intervention. These techniques include multi-class share structures whereby a company founder's shares are typically entitled to multiple votes per share; "poison pill" plans allowing the issuance of shares at a deep discount, which causes significant economic and voting dilution; staggered board provisions whereby a portion of the board members are not elected at annual shareholders meetings and hence cannot all be replaced simultaneously; and charter and bylaw provisions and amendments.

Typical Activist Targets

Activist investors look for specific characteristics in deciding which companies to target. Exhibit 21 shows the steps of identifying an activist investment target company.[10] Target companies feature slower revenue and earnings growth than the market, suffer negative share price momentum, and have weaker-than-average corporate governance.[11] By building stakes and initiating change in underperforming companies, activists hope to unlock value. In addition, by targeting such companies, activist investors are more likely to win support for their actions from other shareholders and the wider public. Traditionally, the target companies have been small and medium-sized listed stocks. This has changed as a number of larger companies have become subject to activism.[12]

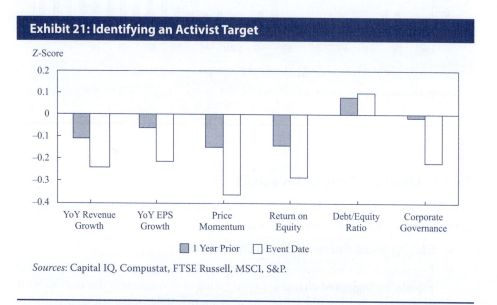

Exhibit 21: Identifying an Activist Target

Sources: Capital IQ, Compustat, FTSE Russell, MSCI, S&P.

DO ACTIVISTS REALLY IMPROVE COMPANY PERFORMANCE?

On average, fundamental characteristics of targeted companies do improve in subsequent years following activists' efforts, with evidence that revenue and earnings growth increase, profitability improves, and corporate governance indicators become more robust. There is evidence, however, that the financial leverage of such companies increases significantly.

DO ACTIVIST INVESTORS GENERATE ALPHA?

Activist hedge funds are among the major activist investors. Based on the HFRX Activist Index, in the aggregate, activist hedge funds have delivered an average annual return of 7.7% with annual volatility of 13.7% and therefore a Sharpe

---

10 The fundamental characteristics of all companies in the investment universe (i.e., the Russell 3000) are standardized using z-scores (by subtracting the mean and dividing by the standard deviation) every month from 1988 until 2015. Thus, we can compare the average exposure to each fundamental characteristic over time.
11 We normalize all target and non-target companies' factor exposures using z-scores (i.e., subtracting the sample mean and dividing by the sample standard deviation).
12 Trian Fund Management proposed splitting PepsiCo into standalone public companies; Third Point called for leadership change at Yahoo!.

ratio of 0.56—slightly higher than the Sharpe ratio of the S&P 500 Index of 0.54 (see Exhibit 22). However, it is difficult to conclude how much value activist investors add because the HFRX index does not include a large enough number of managers. Furthermore, managers themselves vary in their approaches and the risks they take.

Exhibit 22: Performance of HFRX Activist Index vs. S&P 500

Sources: Hedge Fund Research, S&P.

HOW DOES THE MARKET REACT TO ACTIVIST EVENTS?

Investors have generally reacted positively to activism announcements: On average, target company stocks go up by 2% on the announcement day (based on all activist events in the Thomson Reuters Corporate Governance Intelligence database during a discrete 30-year period).[13] Interestingly, the positive reaction comes on top of stock appreciation prior to activism announcements (see Exhibit 23). According to the model of Maug (1998), activist investors trade in a stock prior to the announcement to build up a stake, assert control, and profit from the value creation. It may also be argued that there must be information leakage about the activists' involvement, driving the stock higher even before the first public announcement. There is a modest post-announcement drift: In the month after the activist announcement date, target share prices move up by 0.6%, on average, relative to the market.

---

[13] All returns are excess returns, adjusted for the market and sector. For details, see Jussa, Webster, Zhao, and Luo (2016).

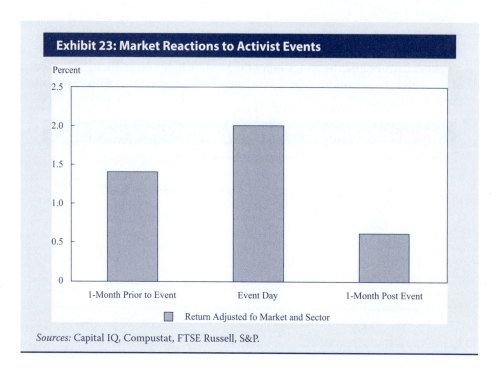

Exhibit 23: Market Reactions to Activist Events

Sources: Capital IQ, Compustat, FTSE Russell, S&P.

EXAMPLE 6

Activist Investing

1. Kendra Cho is an analyst at an investment firm that specializes in activist investing and manages a concentrated portfolio of stocks invested in listed European companies. Cho and her colleagues hope to identify and buy stakes in companies with the potential to increase their value through strategic, operational, or financial change. Cho is considering the following three companies:

   - Company A is a well-established, medium-sized food producer. Its profitability, measured by operating margins and return on assets, is ahead of industry peers. The company is recognised for its high corporate governance standards and effective communication with existing and potential investors. Cho's firm has invested in companies in this sector in the past and made gains on those positions.

   - Company B is a medium-sized engineering business that has experienced a significant deterioration in profitability in recent years. More recently, the company has been unable to pay interest on its debt, and its new management team has recognized the need to restructure the business and negotiate with its creditors. Due to the company's losses, Cho cannot use earnings-based price multiples to assess upside potential, but based on sales and asset multiples, she believes there is significant upside potential in the stock if the company's current difficulties can be overcome and the debt can be restructured.

   - Company C is also a medium-sized engineering business, but its operating performance, particularly when measured by the return on assets, is below that of the rest of the industry. Cho has identified a number of company assets that are underutilised. She believes that the management has significant potential to reduce fixed-asset investments, concentrate production in fewer facilities, and dispose of

> assets, in line with what the company's peers have been doing. Such steps could improve asset turnover and make it possible to return capital to shareholders through special dividends.
>
> Identify the company that is most appropriate for Cho to recommend to the fund managers:
>
> **Solution:**
>
> Company C is the most appropriate choice. The company offers upside potential because of its ability to improve operating performance and cash payout using asset disposals, a strategy being implemented by other companies in its sector. Neither Company A nor Company B offers an attractive opportunity for activist investing: Company A is already operating efficiently, while Company B is more suitable for investors that focus on restructuring and distressed investing.

OTHER ACTIVE STRATEGIES

☐ describe active strategies based on statistical arbitrage and market microstructure

There are many other strategies that active portfolio managers employ in an attempt to beat the market benchmark. In this section, we explain two other categories of active strategies that do not fit neatly into our previous categorizations—namely, statistical arbitrage and event-driven strategies. Both rely on extensive use of quantitative data and are usually implemented in a systematic, rules-based way but can also incorporate the fund manager's judgment in making investment decisions.

Strategies Based on Statistical Arbitrage and Market Microstructure

Statistical arbitrage (or "stat arb") strategies use statistical and technical analysis to exploit pricing anomalies. Statistical arbitrage makes extensive use of data such as stock price, dividend, trading volume, and the limit order book for this purpose. The analytical tools used include (1) traditional technical analysis, (2) sophisticated time-series analysis and econometric models, and (3) machine-learning techniques. Portfolio managers typically take advantage of either mean reversion in share prices or opportunities created by market microstructure issues.

Pairs trading is an example of a popular and simple statistical arbitrage strategy. Pairs trading uses statistical techniques to identify two securities that are historically highly correlated with each other. When the price relationship of these two securities deviates from its long-term average, managers that expect the deviation to be temporary go long the underperforming stock and simultaneously short the outperforming stock. If the prices do converge to the long-term average as forecast, the investors close the trade and realize a profit. This kind of pairs trading therefore bets on a mean-reversion pattern in stock prices. The biggest risk in pairs trading and most other mean-reversion strategies is that the observed price divergence is not temporary; rather, it might be due to structural reasons.[14] Because risk management is critical for the success of such strategies, investors often employ stop-loss rules to exit trades when a loss limit is reached.

The most difficult aspect of a pairs-trading strategy is the identification of the pairs of stocks. This can be done either by using a quantitative approach and creating models of stock prices or by using a fundamental approach to judge the two stocks whose prices should move together for qualitative reasons.

Consider Canadian National Railway (CNR) and Canadian Pacific Railway (CP). These are the two dominant railways in Canada. Their business models are fairly similar, as both operate railway networks and transport goods throughout the country. Exhibit 24 shows that the prices of the two stocks have been highly correlated.[15] The y-axis shows the log price differential, referred to as the spread.[16] The exhibit also shows the moving average of the spread computed on a rolling 130-day window and bands at two standard deviations above and two standard deviations below the moving average. A simple pairs-trading strategy would be to enter into a trade when the spread is more than (or less than) two standard deviations from the moving average. The trade would be closed when the spread reaches the moving average again. Exhibit 24 shows the three trades based on our decision rules. The first trade was opened on 2 October 2014, when the spread between CNR and CP crossed the −2 standard deviation mark.[17] This trade was closed on 18 November 2014, when the spread reached the moving average. The first trade was profitable, and the position was maintained for slightly more than a month. The second trade was also profitable but lasted much longer. After the third trade was entered on 21 July 2015, however, there was a structural break, in that CP's decline further intensified while CNR stayed relatively flat; therefore, the spread continued to narrow. The loss on the third trade could have been significantly greater than the profits made from the first two transactions if the positions had been closed prior to mean reversion in the spring of 2016. This example highlights the risk inherent in mean-reversion strategies.

---

14 For example, the outperformance of one stock might be due to the fact that the company has developed a new technology or product that cannot be easily replicated by competitors.
15 The correlation coefficient between the two stocks was 69% based on daily returns from 2 January 2014 to 26 May 2016.
16 ln(Price of CNR/Price of CP).
17 The position is long CNR and short CP.

Other Active Strategies

Exhibit 24: Pairs Trade between CNR and CP

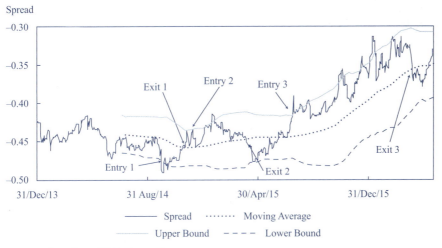

Sources: Bloomberg, Wolfe Research

In the United States, many market microstructure–based arbitrage strategies take advantage of the NYSE Trade and Quote (TAQ) database and often involve extensive analysis of the limit order book to identify very short-term mispricing opportunities. For example, a temporary imbalance between buy and sell orders may trigger a spike in share price that lasts for only a few milliseconds. Only those investors with the analytical tools and trading capabilities for high-frequency trading are in a position to capture such opportunities, usually within a portfolio of many stocks designed to take advantage of very short-term discrepancies.

EXAMPLE 7

An analyst is asked to recommend a pair of stocks to be added to a statistical arbitrage fund. She considers the following three pairs of stocks:

- Pair 1 consists of two food-producing companies. Both are mature companies with comparable future earnings prospects. Both typically trade on similar valuation multiples. The ratio of their share prices shows mean reversion over the last two decades. The ratio is currently more than one standard deviation above its moving average.

- Pair 2 consists of two consumer stocks: One is a food retailer, and the other is a car manufacturer. Although the two companies operate in different markets and have different business models, statistical analysis performed by the analyst shows strong correlation between their share prices that has persisted for more than a decade. The stock prices have moved significantly in opposite directions in recent days. The analyst, expecting mean reversion, believes this discrepancy represents an investment opportunity.

- Pair 3 consists of two well-established financial services companies with a traditional focus on retail banking. One of the companies recently saw the arrival of a new management team and an increase in acquisition activity in corporate and investment banking—both new business areas for the company. The share price fell sharply on news of these changes. The price ratio of the two banks now deviates significantly from the moving average.

> 1. Based on the information provided, select the pair that would be most suitable for the fund.
>
> **Solution:**
>
> Pair 1 is the most suitable for the fund. The companies' share prices have been correlated in the past, with the share price ratio reverting to the moving average. They have similar businesses, and there is no indication of a change in either company's strategies, as there is for Pair 3. By contrast with the price ratio for Pair 1, the past correlation of share prices for Pair 2 may have been spurious and is not described as exhibiting mean reversion.

Event-Driven Strategies

Event-driven strategies exploit market inefficiencies that may occur around corporate events such as mergers and acquisitions, earnings or restructuring announcements, share buybacks, special dividends, and spinoffs.

Risk arbitrage associated with merger and acquisition (M&A) activity is one of the most common examples of an event-driven strategy.

In a cash-only transaction, the acquirer proposes to purchase the shares of the target company for a given price. The stock price of the target company typically remains below the offered price until the transaction is completed. Therefore, an arbitrageur could buy the stock of the target company and earn a profit if and when the acquisition closes.

In a share-for-share exchange transaction, the acquirer uses its own shares to purchase the target company at a given exchange ratio. A risk arbitrage trader normally purchases the target share and simultaneously short-sells the acquirer's stock at the same exchange ratio. Once the acquisition is closed, the arbitrageur uses his or her long positions in the target company to exchange for the acquirer's stocks, which are further used to cover the arbitrageur's short positions.

The first challenge in managing risk arbitrage positions is to accurately estimate the risk of the deal failing. An M&A transaction, for example, may not go through for numerous reasons. A regulator may block the deal because of antitrust concerns, or the acquirer may not be able to secure the approval from the target company's shareholders. If a deal fails, the price of the target stock typically falls sharply, generating significant loss for the arbitrageur. Hence, this strategy has the label "risk arbitrage."

Another important consideration that an arbitrageur has to take into account is the deal duration. At any given point in time, there are many M&A transactions outstanding, and the arbitrageur has to decide which ones to participate in and how to weight each position, based on the predicted premium and risk. The predicted premium has to be annualized to enable the arbitrageur to compare different opportunities. Therefore, estimating deal duration is important for accurately estimating the deal premium.

10. CREATING A FUNDAMENTAL ACTIVE INVESTMENT STRATEGY

☐ describe how fundamental active investment strategies are created

Fundamental (or discretionary) investing remains one of the prevailing philosophies of active management. In the following sections, we discuss how fundamental investors organize their investment processes.

The Fundamental Active Investment Process

The broad goal of active management is to outperform a selected benchmark on a risk-adjusted basis, net of fees and transaction costs. Value can be added at different stages of the investment process. For example, added value may come from the use of proprietary data, from special skill in security analysis and valuation, or from insight into industry/sector allocation.

Many fundamental investors use processes that include the following steps:

1. Define the investment universe and the market opportunity—the perceived opportunity to earn a positive risk-adjusted return to active investing, net of costs—in accordance with the investment mandate. The market opportunity is also known as the investment thesis.

2. Prescreen the investment universe to obtain a manageable set of securities for further, more detailed analysis.

3. Understand the industry and business for this screened set by performing:

    - industry and competitive analysis and
    - analysis of financial reports.

4. Forecast company performance, most commonly in terms of cash flows or earnings.

5. Convert forecasts to valuations and identify *ex ante* profitable investments.

6. Construct a portfolio of these investments with the desired risk profile.

7. Rebalance the portfolio with buy and sell disciplines.

The investment universe is mainly determined by the mandate agreed on by the fund manager and the client. The mandate defines the market segments, regions, and/or countries in which the manager will seek to add value. For example, if an investment mandate specifies Hong Kong's Hang Seng Index as the performance benchmark, the manager's investment universe will be primarily restricted to the 50 stocks in that index. However, an active manager may also include non-index stocks that trade on the same exchange or whose business activities significantly relate to this region. It is important for investors who seek to hold a diversified and well-constructed portfolio to understand the markets in which components of the portfolio will be invested. In addition, a clear picture of the market opportunity to earn positive active returns is important for active equity investment. The basic question is, what is the opportunity and why is it there? The answer to this two-part question can be called the investment thesis. The "why" part involves understanding the economic, financial, behavioral, or other rationale for a strategy's profitability in the future.

Practically, the investment thesis will suggest a set of characteristics that tend to be associated with potentially profitable investments. The investor may prescreen the investment universe with quantitative and/or qualitative criteria to obtain a manageable subset that will be analyzed in greater detail. Prescreening criteria can often be associated with a particular investment style. A value style manager, for example, may first exclude those stocks with high P/E multiples and high debt-to-equity ratios. Growth style managers may first rule out stocks that do not have high enough historical or forecast EPS growth. Steps 3 to 5 cover processes of in-depth analysis described in the Level II CFA Program readings on industry and company analysis and equity valuation. Finally, a portfolio is constructed in which stocks that have high upside potential are overweighted relative to the benchmark and stocks that are expected to underperform the benchmark are underweighted, not held at all, or (where relevant) shorted.[18]

As part of the portfolio construction process (step 6), the portfolio manager needs to decide whether to take active exposures to particular industry groups or economic sectors or to remain sector neutral relative to the benchmark. Portfolio managers may have top-down views on the business trends in some industries. For example, innovations in medical technology may cause an increase in earnings in the health care sector as a whole, while a potential central bank interest rate hike may increase the profitability of the banking sector. With these views, assuming the changed circumstances are not already priced in by the market, a manager could add extra value to the portfolio by overweighting the health care and financial services sectors. If the manager doesn't have views on individual sectors, he or she should, in theory, establish a neutral industry position relative to the benchmark in constructing the portfolio. However, a manager who has very strong convictions on the individual names in a specific industry may still want to overweight the industry that those names belong to. The potential high excess return from overweighting individual stocks can justify the risk the portfolio takes on the active exposure to that industry.

In addition to the regular portfolio rebalancing that ensures that the investment mandate and the desired risk exposures are maintained, a stock sell discipline needs to be incorporated into the investment process. The stock sell discipline will enable the portfolio to take profit from a successful investment and to exit from an unsuccessful investment at a prudent time.

In fundamental analysis, each stock is typically assigned a target price that the analyst believes to be the fair market value of the stock. The stock will be reclassified from undervalued to overvalued if the stock price surpasses this target price. Once this happens, the upside of the stock is expected to be limited, and holding that stock may not be justified, given the potential downside risk. The sell discipline embedded within an investment process requires the portfolio manager to sell the stock at this point. In practice, recognizing that valuation is an imprecise exercise, managers may continue to hold the stock or may simply reduce the size of the position rather than sell outright. This flexibility is particularly relevant when, in relative valuation frameworks where the company is being valued against a peer group, the valuations of industry peers are also changing. The target price of a stock need not be a constant but can be updated by the analyst with the arrival of new information. Adjusting the target price downward until it is lower than the current market price would also trigger a sale or a reduction in the position size.

Other situations could arise in which a stock's price has fallen and continues to fall for what the analyst considers to be poorly understood reasons. If the analyst remains positive on the stock, he or she should carefully consider the rationale for maintaining the position; if the company fundamentals indeed worsened, the analyst must also consider his or her own possible behavioral biases. The portfolio manager needs to have the discipline to take a loss by selling the stock if, for example, the price touches some pre-defined stop-loss trigger point. The stop-loss point is intended to set the maximum loss for each asset, under any conditions, and limit such behavioral biases.

---

18 A portfolio that is benchmarked against an index that contains hundreds or thousands of constituents will most likely have zero weighting in most of them.

Creating a Fundamental Active Investment Strategy

EXAMPLE 8

Fundamental Investing

1. A portfolio manager uses the following criteria to prescreen his investment universe:

    1. The year-over-year growth rate in earnings per share from continuing operations has increased over each of the last four fiscal years.
    2. Growth in earnings per share from continuing operations over the last 12 months has been positive.
    3. The percentage difference between the actual announced earnings and the consensus earnings estimate for the most recent quarter is greater than or equal to 10%.
    4. The percentage change in stock price over the last four weeks is positive.
    5. The 26-week relative price strength is greater than or equal to the industry's 26-week relative price strength.
    6. The average daily volume for the last 10 days is in the top 50% of the market.

    Describe the manager's investment mandate.

Solution:

The portfolio manager has a growth orientation with a focus on companies that have delivered EPS growth in recent years and that have maintained their earnings and price growth momentum. Criterion 1 specifies accelerating EPS growth rates over recent fiscal years, while criterion 2 discards companies for which recent earnings growth has been negative. Criterion 3 further screens for companies that have beaten consensus earnings expectations—have had a positive earnings surprise—in the most recent quarter. A positive earnings surprise suggests that past earnings growth is continuing. Criteria 4 and 5 screen for positive recent stock price momentum. Criterion 6 retains only stocks with at least average market liquidity. Note the absence of any valuation multiples among the screening criteria: A value investor's screening criteria would typically include a rule to screen out issues that are expensively valued relative to earnings or assets.

Pitfalls in Fundamental Investing

Pitfalls in fundamental investing include behavioral biases, the value trap, and the growth trap.

Behavioral Bias

Fundamental, discretionary investing in general and stock selection in particular depend on subjective judgments by portfolio managers based on their research and analysis. However, human judgment, though potentially more insightful than a purely quantitative method, can be less rational and is often susceptible to human biases. The CFA Program curriculum readings on behavioral finance divide behavioral biases into two broad groups: cognitive errors and emotional biases. Cognitive errors are basic statistical, information-processing, or memory errors that cause a decision to deviate from the rational decisions of traditional finance, while emotional biases arise spontaneously as a result of attitudes and feelings that can cause a decision to deviate from the rational decisions of traditional finance. Several biases that are relevant to active fundamental equity management are discussed here.

Confirmation Bias

A cognitive error, confirmation bias—sometimes referred to as "stock love bias"—is the tendency of analysts and investors to look for information that confirms their existing beliefs about their favorite companies and to ignore or undervalue any information that contradicts their existing beliefs. This behavior creates selective exposure, perception, and retention and may be thought of as a selection bias. Some of the consequences are a poorly diversified portfolio, excessive risk exposure, and holdings in poorly performing securities. Actively seeking out the opinions of other investors or team members and looking for information from a range of sources to challenge existing beliefs may reduce the risk of confirmation bias.

Illusion of Control

The basic philosophy behind active equity management is that investors believe they can control or at least influence outcomes. Skilled investors have a healthy confidence in their own ability to select stocks and influence outcomes, and they expect to outperform the market. The illusion of control bias refers to the human tendency to overestimate these abilities. Langer (1983) defines the illusion of control bias as "an expectancy of a personal success probability inappropriately higher than the objective probability would warrant." The illusion of control is a cognitive error.

Having an illusion of control could lead to excessive trading and/or heavy weighting on a few stocks. Investors should seek contrary viewpoints and set and enforce proper trading and portfolio diversification rules to try to avoid this problem.

Availability Bias

Availability bias is an information-processing bias whereby individuals take a mental shortcut in estimating the probability of an outcome based on the availability of the information and how easily the outcome comes to mind. Easily recalled outcomes are often perceived as being more likely than those that are harder to recall or understand. Availability bias falls in the cognitive error category. In fundamental equity investing, this bias may reduce the investment opportunity set and result in insufficient diversification as the portfolio manager relies on familiar stocks that reflect a narrow range of experience. Setting an appropriate investment strategy in line with the investment horizon, as well as conducting a disciplined portfolio analysis with a long-term focus, will help eliminate any short-term over-emphasis caused by this bias.

Loss Aversion

Loss aversion is an emotional bias whereby investors tend to prefer avoiding losses over achieving gains. A number of studies on loss aversion suggest that, psychologically, losses are significantly more powerful than gains. In absolute value terms, the utility derived from a gain is much lower than the utility given up in an equivalent loss.

Loss aversion can cause investors to hold unbalanced portfolios in which poorly performing positions are maintained in the hope of potential recovery and successful investments are sold (and the gains realized) prematurely in order to avoid further risk. A disciplined trading strategy with firmly established stop-loss rules is essential to prevent fundamental investors from falling into this trap.

Overconfidence Bias

Overconfidence bias is an emotional bias whereby investors demonstrate unwarranted faith in their own intuitive reasoning, judgment, and/or cognitive abilities. This overconfidence may be the result of overestimating knowledge levels, abilities, and access to information. Unlike the illusion of control bias, which is a cognitive error,

Creating a Fundamental Active Investment Strategy

overconfidence bias is an illusion of exaggerated knowledge and abilities. Investors may, for example, attribute success to their own ability rather than to luck. Such bias means that the portfolio manager underestimates risks and overestimates expected returns. Regularly reviewing actual investment records and seeking constructive feedback from other professionals can help investors gain awareness of such self-attribution bias.

Regret Aversion Bias

An emotional bias, regret aversion bias causes investors to avoid making decisions that they fear will turn out poorly. Simply put, investors try to avoid the pain of regret associated with bad decisions. This bias may actually prevent investors from making decisions. They may instead hold on to positions for too long and, in the meantime, lose out on profitable investment opportunities.

A carefully defined portfolio review process can help mitigate the effects of regret aversion bias. Such a process might, for example, require investors to periodically review and justify existing positions or to substantiate the decision not to have exposure to other stocks in the universe.

Value and Growth Traps

Value- and growth-oriented investors face certain distinctive risks, often described as "traps."

The Value Trap

A value trap is a stock that appears to be attractively valued—with a low P/E multiple (and/or low price-to-book-value or price-to-cash-flow multiples)—because of a significant price fall but that may still be overpriced given its worsening future prospects. For example, the fact that a company is trading at a low price relative to earnings or book value might indicate that the company or the entire sector is facing deteriorating future prospects and that stock prices may stay low for an extended period of time or decline even further. Often, a value trap appears to be such an attractive investment that investors struggle to understand why the stock fails to perform. Value investors should conduct thorough research before investing in any company that appears to be cheap so that they fully understand the reasons for what appears to be an attractive valuation. Stock prices generally need catalysts or a change in perceptions in order to advance. If a company doesn't have any catalysts to trigger a reevaluation of its prospects, there is less of a chance that the stock price will adjust to reflect its fair value. In such a case, although the stock may appear to be an attractive investment because of a low multiple, it could lead the investor into a value trap.

HSBC Holdings is a multinational banking and financial services holding company headquartered in London. It has a dual primary listing on the Hong Kong Stock Exchange (HKSE) and the London Stock Exchange (LSE) and is a constituent of both the Hang Seng Index (HSI) and the FTSE 100 Index (UKX).

The stock traded on the HKSE at a price of over HKD 80 at the end of 2013 and dropped below HKD 41 at the end of 2020. It declined by 48.7% in seven years, while the industry index (the Hang Seng Financial Index) gained 16.0% over the same period. At the start of the period, HSBC Holdings looked cheap compared to peers and its own history, with average P/E and P/B multiples of 10.9x and 0.9x, respectively. Despite appearing undervalued, the stock performed poorly over the subsequent seven-year period (see Exhibit 25) for reasons that included the need for extensive cost cutting. The above scenario is an illustration of a value trap.

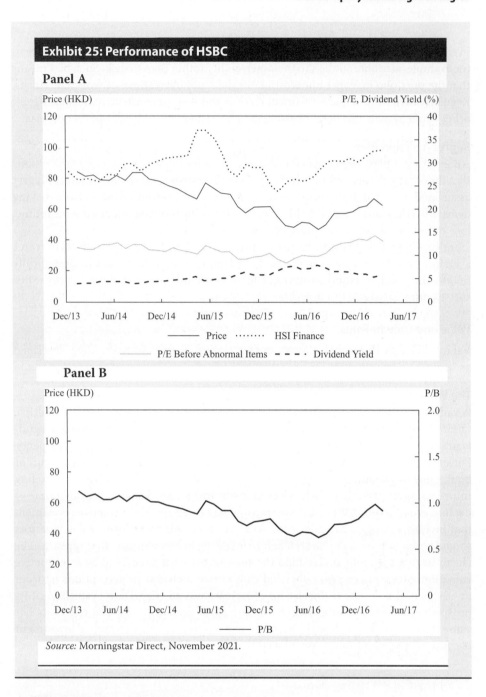

The Growth Trap

Investors in growth stocks do so with the expectation that the share price will appreciate when the company experiences above-average earnings (or cash flow) growth in the future. However, if the company's results fall short of these expectations, stock performance is affected negatively. The stock may also turn out to have been overpriced at the time of the purchase. The company may deliver above-average earnings or cash flow growth, in line with expectations, but the share price may not move any higher due to its already high starting level. The above circumstances are known as a growth trap. As with the value trap in the case of value stocks, the possibility of a growth trap should be considered when investing in what are perceived to be growth stocks.

Investors are often willing to justify paying high multiples for growth stocks in the belief that the current earnings are sustainable and that earnings are likely to grow fast in the future. However, neither of these assumptions may turn out to be true: The company's superior market position may be unsustainable and may last only until its competitors respond. Industry-specific variables often determine the pace at which new entrants or existing competitors respond and compete away any supernormal profits. It is also not uncommon to see earnings grow quickly from a very low base only to undergo a marked slowdown after that initial expansion.

CREATING A QUANTITATIVE ACTIVE INVESTMENT STRATEGY

☐ describe how quantitative active investment strategies are created

Quantitative active equity investing began in the 1970s and became a mainstream investment approach in the subsequent decades. Many quantitative equity funds suffered significant losses in August 2007, an event that became known as the "quant meltdown." The subsequent global financial crisis contributed to growing suspicions about the sustainability of quantitative investing. However, both the performance and the perception of quantitative investing have recovered significantly since 2012 as this approach has regained popularity.

Creating a Quantitative Investment Process

Quantitative (systematic, or rules-based) investing generally has a structured and well-defined investment process. It starts with a belief or hypothesis. Investors collect data from a wide range of sources. Data science and management are also critical for dealing with missing values and outliers. Investors then create quantitative models to test their hypothesis. Once they are comfortable with their models' investment value, quantitative investors combine their return-predicting models with risk controls to construct their portfolios.

Defining the Market Opportunity (Investment Thesis)

Like fundamental active investing, quantitative active investing is based on a belief that the market is competitive but not necessarily efficient. Fund managers use publicly available information to predict future returns of stocks, using factors to build their return-forecasting models.

Acquiring and Processing Data

Data management is probably the least glamorous part of the quantitative investing process. However, investors often spend most of their time building databases, mapping data from different sources, understanding the data availability, cleaning up the data, and reshaping the data into a usable format. The most commonly used data in quantitative investing typically fall into the following categories:

- **Company mapping** is used to track many companies over time and across data vendors. Each company may also have multiple classes of shares. New companies go public, while some existing companies disappear due to bankruptcies, mergers, or takeovers. Company names, ticker symbols, and other identifiers can also change over time. Different data vendors have their own unique identifiers.

- **Company fundamentals** include company demographics, financial statements, and other market data (e.g., price, dividends, stock splits, trading volume). Quantitative portfolio managers almost never collect company fundamental data themselves. Instead, they rely on data vendors, such as Capital IQ, Compustat, Worldscope, Reuters, FactSet, and Bloomberg.
- **Survey data** include details of corporate earnings, forecasts and estimates by various market participants, macroeconomic variables, sentiment indicators, and information on funds flow.
- **Unconventional data,** or unstructured data, include satellite images, measures of news sentiment, customer–supplier chain metrics, and corporate events, among many other types of information.

Data are almost never in the format that is required for quantitative investment analysis. Hence, investors spend a significant amount of time checking data for consistency, cleaning up errors and outliers, and transforming the data into a usable format.

Back-testing the Strategy

Once the required data are available in the appropriate form, strategy back-testing is undertaken. Back-testing is a simulation of real-life investing. For example, in a standard monthly back-test, one can build a portfolio based on a value factor as of a given month-end—perhaps 10 years ago—and then track the return of this portfolio over the subsequent month. Investors normally repeat this process (i.e., rebalance the portfolio) according to a predefined frequency or rule for multiple years to evaluate how such a portfolio would perform and assess the effectiveness of a given strategy over time.

Information Coefficient

Under the assumption that expected returns are linearly related to factor exposures, the correlation between factor exposures and their holding period returns for a cross section of securities has been used as a measure of factor performance in quantitative back-tests. This correlation for a factor is known in this context as the factor's information coefficient (IC). An advantage of the IC is that it aggregates information about factors from all securities in the investment universe, in contrast to an approach that uses only the best and worst deciles (a quantile-based approach), which captures only the top and bottom extremes.

The Pearson IC is the simple correlation coefficient between the factor scores (essentially standardized exposures) for the current period's and the next period's stock returns. As it is a correlation coefficient, its value is always between −1 and +1 (or, expressed in percentage terms, between −100% and +100%). The higher the IC, the higher the predictive power of the factor for subsequent returns. As a simple rule of thumb, in relation to US equities, any factor with an average monthly IC of 5%–6% is considered very strong. The coefficient is sensitive to outliers, as is illustrated below.

A similar but more robust measure is the Spearman rank IC, which is often preferred by practitioners. The Spearman rank IC is essentially the Pearson correlation coefficient between the ranked factor scores and ranked forward returns.

In the example shown in Exhibit 26 for earnings yield, the Pearson IC is negative at −0.8%, suggesting that the signal did not perform well and was negatively correlated with the subsequent month's returns. Looking more carefully, however, we can see that the sample factor is generally in line with the subsequent stock returns, with the exception of Stock I, for which the factor predicts the highest return but which turns out to be the worst performer. A single outlier can therefore turn what may actually be a good factor into a bad one, as the Pearson IC is sensitive to outliers. In contrast, the Spearman rank IC is at 40%, suggesting that the factor has strong predictive power for subsequent returns. If three equally weighted portfolios had been constructed, the long basket (Stocks G, H, and I) would have outperformed the short basket (Stocks A, B, and C) by 56 bps in this period.

Exhibit 26: Pearson Correlation Coefficient IC and Spearman Rank IC

Stock	Factor Score	Subsequent Month Return (%)	Rank of Factor Score	Rank of Return
A	−1.45	−3.00%	9	8
B	−1.16	−0.60%	8	7
C	−0.60	−0.50%	7	6
D	−0.40	−0.48%	6	5
E	0.00	1.20%	5	4
F	0.40	3.00%	4	3
G	0.60	3.02%	3	2
H	1.16	3.05%	2	1
I	1.45	−8.50%	1	9
Mean	0.00	−0.31%		
Standard deviation	1.00	3.71%		
Pearson IC		−0.80%		
Spearman rank IC				40.00%
Long/short tercile portfolio return				0.56%

Note: The portfolio is split into terciles, with each tercile containing one-third of the stocks.
Source: QES (Wolfe Research).

Creating a Multifactor Model

After studying the efficacy of single factors, managers need to decide which factors to include in a multifactor model. Factor selection and weighting is a fairly complex subject. Managers can select and weight each factor using either qualitative or systematic processes. For example, Qian, Hua, and Sorensen (2007) propose treating each factor as an asset; therefore, factor weighting becomes an asset allocation decision. A standard mean–variance optimization can also be used to weight factors. Deciding on which factors to include and their weight is a critical piece of the strategy. Investors should bear in mind that factors may be effective individually but not add material value to a factor model because they are correlated with other factors.

Evaluating the Strategy

Once back-testing is complete, the performance of the strategy can be evaluated. An out-of-sample back-test, in which a different set of data is used to evaluate the model's performance, is generally done to confirm model robustness. However, even strategies with great out-of-sample performance may perform poorly in live trading. Managers generally compute various statistics—such as the *t*-statistic, Sharpe ratio, Sortino ratio, VaR, conditional VaR, and drawdown characteristics—to form an opinion on the outcome of their out-of-sample back-test.

Portfolio Construction Issues in Quantitative Investment

Most quantitative managers spend the bulk of their time searching for and exploring models that can predict stock returns, and may overlook the importance of portfolio construction to the quantitative investment process. While portfolio construction is covered in greater detail in other readings, the following aspects are particularly relevant to quantitative investing:

- **Risk models:** Risk models estimate the variance–covariance matrix of stock returns—that is, the risk of every stock and the correlation among stocks. Directly estimating the variance–covariance matrix using sample return data typically is infeasible and suffers from significant estimation errors.[19] Managers generally rely on commercial risk model vendors[20] for these data.

- **Trading costs:** There are two kinds of trading costs—explicit (e.g., commissions, fees, and taxes) and implicit (e.g., bid–ask spread and market impact). When two stocks have similar expected returns and risks, normally the one with lower execution costs is preferred.[21]

UNCONVENTIONAL BIG DATA AND MACHINE-LEARNING TECHNIQUES

Rohal, Jussa, Luo, Wang, Zhao, Alvarez, Wang, and Elledge (2016) discuss the implications and applications of big data and machine-learning techniques in investment management. The rapid advancement in computing power today allows for the collection and processing of data from sources that were traditionally impossible or overly expensive to access, such as satellite images, social media, and payment-processing systems.

Investors now have access to data that go far beyond the traditional company fundamentals metrics. There are also many data vendors providing increasingly specialized or unique data content. Processing and incorporating unconventional data into existing investment frameworks, however, remains a challenge. With the improvements in computing speed and algorithms, significant successes in machine-learning techniques have been achieved. Despite concerns about data mining, machine learning has led to significant improvement in strategy performance.

Pitfalls in Quantitative Investment Processes

All active investment strategies have their pros and cons. There are many pitfalls that investors need to be aware of when they assess any quantitative strategy. Wang, Wang, Luo, Jussa, Rohal, and Alvarez (2014) discuss some of the common issues in quantitative investing in detail.

Survivorship Bias, Look-Ahead Bias, Data Mining, and Overfitting

Survivorship bias is one of the most common issues affecting quantitative decision making. While investors are generally aware of the problem, they often underestimate its significance. When back-tests use only those companies that are currently in business today, they ignore the stocks that have left the investment universe due

---

[19] One problem with a sample covariance matrix is the curse of dimensionality. For a portfolio of N assets, we need to estimate $N \times (N + 1)/2$ parameters—that is, $N \times (N - 1)/2$ covariance parameters and N estimates of stock-specific risk. For a universe of 3,000 stocks, we would have to estimate about 4.5 million parameters.
[20] MSCI Barra and Axioma are examples of data providers.
[21] Trading costs are covered in depth in separate curriculum readings.

Creating a Quantitative Active Investment Strategy

to bankruptcy,[22] delisting, or acquisition. This approach creates a bias whereby only companies that have survived are tested and it is assumed that the strategy would never have invested in companies that have failed. Survivorship bias often leads to overly optimistic results and sometimes even causes investors to draw wrong conclusions.

The second major issue in back-testing is look-ahead bias. This bias results from using information that was unknown or unavailable at the time an investment decision was made. An example of this bias is the use of financial accounting data for a company at a point in time before the data were actually released by the company.

In computer science, data mining refers to automated computational processes for discovering patterns in large datasets, often involving sophisticated statistical techniques, computation algorithms, and large-scale database systems. In finance, data mining can refer to such a process and can introduce a bias that results in model overfitting. It can be described as excessive search analysis of past financial data to uncover patterns and to conform to a pre-determined model for potential use in investing.

Turnover, Transaction Costs, and Short Availability

Back-testing is often conducted in an ideal, but unrealistic world without transaction costs, constraints on turnover, or limits on the availability of long and short positions. In reality, managers may face numerous constraints, such as limits on turnover and difficulties in establishing short positions in certain markets. Depending on how fast their signal decays, they may or may not be able to capture their model's expected excess return in a live trading process.

More importantly, trading is not free. Transaction costs can easily erode returns significantly. An example is the use of short-term reversal as a factor: Stocks that have performed well recently (say, in the last month) are more likely to revert (underperform) in the subsequent month. This reversal factor has been found to be a good stock selection signal in the Japanese equity market (before transaction costs). As shown in Exhibit 27, in a theoretical world with no transaction costs, a simple long/short strategy (buying the top 20% dividend-paying stocks in Japan with the worst performance in the previous month and shorting the bottom 20% stocks with the highest returns in the previous month) has generated an annual return of 12%, beating the classic value factor of price to book. However, if the transaction cost assumption is changed from 0 bps to 30 bps per trade, the return of the reversal strategy drops sharply, while the return of the price-to-book value strategy drops only modestly.

---

[22] In the United States, companies may continue to trade after filing for bankruptcy as long as they continue to meet listing requirements. However, their stocks are normally removed from most equity indexes.

Exhibit 27: Annualized Returns with Different Transaction Cost Assumptions

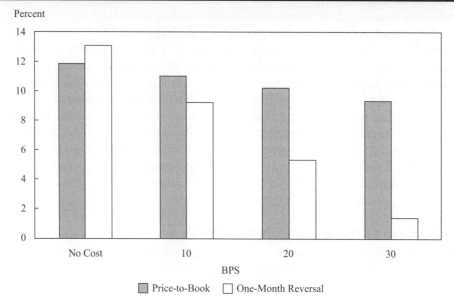

Sources: Compustat, Capital IQ, Thomson Reuters.

QUANT CROWDING

In the first half of 2007, despite some early signs of the US subprime crisis, the global equity market was relatively calm. Then, in August 2007, many of the standard factors used by quantitative managers suffered significant losses,[23] and quantitative equity managers' performance suffered. These losses have been attributed to crowding among quantitative managers following similar trades (see Khandani and Lo 2008). Many of these managers headed for the exit at the same time, exacerbating the losses.

How can it be concluded that the August 2007 quant crisis was due to crowding? More importantly, how can crowding be measured so that the next crowded trade can be avoided? Jussa et al (2016a) used daily short interest data from Markit's securities finance database to measure crowding. They proposed that if stocks with poor price momentum are heavily shorted[24] relative to outperforming stocks, it indicates that many investors are following a momentum style. Hence, momentum as an investment strategy might get crowded. A measure of crowding that may be called a "crowding coefficient" can be estimated by regressing short interest on price momentum. Details of such regression analysis are beyond the scope of this reading.[25] As shown in Exhibit 28, the level of crowding for momentum reached a local peak in mid-2007. In the exhibit, increasing values of the crowding coefficient indicate greater crowding in momentum strategies.

---

23 The average performance of many common factors was strong and relatively stable in 2003–2007. Actually, value and momentum factors suffered more severe losses in late 2002 and around March 2009.
24 Short interest can be defined as the ratio of the number of stocks shorted to the number of stocks in the available inventory for lending.
25 For more on this subject, see Jussa, Rohal, Wang, Zhao, Luo, Alvarez, Wang, and Elledge (2016) and Cahan and Luo (2013).

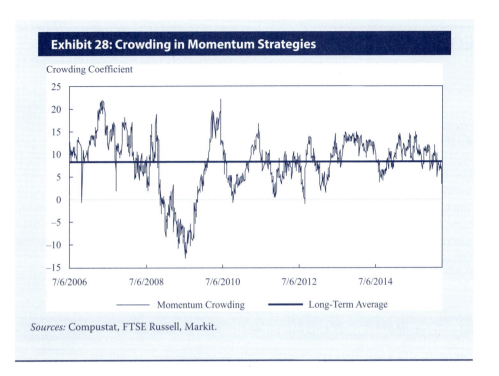

Exhibit 28: Crowding in Momentum Strategies

Sources: Compustat, FTSE Russell, Markit.

EXAMPLE 9

How to Start a Quantitative Investment Process

1. An asset management firm that traditionally follows primarily a fundamental value investing approach wants to diversify its investment process by incorporating a quantitative element. Discuss the potential benefits and hurdles involved in adding quantitative models to a fundamental investment approach.

Solution:

Quantitative investing is based on building models from attributes of thousands of stocks. The performance of quantitative strategies is generally not highly correlated with that of fundamental approaches. Therefore, in theory, adding a quantitative overlay may provide some diversification benefit to the firm.

In practice, however, because the processes behind quantitative and fundamental investing tend to be quite different, combining these two approaches is not always straightforward. Quantitative investing requires a large upfront investment in data, technology, and model development. It is generally desirable to use factors and models that are different from those used by most other investors to avoid potential crowded trades.

Managers need to be particularly careful with their back-testing so that the results do not suffer from look-ahead and survivorship biases. Transaction costs and short availability (if the fund involves shorting) should be incorporated into the back-testing.

12 EQUITY INVESTMENT STYLE CLASSIFICATION

> discuss equity investment style classifications

An investment style classification process generally splits the stock universe into two or three groups, such that each group contains stocks with similar characteristics. The returns of stocks within a style group should therefore be correlated with one another, and the returns of stocks in different style groups should have less correlation. The common style characteristics used in active management include value, growth, blend (or core), size, price momentum, volatility, income (high dividend), and earnings quality. Stock membership in an industry, sector, or country group—for example, the financial sector or emerging markets—is also used to classify the investment style. Exhibit 29 lists a few mainstream categories of investment styles in use today.

Exhibit 29: Examples of Investment Styles

Characteristics based	Value, Growth or Blend/Core
	Capitalization
	Volatility
Membership based	Sector
	Country
	Market (developed or emerging)
Position based	Long/short (net long, short, or neutral)

Investment style classification is important for asset owners who seek to select active strategies. It allows active equity managers with similar styles to be compared with one another. Further, comparing the active returns or positions of a manager with those of the right style index can provide more information about the manager's active strategy and approach. A manager's portfolio may appear to have active positions when compared with the general market benchmark index; however, that manager may actually follow a style index and do so passively. Identifying the actual investment style of equity managers is important for asset owners in their decision-making process.

Different Approaches to Style Classification

Equity styles are defined by pairs of common attributes, such as value and growth, large cap and small cap, high volatility and low volatility, high dividend and low dividend, or developed markets and emerging markets. Style pairs need not be mutually exclusive. Each pair interprets the stock performance from a different perspective. A combination of several style pairs may often give a more complete picture of the sources of stock returns.

Identifying the investment styles of active managers helps to reveal the sources of added value in the portfolio. Modern portfolio theory advocates the use of efficient portfolio management of a diversified portfolio of stocks and bonds. Gupta, Skallsjö, and Li (2016) detail how the concept of diversification, when extended to different strategies and investment processes, can have a significant impact on the risk and reward of an investor's portfolio. A portfolio's risk–return profile is improved not only by including multiple asset classes but also by employing managers with different

Equity Investment Style Classification

investment styles. An understanding of the investment style of a manager helps in evaluating the manager and confirming whether he or she sticks with the claimed investment style or deviates from it.

Two main approaches are often used in style analysis: a holdings-based approach and a returns-based approach. Each approach has its own strengths and weaknesses.

Holdings-Based Approaches

An equity investment style is actually the aggregation of attributes from individual stocks in the portfolio. Holdings-based approaches to style analysis are done bottom-up, but they are executed differently by the various commercial investment information providers. Using different criteria or different sources of underlying value and growth numbers may lead to slightly different classifications for stocks and therefore may result in different style characterizations for the same portfolio. In the style classification process followed by Morningstar and Thomson Reuters Lipper, the styles of individual stocks are clearly defined in that a stock's attribute for a specific style is 1 if it is included in that style index; otherwise, it is 0. The methodology used by MSCI and FTSE Russell, on the other hand, assumes that a stock can have characteristics of two styles, such as value and growth, at the same time. This methodology uses a multifactor approach to assign style inclusion factors to each stock. So a particular stock can belong to both value and growth styles by a pre-determined fraction. A portfolio's active exposure to a certain style equals the sum of the style attributes from all the individual stocks, weighted by their active positions.

THE MORNINGSTAR STYLE BOX

The Morningstar Style Box first appeared in 1992 to help investors and advisers determine the investment style of a fund. In a style box, each style pair splits the stock universe into two to three groups, such as value, core (or "blend"), and growth. The same universe can be split by another style definition—for example, large cap, mid cap, and small cap. The Morningstar Style Box splits the stock universe along both style dimensions, creating a grid of nine squares. It uses holdings-based style analysis and classifies about the same number of stocks in each of the value, core, and growth styles. Morningstar determines the value and growth scores by using five stock attributes (see Exhibit 31). The current Morningstar Style Box, as shown in Exhibit 30, is a nine-square grid featuring three stock investment styles for each of three size categories: large, mid, and small. Two of the three style categories are "value" and "growth," common to both stocks and funds. However, the third, central column is labeled "core" for stocks (i.e., those stocks for which neither value nor growth characteristics dominate) and "blend" for funds (meaning that the fund holds a mixture of growth and value stocks).

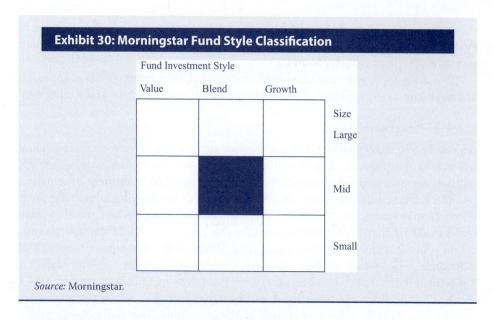

Large-Cap, Mid-Cap, and Small-Cap Classifications

The size classification is determined by the company's market capitalization. There is no consensus on what the size thresholds for the different categories should be, and indeed, different data and research providers use different criteria for size classification purposes. Large-cap companies tend to be well-established companies with a strong market presence, good levels of information disclosure, and extensive scrutiny by the investor community and the media. While these attributes may not apply universally across different parts of the world, large-cap companies are recognized as being lower risk than smaller companies and offering more limited future growth potential. Small-cap companies, on the other hand, tend to be less mature companies with potentially greater room for future growth, higher risk of failure, and a lower degree of analyst and public scrutiny.

Mid-cap companies tend to rank between the two other groups on many important parameters, such as size, revenues, employee count, and client base. In general, they are in a more advanced stage of development than small-cap companies but provide greater growth potential than large-cap companies.

There is no consensus on the boundaries that separate large-, mid-, and small-cap companies. One practice is to define large-cap stocks as those that account for the top ~70% of the capitalization of all stocks in the universe, with mid-cap stocks representing the next ~20% and small-cap stocks accounting for the balance.

Measuring Growth, Value, and Core Characteristics

Equity style analysis starts with assigning a style score to each individual stock. Taking the value/growth style pair as an example, each stock is assigned a value score based on the combination of several value and growth characteristics or factors of that stock. The simplest value scoring model uses one factor, price-to-book ratio, to rank the stock. The bottom half of the stocks in this ranking (smaller P/Bs) constitute the value index, while the stocks ranked in the top half (higher P/Bs) constitute the growth index. Weighting the stocks by their market capitalization thus creates both a value index and a growth index, with the condition that each style index must represent 50% of the market capitalization of all stocks in the target universe. A comprehensive value scoring model may use more factors in addition to price to book, such as price to earnings, price to sales, price to cash flow, return on equity, dividend yield, and so on. The combination of these factors through a predefined process, such as assigning a fixed weight to each selected factor, generates the value score. The value score is usually a number between 0 and 1, corresponding to 0% and 100% contribution to

Equity Investment Style Classification

the value index. Depending on the methodologies employed by the vendors, the value score may be a fraction. A security with a value score of 0.6 will have 60% of its market capitalization allocated to the value index and the remaining 40% to the growth index.

MORNINGSTAR'S CLASSIFICATION CRITERIA FOR VALUE STOCKS

For each stock, Morningstar assigns a growth score and a value score, each based on five components that are combined with pre-determined weights, as shown in Exhibit 31.

Exhibit 31: Morningstar Value and Growth Scoring Scheme

Value Score Components and Weights		Growth Score Components and Weights	
Forward-looking measures	**50.0%**	*Forward-looking measures*	**50.0%**
*Price to projected earnings		*Long-term projected earnings growth	
Historical measures	**50.0%**	*Historical measures*	**50.0%**
*Price to book	12.5%	*Historical earnings growth	12.5%
*Price to sales	12.5%	*Sales growth	12.5%
*Price to cash flow	12.5%	*Cash flow growth	12.5%
*Dividend yield	12.5%	*Book value growth	12.5%

The scores are scaled to a range of 0 to 100, and the difference between the stock's growth and value scores is called the net style score. If this net style score is strongly negative, approaching −100, the stock's style is classified as value. If the result is strongly positive, the stock is classified as growth. If the scores for value and growth are similar in strength, the net style score will be close to zero and the stock will be classified as core. On average, value, core, and growth stocks each account for approximately one-third of the total capitalization in a given row of the Morningstar Style Box.

MSCI WORLD VALUE AND GROWTH INDEXES

MSCI provides a range of indexes that include value and growth. In order to construct those indexes, the firm needs to establish the individual stocks' characteristics. The following (simplified) process is used to establish how much of each stock's market capitalization should be included in the respective indexes.

The value investment style characteristics for index construction are defined using three variables: book-value-to-price ratio, 12-month forward-earnings-to-price ratio, and dividend yield. The growth investment style characteristics for index construction are defined using five variables: long-term forward EPS growth rate, short-term forward EPS growth rate, current internal growth rate, long-term historical EPS growth trend, and long-term historical sales-per-share growth trend. Z-scores for each variable are calculated and aggregated for each security to determine the security's overall style characteristics. For example, a stock is assigned a so-called "value inclusion factor" of 0.6, which means that the stock could have both value and growth characteristics and contributes to the performance of the value and growth indexes by 60% and 40%, respectively. Exhibit 32 shows the cumulative return of the MSCI World Value and MSCI World Growth indexes since 1975.

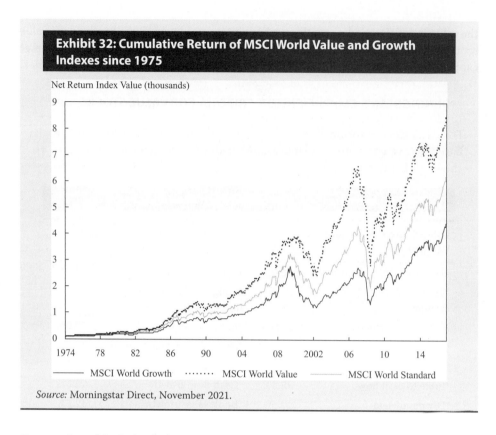

Exhibit 32: Cumulative Return of MSCI World Value and Growth Indexes since 1975

Source: Morningstar Direct, November 2021.

Returns-Based Style Analysis

Many investment managers do not disclose the full details of their portfolios, and therefore a holdings-based approach cannot be used to assess their strategies. The investment style of these portfolio managers is therefore analyzed by using a returns-based approach to compare the returns of the employed strategy to those of a set of style indexes.

The objective of a returns-based style analysis is to find the style concentration of underlying holdings by identifying the style indexes that provide significant contributions to fund returns with the help of statistical tools. Such an analysis attributes fund returns to selected investment styles by running a constrained multivariate regression:[26]

$$r_t = \alpha + \sum_{s=1}^{m} \beta^s R_t^s + \varepsilon_t$$

where

r_t = the fund return within the period ending at time t

R_t^s = the return of style index s in the same period

β^s = the fund exposure to style s (with constraints $\sum_{s=1}^{m} \beta^s = 1$ and $\beta^s > 0$ for a long-only portfolio)

α = a constant often interpreted as the value added by the fund manager

ε_t = the residual return that cannot be explained by the styles used in the analysis

The key inputs to a returns-based style analysis are the historical returns for the portfolio and the returns for the style indexes. The critical part, however, is the selection of the styles used, as stock returns can be highly correlated within the same

---

26 Sharpe (1992).

Equity Investment Style Classification

sector, across sectors, and even across global markets. If available, the manager's own description of his or her style is a good starting point for determining the investment styles that can be used.

Commercial investment information providers, such as Thomson Reuters Lipper and Morningstar, perform the role of collecting and analyzing fund data and classifying the funds into style groups.

> **DATA SOURCES**
>
> The success of a returns-based style analysis depends, to some extent, on the choice of style indexes. The component-based style indexes provided by investment information providers enable analysts to identify the style that is closest to the investment strategy employed by the fund manager.
>
> Thomson Reuters Lipper provides mutual and hedge fund data as well as analytical and reporting tools to institutional and retail investors. All funds covered by Lipper are given a classification based on statements in the funds' prospectuses. Funds that are considered "diversified," because they invest across economic sectors and/or countries, also have a portfolio-based classification. Exhibit 33 shows the Lipper fund classifications for US-listed open-end equity funds.

Exhibit 33: Lipper's Style Classification

	OPEN-END EQUITY FUNDS		
	General Domestic Equity	**World Equity**	**Sector Equity**
Prospectus-Based Classifications	**All** prospectus-based classifications in this group are considered diversified.	**Some** prospectus-based classifications in this group are considered diversified (global and international types only).	**No** prospectus-based classifications in this group are considered diversified.
	Capital Appreciation	Gold	Health/Biotech
	Growth	European Region	Natural Resources
	Micro Cap	Pacific Region	Technology
	Mid Cap	Japan	Telecom
	Small Cap	Pacific ex-Japan	Utilities
	Growth & Income	China	Financial Services
	S&P 500	Emerging Markets	Real Estate
	Equity	Latin America	Specialty & Miscellaneous
	Income	Global	
		Global Small Cap	
		International	
		International Small Cap	

Equity Investment Style Classification

	OPEN-END EQUITY FUNDS		
	General Domestic Equity	**World Equity**	**Sector Equity**
Portfolio-Based Classifications	Large-Cap Growth	Global Large-Cap Growth	
	Large-Cap Core	Global Large-Cap Core	
	Large-Cap Value	Global Large-Cap Value	
	Multi-Cap Growth	Global Multi-Cap Growth	
	Multi-Cap Core	Global Multi-Cap Core	
	Multi-Cap Value	Global Multi-Cap Value	
	Mid-Cap Growth	Global Small-/Mid-Cap Growth	
	Mid-Cap Core	Global Small-/Mid-Cap Core	
	Mid-Cap Value	Global Small-/Mid-Cap Value	
	Small-Cap Growth	International Large-Cap Growth	
	Small-Cap Core	International Large-Cap Core	
	Small-Cap Value	International Large-Cap Value	
	S&P 500	International Multi-Cap Growth	
	Equity Income	International Multi-Cap Core	
		International Multi-Cap Value	
		International Small-/Mid-Cap Growth	
		International Small-/Mid-Cap Core	
		International Small-/Mid-Cap Value	

Source: Thomson Reuters Lipper.

Manager Self-Identification

Equity strategy investment styles result from the active equity manager's employment of a particular strategy to manage the fund. The fund's investment strategy is usually described in the fund prospectus and can be used to identify the fund's investment objective. This objective can be regarded as the manager's self-identification of the investment style.

Returns-based or holdings-based style analysis is commonly used to identify the investment style—such as value/growth or large cap/small cap—and to determine whether it corresponds to the manager's self-identified style. Some other styles, however, cannot be easily identified by such methods. For example, the styles of equity hedge funds, equity income funds, and special sector funds can be more efficiently identified using a combination of manager self-identification and holdings- or returns-based analysis.

Some equity hedge fund styles are non-standard and do not fit into any of the established style categories. Examples include long/short equity, equity market neutral, and dedicated short bias. For such funds, the investment objective is often laid out in the prospectus, which explains the fund's investment strategy. The prospectus becomes the key source of information for those assigning styles to such funds.

Strengths and Limitations of Style Analysis

Holdings-based style analysis is generally more accurate than returns-based analysis because it uses the actual portfolio holdings. Portfolio managers (and those who assess their strategies and performance) can see how each portfolio holding contributes to the portfolio's style, verify that the style is in line with the stated investment philosophy, and take action if they wish to prevent the portfolio's style from moving away from its intended target. Unlike returns-based style analysis, holdings-based style analysis is able to show the styles that any portfolio is exposed to, thus providing input for style allocation decisions.

Holdings-based style analysis requires the availability of all the portfolio constituents as well as the style attributes of each stock in the portfolio. While this information may be accessible for current portfolios, an analyst who wants to track the historical change in investment styles may face some difficulty. In this case, point-in-time databases are required for both the constituents of the fund and the stocks' style definitions.

As investment style research uses statistical and empirical methods to arrive at conclusions, it can produce inaccurate results due to limitations of the data or flaws in the application design. Kaplan (2011) argued that most returns-based style analysis models impose unnecessary constraints that limit the results within certain boundaries, making it difficult to detect more aggressive positions, such as deep value or micro cap. Furthermore, the limited availability of data on derivatives often makes holdings-based style analysis less effective for funds with substantial positions in derivatives. It is therefore important to understand the strengths and limitations of style analysis models in order to interpret the results correctly. Morningstar studies have concluded that holdings-based style analysis generally produces more accurate results than returns-based style analysis, although there may be exceptions. Ideally, practitioners should use both approaches: Returns-based models can often be more widely applied, while holdings-based models allow deeper style analysis.

> **VARIATION OF FUND CHARACTERISTICS WITHIN A STYLE CLASSIFICATION**
>
> Consider the Morningstar Style Box, in which funds are classified along two dimensions: value/growth and size (market capitalization). Within the same value style box, funds can be classified as large cap or small cap. To keep the classification map simple and concise, Morningstar omits other styles and characteristics, such as performance volatility and sector or market/region exposure. It is important to note that style classification provides only a reference to the key investment styles that may contribute to performance. The funds within the same style classification can be quite different in other characteristics, which may also contribute to fund returns and lead to differences in performance.

Equity Investment Style Classification

> **EXAMPLE 10**
>
> ## Equity Investment Styles
>
> 1. Consider an actively managed equity fund that has a five-year track record. An analyst performed both holdings-based and returns-based style analysis on the portfolio. She used the current portfolio holdings to perform the holdings-based style analysis and five-year historical monthly returns to carry out the returns-based analysis. The analyst found the following:
>
>   - Holdings-based style analysis on the current portfolio shows that the fund has value and growth exposures of 0.85 and 0.15, respectively.
>   - Returns-based style analysis with 60 months' historical returns shows that the value and growth exposures of the fund are equal to 0.4 and 0.6, respectively.
>
>   Explain possible reason(s) for the inconsistency between the holdings-based and returns-based style analyses.
>
> ## Solution:
>
> Some active equity managers may maintain one investment style over time in the belief that that particular style will outperform the general market. Others may rotate or switch between styles to accommodate the then-prevailing investment thesis. Returns-based style analysis regresses the portfolio's historical returns against the returns of the corresponding style indexes (over 60 months in this example). Its output indicates the average effect of investment styles employed during the period. While the holdings-based analysis suggests that the current investment style of the equity fund is value oriented, the returns-based analysis indicates that the style actually employed was likely in the growth category for a period of time within the past five years.

SUMMARY

This reading discusses the different approaches to active equity management and describes how the various strategies are created. It also addresses the style classification of active approaches.

- Active equity management approaches can be generally divided into two groups: fundamental (also referred to as discretionary) and quantitative (also known as systematic or rules-based). Fundamental approaches stress the use of human judgment in arriving at an investment decision, whereas quantitative approaches stress the use of rules-based, quantitative models to arrive at a decision.
- The main differences between fundamental and quantitative approaches include the following characteristics: approach to the decision-making process (subjective versus objective); forecast focus (stock returns versus factor returns); information used (research versus data); focus of the analysis

(depth versus breadth); orientation to the data (forward looking versus backward looking); and approach to portfolio risk (emphasis on judgment versus emphasis on optimization techniques).

- The main types of active management strategies include bottom-up, top-down, factor-based, and activist.
- Bottom-up strategies begin at the company level, and use company and industry analyses to assess the intrinsic value of the company and determine whether the stock is undervalued or overvalued relative to its market price.
- Fundamental managers often focus on one or more of the following company and industry characteristics: business model and branding, competitive advantages, and management and corporate governance.
- Bottom-up strategies are often divided into value-based approaches and growth-based approaches.
- Top-down strategies focus on the macroeconomic environment, demographic trends, and government policies to arrive at investment decisions.
- Top-down strategies are used in several investment decision processes, including the following: country and geographic allocation, sector and industry rotation, equity style rotation, volatility-based strategies, and thematic investment strategies.
- Quantitative equity investment strategies often use factor-based models. A factor-based strategy aims to identify significant factors that drive stock prices and to construct a portfolio with a positive bias towards such factors.
- Factors can be grouped based on fundamental characteristics—such as value, growth, and price momentum—or on unconventional data.
- Activist investors specialize in taking meaningful stakes in listed companies and influencing those companies to make changes to their management, strategy, or capital structures for the purpose of increasing the stock's value and realizing a gain on their investment.
- Statistical arbitrage (or "stat arb") strategies use statistical and technical analysis to exploit pricing anomalies and achieve superior returns. Pairs trading is an example of a popular and simple statistical arbitrage strategy.
- Event-driven strategies exploit market inefficiencies that may occur around corporate events such as mergers and acquisitions, earnings announcements, bankruptcies, share buybacks, special dividends, and spinoffs.
- The fundamental active investment process includes the following steps: define the investment universe; prescreen the universe; understand the industry and business; forecast the company's financial performance; convert forecasts into a target price; construct the portfolio with the desired risk profile; and rebalance the portfolio according to a buy and sell discipline.
- Pitfalls in fundamental investing include behavioral biases, the value trap, and the growth trap.
- Behavioral biases can be divided into two groups: cognitive errors and emotional biases. Typical biases that are relevant to active equity management include confirmation bias, illusion of control, availability bias, loss aversion, overconfidence, and regret aversion.
- The quantitative active investment process includes the following steps: define the investment thesis; acquire, clean, and process the data; backtest the strategy; evaluate the strategy; and construct an efficient portfolio using risk and trading cost models.

- The pitfalls in quantitative investing include look-ahead and survivorship biases, overfitting, data mining, unrealistic turnover assumptions, transaction costs, and short availability.
- An investment style generally splits the stock universe into two or three groups, such that each group contains stocks with similar characteristics. The common style characteristics used in active management include value, size, price momentum, volatility, high dividend, and earnings quality. A stock's membership in an industry, sector, or country group is also used to classify the investment style.
- Two main approaches are often used in style analysis: a returns-based approach and a holdings-based approach. Holdings-based approaches aggregate the style scores of individual holdings, while returns-based approaches analyze the investment style of portfolio managers by comparing the returns of the strategy to those of a set of style indexes.

REFERENCES

Basu, S. 1977. "Investment Performance of Common Stocks in Relation to Their Price-Earnings Ratios: A Test of the Efficient Market Hypothesis." *Journal of Finance* 32 (3): 663–82. 10.1111/j.1540-6261.1977.tb01979.x

Cahan, R. and Y. Luo. 2013. "Standing Out From the Crowd: Measuring Crowding in Quantitative Strategies." *Journal of Portfolio Management* 39 (4): 14–23. 10.3905/jpm.2013.39.4.014

Fama, E. and K. R. French. 1992. "The Cross-Section of Expected Stock Returns." *Journal of Finance* 47 (2): 427–65. 10.1111/j.1540-6261.1992.tb04398.x

Fama, E. and K. R. French. 1993. "Common Risk Factors in the Returns on Stocks and Bonds." *Journal of Financial Economics* 33 (1): 3–56. 10.1016/0304-405X(93)90023-5

Fama, E. and K. R. French. 1996. "Multifactor Explanations of Asset Pricing Anomalies." *Journal of Finance* 51 (1): 55–84. 10.1111/j.1540-6261.1996.tb05202.x

Graham, B. and D. L. Dodd. 1934. *Security Analysis.* New York: McGraw-Hill.

Greenblatt, J. 2010. *The Little Book That Still Beats the Market.* Hoboken, NJ: John Wiley & Sons.

Greenwald, B., J. Kahn, P. Sonkin, and M. Biema. 2001. *Value Investing: From Graham to Buffett and Beyond.* Hoboken, NJ: John Wiley & Sons.

Gupta, P., S. Skallsjö, and B. Li. 2016. *Multi-Asset Investing: A Practitioner's Framework.* Chichester, UK: John Wiley & Sons. 10.1002/9781119241614

Jegadeesh, N. and S. Titman. 1993. "Returns to Buying Winners and Selling Losers: Implications for Stock Market Efficiency." *Journal of Finance* 48 (1): 65–91. 10.1111/j.1540-6261.1993.tb04702.x

Jussa, J., G. Rohal, S. Wang, G. Zhao, Y. Luo, M. Alvarez, A. Wang, and D. Elledge. 2016a. "Strategy Crowding." Deutsche Bank (16 May).

Kaplan, P. 2011. *Frontiers of Modern Asset Allocation.* Hoboken, NJ: John Wiley & Sons.

Khandani, A. and A. Lo. 2008. "What Happened to the Quants in August 2007? Evidence from Factors and Transactions Data." NBER Working Paper 14465. 10.3386/w14465

Lakonishok, J., A. Shleifer, and R. W. Vishny. 1994. "Contrarian Investment, Extrapolation, and Risk." *Journal of Finance* 49 (5): 1541–78. 10.1111/j.1540-6261.1994.tb04772.x

Langer, E. J. 1983. *The Psychology of Control.* Beverly Hills, CA: Sage Publications.

Maug, E. 1998. "Large Shareholders as Monitors: Is There a Trade-Off between Liquidity and Control?" *Journal of Finance* 53 (1): 65–98. 10.1111/0022-1082.35053

Qian, E. E., R. H. Hua, and E. H. Sorensen. 2007. *Quantitative Equity Portfolio Management: Modern Techniques and Applications.* Boca Raton, FL: Chapman & Hall/CRC.

Rohal, G., J. Jussa, Y. Luo, S. Wang, G. Zhao, M. Alvarez, A. Wang, and D. Elledge. 2016. "Big Data in Investment Management." Deutsche Bank (17 February).

Sharpe, W. F. 1992. "Asset Allocation, Management Style, and Performance Measurement." *Journal of Portfolio Management* 18 (2): 7–19. 10.3905/jpm.1992.409394

Sloan, R. G. 1996. "Do Stock Prices Fully Reflect Information in Accruals and Cash Flows about Future Earnings?" *Accounting Review* 71 (3): 289–315.

Wang, S., A. Wang, Y. Luo, J. Jussa, G. Rohal, and M. Alvarez. 2014. *Seven Sins of Quantitative Investing.* Deutsche Bank Market Research (September).

PRACTICE PROBLEMS

The following information relates to questions 1-6

James Leonard is a fund-of-funds manager with Future Generation, a large sovereign fund. He is considering whether to pursue more in-depth due diligence processes with three large-cap long-only funds proposed by his analysts. Although the funds emphasize different financial metrics and use different implementation methodologies, they operate in the same market segment and are evaluated against the same benchmark. The analysts prepared a short description of each fund, presented in Exhibit 1.

Exhibit 1: Description of Each Candidate Fund

Fund	Description
Furlings	Furlings Investment Partners combines sector views and security selection. The firm's head manager uses several industry and economic indicators identified from his own experience during the last two decades, as well as his personal views on market flow dynamics, to determine how to position the fund on a sector basis. Sector deviations from the benchmark of 10% or more are common and are usually maintained for 12 to 24 months. At the same time, sector managers at Furlings use their expertise in dissecting financial statements and their understanding of the corporate branding and competitive landscape within sectors to build equally weighted baskets of securities within sectors. Each basket contains their 7 to 10 highest-conviction securities, favoring firms that have good governance, strong growth potential, competitive advantages such as branding, and attractive relative valuations. The Furlings master fund holds approximately 90 securities.
Asgard	Asgard Investment Partners is a very large asset manager. It believes in investing in firms that have a strong business model and governance, reasonable valuations, solid capital structures with limited financial leverage, and above-average expected earnings growth for the next three years. Although the Asgard master fund invests in fewer than 125 securities, each sector analyst builds financial models that track as many as 50 firms. To support them in their task, analysts benefit from software developed by the Asgard research and technology group that provides access to detailed market and accounting information on 5,000 global firms, allowing for the calculation of many valuation and growth metrics and precise modeling of sources of cash-flow strengths and weaknesses within each business. Asgard analysts can also use the application to back-test strategies and build their own models to rank securities' attractiveness according to their preferred characteristics. Security allocation is determined by a management team but depends heavily on a quantitative risk model developed by Asgard. Asgard has a low portfolio turnover.
Tokra	Tokra Capital uses a factor-based strategy to rank securities from most attractive to least attractive. Each security is scored based on three metrics: price to book value (P/B), 12-month increase in stock price, and return on assets. Tokra's managers have a strong risk management background. Their objective is to maximize their exposure to the most attractive securities using a total scoring approach subject to limiting single-security concentration below 2%, sector deviations below 3%, active risk below 4%, and annual turnover less than 40%, while having a market beta close to 1. The master fund holds approximately 400 positions out of a possible universe of more than 2,000 securities evaluated.

When Leonard's analysts met with Asgard, they inquired whether its managers engage in activist investing because Asgard's portfolio frequently holds significant positions, because of their large asset size, and because of their emphasis on strong governance and their ability to model sources of cash-flow strengths and weaknesses within each business. The manager indicated that Asgard engages with companies from a long-term shareholder's perspective, which is consistent with the firm's low portfolio turnover, and uses its voice, and its vote, on matters that can influence companies' long-term value.

Leonard wants to confirm that each manager's portfolios are consistent with its declared style. To this end, Exhibit 2 presents key financial information associated with each manager's portfolio and also with the index that all three managers use.

Exhibit 2: Key Financial Data

Fund	Index	Furlings	Asgard	Tokra
Dividend/price (trailing 12-month)	2.3%	2.2%	2.2%	2.6%
P/E (trailing 12-month)	26.5	24.7	26.6	27.3
Price/cash flows (12-month forward)	12.5	13.8	12.5	11.6
P/B	4.8	4.30	4.35	5.4
Average EPS growth (three to five years forward)	11.9%	11.0%	13.1%	10.8%
Net income/assets	2.8%	4.5%	4.3%	3.2%
Average price momentum (trailing 12 months)	10.5%	14.0%	10.0%	12.0%

1. Which fund manager's investing approach is most consistent with fundamental management?

    A. Furlings

    B. Asgard

    C. Tokra

2. Which of the following statements about the approaches and styles of either Furlings, Asgard, or Tokra is incorrect?

    A. Furlings is a top-down sector rotator with a value orientation within sectors.

    B. Asgard is a bottom-up manager with a GARP (growth at a reasonable price) style.

    C. Tokra is a factor-based manager using value, growth, and profitability metrics.

3. Which manager is most likely to get caught in a value trap?

    A. Furlings

    B. Asgard

    C. Tokra

4. Which activist investing tactic is Asgard *least likely* to use?

    A. Engaging with management by writing letters to management, calling for and explaining suggested changes, and participating in management discussions with analysts or meeting the management team privately

Practice Problems

    B. Launching legal proceedings against existing management for breach of fiduciary duties

    C. Proposing restructuring of the balance sheet to better utilize capital and potentially initiate share buybacks or increase dividends

5. Based on the information provided in Exhibits 1 and 2, which manager's portfolio characteristics is most likely at odds with its declared style?

    A. Furlings

    B. Asgard

    C. Tokra

6. Leonard is looking at the style classification from Asgard as reported by Morningstar and Thomson Reuters Lipper. He is surprised to find that Asgard is classified as a blend fund by Morningstar and a value fund by Lipper. Which of the following statements is correct?

    A. Although the Morningstar methodology classifies securities as either value, growth, or core, the Lipper methodology assumes a stock can have the characteristics of many styles. This approach can result in a different classification for the same portfolio.

    B. The Lipper methodology can only lead to a value or growth classification. It does not offer a core/blend component.

    C. The Morningstar methodology classifies securities as either value, growth, or core by looking at the difference between their respective growth and value scores. It is possible that the Asgard funds hold a balanced exposure to both value and growth and/or core stocks.

The following information relates to questions 7-14

Aleksy Nowacki is a new portfolio manager at Heydon Investments. The firm currently offers a single equity fund, which uses a top-down investment strategy based on fundamentals. Vicky Knight, a junior analyst at Heydon, assists with managing the fund.

Nowacki has been hired to start a second fund, the Heydon Quant Fund, which will use quantitative active equity strategies. Nowacki and Knight meet to discuss distinct characteristics of the quantitative approach to active management, and Knight suggests three such characteristics:

    Characteristic 1   The focus is on factors across a potentially large group of stocks.

    Characteristic 2   The decision-making process is systematic and non-discretionary.

    Characteristic 3   The approach places an emphasis on forecasting the future prospects of underlying companies.

Nowacki states that quantitative investing generally follows a structured and well-defined process. Knight asks Nowacki:

"What is the starting point for the quantitative investment process?"

The new Heydon Quant Fund will use a factor-based strategy. Nowacki assembles a large dataset with monthly standardized scores and monthly returns for the strategy to back-test a new investment strategy and calculates the information coefficient. $FS(t)$ is the factor score for the current month, and $FS(t + 1)$ is the score for the next month. $SR(t)$ is the strategy's holding period return for the current month, and $SR(t + 1)$ is the strategy's holding period return for the next month.

As an additional step in back-testing of the strategy, Nowacki computes historical price/book ratios (P/Bs) and price/earnings ratios (P/Es) using calendar year-end (31 December) stock prices and companies' financial statement data for the same calendar year. He notes that the financial statement data for a given calendar year are not typically published until weeks after the end of that year.

Because the Heydon Quant Fund occasionally performs pairs trading using statistical arbitrage, Nowacki creates three examples of pairs trading candidates, presented in Exhibit 1. Nowacki asks Knight to recommend a suitable pair trade.

Exhibit 1: Possible Pairs Trades Based on Statistical Arbitrage

Stock Pair	Current Price Ratio Compared with Long-Term Average	Historical Price Ratio Relationship	Historical Correlation between Returns
1 and 2	Not significantly different	Mean reverting	High
3 and 4	Significantly different	Mean reverting	High
5 and 6	Significantly different	Not mean reverting	Low

Knight foresees a possible scenario in which the investment universe for the Heydon Quant Fund is unchanged but a new factor is added to its multifactor model. Knight asks Nowacki whether this scenario could affect the fund's investment-style classifications using either the returns-based or holdings-based approaches.

7. Which of the following asset allocation methods would **not** likely be used by Nowacki and Knight to select investments for the existing equity fund?

    A. Sector and industry rotation

    B. Growth at a reasonable price

    C. Country and geographic allocation

8. Relative to Heydon's existing fund, the new fund will *most likely*:

    A. hold a smaller number of stocks.

    B. rebalance at more regular intervals.

    C. see risk at the company level rather than the portfolio level.

9. Which characteristic suggested by Knight to describe the quantitative approach to active management is *incorrect*?

    A. Characteristic 1

Practice Problems

   B. Characteristic 2

   C. Characteristic 3

10. Nowacki's *most appropriate* response to Knight's question about the quantitative investment process is to:

    A. back-test the new strategy.

    B. define the market opportunity.

    C. identify the factors to include and their weights.

11. In Nowacki's back-testing of the factor-based strategy for the new fund, the calculated information coefficient should be based on:

    A. $FS(t)$ and $SR(t)$.

    B. $FS(t)$ and $SR(t + 1)$.

    C. $SR(t)$ and $FS(t + 1)$.

12. Nowacki's calculated price/book ratios (P/Bs) and price/earnings ratios (P/Es), in his back-testing of the new strategy, are a problem because of:

    A. data mining.

    B. look-ahead bias.

    C. survivorship bias.

13. Based on Exhibit 1, which stock pair should Knight recommend as the best candidate for statistical arbitrage?

    A. Stock 1 and Stock 2

    B. Stock 3 and Stock 4

    C. Stock 5 and Stock 6

14. The *most appropriate* response to Knight's question regarding the potential future scenario for the Heydon Quant Fund is:

    A. only the returns-based approach.

    B. only the holdings-based approach.

    C. both the returns-based approach and the holdings-based approach.

The following information relates to questions 15-19

Jack Dewey is managing partner of DC&H, an investment management firm, and Supriya Sardar is an equity analyst with the firm. Dewey recently took over management of the firm's Purity Fund. He is developing a fundamental active investment process for managing this fund that emphasizes financial strength and demonstrated profitability of portfolio companies. At his previous employer,

Dewey managed a fund for which his investment process involved taking active exposures in sectors based on the macroeconomic environment and demographic trends.

Dewey and Sardar meet to discuss developing a fundamental active investment process for the Purity Fund. They start by defining the investment universe and market opportunity for the fund, and then they pre-screen the universe to obtain a manageable set of securities for further, more detailed analysis. Next, Dewey notes that industry and competitive analysis of the list of securities must be performed. He then asks Sardar to recommend the next step in development of the fundamental active management process.

During the next few months, Dewey rebalances the Purity Fund to reflect his fundamental active investment process. Dewey and Sardar meet again to discuss potential new investment opportunities for the fund. Sardar recommends the purchase of AZ Industrial, which she believes is trading below its intrinsic value, despite its high price-to-book value (P/B) relative to the industry average.

Dewey asks Sardar to perform a bottom-up style analysis of the Purity Fund based on the aggregation of attributes from individual stocks in the portfolio. Dewey plans to include the results of this style analysis in a profile he is preparing for the fund.

15. In managing the fund at his previous employer, Dewey's investment process can be *best* described as:

    A. an activist strategy.

    B. a top-down strategy.

    C. a bottom-up strategy.

16. Sardar's recommendation for the next step should be to:

    A. review results from back-testing the strategy.

    B. make recommendations for rebalancing the portfolio.

    C. forecast companies' performances and convert those forecasts into valuations.

17. Based upon Dewey's chosen investment process for the management of the Purity Fund, rebalancing of the fund will *most likely* occur:

    A. at regular intervals.

    B. in response to changes in company-specific information.

    C. in response to updated output from optimization models.

18. Which investment approach is the *most likely* basis for Sardar's buy recommendation for AZ Industrial?

    A. Relative value

    B. High-quality value

    C. Deep-value investing

19. The analysis performed by Sardar on the Purity Fund can be *best* described as

being based on:

A. a holdings-based approach.

B. manager self-identification.

C. a returns-based style analysis.

SOLUTIONS

1. A is correct. Furlings combines a top-down and bottom-up approach, but in both cases, the allocation process is significantly determined according to the managers' discretion and judgement. There is a strong emphasis on understanding financial reporting, and the sector managers focus on a relatively small number for firms. They also extend their analysis to other areas associated with fundamental management, such as valuation, competitive advantages, and governance. Finally, Furlings's top-down process depends largely on the views and experience of its head manager.

    B is incorrect. Asgard has many of the attributes associated with a fundamental manager. It invests in a relatively small number of securities and focuses on the companies' business model, valuations, and future growth prospects. Because of the scope of the securities coverage by each manager, however, Asgard depends heavily on technology and tools to support screening and ranking of securities attractiveness. Each manager can use his judgement to build his own quantitative models. Furthermore, the allocation process, although overlaid by a management team, also depends heavily on technology. Asgard has characteristics of both fundamental and quantitative managers.

    C is incorrect. Tokra exhibits the characteristics of a quantitative manager. The firm uses quantitative metrics to rank securities based on valuation, profitability, and momentum criteria and uses portfolio optimization to determine the final allocation. Tokra holds many positions typical of quantitative approaches.

2. C is an incorrect statement. Although Tokra is a factor manager, and although it uses a value proxy such as P/B and a profitability proxy such as return on assets, it does not use a growth proxy such as earnings growth over the last 12 or 36 months but rather a price momentum proxy.

    A is a correct statement. Furlings is a top-down manager. It makes significant sector bets based on industry and economic indicators derived from the head manager's experience, and it does select its securities within sectors while considering relative valuation.

    B is a correct statement. Asgard favors securities that have reasonable valuations and above-average growth prospects. It has a bottom-up approach and builds its portfolio starting at the security level.

3. C is the correct answer. A value trap occurs when a stock that appears to have an attractive valuation because of a low P/E and/or P/B multiple (or other relevant value proxies) appears cheap only because of its worsening growth prospects. Although a pitfall such as value trap is more common in fundamental investing, a quantitative process that relies on historical information and does not integrate future expectations about cash flows or profitability may be unable to detect a value trap.

    A is an incorrect answer. Although Furlings is a top-down manager, its sector portfolios are built through investing in a small number of high-conviction securities after its analysts have dissected the financial statements and analyzed the competitive landscape and growth prospects. Managers at Furlings are more likely than managers at Tokra to be aware of the significant deteriorating prospects of a security they are considering for investment.

    B is an incorrect answer. One of Asgard's investment criteria is identifying firms that have good potential cash flow growth over the next three years. The firm has access to database and support tools, allowing its analysts to evaluate many potential growth metrics. Managers at Asgard are more likely than managers at

Solutions

Tokra to be aware of the significant deteriorating prospects of a security they are considering for investment.

4. B is the correct answer. Asgard invests in firms that have strong business models and good governance. Also, it approaches investing as a long-term investor looking to use its voice to improve the company's asset management. Asgard is unlikely to use an aggressive posturing or to invest or stay invested in companies with weak governance or where managers may be in breach of fiduciary duties.

   A is an incorrect answer. Engaging in positive conversations with management of companies with which Asgard has invested reflects a use of its voice to improve these companies' long-term value.

   C is an incorrect answer. Because Asgard is strong at modeling sources of cash flows and is known for investing in companies with a strong capital structure, it would be consistent for Asgard to propose ways to optimize the capital structure and shareholders' compensation.

5. C is the correct answer. Tokra indicates that it emphasizes three metrics: P/B, 12-month price momentum, and return on assets. Although the portfolio consists of securities that have stronger momentum than those of the index on average, and although the ratio of net income to assets is also favorable, the average P/B is somehow higher than that of the index. Although this scenario could normally be explained by an emphasis on specific sectors with a higher P/B than other sectors, the low level of sector deviation tolerated within the strategy weakens that explanation. This should be explored with Tokra's managers.

   A is an incorrect answer. Furlings is a top-down sector rotator with a value orientation within sectors. The lower P/B and P/E and higher net income over assets are consistent with a relative value orientation. Because Furlings can take significant positions in specific sectors, however, there could be other circumstances in which the portfolio would have a higher P/B and/or P/E and or a lower net income /assets than the index if the fund were to emphasize sectors having such characteristics. Yet, this would not necessarily imply that the firm does not favor the most attractive relative valuations within sectors.

   B is an incorrect answer. Asgard invests in firms that offer reasonable valuations and above-average expected cash flow growth during the next three years. The data, such as P/B and average expected three-year profit growth, are consistent with its declared style. Again, it is not necessarily inconsistent to emphasize these aspects while investing in a portfolio that has a lower dividend yield, slightly higher P/E, and lower price momentum.

6. C is a correct answer. Morningstar calculates a score for value and growth on a scale of 0 to 100 using five proxy measures for each. The value score is subtracted from the growth score. A strongly positive net score leads to a growth classification, and a strongly negative score leads to a value classification. A score relatively close to zero indicates a core classification. To achieve a blend classification, the portfolio must have a balanced exposure to stocks classified as value and growth, a dominant exposure to stocks classified as core, or a combination of both.

   A is an incorrect answer. Both Morningstar and Lipper classify individual stocks in a specific style category. Neither assumes a security can belong to several styles in specific proportion.

   B is an incorrect answer. The Lipper methodology does have a core classification. It sums the Z-score of six portfolio characteristics over several years to determine an overall Z-score that determines either a value, core, or growth classification.

7. B is correct. The firm currently offers a single equity fund, which uses a top-down investment strategy. Country and geographic allocation and sector and industry

rotation are both top-down strategies that begin at the top or macro level and are consistent with the fund's top-down investment strategy. Growth at a reasonable price (GARP), however—a growth-based approach—is a bottom-up asset selection strategy that begins with data at the company level. Therefore, Nowacki and Knight likely would not use the GARP approach to select investments for the existing equity fund, which uses a top-down investment strategy. A is incorrect because sector and industry rotation is a top-down strategy, consistent with the fund's top-down approach. C is incorrect because country and geography selection is a top-down strategy, consistent with the fund's top-down approach.

8. B is correct. Portfolios managed using a quantitative approach are usually rebalanced at regular intervals, such as monthly or quarterly. In contrast, portfolios managed using a fundamental approach usually monitor the portfolio's holdings continuously and may increase, decrease, or eliminate positions at any time.

   Also, the focus of a quantitative approach is on factors across a potentially large group of stocks, whereas fundamental strategies focus on a relatively small group of stocks. Consequently, Heydon's new quantitative fund will likely hold a larger number of stocks than the existing equity fund.

   Finally, managers following a fundamental approach typically select stocks by performing extensive research on individual companies; thus, fundamental investors see risk at the company level. In contrast, with a quantitative approach, the risk is that factor returns will not perform as expected. Because the quantitative approach invests in baskets of stocks, the risks lie at the portfolio level rather than at the level of specific stocks (company level). Consequently, Nowacki's new quantitative fund will likely see risk at the portfolio level, rather than the company level as the existing equity fund does.

9. C is correct. Quantitative analysis uses a company's history to arrive at investment decisions. The quantitative decision-making process is systematic and non-discretionary (whereas the fundamental decision-making process is more discretionary), and the focus of the quantitative approach is on factors across a potentially large group of stocks (whereas fundamental strategies focus on a relatively small group of stocks). In contrast, fundamental analysis (not quantitative analysis) emphasizes forecasting future prospects, including the future earnings and cash flows of a company.

10. B is correct. The first step in creating a quantitative, active strategy is to define the market opportunity or investment thesis. Then, relevant data is acquired, processed, and transformed into a usable format. This step is followed by back-testing the strategy, which involves identifying the factors to include as well as their weights. Finally, the strategy performance should be evaluated using an out-of-sample back-test.

11. B is correct. The purpose of back-testing is to identify correlations between the current period's factor scores, $FS(t)$, and the next period's holding period strategy returns, $SR(t + 1)$.

12. B is correct. Look-ahead bias results from using information that was unknown or unavailable at the time the investment decision was made. An example of this bias is using financial accounting data for a company at a point before the data were actually released by the company. Nowacki computed historical P/Bs and P/Es using calendar year-end (31 December) stock prices and companies' financial statement data for the same calendar year, even though the financial statement data for that calendar year were likely unavailable at year-end.

   Data mining refers to automated computational procedures for discovering patterns in large datasets, which can introduce a bias known as overfitting. Survivor-

Solutions

ship bias occurs when back-testing uses companies that are in business today but ignores companies that have left the investment universe.

13. B is correct. Knight should recommend the Stock 3 and Stock 4 pair trade. Two stocks make for an ideal pairs trade if (1) the current price ratio differs from its long-term average and shows historical mean reversion and (2) the two stocks' returns are highly correlated. The relationship between Stock 3 and Stock 4 meets these conditions.

14. C is correct. Because the Heydon Quant Fund would be changing its factor model by adding a new factor, the correlations of the fund's returns with the factors would likely change and the returns-based style would change. Even though the investment universe is unchanged, the portfolio holdings would likely change and the holdings-based style classification would also will be affected.

15. B is correct. At his previous firm, Dewey managed a fund for which his investment process involved taking active exposures in sectors based on the macroeconomic environment and demographic trends. An investment process that begins at a top, or macro level, is a top-down strategy. Top-down portfolio strategies study variables affecting many companies or whole sectors, such as the macroeconomic environment, demographic trends, and government policies. This approach differs from bottom-up strategies, which focus on individual company variables in making investment decisions. It also differs from activist strategies, which take stakes in listed companies and advocate changes for the purpose of producing a gain on the investment.

16. C is correct. The steps to developing a fundamental active investment process are as follows:

    1. Define the investment universe and the market opportunity—the perceived opportunity to earn a positive risk-adjusted return to active investing, net of costs—in accordance with the investment mandate. The market opportunity is also known as the investment thesis.
    2. Prescreen the investment universe to obtain a manageable set of securities for further, more detailed analysis.
    3. Understand the industry and business for this screened set by performing industry and competitive analysis and analyzing financial reports.
    4. Forecast company performance, most commonly in terms of cash flows or earnings.
    5. Convert forecasts to valuations and identify *ex ante* profitable investments.
    6. Construct a portfolio of these investments with the desired risk profile.
    7. Rebalance the portfolio with buy and sell disciplines.

    So, Sardar should recommend that the next step in the development of the fundamental active management process be forecasting companies' performances and converting those forecasts into valuations.

17. B is correct. Managers using an active fundamental investment process, like Dewey's, usually monitor the portfolio's holdings continuously and may rebalance at any time. In contrast, portfolios using a quantitative approach are usually rebalanced at regular intervals, such as monthly or quarterly, or in response to updated output from optimization models. A is incorrect because portfolios using a quantitative (not fundamental) active approach are usually rebalanced at regular intervals, such as monthly or quarterly. C is incorrect because construction of a quantitative portfolio (not a fundamental portfolio) typically involves us-

ing a portfolio optimizer, which controls for risk at the portfolio level in arriving at individual stock weights and leads to rebalancing decisions.

18. B is correct. Dewey has developed a fundamental active investment process for the Purity Fund that emphasizes financial strength and demonstrated profitability. High-quality value investors focus on companies' intrinsic values that are supported by attractive valuation metrics, with an emphasis on financial strength and demonstrated profitability. In their view, investors sometimes behave irrationally, making stocks trade at prices very different from intrinsic value based on company fundamentals. A is incorrect because investors who pursue a relative value strategy evaluate companies by comparing their value indicators (e.g., P/E or P/B multiples) with the average valuation of companies in the same industry sector, in an effort to identify stocks that offer value relative to their sector peers. AZ Industrial is trading at a high P/B relative to the industry average, which is contrary to relative value and suggests that the relative value approach was not the basis for Sardar's buy recommendation. C is incorrect because a deep-value investing approach focuses on undervalued companies that are available at extremely low valuation relative to their assets. Such companies are often those in financial distress, which is not reflective of financial strength or demonstrated profitability. Therefore, Sardar's buy recommendation was not based on a deep-value investing orientation.

19. A is correct. Dewey asks Sardar to perform a bottom-up style analysis of the Purity Fund based on the aggregation of attributes from individual stocks in the portfolio, which describes a holdings-based approach to style analysis. The overall equity investment style is an aggregation of attributes from individual stocks in the portfolio, weighted by their positions.

LEARNING MODULE 3

Active Equity Investing: Portfolio Construction

by Jacques Lussier, PhD, CFA, and Marc R. Reinganum, PhD.

Jacques Lussier, PhD, CFA (Canada). Marc R. Reinganum, PhD (USA).

LEARNING OUTCOMES	
Mastery	The candidate should be able to:
☐	describe elements of a manager's investment philosophy that influence the portfolio construction process
☐	discuss approaches for constructing actively managed equity portfolios
☐	distinguish between Active Share and active risk and discuss how each measure relates to a manager's investment strategy
☐	discuss the application of risk budgeting concepts in portfolio construction
☐	discuss risk measures that are incorporated in equity portfolio construction and describe how limits set on these measures affect portfolio construction
☐	discuss how assets under management, position size, market liquidity, and portfolio turnover affect equity portfolio construction decisions
☐	evaluate the efficiency of a portfolio structure given its investment mandate
☐	discuss the long-only, long extension, long/short, and equitized market-neutral approaches to equity portfolio construction, including their risks, costs, and effects on potential alphas

1. INTRODUCTION

Active equity investing is based on the concept that a skilled portfolio manager can both identify and differentiate between the most attractive securities and the least attractive securities—typically relative to a pre-specified benchmark. If this is the case, why is a portfolio—a collection of securities—even necessary? Why shouldn't the portfolio manager just identify the most attractive security and invest all assets in this one security? Or in a long/short context, why not buy the "best" security and sell the "worst" one? Although very simple, this one-stock approach is not likely to be optimal or even feasible. No manager has perfect foresight, and her predictions will likely differ from realized returns. What she predicted would be the "best security" may quite likely turn out *not* to be the best. Active equity portfolio managers, even those with great skill, cannot avoid this risk. Security analysis is the process for ranking the relative attractiveness of securities, whereas portfolio construction is about selecting the securities to be included and carefully determining what percentage of the portfolio is to be held in each security—balancing superior insights regarding predicted returns against some likelihood that these insights will be derailed by events unknown or simply prove to be inaccurate.

Active managers rely on a wide array of investment strategies and methodologies to build portfolios of securities that they expect to outperform the benchmark. The challenges faced by active managers are similar whether they manage long-only traditional strategies, systematic/quantitative strategies, or long/short opportunistic strategies. Managers may differ in their investment style, operational complexity, flexibility of investment policy, ability to use leverage and short positions, and implementation methodologies, but predictions about returns and risk are essential to most active equity management styles.

In Section 2, we introduce the "building blocks" of portfolio construction, and in Sections 3–5, we discuss the different approaches to portfolio construction. In Sections 6–9, we discuss risk budgeting concepts relevant to portfolio construction and the measures used to evaluate portfolio risk. Section 10 looks at how issues of scale may affect portfolio construction. Section 11 addresses the attributes of a well-constructed portfolio. Section 12 looks at certain specialized equity strategies and how their approaches to portfolio construction may differ from a long-only equity strategy. The reading concludes with a summary.

2. BUILDING BLOCKS OF ACTIVE EQUITY PORTFOLIO CONSTRUCTION

☐ describe elements of a manager's investment philosophy that influence the portfolio construction process

Investors who pursue active management are looking to generate portfolio returns in excess of benchmark returns (adjusted for all costs) for an appropriate level of risk. The excess return—also called **active return** (R_A)—of an actively managed portfolio is driven by the difference in weights between the active portfolio and the benchmark. It can be mathematically expressed as

$$R_A = \sum_{i=1}^{N} \Delta W_i R_i \tag{1}$$

where

R_i = the return on security i and

ΔW_i = the difference between the portfolio weights W_{Pi} and the benchmark weights W_{Bi}. ΔW_i is also referred to as the active weight.

An active manager will generate positive active returns if:

Building Blocks of Active Equity Portfolio Construction

The gains generated by		The losses generated by
▪ overweighting the securities that outperform the benchmark and	are, on average, >	▪ underweighting the securities that outperform the benchmark and
▪ underweighting the securities that underperform the benchmark.		▪ overweighting the securities that underperform the benchmark.

Fundamentals of Portfolio Construction

Conceptually, a manager can generate active returns by

- strategically adjusting the active weights of the securities to create long-term exposures to rewarded risks that are different from those of his benchmark;
- tactically adjusting the active weights of the securities using his skills/expertise in identifying mispricing in securities, sectors, rewarded risks, and so on, to generate alpha that cannot be explained by long-term exposure to rewarded risks; and
- assuming excessive idiosyncratic risk that may result in lucky or unlucky returns.

Historically, any excess return over the benchmark was often termed "alpha." More sophisticated investors then moved to evaluating managers on the basis of excess *risk-adjusted* returns, where risk was assessed relative to a cap-weighted index. The information ratio became an important measure of the manager's value-added. Today, research supports the argument that much of what was historically viewed as alpha is, in fact, "alternative beta"—exposure to rewarded risks (often referred to as "priced factors" or "rewarded factors") that can be obtained at much lower cost.[1] In this reading, we use "rewarded factors" as a generic term that refers specifically to investment risks for which investors expect to be compensated through a long-run return premium, such as exposure to market risk and liquidity risk. The existence of numerous rewarded factors is well documented in the literature and supported by strong empirical evidence. The recognition of this phenomenon is fundamentally altering the investment management industry, with large asset owners negotiating fee structures that compensate active managers for returns above and beyond those that can be generated by simple exposure to rewarded factors.[2]

These three sources of active return remain the same whether a manager follows a fundamental/discretionary or quantitative/systematic approach, a bottom-up or top-down strategy, or a style such as value or growth at a reasonable price. Of course, the proportion of return sourced from exposure to rewarded factors, alpha, and luck will vary among managers and portfolio management approaches. Equation 2 expresses the decomposition of *ex post* active returns in terms of these components:

$$R_A = \sum \left(\beta_{pk} - \beta_{bk}\right) \times F_k + (\alpha + \varepsilon) \qquad (2)$$

---

[1] Kahn and Lemmon (2016); Bender, Hammond, and Mok (2014).
[2] Rewarded factors were discussed in the Level II reading "An Introduction to Multifactor Models." For example, Fama and French (1992) introduced a three-factor model that includes Market, Size, and Value, which was complemented with Momentum by Carhart (1997). However, there are potentially many more factors, such as liquidity, low beta, and credit. There are also factors related to surprises in macroeconomic variables, such as interest rates, inflation, and business cycles, although academicians have had much more difficulty identifying reliable return premiums to these types of macroeconomic factors.

where

β_{pk} = the sensitivity of the portfolio (*p*) to each rewarded factor (*k*)

β_{bk} = the sensitivity of the benchmark to each rewarded factor[3]

F_k = the return of each rewarded factor

$(\alpha + \varepsilon)$ = the part of the return that cannot be explained by exposure to rewarded factors. The volatility of this component is very much dependent on how a manager sizes individual positions in his portfolio. The alpha (α) is the active return of the portfolio that can be attributed to the specific skills/strategies of the manager—skills such as security selection and factor timing. ε is the idiosyncratic return, often resulting from a random shock, such as a company announcing unexpected earnings. It could also be called noise or luck (good or bad). Although managers generate returns above or below those that can be explained by the exposure to rewarded factors, it is very difficult to isolate how much of this return differential can be attributed to alpha/skill or to noise/luck.[4]

Although not all active managers expressly employ a factor methodology in creating active returns, the growth of exchange-traded funds, coupled with the disappointing after-fee performance of many active managers, is expanding the factor-based view of the investment landscape. It is important to understand the components of active returns (exposure to rewarded risks, alpha, and luck) and how Equation 2 explicitly or implicitly relates to various management styles and approaches.

To illustrate, let's consider two hypothetical managers: a systematic manager (Quanto) and a discretionary manager (Evolo). Each claims to have a "Value" orientation.

Quanto estimates the "Value" characteristics of each security in his investment universe using such proxies as the ratios of price to book and forward earnings to price. He then uses a systematic allocation methodology that determines the specific active weights that can be expected to deliver the desired exposure to the Value factor. Quanto holds a large number of securities to limit the impact of idiosyncratic risks on performance. Quanto attempts to outperform the benchmark by choosing factor exposures that differ from those of the benchmark.

Evolo has developed a comprehensive measure of value using a forward-looking free cash flow model. This allows Evolo to compare her own estimates of security valuation to the current market price for each security covered by the firm. The manager uses her judgment to determine the appropriate active weights based on her own level of confidence in each estimate. She runs a concentrated portfolio because she believes she has an edge in setting the appropriate active weights.

Although Evolo is not using a systematic approach to determine the active security weights and the overall portfolio exposure to the Value factor, she is driven by a Value philosophy and is exposed to the Value factor. Her returns will be driven in part by this factor exposure, even if she has never seen Equation 2. Indeed, if her portfolio is not exposed to the Value factor, clients and consultants may question her claim to run a value-oriented portfolio. If Evolo has developed a better Value proxy than her competitors and if she is skilled at identifying the best and worst securities and setting

---

3 Because the investable universe as a whole (the market) is usually much larger than the investment universe defined by any single benchmark, most benchmarks have an inherent exposure to the Market factor different from one and some net exposure (different from zero) to other rewarded factors.

4 If one observes only a small number of active returns, it may be difficult to infer whether the active return is zero or significantly different from zero given the likely volatility of realized active returns.

appropriate active weights, part of her active return will be attributed to her alpha skills. Because Evolo runs a more concentrated portfolio, the portion of her active performance attributed to idiosyncratic risk will likely be greater.

Building Blocks Used in Portfolio Construction

This section introduces the three main building blocks of portfolio construction—*rewarded factor weightings*, *alpha skills*, and *position sizing* (shown in Exhibit 1)—and explains how each relates to the three broad sources of active returns. A fourth critical component of portfolio construction, *breadth of expertise*, is necessary to assemble these three building blocks into a successful portfolio construction process.

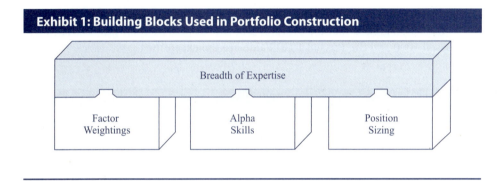

Exhibit 1: Building Blocks Used in Portfolio Construction

First Building Block: Overweight or Underweight Rewarded Factors

Let's begin by considering the market portfolio as our benchmark. The market portfolio encompasses all securities, and the weight of each security is proportional to its market capitalization. Our benchmark would have an exposure (or beta, β) of 1 to the Market factor and no net exposure to other rewarded factors, such as Size, Value, and Momentum.[5]

However, most individual securities have a β less than or greater than 1 to the Market factor and most will also have a non-zero exposure to the other factors. Indeed, one way an active manager can try to add value over and above the market portfolio is to choose, explicitly or implicitly, exposures to rewarded risks that differ from those of the market.

Practically speaking, most investors use narrower market proxies as a benchmark: the S&P 500 Index for a US mandate, the FTSE 100 Index for a UK mandate, or the MSCI All Country World Index (ACWI)[6] for a global mandate, for example. These indexes, although quite broad, do not include all securities that are publicly traded. Thus, these well-known indexes may not have a β of exactly 1 to the Market factor and could very well have a net exposure to other rewarded factors. For example, although most large-cap indexes usually have a β close to 1 to the Market factor, they usually have a negative sensitivity to the Size factor, indicating their large-cap tilt. When a manager is creating an exposure to a rewarded risk, the exposure must be established relative to that of his benchmark to achieve an expected excess return.

---

5 Market is a long-only factor, whereas other factors, such as Size and Value, are defined as long/short factors. Hence, the exposure of the market portfolio to the Market factor should be 1, whereas the exposure of the market portfolio to other factors should be 0.
6 The MSCI ACWI is a cap-weighted index that represents sources of equity returns from 23 developed and 24 emerging markets.

The growing understanding of rewarded factors is profoundly changing the view of active and passive investing. There are many investment products that allow investors to directly access such factors as Value, Size, Momentum, and Quality, and the bar for active managers is rising: An active value manager not only needs to outperform a passive value benchmark but may also need to outperform a rules-based value-tilted product. In the following discussion, we illustrate the concept of returns to factors and the application of this concept to portfolio management.

Exhibit 2 illustrates the factor exposures of the Russell 1000 Index, the Russell 1000 Value Index, and a discretionary mid-cap value fund (using the four Fama–French and Carhart factors) over a discrete 26-year period. The performance of the actively managed fund is presented before the deduction of fees to make the comparison with benchmark returns fair.

The average monthly performance of each factor is specified in the last column.[7] All four factors showed positive returns over the period. Most regression coefficients are statistically significant at the 5% level (not shown); the momentum coefficients of the Russell 1000 and the Russell 1000 Value are the exceptions.

Exhibit 2: Risk Factor Exposure

	Russell 1000 Index	Russell 1000 Value Index	Value Fund	Factor Performance US Market
Monthly performance in excess of the risk-free rate	0.64%	0.66%	0.40%	—
β to specified factor:				
Market*	0.99	0.92	0.90	0.64%
Size	−0.16	−0.23	0.13	0.16%
Value	0.02	0.41	0.59	0.18%
Momentum	−0.01	0.13	0.09	0.61%
"Alpha" (monthly)	0.05%	−0.05%	−0.35%	—
R^2	0.99	0.95	0.74	

* As mentioned in footnote 3, the Market factor is built from a much larger universe of securities than are traditional benchmarks, such as the Russell 1000. Therefore, we should not expect the β of indexes to the Market factor to be necessarily equal to one.
Note: All data are measured in US dollars.
Sources: Factor data for the United States are from AQR Capital Management, market data are from Bloomberg, and calculations are from the authors.

The Russell 1000 Index has a Market β close to 1, a negative exposure to the Size factor (indicating it has a large-cap tilt), and almost no sensitivity to the Value and Momentum factors. This is what we would expect for a capitalization-weighted large-cap index. In comparison, the Russell 1000 Value Index has a lower Market β and a significant exposure to the Value factor, also in line with expectations. Finally, the mid-cap value fund has positive exposure to the Size factor (consistent with its mid-cap tilt) and a very significant exposure to the Value factor.

In these regression specifications, there is still a component of return that cannot be explained by the rewarded factors alone. It is often labeled "alpha." This may be true alpha, or it may be simply noise/luck. The two indexes have a relatively small alpha,

---

7 Pricing and accounting data used by AQR are from the union of the CRSP tape and the Compustat/Xpressfeed Global database. The data include all available common stocks in the merged CRSP/Xpressfeed data.

whereas the value fund has a significantly negative alpha of −0.35% per month. An alpha of this magnitude is unlikely to be explained by a small misspecification in the factor model. An investor considering this fund would need to investigate the causes of this negative alpha.

In Exhibit 3, we show the sources of performance of each product in terms of its exposure to each of the four factors and its respective alpha. In all cases, the Market factor is the dominant source of performance. The Value and Momentum factors did contribute positively to performance for the Russell 1000 Value, but much of this performance was lost because of the large-cap tilt and the negative alpha. The value fund did get a significant performance boost from the Value tilt, but much of it was lost to the very poor alpha in this period.

Exhibit 3: Sources of Performance (February 1990–December 2016)

Source of Performance	Russell 1000	Russell 1000 Value	Value Fund
Market	0.63%	0.59%	0.57%
Size	−0.03%	−0.04%	0.02%
Value	0.00%	0.08%	0.11%
Momentum	−0.01%	0.08%	0.05%
Alpha	0.05%	−0.05%	−0.35%
Total monthly performance	0.64%	0.66%	0.40%

Source: Calculations by authors.

These examples illustrate the components of Equation 2. Irrespective of the manager's investment approach—whether she explicitly targets factors or focuses only on securities she believes to be attractively priced—her portfolio performance can be analyzed in terms of factors. Some portion of returns will not be explained by factors, which may be attributable to

- the unique skills and strategies of the manager (alpha),
- an incomplete factor model that ignores relevant factors, or
- exposure to idiosyncratic risks that either helped or hurt performance.

The next section discusses the alpha skills building block.

Second Building Block: Alpha Skills

In principle, there are many approaches that can be used to generate alpha, but in practice, generating positive alpha in a zero-sum game environment (before fees) is a challenge.[8] Furthermore, the alpha generated by active managers must be sufficient to cover the higher fees usually associated with active management.

Let's initially consider rewarded factors. With exposures to rewarded factors increasingly accessible via rule-based indexes, simple static exposure to known rewarded factors is no longer widely considered a source of alpha. However, successfully timing that exposure *would* be a source of alpha. For example, some managers

---

[8] Investing is often considered a zero-sum game (before fees) because all investors in aggregate own the market. Assuming all investors in a specific market (such as US equity) have a similar and appropriate benchmark, for each investor that outperforms the benchmark by $1, there would be another investor or group of investors that underperforms the benchmark by $1. Hence, in a zero-sum game, we can outperform only at the expense of someone else. The average level of expertise of market participants in that market does not change this observation. Although beyond the scope of this reading, if different investors use different benchmarks, the zero-sum game analogy may not be appropriate.

believe part of their skill emanates from an understanding of when rewarded factor returns might be greater than or less than their average returns (factor timing). Hence, in periods when the market return is negative, a manager with an exposure (β) to the Market factor substantially less than 1 will outperform the market and will probably also outperform many other managers. Similarly, a beta greater than 1 in a rising market would drive strong portfolio performance relative to the market. Exposure to the Market factor can be adjusted by investing in securities having, on average, Market betas less than or greater than 1.

Exhibit 4 shows the cumulative value of $100 invested in both the Russell 1000 Growth Index and the Russell 1000 Value Index over a 10-year period ending in 2020. The Growth index produced superior performance over the full 10-year time span.[9]

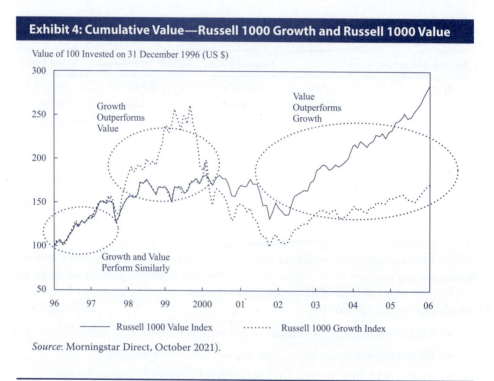

Exhibit 4: Cumulative Value—Russell 1000 Growth and Russell 1000 Value

Source: Morningstar Direct, October 2021).

In principle, alpha can also be generated from timing exposure to *unrewarded* factors, such as regional exposure, sector exposure, the price of commodities, or even security selection. For example, there is no theoretical basis supporting an expectation that a portfolio with greater-than-benchmark sensitivity to oil prices will be rewarded in the long term. Oil price fluctuations are certainly a risk, but oil price is not a rewarded factor. However, a manager who held a very specific view about the future of oil prices and correctly anticipated the decline in the price of oil that started in June 2014 and ended in March 2016 would have had a strong incentive to reduce his exposure to the energy sector and especially to smaller, less integrated, and more indebted energy companies, which performed poorly as a result of the price movement. A discretionary manager might refer to these as *thematic exposures*. Although oil prices are not a rewarded "factor," his skill in timing that exposure would have been amply rewarded. The literature thus far has found little evidence of an ability to consistently time rewarded factors, but it is conceivable that a skillful manager could have identified a factor that has yet to be recognized by the academic or investment community.

---

9 See Asness (2017).

Building Blocks of Active Equity Portfolio Construction

In summary, active returns arising from skillful timing of exposure to rewarded factors, unrewarded factors, or even other asset classes (such as cash) constitute a manager's alpha—the second building block.

Third Building Block: Sizing Positions

Position sizing is about balancing managers' confidence in their alpha and factor insights while mitigating idiosyncratic risks. Although position sizing influences all three components of Equation 2, its most dramatic impact is often on idiosyncratic risk. For example, consider a manager seeking to create a greater exposure to the Value and Size factors. She could achieve the same average exposure (beta) to these factors by allocating her portfolio to 20 securities or 200 securities. However, the level of idiosyncratic risk and the potential impact of luck on performance will be much greater in the concentrated portfolio. In concentrated portfolios, the volatility of the active return $\left(\sigma_{R_A}\right)$ attributed to idiosyncratic risks (σ_ε) will likely be more significant.

In other words, there may be greater deviations between realized portfolio returns and expected returns.

A manager's choices with respect to portfolio concentration are a function of his beliefs regarding the nature of his investment skill. The factor-oriented manager believes that she is skilled at properly setting and balancing her exposure to rewarded factors. She targets specific exposure to factors (the $\Sigma \left(\beta_{pk} - \beta_{bk}\right) \times F_k$ part of Equation 2) and maintains a diversified portfolio to minimize the impact of idiosyncratic risk. The stock picker believes that he is skilled at forecasting security-specific performance over a specific horizon and expresses his forward-looking views using a concentrated portfolio, assuming a higher degree of idiosyncratic risk (the α + ε part of Equation 2).

DIVERSIFICATION, VOLATILITY, AND IDIOSYNCRATIC RISK

The stock picker must carefully consider influences that can substantially alter the absolute or relative risk profile of his portfolio. Consider, for example, the absolute volatility of the Russell 1000 Index and its underlying securities over the 12 months ending in October 2016. During this period:

- the index had an annualized daily volatility of 15.7%;
- the weighted average volatility of all securities in the index was substantially higher, about 26.7%;
- the average volatility of the 100 smallest securities in the index was approximately 41%;
- the average volatility of the 100 largest securities in the index was approximately 24%.

This disparity in individual stock volatility illustrates the potential of diversification. A concentrated portfolio is unlikely to achieve the low volatility of the Russell 1000 unless the manager specifically emphasizes investing in stocks that have a lower average volatility than that of the average security in the index.

Exhibit 5 illustrates the effect of diversification on total portfolio risk at two different levels of average individual stock volatility. (We use the standard deviation of returns as our measure of risk here.) Total portfolio volatility is a function of the average individual stock volatility and the number of securities in the portfolio. The calculations assume an average cross correlation of 0.24, consistent with the historical average correlation for Russell 1000 securities since 1979.

Exhibit 5: Total Portfolio Volatility as a Function of Concentration and Single Stock Volatility[10]

	Single Stock Volatility	
	25%	30%
Number of Securities	Portfolio Volatility	
10	14.1%	16.9%
30	12.9%	15.5%
50	12.6%	15.2%
100	12.4%	14.9%
500	12.3%	14.7%

Examining this table closely, we can see that diversification is a powerful tool but that it has its limitations. Even the most diversified portfolio of high-volatility stocks (the 500-stock portfolio with an average single-stock volatility of 30%) cannot achieve the same level of volatility inherent in the portfolios of lower-volatility stocks. Even the most concentrated portfolio of lower-volatility stocks displays a portfolio volatility lower than that of the highly diversified portfolio of higher-volatility stocks.

The concentrated portfolio, however, bears higher idiosyncratic risk, which can substantially influence portfolio performance. The manager's choices with respect to the magnitude of his active weights and the volatility of the securities with the highest active weights will be significant determinants of the portfolio's active return and active risk.

Active risk is a measure of the volatility of portfolio returns relative to the volatility of benchmark returns. It is expressed as follows:

$$\text{Active risk } \left(\sigma_{R_A}\right) = \sqrt{\frac{\sum_{t=1}^{T}(R_{At})^2}{T-1}} \quad (3)$$

where R_{At} represents the active return at time t and T equals the number of return periods. Active risk is often referred to as "tracking error."

All else being equal, a 1.0% allocation to a security that has a 0.2% weighting in the benchmark (Security A) will have a greater effect on the active risk of the portfolio than a 2.0% allocation to a security that has a 2.5% weighting in the benchmark (Security B). Despite the overall smaller position size of Security A, the active decision the manager made with respect to the weighting of Security A (an 80 bp difference from the benchmark weight) is significantly larger than the active decision with respect to the weight of Security B (a 50 bp difference). If Security A also has a higher volatility than Security B, the effect of the active decision will be magnified.

---

[10] This is a simplified example of Markowitz portfolio diversification where securities are equally weighted and all securities have the same volatility and cross correlation:

$$\sigma_p = \sqrt{\frac{1}{n}\sigma^2 + \frac{(n-1)}{n}\sigma^2 C},$$

where n is the number of securities, σ^2 is the equal variance of all securities, and C is the cross correlation between them.

> Similarly, all else equal, an active weight of 1.0% on a single security will have a greater impact on active risk than will an active weight of 0.2% on five separate securities. The imperfect cross correlations of active returns of the basket of five stocks would contribute to lowering the level of active risk.

To summarize, a manager's choice with respect to position sizing is influenced by her investment approach and the level of confidence she places on her analytic work. On the one hand, the stock picker with high confidence in her analysis of individual securities may be willing to assume high levels of idiosyncratic risk. This is consistent with her emphasis on the "α + ε" part of Equation 2. On the other hand, a manager focused on creating balanced exposures to rewarded factors is unlikely to assume a high level of idiosyncratic risk and is, therefore, quite likely to construct a highly diversified portfolio of individual securities.

Integrating the Building Blocks: Breadth of Expertise

The three foregoing building blocks encompass all of Equation 2, which we used to describe the sources of a manager's active returns:

- exposure to rewarded risks,
- timing of exposures to rewarded and unrewarded risks, and
- position sizing and its implications for idiosyncratic risk.

A manager may be more or less successful at combining these three sources of return into a portfolio. Success is a function of a manager's breadth of expertise. Broader expertise may increase the manager's likelihood of generating consistent, positive active returns.

The importance of breadth of expertise is implicit in the fundamental law of active management (covered extensively in the Level II reading "Analysis of Active Portfolio Management"), which implies that confidence in a manager's ability to outperform his benchmark increases when that performance can be attributed to a larger sample of independent decisions. Independent decisions are not the same thing as individual securities. Independent decisions are uncorrelated decisions, much like two uncorrelated stocks are diversifying. Thus, overweighting both General Motors and Toyota, two auto companies, relative to their benchmark weights are not fully independent decisions because much of their respective returns are driven by common influences—the strength of consumer spending, the price of gasoline, and the price of steel and aluminum, for example. In evaluating portfolio construction, one must distinguish between the nominal number of decisions a manager makes about his active weights and the effective number of independent decisions. Without truly independent decisions, performance may be influenced more significantly by common exposures to specific factors.[11] According to the fundamental law, the expected active portfolio return $E(R_A)$ is determined by the following:[12]

$$E(R_A) = IC\sqrt{BR}\,\sigma_{R_A}TC \tag{4}$$

---

[11] Although the fundamental law is an interesting concept for illustrating the main drivers of positive expected active returns, investment decisions are rarely truly independent. When using specific metrics to determine how to allocate to securities, managers emphasize securities that have common characteristics they deem to be relevant. The process by which managers determine their allocation to securities will affect the degree of independence of investment decisions. In other words, investing in the 100 securities among 1,000 that have the lowest price-to-book ratio does not lead to 100 independent decisions. Furthermore, we should not assume that the information coefficient of the manager is insensitive to the number of securities in his portfolio.

[12] The basic fundamental law was initially introduced by Grinold (1989) but was further expanded into the full fundamental law with the addition of the transfer coefficient by Clarke, de Silva, and Thorley (2002).

where

> IC = Expected **information coefficient** of the manager—the extent to which a manager's forecasted active returns correspond to the managers realized active returns
>
> BR = **Breadth**—the number of truly independent decisions made each year
>
> TC = **Transfer coefficient**, or the ability to translate portfolio insights into investment decisions without constraint (a truly unconstrained portfolio would have a transfer coefficient of 1)
>
> σ_{R_A} = the manager's active risk

For example, assuming an active risk of 6% (which many institutional investors would consider to be high), a transfer coefficient of 0.25 (representative of a constrained long-only investor), and an information coefficient of 0.10, the manager could expect to generate an active return of 15 bps yearly, on average, if she makes a single independent decision. If the manager wanted to achieve excess return of 1%, she would need to make approximately 40 fully independent decisions. Even if a manager does have positive information and transfer coefficients, it does not necessarily follow that excess return will be positive every year. A horizon of many years is required to have a reasonable probability of generating the expected excess return. However, a larger number of independent decisions will increase the probability of outperforming over a shorter horizon.

What is the implication of making multiple independent decisions? Assume two managers hold similarly diversified portfolios in terms of the number of securities and that both managers have outperformed the market over a specific period. Manager A has a pure value style and favors securities that have a low price-to-book ratio (a single valuation metric), whereas Manager B has a multidimensional, factor-based approach. Manager B's approach includes considerations related to valuation, price momentum, growth, balance sheet sustainability, quality of management, and so on, and considers a much larger set of metrics for each dimension (such as several metrics for valuation). Manager A's performance is largely attributed to a single dimension: his narrowly defined value bias. Although he holds 100 securities, he did not make 100 independent decisions.[13]

Manager B may not have 100 independent decisions embedded in her portfolio, but she likely has more than Manager A. Thus, the historical performance of Manager B may be a more reliable indicator of her ability to outperform in the future because her portfolio construction process integrates several dimensions and metrics, as well as their interactions. Her performance is less likely to be explained by how the market has recently favored a specific management style.

Let's take this example a bit further. Suppose Manager A makes 20 independent decisions and Manager B makes 40 independent decisions. Assume they both have the same information coefficient (0.2), the same active risk (4%), and the same transfer coefficient (0.6). What would be the expected active return of each manager? Using Equation 4:

Manager A: $0.2 \times \sqrt{20} \times 4\% \times 0.6 = 2.15\%$

Manager B: $0.2 \times \sqrt{40} \times 4\% \times 0.6 = 3.04\%$

---

[13] Consider an active manager who has a value and momentum style. Value is measured by the price-to-book ratio, and momentum is measured over a single historical period, such as $P_{t-1month}/P_{t-12months}$. Assume that his exposure to these two factors explains more than 60% of his excess return (consistent with a study by Bender, Hammond, and Mok, 2014). The portfolio exposure to these two risk factors has, therefore, had greater bearing on excess returns than have the security selection skills of the manager.

What if Manager A's information coefficient was only 0.1? How many independent decisions would the manager need to make to generate the same 2.15% expected active return?

Manager A: $0.1 \times \sqrt{x} \times 4\% \times 0.6 = 2.15\%$

$x \approx 80$

Assuming Manager A maintains a concentrated portfolio of twenty securities, what information coefficient would be required for Manager A to match the expected performance of Manager B?

Manager A: $x \times \sqrt{20} \times 4\% \times 0.6 = 3.04\%$

$x \approx 0.28$

Equation 4 illustrates the importance of breadth of expertise. As a practical matter, long-term success is not achieved by being right all the time but, rather, by being right often through small victories achieved consistently over long periods.

EXAMPLE 1

The Building Blocks of Asset Management

1. Proteus was launched as an asset management firm 20 years ago, after receiving assets of $100 million from a seed investor. Today, the firm has grown into a large organization with more than $30 billion in assets. Although the investment process has evolved, the firm has remained true to its core philosophy. It has also delivered strong risk-adjusted performance to its investors.

   Proteus's emphasis has always been to invest in quality companies, appropriately priced, which are benefiting from positive and sustained price momentum. Although fairly agnostic in terms of portfolio weights compared with benchmark weights, the managers of Proteus believe in avoiding extreme views. For example, sector deviations are limited to between 80% and 120% of benchmark weights plus or minus 500 bps; for example, a sector with a 20% weight in the index could have a weight in the portfolio ranging from 11% [(0.8 × 20%) − 5%] to 29% [(1.2 × 20%) + 5%]. An individual security position can be no more than the lesser of (1) 10 times its weight in the index or (2) its weight in the index + 1%. On average, Proteus's portfolios hold between 120 and 150 securities. The active risk is above 5%.

   As the firm grew in experience, research, and resources, the process of defining and measuring what is a quality company, appropriately priced, and benefiting from positive momentum evolved. Initially, the firm avoided companies that were the most indebted within their sector and favored those that generated strong cash flows to sales. It also favored companies that had a lower price-to-book value and had positive price momentum in the last 12 months.

   Today, Proteus still emphasizes quality, valuation, and price momentum but has considerably improved how those characteristics are measured and weighed. It now evaluates 45 metrics related to the financial health of the companies, the quality of its financial reporting, its valuation within its sector, and its short- and medium-term price momentum. It also developed its own weighting mechanism to appropriately weight each metric. The managers at Proteus believe their competitive advantage is the effort they invest in identifying, measuring, and weighing these metrics.

Discuss the contributions of rewarded factors, alpha skills, position sizing, and breadth of expertise for Proteus.

Solution:

Overall, Proteus has integrated all the primary dimensions of the investment process.

- Rewarded factors: Proteus recognizes the existence of rewarded factors, and it has significantly enhanced its measures of Quality, Value, and Momentum over time.
- Alpha skills: Given the commercial success of Proteus as a firm, we might safely assume that there is an alpha component in the process.
- Position sizing: Position size limits are integrated into the investment process to ensure diversification limits idiosyncratic risks.
- Breadth of expertise: Proteus has 20 years of experience refining and improving an investment process based on a consistent investment philosophy.

3. PORTFOLIO CONSTRUCTION APPROACHES

discuss approaches for constructing actively managed equity portfolios

Portfolio construction is part art and part science. It is about investment philosophy and the implementation of that philosophy. It requires an understanding of the technical principles of portfolio construction, filtered through a manager's core beliefs regarding her ability to add value using the building blocks discussed earlier:

- *Factor exposures:* How does she create her factor exposures? Does the manager believe she is skilled at extracting return premiums from rewarded factors? Or are her exposures to rewarded factors a residual of her in-depth research into the securities' fundamentals?
- *Timing:* Does she believe that she has skill in generating alpha through timing of portfolio exposures to rewarded and unrewarded factors or to security selection uncorrelated with exposures to either rewarded or unrewarded factors?
- *Position sizing:* How does she size portfolio positions? Is she confident about her expected return forecasts, and therefore runs a high-conviction portfolio? Or does she seek to reduce idiosyncratic risk by running a highly diversified portfolio?
- *Breadth or depth:* Does she rely on a specialized but narrower skill set or on a greater breadth of expertise?

A manager's portfolio construction process should reflect her beliefs with respect to the nature of her skills in each of these areas. The majority of investment approaches can be classified as either

- *systematic or discretionary* (the degree to which a portfolio construction process is subject to a set of predetermined rules or is left to the discretionary views of the manager)

and

- *bottom-up or top-down* (the degree to which security-specific factors, rather than macroeconomic factors, drive portfolio construction).

In addition, these approaches can vary in the extent to which they are *benchmark aware* versus *benchmark agnostic*. Each manager's investment approach is implemented within a framework that specifies the acceptable levels of active risk and **Active Share** relative to a clearly articulated benchmark. (Active Share is a measure of how similar a portfolio is to its benchmark.) A manager may emphasize these dimensions to varying degrees as he attempts to differentiate his portfolio from the benchmark.

The Implementation Process: The Choice of Portfolio Management Approaches

We previously identified three primary building blocks that managers can use in constructing a portfolio that reflects their core beliefs. Let's look at these in a little more detail, beginning with the systematic–discretionary continuum.

Systematic vs. Discretionary

How are a manager's beliefs regarding rewarded factor exposures, timing of factor exposures, exposure to unrewarded factors, and willingness to assume idiosyncratic risk reflected in a systematic investment process and in a discretionary investment process?

- Systematic strategies are more likely to be designed around the construction of portfolios seeking to extract return premiums from a balanced exposure to known, rewarded factors.
- Discretionary strategies search for active returns by building a greater depth of understanding of a firm's governance, business model, and competitive landscape, through the development of better factor proxies (e.g., a better definition of Quality), or through successful timing strategies. Factor timing is a challenging endeavor, and few factor-based systematic strategies have integrated a factor timing approach.
- Systematic strategies typically incorporate research-based rules across a broad universe of securities. For example, a simple systematic value methodology could filter out the 50% of securities that have the highest price-to-book ratio and then equally weight the remaining securities, leading to small individual portfolio positions. A more comprehensive approach might integrate a much larger number of considerations and balance total portfolio risk equally across them.
- Discretionary strategies integrate the judgment of the manager, usually on a smaller subset of securities. While a discretionary value manager might also rely on financial metrics to estimate the value characteristics of each security, she is likely to use her judgment to evaluate the relative importance of this information and assign appropriate weights to each security. A discretionary manager is also likely to integrate nonfinancial variables to

the equation, such as the quality of management, the competitive landscape, and the pricing power of the firm. (Systematic strategies also integrate judgment, but their judgment is largely expressed up front through the design of the strategy and the learning process that comes with its implementation.)

- Systematic strategies seek to reduce exposure to idiosyncratic risk and often use broadly diversified portfolios to achieve the desired factor exposure while minimizing security-specific risk.
- Discretionary strategies are generally more concentrated portfolios, reflecting the depth of the manager's insights on company characteristics and the competitive landscape.
- Systematic strategies are typically more adaptable to a formal portfolio optimization process. The systematic manager must, however, carefully consider the parameters of that optimization. What objective function is he seeking to maximize (information ratio, Sharpe ratio, index or factor exposure, etc.) or minimize (volatility, downside risk, etc.)? Will elements of his investment style (such as performance and valuation metrics) be incorporated into the objective function or into the constraints?
- Discretionary portfolio managers typically use a less formal approach to portfolio construction, building a portfolio of securities deemed attractive, subject to a set of agreed-upon risk constraints.

> **BRIDGING THE DIVIDE**
>
> The philosophical divide between systematic and discretionary managers seems to be shrinking. Systematic and discretionary strategies were commonly differentiated in terms of their breadth and depth (discretionary managers conducting more in-depth research on a sub-set of the securities universe) and systematic managers having more breadth (less in-depth research across the entire universe of securities). Although this remains generally true today, research and technology have been narrowing the gap. Advancements in and the accessibility of technology, together with the greater range of quality data available, are allowing discretionary managers to extend their in-depth analyses across a broader universe of securities. Technology also allows systematic managers to design strategies that can capture risk premiums in rewarded factors, a source of active returns that was previously considered to be part of the alpha of discretionary managers.

Bottom-Up vs. Top-Down

A top-down approach seeks to understand the overall geo-political, economic, financial, social, and public policy environment and then project how the expected environment will affect countries, asset classes, sectors, and then securities. An investment manager who projects that growth companies will outperform value companies, that financials will outperform industrials, that the US market will outperform the European market, that oil prices will increase, or that cash will outperform equity and then targets individual securities and/or a cash/stock allocation to reflect these views is following a top-down approach.

A manager following a bottom-up approach develops his understanding of the environment by first evaluating the risk and return characteristics of individual securities. The aggregate of these risk and return expectations implies expectations for the overall economic and market environment. An investment manager who expects Ford to outperform GM, AstraZeneca (a bio-pharmaceutical company) to outperform Ford, and Sony to outperform AstraZeneca and builds a portfolio based on these stock-specific forecasts is following a bottom-up approach. Although the resulting portfolio will contain an implicit expectation for sector, style, and country performance, this is nonetheless a bottom-up approach.

- Both top-down and bottom-up strategies typically rely on returns from factors. However, top-down managers are more likely to emphasize macro factors, whereas bottom-up managers emphasize security-specific factors.
- A top-down investment process contains an important element of factor timing. A manager who opportunistically shifts the portfolio to capture returns from rewarded or unrewarded factors, such as country, sectors, and styles, is following a top-down investment process. They may also embrace the same security characteristics sought by bottom-up managers as they translate their macro views into security-specific positions. A top-down investment process is also more likely to raise cash opportunistically when the overall view of the Market factor is unfavorable.
- Bottom-up managers may embrace such styles as Value, Growth at Reasonable Price, Momentum, and Quality. These strategies are often built around documented rewarded factors, whether explicitly or implicitly.
- A top-down manager is likely to run a portfolio concentrated with respect to macro factor exposures. Bottom-up managers and top-down managers can run portfolios that are either diversified or concentrated in terms of securities. Both a bottom-up stock picker and a top-down sector rotator can run concentrated portfolios. Both a bottom-up value manager and a top-down risk allocator can run diversified portfolios.

Some managers will incorporate elements of both top-down and bottom-up investment approaches.

A Summary of the Different Approaches

While most managers make some use of all the building blocks, we can make some general assertions about the relative importance and use of these building blocks to each of the implementation choices. They are summarized in the four quadrants of Exhibit 6.

Exhibit 6: Approaches and Their Use of Building Blocks

	Top-Down	
Systematic	• Emphasizes macro factors • Factor timing • Diversified	• Emphasizes macro factors • Factor timing • Diversified or concentrated depending on strategy and style
	• Emphasizes security specific factors • No factor timing • Diversified	• Emphasizes firm specific characteristics or factors • Potential factor timing • Diversified or concentrated depending on strategy and style
	Bottom-Up	Discretionary

- Exposure to rewarded factors can be achieved with either a systematic or discretionary approach.
- Bottom-up managers first emphasize security-specific factors, whereas top-down managers first emphasize macro factors.
- Factor timing is more likely to be implemented among discretionary managers, especially those with a top-down approach.
- Systematic managers are unlikely to run concentrated portfolios. Discretionary managers can have either concentrated or diversified portfolios, depending on their strategy and portfolio management style.
- In principle, a systematic top-down manager would emphasize macro factors and factor timing and would have diversified portfolios. However, there are few managers in this category.

4   MEASURES OF BENCHMARK-RELATIVE RISK

☐ discuss approaches for constructing actively managed equity portfolios

☐ distinguish between Active Share and active risk and discuss how each measure relates to a manager's investment strategy

Managers have very specific beliefs about the level of security concentration and the absolute or relative risk that they (and their investors) are willing to tolerate. Relative risk is measured with respect to the benchmark that the manager has adopted as representative of his investment universe. We know that a manager must have active weights different from zero in order to outperform his benchmark. How do we measure these weights?

Measures of Benchmark-Relative Risk

There are two measures of benchmark-relative risk used to evaluate a manager's success—Active Share and active risk—and they do not always move in tandem. A manager can pursue a higher Active Share without necessarily increasing active risk (and vice versa).

Active Share is easier to calculate than active risk; one only needs to know the weight of each security in the portfolio and the weight of the security in the benchmark. The formula for Active Share is shown in Equation 5. It measures the extent to which the number and sizing positions in a manager's portfolio differ from the benchmark.

$$\text{Active Share} = \frac{1}{2}\sum_{i=1}^{n}\left|\text{Weight}_{portfolio,i} - \text{Weight}_{benchmark,i}\right| \tag{5}$$

where n represents the total number of securities that are in either the portfolio or the benchmark.

The Active Share calculation involves no statistical analysis or estimation; it is simple arithmetic. Active Share is a measure of the differentiation of the holdings of a portfolio from the holdings of a chosen benchmark portfolio. It measures the proportion of a portfolio's holdings that is different from the benchmark for that portfolio. The Active Share is 0 for a portfolio that matches the benchmark and 100% for a portfolio that shares no investments with those of the benchmark. The percentage of portfolio assets deployed in the same way as the benchmark is equal to 100% minus the portfolio's Active Share. For example, an Active Share of 80% implies that 20% of the portfolio capital was invested in a similar way as the index. There are only two sources of Active Share:

- Including securities in the portfolio that are not in the benchmark
- Holding securities in the portfolio that are in the benchmark but at weights different than the benchmark weights

If two portfolios are managed against the same benchmark (and if they invest only in securities that are part of the benchmark), the portfolio with fewer securities will have a higher level of Active Share than the highly diversified portfolio. A portfolio manager has complete control over his Active Share because he determines the weights of the securities in his portfolio.

Active risk is a more complicated calculation. Like Active Share, active risk depends on the differences between the security weights in the portfolio and the security weights in the benchmark. There are two different measures of active risk. One is realized active risk, which is the actual, historical standard deviation between the portfolio return and the benchmark return as described in Equation 3. This number relies on historical returns and is easy to calculate. But portfolio construction is a forward-looking exercise, and in this context, the relevant measure is predicted active risk, which requires a forward-looking estimate of correlations and variances.[14] As the accuracy of the forward-looking estimates of correlations and variances improves, the likelihood of better portfolio outcomes also improves.

The variance–covariance matrix of returns is very important in the calculation of active risk. Although portfolios that have higher active risk tend to have higher Active Share (and vice versa), this is not always the case. For example, underweighting one

---

[14] To generate estimates of future volatility and correlations, different levels of sophistication can be considered. Although several methodologies are available, two dominant methodologies are exponentially weighted moving average (EWMA) and generalized autoregressive conditional heteroskedasticity (GARCH). EWMA applies greater weights to recent return observations, allowing for a more accurate representation of the near-term volatility environment. However, EWMA does not allow for regression to the mean to occur. More specifically, abnormally high or low levels of volatility in financial markets are expected to eventually normalize toward a long-term mean. The family of GARCH models integrates the benefits of EWMA and regression to the mean. The efficiency of risk forecasting and its implementation are illustrated in Langlois and Lussier (2017, pp. 82–85).

bank stock to overweight another bank stock will likely have less effect on active risk than underweighting one bank stock and overweighting an information technology stock. Active risk is affected by the degree of cross correlation, but Active Share is not. Active Share is not concerned with the efficiency of diversification.[15] If the extent of underweighting and overweighting is the same in the bank/bank over-/underweight and in the bank/technology over-/underweight, the effect on Active Share would be identical. The effect on active risk would be different, however, because the correlation of the bank/technology pair is most likely lower than the correlation of the bank/bank pair. This highlights an important difference in Active Share versus active risk. A portfolio manager can completely control Active Share, but she cannot completely control active risk because active risk depends on the correlations and variances of securities that are beyond her control. Recall that in Equation 2, we decomposed active return into returns to factors, alpha, and idiosyncratic risk.

$$\sigma_{R_A} = \sqrt{\sigma^2 \left(\Sigma \left(\beta_{pk} - \beta_{bk} \right) \times F_k \right) + \sigma_e^2} \qquad (6)$$

Here, we show that the active *risk* of a portfolio $\left(\sigma_{R_A} \right)$ is a function of the *variance* attributed to the factor exposure $\sigma^2 \left(\Sigma \left(\beta_{pk} - \beta_{bk} \right) \times F_k \right)$ and of the *variance* attributed to the idiosyncratic risk $\left(\sigma_e^2 \right)$.[16] Although realized active risk will almost never be identical to predicted active risk, existing risk forecasting methodologies allow the manager to predict active risk over a short horizon with a high level of accuracy. Managers can then control the level of active risk through portfolio structure.

Sapra and Hunjan (2013) derived a relationship between active risk, Active Share, and factor exposure for an unconstrained investor, assuming a single-factor model. They found that

- high net exposure to a risk factor will lead to a high level of active risk, irrespective of the level of idiosyncratic risk;
- if the factor exposure is fully neutralized, the active risk will be entirely attributed to Active Share;
- the active risk attributed to Active Share will be smaller if the number of securities is large and/or average idiosyncratic risk is small; and
- the level of active risk will rise with an increase in factor and idiosyncratic volatility (such as occurred in 2008).[17]

These observations are very intuitive: Active risk increases when a portfolio becomes more uncorrelated with its benchmark. As discussed previously, although overweighting or underweighting GM relative to Ford will generate some Active Share, it will typically not generate much active risk. However, overweighting or underweighting energy firms versus financial firms, small-cap firms versus large-cap firms, or growth firms versus value firms will certainly contribute more to active risk.

---

15 Active Share is often used to determine how much fees an investor is paying for active management. For example, if two managers charge asset management fees of 0.5%, the manager with an Active Share of 0.80 offers twice as much "active" management per unit of fees as a manager with an Active Share of 0.40.
16 The variance attributed to alpha returns is embedded in the variance of idiosyncratic risks.
17 In 2008, markets were faced with the worst crisis of confidence and liquidity since the Great Depression. This situation triggered a deep global recession and rising unemployment and debt levels. The Market factor performed poorly, but the onset of the economic decline, the Lehman Brothers' bankruptcy on 15 September 2008, and the exposure of financial firms to weak mortgage and leveraged credit led to poor performance of value stocks and, consequently, of the Value factor. Furthermore, the forced deleveraging of many trades/strategies led to the biggest decline of the Momentum factor in more than 70 years.

Measures of Benchmark-Relative Risk

So how do we use these two measures to discriminate between different portfolio management approaches and management styles? Using the observations from Sapra and Hunjan (2013), we could characterize a manager as

- factor neutral, factor diversified, or factor concentrated and as
- diversified (with low security concentration and low idiosyncratic risk) or concentrated (with high security concentration and high idiosyncratic risk).[18]

Exhibit 7 illustrates how various combinations of factor exposure and idiosyncratic risk affect Active Share and active risk.[19]

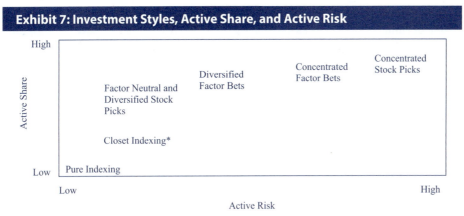

*A **closet indexer** is defined as a fund that advertises itself as being actively managed but is substantially similar to an index fund in its exposures.

Using this framework, we can classify most equity strategies in terms of active risk and Active Share by analyzing the specific management style of the manager. For example, most multi-factor products have a low concentration among securities, often holding more than 250 positions (the purpose of these products is to achieve a balanced exposure to risk factors and minimize idiosyncratic risks). They are diversified across factors and securities. Thus, they typically have a high Active Share, such as 0.70, but they have reasonably low active risk (tracking error), often in the range of ±3%.

The concentrated stock picker, in contrast, has both a high Active Share (typically above 0.90) and a high active risk (such as 8%–12% or higher).[20] (The average active manager owns about 100 stocks, and fewer than 20% of managers own more than 200 stocks.) It follows, then, that the level of idiosyncratic risk in the average active discretionary portfolio is greater than that of the average multi-factor fund, with its 250+ positions. Therefore, on average, we could expect the portfolio of a typical discretionary manager to display higher active risk.

Consequently, a manager can increase his degree of control over the level of Active Share and/or active risk in his portfolio by decreasing his security concentration. For example, it would not be uncommon for a sector rotator—typically a high-active-risk

---

18 See Ceria (2015).
19 Factor portfolios usually have low security concentration.
20 See Yeung, Pellizzari, Bird, and Abidin (2012).

strategy—to have an active risk above 8%. If he chooses to run a concentrated portfolio, he might also have high Active Share. Or he can diversify his portfolio and reduce his Active Share.[21]

Petajisto (2013) provided examples of funds of different styles and their corresponding active risk and Active Share; see Exhibit 8. The risk tolerance and portfolio construction approach of each manager is partially revealed by his Active Share and active risk. Exhibit 9 presents the same information but plots it in the Active Share/active risk dimension using the format of Exhibit 7.

Exhibit 8: Active Risk, Active Share, and Portfolio Styles Examples

Name of Fund	Style/Comments	Active Risk	Active Share
Vanguard Index Fund	Indexed	0.0%	0.00
RiverSource Disciplined Equity Fund	Large-Cap Growth (Small active weight, limited factor timing)	4.4%	0.54
T. Rowe Price Mid-Cap Value Fund	Mid-Cap Value (Limited active weights on sectors but significant stock picking)	5.4%	0.93
AIM Constellation Fund	Large-Cap Growth (Significant sector bets)	9.7%	0.66
GMO Quality Fund	Mega-Cap Core (Timing on a number of factors and cash)	12.9%	0.65
Sequoia	Stock Picker (Highly concentrated positions)	14.1%	0.97

Source: Petajisto (2013).

Exhibit 9: Active Risk, Active Share, and Portfolio Styles

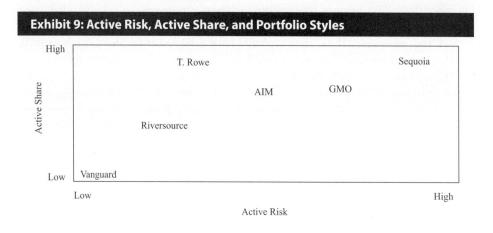

---

21 It is important to use an appropriate index when calculating the level of Active Share. A manager whose investment universe is the S&P 500 could see her Active Share increase by approximately 12% if the Russell 1000 index was used to compute the Active Share. By default, a portfolio of 500 stocks will have high Active Share if Active Share is measured against the Russell 1000 Index.

Measures of Benchmark-Relative Risk

Active risk and Active Share provide information about the level of managers' activism against their benchmark, but there is little research on the relative efficiency of different asset management styles translating higher active risk or Active Share into higher active returns. However, many investors are using Active Share to assess the fees that they pay per unit of active management. For example, a fund with an Active Share of 0.25 (a closet indexer) would be considered expensive relative to a fund with an Active Share of 0.75 if both funds were charging the same fees.

Not all investment products neatly fall into the categorization we have just presented. Niche equity strategies, such as statistical arbitrage, event-driven investing, and activist investing, focus on generating alpha returns generally without regard to factor exposures or factor timing. These strategies do, however, typically assume a high level of idiosyncratic risk.

EXAMPLE 2

Portfolio Construction—Approaches and Return Drivers

1. You are evaluating two equity managers. Explain how Manager A, with his high level of Active Share, is able to achieve such a low active risk. What are the implications for Manager B's performance relative to that of Manager A?

	Manager A	Manager B
Active Share	0.73	0.71
Active risk	2.8%	6.0%
Number of positions	120	125

Solution:

Managers A and B have a similar number of positions and similar Active Share. Manager B has much higher active risk. A high Active Share says only that a manager's security-level weights are quite different from those of the index. A 0.5% underallocation to one security and a 0.5% over-allocation to another security will have the same impact on Active Share whether these two securities are in the same sector or in different sectors. Given similar levels of Active Share, it is likely that Manager B's active risk is driven by active decisions at the sector level rather than at the security level. Clearly, they implement very different investment strategies. Although we cannot draw a direct conclusion about the ability of Manager B to outperform Manager A, we can assume that the realized outcomes of Manager B are likely to be much more dispersed about the benchmark (both in positive and negative directions) given the higher level of active risk.

2. Discuss the drivers of return for Managers A and B.

	Manager A	Manager B	Factor Returns
Monthly performance in excess of the risk-free rate	0.65%	0.65%	
"Alpha" (monthly)	0.00%	0.20%	
Beta to:			
Market*	0.99	1.05	0.45%
Size	0	−0.2	0.20%

	Manager A	Manager B	Factor Returns
Value	0.15	0.05	0.35%
Momentum	0.25	0	0.60%
R-squared	0.99	0.78	

Market factor is built from a much larger universe of securities than traditional benchmarks such as the Russell 1000. Therefore, we should not expect the β of indexes to the Market factor to be necessarily equal to one.

Solution:

Both managers generated the same absolute return, but they achieved their performance in very different ways. All of Manager A's performance can be explained from exposure to rewarded factors. There is no alpha, and the high R^2 shows that the four factors explain much of the monthly variability in returns. Manager A did outperform the Market factor by 20 bps (0.65% − 0.45%). The excess return can be attributed to the significant exposure (0.25) to the strong-performing Momentum factor (0.60%). Exposure to the Value factor explains the balance.

Manager B generated significant alpha (20 bps per month). The relatively low R^2 indicates that much of the variability of returns is unexplained by the factors. Manager B's performance must, therefore, be attributed to either her alpha skills or idiosyncratic risks that favored the manager's investment approach during the period.

3. Based on the information provided below regarding four managers benchmarked against the MSCI World Index, identify the manager most likely to be a:

   a. closet indexer.
   b. concentrated stock picker.
   c. diversified multi-factor investor.
   d. sector rotator.

   Justify your response.

Manager Constraints:	A	B	C	D
Target active risk	10%	1%	4%	7%
Max. sector deviations	0%	3%	10%	15%
Max. risk contribution, single security	5%	1%	1%	3%

Solution:

Manager B is a closet indexer. The low targeted active risk combined with the narrow sector deviation constraint indicates that the manager is making very few active bets.

Manager A is likely a concentrated stock picker. The 10% active risk target indicates a willingness to tolerate significant performance deviations from the market. The 5% limit on a single security's contribution to portfolio risk indicates he is willing to run a concentrated portfolio. The unwillingness to take sector deviations combined with the high tolerance for idiosyncratic risk indicates that the manager likely focuses on stock selection and is, therefore, a stock picker.

Manager C limits single-security risk contribution to no more than 1%, which implies a highly diversified portfolio. The significant sector deviations despite this high diversification are often indicative of a multi-factor manager. The relatively low tracking error further supports the argument that Manager C is a multi-factor manager.

Manager D has characteristics consistent with a sector rotator. The significant active risk and high tolerance for sector deviations and security concentration are what one would expect to find with a sector rotator.

4. Discuss the main differences between top-down and bottom-up portfolio management approaches and how they relate to two of the building blocks: exposure to rewarded factors and alpha.

Solution:

Factor exposure.

Bottom-up managers look at characteristics of securities to build their portfolios. The factor exposure inherent in their portfolios may be intentional, or it may be a by-product of their security selection process. Top-down managers articulate a macro view of the investment universe and build a portfolio emphasizing the macro factors that reflect those views. Although their macro views could then be translated into security views using a bottom-up approach, their performance will likely be dominated by their macro-level factor exposures.

Alpha.

In the context of Equation 2, the alpha of bottom-up managers is most likely attributable to their security selection skills. Some portion of their active return can also be explained through exposure to rewarded factors. Top-down managers' alphas are largely derived from factor timing.

OBJECTIVES AND CONSTRAINTS 5

☐ discuss approaches for constructing actively managed equity portfolios

☐ distinguish between Active Share and active risk and discuss how each measure relates to a manager's investment strategy

The simplest conceptual way to think about portfolio construction is to view it as an optimization problem. A standard optimization problem has an objective function and a set of constraints. The objective function defines the desired goal while the constraints limit the actions one can take to achieve that goal. Portfolio managers are trying to achieve desirable outcomes within the bounds of permissible actions. The nature of the objective function and the nature and specifics of the constraints can be indicative of an investment manager's philosophy and style.

A common objective function in portfolio management is to maximize a risk-adjusted return. If risk is being measured by predicted active risk, then the objective function is seeking to maximize the information ratio (the ratio of active return to active risk). If risk is being measured by predicted portfolio volatility, then the objective function is seeking to maximize the Sharpe ratio (the ratio of return in excess of the risk-free rate to portfolio volatility). Ideally, these objective functions would specify *net* returns—adjusted for the costs associated with implementation.

Typical constraints in the portfolio optimization problem may include limits on geographic, sector, industry, and single-security exposures and may also specify limits on transaction costs (to limit turnover and/or help manage liquidity issues). They may also include limits on exposure to specific factors; for example, the investment process may specify a required minimum market capitalization for any single security or a minimum weighted average capitalization for the portfolio as a whole. Or it may specify a maximum price-to-book ratio for any single security or a maximum weighted average price-to-book ratio for the portfolio. Constraints can be defined relative to the benchmark or without regard to it. Setting constraints that properly express the risk dimensions being monitored, the desired level of risk taking, and the preferred portfolio structure while still allowing sufficient flexibility to achieve the risk and return goals is a challenging task. In principle, the active equity manager's portfolio is the final blend that maximizes the objective function subject to the portfolio constraints.

Not all portfolio managers engage in such a formalistic, scientific approach to portfolio construction. The objectives and constraints of systematic managers are explicitly specified, whereas those of discretionary managers are less explicitly specified. However, most managers at least conceptually optimize their portfolios using the expected returns for each security, their own view of risk, and constraints imposed by the stated portfolio construction process or by the client. For our purposes, it is useful to frame the problem in this technical manner to provide a framework for discussion of the portfolio construction process.

Objectives and constraints may be stated in absolute terms or relative to a benchmark. Exhibit 10 illustrates two generic objective functions—one that is absolute and one that is relative. Each is subject to a few specific constraints.

Exhibit 10: Objective Functions and Constraints

	Absolute Framework	Relative Framework
Objective Function:	Maximize Sharpe Ratio	Maximize Information Ratio
Constraint		
Individual security weights (w)	$w_i \leq 2\%$	$|w_{ip} - w_{ib}| \leq 2\%$
Sectors weights (S)	$S_i \leq 20\%$	$|S_{ip} - S_{ib}| \leq 10\%$
Portfolio volatility (σ)	$\sigma_p < 0.9\,\sigma_b$	—
Active risk (TE)	—	$TE \leq 5\%$
Weighted average capitalization (Z)	$Z \geq 20\text{bn}$	$Z \geq 20\text{bn}$

- The absolute approach seeks to maximize the Sharpe ratio; the relative approach seeks to maximize the information ratio.
- The absolute approach limits any single security position to no more than 2% of the portfolio and any single sector to no more than 20% of the portfolio; the relative approach imposes a constraint that a security must remain within ±2% of its index weight and sector weights must remain within ±10% of the index weights.

Objectives and Constraints

- The absolute approach imposes a portfolio volatility limit equal to 90% of the estimated benchmark volatility and imposes a minimum weighted average security capitalization of $20 billion; the relative approach imposes a 5% active risk limit and the same capitalization constraint.
- Managers can also combine relative and absolute constraints in the same framework, such as limiting sector deviations against a benchmark while imposing absolute limits on security positions.

Other optimization approaches specify their objectives in terms of the risk metrics, such as portfolio volatility, downside risk, maximum diversification, and drawdowns. These approaches do not integrate an explicit expected return component. However, they do implicitly create an exposure to risk factors. For example, products built using a risk-based objective function (such as minimum variance or maximum diversification)[22] often exhibit a Market beta below 1.0 and have a statistically significant exposure to the Value factor and to the low-minus-high-β factor.[23] This occurs because an objective function that seeks to manage or minimize risk will tend to favor value and low-beta securities.

Finally, not all objective functions are explicitly concerned with risk or returns. For example, Equation 7 shows an explicit objective function that might be specified by a quantitative manager seeking to maximize exposure to rewarded factors:

$$\text{MAX} \left(\sum_{i=1}^{N} \tfrac{1}{3}\text{Size}_i + \tfrac{1}{3}\text{Value}_i + \tfrac{1}{3}\text{Momentum}_i \right) \tag{7}$$

where Size_i, Value_i, and Momentum_i are standardized[24] proxy measures of Size, Value, and Momentum for security i.[25] The portfolio may also be subject to additional constraints similar to those in Exhibit 10.

Of course, articulating an explicit objective of maximizing the Sharpe ratio or the information ratio or minimizing a given risk measure implies that we have information about expected returns and expected risk. Some managers—typically discretionary managers—do not make explicit return and risk forecasts and instead seek to "maximize" their exposure to securities having specific characteristics. Embedded in their investment process is an implicit return-to-risk objective.

For example, the objective function of a discretionary manager may be expressed in a mission statement such as: "We are a deep value manager in large-cap US equity with a concentrated, best ideas style." They then identify securities possessing deep value characteristics (as they define value). The portfolio construction process will balance security concentration and sector exposure as the manager seeks to maximize the return at an acceptable level of risk. The allocation may be driven by the manager's judgment about the risk and return trade-offs, or a formal risk management protocol may be used to drive the allocation process, or a feedback mechanism may be put in place to ensure that constraints are being respected as the portfolio is being assembled or rebalanced by the manager.

---

22 The maximum diversification concept seeks to maximize the ratio of the average volatility of securities within a portfolio to portfolio volatility. It does not seek to achieve the lowest volatility, but rather, it seeks to maximize the benefits that diversification can bring.

23 The low-minus-high-β factor compensation is justified as a structural impediment. Frazzini and Pedersen (2014) expanded on an idea raised by Fischer Black (1972). They made the argument that investors looking for higher returns but who are constrained by borrowing limits bid up the prices of high-β securities.

24 Because it can be unwise to compare securities of different size, price-to-book ratio, and other metrics across sectors or countries, proxies of factors are often standardized by sectors or countries.

25 For example, a manager could rank securities per these three measures and determine a score for each security. For example, a small firm with a high book-to–price ratio and positive price momentum would score higher than a large firm with a low book-to-price ratio and negative price momentum. Other approaches could be used to attribute scores on each factor.

When an explicit objective function is not used, many heuristic methodologies can be considered to determine security weighting in a portfolio. We list a few examples below.

- Identify securities that have the desired characteristics and weight them relative to their scoring on these characteristics. For example, a security with a price-to-book ratio of 8 would have half the weight of a security with a price-to-book ratio of 4.
- Identify securities that have the desired characteristics and weight them per their ranking or risk on these characteristics. For example, if there are five securities ranked on their price-to-book ratios, the security with the lowest price-to-book ratio would constitute 33% of the portfolio value [5/(5 + 4 + 3 + 2 + 1)] and the security with the highest price-to-book ratio would constitute 6.7% of the portfolio value [1/(5 + 4 + 3 + 2 + 1)].
- Identify stocks that have the desired characteristics, rank them according to how strongly they adhere to these characteristics, select the top x% of these stocks, and assign them portfolio weights based on one of several methodologies, such as equal weight, equal risk, scoring, or ranking on these characteristics. For example, if there are 1,000 securities in an index, the 500 securities with the lowest price-to-book ratios could be selected. Each security would then be weighted using the chosen methodology.

Although these alternative methodologies may be intuitively appealing, they may not allocate active risk as efficiently as a formal optimization framework would. The constraints and objective function will be strongly reflective of the philosophy and style of a manager. For example, a stock picker is likely to have fewer and more permissive constraints on security weights than a multi-factor manager seeking to minimize idiosyncratic risks. A manager specializing in sector rotation will have more permissive constraints with respect to sector concentration than a value manager.

> **EXAMPLE 3**
>
> ## Approaches to Portfolio Construction
>
> 1. Marc Cohen is a portfolio manager whose primary skill is based on having a good understanding of rewarded sources of risk. He does not believe in factor timing. Sophie Palmer is a portfolio manager who believes she has skill in anticipating shifts in sector performance. She does not profess to have skill in individual security selection but tolerates significant deviations in sector exposure. Sean Christopher is a stock picker running a high-turnover strategy based on recent movements in market price among the Russell 1000 stock universe. He is highly sector and size agnostic and has significant active risk. Discuss the expected profile of each manager in terms of
>
>   - the sensitivity of their performance to risk factors,
>   - the level of security concentration, and
>   - the contribution of idiosyncratic risk to the total active risk of their portfolios.
>
> ### Solution:
>
> We should be able to explain a large part of Cohen's excess return using the performance of rewarded factors. We would not expect alpha to be a significant component of his performance. His exposure to risk factors would be relatively stable across time periods because he does not believe in factor

timing. Because his primary emphasis is on long-term exposure to risk factors, he would hold a highly diversified portfolio to minimize idiosyncratic risk. As a multi-factor manager running a diversified portfolio, his active risk should be relatively low.

Palmer's performance is likely to be explained by tactical exposures to sectors, which we have said are unrewarded risks, rather than static exposures to known rewarded factor returns. Her excess performance against her benchmark will likely be attributed to alpha. With no professed skill in security selection, she is likely to hold a large number of securities in each sector to minimize idiosyncratic risk. The active risk arising from her sector weightings will overshadow the active risk from security weightings. Her active risk is likely to be higher than that of Marc Cohen.

Christopher's portfolio is more difficult to assess. His focus on recent price movements indicates a sensitivity to the Momentum factor, although the sensitivity to this factor may depend on the time horizons and methodologies he uses to measure price momentum. He is size agnostic and may at times have exposure to the Size factor, a smaller-cap bias. With the information given, we cannot make an inference regarding the diversification of his portfolio. As a discretionary manager, he is to run a concentrated portfolio in order to more closely monitor his positions. However, if he makes extensive use of quantitative tools in monitoring his portfolio, he may be able to hold a more diversified portfolio. His active risk will be high, and his performance is likely to have a significant alpha component, whether positive or negative.

EXAMPLE 4

Approaches to Portfolio Construction

1. *Manager A* uses a scoring process and seeks to maximize the portfolio score based on the factor characteristics of individual securities. His purpose is not to time factor exposure but to achieve an appropriate diversification of factor risks. His approach is fully systematic, and he has a tracking error constraint of less than 4%. No one position can be greater than 2%, irrespective of its benchmark weight.

   Manager B has a strong fundamental process based on a comprehensive understanding of the business model and competitive advantages of each firm. However, Manager B also uses sophisticated models to make explicit three-year forecasts of the growth of free cash flow to determine the attractiveness of each security's current valuation. A committee of portfolio managers meets once a month to debate the portfolio allocation. The manager has a large staff of portfolio managers and analysts and thus can maintain wide coverage of companies within each industry. Individual positions are constrained to the lower of (1) benchmark weight + 2% or (2) five times the benchmark weight.

   Manager C specializes in timing sector exposure and has little appetite for idiosyncratic risks within sectors. Using technical analyses and econometric methodologies, she produces several types of forecasts. The manager uses this information to determine appropriate sector weights. The risk contribution from any single sector is limited to 30% of total portfolio risk. The final decision on sector allocations rests with the manager.

Discuss each manager's implementation approach, security selection approach, portfolio concentration, objective function, and constraints.

Solution:

Manager A is best characterized as a systematic, bottom-up manager.

- *Implementation approach.* An implementation approach that is fully quantitative (allocations are unaffected by a portfolio manager's judgment) is systematic.
- *Security selection approach.* A scoring process that ranks individual securities based on their factor characteristics is a bottom-up approach.
- *Concentration.* Although the limit of no more than 2% of the portfolio in any single position means the portfolio could hold as few as 50 securities, the tracking error constraint of 4% indicates that the portfolio is likely diversified.
- *Objective function.* A process that aims to maximize the portfolio's score based on the factor characteristics of single securities is an example of an explicit objective function.
- *Constraints.* The tracking error constraint of less than 4% is a relative constraint function. The limit on any single position to no more than 2% of the portfolio is an absolute—not a relative—constraint. It does not depend on benchmark weights.

The following table summarizes this information for all three managers:

	Manager A	Manager B	Manager C
Implementation approach	Systematic	Discretionary	Discretionary
Security selection approach	Bottom-up	Bottom-up	Top-down
Portfolio concentration	Diversified	Diversified	Security diversified Factor concentrated
Objective function	Explicit	Explicit	Explicit
Constraints	Relative and absolute	Relative	Absolute

ABSOLUTE VS. RELATIVE MEASURES OF RISK

☐ discuss the application of risk budgeting concepts in portfolio construction

☐ discuss risk measures that are incorporated in equity portfolio construction and describe how limits set on these measures affect portfolio construction

Risk budgeting is a process by which the total risk appetite of the portfolio is allocated among the various components of portfolio choice. As an example, if the portfolio manager has an *ex ante* active risk budget explicitly provided by the client, with risk budgeting, she seeks to optimize the portfolio's exposures relative to the benchmark to ensure that the choices she makes among stocks, sectors, or countries make efficient use of the active risk budget. But *ex ante* active risk is just one possible measure of risk. An effective risk management process requires that the portfolio manager do the following:

- Determine which type of risk measure is most appropriate to her strategy.
  - For example, a long/short equity manager benchmarked against a cash plus target will usually prefer an absolute risk measure (such as total volatility of portfolio returns), whereas a long-only equity manager benchmarked against a capitalization-weighted index may prefer a relative risk measure (such as active risk).
- Understand how each aspect of the strategy contributes to its overall risk.
  - Total portfolio variance may be dominated by exposure to rewarded risk factors or by allocations to countries, sectors, or securities. If these exposures are dynamic, the timing of portfolio exposures also introduces risk. An important step in risk budgeting is to understand what drives a portfolio's risk and to ensure the portfolio has the right kinds of specific risks.
- Determine what level of risk budget is appropriate.
  - Targeted levels of risk vary widely among managers and strategies. Although there are general principles that limit the level of advisable risk in a specific strategy, it is also very much a policy issue.
- Properly allocate risk among individual positions/factors.
  - Whether the risk measure is absolute or relative, managers must efficiently allocate their targeted risk budget.

Absolute vs. Relative Measures of Risk

The choice between an absolute and a relative risk portfolio management orientation is driven by the mandate of the manager and the goals of investors. If the mandate is to outperform a market index over a horizon, such as three years, then the manager will focus on active risk. If the investment objective is expressed in terms of total returns, then the manager will likely focus on the volatility of portfolio returns.

Managers' beliefs about how they add value can influence the choice between an absolute and a relative risk measure. Some managers may believe that the benchmark-relative constraints so common in the world of investment management today inhibit the ability of their investment approach to realize its full potential. To address this issue, they may prefer either an absolute risk measure or a relative risk measure with a wide range of allowed deviations. An absolute risk measure is just that: Whatever the risk threshold, the portfolio risk must remain at or below that level. The manager is free to construct his portfolio without regard to the characteristics of the benchmark. A relative risk measure with wide bands around a central target implies a benchmark-relative approach with significant degrees of freedom to diverge from the characteristics of the benchmark. Ultimately, however, risk and reward will be measured relative to that benchmark. Although some large institutional investors have adopted investment strategies in recent years that are agnostic to the benchmark (an absolute/total return approach) or have had a very high active risk target in a benchmark-relative framework, most assets under management are managed under benchmark-relative mandates. Irrespective of whether a manager focuses on absolute risk or relative risk, the risks he chooses to take should be related to his perceived skills. All other risk should be diversified or minimized. For example,

- market timers should be concerned with timing their factor exposure,
- sector rotators should be concerned with timing their sector exposure, and
- multi-factor managers should be concerned with balancing their factor exposure.

The first step in determining how risk should be allocated is understanding the generic drivers of absolute and relative portfolio risk.

Causes and Sources of Absolute Risk

We start with the following fundamental principles:

- If a manager adds a new asset (such as a security) to his portfolio that has a higher covariance with the portfolio than most current securities, total portfolio risk will rise. (A high covariance with the existing portfolio can be driven by a high variance or a higher correlation of the new security with the portfolio.)
- If a manager replaces an existing security with another security that has a higher covariance with the portfolio than that of the security being replaced, total portfolio risk will rise.

These principles also work in reverse. Consider the three-asset portfolio in Exhibit 11.

Exhibit 11: Absolute Risk Attribution

	Portfolio Weight	Standard Deviation	Correlation Asset A	Correlation Asset B	Correlation Asset C	Contribution to Portfolio Variance Absolute	Contribution to Portfolio Variance %
Asset A	40%	20%	1	0.40	0.20	0.008416	59.22%
Asset B	50%	12%	0.40	1	0.20	0.005592	39.35%

Absolute vs. Relative Measures of Risk

	Portfolio Weight	Standard Deviation	Correlation			Portfolio Risk Attribution	
			Asset A	Asset B	Asset C	Contribution to Portfolio Variance	
						Absolute	%
Asset C	10%	6%	0.20	0.20	1	0.000204	1.44%
Portfolio	100%	11.92%	0.88	0.78	0.20	0.014212	100%

	Covariance		
	Asset A	Asset B	Asset C
Asset A	0.040000	0.009600	0.002400
Asset B	0.009600	0.014400	0.001440
Asset C	0.002400	0.001440	0.003600
Portfolio	**0.020926**	**0.011129**	**0.001427**

Portfolio variance is a function of the individual asset returns and the covariance of returns between assets. In this example, the total variance is 0.014212, which equates to a portfolio standard deviation of 11.92%. Equation 8 expresses the calculation of total portfolio variance (V_p), and Equation 9 determines the contribution of each asset to portfolio variance (CV_i).

$$V_p = \sum_{i=1}^{n}\sum_{j=1}^{n} x_i x_j C_{ij} \qquad (8)$$

$$CV_i = \sum_{j=1}^{n} x_i x_j C_{ij} = x_i C_{ip} \qquad (9)$$

where

x_j = the asset's weight in the portfolio

C_{ij} = the covariance of returns between asset i and asset j

C_{ip} = the covariance of returns between asset i and the portfolio

In other words, the contribution of an asset to total portfolio variance is equal to the product of the weight of the asset and its covariance with the entire portfolio. For example, Asset A's contribution to total portfolio variance is calculated as follows:

Weight of Asset A × Weight of Asset A × Covariance of Asset A with Asset A	0.40 × 0.40 × 0.04
+ Weight of Asset A × Weight of Asset B × Covariance of Asset B with Asset A	+ 0.40 × 0.50 × 0.0096
+ Weight of Asset A × Weight of Asset C × Covariance of Asset C with Asset A	+ 0.40 × 0.10 × 0.0024
= Asset A's contribution to total portfolio variance	= 0.008416

The proportion of total portfolio variance contributed by Asset A is, therefore, 0.008416/0.014212 = 59.22%. Asset A, which has an allocation of 40%, accounts for nearly 60% of total portfolio variance. This is not surprising, because the correlation of Asset A with the portfolio is 0.88. Asset B contributes 39.35% of total portfolio variance, and Asset C contributes 1.44%.

As you read the foregoing discussion, you naturally thought of Assets A, B, and C as securities, but the "assets" might also be sectors, countries, or pools of assets representing risk factors (Value versus Growth, Small versus Large). Hence, if a manager specializes in sector rotation and replaces an allocation to one sector with an allocation to another sector having a higher covariance with the portfolio, total portfolio risk will increase.

We have explained risk by looking at how a single asset contributes to total portfolio variance, but a manager might also seek to understand how his portfolio variance can be attributed to factor exposures versus that which is unexplained by these factors. As we noted earlier, the risks a manager chooses to take should be related to his perceived skills. If the manager's skills can be attributed to certain factors, then he would want to minimize the level of portfolio risk not explained by those factors. The segmentation of absolute portfolio variance into these two components—variance attributed to factor exposure and variance unexplained—is expressed by Equation 10:[26]

$$V_p = \text{Var}\left(\sum_{i=1}^{K}\left(\beta_{ip} \times F_i\right)\right) + \text{Var}\left(\varepsilon_p\right) \qquad (10)$$

If the manager's portfolio were the market portfolio, all the variance of the portfolio returns would be explained by a beta of 1 to the Market factor. Idiosyncratic risks would be fully diversified. However, as we move away from the market portfolio, total portfolio variance will be influenced by other factor exposures and other risks unexplained by factors.[27]

Exhibit 12 presents the risk factor attribution (as measured by the variance of returns) of the three products presented earlier in Exhibit 2: the Russell 1000 Index, the Russell 1000 Value Index, and a Value fund. Exhibit 12 shows that more than 100% of the absolute risk of the Russell 1000 Index is explained by the Market factor. The size exposure (the large-cap tilt of the Russell 1000 relative to the market) has a slight negative contribution to total risk.

The risk of the Russell 1000 Value Index is also dominated by the Market factor, and unsurprisingly, the Value factor explains 12.5% of total risk.

The Value fund appears to have much idiosyncratic risk. Its sensitivity to the Market factor is only 57.7%, whereas the Value factor accounts for 18.1% of total risk. Overall, the four factors account for slightly more than 74% of total portfolio risk, and almost 26% remains unexplained. The percentage of total variance that is explained corresponds to the R^2 of the regressions as reported in Exhibit 2.

Exhibit 12: Absolute Risk Factor Attribution[28]

	Russell 1000 Index	Russell 1000 Value Index	Value Fund
Market	100.4%	88.9%	57.7%
Size	−1.8%	−1.6%	1.8%
Value	0.2%	12.5%	18.1%
Momentum	0.5%	−5.2%	−3.5%

---

26 Equation 10 is the same general formulation as Equation 1. However, Equation 6 was concerned with active risk.

27 There are two ways of determining the portion of the variance of returns attributed to factors versus idiosyncratic risk. One approach consists of simply calculating each period's returns attributed to factors (the sum of the product of factor coefficients and the factor returns, which is the first term of Equation 10) and then calculating the variance of the calculated return series. This is variance attributed to factors. It can then be compared with the actual portfolio variance. A second approach identifies the variance contribution of each individual factor. However, it requires the variance–covariance matrix of factors and the vector of factor coefficients.

28 The Market factor is built from a much larger universe of securities than traditional benchmarks, such as the Russell 1000. Therefore, we should not expect the β of indexes to the Market factor to necessarily equal one.

Absolute vs. Relative Measures of Risk

	Russell 1000 Index	Russell 1000 Value Index	Value Fund
Total explained risk	99.3%	94.6%	74.1%
Total unexplained risk	0.7%	5.4%	25.9%
Total absolute risk (standard deviation annualized)	14.5%	14.2%	18.0%

Source: Calculations by authors.

Causes and Sources of Relative/Active Risk

Relative risk becomes an appropriate measure when the manager is concerned with her performance relative to a benchmark. One measure of relative risk is the variance of the portfolio's active return (AV_p):

$$AV_p = \sum_{i=1}^{n}\sum_{j=1}^{n} (x_i - b_i)(x_j - b_j) RC_{ij} \tag{11}$$

where

x_i = the asset's weight in the portfolio

b_i = the benchmark weight in asset i

RC_{ij} = the covariance of relative returns between asset i and asset j

The contribution of each asset to the portfolio active variance (CAV_i) is

$$CAV_i = (x_i - b_i) RC_{ip} \tag{12}$$

where RC_{ip} is the covariance of relative returns between asset i and the portfolio.

If you are assessing risk using a relative risk construct, you can no longer assume that a lower-risk asset reduces active risk or that a higher-risk asset increases it. In fact, depending on the composition of the benchmark, a lower-risk asset could increase active risk whereas a higher-risk asset might reduce it.

Let's consider a simple example. Assume a benchmark is composed of a 50/50 allocation to two equity indexes. The portfolio is composed of allocations to these two indexes and to a third asset—cash. What happens to the active risk of the portfolio if, instead of a 50/50 allocation to the two indexes, the portfolio allocation is 40/40 and 20% in cash? The benchmark is still 50/50. Let's look at the contribution of the active weights to the active variance of the portfolio. Exhibit 13 presents the relevant information and the results.

Exhibit 13: Relative Risk Attribution

	Benchmark Weight	Portfolio Weight	Standard Deviation	Active Risk	Correlation of Active Returns — Index A	Index B	Cash	Variance of Active Returns Attributed to Each Asset
Index A	50%	40%	16%	5.0%	1.00	−1.00	−0.69	14.3%
Index B	50%	40%	10%	5.0%	−1.00	1.00	0.69	−14.3%
Cash	0%	20%	0.5%	12.0%	−0.69	0.69	1.00	100%
Total	100%	100%		2.4%	−0.69	0.69	1.00	100%

Index A and Index B have absolute volatilities of 16% and 10%, respectively, whereas cash has a very low volatility. The manager is concerned with active risk, however, not portfolio volatility. Both Index A and Index B have an active risk of 5% against the 50/50 benchmark. Cash has higher active risk because it has a low correlation with the equity benchmark.

Exhibit 13 shows that the correlations of active returns between the benchmark and Index A and between the benchmark and Index B are both −1.0. This is not a coincidence; it must be so. Because the benchmark comprises just these two indexes, any outperformance of one index relative to the benchmark must be offset by underperformance of the other index. Similarly, cash has a positive correlation of relative returns with one index and a negative relative correlation with the other.

This example illustrates that this portfolio's risk (defined here as variance of active returns) can be attributed entirely to the allocation to cash, which is a low-risk asset—in an absolute sense. Hence, in the context of relative measures of risk, what matters is not the volatility of an asset but its relative (active) volatility. Introducing a low-volatility asset within a portfolio benchmarked against a high-volatility index would increase the active risk. Similarly, introducing a high-volatility asset to a portfolio might lower the active risk if the asset has a high covariance with the benchmark. These principles hold whether allocating among countries, sectors, securities, or other factors.

Exhibit 14 is similar to Exhibit 12, but it considers the attribution of active risk rather than absolute risk. It shows how much of the active risk of each product can be attributed to the four factors and how much remains unexplained. The Russell 1000 Index has some active risk (though very low, at 2% annualized). The active risk of the Russell 1000 Value Index and the Value fund are higher, at 6.0% and 11.4%, respectively.[29]

The Market factor does not explain much of the active risk; the very action of building a portfolio that is structurally different from the market creates the active risk. The two indexes have a significant portion of their active risk explained by the four rewarded factors. More than half of the active risk of the Russell 1000 Index is generated from the larger-cap tilt of the index. About 37% of the active risk remains unexplained. More than half of the active risk of the Russell 1000 Value Index is generated from the value tilt of the index. About 31% of the active risk remains unexplained. Finally, the Value fund has significant active risk (11.4%). Virtually all of this risk can be attributed the Value factor. In this case, though, nearly two-thirds of the active risk remains unexplained. An investor would want to investigate more carefully what is driving the active risk of the value manager.

Exhibit 14: Active Risk Factor Attribution

	Russell 1000	Russell 1000 Value	Value Fund
Total active risk	2.0%	6.0%	11.4%
Risk Factor Contribution to Active Risk			
Market	3.0%	6.0%	1.2%
Size	56.4%	15.4%	0.8%
Value	3.0%	53.9%	38.4%
Momentum	0.5%	−5.4%	−4.1%
Total explained risk	62.8%	69.9%	36.4%
Total unexplained risk	37.2%	31.1%	63.6%

Source: Calculations by authors.

---

29 For a detailed explanation of risk decomposition, see MacQueen (2007).

DETERMINING THE APPROPRIATE LEVEL OF RISK

☐ discuss the application of risk budgeting concepts in portfolio construction

☐ discuss risk measures that are incorporated in equity portfolio construction and describe how limits set on these measures affect portfolio construction

Listed below are representative examples of risk targets for different mandates:

- a market-neutral hedge fund targeting an absolute risk of 10%,
- a long-only equity manager targeting an active risk of something less than 2% (a closet indexer),
- a long-only manager targeting active risk of 6%–10% (benchmark agnostic), and
- a benchmark-agnostic equity manager targeting an absolute risk equal to 85% of the index risk.

Establishing the appropriate level of absolute or relative risk is a subjective exercise, highly sensitive to managers' investment style and their conviction in their ability to add value using the various levers at their disposal. Managers with similar investment approaches may have very different risk appetites. This has implications for portfolio structure, portfolio turnover, and other facets of portfolio implementation. Managers must clearly communicate to investors their overall risk orientation, and investors must understand the implications of this risk orientation. This does not mean that a strategy can or should be executed at any level of risk. Here are three scenarios that give some insights into practical risk limits:

- portfolios may face implementation constraints that degrade the information ratio if active risk increases beyond a specific level;
- portfolios with high absolute risk targets face limited diversification opportunities, which may lead to a decrease in the Sharpe ratio; and
- there is a level of leverage beyond which volatility reduces expected compounded returns.

Implementation Constraints

Consider two managers (A and B), each with a relative risk focus. Irrespective of the targeted level of active risk, the managers seek to use that risk efficiently. They are concerned with the ratio of active return to active risk—the information ratio. Assume that their portfolios have the same information ratio but different levels of active risk. If the investor is willing to tolerate the higher level of active risk, Manager A might proportionately scale up his active risk to match the active risk level of Manager B. He would accomplish this by scaling up his active weights, which would increase Manager A's excess returns while maintaining the same information ratio. This scenario is illustrated in Exhibit 15.

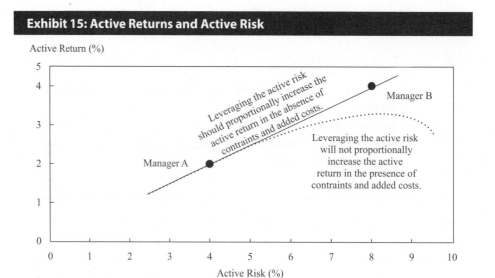

However, there may be constraints that prevent Manager A from scaling his active weights. For example, if the investment policy does not allow short positions, he may be unable to increase underweights. If the policy does not allow leverage, he may be unable to increase overweights. If some of the security positions have poor liquidity, leveraging these positions may be imprudent and may also have a trading cost impact. If the policy restricts maximum position sizes, Manager A may be unable to proportionately scale his active risk.[30]

Limited Diversification Opportunities

Consider a manager with a high absolute risk target. Despite his higher risk tolerance, he still strives to use risk efficiently. We know, though, that twice the absolute risk will not lead to twice the return: The mathematics of the Markowitz efficient investment frontier clearly shows that the relationship between return and risk is concave. Expected returns increase with risk but at a declining pace. Portfolios with higher risk/return targets eventually run out of high-return investment opportunities and lose the ability to diversify efficiently, thereby reducing the Sharpe ratio.

Leverage and its Implications for Risk

Sharpe demonstrated that if there is a risk-free rate at which investors can borrow or lend, there is a linear relationship between absolute risk and return in a one-period setting. Managers can scale expected returns and absolute risk up or down proportionately and maintain a constant, optimal Sharpe ratio. A manager could choose to leverage her portfolio to extend the implementation limits of a strategy. However, as we show below, leverage eventually leads to a reduction of expected compounded return in a multi-period setting.

---

30 This constraint is also implicit in the full fundamental law of active management, which expresses the main sources of active returns. The transfer coefficient represents the ability to translate portfolio insights into investment decisions without constraint. If a manager is limited in his ability to implement his strategy, the transfer coefficient will decline. If he attempts to maintain the same level of active risk, his information ratio will also decline. In this case, there is an optimal/maximum level of active risk.

We know that the expected compounded/geometric return of an asset (R_g) is approximately related to its expected arithmetic/periodic return (R_a) and its expected volatility (σ):[31]

$$R_g = R_a - \sigma^2/2 \qquad (13)$$

For example, let's consider again the performance of the Russell 1000 over a discrete 26-year period. The average monthly compounded return was 0.789%, the monthly arithmetic return was 0.878%, and the volatility, as measured by the standard deviation of return, was 4.199%. Applying Equation 13, we obtain the compounded return as follows:

$$R_g = 0.878\% - \frac{4.199\%^2}{2} = 0.790\%$$

which is very close to the realized compounded return. Now, what happens to the relationship between the arithmetic return and the compounded return when leverage is used? Let's consider an asset with a 20% standard deviation and a 10% expected arithmetic return. This asset has an expected compounded return of 8%:

$$10\% - 20\%^2/2 = 8\%$$

Ignoring the cost of funding, if we leverage the asset by a factor of 2, the expected compounded return increases to 12%:

$$2 \times 10\% - (2 \times 20\%)^2/2 = 12\%$$

If we leverage the asset by a factor of 3, however, there is no additional improvement in return:

$$3 \times 10\% - (3 \times 20\%)^2/2 = 12\%$$

If we incorporate the cost of funding leverage, the active return is reduced while the volatility remains proportional to the amount of leverage. The Sharpe ratio will decline even faster. For example, using the same example, we could show that a portfolio with a leverage of 3× would have the same expected return as an unlevered portfolio if the cost of funding leverage were 2%:

$$(3 \times 10\% - 2 \times 2\%) - (3 \times 20\%)^2/2 = 8\%$$

Furthermore, if the realized volatility is significantly greater than expected, such as in crisis time, the combined impact of volatility and leverage on compounded return could be dramatic.

The information ratio and the Sharpe ratio will not always be degraded by a reasonable rise in active or absolute risk, and a reasonable level of leverage can increase expected compounded return. The appropriate tactics must be evaluated by the manager in the context of his investment approach and investors' expectations.

ALLOCATING THE RISK BUDGET

8

- ☐ discuss the application of risk budgeting concepts in portfolio construction
- ☐ discuss risk measures that are incorporated in equity portfolio construction and describe how limits set on these measures affect portfolio construction

---

31 The arithmetic return and the geometric returns are the same only when there is no volatility.

We have explained how absolute and relative risk are determined by the position sizing of assets/factors (absolute or relative) and by the covariance of assets/factors with the portfolio (absolute or relative). By understanding both components (position sizing and covariance), a manager can determine the contribution of each position (whether a factor, country, sector, or security) to the portfolio's variance or active variance.

Let's consider a benchmark-agnostic US sector rotator. Although he himself is benchmark agnostic, his client is going to evaluate his performance relative to *some* benchmark—one that represents the universe of securities he typically draws from. The nature of his strategy indicates that he will likely exhibit a high level of active risk. In assessing whether he has effectively used this risk budget, the client will look to decompose the sources of realized risk: How much is attributable to market risk and other risk factors? How much is attributable to other decisions, such as sector and security allocation? If the manager runs a concentrated portfolio, we should expect sector and security allocation to be the main source of active risk. Although all these aspects may not be explicit elements of his portfolio construction process, because his effectiveness will be evaluated using these metrics, he would be well served to understand their contributions to his risk and return.

A fund's style and strategy will also dictate much of the structure of its risk budget. We explore this further with an examination of the three US equity managers presented in Exhibit 16. All managers draw their securities from a universe of large-cap and mid-cap securities defined by the Russell 1000 index, which has a weighted average market capitalization of approximately $446.1 billion as of January 31, 2021. The first two managers believe their skill is their ability to create balanced exposures to rewarded risk factors. The third specializes in sector timing, but he also makes significant use of cash positions. The first two managers have many securities in their portfolios, which suggests that their active risk is unlikely to be driven by idiosyncratic risks related to security concentration. Their low level of security concentration is consistent with their respective investment style.

The third manager runs a highly concentrated portfolio. As a sector rotator, he is exposed to significant unrewarded risk related to his sector views and to idiosyncratic risk related to his security views. A sector rotator could choose to run either a diversified portfolio or a highly concentrated portfolio within sectors. Manager C chose the latter. A greater concentration of risk implicitly leads to a greater sensitivity to unrewarded factors and idiosyncratic risks.

Exhibit 16: Comparative Sources of Risk, Drivers of Return

	Manager A	Manager B	Manager C
Investment Approach:	Factor Diversified	Factor Diversified	Sector Rotator
Number of securities	251	835	21
Weight of top 5 securities	6.54%	3.7%	25.1%
Cash and bond position	0.8%	0.0%	21.3%
Weighted average capitalization ($ billions)	33.7	21.3	164.0
Market beta	0.90	0.97	1.28
Absolute risk	10.89%	10.87%	11.69%
Active risk	3.4%	3.6%%	4.5%
Active Share	0.76	0.63	0.87
Average sector deviation	3.6%	3.9%	5.6%
Source of risk: Market	98.0%	99.2%	69.2%

Allocating the Risk Budget

	Manager A	Manager B	Manager C
Source of risk: Sectors	−0.8%	−3.8%	11.6%
Source of risk: Styles	1.8%	4.2%	9.7%
Unexplained	1.0%	0.4%	9.5%

Note: Manager C owns 49 positions, but several of these positions are cash and bond related.
Source: Bloomberg.

None of the managers is tightly tracking the benchmark; active risk exceeds 3% for all three. Somewhat surprisingly, the active risk of the sector rotator (4.5%) is only slightly greater than that for the other managers, especially given that the rotator has 25.1% of his portfolio invested in the top five positions and holds 21.3% in cash and bonds.[32] The large position in cash and bonds may also explain why the absolute volatility is not higher. We can see, however, that the sector rotator is taking less of a size bet: The weighted average capitalization of his portfolio is close to that of the index, whereas the weighted average capitalization of the two factor managers is quite low. This smaller size bet is likely what has constrained the active risk of the sector rotator.

Although managers may view their investment process and evaluation of securities as benchmark agnostic, the outcomes may, in fact, be similar to the benchmark along critical dimensions, such as active risk. The portfolio construction process of multi-factor managers often leads to a balanced exposure to risk factors, constraining active risk. The sector rotator has a higher level of active risk, but not dramatically so. The returns of the sector rotator are more driven by concentrated sector and style exposures than are the returns of the multi-factor managers. These differences are likely to influence returns over shorter horizons. Two strategies with similar active risk may have very different patterns of realized returns. When evaluating an investment manager, the asset owner needs to understand the drivers of active risk that can lead to differences in realized portfolio returns over time.

The strategy and portfolio structure of Manager C is also revealed by the sources of absolute risk. The risk attribution in Exhibit 16 not only considers the Market factor but also adds a sector factor and a style factor.

The exposures of Managers A and B are dominated by the Market factor. Manager B's active risk, however, can be explained in part by the sector and style factors: The sector exposure reduces risk by 3.8%, and the style exposure increases it by 4.2%.

Let's look more closely at the risk profile of Manager C in Exhibit 17.

Exhibit 17

		Manager C
Investment Approach:	**Sector Rotator**	**Risk Positioning Relative to Managers A and B**
Number of securities	21	Very concentrated; high levels of security-specific risk
Weight of top 5 securities	25.1%	
Cash and bond position	21.3%	Large cash position dampens overall portfolio volatility
Weighted average capitalization ($ billions)	164.0	Much closer to the capitalization of the index
Market beta	1.28	Significantly higher, consistent with the absolute risk measures

---

32 The active risk is calculated from daily data over a one-year horizon. This calculation usually leads to a lower active risk than would be obtained from monthly data over a longer period.

	Manager C	
Investment Approach:	Sector Rotator	Risk Positioning Relative to Managers A and B
Absolute risk	11.69%	Absolute risk only slightly higher, likely dampened by the large cash position
Active risk	4.5%	Higher
Active Share	0.87	High, consistent with the level of security concentration
Average sector deviation	5.6%	Higher, consistent with willingness to take sector bets
Source of risk: Market	69.2%	Significantly less exposure to the Market factor, consistent with a concentrated, high-Active-Share manager
Source of risk: Sectors	11.6%	Significantly more Sector risk
Source of risk: Styles	9.7%	Significantly more Style risk
Unexplained	9.5%	Significantly higher proportion of risk is unexplained

Taken together, these measures indicate a benchmark-agnostic strategy with significant and concentrated security, sector, and style exposures.

EXAMPLE 5

Application of Risk Budgeting Concepts

1. Using the information in Exhibit 16, discuss key differences in the risk profiles of Manager A and Manager C.

Solution:

Manager C holds significantly fewer positions than Manager A, and the weight of his top five securities is nearly four times that of Manager B. This indicates a willingness to assume a much higher level of idiosyncratic risk. This observation is reinforced by Manager C's higher Active Share and higher proportion of unexplained risk. The Market beta of Manager C is significantly greater, and the risk decomposition indicates that Manager C appears more willing to make sector and style bets. Finally, the absolute risk of Manager's C portfolio is higher, even though it appears that he makes greater use of lower-risk bond and cash positions.

2. The table below presents the risk factor coefficients of a four-factor model and the factor variance–covariance matrix of a manager running a low-risk strategy. All data are monthly. The monthly standard deviation of the manager's return is 3.07%. What portion of the total portfolio risk is explained by the Market factor?

		Variance/Covariance of Returns			
	Coefficients	Market	Size	Value	Momentum
Market	0.733	0.00178	0.00042	0.00066	−0.00062
Size	−0.328	0.00042	0.00048	0.00033	−0.00035
Value	0.045	0.00066	0.00033	0.00127	−0.00140
Momentum	0.042	−0.00062	−0.00035	−0.00140	0.00214

Allocating the Risk Budget

Solution:

91% of total portfolio risk is explained by the Market factor. From Equation 9 (repeated below), the contribution of an asset to total portfolio variance is equal to the product of the weight of the asset and its covariance with the entire portfolio. To calculate the variance attributed to the Market factor,

$$CV_i = \sum_{j=1}^{n} x_i x_j C_{ij} = x_i C_{ip} \qquad (14)$$

where

x_j = the asset's weight in the portfolio

C_{ij} = the covariance of returns between asset i and asset j

C_{ip} = the covariance of returns between asset i and the portfolio

Therefore, the variance attributed to the Market factor is

$(0.733 \times 0.00178 \times 0.733) + (0.733 \times 0.00042 \times -0.328) + (0.733 \times 0.00066 \times 0.045) + (0.733 \times -0.00062 \times 0.042)$

$= 0.000858$

Divide this result by the portfolio variance of returns:

$0.000858/3.07\%^2 = 0.000858/0.000942$

$= 91\%$ of total portfolio variance is explained by the Market factor.

3. If a manager benchmarked against the FTSE 100 makes a significant allocation to cash, how will that allocation affect the portfolio's absolute risk and active risk?

Solution:

Cash has a low volatility and a low correlation of returns with any asset. Therefore, it will contribute to a reduction in absolute risk. However, because cash has a low correlation with other assets, it will contribute to an increase in active risk.

4. Manager A has been running a successful strategy achieving a high information ratio with a relatively low active risk of 3.4%. The manager is considering offering a product with twice the active risk. What are the obstacles that may make it difficult for the manager to maintain the same information ratio?

Solution:

If the manager is running a long-only portfolio without leverage, she is likely able to increase her exposure to securities she wants to overweight, but she may be limited in her ability to reduce exposure to securities she wishes to avoid or underweight. Increased exposure to the most desirable securities (in her view) will lead to increased security concentration and may substantially increase active risk. The manager risks a degradation of her information ratio if there is not a corresponding increase in her active return. If the manager can short, she will be able to increase underweighting when desired (assuming the securities can be easily borrowed). Although leverage can increase total exposure and reduce concentration issues, its impact on volatility may be substantial, and the additional return enabled by leverage

> may be eroded by the impact of the increased volatility on compounded returns and the other associated costs.

9. ADDITIONAL RISK MEASURES

> ☐ discuss the application of risk budgeting concepts in portfolio construction
>
> ☐ discuss risk measures that are incorporated in equity portfolio construction and describe how limits set on these measures affect portfolio construction

Risk constraints imposed as part of the portfolio construction process may be either formal or heuristic. Heuristic constraints appear as controls imposed on the permissible portfolio composition through some exogenous classification structure. Such constraints are often based on experience or practice, rather than empirical evidence of their effectiveness. These risk controls may be used to limit

- exposure concentrations by security, sector, industry, or geography;
- net exposures to risk factors, such as beta, size, value, and momentum;
- net exposures to currencies;
- degree of leverage;
- degree of illiquidity;
- turnover/trading-related costs;
- exposures to reputational and environmental risks, such as actual or potential carbon emissions; and
- other attributes related to an investor's core concerns.

A major concern of any portfolio manager is a risk that is unknown or unexpected. Risk constraints are one way that managers try to limit the portfolio losses from unexpected events. Listed below are sample heuristic constraints that may be used by a portfolio manager:

- Any single position is limited to the lesser of
  - five times the weight of the security in the benchmark or
  - 2%.
- The portfolio must have a weighted average capitalization of no less than 75% of that of the index.
- The portfolio may not size any position such that it exceeds two times the average daily trading volume of the past three months.
- The portfolio's carbon footprint must be limited to no more than 75% of the benchmark's exposure.

Such heuristic constraints as these may limit active managers' ability to fully exploit their insights into expected returns, but they might also be viewed as safeguarding against overconfidence and hubris.

Managing risk through portfolio characteristics is a "bottom-up" risk management process. Managers that rely on such an approach express their risk objectives through the heuristic characteristics of their portfolios. The resulting statistical risk measures

Additional Risk Measures

of such portfolios do not drive the portfolio construction process but are an outcome of those heuristic characteristics. For example, if a manager imposes maximum sector deviations of ±3% and limits security concentration to no more than the index weight + 1% or twice the weight of any security in the index, then we could expect the active risk of that portfolio to be small even if no constraint on active risk is explicitly imposed. The portfolio construction process ensures that the desired heuristic risk is achieved. Continuous monitoring is necessary to determine whether the evolution of market prices causes a heuristic constraint to be breached or nearly breached.

Managers will often impose constraints on the heuristic characteristics of their portfolios even if they also use more formal statistical measures of risk. The investment policy of most equity products, for example, will usually specify constraints on allocations to individual securities and to sectors or, for international mandates, regions. Some may also have constraints related to liquidity and capitalization. Even managers with a low-volatility mandate will have security and sector constraints to avoid unbalanced and concentrated portfolio solutions that may have significant idiosyncratic risk or allocations that are unduly influenced by estimation error.

Formal Constraints

Formal risk measures are distinct from these heuristic controls. They are often statistical in nature and directly linked to the distribution of returns for the portfolio.

Formal measures of risk include the following:

- Volatility
- Active risk
- Skewness
- Drawdowns
- Value at risk (VaR)
- Conditional Value at risk (CVaR)
- Incremental Value at risk (IVaR)
- Marginal Value at risk (MVaR)

A major difference between formal and heuristic risk measures is that formal measures require a manager to estimate or predict risk. For example, a formal risk measure might be that predicted active risk be no more than, say, 5%. With the benefit of hindsight, one can always calculate the historical active risk, but in portfolio construction, the forward-looking view of risk and active risk is what matters: Portfolio decisions are based on these forward-looking estimates. If predicted risk deviates substantially from realized risk, it is likely that portfolio performance will be quite different than expected. In times of crisis or financial stress, predicted and realized risks could diverge very significantly.

Exhibit 18 presents five different risk measures for the same three products discussed in Exhibit 16. Four one-day VaR measures are presented: VaR and CVaR at two different levels of probability (1% and 5%).

Exhibit 18: Risk Measures

Risk Measure	Manager A Factor Diversified	Manager B Factor Diversified	Manager C Sector Rotator
Absolute risk	10.89%	10.87%	11.69%
Active risk	3.4%	3.6%%	4.5%
VaR (5%)	1.08%	1.11%	1.20%
VaR (1%)	1.77%	1.77%	1.87%
CVaR (5%)	1.50%	1.53%	1.65%
CVaR (1%)	2.21%	2.24%	2.41%

Source: Bloomberg.

In this example, Manager A has a 5% probability of realizing a one-day loss greater than 1.08% and a 1% probability of a loss greater than 1.77%. If we look at the distribution of losses beyond the 5% and 1% probability levels, the averages of the tail losses (CVaR) are 1.50% and 2.21%, respectively. Despite the high security concentration, the loss estimates of Manager C are not much higher than those of Managers A and B, most likely because of the large position in cash and bonds.

Risk Measures

- Volatility is the standard deviation of portfolio returns.
- Active risk is the standard deviation of the differences between a portfolio's returns and its benchmark's returns. It is also called *tracking error* or *tracking risk*.
- Skewness is a measure of the degree to which return expectations are non-normally distributed. If a distribution is positively skewed, the mean of the distribution is greater than its median (more than half of the deviations from the mean are negative and less than half are positive) and the average magnitude of positive deviations is larger than the average magnitude of negative deviations. Negative skew indicates that the mean of the distribution lies below its median and the average magnitude of negative deviations is larger than the average magnitude of positive deviations.
- Drawdown measures the portfolio loss from its high point until it begins to recover.
- VaR is the minimum loss that would be expected a certain percentage of the time over a specific period of time (e.g., a day, a week, a month) given the modeled market conditions. It is typically expressed as the minimum loss that can be expected to occur 5% of the time.
- CVaR is the average loss that would be incurred if the VaR cutoff is exceeded. It is also sometimes referred to as the **expected tail loss** or **expected shortfall**. It is not technically a VaR measure.
- IVaR is the change in portfolio VaR when adding a new position to a portfolio, thereby reducing the position size of current positions.

Additional Risk Measures

- MVaR reflects the effect of a very small change in the position size. In a diversified portfolio, marginal VaR may be used to determine the contribution of each asset to the overall VaR.

Formal risk constraints may be applied as part of a portfolio optimization process (as is common with systematic strategies) or using an iterative feedback mechanism to determine whether the portfolio would remain within the risk tolerance limits given the proposed change (an approach more common among discretionary managers).

All risk measures, whether formal or heuristic, can be expressed on an absolute basis or relative to a benchmark. For example, a benchmark-aware long-only equity manager may limit sector deviations to 5%, whereas a long/short hedge fund manager concerned with the overall diversification of his portfolio may limit any given sector exposure to no more than 30% of his gross exposure. Similarly, a long-only equity manager may limit active risk to 5%, whereas a long/short equity manager may limit overall portfolio volatility to 10%. In many cases, the investment policy imposes both formal and heuristic constraints on a portfolio. Exhibit 19 illustrates a product for which the investment policy statement considers constraints on both types of risk measures.

Exhibit 19: Sample Investment Policy Risk Constraints

The MSCI Diversified Multi-Factor Index

This index uses an optimization process to maximize the exposure score to several risk factors. The index seeks to achieve this objective while controlling for several portfolio and risk characteristics, such as the following:

- Weight of index constituents: maximum of weight in the parent (capitalization-weighted) index + 2% or 10 times weight in the parent index
- Sector weights: restricted to a 5% deviation against the parent index
- Exposure to style factors, such as growth and liquidity: restricted to a 0.25 standard deviation from the parent index
- Limit on volatility: restricted to a 0.25 standard deviation from the parent index

The Risks of Being Wrong

The consequences of being wrong about risk expectations can be significant but even more so when a strategy is leveraged. In 2008, for example, a hedge fund owned a two-times levered portfolio of highly rated mortgage-related securities. Although the specific securities were not materially exposed to subprime mortgages, concerns about the economy and poor market liquidity led to a steep decline in the prices of these securities. Prices quickly recovered, but the presence of the 2× leverage combined with an unprecedented price decline led to a forced liquidation of the assets just a few days before prices recovered. The manager and his investors lost all capital.

Similarly, a pension fund created an indexed equity position by combining an investment of short-term highly rated (AAA) commercial paper with an equivalent notional position in equity derivatives (a receiver swap on a large-cap equity index), creating a synthetic indexed equity position. In principle, this pension fund believed it owned the equivalent of an index equity position. However, as the liquidity crisis worsened in 2008 and early 2009, the pension fund was faced with a substantial decline in equity markets *and* a simultaneous spike in the perceived riskiness of the short-term commercial paper. The equity derivatives position and the commercial paper each lost 50% of their value, creating a paper loss equivalent to 100% of the invested capital. Although both components eventually recovered, such unexpected losses can lead to a forced liquidation of all or part of the portfolio in an unfavorable market environment, crystalizing the losses.

Exhibit 20 illustrates the time-varying volatility of the S&P 500 from 1995-2020. Although volatility remains in a range of 10%–20% most of the time, periods of much higher volatility are observed: in 2000–2002 when technology stocks collapsed, in the 2008-2009 the Global Financial Crisis, and in 2020 during the COVID-19 pandemic.. Effective risk management requires the manager to account for the fact that unexpected volatility can derail the investment strategy. Furthermore, spikes in volatility can also be sector specific—the technology sector in the early 2000s and the energy sector in 2014 and 2015. Therefore, what may seem to be an acceptable sector deviation limit in normal times may be the source of significant active losses in a different environment. Some managers may tighten risk constraints in more volatile periods to protect the portfolio against excessive variability.

Despite these "tail events," risk can usually be managed efficiently. The dotted line in Exhibit 20[33] shows the realized volatility of a portfolio dynamically allocated between the S&P 500 Index and short-term bonds. The portfolio targets a 10% annualized volatility.[34] The realized volatility stayed very close to the target.

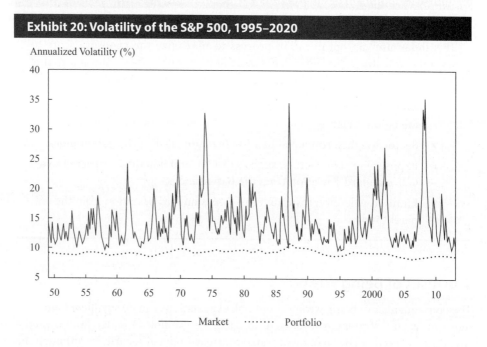

Exhibit 20: Volatility of the S&P 500, 1995–2020

The statistical risk measures used in equity portfolio construction often depend on the style of management. A benchmark-agnostic manager with an absolute return philosophy is less likely to be concerned with active risk but is much more likely to be concerned with drawdowns. A long/short equity manager who neutralizes market risk but is exposed to other risk premiums is likely to target a volatility within a specific range.

---

33 Langlois and Lussier (2017).
34 The management of this portfolio required forecasts of volatility and correlation for both assets. The same general techniques described in footnote 15 were used.

Additional Risk Measures

Portfolios with a very limited number of securities may be more difficult to manage using formal risk measures because estimation errors in portfolio risk parameters are likely to be higher: The dispersion in possible outcomes may be wide, and the distributions may not easily conform to standard assumptions underlying many of the formal risk measures.

This does not mean, however, that these measures cannot be used on an *ex ante* basis. It merely suggests that they should be used with an understanding of their limitations. For example, VaR is particularly useful to a pension plan sponsor that has a multi-asset-class portfolio and needs to measure its exposure to a variety of risk factors (Simons, 2000). However, this information may be less useful to an equity manager holding only 40 equity positions. Measures of risk and their efficacy must be appropriate to the nature and objective of the portfolio mandate.

Formal, statistical measures of risk are often not outlined in investment policy statements even if the manager is actively tracking such risks and using such measures to adjust security weights. One reason may be the difficulty in measuring and forecasting such measures as volatility and value at risk. The resultant answers are likely to be different depending on what methodology is used. Even if the historical measures were in alignment with one another, what happened in the past will not necessarily be indicative of what is to come. When formal, statistical measures of risk are used by managers, they are typically expressed as a soft target, such as, "We are targeting a 10%–12% annualized volatility."

Calibrating risk is as much an art as it is a science. If an active manager imposes restrictions that are too tightly anchored to her investment benchmark (or perhaps these restrictions are imposed by the investor), the resulting portfolio may have performance that too closely mirrors that of the benchmark.

EXAMPLE 6

Risk Measures in Portfolio Construction

Matthew Rice runs a discretionary equity strategy benchmarked on the Russell 1000 Index. His fund contains approximately 80 securities and has recently passed $2 billion in assets. His strategy emphasizes quality companies that are attractively priced within their sector. This determination is based on careful analyses of the balance sheet, free cash flows, and quality of management of the companies they invest in. Rice is not benchmark agnostic, but his strategy does require the ability to tolerate some sector deviations because attractive positions are sometimes concentrated in three or four sectors. Rice is supported by a team of six analysts but makes all final allocation decisions. Historically, no single position or bet has dominated the performance of the fund. However, Rice believes there is no point in holding a position so small that it will barely affect excess returns even if it is successful. Rice does not believe in taking aggressive views. His investors do not expect him to have the active risk of a sector rotator. The portfolio has lower turnover than that of most of his peers. Single positions can easily remain in the portfolio for two or three years.

1. What heuristic constraints could be appropriate for such a fund?

Solution:

Because no single position or bet has dominated historical returns, a heuristic constraint on maximum position size is a logical one. Given that his portfolio is built around a relatively small number of positions (80), single positions might be constrained to no more than 3%. Given his view on small position sizes, a minimum position size of 0.5% might also be appropriate.

Rice's strategy requires some active risk, but he could not tolerate the sector deviations taken by a sector rotator. A sector constraint in the range of ±5%–7.5% relative to the index is appropriate for his strategy.

The fund's benchmark incorporates many mid-cap securities. With $2 billion in assets, a single position can be as small as $10 million (0.5%) but as high as perhaps $60 million (3%). Positions on the higher end of this range could represent a large portion of the average daily trading of some mid-cap securities, which range in size from $2 billion to $10 billion. The fund's long investment horizon means that trading into and out of a position can be stretched over days or even weeks. Nevertheless, it could make sense to consider a constraint that accounts for the size (capitalization) of individual securities and their trading volume, such as not owning more than five times the capitalization weight in the index of any security.

2. What role might such statistical measures as VaR or active risk play in the management of Rice's fund?

Solution:

Discretionary managers usually do not use statistical measures as hard constraints, but they can be used as guidelines in the portfolio management process. A fund that contains only 80 positions out of a universe of 1,000 possible securities and takes views across capitalization and sectors is likely to see significant variability in its active risk or VaR over time. Although Rice is not very sensitive to what happens in the short run (he is a long-term investor), statistical measures can be used to monitor changes in the risks within his portfolio. If these risk exposures deviate from his typical risk exposures, it might signal a need to investigate the sources of such changes and initiate some portfolio changes if those exposures are unwanted.

10. IMPLICIT COST-RELATED CONSIDERATIONS

> discuss how assets under management, position size, market liquidity, and portfolio turnover affect equity portfolio construction decisions

There are numerous costs that can affect the net performance of an investment product. The same investment strategy can easily cost twice as much to manage if a manager is not careful with her implementation approach. Assets under management (AUM) will affect position size. Position size and the liquidity of the securities in the portfolio will affect the level of turnover that can be sustained at an acceptable level of costs.[35] Although smaller-AUM funds may pay more in explicit costs (such as broker commissions), these funds may incur lower implicit costs (such as delay and market

---

35 The portfolio turnover ratio is a measure of the fund's trading activity. It is computed by taking the lesser of purchases or sales and dividing by average monthly net assets.

impact) than large-AUM funds. Overall, smaller funds may be able to sustain greater turnover and still deliver superior performance. A manager needs to carefully weigh both explicit and implicit costs in his implementation approach.

Thoughtful portfolio management requires a manager to balance the potential benefits of turnover against the costs of turnover. When considering a rebalancing or restructuring of the portfolio, the benefits of the post-trade risk/return position must justify the costs of getting there.

This section concerns the implicit costs of implementing an active strategy and implementation issues related to asset under management, position sizing, turnover, and market liquidity. Explicit costs, such as broker commissions, financial transaction taxes, custody/safekeeping fees, and transaction processing, are covered in other parts of the CFA Program curriculum.

Implicit Costs—Market Impact and the Relevance of Position Size, Assets under Management, and Turnover

The price movement (or market impact) resulting from a manager's purchase or sale of a security can materially erode a manager's alpha. Market impact is a function of the liquidity and trade size of the security. A manager's investment approach and style will influence the extent to which he is exposed to market impact costs. A manager whose strategy demands immediacy in execution or requires a higher portfolio turnover is likely to incur higher market impact costs relative to a manager who patiently trades into a position. A manager who believes her investment insights will be rewarded over a longer-term investment horizon may be able to mitigate market impact costs by slowly building up positions as liquidity becomes available. A manager whose trades contain "information" is more vulnerable to market impact costs. A trade contains information when the manager's decision to buy or sell the security signals to the market that something has changed. If a discretionary manager with sizable assets under management begins to buy a stock, the trade signals to other market participants that there is likely to be upward pressure on the stock price as the manager builds the position. Some market participants may try to "front-run" the manager, buying up known supply to sell it to the manager at a higher price. If that same manager begins to sell his position following a company "event," it signals to the market that the manager's view on the stock has changed and he is likely to be selling off his position, putting downward pressure on the price. Assets under management, portfolio turnover, and the liquidity of the underlying assets all affect the potential market impact costs.

Consider the relationship between the size of a security, as measured by its capitalization, and a manager's ability to trade in this security, as measured by its average daily trading volume. Exhibit 21 presents the capitalization and average daily trading volume of the Russell 1000 companies in declining order of their capitalization. The figure is built using a moving average of the capitalization of groups of 20 companies. The first point on the graph shows the average capitalization and trading volume of the largest 20 companies by capitalization. The next point on the graph presents the same information for the averages of the companies ranking 2nd to 21st in terms of capitalization, and so on.

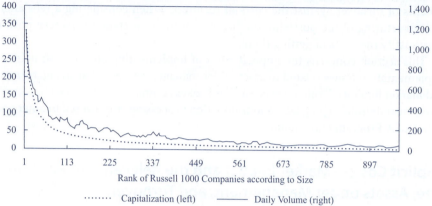

Exhibit 21: Capitalization and Trading Volume (in $) of the Russell 1000 Companies in Declining Order of Capitalization

Source: Data from Bloomberg.

Two observations are warranted. First, the distribution of market cap is skewed: The average capitalization declines quickly. The combined capitalization of the top 500 companies is more than seven times that of the bottom 500 companies. Second, smaller-capitalization companies have lower daily trading volume (in dollars). However, smaller-cap companies trade a greater percentage of their capitalization. The smallest 900 companies within the index trade nearly two times more volume—as a percentage of their market capitalization—than the 100 largest companies (e.g., the 900 smallest companies on average trade 1% of their market cap daily, whereas the 100 largest companies trade 0.5% of their market cap daily). Nevertheless, the lower absolute level of average trading volume of the smaller securities can be a significant implementation hurdle for a manager running a strategy with significant assets under management and significant positive active weights on smaller companies.

For example, let's assume the smallest company within an index has a capitalization of $2 billion and that 1% of its capitalization trades each day on average—about $20 million. Let's also assume that a manager has a policy not to own a position that constitutes more than 10% of the average trading volume of a security and that no position in the portfolio can be larger than 2% of total assets. If this manager has $200 million under management, the allocation constraint indicates that he could own as much as $4 million of that security ($200 million × 2% = $4 million), but the liquidity constraint limits the position to $2 million ($20 million × 10%). Thus, the position size is limited to about 1.0% of the fund's assets. A $1 billion fund with similar constraints would be limited to the same $2 million position, a much smaller position size relative to his total portfolio.

A $100 million fund can typically implement its strategy with very few obstacles arising from trading volume and position size constraints. However, the manager of a $5 billion fund could not effectively operate with the same constraints. A 2% position in a $5 billion fund is $100 million, yet only approximately 35% of the securities in the Russell 1000 have an average daily trading volume greater than $100 million. The trading volume constraint significantly limits the manager's opportunity set. A large-AUM fund can address this issue in several ways:

- It may establish position limits on individual securities that consider their respective market-cap weights on both an absolute and relative basis. For example, it may limit the allocation to the lesser of market-cap weight + 1%

Implicit Cost-Related Considerations

(100 bps) or 10 times the market-cap weight allocation of the security within the index. In other words, the position limit would be related to the market cap of each security.

- It may establish position limits based on the average daily trading volume of a security. For example, it may limit the position size to, say, no more than 10 days of average trading volume.

- It may build a rebalancing strategy into the investment process that anticipates a longer rebalancing period or that gradually and consistently rebalances over time, assuming the performance of the strategy is not affected by the implementation delay.

The challenges are even greater for small-cap funds. The weighted average capitalization of the Russell 2000 Index is only $2.2 billion, and nearly 60% of the companies in the index have a market capitalization below $1 billion (as of March 2017). The average market cap of companies over this $1 billion market-cap threshold is only $1.2 billion. The average daily volume of these "larger" companies is approximately 2% of their market capitalization—less than $25 million. Approximately 75% of securities within the index have a lower average daily trading volume.

A small-cap manager with the same limits on position size relative to trading volume as the manager above would have an average position size of no more than $2.5 million, based on average daily trading volume. A strategy rooted in a smaller number of securities—say, 40—may find it difficult to run a $100 million fund and may have to concentrate its allocation among the 25% largest securities in the index or accept a lower turnover. Although a strategy with a larger number of securities—say, 200—would be able to support a substantially higher level of AUM, it may still be constrained to concentrate its exposure among the larger and more liquid securities. Small-cap funds with capacities of $1 billion or greater may very well need to hold 400 securities or more.

The strategy of the manager must be consistent with the feasibility of implementing it. A high-turnover strategy with a significant allocation to smaller securities will at some point reach a level of AUM at which the strategy becomes difficult to implement successfully. The level of idiosyncratic risk inherent in the strategy will also play a role in the suitable level of AUM. A manager targeting low levels of idiosyncratic risk in his portfolio is likely to have more securities and smaller position sizes and could, therefore, conceivably support a higher level of AUM.

Estimating the Cost of Slippage

Slippage is often measured as the difference between the execution price and the midpoint of the bid and ask quotes at the time the trade was first entered.[36] It incorporates both the effect of volatility/trend costs and market impact. (Volatility/trend costs are the costs associated with buying in a rising market and selling in a declining market.) This measure provides an estimate of the cost to execute a transaction when the order is executed in a single trade.

When a larger trade is executed in increments over multiple days, the estimate of market impact costs for later trades does not account for the impact of earlier trades on subsequent execution prices. Depending on the size of the trade, the manager's own sell (buy) orders may put downward (upward) pressure on the security's price, thereby increasing the effective cost of implementation. Large institutional investors today will often try to camouflage the potential size of their trade by breaking a trade

---

36 See Taleb (1997).

into many smaller trades or by trading in "unlit" venues. Unlit venues allow buyers and sellers to trade anonymously with one another. Dark pools and crossing networks are examples of unlit venues.[37]

Studies have shown that small-cap stocks have consistently had higher effective trading costs than large-cap stocks and that illiquidity can be very cyclical, increasing prior to the beginning of a recession and decreasing prior to the end of a recession.[38] It is difficult to quantify this cost, but we know intuitively that a given trading volume causes a larger price move for a less liquid asset.[39] The larger a trade size relative to a stock's average daily volume is, the more likely it is that the trade will affect prices. Thus, a fund with a focus on large-cap stocks can support a higher level of AUM than can a similar-strategy fund focused on small-cap stocks. A fund focused on small-cap stocks must either limit its AUM, hold a more diversified portfolio, limit turnover, or devise a trading strategy to mitigate market impact costs.

Exhibit 22 provides estimates of the average slippage for several markets in 2020. There are three conclusions we can draw:

- Slippage costs are usually more important than commission costs.
- Slippage costs are greater for smaller-cap securities than for large-cap securities.
- Slippage costs can vary substantially over time, especially when market volatility is higher.

---

[37] If a large institution wants to sell a big block of stock but doesn't want to alert other market participants about the pending activity, it may choose to trade anonymously. Unlit venues—private trading venues where transactions are completed "in the dark" (without full transparency)—have become a powerful force in financial markets.
[38] Hasbrouck (2009) and Amihud (2002).
[39] Ilmanen (2011).

Implicit Cost-Related Considerations

Exhibit 22: Average Slippage by Cap Size and Country

A. US Market by Cap Size

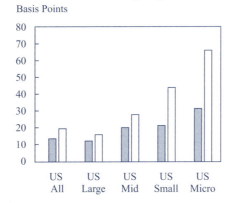

B. By Country

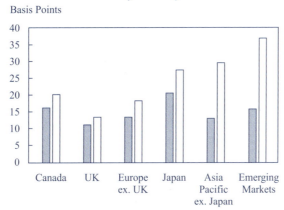

■ 2016   □ Q3 and Q4 2009

Source: ITG, "Global Cost Review Q4/2016" (2017).

Slippage cost can be managed with a strategic approach to implementation. Smaller-AUM managers have an advantage in this respect. For example, two hypothetical $100 million trades were sent to an execution platform that provides estimates of trading costs. The first trade mirrored the Russell 1000. The second trade bought just 250 securities in the same Russell 1000 universe, but the weighted average capitalization was only $26 billion (versus $133 billion for the index). Assuming the trading was accomplished in the course of a single day, the first trade had an estimated implementation cost of just 1 bp, whereas the second trade incurred implementation costs of 3%.

For some strategies, the true cost of slippage may be the opportunity cost of not being able to implement the strategy as assets grow. Investors choose a given fund based on the manager's stated strategy and implementation approach. If this approach is modified as the manager's level of AUM grows, it may have unanticipated consequences for expected risks and returns to investors. In these situations, the manager must either inform investors of changes being made to the strategy and its implementation or they must limit the size of the fund assets—that is, close the fund to new investors or new contributions from existing investors. Managers need to very carefully think about capacity as a new product is launched; although historical results based on a lower level of AUM may attract attention and clients, if the strategy cannot be scaled for the larger AUM, the product delivered to clients may be different from the strategy they thought they were investing in.

A study by AQR Capital Management "Factor Momentum Everywhere", 2019 documents robust persistence in the returns of equity factor portfolios. This persistence is exploitable with a time-series momentum trading strategy that scales factor exposures up and down in proportion to their recent performance. Factor timing in this manner produces economically and statistically large excess performance relative to untimed factors. Taken alongside the evidence of time series momentum in commodity, bond, and currency factors, the findings of momentum among equity factors—in the time series, in the cross section, and around the world—support the conclusion that factor momentum is a pervasive phenomenon in financial markets.[40]

EXAMPLE 7

Issues of Scale

1. Stephen Lo has been the sole portfolio manager of the Top Asia Fund since its inception 20 years ago. He is supported by a group of analysts. The fund has been highly successful as it grew from assets of less than $30 million in his first year to more than $7 billion. As a potential investor in the Top Asia Fund, you have been asked to determine how Lo has been able to generate his performance and whether his style has evolved over the years. You prepared the following analysis of the return and risk characteristics of the fund for its first five years and last five years of existence.

   Discuss the evolution of the fund's characteristics and its implications for Lo's success as a manager.

Top Asia Fund Characteristics	First Five Years	Last Five Years
Average assets ($ millions)	200	5,000
Average number of positions	80	300
Market Beta	0.90	0.91
Size coefficient	0.30	−0.10
Value coefficient	0.25	0.24
Momentum coefficient	0.20	0.10
Portfolio turnover	100%	30%
Alpha (gross of fees)	2.5%	0.40%

Solution:

AUM grew rapidly over the past 20 years. The number of positions in the portfolio nearly quadrupled while assets grew by a factor of 25. Still, there are aspects of his style that have not changed: He is still very much a value manager investing in lower-beta securities. However, the portfolio no longer has a small-cap tilt, and the exposure to the momentum factor has also declined. It is likely that these are both byproducts of the increase in AUM; for example, a large fund has greater difficulty executing in small-cap securities.

---

40 Peter Lynch, while managing the highly successful Magellan Fund, generated a 2% gross *monthly* alpha on average (less than $1 million per month) assets under management of $40 million during his first five years of tenure and a 0.20% alpha per month during his last five years on assets of about $10 billion (more than $20 million per month). It is likely that the portfolio management approach evolved as the asset base grew.

This last point is supported by the decline in portfolio turnover. The decline in alpha indicates that the growth in AUM has altered the implementation of the investment approach.

2. Andrew Isaac runs a $100 million diversified equity portfolio (about 200 positions) using the the Russell 1000 as his investable universe. The total capitalization of the index is approximately $20 trillion. Isaac's strategy is very much size agnostic. He consistently owns securities along the entire size spectrum of permissible securities. The strategy was designed with the following constraints:

- No investment in any security whose index weight is less than 0.015% (approximately 15% of the securities in the index)
- Maximum position size equal to the lesser of 10× the index weight or the index weight plus 150 bps
- No position size that represents more than 5% of the security's average daily trading volume (ADV) over the trailing three months

The smaller securities in Isaac's permissible universe trade about 1% of shares outstanding daily. At what level of AUM is Isaac's strategy likely to be affected by the liquidity and concentration constraints?

Solution:

Based on the index capitalization of $20 trillion, the size constraint indicates that the smallest stocks in his portfolio will have a minimum market cap of about $3 billion (0.015% × $20 trillion). The ADV of the stocks at the lower end of his capitalization constraint would be about $30 million (1% × $3 billion). Because Isaac does not want to represent more than 5% of any security's ADV, the maximum position size for these smaller-cap stocks is about $1.5 million (5% × $30 million). It appears that Isaac's strategy will not be constrained until the portfolio reaches about $1 billion in size ($1.5 million ÷ 0.15% = $1 billion). If the level of AUM exceeds $1 billion, his position size constraints will require the portfolio to hold a larger number of smaller-cap positions. There is room to grow this strategy.

THE WELL-CONSTRUCTED PORTFOLIO

11

evaluate the efficiency of a portfolio structure given its investment mandate

A well-constructed portfolio should deliver results consistent with investors' risk and return expectations. It will not guarantee excess return relative to the appropriate benchmark, especially over a shorter horizon, but it will be designed to deliver the risk characteristics desired by the manager and promised to investors. The well-constructed portfolio possesses

- a clear investment philosophy and a consistent investment process,
- risk and structural characteristics as promised to investors,
- a risk-efficient delivery methodology, and

- reasonably low operating costs given the strategy.

Investors and managers may have different requirements with respect to the characteristics they seek in a well-structured portfolio. For some managers, substantial diversification is required, whereas others seek a high-conviction, less diversified strategy. Some investors require formal and heuristic risk metrics that are tightly constrained, and others tolerate more permissive risk limits. A well-structured portfolio must, at the very least, deliver the promised characteristics in a cost- and risk-efficient way.

Consider the following large-cap US equity products, Product A and Product B. Between January 1999 and September 2016, the two products had similar annualized absolute volatility, 15.1% and 15.2%, and similar active risk, 4.9% and 4.8%. However, they differ on other dimensions. Exhibit 23 presents the factor exposure of each product using a six-factor model. The factors are Market, Size, Value, Momentum, Betting against Beta (BAB), and Quality. The exhibit also shows the volatility of each factor. Exhibit 24 illustrates the contribution to the total variance of each product originating from these factors, as well as the portion of total variance that remains unexplained. Other characteristics are also presented.[41]

Exhibit 23: Factor Exposure, January 1999–September 2016

Factor	Product A	Product B	Factor Volatility
Market	0.92	1.08	15.8%
Size	−0.29	0.04	9.7%
Value	0.33	0.06	14.7%
Momentum	0.04	0.06	19.2%
BAB	0.02	0.09	14.4%
Quality	0.03	0.23	11.4%

Sources: Data are from Bloomberg and AQR.

Exhibit 24: Risk Characteristics

	Factor Risk Contribution	
Factor	Product A	Product B
Market	87.4%	105.9%
Size	−2.3%	0.6%
Value	14.0%	1.2%
Momentum	−2.7%	−2.0%
BAB	−0.4%	−2.0%
Quality	−1.6%	−10.5%

---

41 The style of a particular product may evolve over time because of changes in investment philosophy and even changes in the product management team. Although the two products presented in Exhibit 23 and Exhibit 24 were selected for the consistency of their respective approaches over time, when the period covers several decades, it would be prudent to do factor analyses over several sub periods to determine whether changes in management style did, in fact, occur.

The Well-Constructed Portfolio

| | Factor Risk Contribution ||
Factor	Product A	Product B
Unexplained	5.5%	6.8%
Total	100%	100%

	Other Characteristics	
Number of securities	≈320	≈120
Annualized active risk	4.9%	4.8%
Active Share	0.43	0.80
Annualized volatility	15.1%	15.2%
Maximum drawdown	54.6%	51.8%

Since the two products have similar volatility and active risk, what opinion can we form about the risk efficiency of each product?

Product A exhibits the following relevant characteristics:

- A Market β slightly less than 1
- A large-cap bias (a negative coefficient on the Size factor)
- A very large exposure to the Value factor
- Greater security-level diversification than Product B
- Market risk representing only 87.4% of the total portfolio risk
- A significant portion of the absolute risk attributed to the Value factor

The relevant characteristics for Product B are:

- A Market β slightly more than 1
- A more balanced exposure to all factors
- A large exposure to the Quality factor (although the factor itself has a relatively low volatility)
- Active Share nearly double that of Product A
- Modestly lower drawdowns
- More than 100% of its absolute risk attributed to the Market factor

Thus, Product B's emphasis on quality companies having a high return on equity, a low debt-to-equity ratio, and a low earnings variability is a likely explanation for absolute and relative risk measures that are not significantly different from those of Manager A. That Product B can achieve this level of risk efficiency with less than half the number of securities held by Product A indicates that risk management is an important component of the portfolio construction process of Product B. Although there is no guarantee that a more efficiently risk-structured portfolio will outperform, Product B outperformed Product A by more than 3.1% annually over the period.

In a well-constructed portfolio, we would be looking for risk exposures that are aligned with investor expectations and constraints and low idiosyncratic risk (unexplained) relative to total risk. If two products have comparable factor exposures, the product with a lower absolute volatility and lower active risk will likely be preferred (assuming similar costs). If two products have similar active and absolute risks, the portfolios have similar costs, and the alpha skills of the managers are similar, the product having a higher Active Share is preferable, because it leverages the alpha skills of the manager and will have higher expected returns.

Finally, the "risk efficiency" of any given portfolio approach should be judged in the context of the investor's total portfolio. The active risk of a concentrated stock picker should be higher than that of a diversified factor investor, and the concentrated stock picker may have a lower information ratio. Yet both managers could be building a well-structured portfolio relative to their mandate. It is important to consider the diversification effect of a manager's portfolio on the total portfolio of the investor to arrive at an appropriate solution.

> **EXAMPLE 8**
>
> ### The Well-Structured Portfolio
>
> David Larrabee is CIO of a pension fund with $5 billion in assets. The fund has 60% of its assets invested in equities with more than 10 managers. Larrabee is considering creating a core equity position that would represent 65% of all equity assets. The remaining 35% would then be allocated to approximately five active satellite (non-core) managers. The core position would be invested in a customized passive portfolio designed specifically for the pension fund using a well-documented construction and rebalancing process. The portfolio would be implemented by a known counterparty at a low cost (less than 10 bps). The main specifications for the custom portfolio were the following:
>
> - Investable universe composed of securities within the MSCI World Index
> - Low volatility achieved through an optimization process
> - High payout yield (dividend and share repurchase)
> - No fewer than 250 securities
> - No position greater than 2%
> - Average portfolio turnover less than 50% annually
>
> Larrabee understands that a low-volatility objective usually leads to portfolios with large-cap, Value, and Quality biases.
>
> Exhibit 25 and Exhibit 26 present the results of a pro forma analysis of the custom portfolio. The portfolio was simulated over a period of 12 years. Exhibit 25 presents some key risk and structural characteristics, as well as the average active sector exposure. Exhibit 26 presents the results of factor analyses for both the MSCI World and the custom portfolio.
>
> **Exhibit 25**
>
> | | MSCI World | Custom Portfolio |
> | --- | --- | --- |
> | Return annualized | 7.0% | 8.45% |
> | Volatility annualized | 11.3% | 9.0% |
> | Active risk | — | 6.0% |
> | Number of securities | 1,700 | 325 |
> | Turnover | 2.4% | 35% |
> | Dividend yield | 2.6% | 3.6% |
> | **Average Active Sector Exposure** | | |
> | Energy | — | −2.00% |
> | Materials | — | −1.50% |
> | Industrials | — | −1.50% |

The Well-Constructed Portfolio

	MSCI World	Custom Portfolio
Consumer discretionary	—	3.00%
Consumer staples	—	4.20%
Health care	—	2.40%
Financials	—	–1.00%
Information technology	—	–10.00%
Telecommunication services	—	3.20%
Utilities	—	3.20%

Exhibit 26

	Factor Exposure MSCI World	Factor Exposure Custom Portfolio	Factor Relative Risk Attribution MSCI World	Factor Relative Risk Attribution Custom Portfolio
Alpha (annualized)	–1.0%	–3.1%	—	—
Market	1.00	0.84	103%	105%
Size	–0.13	–0.26	–1%	–1%
Value	0.06	0.30	2%	10%
Momentum	0.02	0.02	–1%	–3%
BAB	0.01	0.32	0%	2%
Quality	0.10	0.54	–4%	–22%
Unexplained	—	—	1%	9%

Larrabee has hired you to advise him on the proposed core product. Considering the information provided,

1. Does the pro forma custom portfolio meet the specifications of a well-structured portfolio, and are there any characteristics of this product that concern you?

Solution:

The proposed solution is aligned with many of the characteristics of a well-constructed portfolio. It is based on a consistent investment process, and it appears to meet the requirements of the investor: It has significantly lower volatility than the MSCI World and a significantly higher dividend yield (although we do not have the information on the payout yield), the portfolio has a low security concentration, and the estimated turnover is lower than the required limit. It can also be implemented at a low cost. The factor analysis also confirms what we could expect from a high-payout/low-volatility portfolio. The Market beta is significantly below 1, the negative Size coefficient indicates a larger-capitalization bias, and finally, the portfolio has a Value and Quality bias. The risk attribution analysis indicates that the exposure to Quality companies is largely responsible for reducing the total risk of the portfolio.

However, there are some aspects of the portfolio that create some concerns. Although the custom portfolio meets all of Larrabee's specified objectives, the portfolio construction process leads to a high tracking error (active risk).

> Given the size of this allocation relative to the total equity portfolio, this poses a problem. Some of this tracking error may be attributed to a significant under-allocation to the information technology sector. Finally, although the portfolio would have generated an excess return on average over the past 12 years, the alpha is negative. Understanding the source of this negative alpha is essential. In this instance, the excess return was achieved largely through a very high and intentional exposure to rewarded factors, such as Value, BAB, and Quality, which may not have been rewarded over the simulated period.

> 2. If the custom portfolio were implemented, what recommendations would you make to Larrabee in terms of the style of the satellite managers or in general?
>
> **Solution:**
>
> The first recommendation would be to investigate further the source of the significant negative alpha. Because the excess performance is so strongly explained by exposure to specific factors, we should be concerned about how the portfolio would perform if factor returns were to decline. Is there a systemic reason that can explain this observation? Secondly, if tracking error is a concern, it is important to identify satellite managers whose active returns have a low correlation with the core mandate, perhaps even a lower active risk. Finally, considering the importance of the information technology sector, it could be prudent to hire a manager that has a strong technology orientation. The objective is not necessarily to maintain a technology exposure equal to that of the MSCI World Index but perhaps to lower the consistent underexposure to a more reasonable level. At the very least, these structural biases should be continuously monitored.

12. LONG/SHORT, LONG EXTENSION, AND MARKET-NEUTRAL PORTFOLIO CONSTRUCTION

> discuss the long-only, long extension, long/short, and equitized market-neutral approaches to equity portfolio construction, including their risks, costs, and effects on potential alphas

Long/short, long extension, and market-neutral portfolio approaches are all variations on a theme: Each is predicated on the belief that research insights can be exploited not only in the pursuit of stocks that are expected to perform well but also to profit from the negative insights gathered during the research process. "Long/short" is the most encompassing term and can include long extension and market-neutral products. Most commonly, the term "long/short" refers to strategies that are relatively unconstrained in the extent to which they can lever both positive and negative insights.

Long extension strategies are constrained long/short strategies. The capital committed by the client is invested similarly to a manager's long-only strategy but levered to some extent to exploit the manager's insights on projected losers as well as winners. A typical long-extension strategy is constrained to have a net exposure of 100%; for example, 130% of the capital is invested long and 30% of the capital is invested short, for a net exposure of 100%—the same as it would be in a long-only portfolio. There may or may not be a relationship between the long and the short portfolios.

Market-neutral strategies are long/short portfolios constructed in a manner to ensure that the portfolio's exposures to a wide variety of risk factors is zero. In addition, these portfolios may be neutralized against a wide variety of other risk factors.

The Merits of Long-Only Investing

An investor's choice of whether to pursue a long-only strategy or some variation of a long/short strategy is likely to be influenced by several considerations:

- Long-term risk premiums
- Capacity and scale (the ability to invest assets)
- Limited legal liability and risk appetite
- Regulatory constraints
- Transactional complexity
- Management costs
- Personal ideology

Long-term risk premiums

A major motivation for investors to be long only is the generally accepted belief that there is a positive long-run premium to be earned from bearing market risk. Investors may also believe that risk premiums can be earned from other sources of risk, such as Size, Value, or Momentum. To capture these risk premiums, investors must over time own (go net "long") the underlying securities that are exposed to these risks. Although risk premiums have been shown to earn a return in the long run, realized risk premium returns can be negative in the short run; the market can and does experience returns less than the risk-free rate, and recall the earlier discussion regarding the cyclicality of the Size, Value, and Momentum factors. For investors with shorter-term investment horizons, the potential benefits of a positive expected risk premium over the long run may not offset the potential risk of market declines or other reversals. These investors may pursue an approach other than strictly long-only investing and may prefer to short-sell some securities.

Capacity and scalability

Long-only investing, particularly strategies that focus on large-cap stocks, generally offers greater investment capacity than other approaches. For example, the MSCI ACWI has a total market cap of nearly $65.8 trillion, and the 10 largest companies are worth $10.4 trillion as of September 30, 2021.[42] For large institutional investors, such as pension plans, there are no effective capacity constraints in terms of the total market cap available for long-only large-cap investing. Long-only strategies may face capacity constraints, however, if they focus on smaller and illiquid stocks or employ a strategy reliant on a high level of portfolio turnover. Unlike long-only strategies, the capacity of short-selling strategies is limited by the availability of securities to borrow.

---

42 Market cap is not necessarily the same as shares available for general investors, because some shares may be closely held and not traded. Most index providers now calculate "float," which represents shares the public can trade.

Limited legal liability

Common stocks are limited liability financial instruments. The lowest a stock price can fall to is zero, so the maximum amount that a long-only investor in a common stock can lose is the amount of money that she invested in the stock. Thus, long-only investing puts a firm floor on how much an investor can lose. In contrast, a short-seller's potential losses are unlimited in principle. The short-seller loses money as the stock price rises, and there is no ceiling limiting the price increase. This type of "naked" short-selling is quite risky. To offset this risk, investors often combine a short-selling strategy with a long-only strategy. Indeed, long/short strategies are often less risky than long-only or short-only strategies.

Regulatory

Some countries ban short-selling activities. Others have temporarily restricted or banned short-selling. For example, on 18 September 2008, the UK Financial Services Authority (FSA) temporarily prohibited the short-selling of financial companies to protect the integrity of the financial system. The US Securities and Exchange Commission (SEC) followed suit the next day. Additionally, many countries that allow short-selling prohibit or restrict naked short-selling, a practice consisting of short-selling a tradable asset without first borrowing the security or ensuring that it can be borrowed.

Transactional complexity

The mechanics of long-only investing are relatively simple and easy to understand. The investment manager instructs a broker (or uses an electronic platform) to buy stock XYZ. The broker executes the trade on the client's behalf and arranges for the security to be delivered to the client's account. Typically, a custodial bank sits between the investment adviser and the client. In this case, the custodian would deliver the cash for the stock and take possession of the shares of XYZ stock. If the shares are held in a custodial bank, the adviser can liquidate the position at any time (a caveat is that to exercise this flexibility completely, the custodian must be instructed not to lend out the shares). In long-only investing, buying and selling stocks are straightforward, intuitive transactions.

A short-selling transaction is more complex. The investor first needs to find shares of stock to borrow. Although many stocks are easy to borrow, others may be hard to locate, and the cost to borrow these shares can be much higher. Investors must also provide collateral to ensure that they can repay the borrowed stock if the price moves up. Borrowed stock may also be recalled at an inopportune time for the short-seller.

In many regions, regulated investment entities must use a custodian for all the transactions. When a custodian is involved, complicated three-party agreements (between the fund, prime broker, and custodian) are required. The agreements govern the buying and selling of securities as well as the management of collateral. An investor who does not use a custodian is exposed to counterparty risk—the collateral is often held in a general operating account of a prime broker. If the prime broker goes bankrupt, the collateral can vanish (which happened to many investors in the Lehman Brothers bankruptcy). Operational risk is significantly greater with long/short investing.

Management costs

Long-only investing is less expensive, both in terms of management fees and from an operational perspective. Managers of long/short products often charge fees that are a multiple of what long-only managers typically charge. Three categories of long/short products are active extension, market neutral, and directional.[43] As of 2021, long/short

---

43 See Pavilion (2011).

hedge funds typically charge hedge fund fixed fees of about 2% and performance fees of about 20%. It follows, then, that the investor in a long/short product must have a high degree of confidence in the manager's ability to extract premiums or generate alpha relative to lower-fee, long-only managers.

Personal ideology

Some investors may express a preference for long-only investment for ideological reasons. They may feel that directly gaining from the losses of others is morally wrong, as might be the case in short-selling. Some investors may believe that short-selling requires significantly greater expertise than long-only investing and that such expertise is not reliably available or consistent. And some might argue that short-selling requires significant leverage to achieve the targeted long-term expected return, and they may be unwilling to assume this risk. In short, some investors may "just say no" to anything other than long-only investing.

Long/Short Portfolio Construction

Investors may be interested in long/short strategies for a variety of reasons. For example, the conviction of negative views can be more strongly expressed when short-selling is permitted than in a long-only approach. In addition, short-selling can help reduce exposures to sectors, regions, or general market movements and allow managers to focus on their unique skill set. Finally, the full extraction of the benefits of risk factors requires a long/short approach (i.e., short large cap and long small cap, short growth and long value, short poor price momentum and long high price momentum, etc.). Long-only investors can profit from only part of the opportunity set.

There are many different styles of long/short strategies, each driven by its own investment thesis. Exhibit 27 presents a range of possible options to structure a long/short portfolio. Implementation of long/short strategies varies with their intended purpose. In a long-only portfolio construction process, the weights assigned to every asset must be greater than or equal to 0 and the weights must sum to 1. In the long/short approach, position weights can be negative and the weights are not necessarily constrained to sum to 1. Some long/short portfolios may even have aggregate exposure of less than 1. The absolute value of the longs minus the absolute value of the shorts is called the portfolio's *net exposure*. The sum of the longs plus the absolute value of the shorts is called the portfolio's *gross exposure*.

A comprehensive use of long/short strategies can also be found in the design of equal-risk-premium products. Such products seek to extract return premiums from rewarded factors, often across asset classes. To do so, the manager must create long/short sub-portfolios extracting these premiums (such as Size, Value, Momentum, and Low Beta) and combine these sub-portfolios using weightings that ensure each component will contribute the same amount of risk to the overall portfolio. The combination may be levered across all sub-portfolios to achieve a specific volatility level. In other words, the manager is using long and short positions as well as leverage (or deleveraging) to achieve the most efficient combination of rewarded factors.

Exhibit 27: Illustrative Long/Short Portfolio Structures (as a percentage of capital)

	Long Positions	Short Positions	Cash	Gross Exposure	Net Exposure
Long only	100	0	0	100	100
130/30 long extension	130	30	0	160	100

	Long Positions	Short Positions	Cash	Gross Exposure	Net Exposure
Market neutral – low risk	50	50	100	100	0
Market neutral – higher risk	100	100	100	200	0
Directional – low risk	80	40	60	120	40
Net short	40	100	160	140	−60

Long/short managers typically define their exposure constraints as part of the portfolio construction process. For example, many equity hedge funds have a strategy of targeting a gross exposure (long plus short) of 150%–200% while targeting a net exposure (long minus short) of 0%–60%. A net exposure greater than zero implies some positive exposure to the Market factor. Regardless of the investment approach, all long/short strategies must establish parameters regarding the desired level of gross and net exposure, and these parameters will provide the investor with meaningful information about the manager's strategy and its expected risk profile.

Long Extension Portfolio Construction

Long extension strategies are a hybrid of long-only and long/short strategies. They are often called "enhanced active equity" strategies. A particular enhanced active equity strategy called "130/30" was popular until the market decline during the global financial crisis.[44] This strategy is making inroads again as investors better understand the potential pitfalls of shorting and are seeking more return in a low interest rate environment. A 130/30 strategy builds a portfolio of long positions worth 130% of the wealth invested in the strategy—that is, 1.3 times the amount of capital. At the same time, the portfolio holds short positions worth 30% of capital. The long and short positions combined equal 100% of capital. In essence, the short positions are funding the excess long positions, and the resulting gross leverage (160% = 130% + 30%) potentially allows for greater alpha and a more efficient exposure to rewarded factors. Unlike leverage incurred via cash borrowing in a long-only portfolio, which can be used only to exploit *long* insights, the long/short approach allows the portfolio to benefit not only from insights on companies that are forecasted to perform well (the long positions) but also from insights on companies forecasted to perform poorly (the short positions). In theory, this strategy offers the opportunity to magnify total returns. Of course, the long/short approach could also lead to greater losses if the manager is simultaneously wrong on both his long and short picks.

Another benefit of the 130/30 strategy is that long-only managers are limited in their ability to underallocate to securities that have a small initial allocation in the benchmark. For example, if Security X has a 0.25% allocation within the benchmark, a long-only manager can express a negative view on the stock only to the extent of its 0.25% benchmark weight by omitting the security from the portfolio. A 130/30 strategy affords the possibility of sizing the underweight in line with the manager's expectations for the stock. This ability allows the strength of the positive and negative views to be expressed more symmetrically.

---

44 130/30 strategies can accentuate losses. For example, Value strategies performed poorly during the financial crisis of 2007–2008, whereas Momentum strategies performed poorly after March 2009, as the equity markets rebounded. Many 130/30 products were built on these rewarded factors and performed poorly.

Market-Neutral Portfolio Construction

Market-neutral portfolio construction is a specialized form of long/short portfolio construction. At a very simple, naive level, one might think that in this strategy, the dollars invested in long securities are identical to the dollars associated with short-selling—that is, a portfolio with zero net investment, often called "dollar neutral." But dollar neutral is not the same thing as market neutral, because the economic drivers of returns for the long side may not be the same as the economic drivers for the short side.

True market-neutral strategies hedge out most market risk. They are often employed when the investor wants to remove the effects of general market movements from returns to explicitly focus on the manager's skill in forecasting returns of stocks, sectors, factors, or geographic regions. In essence, the investor wants to remove the "noise" that market movements can create to better focus on the creation of positive abnormal returns. In isolation, this strategy could be considered risky. For example, if stock prices appreciate rapidly (and historically, stock prices do rise), then the investor would miss out on this appreciation. However, some investors might add this type of strategy to their overall portfolio to increase diversification and at least partially offset losses in other parts of the portfolio when stock prices decline.

Market-neutral portfolio construction attempts to exactly match and offset the systematic risks of the long positions with those of the short positions. For example, if one uses beta as the measure of systematic risk, then a market-neutral portfolio, using longs and shorts, would have a Market beta of zero. A simple example of zero-beta investment would be a fund that is long $100 of assets with a Market beta of 1 and short $80 of assets with a Market beta of 1.25. This concept can be extended to include other systematic factors that influence returns, such as Size, Value, and Momentum. In other words, the market-neutral concept can be implemented for a variety of risk factors. The main constraint is that in aggregate, the targeted beta(s) of the portfolio be zero.

A market-neutral strategy is still expected to generate a positive information ratio. Although market neutral may seek to eliminate market risk and perhaps some other risks on an *ex ante* basis, the manager cannot eliminate all risks. If she could—and did—the expected return would likely be equal to the risk-free rate minus the manager's fees. The objective is to neutralize the risks for which the manager believes she has no comparative forecasting advantage, thus allowing the manager to concentrate on her very specific skills.

Given that market-neutral strategies seek to remove major sources of systematic risk from a portfolio, these strategies are usually less volatile than long-only strategies. They are often considered absolute return strategies because their benchmarks might be fixed-income instruments. Even if a market-neutral strategy is not fully successful in its implementation, the correlation of market-neutral strategies with other types of strategies is typically quite low. Thus, some market-neutral strategies may serve more of a diversification role in a portfolio, rather than a high-return-seeking role.

A specific form of market-neutral strategy is pairs trading, where an investor will go long one security in an industry and short another security in the same industry, trying to exploit what the investor perceives as "mispricing." A more quantitatively oriented form of pairs trading called *statistical arbitrage* ("stat arb") uses statistical techniques to identify two securities that are historically highly correlated with each other. When the price correlation of these two securities deviates from its long-term average (and if the manager believes that the deviation is temporary), the manager will go long the underperforming stock and simultaneously short the outperforming stock. If the prices do converge to the long-term average as forecasted, the manager will close the trade and realize a profit.

In other variations of market-neutral investing, one might find portfolios constructed with hundreds of securities identified using systematic multi-factor models that evaluate all securities in the investable universe. The manager will buy the most favorably ranked securities and short the least favorably ranked ones. The manager may impose constraints on exposures of the longs and the shorts to keep gross and net exposures at the desired levels.

Market-neutral strategies have two inherent limitations:

1. Practically speaking, it is no easy task to maintain a beta of zero. Not all risks can be efficiently hedged, and correlations between exposures are continually shifting.

2. Market-neutral strategies have a limited upside in a bull market unless they are "equitized." Some investors, therefore, choose to index their equity exposure and overlay long/short strategies. In this case, the investor is not abandoning equity-like returns and is using the market-neutral portfolio as an overlay.

Benefits and Drawbacks of Long/Short Strategies

Long/short strategies offer the following benefits:

- Ability to more fully express short ideas than under a long-only strategy
- Efficient use of leverage and of the benefits of diversification
- Greater ability to calibrate/control exposure to factors (such as Market and other rewarded factors), sectors, geography, or any undesired exposure (such as, perhaps, sensitivity to the price of oil)

We've explored the first two benefits of long/short portfolio construction listed above. Let's look more closely at the last one.

A fully invested long-only strategy will be exposed to market risk. To reduce the level of market risk, the manager must either concentrate holdings in low-beta stocks or hold a portion of the assets in cash, an asset that produces minimal return. Conversely, to increase the level of market risk, the long-only manager must own high-beta stocks or use financial leverage; the cost of leverage will reduce future returns. Practically speaking, the portfolio beta of a long-only manager is likely constrained within a range of, say, 0.8–1.2. In contrast, a long/short manager has much more flexibility in adjusting his level of market exposure to reflect his view on the current opportunities.

In long-only portfolios, total portfolio risk is dominated by the Market factor, and the Market factor is a long-only factor. However, all other factor returns can be thought of as long/short portfolios: *Size* is long small cap and short large cap, *Value* is long value and short growth, *Momentum* is long positive momentum and short less positive or negative momentum, and so on. Just like with beta, the ability to tilt a portfolio in favor of these other factors or diversify efficiently across factors is structurally restricted in a long-only portfolio. Because the average of cross correlations among rewarded factors is close to zero or even negative, efficiently allocating across factors could bring significant diversification benefits. But the ability to reduce overall risk and to distribute sources of risk more evenly cannot be optimally achieved without short-selling.

Strategies that short securities contain the following inherent risks, which must be understood:

1. Unlike a long position, a short position will move against the manager if the price of the security increases.

2. Long/short strategies sometimes require significant leverage. Leverage must be used wisely.

Long/Short, Long Extension, and Market-Neutral Portfolio Construction

3. The cost of borrowing a security can become prohibitive, particularly if the security is hard to borrow.
4. Collateral requirements will increase if a short position moves against the manager. In extreme cases, the manager may be forced to liquidate some favorably ranked long positions (and short positions that might eventually reverse) if too much leverage has been used. The manager may also fall victim to a short squeeze. A short squeeze is a situation in which the price of the stock that has been shorted has risen so much and so quickly that many short investors may be unable to maintain their positions in the short run in light of the increased collateral requirements. The "squeeze" is worsened as short-sellers liquidate their short position, buying back the security and possibly pushing the price even higher.

As previously indicated, to short-sell securities, investors typically rely on a prime broker who can help them locate the securities they wish to borrow. But the prime broker will require collateral from the short-sellers to assure the lenders of these securities that their contracts will be honored. The higher the relative amount of short-selling in a portfolio, the greater the amount of collateral required. A portfolio with 20% of capital invested short may be required to put up collateral equal to 40% of the short positions, whereas a portfolio with 100% of capital invested short could be required to put up collateral equal to 200% of the short positions. In addition, different types of assets are weighed differently in the calculation of collateral value. For example, a US Treasury bill may be viewed as very safe collateral and accorded 100% of its value toward the required collateral. In contrast, a high-yield bond or some other asset with restricted liquidity would have only a portion of its market value counted toward the collateral requirement.

These collateral requirements are designed to protect the lender in the event of adverse price movements. When stock prices are rising rapidly, the lender may recall all the borrowed shares, fearing that the borrower's collateral will be wiped out. If this were to happen, the leveraged long/short manager would be forced to close out his short positions at an inopportune time, leaving significant profits on the table. In the end, long/short investing is a compromise between return impacts, sources of risk, and costs, as illustrated in the table below.

Benefits	Costs
▪ Short positions can reduce market risk. ▪ Shorting potentially expands benefits from other risk premiums and alpha. ▪ The combination of long and short positions allows for a greater diversification potential.	▪ Short positions might reduce the market return premium. ▪ Shorting may amplify the active risk (but please note that it does note have to do so). ▪ There are higher implementation costs and greater complexity associated with shorting and leverage relative to a long-only approach.

EXAMPLE 9

Creating a 130/30 Strategy

Alpha Prime has been managing long-only equity portfolios for more than 15 years. The firm has a systematic investment process built around assessing security valuation and price momentum. Each company is attributed a standardized score (F_k) that is based on a combination of quantitative and fundamental metrics. Positions are selected from among those securities with a positive standardized score and are weighted based on the strength of that score. The security weightings within sectors can be significantly different from those of the benchmark, but the portfolio's sector weightings adhere closely to the benchmark weights. Investment decisions are made by the portfolio management team and are re-evaluated monthly. A constrained optimization process is used to guide investment decision making. Listed below are the objective function and the primary constraints used by the firm.

- *Objective function:* Maximize the portfolio factor score
- *Total exposure constraint:* Sum of portfolio weights must = 1
- *Individual security constraint:* Minimum weight of 0% and maximum weight of 3%
- *Sector constraint:* Benchmark weight ±5%
- *Constraint on active risk (TE):* Active risk less than 5%

The managers at Alpha Prime have realized that their investment process can also generate a negative signal, indicating that a security is likely to underperform. However, the signal is not quite as reliable or stable when it is used for this purpose. There is much more noise around the performance of the expected losers than there is around the performance of the winners. Still, the signal has value.

1. You are asked to draft guidelines for the creation of a 130/30 strategy. What changes to the objective function and to each of the constraints would you recommend?

Solution:

- *Objective function:* The objective function would remain the same. Securities with a positive standardized score would be eligible for positive weights, and securities with a negative standardized factor score would receive negative weights (the fund would short these securities).
- *Total exposure constraint:* The portfolio now needs a constraint for gross exposure and one for net exposure. The net exposure constraint in a 130/30 product is constrained to 100%. (The notional value of the longs minus the absolute value of the shorts must be equal to 1.) The portfolio's gross exposure constraint is implicit in the nature of the 130/30 product. (The notional value of the longs plus the absolute value of the shorts cannot exceed 160%.)
- *Individual security constraint:* To take advantage of the negative signals from the model, the portfolio must allow shorting. The minimum weight constraint must be relaxed. Given the issues associated with short-selling, the firm's relative inexperience in this area, and the lower reliability of the short signal, the maximum short position size should be smaller than the maximum long position size. One might recommend that the initial short constraint be set at 1%. Position limits on the long side could stay the same, but that would likely lead to more long positions, given the increase in long exposure to 130%. The manager must assess whether to expand the number of securities held in the portfolio or to raise the maximum position size limit.
- *Sector constraint:* There is no need to change the aggregate sector constraint. The manager now has the ability to offset any overweight on the long side with a short position that would bring the portfolio's exposure to that sector back within the current constraint.

- *Tracking error target:* Sector deviations have a greater bearing on active risk than do security-level differences. Alpha Prime's sector bets are very limited; thus, no change in the tracking error constraint is necessary. The ability to short gives them greater opportunity to exploit investment ideas without changing the firm's approach to sector weightings.

2. Discuss the potential challenges of incorporating short positions into the portfolio strategy.

Solution:

Shorting adds complexity to both the operational and the risk aspects of portfolio management. Operationally, the firm must establish relationships with one or more prime brokers and ensure that adequate collateral for the short positions remains available. Some securities can be difficult to borrow, and the cost of borrowing some stocks can be prohibitive. This may inhibit Alpha Prime's ability to implement its short ideas and will raise the operational costs of running the portfolio. In addition, shorting introduces a new type of risk: A short transaction has no loss limit. If the stock moves against the manager in the short run, the manager may have to close the position before he is proven right.

EXAMPLE 10

Long Only vs. Long/Short

Marc Salter has been running a long-only unlevered factor-based strategy in the US market for more than five years. He has delivered a product that has all the expected exposure to rewarded risk factors promised to investors. Salter just met with a pension fund investor looking at a multi-factor based approach. However, the pension fund manager indicates they are also considering investing with a competitor that runs a leveraged long/short factor-based strategy. It appears the competitor's product has a significantly higher information ratio. The product of the competitor neutralizes market risk and concentrates on exposure to other rewarded factors.

1. Why would the competitor's long/short product have a higher information ratio?

Solution:

Factor returns are usually built from a long portfolio having the desired factor characteristic against a short portfolio that does not. A long-only factor investor is limited in his ability to short (relative to the benchmark) positions that do not have the desired characteristics. Adding the ability to leverage negative as well as positive research insights should improve the transfer coefficient and increase the potential to generate better excess returns.

In addition, in a long-only strategy, the Market factor dominates all other risks. Adding the ability to short could facilitate a more balanced distribution of risk. Given the similar volatilities and low cross correlations among factors, the more balanced distribution of risk can be expected to reduce the tracking error of the strategy, thereby improving the information ratio.

2. What are its drawbacks?

Solution:

Multi-factor products often contain several hundred securities, some of which may be difficult to borrow. The complexity of shorting across this large number of names combined with higher management fees and implementation costs may necessitate more implementation constraints on the short side.

Removing the risk associated with the Market factor implies that the long/short product would most likely be used as an overlay on long-only mandates. The mandate may also be leveraged (more than 1× long and 1× short) to maximize the potential return per dollar of capital. For example, equal-risk-premium products (that remove the effect of the Market factor) often need three units of leverage long and short to achieve a 10% absolute risk target. Some investors may be uncomfortable with such leverage.

SUMMARY

Active equity portfolio construction strives to make sure that superior insights about forecasted returns get efficiently reflected in realized portfolio performance. Active equity portfolio construction is about thoroughly understanding the return objectives of a portfolio, as well as its acceptable risk levels, and then finding the right mix of securities that balances predicted returns against risk and other impediments that can interfere with realizing these returns. These principles apply to long-only, long/short, long-extension, and market-neutral approaches. Below, we highlight the discussions of this reading.

- The four main building blocks of portfolio construction are the following:
  - Overweight, underweight, or neutralize rewarded factors: The four most recognized factors known to offer a persistent return premium are Market, Size, Value, and Momentum.
  - Alpha skills: Timing factors, securities, and markets. Finding new factors and enhancing existing factors.
  - Sizing positions to account for risk and active weights.
  - Breadth of expertise: A manager's ability to consistently outperform his benchmark increases when that performance can be attributed to a larger sample of independent decisions. Independent decisions are uncorrelated decisions.
- Managers can rely on a combination of approaches to implement their core beliefs:
  - Systematic vs. discretionary
    - Systematic strategies incorporate research-based rules across a broad universe of securities.
    - Discretionary strategies integrate the judgment of the manager on a smaller subset of securities.
  - Bottom up vs. top down

Long/Short, Long Extension, and Market-Neutral Portfolio Construction

- A bottom-up manager evaluates the risk and return characteristics of individual securities. The aggregate of these risk and return expectations implies expectations for the overall economic and market environment.

- A top-down manager starts with an understanding of the overall market environment and then projects how the expected environment will affect countries, asset classes, sectors, and securities.

- Benchmark aware vs. benchmark agnostic

- Portfolio construction can be framed as an optimization problem using an objective function and a set of constraints. The objective function of a systematic manager will be specified explicitly, whereas that of a discretionary manager may be set implicitly.

- Risk budgeting is a process by which the total risk appetite of the portfolio is allocated among the various components of portfolio choice.

- Active risk (tracking error) is a function of the portfolio's exposure to systematic risks and the level of idiosyncratic, security-specific risk. It is a relevant risk measure for benchmark-relative portfolios.

- Absolute risk is the total volatility of portfolio returns independent of a benchmark. It is the most appropriate risk measure for portfolios with an absolute return objective.

- Active Share measures the extent to which the number and sizing of positions in a manager's portfolio differ from the benchmark.

- Benchmark-agnostic managers usually have a greater level of Active Share and most likely have a greater level of active risk.

- An effective risk management process requires that the portfolio manager

  - determine which type of risk measure is most appropriate,
  - understand how each aspect of the strategy contributes to its overall risk,
  - determine what level of risk budget is appropriate, and
  - effectively allocate risk among individual positions/factors.

- Risk constraints may be either formal or heuristic. Heuristic constraints may impose limits on

  - concentration by security, sector, industry, or geography;
  - net exposures to risk factors, such as Beta, Size, Value, and Momentum;
  - net exposures to currencies;
  - the degree of leverage;
  - the degree of illiquidity;
  - exposures to reputational/environmental risks, such as carbon emissions; and
  - other attributes related to an investor's core concerns.

- Formal risk constraints are statistical in nature. Formal risk measures include the following:

  - Volatility—the standard deviation of portfolio returns
  - Active risk—also called *tracking error* or *tracking risk*
  - Skewness—a measure of the degree to which return expectations are non-normally distributed

- Drawdown—a measure of portfolio loss from its high point until it begins to recover
- Value at risk (VaR)—the minimum loss that would be expected a certain percentage of the time over a certain period of time given the modeled market conditions, typically expressed as the minimum loss that can be expected to occur 5% of the time
- CVaR (expected tail loss or expected shortfall)—the average loss that would be incurred if the VaR cutoff is exceeded
- IVaR—the change in portfolio VaR when adding a new position to a portfolio
- MVaR—the effect on portfolio risk of a change in the position size. In a diversified portfolio, it may be used to determine the contribution of each asset to the overall VaR.

- Portfolio management costs fall into two categories: explicit costs and implicit costs. Implicit costs include delay and slippage.
- The costs of managing assets may affect the investment strategy and the portfolio construction process.

  - Slippage costs are significantly greater for smaller-cap securities and during periods of high volatility.
  - A strategy that demands immediate execution is likely to incur higher market impact costs.
  - A patient manager can mitigate market impact costs by slowly building up positions as liquidity becomes available, but he exposes himself to greater volatility/trend price risk.

- A well-constructed portfolio exhibits

  - a clear investment philosophy and a consistent investment process,
  - risk and structural characteristics as promised to investors,
  - a risk-efficient delivery methodology, and
  - reasonably low operating costs.

- Long/short investing is a compromise between

  - reducing risk and not capturing fully the market risk premium,
  - expanding the return potential from alpha and other risk premiums at the potential expense of increasing active risk, and
  - achieving greater diversification and higher costs and complexity.

REFERENCES

Amihud, Yakov. 2002. "Illiquidity and Stock Returns: Cross-Section and Time-Series Effects." *Journal of Financial Markets* 5, vol. , no. 1: 31–56. 10.1016/S1386-4181(01)00024-6

Asness, Cliff. 2017. "Factor Timing Is Hard." *Cliff's Perspective*, AQR.

Bender, Jennifer, P. Brett Hammond, and William Mok. 2014. "Can Alpha Be Captured by Risk Premia?" *Journal of Portfolio Management* 40, vol. , no. 2 (Winter): 18–29. 10.3905/jpm.2014.40.2.018

Black, Fischer. 1972. "Capital Market Equilibrium with Restricted Borrowing." *Journal of Business* 45, vol. , no. 3: 444–455. 10.1086/295472

Carhart, Mark M. 1997. "On Persistence in Mutual Fund Performance." *Journal of Finance* 52, vol. : 57–82. 10.1111/j.1540-6261.1997.tb03808.x

Ceria, Sebastian. 2015. "Active Is as Active Does: Active Share vs. Tracking Error." FactSet 2015 Symposium (March).

Clarke, Roger, Harindra de Silva, and Steven Thorley. 2002. "Portfolio Constraints and the Fundamental Law of Active Management." *Financial Analysts Journal* 58, vol. , no. 5 (September/October): 48–66. 10.2469/faj.v58.n5.2468

Fama, Eugene F. and Kenneth French. 1992. "The Cross-Section of Expected Stock Returns." *Journal of Finance* 47, vol. , no. 2 (June): 427–465. 10.1111/j.1540-6261.1992.tb04398.x

Frazzini, Andrea, Ronen Israel, and Tobias Moskowitz. 2012. "Trading Costs of Asset Pricing Anomalies." Fama–Miller Center for Research in Finance, University of Chicago Booth School of Business Paper 14–05.

Grinold, R.C. 1989. "The Fundamental Law of Active Management." *Journal of Portfolio Management* 15, vol. : 30–37. 10.3905/jpm.1989.409211

Hasbrouck, Joel. 2009. "Trading Costs and Returns for US Equities: Estimating Effective Costs from Daily Date." *Journal of Finance* 64, vol. , no. 3: 1445–1477. 10.1111/j.1540-6261.2009.01469.x

Ilmanen, Antti. 2011. *Expected Returns: An Investor's Guide to Harvesting Market Rewards*. New York: John Wiley & Sons.

Kahn, Ronald N. and Michael Lemmon. 2016. "The Asset Manager's Dilemma: How Smart Beta Is Disrupting the Investment Management Industry." *Financial Analysts Journal* 72, vol. , no. 1 (January/February): 15–20. 10.2469/faj.v72.n1.1

Langlois, Hugues and Jacques Lussier. 2017. *Rational Investing: The Subtleties of Asset Management*. New York: Columbia Business School Publishing.

MacQueen, Jason. 2007. "Portfolio Risk Decomposition (and Risk Budgeting)." Series of talks presented by R-Squared Risk Management Limited.

Petajisto, Antti. 2013. "Active Share and Mutual Fund Performance." *Financial Analysts Journal* 69, vol. , no. 4 (July/August): 73–93. 10.2469/faj.v69.n4.7

Sapra, Steve and Manny Hunjan. 2013. "Active Share, Tracking Error and Manager Style." PIMCO Quantitative Research and Analytics (October).

Simons, Katerina. 2000. "The Use of Value at Risk by Institutional Investors." *New England Economic Review*, November/December: 21–30.

Taleb, Nassim Nicolas. 1997. *Dynamic Hedging: Managing Vanilla and Exotic Options*. New York: John Wiley & Sons.

Yeung, Danny, Paolo Pellizzari, Ron Bird, and Sazali Abidin. 2012. "Diversification versus Concentration . . . and the Winner Is?" Working Paper 18, University of Technology, Sydney (September).

PRACTICE PROBLEMS

The following information relates to questions 1-8

Monongahela Ap is an equity fund analyst. His manager asks him to evaluate three actively managed equity funds from a single sponsor, Chiyodasenko Investment Corp. Ap's assessments of the funds based on assets under management (AUM), the three main building blocks of portfolio construction, and the funds' approaches to portfolio management are presented in Exhibit 1. Selected data for Fund 1 is presented in Exhibit 2.

Exhibit 1: Ap's Assessments of Funds 1, 2, and 3

Fund	Fund Category	Fund Size (AUM)	Number of Securities	Description
1	Small-cap stocks	Large	Small	Fund 1 focuses on skillfully timing exposures to factors, both rewarded and unrewarded, and to other asset classes. The fund's managers use timing skills to opportunistically shift their portfolio to capture returns from factors such as country, asset class, and sector. Fund 1 prefers to make large trades.
2	Large- cap stocks	Large	Large	Fund 2 holds a diversified portfolio and is concentrated in terms of factors. It targets individual securities that reflect the manager's view that growth firms will outperform value firms. Fund 2 builds up its positions slowly, using unlit venues when possible.
3	Small- cap stocks	Small	Large	Fund 3 holds a highly diversified portfolio. The fund's managers start by evaluating the risk and return characteristics of individual securities and then build their portfolio based on their stock-specific forecasts. Fund 3 prefers to make large trades.

Exhibit 2: Selected Data for Fund 1

Factor	Market	Size	Value	Momentum
Coefficient	1.080	0.098	−0.401	0.034
Variance of the market factor return and covariances with the market factor return	0.00109	0.00053	0.00022	−0.00025
Portfolio's monthly standard deviation of returns				3.74%

Ap learns that Chiyodasenko has initiated a new equity fund. It is similar to Fund 1 but scales up active risk by doubling all of the active weights relative to Fund 1. The new fund aims to scale active return linearly with active risk, but implementation is problematic. Because of the cost and difficulty of borrowing some securities, the new fund cannot scale up its short positions to the same extent that it can scale up its long positions.

Practice Problems

Ap reviews quarterly holdings reports for Fund 3. In comparing the two most recent quarterly reports, he notices differences in holdings that indicate that Fund 3 executed two trades, with each trade involving pairs of stocks. Initially, Fund 3 held active positions in two automobile stocks—one was overweight by 1 percentage point (pp), and the other was underweight by 1pp. Fund 3 traded back to benchmark weights on those two stocks. In the second trade, Fund 3 selected two different stocks that were held at benchmark weights, one energy stock and one financial stock. Fund 3 overweighted the energy stock by 1pp and underweighted the financial stock by 1pp.

In Fund 3's latest quarterly report, Ap reads that Fund 3 implemented a new formal risk control for its forecasting model that constrains the predicted return distribution so that no more than 60% of the deviations from the mean are negative.

1. Based on Exhibit 1, the main building block of portfolio construction on which Fund 1 focuses is *most likely*:

    A. alpha skills.

    B. position sizing.

    C. rewarded factor weightings.

2. Which fund in Exhibit 1 *most likely* follows a bottom-up approach?

    A. Fund 1

    B. Fund 2

    C. Fund 3

3. Which fund in Exhibit 1 *most likely* has the greatest implicit costs to implement its strategy?

    A. Fund 1

    B. Fund 2

    C. Fund 3

4. Based on Exhibit 2, the portion of total portfolio risk that is explained by the market factor in Fund 1's existing portfolio is *closest* to:

    A. 3%.

    B. 81%.

    C. 87%.

5. Relative to Fund 1, Chiyodasenko's new equity fund will *most likely* exhibit a lower:

    A. information ratio.

    B. idiosyncratic risk.

    C. collateral requirement.

6. As a result of Fund 3's two trades, the portfolio's active risk *most likely*:

    A. decreased.

B. remained unchanged.

C. increased.

7. What was the effect of Fund 3's two trades on its active share? Fund 3's active share:

   A. decreased.

   B. remained unchanged.

   C. increased.

8. Which risk measure does Fund 3's new risk control explicitly constrain?

   A. Volatility

   B. Skewness

   C. Drawdown

The following information relates to questions 9-15

Ayanna Chen is a portfolio manager at Aycrig Fund, where she supervises assistant portfolio manager Mordechai Garcia. Aycrig Fund invests money for high-net-worth and institutional investors. Chen asks Garcia to analyze certain information relating to Aycrig Fund's three sub-managers, Managers A, B, and C.

Manager A has $250 million in assets under management (AUM), an active risk of 5%, an information coefficient of 0.15, and a transfer coefficient of 0.40. Manager A's portfolio has a 2.5% expected active return this year.

Chen directs Garcia to determine the maximum position size that Manager A can hold in shares of Pasliant Corporation, which has a market capitalization of $3.0 billion, an index weight of 0.20%, and an average daily trading volume (ADV) of 1% of its market capitalization.

Manager A has the following position size policy constraints:

- Allocation: No investment in any security may represent more than 3% of total AUM.
- Liquidity: No position size may represent more than 10% of the dollar value of the security's ADV.
- Index weight: The maximum position weight must be less than or equal to 10 times the security's weight in the index.

Manager B holds a highly diversified portfolio that has balanced exposures to rewarded risk factors, high active share, and a relatively low active risk target.

Selected data on Manager C's portfolio, which contains three assets, is presented in Exhibit 1.

Practice Problems

Exhibit 1: Selected Data on Manager C's Portfolio

	Portfolio Weight	Standard Deviation	Covariance Asset 1	Covariance Asset 2	Covariance Asset 3
Asset 1	30%	25.00%	0.06250	0.01050	0.00800
Asset 2	45%	14.00%	0.01050	0.01960	0.00224
Asset 3	25%	8.00%	0.00800	0.00224	0.00640

Chen considers adding a fourth sub-manager and evaluates three managers' portfolios, Portfolios X, Y, and Z. The managers for Portfolios X, Y, and Z all have similar costs, fees, and alpha skills, and their factor exposures align with both Aycrig's and investors' expectations and constraints. The portfolio factor exposures, risk contributions, and risk characteristics are presented in Exhibits 2 and 3.

Exhibit 2: Portfolio Factor Exposures and Factor Risk Contribution

	Factor Exposure Portfolio X	Factor Exposure Portfolio Y	Factor Exposure Portfolio Z	Factor Risk Contribution Portfolio X	Factor Risk Contribution Portfolio Y	Factor Risk Contribution Portfolio Z
Market	1.07	0.84	1.08	103%	82%	104%
Size	−0.13	0.15	−0.12	−2%	7%	−3%
Value	0.04	0.30	0.05	−5%	18%	−6%
Momentum	0.08	0.02	0.07	7%	−3%	7%
Quality	0.10	0.35	0.11	−4%	−21%	−5%
Unexplained	—	—	—	1%	17%	3%
Total	n/a	n/a	n/a	100%	100%	100%

Exhibit 3: Portfolio Risk Characteristics

	Portfolio X	Portfolio Y	Portfolio Z
Annualized volatility	10.50%	13.15%	15.20%
Annualized active risk	2.90%	8.40%	4.20%
Active share	0.71	0.74	0.63

Chen and Garcia next discuss characteristics of long–short and long-only investing. Garcia makes the following statements about investing with long–short and long-only managers:

Statement 1 A long–short portfolio allows for a gross exposure of 100%.

Statement 2 A long-only portfolio generally allows for greater investment capacity than other approaches, particularly when using strategies that focus on large-cap stocks.

Chen and Garcia then turn their attention to portfolio management approaches. Chen prefers an approach that emphasizes security-specific factors, engages in factor timing, and typically leads to portfolios that are generally more concentrated than those built using a systematic approach.

9. The number of truly independent decisions Manager A would need to make in order to earn her expected active portfolio return this year is *closest* to:
   A. 8.
   B. 11.
   C. 69.

10. Which of the following position size policy constraints is the most restrictive in setting Manager A's maximum position size in shares of Pasliant Corporation?
    A. Liquidity
    B. Allocation
    C. Index weight

11. Manager B's portfolio is *most likely* consistent with the characteristics of a:
    A. pure indexer.
    B. sector rotator.
    C. multi-factor manager.

12. Based on Exhibit 1, the contribution of Asset 2 to Manager C's portfolio variance is *closest to*:
    A. 0.0025.
    B. 0.0056.
    C. 0.0088.

13. Based on Exhibits 2 and 3, which portfolio *best* exhibits the risk characteristics of a well-constructed portfolio?
    A. Portfolio X
    B. Portfolio Y
    C. Portfolio Z

14. Which of Garcia's statements regarding investing with long–short and long-only managers is correct?
    A. Only Statement 1
    B. Only Statement 2
    C. Both Statement 1 and Statement 2

15. Chen's preferred portfolio management approach would be *best* described as:
    A. top down.
    B. systematic.

C. discretionary.

SOLUTIONS

1. A is correct. The three main building blocks of portfolio construction are alpha skills, position sizing, and rewarded factor weightings. Fund 1 generates active returns by skillfully timing exposures to factors, both rewarded and unrewarded, and to other asset classes, which constitute a manager's alpha skills.

2. C is correct. Bottom-up managers evaluate the risk and return characteristics of individual securities and build portfolios based on stock-specific forecasts; Fund 3 follows this exact approach. Example views of bottom-up managers include expecting one auto company to outperform another, expecting a pharmaceutical company to outperform an auto company, and expecting a technology company to outperform a pharmaceutical company. Both bottom-up and top-down managers can be either diversified or concentrated in terms of securities.

3. A is correct. Because Fund 1 has a large AUM but focuses on small-cap stocks, holds a relatively small number of securities in its portfolio, and prefers to make large trades, Fund 1 likely has the highest implicit costs. Each of these characteristics serves to increase the market impact of its trades. Market impact is a function of the security's liquidity and trade size. The larger a trade size relative to a stock's average daily volume, the more likely it is that the trade will affect prices. The relatively low level of trading volume of small-cap stocks can be a significant implementation hurdle for a manager running a strategy with significant assets under management and significant positive active weights on smaller companies.

4. C is correct. The portion of total portfolio risk explained by the market factor is calculated in two steps. The first step is to calculate the contribution of the market factor to total portfolio variance as follows:

$$CV\text{market factor} = \sum_{j=1}^{n} x_{marketfactor} x_j C_{mf,j} = x_{marketfactor} \sum_{j=1}^{n} x_j C_{mf,j}$$

where

$CV_{market\ factor}$ = contribution of the market factor to total portfolio variance

$x_{market\ factor}$ = weight of the market factor in the portfolio

x_j = weight of factor j in the portfolio

$C_{mf,j}$ = covariance between the market factor and factor j

The variance attributed to the market factor is as follows:

$CV_{market\ factor}$ = (1.080 × 0.00109 × 1.080) + (1.080 × 0.00053 × 0.098) + (1.080 × 0.00022 × −0.401) + (1.080 × −0.00025 × 0.034)

$CV_{market\ factor}$ = 0.001223

The second step is to divide the resulting variance attributed to the market factor by the portfolio variance of returns, which is the square of the standard deviation of returns:

Portion of total portfolio risk explained by the market factor = $0.001223/(0.0374)^2$

Portion of total portfolio risk explained by the market factor = 87%

5. A is correct. As the new fund scales up active risk by doubling active weights,

Solutions

it will face implementation constraints that will prevent it from increasing the weights of many of its short positions. The information ratio (IR) is defined as the ratio of active return to active risk. If there were no constraints preventing the new fund from scaling up active weights, it could scale up active risk by scaling up active weights, proportionally increase active return, and keep the IR unchanged. Implementation constraints experienced by the new fund, however, such as the cost and difficulty in borrowing securities to support the scaled-up short positions, will prevent the active return from proportionally increasing with the active risk. Therefore, the IR would most likely be lower for the new fund than for Fund 1. As the following chart illustrates, as active risk is scaled up, implementation constraints create diminishing returns to scale for active returns, thereby degrading the IR.

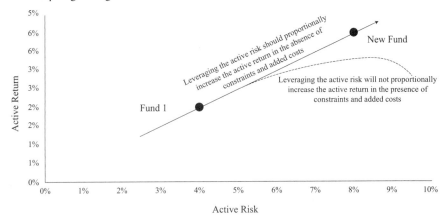

6. C is correct. Active risk is affected by the degree of cross-correlation. The correlation of two stocks in different sectors is most likely lower than the correlation of two stocks in the same sector. Therefore, the correlation of the energy/financial pair is most likely lower than that of the automobile/automobile pair. Because both positions were implemented as an overweight and underweight, the lower correlation of the two stocks in the new position should contribute more to active risk than the two-stock position that it replaced.

7. B is correct. Active share changes only if the total of the absolute values of the portfolio's active weights changes. For the two trades in Fund 3, both the initial position and the new position involved two stocks such that one was 1pp underweighted and the other was 1pp overweighted. Although the active weights of particular securities did change between the initial position and the new position, the total absolute active weights did not change. Therefore, the portfolio's active share did not change.

8. B is correct. Skewness measures the degree to which return expectations are non-normally distributed. If a distribution is positively skewed, the mean of the distribution is greater than its median—more than half of the deviations from the mean are negative and less than half are positive—and the average magnitude of positive deviations is larger than the average magnitude of negative deviations. Negative skew indicates that that the mean of the distribution lies below its median, and the average magnitude of negative deviations is larger than the average magnitude of positive deviations. Fund 3's new risk control constrains its model's predicted return distribution so that no more than 60% of the deviations from the mean are negative. This is an explicit constraint on skewness.

9. C is correct. The breadth (number of truly independent decisions made each year by the manager) required to earn the expected portfolio active return of 2.5% per year is approximately 69 decisions, calculated as follows:

$$E(R_A) = IC \times \sqrt{BR} \times \sigma_{R_A} \times TC$$
$$E(R_A) = 0.15 \times \sqrt{BR} \times 5\% \times 0.40 = 2.5\%$$
$$2.5\% = 0.15 \times \sqrt{BR} \times 5\% \times 0.40$$
$$\sqrt{BR} = \frac{2.5\%}{0.3\%} = 8.33$$
$$BR = 69.44$$

10. A is correct. The maximum position size in shares of Pasliant Corporation (PC) is determined by the constraint with the lowest dollar amount. The maximum position size for PC under each constraint is calculated as follows:

    Liquidity Constraint

    Dollar value of PC traded daily = PC market cap × Average daily trading volume

    Dollar value of PC traded daily = $3 billion × 1.0% = $30 million

    Liquidity constraint = Dollar value of PC traded daily × Liquidity % threshold

    Liquidity constraint = $30 million × 10% = $3 million

    Allocation Constraint

    Allocation constraint = AUM × Maximum position size threshold

    Allocation constraint = $250 million × 3.0% = $7.5 million

    Index Weight Constraint

    Index weight constraint = AUM × (Index weight × 10)

    Index weight constraint = $250 million × (0.20% × 10) = $5.0 million

    The liquidity constraint of $3.0 million is less than both the $5.0 million index weight constraint and the $7.5 million allocation constraint. Therefore, the maximum allowable position size that Manager A may take in PC is $3.0 million.

11. C is correct. Most multi-factor products are diversified across factors and securities and typically have high active share but have reasonably low active risk (tracking error), often in the range of 3%. Most multi-factor products have a low concentration among securities in order to achieve a balanced exposure to risk factors and minimize idiosyncratic risks. Manager B holds a highly diversified portfolio that has balanced exposures to rewarded risk factors, a high active share, and a relatively low target active risk—consistent with the characteristics of a multi-factor manager.

12. B is correct. The contribution of an asset to total portfolio variance equals the summation of the multiplication between the weight of the asset whose contribution is being measured, the weight of each asset (x_j), and the covariance between the asset being measured and each asset (C_{ij}), as follows:

    $$\text{Contribution of each asset to portfolio variance} = CV_i = \sum_{j=1}^{n} x_i x_j C_{ij}$$

    The contribution of Asset 2 to portfolio variance is computed as the sum of the following products:

Solutions

Weight of Asset 2 × Weight of Asset 1 × Covariance of asset 2 with Asset 1, plus	0.45 × 0.30 × 0.01050
Weight of Asset 2 × Weight of Asset 2 × Covariance of Asset 2 with Asset 2, plus	0.45 × 0.45 × 0.01960
Weight of Asset 2 × Weight of Asset 3 × Covariance of Asset 2 with Asset 3	0.45 × 0.25 × 0.00224
= Asset 2's contribution to total portfolio variance	0.005639

13. A is correct. Well-constructed portfolios should have low idiosyncratic (unexplained) risk relative to total risk. Portfolio Y exhibits extremely high unexplained risk relative to total risk, and Portfolios X and Z have low unexplained risk relative to total risk. Therefore, Portfolio Y may be eliminated.

    Portfolios X and Z have comparable factor exposures. In comparing portfolios with comparable factor exposures, the portfolio with lower absolute volatility and lower active risk will likely be preferred, assuming similar costs. Portfolio X has lower absolute volatility and lower active risk than Portfolio Z, although both have similar costs.

    Finally, for managers with similar costs, fees, and alpha skills, if two products have similar active and absolute risks, the portfolio having a higher active share is preferred. Portfolio X has lower absolute volatility, lower active risk, and higher active share than Portfolio Z. As a result, Portfolio X best exhibits the risk characteristics of a well-constructed portfolio.

14. C is correct. Both Statement 1 and Statement 2 are correct.

    Statement 1 is correct because, similar to a long-only portfolio, a long–short portfolio can be structured to have a gross exposure of 100%. Gross exposure of the portfolio is calculated as the sum of the long positions and the absolute value of the short positions, expressed as percentages of the portfolio's capital.

    Gross exposure = Long positions + |Short positions|

    Gross exposure long-only portfolio = 100% (Long positions) + 0% (Short positions)

    = 100%

    Gross exposure long–short portfolio = 50% (Long positions) + |−50%| (Short positions)

    = 100%

    Statement 2 is correct because long-only investing generally offers greater investment capacity than other approaches, particularly when using strategies that focus on large-cap stocks. For large institutional investors such as pension plans, there are no effective capacity constraints in terms of the total market cap available for long-only investing.

15. C is correct. Chen prefers an approach that emphasizes security-specific factors, engages in factor timing, and typically leads to portfolios that are generally more concentrated than those built using a systematic approach. These characteristics reflect a discretionary bottom-up portfolio management approach.

LEARNING MODULE 4

Liability-Driven and Index-Based Strategies

by James F. Adams, PhD, CFA, and Donald J. Smith, PhD.

James F. Adams, PhD, CFA, is at New York University (USA). Donald J. Smith, PhD, is at Boston University Questrom School of Business (USA).

LEARNING OUTCOMES

Mastery	The candidate should be able to:
☐	evaluate strategies for managing a single liability
☐	compare strategies for a single liability and for multiple liabilities, including alternative means of implementation
☐	evaluate liability-based strategies under various interest rate scenarios and select a strategy to achieve a portfolio's objectives
☐	explain risks associated with managing a portfolio against a liability structure
☐	discuss bond indexes and the challenges of managing a fixed-income portfolio to mimic the characteristics of a bond index
☐	compare alternative methods for establishing bond market exposure passively
☐	discuss criteria for selecting a benchmark and justify the selection of a benchmark

INTRODUCTION

Fixed-income instruments make up nearly three-quarters of all global financial assets by market value available to investors. It is thus not surprising that bonds are a critical component of most investment portfolios. In our coverage of structured and passive total return fixed-income investment strategies, we explain that "passive" does not simply mean "buy and hold." The primary strategies discussed—**immunization** and indexation—can entail frequent rebalancing of the bond portfolio. We also note that "passive" stands in contrast to "active" fixed-income strategies that are based on the asset manager's particular view on the interest rate and credit market conditions. We pay particular attention to the Macaulay duration measure to illustrate how it can be utilized to protect a bond portfolio from interest rate risk in different interest rate scenarios. This immunization strategy may be viewed simply as a special case of interest rate hedging.

We then turn our attention to index-based investment strategies, through which investors gain a broader exposure to fixed-income markets, rather than tailoring investments to match a specific liability profile. We explain the advantages of index-based investing, such as diversification, but we also note that the depth and breadth of bond markets make both creating and tracking an index more challenging than in the equity markets. We also explore a variety of alternatives for matching a bond index, from full replication to enhanced indexing using primary risk factors. Finally, we explain that it is critical to select a benchmark that is most relevant to a specific investor based on such factors as the targeted duration profile and risk appetite.

2. MANAGING THE INTEREST RATE RISK OF A SINGLE LIABILITY

☐ evaluate strategies for managing a single liability

Liability-driven investing in most circumstances is used to manage the interest rate risk on multiple liabilities. In this section, we focus on only a single liability to demonstrate the techniques and risks of the classic investment strategy known as interest rate immunization. Immunization is the process of structuring and managing a fixed-income bond portfolio to minimize the variance in the realized rate of return over a known time horizon. This variance arises from the volatility of future interest rates. Default risk is neglected at this point because the portfolio bonds are assumed to have default probabilities that approach zero.

The most obvious way to immunize the interest rate risk on a single liability is to buy a zero-coupon bond that matures on the obligation's due date. The bond's face value matches the liability amount. There is no cash flow reinvestment risk because there are no coupon payments to reinvest, and there is no price risk because the bond is held to maturity. Any interest rate volatility over the bond's lifetime is irrelevant in terms of the asset's ability to pay off the liability. The problem is that in many financial markets, zero-coupon bonds are not available. Nevertheless, the perfect immunization provided by a zero-coupon bond sets a standard to measure the performance of immunizing strategies using coupon-bearing bonds.

Exhibit 1 and Exhibit 2 illustrate the connection between immunization and the duration of a traditional coupon-bearing fixed-income bond.

Managing the Interest Rate Risk of a Single Liability

Exhibit 1: Immunization with a Single Bond: Rate Rise Scenario

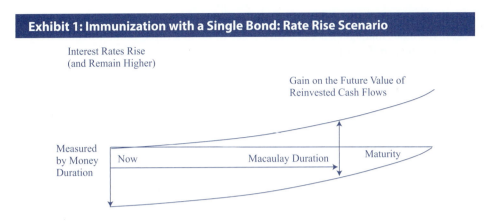

Assume that the bond is currently priced at par value. Then, an instantaneous, one-time, upward (parallel) shift occurs in the yield curve. The bond's value falls. That drop in value is estimated by the money duration of the bond. Recall that the money duration is the bond's modified duration statistic multiplied by the price. Subsequently, the bond price will be "pulled to par" as the maturity date nears (assuming no default, of course). But another factor is at work. Assuming interest rates remain higher, the future value of reinvested coupon payments goes up. It is shown by the rising line as more and more payments are received and reinvested at the higher interest rates.

The key detail to note in Exhibit 1 is that at some point in time, the two effects—the price effect and the coupon reinvestment effect—cancel each other out. The remarkable result is that this point in time turns out to be the bond's Macaulay duration (for a zero-coupon bond, its Macaulay duration is its maturity). Therefore, an investor having an investment horizon equal to the bond's Macaulay duration is effectively protected, or immunized, from interest rate risk in that price, and coupon reinvestment effects offset for either higher or lower rates. Exhibit 2 shows the same effect for an immediate downward shift in interest rates.

Exhibit 2: Immunization: Interest Rate Fall Scenario

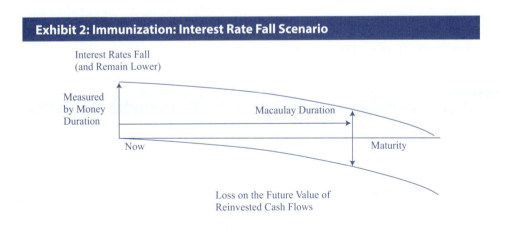

A Numerical Example of Immunization

We now show that the strategy of matching the Macaulay duration to the investment horizon works for a bond portfolio as well as for an individual security. Suppose that some entity has a single liability of EUR250 million due 15 February 2027. Further assume that the current date is 15 February 2021, so the investment horizon is six years. The asset manager for the entity seeks to build a three-bond portfolio to earn a rate of return sufficient to pay off the obligation.

Portfolio Features

Exhibit 3 reports the prices, yields, risk statistics (Macaulay duration and convexity), and par values for the chosen portfolio. The portfolio's current market value is EUR200,052,250 (= EUR47,117,500 + EUR97,056,750 + EUR55,878,000). The semi-annual coupon payments on the bonds occur on 15 February and 15 August of each year (note that we have chosen to use bonds that pay coupons semi-annually, which is not always the case). The price is per 100 of par value, and the yield to maturity is on a street-convention semi-annual bond basis (meaning an annual percentage rate having a periodicity of two). Both the Macaulay duration and the convexity are annualized. (Note that in practice, some bond data vendors report the convexity statistic divided by 100.)

Exhibit 3: The Bond Portfolio to Immunize the Single Liability

	2.5-Year Bond	7-Year Bond	10-Year Bond
Coupon rate	1.50%	3.25%	5.00%
Maturity date	15 August 2023	15 February 2028	15 February 2031
Price	100.25	99.75	100.50
Yield to maturity	1.3979%	3.2903%	4.9360%
Par value	47,000,000	97,300,000	55,600,000
Market value	47,117,500	97,056,750	55,878,000
Macaulay duration	2.463	6.316	7.995
Convexity	7.253	44.257	73.747
Allocation	23.55%	48.52%	27.93%

Exhibit 4 shows the cash flows and calculations used to obtain the relevant portfolio statistics. The third column aggregates the coupon and principal payments received for each date from the three bonds.

Exhibit 4: Portfolio Statistics

Time	Date	Cash Flow	PV of Cash Flow	Weight	Time × Weight	Dispersion	Convexity
0	15-Feb-21	−200,052,250					
1	15-Aug-21	3,323,625	3,262,282	0.0163	0.0163	1.9735	0.0326
2	15-Feb-22	3,323,625	3,202,071	0.0160	0.0320	1.6009	0.0960
3	15-Aug-22	3,323,625	3,142,971	0.0157	0.0471	1.2728	0.1885
4	15-Feb-23	3,323,625	3,084,962	0.0154	0.0617	0.9871	0.3084
5	15-Aug-23	50,323,625	45,847,871	0.2292	1.1459	11.2324	6.8754
6	15-Feb-24	2,971,125	2,656,915	0.0133	0.0797	0.4782	0.5578
7	15-Aug-24	2,971,125	2,607,877	0.0130	0.0913	0.3260	0.7300
8	15-Feb-25	2,971,125	2,559,744	0.0128	0.1024	0.2048	0.9213
9	15-Aug-25	2,971,125	2,512,500	0.0126	0.1130	0.1131	1.1303

Managing the Interest Rate Risk of a Single Liability

Time	Date	Cash Flow	PV of Cash Flow	Weight	Time × Weight	Dispersion	Convexity
10	15-Feb-26	2,971,125	2,466,127	0.0123	0.1233	0.0493	1.3560
11	15-Aug-26	2,971,125	2,420,610	0.0121	0.1331	0.0121	1.5972
12	15-Feb-27	2,971,125	2,375,934	0.0119	0.1425	0.0000	1.8527
13	15-Aug-27	2,971,125	2,332,082	0.0117	0.1515	0.0116	2.1216
14	15-Feb-28	100,271,125	77,251,729	0.3862	5.4062	1.5434	81.0931
15	15-Aug-28	1,390,000	1,051,130	0.0053	0.0788	0.0473	1.2610
16	15-Feb-29	1,390,000	1,031,730	0.0052	0.0825	0.0825	1.4028
17	15-Aug-29	1,390,000	1,012,688	0.0051	0.0861	0.1265	1.5490
18	15-Feb-30	1,390,000	993,997	0.0050	0.0894	0.1788	1.6993
19	15-Aug-30	1,390,000	975,651	0.0049	0.0927	0.2389	1.8533
20	15-Feb-31	56,990,000	39,263,380	0.1963	3.9253	12.5585	82.4316
			200,052,250	1.0000	12.0008	33.0378	189.0580

For instance, EUR3,323,625 is the sum of the coupon payments for the first four dates:

(1.50% × 0.5 × EUR47,000,000) + (3.25% × 0.5 × EUR97,300,000) + (5.00% × 0.5 × EUR55,600,000) = EUR352,500 + EUR1,581,125 + EUR1,390,000

= EUR3,323,625.

On 15 August 2023, the principal of EUR47,000,000 is redeemed so that the total cash flow is EUR50,323,625. The next eight cash flows represent the coupon payments on the second and third bonds, and so forth.

The internal rate of return on the cash flows in column 3 for the 20 semi-annual periods, including the portfolio's initial market value on 15 February 2021, is 1.8804%. Annualized on a semi-annual bond basis, the portfolio's cash flow yield is 3.7608% (= 2 × 1.8804%). This yield is significantly higher than the market value-weighted average of the individual bond yields-to-maturity presented in Exhibit 3, which equals 3.3043%.

(1.3979% × 0.2355) + (3.2903% × 0.4852) + (4.9360% × 0.2793) = 3.3043%.

This difference arises because of the steepness in the yield curve. The key point is that the goal of the immunization strategy is to achieve a rate of return close to 3.76%, not 3.30%.

The fourth column in Exhibit 4 shows the present values for each of the aggregate cash flows, calculated using the internal rate of return per period (1.8804%) as the discount rate. For example, the combined payment of EUR100,271,125 due on 15 February 2028 has a present value of EUR77,251,729. (*Note: Calculations are carried out on a spreadsheet that preserves precision. For readability and to avoid clutter, the exhibits and text report rounded results. For example, the following calculation gives 77,251,498 with the numbers shown on the left-hand side, but it gives 77,251,729, the amount shown on the right-hand side, when the precise semi-annual cash flow yield, 1.0188037819%, is used.*)

$$\frac{100,271,125}{(1.018804)^{14}} = 77,251,729.$$

The sum of the present values in column 4 of Exhibit 4 is EUR200,052,250, the current market value for the bond portfolio.

Portfolio Duration

The sixth column of Exhibit 4 is used to obtain the portfolio's Macaulay duration. This duration statistic is the weighted average of the times to the receipt of cash flow, whereby the share of total market value for each date is the weight. Column

5 shows the weights, which are the PV of each cash flow divided by the total PV of EUR200,052,250. The times to receipt of cash flow (the times from column 1) are multiplied by the weights and then summed. For example, the contribution to total portfolio duration for the second cash flow on 15 February 2022 is 0.0320 (= 2 × 0.0160). The sum of column 6 is 12.0008. That is the Macaulay duration for the portfolio in terms of semi-annual periods. Annualized, it is 6.0004 (= 12.0008/2). It is now clear why the asset manager for the entity chose this portfolio: The portfolio Macaulay duration matches the investment horizon of six years.

In practice, it is common to estimate the portfolio duration using the market value-weighted average of the individual durations for each bond. Exhibit 3 shows those individual durations and the allocation percentages for each bond. The average Macaulay duration is (2.463 × 0.2355) + (6.316 × 0.4852) + (7.995 × 0.2793) = 5.8776.

The difference, as with the cash flow yield and the market value-weighted average yield, arises because the yield curve is not flat. When the yield curve is upwardly sloped, average duration (5.8776) is less than the portfolio duration (6.0004). This difference in duration statistics is important because using the average duration in building the immunizing portfolio instead of the portfolio duration would introduce model risk to the strategy, as we will see later.

Portfolio Dispersion

The sum of the seventh column in Exhibit 4 is the portfolio dispersion statistic. Recall that whereas Macaulay duration is the weighted *average* of the times to receipt of cash flow, dispersion is the weighted *variance*. It measures the extent to which the payments are spread out around the duration. For example, the contribution to total portfolio dispersion for the fifth cash flow on 15 August 2023 is 11.2324: $(5 - 12.0008)^2 \times 0.2292 = 11.2324$.

This portfolio's dispersion is 33.0378 in terms of semi-annual periods. Annualized, it is 8.2594 (= 33.0378/4). The Macaulay duration statistic is annualized by dividing by the periodicity of the bonds (two payments per year); dispersion (and convexity, which follows) is annualized by dividing by the periodicity squared (i.e., $2^2 = 4$ for semi-annual payment bonds).

Portfolio Convexity

The portfolio convexity is calculated with the eighth column. It is the sum of the times to the receipt of cash flow, multiplied by those times plus one, multiplied by the shares of market value for each date (weight), and all divided by one plus the cash flow yield squared. For example, the contribution to the sum for the 14th payment on 15 February 2028 is 81.0931 (= 14 × 15 × 0.3862). The sum of the column is 189.0580. The convexity in semi-annual periods is 182.1437:

$$\frac{189.0580}{(1.018804)^2} = 182.1437.$$

The annualized convexity for the portfolio is 45.5359 (= 182.1437/4). This result is slightly higher than the market value-weighted average of the individual convexity statistics (for each bond) reported in Exhibit 3:

(7.253 × 0.2355) + (44.257 × 0.4852) + (73.747 × 0.2793) = 43.7786.

As with the average yield and duration, this difference results from the slope of the yield curve. The convexity statistic can be used to improve the estimate for the change in portfolio market value following a change in interest rates than is provided by duration alone. That is, convexity is the second-order effect, whereas duration is the first-order effect.

There is an interesting connection among the portfolio convexity, Macaulay duration, dispersion, and cash flow yield in immunized portfolio convexity, also known as the "portfolio convexity statistic":

Managing the Interest Rate Risk of a Single Liability

$$\text{Immunized portfolio convexity} = \frac{\text{MacDur}^2 + \text{MacDur} + \text{Dispersion}}{(1 + \text{Cash flow yield})^2}. \quad (1)$$

In terms of semi-annual periods, the Macaulay duration for this portfolio is 12.0008, the dispersion is 33.0378, and the cash flow yield is 1.8804%.

$$\text{Immunized portfolio convexity} = \frac{12.0008^2 + 12.0008 + 33.0378}{(1.018804)^2} = 182.1437.$$

The portfolio dispersion and convexity statistics are used to assess the **structural risk** to the interest rate immunization strategy. Structural risk arises from the potential for shifts and twists to the yield curve. This risk is discussed later.

Investment Horizon and Immunization

We now demonstrate how matching the Macaulay duration for the portfolio to the investment horizon leads to interest rate immunization. The first three columns of Exhibit 5, shown later, are identical to the ones in Exhibit 4.

The fourth column shows the values of the cash flows as of the horizon date of 15 February 2027, assuming that the cash flow yield remains unchanged at 3.7608%. For instance, the future value of the EUR3,323,625 in coupon payments received on 15 August 2021 is EUR4,079,520:

$$3,323,625 \times \left(1 + \frac{0.037608}{2}\right)^{11} = 4,079,520.$$

The value of the last cash flow for EUR56,990,000 on 15 February 2031 is EUR49,099,099 as of the horizon date of 15 February 2027:

$$\frac{56,990,000}{\left(1 + \frac{0.037608}{2}\right)^8} = 49,099,099.$$

We assume that all the payments received before the horizon date are reinvested at the cash flow yield. All the payments received after the horizon date are sold at their discounted values. The sum of the fourth column in Exhibit 5 is EUR250,167,000, which is more than enough to pay off the EUR250 million liability. The six-year holding period rate of return (ROR), also called the horizon yield, is 3.7608%. It is based on the original market value and the total return and is the solution for ROR:

$$200,052,250 = \frac{250,167,000}{\left(1 + \frac{\text{ROR}}{2}\right)^{12}}.$$

ROR = 0.037608.

The holding period rate of return equals the cash flow yield for the portfolio. This equivalence is the multi-bond version of the well-known result for a single bond: The realized rate of return matches the yield to maturity only if coupon payments are reinvested at that same yield and if the bond is held to maturity or sold at a point on the constant-yield price trajectory.

Exhibit 5: Interest Rate Immunization

Time	Date	Cash Flow	Total Return at 3.7608%	Total Return at 2.7608%	Total Return at 4.7608%
0	15-Feb-21	−200,052,250			
1	15-Aug-21	3,323,625	4,079,520	3,864,613	4,305,237
2	15-Feb-22	3,323,625	4,004,225	3,811,992	4,205,138
3	15-Aug-22	3,323,625	3,930,319	3,760,088	4,107,366

Time	Date	Cash Flow	Total Return at 3.7608%	Total Return at 2.7608%	Total Return at 4.7608%
4	15-Feb-23	3,323,625	3,857,777	3,708,891	4,011,868
5	15-Aug-23	50,323,625	57,333,230	55,392,367	59,332,093
6	15-Feb-24	2,971,125	3,322,498	3,225,856	3,421,542
7	15-Aug-24	2,971,125	3,261,175	3,181,932	3,341,989
8	15-Feb-25	2,971,125	3,200,984	3,138,607	3,264,286
9	15-Aug-25	2,971,125	3,141,904	3,095,871	3,188,390
10	15-Feb-26	2,971,125	3,083,914	3,053,718	3,114,258
11	15-Aug-26	2,971,125	3,026,994	3,012,138	3,041,850
12	15-Feb-27	2,971,125	2,971,125	2,971,125	2,971,125
13	15-Aug-27	2,971,125	2,916,287	2,930,670	2,902,045
14	15-Feb-28	100,271,125	96,603,888	97,559,123	95,662,614
15	15-Aug-28	1,390,000	1,314,446	1,333,991	1,295,282
16	15-Feb-29	1,390,000	1,290,186	1,315,827	1,265,166
17	15-Aug-29	1,390,000	1,266,373	1,297,911	1,235,750
18	15-Feb-30	1,390,000	1,242,999	1,280,238	1,207,018
19	15-Aug-30	1,390,000	1,220,058	1,262,806	1,178,955
20	15-Feb-31	56,990,000	49,099,099	51,070,094	47,213,270
			250,167,000	250,267,858	250,265,241

A Drop in the Cash Flow Yield Scenario

The fifth column in Exhibit 5 repeats the calculations for the assumption of an instantaneous, one-time, 100 bp drop in the cash flow yield on 15 February 2021. The future values of all cash flows received are now lower because they are reinvested at 2.7608% instead of 3.7608%. For example, the payment of EUR50,323,625 on 15 August 2023, which contains the principal redemption on the 2.5-year bond, grows to only EUR55,392,367:

$$50,323,625 \times \left(1 + \frac{0.027608}{2}\right)^7 = 55,392,367.$$

The value of the last cash flow is now higher because it is discounted at the lower cash flow yield:

$$\frac{56,990,000}{\left(1 + \frac{0.027608}{2}\right)^8} = 51,070,094.$$

The important result is that the total return as of the horizon date is EUR250,267,858, demonstrating that the cash flow reinvestment effect is balanced by the price effect, as illustrated for a single bond in Exhibit 1. The holding-period rate of return is 3.7676%:

$$200,052,250 = \frac{250,267,858}{\left(1 + \frac{ROR}{2}\right)^{12}}.$$

ROR = 0.037676.

An Increase in the Cash Flow Yield Scenario

To complete the example, the sixth column in Exhibit 5 reports the results for an instantaneous, one-time, 100 bp jump in the cash flow yield, up to 4.7608% from 3.7608%. In this case, the future values of the reinvested cash flows are higher and the discounted values of cash flows due after the horizon date are lower. Nevertheless, the total return of EUR250,265,241 for the six-year investment horizon is enough to pay off the liability. The horizon yield is 3.7674%:

$$200,052,250 = \frac{250,265,241}{\left(1 + \frac{ROR}{2}\right)^{12}}.$$

ROR = 0.037674.

This numerical exercise demonstrates interest rate immunization using a portfolio of fixed-income bonds. The total returns and holding period rates of return are virtually the same—in fact, slightly higher because of convexity—whether the cash flow yield goes up or down.

Immunization and Rebalancing

Exhibit 4 is somewhat misleading, however, because it suggests that immunization is a buy-and-hold passive investment strategy. It suggests that the entity will (a) hold on the horizon date of 15 February 2027 the same positions in what then will be one-year, 3.25% and four-year, 5% bonds and (b) sell the bonds on that date. This suggestion is misleading because the portfolio must be frequently rebalanced to stay on its target duration. As time passes, the portfolio's Macaulay duration changes but not in line with the change in the remainder of the investment horizon. For example, after five years, the investment horizon as of 15 February 2026 is just one remaining year. The portfolio Macaulay duration at that time needs to be 1.000. The asset manager will have had to execute some trades by then, substantially reducing the holdings in what is then the five-year, 5% bond.

Exhibit 6 offers another way to illustrate interest rate immunization. An immunization strategy is essentially "zero replication." We know that the perfect bond to lock in the six-year holding period rate of return is a six-year zero-coupon bond having a face value that matches the EUR250 million liability. The idea is to originally structure and then manage over time a portfolio of coupon-bearing bonds that replicates the period-to-period performance of the zero-coupon bond. Therefore, immunization is essentially just an interest rate hedging strategy. As the yield on the zero-coupon bond rises and falls, there will be unrealized losses and gains. In Exhibit 6, this is illustrated by the zero-coupon bond's value deviating from the direction of the constant-yield price trajectory. Two paths for the zero-coupon yield are presented: Path A for generally lower rates (and higher values) and Path B for higher rates (and lower values). Regardless, the market value of the zero-coupon bond will be "pulled to par" as maturity nears.

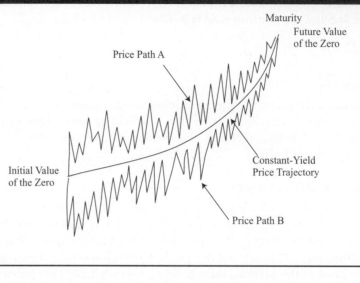

Exhibit 6: Interest Rate Immunization as Zero Replication

Immunizing with coupon-bearing bonds entails continuously matching the portfolio Macaulay duration with the Macaulay duration of the zero-coupon bond over time and as the yield curve shifts, even though the zero-coupon bond could be hypothetical and may not exist. Also, to fully match the liability, the bond portfolio's initial market value has to match or exceed the present value of the zero-coupon bond. The Macaulay duration of that, perhaps hypothetical, zero-coupon bond always matches the investment horizon. Immunization will be achieved if any ensuing change in the cash flow yield on the bond portfolio is equal to the change in the yield to maturity on the zero-coupon bond. That equivalence will ensure that the change in the bond portfolio's market value is close to the change in the market value of the zero-coupon bond. Therefore, at the end of the six-year investment horizon, the bond portfolio's market value should meet or exceed the face value of the zero-coupon bond, regardless of the path for interest rates over the six years.

Immunization and Shifts in the Yield Curve

The key assumption to achieve immunization is the statement that "any ensuing change in the cash flow yield on the bond portfolio is equal to the change in the yield to maturity on the zero-coupon bond." A *sufficient*, but not *necessary*, condition for that statement is a parallel (or shape-preserving) shift to the yield curve whereby all yields change by the same amount. *Sufficient* means that if the yield curve shift is parallel, the change in the bond portfolio's cash flow yield will equal the change in yield to maturity of the zero-coupon bond, which is enough to ensure immunization. To achieve immunization, however, it is not *necessary* that the yield curve shifts in a parallel manner. That is, in some cases, the immunization property can prevail even with non-parallel yield curve movements, such as an upward and steepening shift (sometimes called a "bear steepener"), an upward and flattening shift (a "bear flattener"), a downward and steepening shift (a "bull steepener"), or a downward and flattening shift (a "bull flattener").

Exhibit 7 and Exhibit 8 demonstrate this observation. Exhibit 7 presents three different upward yield curve shifts. The first is a parallel shift of 102.08 bps for each of the three bond yields. The second is a steepening shift of 72.19 bps for the 2.5-year bond, 94.96 bps for the 7-year bond, and 120.82 bps for the 10-year bond. The third is a flattening shift, whereby the yields on the three bonds increase by 145.81 bps, 109.48 bps, and 79.59 bps, respectively. The key point is that each of these yield curve shifts

Managing the Interest Rate Risk of a Single Liability

results in the same 100 bp increase in the cash flow yield from 3.7608% to 4.7608%. Moreover, each shift in the yield curve produces virtually the same reduction in the portfolio's market value.

Exhibit 7: Some Upward Yield Curve Shifts That Achieve Interest Rate Immunization

	Change in 2.5-Year Yield	Change in 7-Year Yield	Change in 10-Year Yield	Change in Cash Flow Yield	Change in Market Value
Upward and parallel	+102.08 bps	+102.08 bps	+102.08 bps	+100 bps	−11,340,537
Upward and steepening	+72.19 bps	+94.96 bps	+120.82 bps	+100 bps	−11,340,195
Upward and flattening	+145.81 bps	+109.48 bps	+79.59 bps	+100 bps	−11,340,183

Exhibit 8 shows the results for three downward shifts in the yield curve. The first is a parallel shift of 102.06 bps. The second and third are downward and steepening (−129.00 bps, −104.52 bps, and −92.00 bps for the 2.5-year, 7-year, and 10-year bonds) and downward and flattening (−55.76 bps, −86.32 bps, and −134.08 bps). Each shift results in the same 100 bp decrease in the cash flow yield from 3.7608% to 2.7608% and virtually the same increase in the market value of the portfolio.

Exhibit 8: Some Downward Yield Curve Shifts That Achieve Interest Rate Immunization

	Change in 2.5-Year Yield	Change in 7-Year Yield	Change in 10-Year Yield	Change in Cash Flow Yield	Change in Market Value
Downward and parallel	−102.06 bps	−102.06 bps	−102.06 bps	−100 bps	12,251,212
Downward and steepening	−129.00 bps	−104.52 bps	−92.00 bps	−100 bps	12,251,333
Downward and flattening	−55.76 bps	−86.32 bps	−134.08 bps	−100 bps	12,251,484

Notice that the interest rate immunization property shown in Exhibit 5 rests only on the change in the cash flow yield going up or down by 100 bps. It is not necessary to assume that the change in the value of the immunizing portfolio arises only from a parallel shift in the yield curve. In the same manner, the immunization property illustrated in Exhibit 6 requires only that the change in the value of the immunizing portfolio, one that has a Macaulay duration matching the investment horizon, is close to the change in the value of the zero-coupon bond that provides perfect immunization. Exhibit 7 and Exhibit 8 demonstrate that some non-parallel as well as parallel shifts can satisfy those conditions. Of course, there are many other non-parallel shifts for which those conditions are not met.

In general, the interest rate risk to an immunization strategy is that the change in the cash flow yield on the portfolio is not the same as on the ideal zero-coupon bond. This difference can occur with twists to the shape of the yield curve, in addition to some non-parallel shifts.

Exhibit 9 and Exhibit 10 portray two such twists. To exaggerate the risk, assume that the immunizing portfolio has a "barbell" structure in that it is composed of half short-term bonds and half long-term bonds. The portfolio Macaulay duration for the barbell is six years. The zero-coupon bond that provides perfect immunization has a maturity (and Macaulay duration) also of six years.

Exhibit 9 shows a steepening twist to the yield curve. The twist is assumed to occur at the six-year point to indicate that the value of the zero-coupon bond does not change. Short-term yields go down and long-term yields go up by approximately the same amount. The value of the barbell portfolio goes down because the losses on the long-term positions exceed the gains on the short-term holdings because of the difference in duration between the holdings and the equivalence in the assumed changes in yield. Therefore, this portfolio does not track the value of the zero-coupon bond for such a scenario.

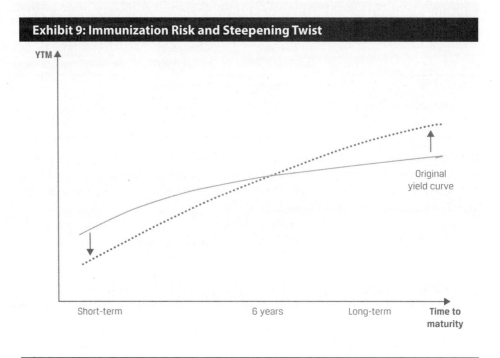

Exhibit 9: Immunization Risk and Steepening Twist

Exhibit 10 illustrates a dramatic twist in the shape of the yield curve. Short-term and long-term yields go up while the six-year yields go down. This type of twist is a butterfly movement, in this case a "positive butterfly." (In a "negative butterfly" twist, short-term and long-term yields go down and intermediate-term yields go up.) The immunizing portfolio decreases in value as its yields go up and the zero-coupon bond goes up in value. Again, for this scenario, the portfolio does not track the change in the value of the bond that provides perfect immunization. Fortunately for those entities that pursue interest rate immunization, these types of twists are rare. Most yield curve shifts are generally parallel, with some steepening and flattening, especially for maturities beyond a few years.

Exhibit 10: Immunization Risk and a Butterfly Yield Curve Movement

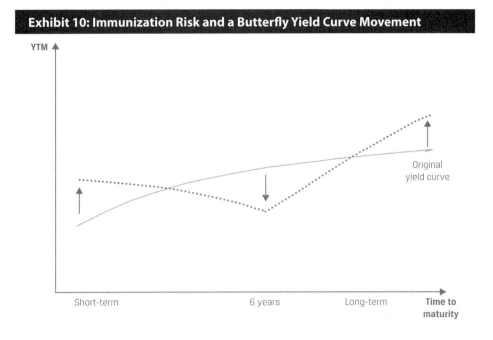

Structural Risk in Immunization Strategy

Exhibit 9 and Exhibit 10 also illustrate how to reduce structural risk to an immunizing strategy. Structural risk arises from portfolio design, particularly the choice of the portfolio allocations. The risk is that yield curve twists and non-parallel shifts lead to changes in the cash flow yield that do not match the yield to maturity of the zero-coupon bond that provides for perfect immunization. Structural risk is reduced by minimizing the dispersion of the bond positions, going from a barbell design to more of a bullet portfolio that concentrates the component bonds' durations around the investment horizon. At the limit, a zero-coupon bond that matches the date of the single obligation has, by design, no structural risk.

Equation 1 (immunized portfolio convexity) indicates that minimizing portfolio dispersion is the same as minimizing the portfolio convexity for a given Macaulay duration and cash flow yield. An advantage to using convexity to measure the extent of structural risk is that the portfolio statistic can be approximated by the market value-weighted average of the individual bonds' convexities. A problem with estimating portfolio dispersion using the weighted average of dispersion statistics for individual bonds is that it can be misleading. Consider a portfolio of all zero-coupon bonds of varying maturities. Each individual bond has zero dispersion (because it has only one payment), so the market value-weighted average is also zero. Clearly, the portfolio overall can have significant (non-zero) dispersion.

In summary, the characteristics of a bond portfolio structured to immunize a single liability are that it:

- has an initial market value that equals or exceeds the present value of the liability.
- has a portfolio Macaulay duration that matches the liability's due date.
- minimizes the portfolio convexity statistic.

This portfolio must be regularly rebalanced over the horizon to maintain the target duration, because the portfolio Macaulay duration changes as time passes and as yields change. The portfolio manager needs to weigh the trade-off between incurring transaction costs from rebalancing and allowing some duration gap. This and other risks to immunization—for instance, those arising from the use of interest rate derivatives to match the duration of assets to the investment horizon—are covered later.

CASE STUDY

An institutional client asks a fixed-income investment adviser to recommend a portfolio to immunize a single 10-year liability. It is understood that the chosen portfolio will need to be rebalanced over time to maintain its target duration. The adviser proposes two portfolios of coupon-bearing government bonds because zero-coupon bonds are not available. The portfolios have the same market value. The institutional client's objective is to minimize the variance in the realized rate of return over the 10-year horizon. The two portfolios have the following risk and return statistics:

	Portfolio A	Portfolio B
Cash flow yield	7.64%	7.65%
Macaulay duration	9.98	10.01
Convexity	107.88	129.43

These statistics are based on aggregating the interest and principal cash flows for the bonds that constitute the portfolios; they are not market value-weighted averages of the yields, durations, and convexities of the individual bonds. The cash flow yield is stated on a semi-annual bond basis, meaning an annual percentage rate having a periodicity of two; the Macaulay durations and convexities are annualized.

1. Indicate the portfolio that the investment adviser should recommend, and explain the reasoning.

   Solution:

   The adviser should recommend Portfolio A. First, notice that the cash flow yields of both portfolios are virtually the same and that both portfolios have Macaulay durations very close to 10, the horizon for the liability. It would be wrong and misleading to recommend Portfolio B because it has a "higher yield" and a "duration closer to the investment horizon of 10 years." In practical terms, a difference of 1 bp in yield is not likely to be significant, nor is the difference of 0.03 in annual duration.

   Given the fact that the portfolio yields and durations are essentially the same, the choice depends on the difference in convexity. The difference between 129.43 and 107.88, however, is meaningful. In general, convexity is a desirable property of fixed-income bonds. All else being equal (meaning the same yield and duration), a more convex bond gains more if the yield goes down and loses less if the yield goes up than a less convex bond.

   The client's objective, however, is to minimize the variance in the realized rate of return over the 10-year horizon. That objective indicates a conservative immunization strategy achieved by building the duration-matching portfolio and minimizing the portfolio convexity. Such an approach minimizes the dispersion of cash flows around the Macaulay duration and makes the portfolio closer to the zero-coupon bond that would provide perfect immunization; see Equation 1.

   The structural risk to the immunization strategy is the potential for non-parallel shifts and twists to the yield curve, which lead to changes in the cash flow yield that do not track the change in the yield on the zero-coupon

> bond. This risk is minimized by selecting the portfolio with the lower convexity (and dispersion of cash flows).
>
> Note that default risk is neglected in this discussion because the portfolio consists of government bonds that presumably have default probabilities approaching zero.

MANAGING THE INTEREST RATE RISK OF MULTIPLE LIABILITIES

3

- ☐ compare strategies for a single liability and for multiple liabilities, including alternative means of implementation
- ☐ evaluate liability-based strategies under various interest rate scenarios and select a strategy to achieve a portfolio's objectives

The principle of interest rate immunization applies to multiple liabilities in addition to a single liability. For now, we continue to assume that these are Type I cash flows in that the scheduled amounts and payment dates are known to the asset manager. In particular, we assume that the same three bonds from Exhibits 4 and 5, which were assets in the single-liability immunization, are now themselves liabilities to be immunized. This assumption allows us to use the same portfolio statistics as in the previous section. The entity in the examples that follow seeks to immunize the cash flows in column 3 (the cash flow column) of Exhibit 5 from Dates 1 through 20, and so it needs to build a portfolio of assets that will allow it to pay those cash flows. The present value of the (now) corporate debt liabilities is EUR200,052,250. The cash flow yield is 3.76%; the Macaulay duration is 6.00; and the convexity is 45.54. We use the portfolio statistics rather than the market value-weighted averages because they better summarize Type I liabilities.

In this section, we discuss several approaches to manage these liabilities:

- *Duration matching*, which extends the ideas of the previous section to a portfolio of debt liabilities.
- *Derivatives overlay*, in particular using futures contracts on government bonds in the immunization strategy; and
- *Contingent immunization*, which allows for active bond portfolio management as long as the surplus is above a designated threshold.

Duration Matching

Duration matching to immunize multiple liabilities is based on similar principles to those covered earlier in relation to a single liability. A portfolio of fixed-income bonds is structured and managed to track the performance of the zero-coupon bonds that would perfectly lock in the rates of return needed to pay off the corporate debt liabilities identified in Exhibit 5. Recall that in the case of a single liability, the immunization strategy is to match the portfolio Macaulay duration with the investment horizon. Also, the initial investment needs to match (or exceed) the present value of the liability. These two conditions can be combined to prescribe that the money duration of the immunizing portfolio matches the money duration of the debt liabilities. Money duration, or "dollar duration," is the portfolio modified duration multiplied by the market value (recall that modified duration is the portfolio Macaulay duration divided by one plus the cash flow yield per period). With multiple liabilities, matching money durations is useful because the market values and cash flow yields of the assets and liabilities are not necessarily equal.

The money duration for the debt liabilities is EUR1,178,237,935:

$$\left[\frac{\text{Portfolio MacDur}}{\left(1 + \frac{\text{Annualized CF yield}}{2}\right)}\right] \times \text{PV of debt liabilities}$$

$$= \left[\frac{6.0004}{\left(1 + \frac{0.037608}{2}\right)}\right] \times 200,052,250 = 1,178,237,935.$$

The term in brackets is the annualized modified duration for the bond portfolio. To keep the numbers manageable, we use the basis point value (BPV) measure for money duration. This measure is the money duration multiplied by 1 bp. The BPV is EUR117,824 (= EUR1,178,237,935 × 0.0001). For each 1 bp change in the cash flow yield, the market value changes by approximately EUR117,824. It is an approximation because convexity is not included. A closely related risk measure is the present value of a basis point (PVBP), also called the PV01 (present value of an "01," meaning 1 bp) and, in North America, the DV01 (dollar value of an "01").

Exhibit 11 shows the three bonds purchased by the asset manager on 15 February 2021. The total cash outlay on that date is EUR202,224,094 (= EUR41,772,719 + EUR99,750,000 + EUR60,701,375 = the market values of the three bonds). Exhibit 12 presents the table used to calculate the cash flow yield and the risk statistics. The annualized cash flow yield is 3.5822%. It is the internal rate of return on the cash flows in the third column of Exhibit 12, multiplied by two. The annualized Macaulay duration for the portfolio is 5.9308 (= 11.8615/2), and the modified duration is 5.8264 (= 5.9308/[1 + 0.035822/2]). The annualized dispersion and convexity statistics are 12.3048 (= 49.2194/4) and 48.6846 (= {201.7767/[1 + 0.035822/2]^2}/4), respectively. Notice that the first few cash flows for the assets in Exhibit 12 are less than the liability payments shown earlier in Exhibit 4. For example, as of 15 August 2021, the asset cash flow of EUR 3,009,000 in column 3 of Exhibit 12 is less than the liability payment of EUR 3,323,625 in Column 3 of Exhibit 4. That disparity indicates that some of the bonds held in the asset portfolio will need to be sold to meet the obligations.

Exhibit 11: The Bond Portfolio to Immunize the Multiple Liabilities

	1.5-Year Bond	6-Year Bond	11.5-Year Bond
Coupon rate	1.00%	2.875%	4.50%
Maturity date	15 August 2022	15 February 2027	15 August 2032
Price	99.875	99.75	100.25
Yield to maturity	1.0842%	2.9207%	4.4720%
Par value	41,825,000	100,000,000	60,550,000
Market value	41,772,719	99,750,000	60,701,375
Macaulay duration	1.493	5.553	9.105
Convexity	2.950	34.149	96.056
Allocation	20.657%	49.326%	30.017%

Managing the Interest Rate Risk of Multiple Liabilities

Exhibit 12: Portfolio Statistics

Time	Date	Cash Flow	PV of Cash Flow	Weight	Time × Weight	Dispersion	Convexity
0	15-Feb-21	−202,224,094					
1	15-Aug-21	3,009,000	2,956,054	0.0146	0.0146	1.7245	0.0292
2	15-Feb-22	3,009,000	2,904,040	0.0144	0.0287	1.3966	0.0862
3	15-Aug-22	44,834,000	42,508,728	0.2102	0.6306	16.5068	2.5225
4	15-Feb-23	2,799,875	2,607,951	0.0129	0.0516	0.7970	0.2579
5	15-Aug-23	2,799,875	2,562,062	0.0127	0.0633	0.5965	0.3801
6	15-Feb-24	2,799,875	2,516,981	0.0124	0.0747	0.4276	0.5228
7	15-Aug-24	2,799,875	2,472,692	0.0122	0.0856	0.2890	0.6847
8	15-Feb-25	2,799,875	2,429,183	0.0120	0.0961	0.1791	0.8649
9	15-Aug-25	2,799,875	2,386,440	0.0118	0.1062	0.0966	1.0621
10	15-Feb-26	2,799,875	2,344,449	0.0116	0.1159	0.0402	1.2753
11	15-Aug-26	2,799,875	2,303,196	0.0114	0.1253	0.0085	1.5034
12	15-Feb-27	102,799,875	83,075,901	0.4108	4.9297	0.0079	64.0865
13	15-Aug-27	1,362,375	1,081,607	0.0053	0.0695	0.0069	0.9734
14	15-Feb-28	1,362,375	1,062,575	0.0053	0.0736	0.0240	1.1034
15	15-Aug-28	1,362,375	1,043,878	0.0052	0.0774	0.0508	1.2389
16	15-Feb-29	1,362,375	1,025,510	0.0051	0.0811	0.0869	1.3794
17	15-Aug-29	1,362,375	1,007,465	0.0050	0.0847	0.1315	1.5245
18	15-Feb-30	1,362,375	989,738	0.0049	0.0881	0.1844	1.6738
19	15-Aug-30	1,362,375	972,323	0.0048	0.0914	0.2450	1.8271
20	15-Feb-31	1,362,375	955,214	0.0047	0.0945	0.3129	1.9839
21	15-Aug-31	1,362,375	938,406	0.0046	0.0974	0.3875	2.1439
22	15-Feb-32	1,362,375	921,894	0.0046	0.1003	0.4686	2.3067
23	15-Aug-32	61,912,375	41,157,805	0.2035	4.6811	25.2505	112.3462
			202,224,094	1.0000	11.8615	49.2194	201.7767

The market value of the immunizing fixed-income bonds is EUR202,224,094. That amount is higher than the value of the liabilities, which is EUR200,052,250. The reason for the difference in market values as of 15 February 2021 is the difference in the cash flow yields. The high-quality assets needed to immunize the corporate liabilities have a cash flow yield of 3.5822%, which is lower than the cash flow yield of 3.7608% on the debt obligations. The assets grow at a lower rate and, therefore, need to start at a higher level. If we discount the debt liabilities scheduled in the third column of Exhibit 12 at 3.5822%, the present value is EUR202,170,671, indicating that initially, the immunizing portfolio is slightly overfunded. Importantly, the asset portfolio BPV is EUR117,824 (= 202,224,094 × 5.8264 × 0.0001), matching the BPV for the debt liabilities.

There is another meaningful difference in the structure of the asset and liability portfolios. Although the money durations are the same, the dispersion and convexity statistics for the assets are greater than for the liabilities—12.30 compared with 8.26 for dispersion, and 48.68 compared with 45.54 for convexity. This difference is required to achieve immunization for multiple liabilities. (Mathematically, in the optimization problem, to minimize the difference in the change in the values of assets and liabilities, the first derivative leads to matching money duration, or BPV, and the second derivative to having higher dispersion.) Intuitively, this condition follows from the general result that, for equal durations, a more convex portfolio generally outperforms a less convex portfolio (higher gains if yields fall, lower losses if yields rise). But, as in the case of immunizing a single liability, the dispersion of the assets should be as low as possible subject to being greater than or equal to the dispersion of the liabilities to mitigate the effect of non-parallel shifts in the yield curve. Note that from Equation 1, higher dispersion implies higher convexity when the Macaulay durations and cash flow yields are equal.

Duration Matching—Parallel Shift Example

Some numerical examples are useful to illustrate that immunization of multiple liabilities is essentially an interest rate risk hedging strategy. The idea is that changes in the market value of the asset portfolio closely match changes in the debt liabilities whether interest rates rise or fall. Exhibit 13 through Exhibit 16 demonstrate this dynamic.

First, we allow the yield curve to shift upward in a parallel manner. The yields on the bonds in Exhibit 11 go up instantaneously by 25 bps on 15 February 2021, immediately after the asset portfolio is purchased. That increase results in a drop in market value of EUR2,842,408. The yields on the debt liabilities in Exhibit 13 also go up by 25 bps, dropping the market value by EUR2,858,681. The difference is EUR16,273, a small amount given that the size of portfolios exceeds EUR200 million. This scenario implicitly assumes no change in the corporate entity's credit risk.

Exhibit 13: Immunizing Multiple Liabilities: Upward Parallel Shift

	Immunizing Assets	Debt Liabilities	Difference
ΔMarket value	−2,842,408	−2,858,681	16,273
ΔCash flow yield	0.2437%	0.2449%	−0.0012%
ΔPortfolio BPV	−2,370	−2,207	−163

Next, we shift the yield curve downward by 25 bps (see Exhibit 14). Both the asset and liability portfolios gain market value by almost the same amount. The difference is only EUR12,504.

Exhibit 14: Immunizing Multiple Liabilities: Downward Parallel Shift

Downward Parallel Shift	Immunizing Assets	Debt Liabilities	Difference
ΔMarket value	2,900,910	2,913,414	−12,504
ΔCash flow yield	−0.2437%	−0.2449%	0.0012%
ΔPortfolio BPV	2,429	2,256	173

The driving factor behind the success of the strategy given these upward and downward shifts is that the portfolio durations are matched and changes in the cash flow yields are very close: 24.37 bps for the assets and 24.49 bps for the liabilities. In Exhibit 14, the asset portfolio rises slightly less than the liabilities when the yield curve shifts down in a parallel manner by 25 bps. Hence, the loss is EUR12,504 despite the greater convexity of the assets. That disparity is explained by the slightly higher decrease in the cash flow yield on the liabilities. As explained previously, a parallel shift is a sufficient but not necessary condition for immunization. Although not shown in the exhibits, an upward non-parallel shift of 15.9 bps in the 1.5-year bond, 23.6 bps in the 6-year bond, and 27.5 bps in the 11.5-year bond leads to virtually the same change in market value (EUR2,842,308) as the 25 bp parallel shift. Those changes are chosen because they result in the same change in the cash flow yield of 24.37 bps.

Duration Matching—Yield Curve Twist Scenario

The structural risk to the immunization strategy is apparent in Exhibit 15. This scenario is the steepening twist in which short-term yields on high-quality bonds go down while long-term yields go up. The 1.5-year yield is assumed to drop by 25 bps. The 6-year yield remains the same, and the 11.5-year yield goes up by 25 bps. These changes lead to a loss of EUR1,178,071 in the asset portfolio as the cash flow yield increases by 10.04 bps. The maturities of the debt liabilities differ from those of the assets. For simplicity, we assume that those yields change in proportion to the differences in maturity around the six-year pivot point for the twist. The 2.5-year yield drops by 19.44 bps (= 25 bps × 3.5/4.5), the 7-year yield goes up by 4.55 bps (= 25 bps × 1/5.5), and the 10-year goes up by 18.18 bps (= 25 bps × 4/5.5). The market value of the liabilities drops by only EUR835,156 because the cash flow yield increases by only 7.11 bps. The value of the assets goes down by more than the liabilities—the difference is EUR342,915. The steepening twist to the shape of the yield curve is the source of the loss.

Exhibit 15: Immunizing Multiple Liabilities: Steepening Twist

	Immunizing Assets	Debt Liabilities	Difference
ΔMarket value	−1,178,071	−835,156	−342,915
ΔCash flow yield	0.1004%	0.0711%	0.0293%
ΔPortfolio BPV	−984	−645	−339

The results of the fourth scenario show that a flattening twist can lead to a comparable gain if long-term high-quality yields fall while short-term yields rise (Exhibit 16). We make the same assumptions about proportionate changes in the yields. In this case, the cash flow yield of the assets goes down more and the market value rises higher than the debt liabilities. Clearly, an entity that pursues immunization of multiple liabilities hopes that steepening twists are balanced out by flattening twists and that most yield curve shifts are more or less parallel.

Exhibit 16: Immunizing Multiple Liabilities: Flattening Twist

	Immunizing Assets	Debt Liabilities	Difference
ΔMarket value	1,215,285	850,957	364,328
ΔCash flow yield	−0.1027%	−0.0720%	−0.0307%
ΔPortfolio BPV	1,016	658	358

The previous illustrations (in Exhibit 13–Exhibit 16) also report the changes in the portfolio BPVs for the assets and liabilities. Before the yield curve shifts and twists, the BPVs are matched at EUR117,824. Afterward, there is a small money duration mismatch. In theory, the asset manager needs to rebalance the portfolio immediately. In practice, the manager likely waits until the mismatch is large enough to justify the transaction costs in selling some bonds and buying others. Another method to rebalance the portfolio is to use interest rate derivatives.

CASE STUDY

A Japanese corporation recently sold one of its lines of business and would like to use the cash to retire the debt liabilities that financed those assets. Summary statistics for the multiple debt liabilities, which range in maturity from three to seven years, are market value, JPY110.4 billion; portfolio modified duration, 5.84; portfolio convexity, 46.08; and BPV, JPY64.47 million.

An investment bank working with the corporation offers three alternatives to accomplish the objective:

1. **Bond tender offer.** The corporation would buy back the debt liabilities on the open market, paying a premium above the market price. The corporation currently has a single-A rating and hopes for an upgrade once its balance sheet is improved by retiring the debt. The investment bank anticipates that the tender offer would have to be at a price commensurate with a triple-A rating to entice the bondholders to sell. The bonds are widely held by domestic and international institutional investors.

2. **Cash flow matching.** The corporation buys a portfolio of government bonds that matches, as closely as possible, the coupon interest and principal redemptions on the debt liabilities. The investment bank is highly confident that the corporation's external auditors will agree to **accounting defeasement** because the purchased bonds are government securities. That agreement will allow the corporation to remove both the defeasing asset portfolio and the liabilities from the balance sheet.

3. **Duration matching.** The corporation buys a portfolio of high-quality corporate bonds that matches the duration of the debt liabilities. Interest rate derivatives contracts will be used to keep the duration on its target as time passes and yields change. The investment bank thinks it is very unlikely that the external auditors will allow this strategy to qualify for accounting defeasement. The corporation can explain to investors and the rating agencies in the management section of its annual report, however, that it is aiming to "effectively defease" the debt. To carry out this strategy, the investment bank suggests three different portfolios of investment-grade corporate bonds that range in maturity from 2 years to 10 years. Each portfolio has a market value of about JPY115 billion, which is considered sufficient to pay off the liabilities.

	Portfolio A	Portfolio B	Portfolio C
Modified duration	5.60	5.61	5.85
Convexity	42.89	50.11	46.09
BPV (in millions)	JPY64.50	JPY64.51	JPY67.28

After some deliberation and discussion with the investment bankers and external auditors, the corporation's CFO chooses Strategy 3, duration matching.

1. Indicate the likely trade-offs that led the corporate CFO to choose the duration-matching strategy over the tender offer and cash flow matching.

Solution:

The likely trade-offs are between removing the debt liabilities from the balance sheet, either by directly buying the bonds from investors or by account-

Managing the Interest Rate Risk of Multiple Liabilities

> ing defeasement via cash flow matching, and the cost of the strategy. The tender offer entails buying the bonds at a triple-A price, which would likely be considerably higher than at a single-A price. Cash flow matching entails buying even more expensive government bonds. The duration-matching strategy can be implemented at a lower cost because the asset portfolio consists of less expensive investment-grade bonds. The CFO has chosen the lowest-cost strategy, even though the debt liabilities will remain on the balance sheet.
>
> 2. Indicate the portfolio that the corporation should choose to carry out the duration-matching strategy.
>
> **Solution:**
>
> The corporation should recommend Portfolio B. Portfolio C closely matches the modified duration (as well as the convexity) of the liabilities. Duration matching when the market values of the assets and liabilities differ, however, entails matching the money durations, in particular the BPVs. The choice then comes down to Portfolios A and B. Although both have BPVs close to the liabilities, it is incorrect to choose A based on its BPV being "closer."
>
> The important difference between Portfolios A and B lies in the convexities. To immunize multiple liabilities, the convexity (and dispersion of cash flows) of the assets needs to be greater than the liabilities. Therefore, Portfolio A does not meet that condition.
>
> Recall that in an earlier exercise, the correct immunizing portfolio is the one with the lower convexity, which minimizes the structural risk to the strategy. But, that bond portfolio still has a convexity greater than the zero-coupon bond that would provide perfect immunization. This greater convexity of the immunizing portfolio is because the dispersion of the zero-coupon bond is zero and the durations are the same. As seen in Equation 1, that dispersion implies a lower convexity statistic.

Derivatives Overlay

Interest rate derivatives can be a cost-effective method to rebalance the immunizing portfolio to keep it on its target duration as the yield curve shifts and twists and as time passes. Suppose that in the duration-matching example shown earlier, there is a much larger instantaneous upward shift in the yield curve on 15 February 2021. All yields shift up by 100 bps. Because yields and duration are inversely related, the portfolio duration statistics go down, as does the market value. The BPV of the immunizing asset portfolio decreases from EUR117,824 to EUR108,679, a drop of EUR9,145. The BPV for the debt liabilities goes down to EUR109,278, a drop of EUR8,546. There is now a money duration gap of −EUR599 (= EUR108,679 − EUR109,278). The asset manager could sell some of the 1%, 1.5-year bonds and buy some more of the 4.50%, 11-year bonds to close the money duration gap. A more efficient and lower-cost rebalancing strategy, however, is likely to buy, or go long, a few interest rate futures contracts to rebalance the portfolio.

To address the question of the required number of contracts to close, or reduce, a duration gap, we change the example from euros to US dollars. Doing so allows us to illustrate the calculations for the required number of futures contracts using the actively traded 10-year US Treasury note futures contract offered at the CME Group. The present value of corporate debt liabilities shown in Exhibits 3 and 4 now is assumed to be USD200,052,250. Risk and return statistics are invariant to currency denomination, so the portfolio Macaulay duration is still 6.0004 and the BPV is USD117,824.

In the previous example for duration matching of multiple liabilities, the asset manager purchased three bonds with maturities of 1, 6, and 11 years. In this next scenario, we assume that the asset manager buys a portfolio of high-quality, short-term bonds. This portfolio has a market value of USD222,750,000, Macaulay duration of 0.8532, and cash flow yield of 1.9804%. Discounting the debt liabilities in the third column of Exhibit 5 at 1.9804% gives a present value of USD222,552,788. This value indicates that the immunizing portfolio is overfunded on 15 February 2021. The BPV for the asset portfolio is USD18,819:

$$\left[\frac{0.8532}{\left(1 + \frac{0.019804}{2}\right)} \right] \times 222{,}750{,}000 \times 0.0001 = 18{,}819.$$

The asset manager might elect to hold a portfolio of short-term bonds rather than intermediate-term and long-term securities for a number of reasons, including greater liquidity, perception of finer pricing in the short-term market, or that the entity faces liquidity constraints and needs to hold these short-term bonds to meet regulatory requirements. A derivatives overlay strategy is then used to close the duration gap while keeping the underlying portfolio unchanged. In general, a derivatives overlay transforms some aspect of the underlying portfolio—the currency could be changed with foreign exchange derivatives or the credit risk profile with credit default swap contracts. Here, interest rate derivatives are used to change the interest rate risk profile, increasing the portfolio BPV from USD18,819 to USD117,824.

Details of interest rate futures contracts are covered elsewhere. Here we note some specific features of the 10-year US Treasury note contract traded at the CME Group relevant for this example. Each contract is for USD100,000 in par value and has delivery dates in March, June, September, and December.

Conversion factors that are used to make the qualifying T-notes roughly equivalent for delivery by the contract seller, or short position are based on an arbitrary yield to maturity of 6.00%. If the eligible T-note has a coupon rate below (above) 6.00%, the conversion factor is less (more) than 1.0000. The invoice price paid by the buyer of the contract, the long position, at the expiration of the contract is the futures price multiplied by the conversion factor, plus accrued interest. The logic of this design is that if the contract seller chooses to deliver a qualifying T-note having a lower (higher) coupon rate than 6.00%, the buyer pays a lower (higher) price.

The key point is that, although the eligible T-notes are roughly equivalent, one will be identified as the cheapest-to-deliver (CTD) security. Importantly, the duration of the 10-year T-note futures contract is assumed to be the duration of the CTD T-note. A factor in determining the CTD T-note is that the conversion factors for each qualifying security are based on the arbitrary assumption of a 6.00% yield to maturity. In practice, when yields are below 6.00% the CTD security typically is the qualifying T-note having the lowest duration. Therefore, the 10-year T-note futures contract essentially has been acting as a 6.5-year contract. (That explains the motivation for introducing the Ultra 10-year contract—to provide a hedging instrument more closely tied to the 10-year T-note traded in the cash market.)

To illustrate the importance of using the risk statistics for the CTD T-note, Exhibit 17 reports two hypothetical qualifying securities for the March 2021 10-year futures contract. One is designated the 6.5-year T-note. It has a coupon rate of 2.75% and matures on 15 November 2027. As of 15 February 2021, it is assumed to be priced to yield 3.8088%. Its BPV per USD100,000 in par value is USD56.8727, and its conversion factor is 0.8226. The other is the on-the-run 10-year T-note. Its coupon rate is 4.00%, and it matures on 15 February 2031. Its BPV is USD81.6607, and its conversion factor is 0.8516.

Managing the Interest Rate Risk of Multiple Liabilities

Exhibit 17: Two Qualifying T-Notes for the March 2021 10-Year T-Note Futures Contract as of 15 February 2021 (hypothetical example)

	6.5-Year T-Note	10-Year T-Note
Coupon rate	2.75%	4.00%
Maturity date	15 November 2027	15 February 2031
Full price per 100,000 in par value	USD94,449	USD99,900
Yield to maturity	3.8088%	4.0122%
Modified duration	6.0215	8.1742
BPV per 100,000 in par value	56.8727	81.6607
Conversion factor	0.8226	0.8516

The calculation of the required number of futures contract, denoted N_f, comes from this relationship:

$$\text{Asset portfolio BPV} + (N_f \times \text{Futures BPV}) = \text{Liability portfolio BPV}. \qquad (2)$$

Inherent in this expression is the important idea that although futures contracts have a market value of zero as a result of daily mark-to-market valuation and settlement, they can add to or subtract from the asset portfolio BPV. This equation can be rearranged to isolate N_f:

$$N_f = \frac{\text{Liability portfolio BPV} - \text{Asset portfolio BPV}}{\text{Futures BPV}}. \qquad (3)$$

If N_f is a positive number, the asset manager buys, or goes long, the required number of futures contracts. Doing so raises the money duration of the assets to match that of the liabilities. If N_f is a negative number, the asset manager sells, or goes short, futures contracts to reduce the money duration. In our problem, the asset portfolio BPV is USD18,819 and the liability portfolio BPV is USD117,824. Therefore, N_f is a large positive number and depends on the BPV for the futures contract. The exact formulation for the futures BPV is complicated, however, and goes beyond the scope of our coverage. It involves such details as the number of days until the expiration of the contract, the interest rate for that period, and the accrued interest on the deliverable bond. To simplify, we use an approximation formula that is common in practice:

$$\text{Futures BPV} \approx \frac{\text{BPV}_{CTD}}{\text{CF}_{CTD}}, \qquad (4)$$

where CF_{CTD} is the conversion factor for the CTD security.

If the CTD security is the 6.5-year T-note shown in Exhibit 17, the futures BPV is estimated to be USD69.1377 (= 56.8727/0.8226). Then, the required number of contracts is approximately 1,432:

$$\frac{117,824 - 18,819}{69.1377} = 1,432.$$

But if the CTD security is the 10-year T-note, the futures BPV is USD95.8909 (= 81.6607/0.8516). To close the money duration gap, the required number of contracts is only 1,032:

$$\frac{117,824 - 18,819}{95.8909} = 1,032.$$

Clearly, the asset manager must know the CTD T-note to use in the derivatives overlay strategy. The difference of 400 futures contracts is significant.

The asset manager has established a synthetic "barbell" strategy: having positions in the short-term and longer-term segments of the yield curve. The term "synthetic" means "created with derivatives." The underlying asset portfolio is concentrated in the short-term market. The derivatives portfolio is either at the 6.5-year or 10-year segment of the yield curve. CME Group also has actively traded two-year and five-year Treasury futures contracts. Therefore, the asset manager could choose to spread out the futures contracts across other segments of the yield curve. That diversification reduces the structural risk to the immunization strategy arising from non-parallel shifts and twists to the curve.

CASE STUDY

A Frankfurt-based asset manager uses the Long Bund contract traded at the Intercontinental Exchange (ICE) futures exchange to manage the gaps that arise from "duration drift" in a portfolio of German government bonds that are used to immunize a portfolio of corporate debt liabilities. This futures contract has a notional principal of EUR100,000 and is based on a 6% coupon rate. The German government bonds that are eligible for delivery have maturities between 8.5 years and 10.5 years.

Currently, the corporate debt liabilities have a market value of EUR330,224,185, a modified duration of 7.23, and a BPV of EUR238,752. The asset portfolio has a market value of EUR332,216,004, a modified duration of 7.42, and a BPV of EUR246,504. The duration drift has arisen because of a widening spread between corporate and government bond yields as interest rates in general have come down. The lower yields on government bonds have increased the modified durations relative to corporates.

Based on the deliverable bond, the asset manager estimates that the BPV for each futures contract is EUR65.11.

1. Does the asset manager go long (buy) or go short (sell) the futures contract?

   Solution:

   The asset manager needs to go short (or sell) Long Bund futures contracts. The money duration of the assets, as measured by the BPV, is greater than the money duration of debt liabilities. This relationship is true of the modified duration statistics as well, but the money duration is a better measure of the gap because the market values differ.

2. How many contracts does the manager buy or sell to close the duration gap?

   Solution:

   Use Equation 3 to get the requisite number of futures contracts to sell.

   $$N_f = \frac{\text{Liability portfolio BPV} - \text{Asset portfolio BPV}}{\text{Futures BPV}},$$

   where Liability portfolio BPV = 238,752, Asset portfolio BPV = 246,504, and Futures BPV = 65.11.

   $$N_f = \frac{238,752 - 246,504}{65.11} = -119.06.$$

   The minus sign indicates the need to go short (or sell) 119 contracts to close the duration gap.

Contingent Immunization

We have seen that the initial market value for the immunizing asset portfolio can vary according to the strategy chosen by the asset manager. Earlier, in the duration-matching example, the initial market value of the asset portfolio was EUR202,224,094, while the liabilities were EUR200,052,250. The derivatives overlay example is to hold a portfolio of short-term bonds having a market value of USD222,750,000 and 1,432 10-year futures contracts (assuming that the CTD eligible security is the 6.5-year T-note) to immunize the liability of USD200,052,250.

The difference between the market values of the assets and liabilities is the **surplus**. The initial surplus in the duration-matching example is EUR2,171,844 (= EUR202,224,094 − EUR200,052,250); the surplus in the derivatives overlay example is USD22,697,750 (= EUR222,750,000 −EUR200,052,250). The presence of a significant surplus allows the asset manager to consider a hybrid passive–active strategy known as **contingent immunization**. The idea behind contingent immunization is that the asset manager can pursue active investment strategies, as if operating under a total return mandate, if the surplus is above a designated threshold. If the actively managed assets perform poorly, however, and the surplus evaporates, the mandate reverts to the purely passive strategy of building a duration-matching portfolio and then managing it to remain on duration target.

In principle, when the surplus is above a sufficient threshold, the manager may increase portfolio risk in any asset category, including equity, fixed income, and alternative investments. The manager could also buy out-of-the-money commodity options contracts or credit default swaps. The objective is to attain portfolio gains to reduce the cost of retiring the debt obligations without falling below the minimum funding threshold. Obviously, liquidity is an important criterion in selecting the investments because the positions will need to be unwound if losses cause the surplus to near the threshold.

A natural setting for contingent immunization is in the fixed-income derivatives overlay strategy. Instead of buying, or going long, 1,432 10-year T-note futures contracts, the asset manager could intentionally over-hedge or under-hedge, depending on the held view on rate volatility at the 6.5-year segment of the Treasury yield curve. That segment matters because the 10-year T-note futures contract price responds to changes in the yield of the CTD security. The asset manager could buy more (less) than 1,432 contracts if she expects the 6.5-year Treasury yield to go down (up) and the futures price to go up (down).

Suppose that on 15 February 2021, the price of the March 10-year T-note futures contract is quoted to be 121-03. The price is 121 and 3/32 percent of USD100,000, which is the contract size. Therefore, the delivery price in March would be USD121,093.75 multiplied by the conversion factor, plus the accrued interest. What matters to the asset manager is the change in the settlement futures price from day to day. For each futures contract, the gain or loss is USD31.25 for each 1/32nd change in the futures price, calculated as 1/32 percent of USD100,000.

Now suppose that the asset manager anticipates an upward shift in the yield curve. Such a shift would cause bond prices to drop in both the Treasury cash and futures markets. Suppose that the quoted March futures price drops from 121-03 to 119-22. That is a 45/32nd change in the price and causes a loss of USD1,406.25 (= 45 × USD31.25) per contract. If the asset manager holds 1,432 long contracts, the loss that day is USD2,013,750 (= USD1,406.25 × 1,432). But if the asset manager is allowed to under-hedge, he could have dramatically reduced the number of long futures contracts and maybe even gone short in anticipation of the upward shift. The presence of the surplus allows the manager the opportunity to take a view on interest rates and save some of the cost of the strategy to retire the debt liabilities. The objective is to be over-hedged when yields are expected to fall and under-hedged when they are expected to rise.

CASE STUDY

An asset manager is asked to build and manage a portfolio of fixed-income bonds to retire multiple corporate debt liabilities. The debt liabilities have a market value of GBP50,652,108, a modified duration of 7.15, and a BPV of GBP36,216.

The asset manager buys a portfolio of British government bonds with a market value of GBP64,271,055, a modified duration of 3.75, and a BPV of GBP24,102. The initial surplus of GBP13,618,947 and the negative duration gap of GBP12,114 are intentional. The surplus allows the manager to pursue a contingent immunization strategy to retire the debt at, hopefully, a lower cost than a more conservative duration-matching approach. The duration gap requires the manager to buy, or go long, interest rate futures contracts to close the gap. The manager can choose to over-hedge or under-hedge, however, depending on market circumstances.

The futures contract that the manager buys is based on 10-year gilts having a par value of GBP100,000. It is estimated to have a BPV of GBP98.2533 per contract. Currently, the asset manager has purchased, or gone long, 160 contracts.

1. Which statement *best* describes the asset manager's hedging strategy and the held view on future 10-year gilt interest rates? The asset manager is:

    A. over-hedging because the rate view is that 10-year yields will be rising.

    B. over-hedging because the rate view is that 10-year yields will be falling.

    C. under-hedging because the rate view is that 10-year yields will be rising.

    D. under-hedging because the rate view is that 10-year yields will be falling.

Solution:

B is correct. The asset manager is over-hedging because the rate view is that 10-year yields will be falling. First calculate the number of contracts (N_f) needed to fully hedge (or immunize) the debt liabilities. The general relationship is Equation 2: Asset portfolio BPV + (N_f × Futures BPV) = Liability portfolio BPV.

Asset portfolio BPV is GBP24,102, Futures BPV is GBP98.2533, and Liability portfolio BPV is GBP36,216.

$24{,}102 + (N_f \times 98.2533) = 36{,}216$.

$N_f = 123.3$.

The asset manager is over-hedging because a position in 160 long futures contracts is more than what is needed to close the duration gap. Long, or purchased, positions in interest rate futures contracts gain when futures prices rise, and rates go down. The anticipated gains from the strategic decision to over-hedge in this case further increase the surplus and reduce the cost of retiring the debt liabilities.

EXAMPLE: DEFINED BENEFIT PENSION PLAN

Earlier we introduced four types of liabilities: Types I, II, III, and IV. Defined benefit (DB) pension plan obligations are a good example of Type IV liabilities for which both the aggregate amounts and dates are uncertain. An LDI strategy for this entity starts with a model for these liabilities. We first explain the model assumptions and then calculate future liabilities.

Model Assumptions

We reveal some of the assumptions that go into this complex financial modeling problem by assuming the work history and retirement profile for a representative employee covered by the pension plan. We assume that this employee has worked for G years, a sufficient length of time to ensure that the retirement benefits are vested. The employee is expected to work for another T years and then to retire and live for Z years. Exhibit 18 illustrates this timeline.

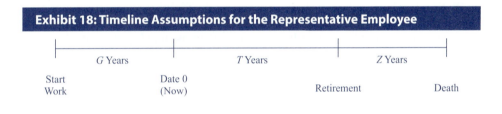

In this final pay DB example, the retired employee receives a fixed lifetime annuity based on her wage at the time of retirement, denoted W_T. Some pension plans index the annual retirement benefit to inflation. Our example assumes an annuity fixed in nominal terms, calculated as the final wage, W_T, multiplied by a multiplier, m, multiplied by the total number of years worked, $G + T$.

There are two general measures of the retirement obligations as of Time 0—the accumulated benefit obligation (ABO) and the projected benefit obligation (PBO). The ABO calculates the liability based on the G years worked and the current annual wage, denoted W_0, even though the annuity paid in retirement is based on W_T (final wage) and $G + T$ years. The use of the current annual wage and the number of years worked is because the ABO represents the *legal liability* today of the plan sponsor if the plan were to be closed or converted to another type of plan, such as a defined contribution (DC) plan. The ABO is the present value of the projected annuity, discounted at an annual rate r on high-quality corporate bonds (most government regulators and accounting authorities allow high-quality corporate bonds to be used to discount the future liabilities), which for simplicity we assume applies for all periods (a flat yield curve).

$$\text{ABO} = \frac{1}{(1+r)^T} \times \left[\frac{m \times G \times W_0}{1+r} + \frac{m \times G \times W_0}{(1+r)^2} + \cdots + \frac{m \times G \times W_0}{(1+r)^Z} \right].$$

The term in brackets is the value of the Z-year annuity as of year T, and that sum is discounted back over T years to Time 0.

The PBO liability measure uses the projected wage for year T instead of the current wage in the Z-year annuity.

$$\text{PBO} = \frac{1}{(1+r)^T} \times \left[\frac{m \times G \times W_T}{1+r} + \frac{m \times G \times W_T}{(1+r)^2} + \cdots + \frac{m \times G \times W_T}{(1+r)^Z} \right].$$

Although the ABO is the legal obligation to the plan sponsor, the PBO is the liability reported in financial statements and used to assess the plan's funding status. The plan is over-funded (under-funded) if the current fair value of assets is more (less) than the present value of the promised retirement benefits.

The next step is to consider how wages evolve between dates 0 and T. We denote w to be the average annual wage growth rate for the employee's remaining work life of T years. Therefore, the relationship between W_0 and W_T is $W_T = W_0 \times (1 + w)^T$.

After some algebraic manipulation and substitution, the two liability measures can be written more compactly as follows:

$$\text{ABO} = \frac{m \times G \times W_0}{(1+r)^T} \times \left[\frac{1}{r} - \frac{1}{r \times (1+r)^Z}\right], \text{ and}$$

$$\text{PBO} = \frac{m \times G \times W_0 \times (1+w)^T}{(1+r)^T} \times \left[\frac{1}{r} - \frac{1}{r \times (1+r)^Z}\right].$$

Note that the PBO always will be larger than the ABO by the factor of $(1 + w)^T$, assuming positive wage growth in nominal terms.

We see in this simple model several of the important assumptions that go into using an LDI strategy to manage these Type IV liabilities. The assumed post-retirement lifetime (Z years) is critical. A higher value for Z increases both the ABO and PBO measures of liability. The pension plan faces *longevity risk*, which is the risk that employees live longer in their retirement years than assumed in the models. Some plans have become under-funded and have had to increase assets because regulators required that they recognize longer life expectancies. Another important assumption is the time until retirement (T years). In the ABO measure, increases in T reduce the liability. That result also holds for the PBO as long as wage growth (w) is lower than the discount rate (r). Assuming w is less than r is reasonable if it can be assumed that employees over time generally are compensated for price inflation and some part of real economic growth, as well as for seniority and productivity improvements. Generally, the labor income growth rate does not quite keep pace with the nominal return on high-quality financial assets over long periods of time.

Model Inputs

We now use a numerical example to show how the effective durations of ABO and PBO liability measures are calculated. Assume that $m = 0.02$, $G = 25$, $T = 10$, $Z = 17$, $W_0 = \text{USD}50{,}000$, and $r = 0.05$. We also assume that the wage growth rate w is an arbitrarily chosen constant fraction of the yield on high-quality corporate bonds r—in particular, that $w = 0.9 \times r$ so that $w = 0.045$ (= 0.9 × 0.05). Based on these assumptions, the ABO and PBO for the representative employee are USD173,032 and USD268,714, respectively.

$$\text{ABO} = \frac{m \times G \times W_0}{(1+r)^T} \times \left[\frac{1}{r} - \frac{1}{r \times (1+r)^Z}\right]$$

$$= \frac{0.02 \times 25 \times 50{,}000}{(1.05)^{10}} \times \left[\frac{1}{0.05} - \frac{1}{0.05 \times (1.05)^{17}}\right] = 173{,}032.$$

$$\text{PBO} = \frac{m \times G \times W_0 \times (1+w)^T}{(1+r)^T} \times \left[\frac{1}{r} - \frac{1}{r \times (1+r)^Z}\right]$$

$$= \frac{0.02 \times 25 \times 50{,}000 \times (1.045)^{10}}{(1.05)^{10}} \times \left[\frac{1}{0.05} - \frac{1}{0.05 \times (1.05)^{17}}\right] = 268{,}714.$$

If the plan covers 10,000 similar employees, the total liability is approximately USD1.730 billion ABO and USD2.687 billion PBO. Assuming that the pension plan has assets with a market value of USD2.700 billion, the plan currently is overfunded by both measures of liability.

Example: Defined Benefit Pension Plan

Calculating Durations

Recall that in general, the effective durations for assets or liabilities are obtained by raising and lowering the assumed yield curve in the valuation model and recalculating the present values.

$$\text{Effective duration} = \frac{(PV_-) - (PV_+)}{2 \times \Delta \text{Curve} \times (PV_0)}.$$

PV_0 is the initial value, PV_- is the new value after the yield curve is lowered by ΔCurve, and PV_+ is the value after the yield curve is raised. In this simple model with a flat yield curve, we raise r from 0.05 to 0.06 (and w from 0.045 to 0.054) and lower r from 0.05 to 0.04 (and w from 0.045 to 0.036); therefore, ΔCurve = 0.01.

Given our assumptions, ABO_0 is USD173,032. Redoing the calculations for the higher and lower values for r and w gives USD146,261 for ABO_+ and USD205,467 for ABO_-. The ABO effective duration is 17.1.

$$\text{ABO duration} = \frac{(PV_-) - (PV_+)}{2 \times \Delta \text{Curve} \times (PV_0)} = \frac{205{,}467 - 146{,}261}{2 \times 0.01 \times 173{,}032} = 17.1.$$

Repeating the calculations for the PBO liability measure gives USD247,477 for PBO_+ and USD292,644 for PBO_-. Given that PBO_0 is 268,714, the PBO duration is 8.4.

$$\text{PBO} = \frac{292{,}644 - 247{,}477}{2 \times 0.01 \times 268{,}714} = \frac{(PV_-) - (PV_+)}{2 \times \Delta \text{Curve} \times (PV_0)} = 8.4.$$

These calculations indicate the challenge facing the fund manager. There is a significant difference between having liabilities of USD1.730 billion and an effective duration of 17.1, as measured by the ABO, and liabilities of USD2.687 billion and an effective duration of 8.4, as measured by the PBO. The ABO BPV is USD2,958,300 (= USD1.730 billion × 17.1 × 0.0001), and the PBO BPV is USD2,257,080 (= USD2.687 billion × 8.4 × 0.0001). The plan sponsor must decide which liability measure to use for risk management and asset allocation. For example, if the corporation anticipates that it might be a target for an acquisition and that the acquirer likely would want to convert the retirement plan from defined benefit to defined contribution, the ABO measure matters more than the PBO.

We assume that the corporate sponsor sees itself as an ongoing independent institution that preserves the pension plan's current design. Therefore, PBO is the appropriate measure for pension plan liabilities. The plan is fully funded in that the market value of assets, assumed to be USD2.700 billion, exceeds the PBO of USD2.687 billion, giving a surplus of only USD13 million. That surplus disappears quickly if yields on high-quality corporate bonds that are used to discount the projected benefits drop by about 5 bps to 6 bps. Note that the surplus divided by the PBO BPV is 5.76 (= 13,000,000/2,257,080). Interest rate risk is a major concern to the plan sponsor because changes in the funding status flow through the income statement, thereby affecting reported earnings per share.

Lower yields also raise the market value of assets depending on how those assets are allocated. We assume that the current asset allocation is 50% equity, 40% fixed income, and 10% alternatives. The fixed-income portfolio is managed to track an index of well-diversified corporate bonds—such indexes are covered later. Relevant at this point is that the chosen bond index reports a modified duration of 5.5.

The problem is to assign a duration for the equity and alternative investments. To be conservative, we assume that there is no stable and predictable relationship between valuations on those asset classes and market interest rates. Therefore, equity duration and alternatives duration are assumed to be zero. Assuming zero duration does not imply that equity and alternatives have no interest rate risk. Effective duration estimates the percentage change in value arising from a change in nominal interest rates. The effect on equity and alternatives depends on *why* the nominal rate changes, especially if that rate change is not widely anticipated in the market. Higher or lower interest rates can arise from a change in expected inflation, a change in monetary policy, or a change in macroeconomic conditions. Only fixed-income securities have a well-defined connection between market values and the yield curve. Nevertheless, assumptions are a source of model risk, as discussed in the next section.

Given these assumptions, we conclude that the asset BPV is USD594,000 = USD2.700 billion × [(0.50 × 0) + (0.40 × 5.5) + (0.10 × 0)] × 0.0001. The term in brackets is the estimated effective duration for the asset portfolio, calculated using the shares of market value as the weights. Clearly, the pension plan is running a significant duration gap—the asset BPV of USD594,000 is much lower than the liability BPV of USD2,257,080, using the PBO measure. If all yields go down by 10 bps, the market value of assets goes up by approximately USD5.940 million and the present value of liabilities goes up by USD22.571 million. The pension plan would have a deficit and be deemed under-funded.

Addressing the Duration Gap

The pension fund manager can choose to reduce, or even eliminate, the duration gap using derivatives. We consider several scenarios, starting with futures. We then consider the use of swaps and options to enter an interest rate swap.

Using Futures to Reduce the Duration Gap

For example, suppose the Ultra 10-year Treasury futures contract at the Chicago Mercantile Exchange has a BPV of USD95.8909 because the on-the-run T-note is the CTD security. Using Equation 3, the pension plan would need to buy, or go long, 17,343 contracts to fully hedge the interest rate risk created by the duration gap:

$$N_f = \frac{\text{Liability portfolio BPV} - \text{Asset portfolio BPV}}{\text{Futures BPV}}$$

$$= \frac{2,257,080 - 594,000}{95.8909} = 17,343.$$

One concern with hedging with futures is the need for daily oversight of the positions. That need arises because futures contracts are marked to market and settled at the end of each trading day into the margin account. Suppose that the fund did buy 17,343 futures contracts and 10-year Treasury yields go up by 5 bps. Given that the futures BPV is USD95.8909 per contract, the *realized* loss that day is more than USD8.315 million: USD95.8909 × 5 × 17,343 = 8,315,179. That amount is offset by the *unrealized* reduction in the present value of liabilities. Such a large position in futures contracts would lead to significant daily cash inflows and outflows. For that reason, such hedging problems as the one facing the pension fund often are addressed with over-the-counter interest rate swaps rather than exchange-traded futures contracts.

Using Interest Rate Swaps to Reduce Duration Gap

Suppose that the pension fund manager can enter a 30-year, receive-fixed interest rate swap against the three-month market reference rate (MRR). The fixed rate on the swap is 4.16%. Assume its effective duration is +16.73, and its BPV is +0.1673 per USD100 of notional principal. Exhibit 19 illustrates this swap.

Example: Defined Benefit Pension Plan

Exhibit 19: Interest Rate Swap

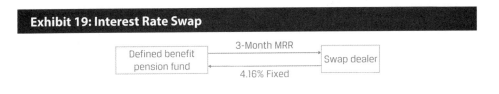

The risk statistics for an interest rate swap can be obtained from interpreting the contract as a combination of bonds. From the pension fund's perspective, the swap is viewed as buying a 30-year, 4.16% fixed-rate bond from the swap dealer and financing that purchase by issuing a 30-year floating-rate note (FRN) that pays the three-month MRR.

> Swaps are typically quoted as a fixed rate against the MRR flat, meaning no spread. The spread over the MRR is put into the fixed rate. For instance, a swap of 4.00% against the MRR flat is the same as a swap of 4.25% against MRR + 0.25%. The swap's money duration is taken to be the (high) duration of the fixed-rate bond minus the (low) duration of the FRN. That explains why a receive-fixed swap has positive duration. From the swap dealer's perspective, the contract is viewed as purchasing a (low duration) FRN that is financed by issuing a (high duration) fixed-rate bond. Hence, the swap has negative duration to the dealer.

The notional principal (NP) on the interest rate swap needed to close the duration gap to zero can be calculated with this expression:

$$\text{Asset BPV} + \left[NP \times \frac{\text{Swap BPV}}{100} \right] = \text{Liability BPV}. \quad (5)$$

This is similar to Equation 2 for futures contracts. Given that the Asset BPV is USD594,000 and the Liability BPV is USD2,257,080 using the PBO measure, the required notional principal for the receive-fixed swap having a BPV of 0.1673 is about USD994 million.

$$594{,}000 + \left[NP \times \frac{0.1673}{100} \right] = 2{,}257{,}080 \;; NP = 994{,}070{,}532.$$

Exhibit 20 shows the simplified payoff from entering the receive-fixed swap with a break-even interest rate of 4.16.

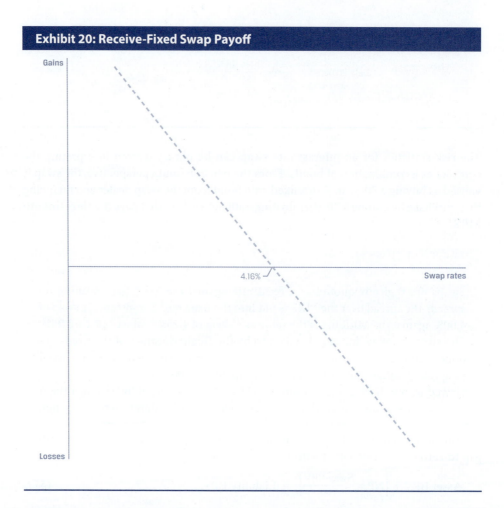

We use the term "hedging ratio" (or "interest rate hedging ratio," since the focus is on reducing interest rate risk) to indicate the extent of interest rate risk management. A hedging ratio of 0% indicates no hedging at all. The pension plan retains the significant negative duration gap and the risk of lower corporate bond yields if it does not hedge. A hedging ratio of 100% indicates an attempt to fully balance, or to immunize, the assets and liabilities. In this case, the plan manager enters the receive-fixed swap for a notional principal of USD994 million. In practice, partial hedges are common; the manager's task is to select the hedging ratio between 0% and 100%. The initial use of derivatives entails moving up a substantial learning curve. It is important that all stakeholders to the retirement plan understand the hedging strategy. These stakeholders include the plan sponsor, the regulatory authorities, the auditors, the employees covered by the plan, and perhaps even the employees' union representatives. Interest rate swaps typically have a value of zero at initiation. If swap rates rise, the value of the receive-fixed swap becomes negative, and stakeholders will need an explanation of those losses. If the contract is collateralized, the pension fund will have to post cash or marketable securities with the swap dealer. We discuss collateralization further in the next section. The key point is that likely, the prudent course of action for the plan manager is to use a partial hedge rather than attempt to reduce the duration gap to zero.

One possibility is that the plan sponsor allows the manager some flexibility (called "strategic hedging") in selecting the hedging ratio. For example, the mandate could be to stay within a range of 25% to 75%. When the manager anticipates lower market rates and gains on receive-fixed interest rate swaps, the manager prefers to be at the top of an allowable range. On the other hand, if market (swap) rates are expected to go up, the manager could reduce the hedging ratio to the lower end of the range. The performance of the strategic hedging decisions can be measured against a strategy of maintaining a preset hedging ratio, for instance, 50%. That strategy means entering the receive-fixed swap for a notional principal of USD497 million, which is about half of the notional principal needed to attempt to immunize the plan from interest rate risk.

Using Options to Reduce Duration Gap

Another consideration for the plan manager is whether to use an option-based derivatives overlay strategy. Instead of entering a 30-year, receive-fixed interest rate swap against the three-month MRR, the pension fund could purchase an option to enter a similar receive-fixed swap. This contract is called a receiver swaption. The cost is a known amount paid upfront. Suppose that the strike rate on the swaption is 3.50%. Given that the current 30-year swap fixed rate is assumed to be 4.16%, this receiver swaption is out of the money. The swap rate would have to fall by 66 bps (= 4.16% − 3.50%) for the swap contract to have intrinsic value. Suppose that the swaption premium is 100 bps, an amount based on the assumed level of interest rate volatility and the time to expiration (the next date that liabilities are measured and reported). Given a notional principal of USD497 million, the pension plan pays USD4.97 million (= USD497 million × 0.0100) up front to buy the swaption. (This example neglects that the 3.50% swap has a somewhat higher effective duration and BPV than the 4.16% swap.) Exhibit 21 shows the payoff profile of the receiver swaption.

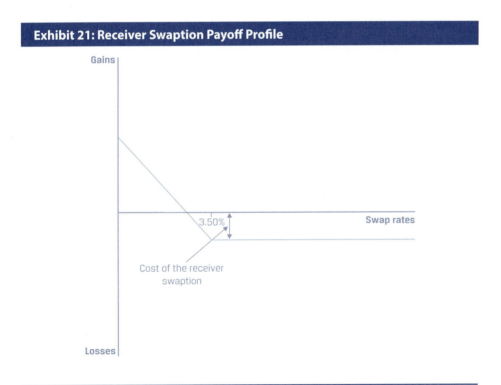

Exhibit 21: Receiver Swaption Payoff Profile

When the expiration date arrives, the plan exercises the swaption if 30-year swap rates are below 3.50%. The plan could "take delivery" of the swap and receive what has become an above-market fixed rate for payment of the three-month MRR. Or the plan could close out the swap with the counterparty to capture the present value of the annuity based on the difference between the contractual fixed rate of 3.50% and the fixed rate in the swap market, multiplied by the notional principal. This gain partially offsets the loss incurred on the higher value for the pension plan liabilities. If 30-year swap rates are equal to or above 3.50% at expiration, the plan lets the swaption expire.

Using a Swaption Collar

Another derivatives overlay is a swaption collar. The plan buys the same receiver swaption, but instead of paying the premium of USD4.97 million in cash, the plan writes a payer swaption. Suppose that a strike rate of 5.00% on the payer swaption generates an upfront premium of 100 bps. Therefore, the combination is a "zero-cost" collar, at least in terms of the initial expense. If 30-year swap rates are below 3.50% at expiration, the purchased receiver swaption is in the money and the option is exercised. If the swap rate is between 3.50% and 5.00%, both swaptions are out of the money. But if the swap rate exceeds 5.00%, the payer swaption is in the money to the counterparty. As the writer of the contract, the pension plan is obligated to receive a fixed rate of only 5.00% when the going market rate is higher. The plan could continue with the swap but, in practice, would more likely seek to close it out by making a payment to the counterparty for the fair value of the contract. Note that potential losses on the receive-fixed swap and swaption collar are *time-deferred* and *rate-contingent* and therefore are uncertain. Exhibit 22 illustrates the payoff profile of the swaption collar.

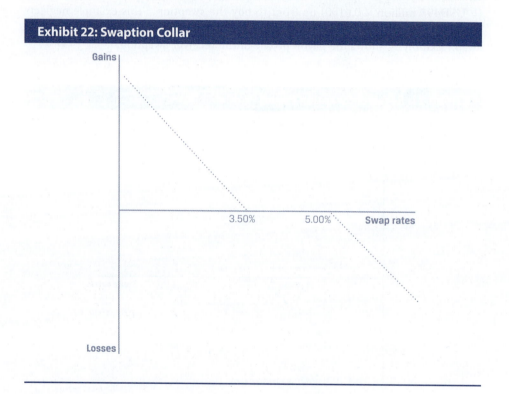

Exhibit 22: Swaption Collar

Selecting a Suitable Hedging Strategy

Hedging decisions involve several factors, including accounting and tax treatment for the derivatives used in the overlay strategy. An important consideration is the various stakeholders' sensitivity to losses on the derivatives. Obviously, the plan manager is a "hero" if yields suddenly go down and if any of the three strategies—enter the receive-fixed swap, buy the receiver swaption, or enter the swaption collar—are undertaken. Note that swap rates do not need to go below 3.50% for the receiver swaption to generate an immediate gain. Its market value would go up if market rates fall (an increase in the value of the option), and it could be sold for more than the purchase price. The problem for the manager, however, occurs if yields suddenly and unexpectedly go up, leading to a significant loss on the hedge. Will being hedged be deemed a managerial mistake by some of the stakeholders?

Example: Defined Benefit Pension Plan

A factor in the choice of derivatives overlay is the plan manager's view on future interest rates, particularly on high-quality corporate bond yields at the time of the next reporting for liabilities. An irony to interest rate risk management is that the view on rates is part of decision making even when uncertainty about future rates is the motive for hedging. Exhibit 23 brings together the payoffs on the three derivatives and the breakeven rates that facilitate the choice of contract.

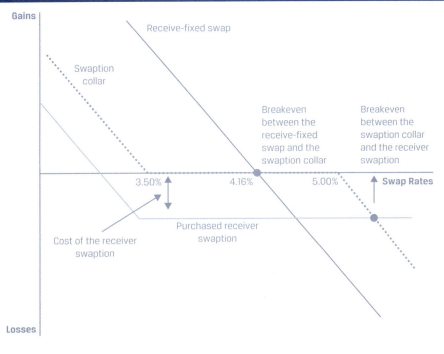

Exhibit 23: Payoffs on Received-Fixed Swap, Receiver Swaption, and Swaption Collar

Consider first the receive-fixed swap payoff. We assume it has a notional principal of USD497 million (a 50% hedging ratio). There are gains (losses) if rates on otherwise comparable 30-year swaps are below (above) 4.16%. The payoff line is not linear as shown in the exhibit. Suppose the swap rate moves down to 4.10%. The gain is the present value of the 30-year annuity of USD149,100 (= [0.0416 − 0.0410] × 0.5 × USD497,000,000) per period, assuming semi-annual payments. If 4.10% is the correct rate for discounting, the gain is about USD5.12 million:

$$\frac{149,100}{\left(1+\frac{0.0410}{2}\right)^1} + \frac{149,100}{\left(1+\frac{0.0410}{2}\right)^2} + \cdots + \frac{149,100}{\left(1+\frac{0.0410}{2}\right)^{60}} = 5,120,670.$$

If the swap rate moves up to 4.22%, the annuity is still USD149,100. But the loss is about USD5.05 million using 4.22% to discount the cash flows.

$$\frac{149,100}{\left(1+\frac{0.0422}{2}\right)^1} + \frac{149,100}{\left(1+\frac{0.0422}{2}\right)^2} + \cdots + \frac{149,100}{\left(1+\frac{0.0422}{2}\right)^{60}} = 5,047,526.$$

The payoffs, including the initial cost, for the purchased 3.50% receiver swaption are shown as the thin line in Exhibit 6. The premium paid at purchase is USD4.97 million, assuming that the quoted price is 100 bps and the notional principal is USD497 million. The dotted line shows the payoffs on the swaption collar. It is composed of the long position in the 3.50% receiver swaption and the short position in the 5.00% payer swaption. There is a gain if the swap rate is below 3.50% and a loss if the rate is above 5.00%.

Decision making is facilitated by breakeven numbers. It is easier to ask "do we expect the rate to be above or below a certain number" than to state a well-articulated probability distribution for the future rate. Exhibit 23 shows two breakeven rates. If the plan manager expects the swap rate to be at or below 4.16%, the receive-fixed swap is preferred. Its gains are higher than the other two derivatives overlays. If the manager expects the swap rate to be above 4.16%, however, the swaption collar is attractive because the swap would be incurring a loss. At some point above 5.00%, the purchased receiver swaption is better because it limits the loss. That breakeven rate can be found by trial-and-error search. The task is to find the swap rate that generates a loss that is more than the USD4.97 million purchase price for the receiver swaption.

Suppose the swap rate goes up to 5.07% on the date that the liabilities are measured and reported. The fair value of the written 5.00% payer swaption starts with the 30-year annuity of USD173,950 [= (0.0507 − 0.0500) × 0.5 × USD497,000,000]. The loss of about USD5.33 million is the present value of that annuity, discounted at 5.07%.

$$\frac{173{,}950}{\left(1+\frac{0.0507}{2}\right)^1} + \frac{173{,}950}{\left(1+\frac{0.0507}{2}\right)^2} + \cdots + \frac{173{,}950}{\left(1+\frac{0.0507}{2}\right)^{60}} = 5{,}333{,}951.$$

Therefore, if the plan manager expects the swap rate to be above 5.07%, the purchased receiver swaption is preferred.

In summary, many decisions go into the LDI strategy for defined benefit pension plans. Given the assumptions that lie behind the calculations of the asset BPV and the liability BPV, including the important choice between the ABO and PBO measure of liabilities, the plan manager faces a significant duration gap. The hedging ratio (the percentage of the duration gap to close) is a key decision that might depend on the held view on future interest rates—in particular, on high-quality corporate bond yields that are used to measure the liabilities. Then, given the determined hedging ratio, the choice of derivatives overlay is made. That decision once again depends on many factors, including the view on future rates.

> **CASE STUDY**
>
> A corporation is concerned about the defined benefit pension plan that it sponsors for its unionized employees. Because of recent declines in corporate bond yields and weak performance in its equity investments, the plan finds itself to be only about 80% funded based on the PBO measure. That fact is raising concerns with its employees as well as with the rating agencies. Currently, the present value of the corporation's retirement obligations is estimated by the plan's actuarial advisers to be about USD1.321 billion using the PBO measure of liabilities. The corporation has no plans to close the defined benefit plan but is concerned about having to report the funding status in its financial statements. The market value of its asset portfolio is USD1.032 billion; the plan is underfunded by USD289 million.
>
> The pension fund's asset allocation is rather aggressive: 70% equity, 10% alternative assets, and 20% fixed income. The fund manager hopes that a recovering equity market will reverse the deficit and ultimately return the plan to a fully funded position. Still, the manager is concerned about tightening corporate spreads as the economy improves. That scenario could lead to lower discount rates that are used to calculate the present value of the liabilities and offset any gains in the stock market. The actuarial advisers to the plan estimate that the effective duration of the liabilities is 9.2, so the BPV is USD1.215 million. The corporate sponsor requires that the manager assume an effective duration of zero on equity and alternative assets. The fixed-income portfolio consists mostly

Example: Defined Benefit Pension Plan

of long-term bonds, including significant holdings of zero-coupon government securities. Its effective duration is estimated to be 25.6. Taken together, the asset BPV is USD528,384. The negative money duration gap is substantial.

The pension plan has hired a qualified professional asset manager (QPAM) to offer advice on derivatives overlay strategies and to execute the contracts with a commercial bank. The QPAM suggests that the pension plan consider the use of interest rate derivatives to partially close the duration gap between its assets and liabilities.

The QPAM has identified three interest rate derivatives strategies that can be executed with the commercial bank. The first is a 30-year, 3.80% receive-fixed swap referencing the three-month MRR. The swap's effective duration is +17.51, and its BPV is 0.1751 per USD100 of notional principal. The second is a receiver swaption having a strike rate of 3.60%. The plan pays a premium of 145 bps upfront to buy the right to enter a 30-year swap as the fixed-rate receiver. The expiration date is set to match the date when the pension plan next reports its funding status. The third is a swaption collar, the combination of buying the 3.60% receiver swaption and writing a 4.25% payer swaption. The premiums on the two swaptions offset, so this is a "zero-cost" collar.

After some discussions with the rates desk at the commercial bank and a conversation with the bank's strategy group, the plan manager instructs the QPAM to select the 3.80% receive-fixed interest rate swap. Moreover, the manager chooses a hedging ratio of 75%.

1. Calculate the notional principal on the interest rate swap to achieve the 75% hedging ratio.

   Solution:

   First calculate the notional principal needed to close the duration gap between assets and liabilities to zero using Equation 4.

   $$\text{Asset BPV} + \left(\text{NP} \times \frac{\text{Swap BPV}}{100}\right) = \text{Liability BPV}$$

   Asset BPV is USD528,384, Swap BPV is 0.1751 per 100 of notional principal, and Liability BPV is USD1.215 million.

   $$528{,}384 + \left(\text{NP} \times \frac{0.1751}{100}\right) = 1{,}215{,}000;$$

   NP = 392,127,927.

   A 100% hedging ratio requires a receive-fixed interest rate swap with a notional principal of about USD392 million. For a hedging ratio of 75%, the notional principal needs to be about USD294 million (= 392 × 0.75).

2. Indicate the plan manager's likely view on future 30-year swap fixed rates given the decision to choose the swap rather than the purchased receiver swaption or the swaption collar.

   Solution:

   The plan manager's likely view is that the 30-year swap rate will be less than 3.80%. Then the gains on the receive-fixed interest rate swap exceed those on the swaption collar (i.e., not profitable until the swap rate falls below 3.60%) and on the purchased receiver swaption (i.e., not profitable until the swap rate falls sufficiently below 3.60% to recover the premium paid). Note that if the 30-year swap rate exceeds 3.80%, then the receive-fixed interest rate swap will begin losing immediately. Losses on the swaption collar will not begin until the rate rises above 4.25%, while losses on the purchased

> receiver swaption (at any swap rate above 3.60%) are limited to the premium paid.
>
> Notice that this rate view is also consistent with the concern about lower corporate bond yields and the relatively high hedging ratio.

5. RISKS IN LIABILITY-DRIVEN INVESTING

> explain risks associated with managing a portfolio against a liability structure

We have mentioned in previous sections some of the risks to LDI strategies for single and multiple liabilities. In this section, we review those risks and introduce some new ones. The essential relationship for full interest rate hedging is summarized in this expression:

$$\text{Asset BPV} \times \Delta\text{Asset yields} + \text{Hedge BPV} \times \Delta\text{Hedge yields} \approx \text{Liability BPV} \times \Delta\text{Liability yields}. \tag{6}$$

ΔAsset yields, ΔHedge yields, and ΔLiability yields are measured in basis points. This equation describes an immunization strategy (a hedging ratio of 100%) whereby the intent is to match the changes in market value on each side of the balance sheet when yields change. Doing so entails matching the money duration of assets and liabilities. We know, however, that entities also choose to partially hedge interest rate risk by selecting a hedging ratio less than 100%. In any case, Equation 6 serves to indicate the source of the risks to LDI. The "approximately equals" sign (≈) in the equation results from ignoring higher-order terms, such as convexity.

Model Risk in Liability-Driven Investing

We encounter model risk in financial modeling whenever assumptions are made about future events and approximations are used to measure key parameters. The risk is that those assumptions turn out to be wrong and the approximations are inaccurate. For example, in our earlier defined benefit pension plan example, we assumed that the effective durations for investments in equity and alternative assets are zero. That assumption introduces the risk that asset BPV is mis-measured if, in fact, those market values change as the yield curve shifts. The modeling problem is that the effect on those asset classes is not predictable or stable because it depends on the reason for the change in nominal interest rates. Unlike fixed-income bonds, an increase in expected inflation can have a very different effect on equity and alternative asset valuations than an increase in the real rate.

Measurement error for asset BPV can even arise in the classic immunization strategy for Type I cash flows, which have set amounts and dates. In practice, it is common to approximate the asset portfolio duration using the weighted average of the individual durations for the component bonds. A better approach to achieve immunization, however, uses the cash flow yield to discount the future coupon and principal payments. This error is minimized when the underlying yield curve is flat or when future cash flows are concentrated in the flattest segment of the curve.

A similar problem arises in measuring hedge BPV. When we illustrated the use of derivatives overlays to immunize, we used a common approximation for the futures BPV. Equation 4 estimates it to be the BPV for the qualifying CTD security divided by its conversion factor. A more developed calculation involving short-term rates and accrued interest, however, could change the number of contracts needed to hedge the interest rate risk. Although the error introduced by using an approximation might not be large, it still can be a source of underperformance in the hedging strategy.

Model risk in obtaining a measure of liability BPV is evident in the earlier defined benefit pension plan example. Measuring a defined benefit pension plan's liability is clearly a difficult financial modeling problem. Even the simple models for the two liability measures (the ABO and PBO) necessarily require many assumptions about the future, including the dates when employees retire and their wage levels at those times. The difficulty in projecting life spans of retirees covered by the pension plan leads to longevity risk. The risk is the sponsor has not provided sufficient assets to make the longer-than-expected payout stream. More, and harder-to-make, assumptions are needed to deal with Type IV liabilities and lead to greater uncertainty regarding the models' outputs.

Implicit in Equation 6 is the assumption that all yields change by the same number of basis points—that is, ΔAsset Yields, ΔHedge Yields, and ΔLiability Yields are equal. That is a strong assumption—and a source of risk—if the fixed-income assets, the derivatives, and the liabilities are positioned at varying points along the benchmark bond yield curve and at varying spreads to that curve. Previously, when we discussed immunizing the interest rate risk on a single liability by structuring and managing a portfolio of fixed-income bonds, we pointed out that a parallel yield curve shift is a sufficient but not necessary condition to achieve the desired outcome. Non-parallel shifts and twists to the yield curve can result in changes to the cash flow yield on the immunizing portfolio that do not match the change in the yield on the zero-coupon bond that provides perfect immunization. Minimizing dispersion of the cash flows in the asset portfolio mitigates this risk.

Generally, the framework for thinking about interest rate risk rests on changes in the benchmark bond yield curve, which usually is the yield curve for government bonds. In practice, however, ΔAsset yield and ΔLiability yield often refer to various classes of corporate bonds. In the pension fund example, the fund holds a portfolio of fixed-income bonds that tracks a well-diversified index of corporate bonds that may include non-investment-grade securities. The present value of retirement benefits, however, depends on yields on high-quality corporate bonds. Therefore, a risk is that the respective spreads on the broad index and the high-quality sector do not move in unison with a shift in the government bond yield curve. A similar spread risk is present in the earlier example of immunizing multiple Type I liabilities. The difference is that the assets in that example are of higher quality than the liabilities.

Spread Risk in Liability-Driven Investing

Spread risk also is apparent in the derivatives overlay LDI strategies. We illustrated how futures contracts can be used to hedge the interest rate risk of the multiple liabilities, either passively or contingently. In particular, the futures contracts are on 10-year US Treasury notes, whereas the liabilities are corporate obligations. Movements in the corporate/Treasury yield spread introduce risk to the hedging strategy. Usually, yields on high-quality corporate bonds are less volatile than on more-liquid Treasuries. Government bonds are used in a wide variety of hedging as well as speculative trading strategies by institutional investors. Also, inflows of international funds typically are placed in government bonds, at least until they are allocated to other asset classes. Those factors lead to greater volatility in Treasury yields than comparable-maturity corporate bonds.

Another source of spread risk is the use of interest rate swap overlays. We showed how receive-fixed swaps, purchased receiver swaptions, and swaption collars can reduce the duration gap between pension plan assets and liabilities. In that example,

ΔHedge yield refers to fixed rates on interest rate swaps referencing the three-month MRR. The spread risk is between high-quality corporate bond yields and swap rates. Typically, there is less volatility in the corporate/swap spread than in the corporate/Treasury spread because both the MRR and corporate bond yields contain credit risk vis-à-vis Treasuries. Therefore, one of the usual advantages to hedging corporate bond risk with interest rate swaps is that those derivatives pose less spread risk than Treasury futures contracts.

Counterparty Credit Risk

Counterparty credit risk is a concern if the interest rate swap overlays are uncollateralized, as was common before the 2008–2009 global financial crisis. Suppose that the interest rate swap portrayed in Exhibit 19 does not have a collateral agreement, or Credit Support Annex (CSA), to the standard International Swaps and Derivatives Association (ISDA) contract. The credit risk facing the pension plan is that the swap dealer defaults at a time when the replacement swap fixed rate is below 4.16%. In the same manner, the credit risk facing the dealer is that the pension plan defaults at the time when the market rate on a comparable swap is above 4.16%. Therefore, credit risk entails the joint probability of default by the counterparties and movement in market rates that results in the swap being valued as an asset.

Since the 2008–2009 global financial crisis, over-the-counter derivatives increasingly include a CSA to the ISDA contract to mitigate counterparty credit risk. Collateral provisions vary. A typical CSA calls for a zero threshold, meaning that only the counterparty for which the swap has negative market value posts collateral, which usually is cash but can be highly marketable securities. The CSA can be one way (only the "weaker" counterparty needs to post collateral when the swap has negative market value from its perspective) or two way (either counterparty is obligated to post collateral when the swap has negative market value). The threshold could be positive, meaning that the swap must have a certain negative value before collateral needs to be exchanged. Another possibility is that one or both counterparties are required to post a certain amount of collateral, called an independent amount, even if the swap has zero or positive value. This provision makes the CSA similar to the use of margin accounts with exchange-traded futures contracts.

Collateralization on derivatives used in an LDI strategy introduces a new risk factor—the risk that available collateral becomes exhausted. That risk is particularly important for the pension plan example, in which the plan would need to enter a sizable derivatives overlay to even use a 50% hedging ratio, let alone to fully hedge the interest rate risk. That is because the duration gap between assets and liabilities is often large, especially for plans having a significant equity allocation. Therefore, the probability of exhausting collateral is a factor in determining the hedging ratio and the permissible range in the ratio if strategic hedging is allowed.

The same concern about cash management and collateral availability arises with the use of exchange-traded futures contracts. These contracts entail daily mark-to-market valuation and settlement into a margin account. This process requires daily oversight because cash moves into or out of the margin account at the close of each trading day. In contrast, the CSA on a collateralized swap agreement typically allows the party a few days to post additional cash or marketable securities. Also, there usually is a *minimum transfer amount* to mitigate the transaction costs for small inconsequential payments.

Asset Liquidity Risk

Asset liquidity becomes a risk factor in strategies that combine active investing to the otherwise passive fixed-income portfolios. This risk is particularly important with contingent immunization. In the presence of a surplus above a sufficient threshold, the manager may increase portfolio risk by using active management. But if losses reduce the surplus to some minimum amount, the positions need to be adjusted to revert to a passive duration-matching fixed-income portfolio of high-quality bonds. Distressed assets that become hard to value, such as tranches of subprime mortgage-backed securities, also become illiquid during financial crises.

In summary, an LDI manager has a fundamental choice between managing interest rate risk with asset allocation and with derivatives overlays. As with all financial management decisions, the choice depends on a thorough evaluation of risk and return trade-offs. In some circumstances, derivatives might be deemed too expensive or risky, particularly regarding available collateral and cash holdings. Then the manager might choose to increase holdings of long-term, high-quality bonds that have high duration statistics. The growth of government zero-coupon bonds, such as US Treasury STRIPS (Separate Trading of Registered Interest and Principal of Securities), facilitates that asset reallocation process.

CASE STUDY

A derivatives consultant, a former head of interest rate swaps trading at a major London bank, is asked by a Spanish corporation to devise an overlay strategy to "effectively defease" a large debt liability. That means that there are dedicated assets to retire the debt even if both assets and the liability remain on the balance sheet. The corporation currently has enough euro-denominated cash assets to retire the bonds, but its bank advises that acquiring the securities via a tender offer at this time will be prohibitively expensive.

The 10-year fixed-rate bonds are callable at par value in three years. This is a one-time call option. If the issuer does not exercise the option, the bonds are then non-callable for the remaining time to maturity. The corporation's CFO anticipates higher benchmark interest rates in the coming years. Therefore, the strategy of investing the available funds for three years and then calling the debt is questionable because the embedded call option might be "out of the money" when the call date arrives. Moreover, it is likely that the cost to buy the bonds on the open market at that time will still be prohibitive.

The corporation has considered a cash flow matching approach by buying a corporate bond having the same credit rating and a call structure (call date and call price) close to the corporation's own debt liability. However, the bank working with the CFO has been unable to identify an acceptable bond. Instead, the bank suggests that the corporation buy a 10-year non-callable, fixed-rate corporate bond and use a swaption to mimic the characteristics of the embedded call option. The idea is to transform the callable bond (the liability) into a non-callable security synthetically using the swaption. Then the newly purchased non-callable bond "effectively" defeases the transformed "non-callable" debt liability.

To confirm the bank's recommendation for the derivatives overlay, the CFO turns to the derivatives consultant, asking if the corporation should (1) buy a payer swaption, (2) buy a receiver swaption, (3) write a payer swaption, or (4) write a receiver swaption. The time frames for the swaptions correspond to the embedded call option. They are "3y7y" contracts, an option to enter a seven-year interest rate swap in three years. The CFO also asks the consultant about the risks to the recommended swaption position.

1. Indicate the swaption position that the derivatives consultant should recommend to the corporation.

   Solution:

   The derivatives consultant should recommend that the corporation choose the fourth option and write a receiver swaption—that is, an option that gives the swaption buyer the right to enter into a swap to receive fixed and pay floating. When the corporation issued the callable bond, it effectively bought the call option, giving the corporation the flexibility to refinance at a lower cost of borrowed funds if benchmark rates and/or the corporation's credit spread narrows. Writing the receiver swaption "sells" that call option, and the corporation captures the value of the embedded call option by means of the premium received. Suppose that market rates in three years are higher than the strike rate on the swaption and the yield on the debt security. Then both options—the embedded call option in the bond liability, as well as the swaption—expire out of the money. The asset and liability both have seven years until maturity and are non-callable. Suppose instead that market rates fall and bond prices go up. Both options are now in the money. The corporation sells the seven-year bonds (the assets) and uses the proceeds to call the debt liabilities at par value. The gain on that transaction offsets the loss on closing out the swaption with the counterparty.

2. Indicate the risks in using the derivatives overlay.

Solution:

Potential risks to using swaptions include (1) credit risk if the swaption is not collateralized, (2) "collateral exhaustion risk" if it is collateralized, and (3) spread risk between swap fixed rates and the corporation's cost of funds. First, suppose the receiver swaption is not collateralized. In general, the credit risk on an option is unilateral, meaning that the buyer bears the credit risk of the writer. That unilateral risk assumes the premium is paid in full upon entering the contract; in other words, the buyer has met their entire obligation. Therefore, the corporation as the swaption writer would have no additional credit exposure to the buyer. Second, assume that the swaption is collateralized. As the writer of the option, the corporation would need to regularly post cash collateral or marketable securities with either the counterparty or a third-party clearinghouse. The risk is that the corporation exhausts its available cash or holdings of marketable securities and cannot maintain the hedge. Spread risk arises because the value of the embedded call option in three years depends on the corporation's cost of funds at that time, including its credit risk. The value of the swaption depends only on seven-year swap fixed rates at that time. In particular, the risk is that the corporate/swap spread widens when benchmark rates are low and both options can be exercised. If the corporate spread over the benchmark rate goes up, the gain in the embedded call option is reduced. If the swap spread over the same benchmark rate goes down, the loss on the swaption increases. Fortunately, corporate and swap spreads over benchmark rates are usually positively correlated, but still the risk of an unexpected change in the spread should be identified.

6. BOND INDEXES

discuss bond indexes and the challenges of managing a fixed-income portfolio to mimic the characteristics of a bond index

Though the need to offset liabilities through immunization requires a specific bond portfolio, many investors seek a broader exposure to the fixed-income universe. These investors may be attracted to the risk versus return characteristics available in bond markets, or they may seek to allocate a portion of their investable assets to fixed income as part of a well-diversified multi-asset portfolio. In either case, an investment strategy based on a bond market index offers an investor the ability to gain broad exposure to the fixed-income universe. Index-based investments generally offer investors the possibility of greater diversification and lower fees as well as avoiding the downside risk from seeking positive excess returns over time from active management.

An investor seeking to offset a specific liability through immunization gauges the success of his strategy based on how closely the chosen bonds offset the future liability or liabilities under different interest rate scenarios. In contrast, an investor seeking to match the returns of a bond market index will gauge an investment strategy's success in terms of how closely the chosen market portfolio mirrors the return of the underlying bond market index. Deviation of returns on the selected portfolio from bond market index returns are referred to as **tracking risk** or **tracking error**. Investors use several methods to match an underlying market index (Volpert 2012). The first of these is **pure indexing**, in which the investor aims to replicate an existing market index by purchasing all of the constituent securities in the index to minimize tracking risk. The purchase of all securities within an index is known as the **full replication approach**. In **enhanced indexing strategy**, the investor purchases fewer securities than the full set of index constituents but matches primary risk factors (discussed later) reflected in the index. This strategy aims to replicate the index performance more efficiently than the full replication of a pure indexing approach by minimizing transaction costs of acquiring a representative portfolio and minimizing problems associated with bonds' unique characteristics, as described further below.

Active management involves taking positions in primary risk factors that deviate from those of the index to generate excess return.

Casual financial market observers usually refer to an equity market index to gauge overall financial market sentiment. Examples often consist of a small set of underlying securities, such as the Dow Jones Industrial Average of 30 US stocks, the CAC 40 traded on Euronext in Paris, or the 50 constituent companies in the Hang Seng Index, which represent more than half the market capitalization of the Hong Kong, SAR stock market. When bond markets are mentioned at all, the price and yield of the most recently issued benchmark government bond is typically referenced rather than a bond market index. This contrast reflects the unwieldy nature of bond markets for both the average investor and financial professionals alike.

Although rarely highlighted in the financial press, investments based on bond market indexes form a very substantial proportion of financial assets held by investors. Fixed-income markets have unique characteristics that make them difficult to track, and investors therefore face significant challenges in replicating a bond market index. These challenges include

- the size and breadth of bond markets,
- the wide array of fixed-income security characteristics,
- unique issuance and trading patterns of bonds versus other securities, and
- the effect of these patterns on index composition and construction, pricing, and valuation.

We will tackle each of these issues and their implications for fixed-income investors.

Size and Breadth of the Fixed-Income Universe

Fixed-income markets are much larger and broader than equity markets, and the number of fixed-income securities outstanding is vastly larger as reflected in broad market indexes. For instance, the MSCI World Index, capturing equities in 23 developed market countries and 85% of the available market capitalization in each market, consists of about 1,600 securities, whereas the Bloomberg Barclays Global Aggregate Index, covering global investment-grade debt from 24 local currency markets, consists of more than 16,000 securities. Those fixed-income issuers represent a much wider range of borrowers than the relatively narrow universe of companies issuing equity securities. For example, the oldest and most widely recognized US bond market index, the Bloomberg Barclays US Aggregate Index (one of four regional aggregate benchmarks that constitute the Bloomberg Barclays Global Aggregate Index), includes US Treasuries, government agency securities, corporate bonds, mortgage-backed securities, asset-backed securities, and commercial mortgage-backed securities. Although the large number of index constituents provides a means of risk diversification, in practice it is neither feasible nor cost-effective for investors to pursue a full replication approach with a broad fixed-income market index.

Array of Characteristics

Different maturities, ratings, call/put features, and varying levels of security and subordination give rise to a much wider array of public and private bonds available to investors. Exhibit 24 illustrates the number of publicly traded fixed-income and equity securities outstanding for a select group of major global issuers.

Exhibit 24: Debt and Equity Securities Outstanding for Select Issuers

Issuer	Fixed-Income Securities	Common Equity Securities	Preferred Equity Securities
Royal Dutch Shell PLC	57	1	0
BHP Billiton Limited	22	1	0
Johnson & Johnson	37	1	0
Ford Motor Company	104	2	2

Source: Bloomberg as of 14 October 2020. Bonds with more than $50 million outstanding included.

As of October 2020, Royal Dutch Shell had 57 bonds outstanding across four currencies, some of which were both fixed and floating rate, with a range of maturities from under a year to bonds maturing in 2052. The existence of many debt securities for a particular issuer suggests that many near substitutes may exist for an investor seeking to pursue an enhanced index strategy. That said, the relative liquidity and performance characteristics of those bonds may differ greatly depending on how recently the bond was issued and how close its coupon is to the yield currently required to price the bond at par.

Unique Issuance and Trading Patterns

Unlike equity securities, which trade primarily over an exchange, fixed-income markets are largely over-the-counter markets that rely on broker/dealers as principals to trade in these securities using a quote-based execution process rather than the order-based trading systems common in equity markets. The rising cost of maintaining risk-weighted assets on dealer balance sheets because of Basel III capital requirements has had an adverse effect on fixed-income trading and liquidity. Broker/dealers have reduced bond inventories because of higher capital costs. With lower trading inventories, dealers have both a limited appetite to facilitate trading at narrow bid–offer spreads and are less willing to support larger "block" trades, preferring execution in smaller trade sizes. Finally, a significant decline in proprietary trading among dealers has had a greater pricing effect on less liquid or "off-the-run" bonds. Although many see these structural changes in fixed-income trading acting as a catalyst for more electronic trading, this trend will likely be most significant for the most liquid fixed-income securities in developed markets, with a more gradual effect on less frequently traded fixed-income securities worldwide. Fixed-income trading in many markets is difficult to track. In some markets, regulators developed systems that facilitate mandatory reporting of over-the-counter transactions in eligible fixed-income securities, such as the US Trade Reporting and Compliance Engine (TRACE) system. All broker/dealers that are Financial Industry Regulatory Authority (FINRA) member firms must report corporate bond transactions within 15 minutes of occurrence. It is important to note the distinct nature of fixed-income trading versus equities. The vast majority of fixed-income securities either do not trade at all or trade only a few times during the year. Only a small fraction trade every business day, according to MarketAxess, a leading electronic trading provider. It is also important to note that the average trade size in dollar terms in the US investment-grade bond market is roughly 70 times the size of the average stock trade.

The illiquid nature of most fixed-income instruments gives rise to pricing and valuation challenges for asset managers. For fixed-income instruments that are not actively traded and therefore do not have an observable price, it is common to use an estimation process known as **matrix pricing** or **evaluated pricing**. Matrix pricing makes use of observable liquid benchmark yields, such as Treasuries of similar maturity and duration, as well as the benchmark spreads of bonds with comparable times to maturity, credit quality, and sector or security type in order to estimate the current market yield and price. In practice, asset managers will typically outsource this function to a global custodian or external vendor. This estimation analysis is another potential source of variation between index performance and portfolio returns.

The complexity of trading and valuing individual fixed-income securities further underscores the challenges associated with managing an index-based bond portfolio. Fixed-income indexes change frequently as a result of both new debt issuance and the maturity of outstanding bonds. Bond index eligibility is also affected by changes in ratings and bond callability. As a result, rebalancing of bond market indexes usually occurs monthly rather than semi-annually or annually as it does for equity indexes. Fixed-income investors pursuing a pure indexing strategy therefore must also incur greater transaction costs associated with maintaining a bond portfolio consistent with the index.

Primary Risk Factors

Given the significant hurdles involved in bond index matching, asset managers typically seek to target the primary risk factors present in a fixed-income index through a diversified portfolio. Volpert (2012) summarized these primary indexing risk factors as follows:

- **Portfolio modified adjusted duration.** Effective duration, or the sensitivity of a bond's price to a change in a benchmark yield curve, is an important primary factor as a first approximation of an index's exposure to interest rate changes. It is important to factor in option-adjusted duration so that the analysis reflects securities with embedded call risk. Larger rate moves should incorporate the second-order convexity adjustment to increase accuracy.

- **Key rate duration.** Although effective duration may be a sufficient measure for small rate changes and parallel yield curve shifts, the **key rate duration** considers rate changes in a specific maturity along the yield curve while holding the remaining rates constant. This measure of duration gauges the index's sensitivity to non-parallel yield curve shifts. By effectively matching the key rate durations between the portfolio and the underlying index, a manager can significantly reduce the portfolio's exposure to changes in the yield curve.

- **Percent in sector and quality.** Index yield is most effectively matched by targeting the same percentage weights across fixed-income sectors and credit quality, assuming that maturity parameters have also been met.

- **Sector and quality spread duration contribution.** The portfolio manager can minimize deviations from the benchmark by matching the amounts of index duration associated with the respective issuer sectors and quality categories. The former refers to the issuer type and/or industry segment of the bond issuer. In the case of the latter, the risk that a bond's price will change in response to an idiosyncratic rate move rather than an overall market yield change is known as spread risk. For non-government fixed-income securities, we separate the yield to maturity into a benchmark yield (typically the most recently issued or on-the-run government bond with the closest time to maturity) and a spread reflecting the difference between the benchmark yield and the security-specific yield. **Spread duration** refers to the change in a non-Treasury security's price given a widening or narrowing of the spread compared with the benchmark. Matching the relative quality between the portfolio and the fixed-income index will minimize this risk.

- **Sector/coupon/maturity call weights.** Asset managers face several challenges in matching price/yield sensitivity beyond the use of effective duration. Although convexity is a useful second-order condition that should be used to improve this approximation, the negative convexity of callable bonds may distort the call exposure of an index and lead to costly rebalancing when rates shift. As a result, managers should seek to match the sector, coupon, and maturity weights of callable bonds by sector. Doing so is particularly important in the mortgage sector because of the refinancing of high-coupon securities with lower-coupon bonds.

- **Issuer exposure.** Concentration of issuers within a portfolio exposes the asset manager to issuer-specific event risk. The manager should therefore seek to match the portfolio duration effect from holdings in each issuer.

Another method used to address a portfolio's sensitivity to rate changes along the yield curve is referred to as the **present value of distribution of cash flows methodology**. This approach seeks to approximate and match the yield curve risk of an index over discrete time periods referred to as cash flow vertices, and it involves several steps, as follows:

1. The manager divides the cash flows for each non-callable security in the index into discrete semi-annual periods, aggregates them, and then adds the cash flows for callable securities in the index based on the probability of call for each given period.

2. The present value of aggregated cash flows for each semi-annual period is computed, with the total present value of all such aggregated cash flows equal to the index's present value. The percentage of the present value of each cash flow vertex is calculated.

3. The time period is then multiplied by the vertex's proportionate share of the index. (The first cash flow at 6 months is equal to 1; the second cash flow at 12 months is equal to 2; the third cash flow at 18 months is equal to 3, etc.) Because each cash flow represents an effective zero-coupon payment in the corresponding period, the time period reflects the duration of the cash flow. For example, if the third vertex represents 3% of all cash flows, the third period's contribution to duration might be 1.5 years × 3.0%, or 0.045.

4. Finally, each period's contribution to duration is added to arrive at a total representing the bond index's duration. The portfolio being managed will be largely protected from deviations from the benchmark associated with yield curve changes by matching the percentage of the portfolio's present value that comes due at specific points in time with that of the index.

The goal of matching these primary indexing risk factors is to minimize tracking error, the standard deviation of a portfolio's active return for a given period, whereby active return is defined as follows:

Active return = Portfolio return − Benchmark index return.

If we assume that returns are normally distributed around the mean, then from a statistical perspective, 68% of those returns will lie within one standard deviation of the mean. Therefore, if a fund's tracking error is 50 bps, then for approximately two-thirds of the time period observations, we would expect the fund's return to be less than 50 bps above or below the index's return.

CASE STUDY

Cindy Cheng, a portfolio manager based in Hong Kong SAR, has established the All Asia Dragon Fund, a fixed-income fund designed to outperform the Markit iBoxx Asian Local Bond Index (ALBI). The ALBI tracks the total return performance of liquid bonds denominated in local currencies in the following markets: Chinese mainland, Hong Kong SAR, India, Indonesia, South Korea, Malaysia, the Philippines, Singapore, the Taiwan region, and Thailand. The index includes both government and non-government bond issues, with constituent selection criteria by government as well as weights designed to balance the desire for liquidity and stability ("Markit iBoxx ALBI Index Guide," January 2016, Markit Ltd).

Individual bond weightings in the index are based on market capitalization, and market weights, reviewed annually, are designed to reflect the investability of developing Asian local currency bonds available to international investors. These weights are driven by local market size and market capitalization, secondary bond market liquidity, accessibility to foreign investors, and development of infrastructure that supports fixed-income investment and trading, such as credit ratings, yield curves, and derivatives products.

Given the large number of bonds in the index, Cheng uses a representative sample of the bonds to construct the fund. She chooses bonds so that the fund's duration, market weights, and sector/quality percentage weights closely match the ALBI. Given the complexity of managing bond investments in these local markets, Cheng is targeting a 1.25% tracking error for the fund.

1. Interpret Cheng's tracking error target for the All Asia Dragon Fund.

   Solution:

   The target tracking error of 1.25% means that assuming normally distributed returns, in 68% or two-thirds of time periods, the All Asia Dragon Fund should have a return that is within 1.25% of the ALBI.

2. One of Cheng's largest institutional investors has encouraged her to reduce tracking error. Suggest steps Cheng could take to minimize this risk in the fund.

   Solution:

   Cheng could further reduce tracking error beyond her choice of duration, market, and sector/quality weightings to mirror the index by using the present value of distribution of cash flows methodology outlined earlier. By doing so, she can better align the contribution to portfolio duration that comes from each market, sector, and issuer type based on credit quality.

   Cheng should consider matching the amount of index duration that comes from each sector, as well as matching the amount of index duration that comes from various quality categories across government and non-government bonds, to minimize tracking error.

   Finally, Cheng should evaluate the portfolio duration coming from each issuer to minimize event risk. Again, this evaluation should occur on a duration basis rather than as a percentage of market value to quantify the exposure more accurately versus the benchmark ALBI.

7. ALTERNATIVE METHODS FOR ESTABLISHING PASSIVE BOND MARKET EXPOSURE

> compare alternative methods for establishing bond market exposure passively

Why is passive bond market exposure attractive for investors? A **passive investment** in the fixed-income market may be defined as one that seeks to mimic the prevailing characteristics of the overall investments available in terms of credit quality, type of borrower, maturity, and duration rather than express a specific market view. This approach is consistent with the efficient markets hypothesis in that the portfolio manager seeks to simply replicate broader fixed-income market performance rather than outperform the market. Stated differently, establishing passive bond market exposure does not require the in-depth economic, market, or security analysis necessary to achieve an above-market return, nor does it require the high trading frequency of active management, which should lead to lower costs for managing and servicing a portfolio. Finally, the stated goal of matching the performance of a broad-based bond index is consistent with the highest degree of portfolio diversification.

Several methods exist for establishing a passive bond market exposure. In what follows, we will explore both full index replication as well as an enhanced indexing strategy and compare the risks, costs, and relative liquidity of these strategies when applied to the bond market.

Full Replication

Bond market index replication is the most straightforward strategy that a manager can use to mimic index performance. Use of full replication reflects the belief or expectation that (i) an active manager cannot consistently outperform the index on a risk-adjusted basis, (ii) the investor cannot identify a skilled manager in advance, or (iii) the investor is not prepared to go through periods of underperformance. Initial index replication does not require manager analysis but rather involves sourcing a wide range of securities in exact proportion to the index, many of which may be thinly traded. The manager's ongoing task under full replication is to purchase or sell bonds when there are changes to the index in addition to managing inflows and outflows for a specific fund. For example, the manager may have to sell when a security no longer meets the index criteria, such as when a security either matures or is downgraded. For the Bloomberg Barclays US Aggregate Bond Index, a fixed-income security becomes ineligible when it either has a maturity of less than one year or is downgraded below an average minimum investment-grade rating. On the other hand, managers must purchase newly issued securities that meet index criteria to maintain full replication, which, depending on the index, may occur quite frequently. Rolling bond maturities, as well as frequent new issuance eligible for inclusion in the index, drive a monthly rebalancing for most fixed-income indexes. The number of purchases and sales required to maintain an exact proportional allocation would be very significant for most bond indexes. As a result, although the large number of index constituents may well provide the best means of risk diversification, in practice it is neither feasible nor cost-effective for investors to pursue full replication for broad-based fixed-income indexes. It is impractical for all but the most narrow indexes. Investors that wish to have exposure to an index would in practice rely on one of many ETFs that exist in this space.

Enhanced Indexing

Many limitations of the full replication approach are addressed by an enhanced indexing strategy. This approach's goal is to mirror the most important index characteristics and still closely track index performance over time while purchasing fewer securities. This general approach is referred to as a **stratified sampling** or **cell approach** to indexing. First, each cell or significant index portfolio characteristic is identified and mapped to the current index. Second, the fixed-income portfolio manager identifies a subset of bonds or bond-linked exposures, such as derivatives, with characteristics that correspond to the index. Finally, the positions in each cell are adjusted over time given changes to the underlying index versus existing portfolio positions. For example, say a fixed-income index contains 1,000 fixed-income securities, 10% of which are AAA rated. The portfolio manager might choose 5–10 AAA rated securities within a cell to mimic the performance of the AAA rated bonds within the index.

Enhanced indexing is also of critical importance to investors who consider environmental, social, or other factors when selecting a fixed-income portfolio. Additional categories include sustainability, which includes companies addressing their ESG risks, and green bonds, which fund projects with direct environmental benefits. There are two main components to incorporating ESG factors in an index. First, a business involvement screen excludes issuers involved in business lines or such activities as alcohol, gambling, tobacco, adult entertainment, nuclear power, and firearms. Second, an ESG rating, provided by one of numerous third-party companies, is applied. MSCI, one such company, provides ratings on an "AAA to CCC" scale using a rules-based methodology according to the companies' exposure to ESG risks and how well they are managed relative to peers. When building a sustainable index, for example, Bloomberg will apply such rules as those previously described and then further filter the constituents for business involvement and an MSCI minimum rating requirement of BBB. Given the proliferation of ESG data providers, there are differences across methodologies and ratings. Consider also that the pillar of ESG that may be most important to an investor may not have the same emphasis in the rating criteria used by the index provider.

Enhancement Strategies

Volpert (2012) outlines a number of enhancement strategies available to portfolio managers seeking to reduce the component of tracking error associated with the expenses and transaction costs of portfolio management as follows:

- **Lower cost enhancements.** The most obvious enhancement is in the area of cost reduction, whether this involves minimizing fund expenses or introducing a more competitive trading process to reduce the bid–offer cost of trading.
- **Issue selection enhancements.** The use of bond valuation models to identify specific issues that are undervalued or "cheap" to their implied value provides another opportunity to enhance return.
- **Yield curve enhancements.** The use of analytical models to gauge and calculate relative value across the term structure of interest rates allows managers to develop strategies to both overweight maturities that are considered undervalued and underweight those that appear to be richly priced.
- **Sector/quality enhancements.** This strategy involves overweighting specific bond and credit sectors across the business cycle to enhance returns. Other sectors are underweighted as a result. This approach may tilt exposure toward corporates given a greater yield spread per unit of duration exposure or shorter maturities, or it may over- or underweight specific sectors or qualities based on analysis of the business cycle.

For example, a manager may increase her allocation to Treasuries over corporates when significant spread widening is anticipated or reverse this allocation if spread narrowing is deemed more likely.

- **Call exposure enhancements.** Because effective duration is a sufficient risk measure only for relatively small rate changes, anticipated larger yield changes may affect bond performance significantly, especially when a bond shifts from trading to maturity to trading to an earlier call date. Large, expected yield changes increase the value of call protection, and any significant differences from index exposure should incorporate potentially large tracking risk implications, as well as the implicit market view that this difference implies. For example, an anticipated drop in yields might cause a callable bond to shift from being priced on a yield-to-maturity basis to a yield-to-call basis. Callable fixed-income securities (priced on a yield-to-call basis) trading above par tend to be less price sensitive for a given effective duration than those priced on a yield-to-maturity basis, suggesting a manager should use metrics other than effective duration in this case when changing exposure.

The stratified sampling approach provides an asset manager the ability to optimize portfolio performance across these characteristics with fewer securities than would be required through full index replication. By matching portfolio performance as closely as possible, investment managers also seek to minimize tracking error, limit the need to purchase or sell thinly traded securities, and/or frequently rebalance the portfolio as would be required when precisely matching the index.

Alternative Methods for Establishing Passive Bond Market Exposure

> **CASE STUDY**
>
> Adelaide Super, a superannuation fund, offers a range of fixed interest (or fixed-income) investment choices to its members. Superannuation funds are Australian government-supported arrangements for Australian workers to save for retirement, which combine a government-mandated minimum percentage of wages contributed by employers with a voluntary employee contribution that offers tax benefits. Superannuation plans are similar to defined contribution plans common in the United States, Europe, and Asia.
>
> Three of the bond fund choices Adelaide Super offers are as follows:
>
> - **Dundee Australian Fixed-Income Fund.** The investment objective is to outperform the Bloomberg AusBond Composite Index in the medium to long term. The index includes investment-grade fixed-interest bonds with a minimum of one month to maturity issued in the Australian debt market under Australian law, including the government, semi-government, credit, and supranational/sovereign sectors. The index includes AUD-denominated bonds only. The investment strategy is to match index duration but add value through fundamental and model-driven return strategies.
>
> - **Newcastleton Australian Bond Fund.** The fund aims to outperform the Bloomberg AusBond Composite Index over any three-year rolling period, before fees, expenses, and taxes, and uses multiple strategies, such as duration, curve positioning, and credit and sector rotation rather than one strategy, allowing the fund to take advantage of opportunities across fixed-income markets under all market conditions.
>
> - **Paisley Fixed-Interest Fund.** The fund aims to provide investment returns after fees in excess of the fund's benchmark, which is the Bloomberg AusBond Bank Bill Index and the Bloomberg AusBond Composite Index (equally weighted) by investing in a diversified portfolio of Australian income-producing assets. Paisley seeks to minimize transaction costs via a buy-and-hold strategy, as opposed to active management. The AusBond Bank Bill Index is based on the bank bill market, which is the short-term market (90 days or less) in which Australian banks borrow from and lend to one another via bank bills.
>
> 1. Rank the three fixed-income funds in order of risk profile and suggest a typical employee for whom this might be a suitable investment.
>
> **Solution:**
>
> The Paisley Fixed-Interest Fund represents the lowest risk of the three fund choices, given both its choice of underlying bond index (half of which is in short-term securities) and lack of active management strategies. The Paisley Fund could be a suitable choice for an investor near retirement who is seeking income with a minimum risk profile.
>
> The Dundee Fund represents a medium risk profile given the choice of the composite benchmark and suggests an enhanced approach to indexing. This fund may be the best choice for a middle-aged worker seeking to add a fixed-income component with moderate risk to his portfolio.
>
> The Newcastleton Fund has the highest risk of the three choices and is an example of an actively managed fund that has a mandate to take positions in primary risk factors, such as duration and credit, that deviate from those

> of the index to generate excess return. This fund could be an appropriate choice for a younger worker who is seeking exposure to fixed income but willing to accommodate higher risk.

Alternatives to Investing Directly in Fixed-Income Securities

Recall that several alternatives to direct investing into bonds are available to investment managers. We have shown earlier that index-based exposure can be obtained through the following traded products, such as ETFs that offer greater liquidity than the underlying securities or other alternatives, such as mutual funds (i.e., pooled investment vehicles whose shares or units represent a proportional share in the ownership of the assets in an underlying portfolio). Investors benefit from greater bond ETF liquidity versus mutual funds given their availability to be purchased or sold throughout the trading day. Recall that ETFs authorized participants—who enter into an agreement with the distributor of the fund, purchasing shares from or selling ETF shares to the fund creation units—would be encouraged to engage in arbitrage to profit from any significant divergence between the market price of the underlying fixed-income securities portfolio and an ETF's net asset value (NAV). That said, the fact that many fixed-income securities are either thinly traded or not traded at all might allow such a divergence to persist.

Another alternative to direct investing in fixed-income securities are index-based total return swaps, common over-the-counter instruments. Recall that similar to an interest rate swap, a **total return swap** involves the periodic exchange of cash flows between two parties for the life of the contract. Unlike an interest rate swap—in which counterparties exchange a stream of fixed cash flows versus a floating-rate benchmark, such as the MRR, to transform fixed assets or liabilities to a variable exposure—a total return swap (TRS) has a periodic exchange based on a reference obligation that is an underlying equity, commodity, or bond index. The total return receiver receives both the cash flows from the underlying index as well as any appreciation in the index over the period in exchange for paying the MRR plus a pre-determined spread. The total return payer is responsible for paying the reference obligation cash flows and return to the receiver but will also be compensated by the receiver for any depreciation in the index or default losses incurred on the portfolio.

A TRS can have some advantages over a direct investment in a bond mutual fund or ETF. As a derivative, it requires less initial cash outlay than direct investment in the bond portfolio for similar performance. A TRS also carries counterparty credit risk, however. As a customized over-the-counter product, a TRS can offer exposure to assets that are difficult to access directly, such as some high-yield and commercial loan investments.

8 BENCHMARK SELECTION

☐ discuss criteria for selecting a benchmark and justify the selection of a benchmark

The choice of a benchmark is perhaps an investment manager's most important decision beyond the passive versus active decision or the form that the investment takes, as described earlier. Benchmark selection is one of the final steps in the broader asset allocation process.

Benchmark Selection

The asset allocation process starts with a clear delineation of the portfolio manager's investment goals and objectives. Examples of such goals might include the protection of funds (especially against inflation), broad market replication, predictable returns within acceptable risk parameters, or maximum absolute returns through opportunistic means. The manager must agree on an investment policy with the asset owners, beneficiaries, and other constituents outlining return objectives, risk tolerance, and constraints to narrow choices available in the broader capital markets to meet these objectives. Recall that a strategic asset allocation targeting specific weightings for each permissible asset class is the result of this process, while a tactical asset allocation range often provides the investment manager some short-term flexibility to deviate from these weightings in response to anticipated market changes.

Bonds figure prominently in most asset allocations given that they represent the largest fraction of global capital markets, capture a wide range of issuers, and, as borrowed funds, represent claims that should involve lower risk than common equity. Choosing a fixed-income benchmark is unique, however, in that the investor usually has some degree of fixed-income exposure embedded within its asset/liability portfolio, as outlined in the foregoing immunization and liability-driven investing examples. The investment manager must therefore consider these implicit or explicit duration preferences when choosing a fixed-income benchmark.

Benchmark selection must factor in the broad range of issuers and characteristics available in the fixed-income markets. In general, the use of an index as a widely accepted benchmark requires clear, transparent rules for security inclusion and weighting, investability, daily valuation and availability of past returns, and turnover. Unlike in equity indexes, fixed-income market dynamics can drive deviation from a stable benchmark sought by investors for several reasons:

- The finite maturity of bonds in a static portfolio implies that duration will drift downward over time.
- Market dynamics and issuer preferences tend to dictate both issuer composition for broad-based indexes as well as maturity selection for narrower indexes. For example, as shown in Exhibit 25, the composition of the Bloomberg Barclays US Aggregate Bond Index changed significantly during the years prior to and after the 2008 global financial crisis, with a large increase in securitized debt pre-crisis and a significant rise in government debt thereafter:

Exhibit 25: Bloomberg Barclays US Aggregate Bond Index Sector Allocation, Selected Years

Year	Government	Corporate	Securitized
1993	53.0%	17.0%	30.0%
1998	46.0%	22.0%	32.0%
2000	38.0%	24.0%	39.0%
2005	40.2%	19.5%	40.2%
2008	38.6%	17.7%	43.7%
2010	45.8%	18.8%	35.5%
2015	44.8%	24.2%	31.0%
2020	43.4%	27.3%	29.3%

Sources: Barclays.

Separately, a corporate debt index investor might find her benchmark choice no longer desirable if issuers refinance maturing bonds for longer maturities and extend overall debt duration.

The dynamics of fixed-income markets require investors to more actively understand and define their underlying duration preferences as well as a desired risk and return profile within their fixed-income allocation when conducting benchmark selection. Expressed differently, the desired duration profile may be considered the portfolio "beta," with the targeted duration equal to an investor's preferred duration exposure. Once these parameters are clear, investors may wish to combine several well-defined sub-benchmark categories into an overall benchmark. Examples of sub-benchmark categories might include Treasuries (or domestic sovereign bonds), US agencies or other asset-backed securities, corporate bonds, high-yield bonds, bank loans, developed markets global debt, or emerging markets debt.

For investors seeking to combine the potential outperformance of active management with a broad exposure to an index, a **smart beta** approach might be suitable. Smart beta involves the use of simple, transparent, rules-based strategies as a basis for investment decisions. The starting point for smart beta investors is an analysis of the well-established, static strategies that tend to drive excess portfolio returns. In theory, asset managers who can isolate and pursue such strategies can capture a significant proportion of these excess returns without the significantly higher fees associated with active management. Although the use of smart beta strategies is more established among equity managers, fixed-income managers are increasing their use of these techniques as well (see Staal, Corsi, Shores, and Woida 2015).

CASE STUDY

Given the significant rise in regional bond issuance following the 2008 global financial crisis, Next Europe Asset Management Limited aims to grow its assets under management by attracting a variety of new local Eurozone investors to the broader set of alternatives available in the current fixed-income market. Several of the indexes that Next Europe offers as a basis for investment are as follows:

- **S&P Eurozone Sovereign Bond Index.** This index consists of fixed-rate, sovereign debt publicly issued by Eurozone national governments for their domestic markets with various maturities including 1 to 3 years, 3 to 5 years, 5 to 7 years, 7 to 10 years, and 10+ years. For example, the 1- to 3-year index had a weighted average maturity of 1.91 years and a modified duration of 1.87 as of 31 July 2020 (www.spglobal.com).

- **Bloomberg EUR Investment Grade European Corporate Bond Index (BERC).** The BERC index consists of local, EUR-based corporate debt issuance in Eurozone countries and had an effective duration of 5.28 as of September 2020.

- **Bloomberg EUR High Yield Corporate Bond Index (BEUH).** This index consists of sub-investment-grade, EUR-denominated bonds issued by Eurozone-based corporations. It had an effective duration of 3.68 as of September 2020 (www.bloombergindexes.com).

- **FTSE Pfandbrief Index.** The Pfandbrief, which represents the largest segment of the German private debt market, is a bond issued by German mortgage banks, collateralized by long-term assets, such as real estate or public sector loans. These securities are also referred to as covered bonds and are being used as a model for similar issuance in other European countries.

Benchmark Selection

> The FTSE Pfandbrief indexes include jumbo Pfandbriefs from German issuers as well as those of comparable structure and quality from other Eurozone countries. The sub-indexes offer a range of maturities, including 1 to 3 years, 3 to 5 years, 5 to 7 years, 7 to 10 years, and 10+ years (www.ftse.com/products/indices).
> Which of the above indexes would be suitable for the following investor portfolios?
>
> 1. A highly risk-averse investor who is sensitive to fluctuations in portfolio value.
>
>   **Solution:**
>
>   Given this investor's high degree of risk aversion, an index with short or intermediate duration with limited credit risk would be most appropriate to limit market value risk. Of the alternatives listed, the S&P Eurozone Sovereign Bond 1–3 Years Index or the FTSE 1–3 Years Pfandbrief Index (given the high credit quality of covered bonds) would be appropriate choices.
>
> 2. A new German private university that has established an endowment with a very long-term investment horizon.
>
>   **Solution**:
>
>   This investor's very long investment horizon suggests that the BERC is an appropriate index, because it has the longest duration of the indexes given. In addition, the long-term S&P Eurozone Sovereign Bond or FTSE Pfandbrief indexes (10+ years) could be appropriate choices as well. Next Europe should consider the trade-off between duration and risk in its discussion with the endowment.
>
> 3. A Danish life insurer relying on the fixed-income portfolio managed by Next Europe to meet both short-term claims as well as offset long-term obligations.
>
>   **Solution:**
>
>   The Danish life insurer faces two types of future obligation, namely a short-term outlay for expected claims and a long-term horizon for future obligations. For the short-term exposure, stability of market value is a primary consideration, and the insurer would seek an index with low market risk. Of the above alternatives, the 1–3 Years S&P Sovereign Bond or the FTSE Pfandbrief 1–3 Years would be the best choices. The longer-term alternatives in the Solution to 2 would be most appropriate for the long-term future obligations.

SUMMARY

- Immunization is the process of structuring and managing a fixed-income portfolio to minimize the variance in the realized rate of return over a known investment horizon.
- In the case of a single liability, immunization is achieved by matching the Macaulay duration of the bond portfolio to the horizon date. As time passes and bond yields change, the duration of the bonds changes and the portfolio

- needs to be rebalanced. This rebalancing can be accomplished by buying and selling bonds or using interest rate derivatives, such as futures contracts and interest rate swaps.
- An immunization strategy aims to lock in the cash flow yield on the portfolio, which is the internal rate of return on the cash flows. It is not the weighted average of the yields to maturity on the bonds that constitute the portfolio.
- The risk to immunization is that as the yield curve shifts and twists, the cash flow yield on the bond portfolio does not match the change in the yield on the zero-coupon bond that would provide for perfect immunization.
- A sufficient, but not necessary, condition for immunization is a parallel (or shape-preserving) shift whereby all yields change by the same amount in the same direction. If the change in the cash flow yield is the same as that on the zero-coupon bond being replicated, immunization can be achieved even with a non-parallel shift to the yield curve.
- Immunization of multiple liabilities can be achieved by structuring and managing a portfolio of fixed-income bonds. Because the market values of the assets and liabilities differ, the strategy is to match the money durations. The money duration is the modified duration multiplied by the market value. The basis point value is a measure of money duration calculated by multiplying the money duration by 0.0001.
- The conditions to immunize multiple liabilities are that (1) the market value of assets is greater than or equal to the market value of the liabilities, (2) the asset basis point value (BPV) equals the liability BPV, and (3) the dispersion of cash flows and the convexity of assets are greater than those of the liabilities.
- A derivatives overlay—for example, interest rate futures contracts—can be used to immunize single or multiple liabilities.
- The number of futures contracts needed to immunize is the liability BPV minus the asset BPV, divided by the futures BPV. If the result is a positive number, the entity buys, or goes long, futures contracts. If the result is a negative number, the entity sells, or goes short, futures contracts. The futures BPV can be approximated by the BPV for the cheapest-to-deliver security divided by the conversion factor for the cheapest-to-deliver security.
- Contingent immunization adds active management of the surplus, which is the difference between the asset and liability market values, with the intent to reduce the overall cost of retiring the liabilities. In principle, any asset classes can be used for the active investment. The entity can choose to over-hedge or under-hedge the number of futures contracts needed for passive immunization.
- Liability-driven investing (LDI) often is used for complex rate-sensitive liabilities, such as those for a defined benefit pension plan. The retirement benefits for covered employees depend on many variables, such as years of employment, age at retirement, wage level at retirement, and expected lifetime. There are different measures for the liabilities: for instance, the accumulated benefit obligation (ABO) that is based on current wages and the projected benefit obligation (PBO) that is based on expected future wages. For each liability measure (ABO or PBO), a model is used to extract the effective duration and BPV.

- Interest rate swap overlays can be used to reduce the duration gap as measured by the asset and liability BPVs. There often is a large gap because pension funds hold sizable asset positions in equities that have low or zero effective durations and their liability durations are high.

- The hedging ratio is the percentage of the duration gap that is closed with the derivatives. A hedging ratio of zero implies no hedging. A hedging ratio of 100% implies immunization—that is, complete removal of interest rate risk.

- Strategic hedging is the active management of the hedging ratio. Because asset BPVs are less than liability BPVs in typical pension funds, the derivatives overlay requires the use of receive-fixed interest rate swaps. Because receive-fixed swaps gain value as current swap market rates fall, the fund manager could choose to raise the hedging ratio when lower rates are anticipated. If rates are expected to go up, the manager could strategically reduce the hedging ratio.

- An alternative to the receive-fixed interest rate swap is a purchased receiver swaption. This swaption confers to the buyer the right to enter the swap as the fixed-rate receiver. Because of its negative duration gap (asset BPV is less than liability BPV), the typical pension plan suffers when interest rates fall and could become underfunded. The gain on the receiver swaption as rates decline offsets the losses on the balance sheet.

- Another alternative is a swaption collar, the combination of buying the receiver swaption and writing a payer swaption. The premium received on the payer swaption that is written offsets the premium needed to buy the receiver swaption.

- The choice among hedging with the receive-fixed swap, the purchased receiver swaption, and the swaption collar depends in part on the pension fund manager's view on future interest rates. If rates are expected to be low, the receive-fixed swap typically is the preferred derivative. If rates are expected to go up, the receiver swaption can become attractive. And if rates are projected to reach a certain threshold that depends on the option costs and the strike rates, the swaption collar can become the favored choice.

- Model risks arise in LDI strategies because of the many assumptions in the models and approximations used to measure key parameters. For example, the liability BPV for the defined benefit pension plan depends on the choice of measure (ABO or PBO) and the assumptions that go into the model regarding future events (e.g., wage levels, time of retirement, and time of death).

- Spread risk in LDI strategies arises because it is common to assume equal changes in asset, liability, and hedging instrument yields when calculating the number of futures contracts, or the notional principal on an interest rate swap, to attain a particular hedging ratio. The assets and liabilities are often on corporate securities, however, and their spreads to benchmark yields can vary over time.

- Investing in a fund that tracks a bond market index offers the benefits of both diversification and low administrative costs. Tracking risk arises when the fund manager chooses to buy only a subset of the index, a strategy called enhanced indexing, because fully replicating the index can be impractical because of the large number of bonds in the fixed-income universe.

- Corporate bonds are often illiquid. Matrix pricing uses available data on comparable securities to estimate the fair value of the illiquid bonds.

- The primary risk factors encountered by an investor tracking a bond index include decisions regarding duration (option-adjusted duration for callable bonds, convexity for possible large yield shifts, and key rate durations for non-parallel shifts) and portfolio weights (assigned by sector, credit quality, maturity, coupon rate, and issuer).

- Index replication is one method to establish a passive exposure to the bond market. The manager buys or sells bonds only when there are changes to the index. Full replication can be expensive, however, as well as infeasible for broad-based fixed-income indexes that include many illiquid bonds.

- Several enhancement strategies can reduce the costs to track a bond index: lowering trading costs, using models to identify undervalued bonds and to gauge relative value at varying points along the yield curve, over/under weighting specific credit sectors over the business cycle, and evaluating specific call features to identify value given large yield changes.

- Investors can obtain passive exposure to the bond market using ETFs or mutual funds. Exchange-traded fund (ETF) shares have the advantage of trading on an exchange throughout the day.

- A total return swap, an over-the-counter derivative, allows an institutional investor to transform an asset or liability from one asset category to another—for instance, from variable-rate cash flows referencing the MRR to the total return on a particular bond index.

- A total return swap (TRS) can have some advantages over a direct investment in a bond mutual fund or ETF. As a derivative, it requires less initial cash outlay than direct investment in the bond portfolio for similar performance. A TRS also carries counterparty credit risk, however. As a customized over-the-counter product, a TRS can offer exposure to assets that are difficult to access directly, such as some high-yield and commercial loan investments.

- Selecting a particular bond index is a major decision for a fixed-income investment manager. Selection is guided by the specified goals and objectives for the investment. The decision should recognize several features of bond indexes: (1) Given that bonds have finite maturities, the duration of the index drifts down over time; (2) the composition of the index changes over time with the business cycle and maturity preferences of issuers.

REFERENCES

Staal, Arne, Marco Corsi, Sara Shores, and Chris Woida. 2015. "A Factor Approach to Smart Beta Development in Fixed Income." *Journal of Index Investing* 6 (1): 98–110. 10.3905/jii.2015.6.1.098

Volpert, Kenneth E. 2012. "Introduction to Bond Portfolio Management." In *Handbook of Fixed-Income Securities*. 8th ed., ed. Fabozzi, Frank J. 1123–1150. New York: McGraw Hill.

PRACTICE PROBLEMS

The following information relates to questions 1-8

Serena is a risk management specialist with Liability Protection Advisors. Trey, chief financial officer of Kiest Manufacturing, enlists Serena's help with three projects. The first project is to defease some of Kiest's existing fixed-rate bonds that are maturing in each of the next three years. The bonds have no call or put provisions and pay interest annually. Exhibit 1 presents the payment schedule for the bonds.

Exhibit 1: Kiest Manufacturing Bond Payment Schedule (as of beginning of Year 1)

Maturity Date	Payment Amount
End of Year 1	$9,572,000
End of Year 2	$8,392,000
End of Year 3	$8,200,000

The second project for Serena is to help Trey immunize a $20 million portfolio of liabilities. The liabilities range from 3.00 years to 8.50 years with a Macaulay duration of 5.34 years, cash flow yield of 3.25%, portfolio convexity of 33.05, and basis point value of $10,505. Serena suggested employing a duration-matching strategy using one of the three AAA rated bond portfolios presented in Exhibit 2.

Exhibit 2: Possible AAA Rated Duration-Matching Portfolios

	Portfolio A	Portfolio B	Portfolio C
Bonds (term, coupon)	4.5 years, 2.63% 7.0 years, 3.50%	3.0 years, 2.00% 6.0 years, 3.25% 8.5 years, 3.88%	1.5 years, 1.25% 11.5 years, 4.38%
Macaulay duration	5.35	5.34	5.36
Cash flow yield	3.16%	3.33%	3.88%
Convexity	31.98	34.51	50.21
BPV	$10,524	$10,506	$10,516

Serena explains to Trey that the underlying duration-matching strategy is based on the following three assumptions.

Assumption 1 Yield curve shifts in the future will be parallel.

Assumption 2 Bond types and quality will closely match those of the liabilities.

Practice Problems

Assumption 3   The portfolio will be rebalanced by buying or selling bonds rather than using derivatives.

The third project for Serena is to make a significant direct investment in broadly diversified global bonds for Kiest's pension plan. Kiest has a young workforce, and thus, the plan has a long-term investment horizon. Trey needs Serena's help to select a benchmark index that is appropriate for Kiest's young workforce. Serena discusses three benchmark candidates, presented in Exhibit 3.

Exhibit 3: Global Bond Index Benchmark Candidates

Index Name	Effective Duration	Index Characteristics
Global Aggregate	7.73	Market cap weighted; Treasuries, corporates, agency, securitized debt
Global Aggregate GDP Weighted	7.71	Same as Global Aggregate, except GDP weighted
Global High Yield	4.18	GDP weighted; sovereign, agency, corporate debt

With the benchmark selected, Trey provides guidelines to Serena directing her to use the most cost-effective method to replicate the benchmark but with an enhanced return objective.

After providing Trey with advice on direct investment, Serena offered him additional information on alternative indirect investment strategies using (1) bond mutual funds, (2) exchange-traded funds (ETFs), and (3) total return swaps. Trey expresses interest in using bond mutual funds rather than the other strategies for the following reasons.

Reason 1   Total return swaps have much higher transaction costs and initial cash outlay than bond mutual funds.

Reason 2   Unlike bond mutual funds, bond ETFs can trade at discounts to their underlying indexes, and those discounts can persist.

Reason 3   Bond mutual funds can be traded throughout the day at the net asset value of the underlying bonds.

1. Based on Exhibit 1, Kiest's liabilities would be classified as:
   A. Type I.
   B. Type II.
   C. Type III.

2. Based on Exhibit 2, the portfolio with the greatest structural risk is:
   A. Portfolio A.
   B. Portfolio B.
   C. Portfolio C.

3. Which portfolio in Exhibit 2 fails to meet the requirements to achieve immuniza-

tion for multiple liabilities?

- A. Portfolio A
- B. Portfolio B
- C. Portfolio C

4. Based on Exhibit 2, relative to Portfolio C, Portfolio B:
   - A. has higher cash flow reinvestment risk.
   - B. is a more desirable portfolio for liquidity management.
   - C. provides less protection from yield curve shifts and twists.

5. Serena's three assumptions regarding the duration-matching strategy indicate the presence of:
   - A. model risk.
   - B. spread risk.
   - C. counterparty credit risk.

6. The global bond benchmark in Exhibit 3 that is *least* appropriate for Kiest to use is the:
   - A. Global Aggregate Index.
   - B. Global High Yield Index.
   - C. Global Aggregate GDP Weighted Index.

7. To meet both of Trey's guidelines for the pension's bond fund investment, Serena should recommend:
   - A. pure indexing.
   - B. enhanced indexing.
   - C. active management.

8. Which of Trey's reasons for choosing bond mutual funds as an investment vehicle is correct?
   - A. 1
   - B. 2
   - C. 3

Practice Problems

The following information relates to questions 9-16

SD&R Capital (SD&R), a global asset management company, specializes in fixed-income investments. Molly, the firm's chief investment officer, is meeting with a prospective client, Leah, of DePuy Financial Company (DFC).

Leah informs Molly that DFC's previous fixed-income manager focused on the interest rate sensitivities of assets and liabilities when making asset allocation decisions. Molly explains that, in contrast, SD&R's investment process first analyzes the size and timing of client liabilities, and then it builds an asset portfolio based on the interest rate sensitivity of those liabilities.

Molly notes that SD&R generally uses actively managed portfolios designed to earn a return higher than that of the benchmark portfolio. For clients interested in passive exposure to fixed-income instruments, SD&R offers two additional approaches.

Approach 1   Seek to fully replicate a small range of benchmarks consisting of government bonds.

Approach 2   Follow an enhanced indexing process for a subset of the bonds included in the Bloomberg Barclays US Aggregate Bond Index. This approach may also be customized to reflect client preferences.

To illustrate SD&R's immunization approach for controlling portfolio interest rate risk, Molly discusses a hypothetical portfolio composed of two non-callable, investment-grade bonds. The portfolio has a weighted average yield-to-maturity of 9.55%, a weighted average coupon rate of 10.25%, and a cash flow yield of 9.85%.

Leah informs Molly that DFC has a single $500 million liability due in nine years, and she wants SD&R to construct a bond portfolio that earns a rate of return sufficient to pay off the obligation. Leah expresses concern about the risks associated with an immunization strategy for this obligation. In response, Molly makes the following statements about liability-driven investing:

Statement 1   Although the amount and date of SD&R's liability is known with certainty, measurement errors associated with key parameters relative to interest rate changes may adversely affect the bond portfolios.

Statement 2   A cash flow matching strategy will mitigate the risk from non-parallel shifts in the yield curve.

Molly provides the four US dollar–denominated bond portfolios in Exhibit 1 for consideration. Molly explains that the portfolios consist of non-callable, investment-grade corporate and government bonds of various maturities because zero-coupon bonds are unavailable.

Exhibit 1: Proposed Bond Portfolios to Immunize SD&R Single Liability

	Portfolio 1	Portfolio 2	Portfolio 3	Portfolio 4
Cash flow yield	7.48%	7.50%	7.53%	7.51%
Average time to maturity	11.2 years	9.8 years	9.0 years	10.1 years

	Portfolio 1	Portfolio 2	Portfolio 3	Portfolio 4
Macaulay duration	9.8	8.9	8.0	9.1
Market value–weighted duration	9.1	8.5	7.8	8.6
Convexity	154.11	131.75	130.00	109.32

The discussion turns to benchmark selection. DFC's previous fixed-income manager used a custom benchmark with the following characteristics:

Characteristic 1 The benchmark portfolio invests only in investment-grade bonds of US corporations with a minimum issuance size of $250 million.

Characteristic 2 Valuation occurs on a weekly basis, because many of the bonds in the index are valued weekly.

Characteristic 3 Historical prices and portfolio turnover are available for review.

Molly explains that to evaluate the asset allocation process, fixed-income portfolios should have an appropriate benchmark. Leah asks for benchmark advice regarding DFC's portfolio of short-term and intermediate-term bonds, all denominated in US dollars. Molly presents three possible benchmarks in Exhibit 2.

Exhibit 2: Proposed Benchmark Portfolios

Benchmark	Index	Composition	Duration
1	Bloomberg Barclays US Bond Index	80% US government bonds 20% US corporate bonds	8.7
2 Index Blend	50% Bloomberg Barclays US Corporate Bond Index	100% US corporate bonds	7.5
	50% Bloomberg Barclays Short-Term Treasury Index	100% short-term US government debt	0.5
3	Bloomberg Barclays Global Aggregate Bond Index	60% EUR-denominated corporate bonds 40% US-denominated corporate debt	12.3

9. The investment process followed by DFC's previous fixed-income manager is *best* described as:

   A. asset-driven liabilities.

   B. liability-driven investing.

   C. asset–liability management.

10. Relative to Approach 1, gaining passive exposure, an advantage of Approach 2 is that it:

    A. minimizes tracking error.

    B. requires less risk analysis.

Practice Problems

    C. is more appropriate for socially responsible investors.

11. The two-bond hypothetical portfolio's immunization goal is to lock in a rate of return equal to:

    A. 9.55%.

    B. 9.85%.

    C. 10.25%.

12. Which of Molly's statements about liability-driven investing is (are) correct?

    A. Statement 1 only

    B. Statement 2 only

    C. Both Statement 1 and Statement 2

13. Based on Exhibit 1, which of the portfolios will *best* immunize SD&R's single liability?

    A. Portfolio 1

    B. Portfolio 2

    C. Portfolio 3

14. Which of the portfolios in Exhibit 1 *best* minimizes the structural risk to a single-liability immunization strategy?

    A. Portfolio 1

    B. Portfolio 3

    C. Portfolio 4

15. Which of the custom benchmark's characteristics violates the requirements for an appropriate benchmark portfolio?

    A. Characteristic 1

    B. Characteristic 2

    C. Characteristic 3

16. Based on DFC's bond holdings and Exhibit 2, Molly should recommend:

    A. Benchmark 1.

    B. Benchmark 2.

    C. Benchmark 3.

The following information relates to questions 17-22

Doug, the newly hired chief financial officer for the City of Radford, asks the deputy financial manager, Hui, to prepare an analysis of the current investment portfolio and the city's current and future obligations. The city has multiple liabilities of different amounts and maturities relating to the pension fund, infrastructure repairs, and various other obligations.

Hui observes that the current fixed-income portfolio is structured to match the duration of each liability. Previously, this structure caused the city to access a line of credit for temporary mismatches resulting from changes in the term structure of interest rates.

Doug asks Hui for different strategies to manage the interest rate risk of the city's fixed-income investment portfolio against one-time shifts in the yield curve. Hui considers two different strategies:

> Strategy 1   Immunization of the single liabilities using zero-coupon bonds held to maturity
>
> Strategy 2   Immunization of the single liabilities using coupon-bearing bonds while continuously matching duration

The city also manages a separate, smaller bond portfolio for the Radford School District. During the next five years, the school district has obligations for school expansions and renovations. The funds needed for those obligations are invested in the Bloomberg Barclays US Aggregate Index. Doug asks Hui which portfolio management strategy would be most efficient in mimicking this index.

A Radford School Board member has stated that she prefers a bond portfolio structure that provides diversification over time, as well as liquidity. In addressing the board member's inquiry, Hui examines a bullet portfolio, a barbell portfolio, and a laddered portfolio.

17. A disadvantage of Strategy 1 is that:
    A. price risk still exists.
    B. interest rate volatility introduces risk to effective matching.
    C. there may not be enough bonds available to match all liabilities.

18. Which duration measure should be matched when implementing Strategy 2?
    A. Key rate
    B. Modified
    C. Macaulay

19. An upward shift in the yield curve on Strategy 2 will *most likely* result in the:
    A. price effect canceling the coupon reinvestment effect.
    B. price effect being greater than the coupon reinvestment effect.
    C. coupon reinvestment effect being greater than the price effect.

20. The effects of a non-parallel shift in the yield curve on Strategy 2 can be reduced

Practice Problems

by:

A. minimizing the convexity of the bond portfolio.

B. maximizing the cash flow yield of the bond portfolio.

C. minimizing the difference between liability duration and bond portfolio duration.

21. Hui's response to Doug's question about the most efficient portfolio management strategy should be:

A. full replication.

B. active management.

C. an enhanced indexing strategy.

22. Which portfolio structure should Hui recommend that would satisfy the school board member's preference?

A. Bullet portfolio

B. Barbell portfolio

C. Laddered portfolio

The following information relates to questions 23-25

Chaopraya is an investment adviser for high-net-worth individuals. One of her clients, Schuylkill, plans to fund her grandson's college education and considers two options:

Option 1 Contribute a lump sum of $300,000 in 10 years.

Option 2 Contribute four level annual payments of $76,500 starting in 10 years.

The grandson will start college in 10 years. Schuylkill seeks to immunize the contribution today.

For Option 1, Chaopraya calculates the present value of the $300,000 as $234,535. To immunize the future single outflow, Chaopraya considers three bond portfolios given that no zero-coupon government bonds are available. The three portfolios consist of non-callable, fixed-rate, coupon-bearing government bonds considered free of default risk. Chaopraya prepares a comparative analysis of the three portfolios, presented in Exhibit 1.

Exhibit 1: Results of Comparative Analysis of Potential Portfolios

	Portfolio A	Portfolio B	Portfolio C
Market value	$235,727	$233,428	$235,306
Cash flow yield	2.504%	2.506%	2.502%

	Portfolio A	Portfolio B	Portfolio C
Macaulay duration	9.998	10.002	9.503
Convexity	119.055	121.498	108.091

Chaopraya evaluates the three bond portfolios and selects one to recommend to Schuylkill.

23. Recommend the portfolio in Exhibit 1 that would *best* achieve the immunization. Justify your response.

24. Schuylkill and Chaopraya now discuss Option 2.

    Chaopraya estimates the present value of the four future cash flows as $230,372, with a money duration of $2,609,700 and convexity of 135.142. She considers three possible portfolios to immunize the future payments, as presented in Exhibit 2.

Exhibit 2: Data for Bond Portfolios to Immunize Four Annual Contributions

	Portfolio 1	Portfolio 2	Portfolio 3
Market value	$245,178	$248,230	$251,337
Cash flow yield	2.521%	2.520%	2.516%
Money duration	2,609,981	2,609,442	2,609,707
Convexity	147.640	139.851	132.865

Determine the *most appropriate* immunization portfolio in Exhibit 2. Justify your decision.

25. After selecting a portfolio to immunize Schuylkill's multiple future outflows, Chaopraya prepares a report on how this immunization strategy would respond to various interest rate scenarios. The scenario analysis is presented in Exhibit 3.

Exhibit 3: Projected Portfolio Response to Interest Rate Scenarios

	Immunizing Portfolio	Outflow Portfolio	Difference
Upward parallel shift			
Δ Market value	−6,410	−6,427	18
Δ Cash flow yield	0.250%	0.250%	0.000%
Δ Portfolio BPV	−9	−8	−1
Downward parallel shift			
Δ Market value	6,626	6,622	4
Δ Cash flow yield	−0.250%	−0.250%	0.000%
Δ Portfolio BPV	9	8	1
Steepening twist			
Δ Market value	−1,912	347	−2,259
Δ Cash flow yield	0.074%	−0.013%	0.087%
Δ Portfolio BPV	−3	0	−3
Flattening twist			

Practice Problems

	Immunizing Portfolio	Outflow Portfolio	Difference
Δ Market value	1,966	−343	2,309
Δ Cash flow yield	−0.075%	0.013%	−0.088%
Δ Portfolio BPV	3	0	3

Discuss the effectiveness of Chaopraya's immunization strategy in terms of duration gaps.

SOLUTIONS

1. A is correct. Type I liabilities have cash outlays with known amounts and timing. The dates and amounts of Kiest's liabilities are known; therefore, they would be classified as Type I liabilities.

2. C is correct. Structural risk arises from the design of the duration-matching portfolio. It is reduced by minimizing the dispersion of the bond positions, going from a barbell structure to more of a bullet portfolio that concentrates the component bonds' durations around the investment horizon. With bond maturities of 1.5 and 11.5 years, Portfolio C has a definite barbell structure compared with those of Portfolios A and B, and it is thus subject to a greater degree of risk from yield curve twists and non-parallel shifts. In addition, Portfolio C has the highest level of convexity, which increases a portfolio's structural risk.

3. A is correct. The two requirements to achieve immunization for multiple liabilities are for the money duration (or BPV) of the asset and liability to match and for the asset convexity to exceed the convexity of the liability. Although all three portfolios have similar BPVs, Portfolio A is the only portfolio to have a lower convexity than that of the liability portfolio (31.98, versus 33.05 for the $20 million liability portfolio), and thus, it fails to meet one of the two requirements needed for immunization.

4. B is correct. Portfolio B is a laddered portfolio with maturities spread evenly over the yield curve. A desirable aspect of a laddered portfolio is liquidity management. Because there is always a bond close to redemption, the soon-to-mature bond can provide emergency liquidity needs. Barbell portfolios, such as Portfolio C, have maturities only at the short-term and long-term ends and thus are much less desirable for liquidity management.

5. A is correct. Serena believes that any shift in the yield curve will be parallel. Model risk arises whenever assumptions are made about future events and approximations are used to measure key parameters. The risk is that those assumptions turn out to be wrong and the approximations are inaccurate. A non-parallel yield curve shift could occur, resulting in a mismatch of the duration of the immunizing portfolio versus the liability.

6. B is correct. Kiest has a young workforce and thus a long-term investment horizon. The Global Aggregate and Global Aggregate GDP Weighted Indexes have the highest durations (7.73 and 7.71, respectively) and would be appropriate for this group. Global High Yield is the least appropriate due to its relatively shorter duration.

7. B is correct. A pure indexing approach for a broadly diversified bond index would be extremely costly because it requires purchasing all the constituent securities in the index. A pure indexing approach wouldn't provide the opportunity for enhanced returns compared to the indexing. A more efficient and cost-effective way to track the index is an enhanced indexing strategy, whereby Serena would purchase fewer securities than the index but would match primary risk factors reflected in the index. Closely matching these risk factors could provide low tracking error.

8. B is correct. Although a significant spread between the market price of the underlying fixed-income securities portfolio and an ETF's NAV should drive an authorized participant to engage in arbitrage, many fixed-income securities are

Solutions

either thinly traded or not traded at all. This situation might allow such a divergence to persist.

9. C is correct. Asset–liability management strategies consider both assets and liabilities in the portfolio decision-making process. Leah notes that DFC's previous fixed-income manager attempted to control for interest rate risk by focusing on both the asset and the liability sides of the company's balance sheet. The previous manager thus followed an asset–liability management strategy.

10. C is correct. Enhanced indexing is especially useful for investors who consider environmental, social, or other factors when selecting a fixed-income portfolio. Environmental, social, and corporate governance (ESG) investing, also called socially responsible investing, refers to the explicit inclusion or exclusion of some sectors, which is more appropriate for an enhanced index strategy relative to a full index replication strategy. In particular, Approach 2 may be customized to reflect client preferences.

11. B is correct. Immunization is the process of structuring and managing a fixed-income portfolio to minimize the variance in the realized rate of return and to lock in the cash flow yield (internal rate of return) on the portfolio, which in this case is 9.85%.

12. C is correct. Molly is correct that measurement error can arise even in immunization strategies for Type 1 cash flows, which have set amounts and set dates. Also, a parallel shift in yield curves is a sufficient but not a necessary condition to achieve the desired outcome. Non-parallel shifts and twists in the yield curve can change the cash flow yield on the immunizing portfolio; however, minimizing the dispersion of cash flows in the asset portfolio mitigates this risk. As a result, both statements are correct.

13. B is correct. In the case of a single liability, immunization is achieved by matching the bond portfolio's Macaulay duration with the horizon date. DFC has a single liability of $500 million due in nine years. Portfolio 2 has a Macaulay duration of 8.9, which is closer to 9 than that of either Portfolio 1 or 3. Therefore, Portfolio 2 will best immunize the portfolio against the liability.

14. C is correct. Structural risk to immunization arises from twists and non-parallel shifts in the yield curve. Structural risk is reduced by minimizing the dispersion of cash flows in the portfolio, which can be accomplished by minimizing the convexity for a given cash flow duration level. Because Portfolio 4 has the lowest convexity compared with the other two portfolios and also has a Macaulay duration close to the liability maturity of nine years, it minimizes structural risk.

15. B is correct. The use of an index as a widely accepted benchmark requires clear, transparent rules for security inclusion and weighting, investability, daily valuation, availability of past returns, and turnover. Because the custom benchmark is valued weekly rather than daily, this characteristic would be inconsistent with an appropriate benchmark.

16. B is correct. DFC has two types of assets, short term and intermediate term. For the short-term assets, a benchmark with a short duration is appropriate. For the intermediate-term assets, a benchmark with a longer duration is appropriate. In this situation, DFC may wish to combine several well-defined sub-benchmark categories into an overall blended benchmark (Benchmark 2). The Bloomberg Barclays Short-Term Treasury Index is an appropriate benchmark for the short-term assets, and SD&R uses a 50% weight for this component. The longer-duration Bloomberg Barclays US Corporate Bond Index is an appropriate

benchmark for the intermediate-term assets, and SD&R uses a 50% weight for this component. As a result, Molly should recommend proposed Benchmark 2.

17. C is correct. It may be impossible to acquire zero-coupon bonds to precisely match liabilities because the city's liabilities have varying maturities and amounts. In many financial markets, zero-coupon bonds are unavailable.

18. C is correct. An investor with an investment horizon equal to the bond's Macaulay duration is effectively protected, or immunized, from the first change in interest rates, because price and coupon reinvestment effects offset for either higher or lower rates.

19. A is correct. An upward shift in the yield curve reduces the bond's value but increases the reinvestment rate, with these two effects offsetting one another. The price effect and the coupon reinvestment effect cancel each other out in the case of an upward shift in the yield curve for an immunized liability.

20. A is correct. Minimizing the convexity of the bond portfolio minimizes the dispersion of the bond portfolio. A non-parallel shift in the yield curve may result in changes in the bond portfolio's cash flow yield. In summary, the characteristics of a bond portfolio structured to immunize a single liability are that it (1) has an initial market value that equals or exceeds the present value of the liability, (2) has a portfolio Macaulay duration that matches the liability's due date, and (3) minimizes the portfolio convexity statistic.

21. C is correct. Under an enhanced indexing strategy, the index is replicated with fewer than the full set of index constituents but still matches the original index's primary risk factors. This strategy replicates the index performance under different market scenarios more efficiently than the full replication of a pure indexing approach.

22. C is correct. The laddered approach provides both diversification over time and liquidity. Diversification over time offers the investor a balanced position between two sources of interest rate risk: cash flow reinvestment and market price volatility. In practice, perhaps the most desirable aspect of a laddered portfolio is liquidity management, because as time passes, the portfolio will always contain a bond close to maturity.

23. Portfolio A is the most appropriate portfolio because it is the only one that satisfies the three criteria for immunizing a single future outflow (liability), given that the cash flow yields are sufficiently close in value:

    1. Market value: Portfolio A's initial market value of $235,727 exceeds the outflow's present value of $234,535. Portfolio B is not appropriate because its market value of $233,428 is less than the present value of the future outflow of $234,535. A bond portfolio structured to immunize a single liability must have an initial market value that equals or exceeds the present value of the liability.

    2. Macaulay duration: Portfolio A's Macaulay duration of 9.998 closely matches the 10-year horizon of the outflow. Portfolio C is not appropriate because its Macaulay duration of 9.503 is furthest away from the investment horizon of 10 years.

Solutions

3. Convexity: Although Portfolio C has the lowest convexity, 108.091, its Macaulay duration does not closely match the outflow amount. Of the remaining two portfolios, Portfolio A has the lower convexity, 119.055; this lower convexity will minimize structural risk.

Default risk (credit risk) is not considered because the portfolios consist of government bonds that presumably have default probabilities approaching zero.

24. Portfolio 2 is the most appropriate immunization portfolio because it is the only one that satisfies the following two criteria for immunizing a portfolio of multiple future outflows:

    1. Money duration: Money durations of all three possible immunizing portfolios match or closely match the money duration of the outflow portfolio. Matching money durations is useful because the market values and cash flow yields of the immunizing portfolio and the outflow portfolio are not necessarily equal.

    2. Convexity: Given that the money duration requirement is met by all three possible immunizing portfolios, the portfolio with the lowest convexity that is above the outflow portfolio's convexity of 135.142 should be selected. The dispersion, as measured by convexity, of the immunizing portfolio should be as low as possible subject to being greater than or equal to the dispersion of the outflow portfolio. This will minimize the effect of non-parallel shifts in the yield curve. Portfolio 3's convexity of 132.865 is less than the outflow portfolio's convexity, so Portfolio 3 is not appropriate. Both Portfolio 1 and Portfolio 2 have convexities that exceed the convexity of the outflow portfolio, but Portfolio 2's convexity of 139.851 is lower than Portfolio 1's convexity of 147.640. Therefore, Portfolio 2 is the most appropriate immunizing portfolio.

    The immunizing portfolio needs to be greater than the convexity (and dispersion) of the outflow portfolio. But the convexity of the immunizing portfolio should be minimized in order to minimize dispersion and reduce structural risk.

25. Chaopraya's strategy immunizes well for parallel shifts, with little deviation between the outflow portfolio and the immunizing portfolio in market value and BPV. Because the money durations are closely matched, the differences between the outflow portfolio and the immunizing portfolio in market value are small and the duration gaps (as shown by the difference in Δ Portfolio BPVs) between the outflow portfolio and the immunizing portfolio are small for both the upward and downward parallel shifts.

    Chaopraya's strategy does not immunize well for the non-parallel steepening and flattening twists (i.e., structural risks) shown in Exhibit 3. In those cases, the outflow portfolio and the immunizing portfolio market values deviate substantially and the duration gaps between the outflow portfolio and the immunizing portfolio are large.

LEARNING MODULE 5

Yield Curve Strategies

by Robert W. Kopprasch, PhD, CFA, and Steven V. Mann, PhD.

Robert W. Kopprasch, PhD, CFA, is at Bates Group, LLC (USA). Steven V. Mann, PhD, is at the University of South Carolina (USA).

LEARNING OUTCOMES

Mastery	The candidate should be able to:
☐	describe the factors affecting fixed-income portfolio returns due to a change in benchmark yields
☐	formulate a portfolio positioning strategy given forward interest rates and an interest rate view that coincides with the market view
☐	formulate a portfolio positioning strategy given forward interest rates and an interest rate view that diverges from the market view in terms of rate level, slope, and shape
☐	formulate a portfolio positioning strategy based upon expected changes in interest rate volatility
☐	evaluate a portfolio's sensitivity using key rate durations of the portfolio and its benchmark
☐	discuss yield curve strategies across currencies
☐	evaluate the expected return and risks of a yield curve strategy

INTRODUCTION

The size and breadth of global fixed-income markets, as well as the term structure of interest rates within and across countries, lead investors to consider numerous factors when creating and managing a bond portfolio. While fixed-income index replication and bond portfolios that consider both an investor's assets and liabilities were addressed earlier in the curriculum, we now turn our attention to active bond portfolio management. In contrast to a passive index strategy, active fixed-income management involves taking positions in primary risk factors that deviate from those of an index in order to generate excess return. Financial analysts who can successfully apply fixed-income concepts and tools to evaluate yield curve changes and position a portfolio based upon an interest rate view find this to be a valuable skill throughout their careers.

Prioritizing fixed-income risk factors is a key first step. In what follows, we focus on the yield curve, which represents the term structure of interest rates for government or benchmark securities, with the assumption that all promised principal and interest payments take place. Fixed-income securities, which trade at a spread above the benchmark to compensate investors for credit and liquidity risk, will be addressed later in the curriculum. The starting point for active portfolio managers is the current term structure of benchmark interest rates and an interest rate view established using macroeconomic variables introduced earlier. In what follows, we demonstrate how managers may position a fixed-income portfolio to capitalize on expectations regarding the level, slope, or shape (curvature) of yield curves using both long and short cash positions, derivatives, and leverage.

2. KEY YIELD CURVE AND FIXED-INCOME CONCEPTS FOR ACTIVE MANAGERS

☐ describe the factors affecting fixed-income portfolio returns due to a change in benchmark yields

The factors comprising an investor's expected fixed-income portfolio returns introduced earlier in the curriculum are summarized in Equation 1:

$E(R) \approx$ Coupon income (1)

+/− Rolldown return

+/− E (Δ Price due to investor's view of benchmark yields)

+/− E (Δ Price due to investor's view of yield spreads)

+/− E (Δ Price due to investor's view of currency value changes)

Sections 2 and 3 will focus on actively managing the first three components of Equation 1, and Section 4 will include changes in currency. Credit strategies driving yield spreads will be discussed in a later lesson. As active management hinges on an investor's ability to identify actionable trades with specific securities, our review of yield curve and fixed-income concepts focuses on these practical considerations.

Yield Curve Dynamics

When someone refers to "the yield curve," this implies that one yield curve for a given issuer applies to all investors. In fact, a yield curve is a stylized representation of the yields-to-maturity available to investors at various maturities for a specific issuer or group of issuers. Yield curve models make certain assumptions that may vary by investor or by the intended use of the curve, raising such issues as the following:

- Asynchronous observations of various maturities on the curve
- Maturity gaps that require interpolation and/or smoothing
- Observations that seem inconsistent with neighboring values

- Use of on-the-run bonds only versus all marketable bonds (i.e., including off-the-run bonds)
- Differences in accounting, regulatory, or tax treatment of certain bonds that may make them look like outliers

As an example, a yield curve of the most recently issued, or on-the-run, securities may differ significantly from one that includes off-the-run securities. Off-the-run bonds are typically less liquid than on-the-run bonds, and hence they have a lower price (higher yield-to-maturity). Inclusion of off-the-run bonds will tend to "pull" the yield curve higher.

This illustrates two key points about yield curves. First, although we often take reported yield curves as a "given," they often do not consist of traded securities and must be derived from available bond yields-to-maturity using some type of model. This is particularly true for constant maturity yields, shown in some of the following exhibits. A constant maturity yield estimates, for example, what a hypothetical 5-year yield-to-maturity would be if a bond were available with exactly five years to maturity. While some derivatives reference the daily constant maturity yield, the current on-the-run 5-year Treasury issued before today has a maturity of less than five years. Estimating a constant maturity 5-year yield typically requires interpolating the yields-to-maturity on actively traded bonds with maturities *near* five years. Different models and assumptions can produce different yield curves. The difference between models becomes more pronounced as yields-to-maturity are converted to spot and forward rates (as spot and forward rate curves amplify yield curve steepness and curvature).

Second, a tradeoff exists between yield-to-maturity and liquidity. Active management strategies must assess this tradeoff when selecting bonds for the portfolio, especially if frequent trading is anticipated. While off-the-run bonds may earn a higher return if held to maturity, buying and selling them will likely involve increased trading costs (especially in a market crisis).

Primary yield curve risk factors are often categorized by three types: a change in (1) level (a parallel "shift" in the yield curve); (2) slope (a flattening or steepening "twist" of the yield curve); and (3) shape or curvature (or "butterfly movement"). Earlier in the curriculum, principal components analysis was used to decompose yield curve changes into these three separate factors. Level, slope, and curvature movements over time accounted for approximately 82%, 12%, and 4%, respectively, of US Treasury yield curve changes. Although based upon a specific historical period, the consistency of these results over time and across global markets underscores the importance of these factors in realizing excess portfolio returns under an active yield curve strategy.

The following exhibits provide historical context for the three yield curve factors using constant maturity US Treasury yields. Exhibit 1 shows US 10-year constant maturity yield levels.

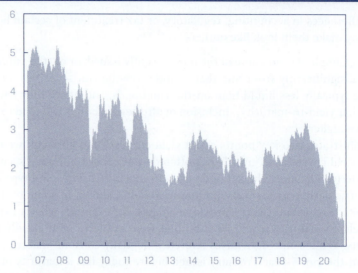

Exhibit 1: 10-Year US Treasury Yield, 2007–2020 (%)

Source: US Federal Reserve.

During the period shown in Exhibit 1, 10-year US Treasury yields-to-maturity demonstrated significant volatility, falling to new lows in 2020 amid a flight to quality during the COVID-19 pandemic. Slower growth and accommodative monetary policy in the form of quantitative easing among global central banks since the 2008 global financial crisis years has driven government yields to zero and below. In 2020, negative yields were common on many Japanese, German, and Swiss government bonds, among others.

A change in yield *level* (or parallel shift) occurs when all yields-to-maturity represented on the curve change by the same number of basis points. Under this assumption, a portfolio manager might use a first-order duration statistic to approximate the impact of an expected yield curve change on portfolio value. This implies that yield curve changes occur only in parallel shifts, which is unreliable in cases where the yield curve's slope and curvature also change. Larger yield curve changes necessitate the inclusion of second-order effects in order to better measure changes in portfolio value.

Yield curve *slope* is often defined as the difference in basis points between the yield-to-maturity on a long-maturity bond and the yield-to-maturity on a shorter-maturity bond. For example, as of July 2020, the slope as measured by the 2s30s spread, or the difference between the 30-year Treasury bond (30s) and the 2-year Treasury note (2s) yields-to-maturity (1.43% and 0.16%, respectively), was 127 bps. Exhibit 2 shows the 2s30s spread for US Treasury constant maturity yields. As this spread increases, or widens, the yield curve is said to steepen, while a decrease, or narrowing, is referred to as a flattening of the yield curve. In most instances, the spread is positive and the yield curve is upward-sloping. If the spread turns negative, as was the case just prior to the 2008 global financial crisis, the yield curve is described as "inverted."

Exhibit 2: 2s30s US Yield Spread, 2007–2020 (%)

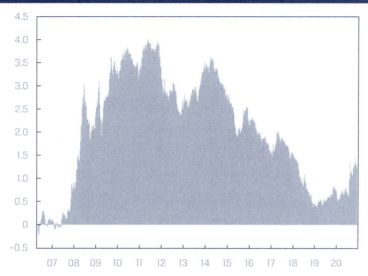

Source: US Federal Reserve.

Yield curve shape or *curvature* is the relationship between yields-to-maturity at the short end of the curve, at a midpoint along the curve (often referred to as the "belly" of the curve), and at the long end of the curve. A common measure of yield curve curvature is the **butterfly spread**:

$$\text{Butterfly spread} = -(\text{Short-term yield}) + (2 \times \text{Medium-term yield}) - \text{Long-term yield} \tag{2}$$

The butterfly spread takes on larger positive values when the yield curve has more curvature. Exhibit 3 displays this measure of curvature for the US Treasury constant maturity yield curve using 2-year, 10-year, and 30-year tenors. Curvature indicates a difference between medium-term yields and a linear interpolation between short-term and long-term yields-to-maturity. A positive butterfly spread indicates a "humped" or concave shape to the midpoint of the curve, while a "saucer" or convex shape indicates the spread is negative. The butterfly spread changes when intermediate-term yield-to-maturity changes are of a different magnitude than those on the wings (the short- and long-end of the curve). Note that as in the case of yield curve slope, the butterfly spread was generally positive until 2020, except for the period just prior to the 2008 global financial crisis.

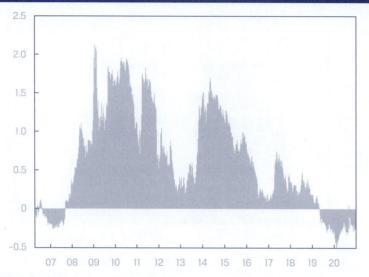

Exhibit 3: US Butterfly Spread (2s/10s/30s), 2007–2020 (%)

Source: US Federal Reserve.

Duration and Convexity

As active managers position their portfolios to capitalize on expected changes in the level, slope, and curvature of the benchmark yield curve, the anticipated change in portfolio value due to yield-to-maturity changes is captured by the third term in Equation 1—namely, the expected change in price due to investor's view of benchmark yields. The price/yield relationship for fixed-income bonds was established earlier in the curriculum as the combination of two factors: a negative, linear first-order factor (*duration*) and a usually positive, non-linear second-order factor (*convexity*), as shown in Exhibit 4.

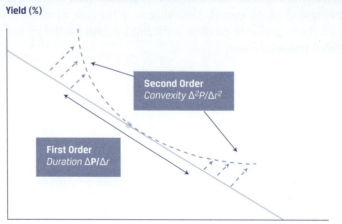

Exhibit 4: Price–Yield Relationship for a Fixed-Income Bond

Key Yield Curve and Fixed-Income Concepts for Active Managers

The third term in Equation 1 (Δ Price due to investor's view of benchmark yield), combines the duration and convexity effects in Equation 3 of the percentage change in the full price (%ΔPV^{Full}) for a single bond as introduced earlier:

$$\%\Delta PV^{\text{Full}} \approx -(\text{ModDur} \times \Delta \text{Yield}) + [\tfrac{1}{2} \times \text{Convexity} \times (\Delta \text{Yield})^2]. \quad (3)$$

Fixed-income portfolio managers often approximate changes in a bond portfolio's present value (PV) by substituting market value (MV)-weighted averages for modified duration and convexity into Equation 3.

$$\text{AvgModDur} = \sum_{j=1}^{J} \text{ModDur}_j \times \left(\frac{\text{MV}_j}{\text{MV}}\right). \quad (4)$$

$$\text{AvgConvexity} = \sum_{j=1}^{J} \text{Convexity}_j \times \left(\frac{\text{MV}_j}{\text{MV}}\right). \quad (5)$$

Active managers focus on the *incremental* effect on these summary statistics for a portfolio by adding or selling bonds in the portfolio or by buying and selling fixed-income derivatives. Duration is a first-order effect that attempts to capture a linear relationship between bond prices and yield-to-maturity. Convexity is a second-order effect that describes a bond's price behavior for larger movements in yield-to-maturity. This additional term is a positive amount on a traditional (option-free) fixed-rate bond for either a yield increase or decrease, causing the yield/price relationship to deviate from a linear relationship. Because duration is a first-order effect, it follows that duration management—accounting for changes in yield curve level—will usually be a more important consideration for portfolio performance than convexity management. This is consistent with our previous discussion of the relative importance of the yield curve level, slope, and curvature. As we shall see later in this lesson, convexity management is more closely associated with yield curve slope and shape changes.

All else equal, positive convexity is a valuable feature in bonds. If a bond has higher positive convexity than an otherwise identical bond, then the bond price increases more if interest rates decrease (and decreases less if interest rates increase) than the duration estimate would suggest. Said another way, the expected price of a bond with positive convexity for a given rate change will be higher than the price change of an identical-duration, lower-convexity bond. This price behavior is valuable to investors; therefore, a bond with higher convexity might be expected to have a lower yield-to-maturity than a similar-duration bond with less convexity. All else equal, bonds with longer durations have higher convexity than bonds with shorter durations. Also, as noted earlier in the curriculum, convexity is affected by the *dispersion* of cash flows—that is, the *variance* of the times to receipt of cash flow. Higher cash flow dispersion leads to an increase in convexity. This is in contrast to Macaulay duration, which measures the weighted *average* of the times to cash flow receipt. Note that throughout this lesson, we will use "raw" versus scaled (or "raw" divided by 100) convexity figures often seen on trading platforms. We can see the convexity effect by comparing two bond portfolios:

EXAMPLE 1

US Treasury Securities Portfolio

Tenor	Coupon	Price	ModDur	Convexity
2y	0.250%	$100	1.994	5.0
5y	0.875%	$100	4.880	26.5
10y	2.000%	$100	9.023	90.8

Consider two $50 million portfolios: Portfolio A is fully invested in the 5-year Treasury bond, and Portfolio B is an investment split between the 2-year (58.94%) and the 10-year (41.06%) bonds. The Portfolio B weights were chosen to (approximately) match the 5-year bond duration of 4.88. How will the value of these portfolios change if all three Treasury yields-to-maturity immediately rise or fall by 50 bps?

Using Equation 3, we can derive the percentage value change for Portfolios A and B as well as the dollar value of each $50 million investment:

Portfolio	+ 50 bps % Δ Price	+ 50 bps Δ Price	− 50 bps % Δ Price	− 50 bps Δ Price
A	−2.407%	($1,203,438)	2.473%	$1,236,563
B	−2.390%	($1,194,883)	2.490%	$1,245,170

For example, for the case of a 50 bp increase in rates:

Portfolio A:

$-2.407\% = (-4.880 \times 0.005) + [0.5 \times 26.5 \times (0.005^2)]$

Portfolio B:

$-2.390\% = 0.5894 \times \{[-1.994 \times 0.005] + [0.5 \times 5 \times (0.005^2)]\} + 0.4106 \times \{[-9.023 \times 0.005] + [0.5 \times 90.8 \times (0.005^2)]\}$

Note that Portfolio B gains *more* ($8,607) than Portfolio A when rates fall 50 bps and loses *less* ($8,555) than Portfolio A when rates rise by 50 bps.

The first portfolio concentrated in a single intermediate maturity is often referred to as a **bullet** portfolio. The second portfolio, with similar duration but combining short- and long-term maturities, is a **barbell** portfolio. Although the bullet and barbell have the same duration, the barbell's higher convexity (40.229 versus 26.5 for the bullet) results in a larger gain as yields-to-maturity fall and a smaller loss when yields-to-maturity rise. Convexity is therefore valuable when interest rate volatility is expected to rise. This dynamic tends to cause investors to bid up prices on more convex, longer-maturity bonds, which drives changes in yield curve shape. As a result, the long end of the curve may decline or even invert (or invert further), increasing the curvature of the yield curve.

EXAMPLE 2

Portfolio Convexity

1. Portfolio convexity is a second-order effect that causes the value of a portfolio to respond to a change in yields-to-maturity in a non-linear manner. Which of the following best describes the effect of positive portfolio convexity for a given change in yield-to-maturity?

    a. Convexity causes a greater increase in price for a decline in yields-to-maturity and a greater decrease in price when yields-to-maturity rise.

    b. Convexity causes a smaller increase in price for a decline in yields-to-maturity and a greater decrease in price when yields-to-maturity rise.

c. Convexity causes a greater increase in price for a decline in yields-to-maturity and a smaller decrease in price when yields-to-maturity rise.

Solution:

The correct answer is c. Note that the convexity component of Equation 3 involves squaring the change in yield-to-maturity, or [½ × Convexity × $(\Delta Yield)^2$], making the term positive as long as portfolio convexity is positive. This adds to the overall portfolio gain when yields-to-maturity decline and reduces the portfolio loss when yields-to-maturity rise.

YIELD CURVE STRATEGIES

- [ ] formulate a portfolio positioning strategy given forward interest rates and an interest rate view that coincides with the market view
- [ ] formulate a portfolio positioning strategy given forward interest rates and an interest rate view that diverges from the market view in terms of rate level, slope, and shape
- [ ] formulate a portfolio positioning strategy based upon expected changes in interest rate volatility
- [ ] evaluate a portfolio's sensitivity using key rate durations of the portfolio and its benchmark

Earlier in the curriculum, we established that yield curves are usually upward-sloping, with diminishing marginal yield-to-maturity increases at longer tenors—that is, flatter at longer maturities. As nominal yields-to-maturity incorporate an expected inflation premium, positively sloped yield curves are consistent with market expectations of rising or stable future inflation and relatively strong economic growth. Investor expectations of higher yields-to-maturity for assuming the increased interest rate risk of long-term bonds also contribute to this positive slope. Active managers often begin with growth and inflation forecasts, which they then translate into expected yield curve level, slope, and/or curvature changes. If their forecasts coincide with today's yield curve, managers will choose active strategies that are consistent with a static or stable yield curve. If their forecasts differ from what today's yield curve implies about these future yield curve characteristics, managers will position the portfolio to generate excess return based upon this divergent view, within the constraints of their investment mandate, using the cash and derivatives strategies we discuss next.

Static Yield Curve

A portfolio manager may believe that bonds are fairly priced and that the existing yield curve will remain unchanged over an investment horizon.

The two basic ways in which a manager may actively position a bond portfolio versus a benchmark index to generate excess return from a static or stable yield curve is to increase risk by adding either duration or leverage to the portfolio. If the yield curve is upward-sloping, longer duration exposure will result in a higher yield-to-maturity over time, while the "repo carry" trade (the difference between a higher-yielding instrument purchased and a lower-yielding (financing) instrument) will also generate excess returns.

Starting with cash-based instruments, "buy-and-hold" is an obvious strategy if the yield curve is upward-sloping. In an active context, this involves buying bonds with duration above the benchmark without active trading during a subsequent period. If the relationship between long- and short-term yields-to-maturity remains stable over this period, the manager is rewarded with higher return from the incremental duration. "Rolling down" the yield curve, a concept introduced previously, differs slightly from the "buy-and-hold" approach in terms of the investment time horizon and expected accumulation. The rolling yield component of Equation 1 (sometimes referred to as "carry-rolldown") incorporates not only coupon income (adjusted over time for any price difference from par) but also additional return from the passage of time and the investor's ability to sell the shorter-maturity bond in the future at a higher price (lower yield-to-maturity due to the upward-sloping yield curve) at the end of the investment horizon. If the yield curve is upward-sloping, buying bonds with a maturity *beyond* the investment horizon offers a total return (higher coupon plus price appreciation) greater than the purchase of a bond with maturity *matching* the investment horizon if the curve remains static. Finally, a common strategy known as a repurchase agreement or repo trade may be used in an expected stable rate environment to add leverage risk to the portfolio. The repo market involves buying a long-term security and financing it at a short-term rate below the long-term yield-to-maturity—that is, earning a positive "repo carry." At the end of the trade, the bond is sold and the repo is unwound. These cash-based strategies are summarized in Exhibit 5 and Exhibit 6.

Exhibit 5: Cash-Based Static Yield Curve Strategies

Strategy	Description	Income	Objective
Buy-and-hold	Constant without active trading	Coupon income	Add duration beyond target given static yield curve view
Rolling down the yield curve	Constant, with Δ Price as maturity shortens	Coupon income +/− Rolldown return	Add duration and increased return if future shorter-term yields are below current yield-to-maturity
Repo carry trade	Finance bond purchase in repo market	(Coupon income +/− Rolldown return)—Financing cost	Generate repo carry return if coupon plus rolldown exceeds financing cost

Yield Curve Strategies

Exhibit 6: Carry, Rolldown, and Buy-and-Hold Strategies under a Static Yield Curve

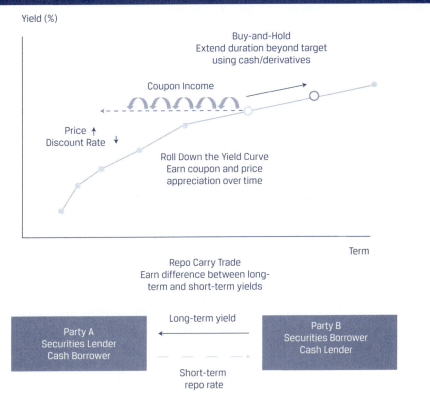

Excess return under these strategies depends upon stable rate levels and yield curve shape. Note that a more nuanced "buy-and-hold" strategy under this scenario could also involve less liquid and higher-yielding government bonds (such as off-the-run bonds). The lack of portfolio turnover may make the strategy seem passive, but in fact it may be quite aggressive as it introduces liquidity risk, a topic addressed in detail later in the curriculum. The ability to benefit from price appreciation by selling a shorter-dated bond at a premium when rolling down (or riding) the yield curve hinges on a reasonably static and upward-sloping yield curve. Not only will the repo carry be maintained under this yield curve scenario, but it also will generate excess return due to the reduced cash outlay versus a term bond purchase.

Active managers whose investment mandate extends to the use of synthetic means to increase risk by adding duration or leverage to the portfolio might consider using the derivatives-based strategies in Exhibit 7 to increase duration exposure beyond a benchmark target. Although the long futures example is similar to rolling down the yield curve, it relies solely on price appreciation rather than bond coupon income. The receive-fixed swap, on the other hand, is similar to the cash-based repo carry trade, but the investor receives the fixed swap rate and pays a market reference rate (MRR), which is often referred to as "swap carry."

Exhibit 7: Derivatives-Based Static Yield Curve Strategies

Strategy	Description	Targeted Return	Goal
Long futures position	Purchase contract for future bond delivery	(Δ Price / Δ Bond yield) − Margin cost	Synthetically increase duration (up-front margin and daily mark-to-market valuation)
Receive-fixed swap	Fixed-rate receiver on an interest rate swap	(Swap rate − MRR) + (Δ Swap mark-to-market / Δ Swap yield)	Synthetically increase portfolio duration (up-front / mark-to-market collateral) +/− Swap carry

As mentioned previously in the curriculum, global exchanges offer a wide range of derivatives contracts across swap, bond, and short-term market reference rates for different settlement dates, and over the counter (OTC) contracts may be uniquely tailored to end user needs. Our treatment here is limited to futures and swaps and will extend to options in a later section.

Although margining was historically limited to exchange-traded derivatives, the advent of derivatives central counterparty (CCP) clearing mandated by regulatory authorities following the 2008 global financial crisis to mitigate counterparty risk has given rise to similar cash flow implications for OTC derivatives. Active managers using both exchange-traded and OTC derivatives must therefore maintain sufficient cash or eligible collateral to fulfill margin or collateral requirements. They must also factor any resulting foregone portfolio return into their overall performance. That said, since the initial cash outlay for a derivative is limited to initial margin or collateral as opposed to the full price for a cash bond purchase, derivatives have a high degree of implicit leverage. That is, a small move in price/yield can have a very large effect on a derivative's mark-to-market value (MTM) relative to the margin posted. Exhibit 8 shows these cash flow mechanics. This outsized price effect makes derivatives effective instruments for fixed-income portfolio management.

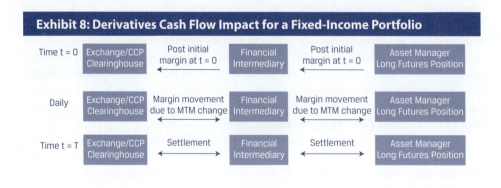

Exhibit 8: Derivatives Cash Flow Impact for a Fixed-Income Portfolio

For example, bond futures involve a contract to take delivery of a bond on a specific future date. Changes in the futures contract value mirror those of the underlying bond's price over time, allowing an investor to create an exposure profile similar to a long bond position by purchasing this contract with a fraction of the outlay of a cash bond purchase. While futures contracts are covered in detail elsewhere in the curriculum, for our purposes here it is important to establish the basis point value (BPV) of a futures contract. Most government bond futures are traded and settled using the least costly or cheapest-to-deliver (CTD) bond among those eligible for future delivery. For example, the CME Group's Ultra 10-Year US Treasury Note Futures contract specifies delivery of an original 10-year issue Treasury security with not less than 9 years, five

Yield Curve Strategies

months and not more than 10 years to maturity with an assumed 6% yield-to-maturity and contract size of $100,000. The "duration" of the bond futures contract is assumed to match that of the CTD security. In order to determine the futures BPV, we use the following approximation introduced previously:

$$\text{Futures BPV} \approx \text{BPV}_{CTD} / \text{CF}_{CTD}, \qquad (6)$$

where CF_{CTD} is the conversion factor for the CTD security. For government bond futures with a fixed basket of underlying bonds, such as Australian Treasury bond futures, the futures BPV simply equals the BPV of an underlying basket of bonds.

The manager in Example 1 can replicate the 10-year Treasury exposure using futures by matching the BPV of the cash bond. As explained elsewhere, the BPV of the $20.53 million (or 41.06% × $50 million) 10-year Treasury position equals the modified duration (9.023) multiplied by the full price (also known as the money duration) times one basis point, or $18,524. If the CTD security under the Ultra 10-Year Futures contract is a Treasury bond also priced at par but with 9.5 years remaining to maturity, modified duration of 8.84, and a conversion factor of 0.684, then each $100,000 futures contract has a BPV of $129.24 ($88.40/0.684). The manager must therefore buy approximately 143 futures contracts ($18,524/$129.24) to replicate the exposure. Note that as shown in Exhibit 8, this will involve an outlay of initial margin and margin movement due to MTM changes rather than investment of full principal.

An interest rate swap involves the net exchange of fixed-for-floating payments, where the fixed rate (swap rate) is derived from short-term market reference rates for a given tenor. As shown in Exhibit 9, the swap contract may be seen as a combination of bonds, namely a fixed-rate bond versus a floating-rate bond of the same maturity.

Exhibit 9: Swaps as a Duration Management Tool

Note the similarities between the "carry" trade in Exhibit 5 and the receive-fixed interest rate swap position on the right in Exhibit 9. The fixed-rate receiver is "long" a fixed-rate term bond and "short" a floating-rate bond, giving rise to an exposure profile that mimics a "long" cash bond position by increasing duration. A swap's BPV may be estimated using Equation 7.

$$\text{Swap BPV} = \text{ModDur}_{Swap} \times \text{Swap Notional}/10{,}000. \qquad (7)$$

The difference between the receive-fixed swap and long fixed-rate bond positions is best understood via an example.

EXAMPLE 3

Calculating Bond versus Swap Returns

Say a UK-based manager seeks to extend duration beyond an index by adding 10-year exposure. The manager considers either buying and holding a 10-year, 2.25% semi-annual coupon UK government bond priced at £93.947, with a corresponding yield-to-maturity of 2.9535%, or entering a new 10-year, GBP receive-fixed interest rate swap at 2.8535% versus the six-month GBP MRR currently set at 0.5925%. The swap has a modified duration of 8.318. We compare the results of both strategies over a six-month time horizon for a £100 million par value during which both the bond yield-to-maturity and swap rates fall 50 bps. We ignore day count details in the calculation.

Position	Income	Price Appreciation/ MTM	Gain in 6 Months
10y UK bond	£1,125,000	£4,337,779	£5,462,778
10y GBP swap	£1,130,500	£4,234,260	£5,364,760

The relevant return components from Equation 1 are income, namely coupon income for the bond versus "carry" for the swap, and E (Δ Price due to investor's view of benchmark yield) in the form of price appreciation for the bond versus an MTM gain for the swap:

10-Year UK Government Bond:

Coupon income = £1,125,000, or (2.25%/2) × £100 million.

Price appreciation = £4,337,779. Using Excel, this is the difference between the 10-year, or [PV (0.029535/2, 20, 1.125, 100)], and the 9.5-year bond at the lower yield-to-maturity, or [PV (0.024535/2, 19, 1.125, 100)] × £1 million.

We can separate bond price appreciation into two components:

Rolldown return: The difference between the 10-year and 9.5-year PV with *no* change in yield-to-maturity of £262,363, or [PV (0.029535/2, 20, 1.125, 100)] – [PV (0.029535/2, 19, 1.125, 100)] × £1 million].

(Δ Price due to investor's view of benchmark yield): The difference in price for a 50 bp shift of the 9.5-year bond of £4,075,415, or [PV (0.029535/2, 19, 1.125, 100)] – [PV (0.024535/2, 19, 1.125, 100)] × £1 million.

10-Year GBP Swap:

Swap carry = £1,130,500, or [(2.8535% – 0.5925%)/2] × £100,000,000.

Swap MTM gain = £4,234,260. The swap MTM gain equals the difference between the fixed leg and floating leg, which is currently at par. The fixed leg equals the 9.5-year swap value given a 50 bp shift in the fixed swap rate, which is £104,234,260, or [PV(0.023535/2, 19, 2.8535/2, 100)] × £1 million, and the floating leg is priced at par and therefore equal to £100,000,000.

We can use Equation 7 to derive an approximate swap MTM change of £4,159,000 by multiplying swap BPV (8.318 × £100 million) by 50 bps. As in the case of a bond future, the cash outlay for the swap is limited to required collateral or margin for the transaction as opposed to the bond's full cash price. Note that for the purposes of this example, we have ignored any interest on the difference between the bond investment and the cash outlay for the swap.

While these strategies are designed to gain from a static or stable interest rate term structure, we now turn to portfolio positioning in a changing yield curve environment.

> **EXAMPLE 4**
>
> **Static Yield Curve Strategies under Curve Inversion**
>
> 1. An investment manager who pursues the cash-based yield curve strategies described in Exhibit 5 faces an inverted yield curve (with a decline in long-term yields-to-maturity and a sharp increase in short-term yields-to-maturity) instead of a static yield curve post implementation. Which of the following is the *least* likely portfolio outcome under this scenario?
>
>   **a.** The manager realizes a loss on a "buy-and-hold" position that extends duration beyond that of the index.
>
>   **b.** The manager faces negative carry when financing a bond purchase in the repo market.
>
>   **c.** The manager is able to reinvest coupon income from a yield curve rolldown strategy at a higher short-term yield-to-maturity.
>
> **Solution:**
>
> The correct answer is a. The fall in long-term yields-to-maturity will lead to price *appreciation* under the "buy-and-hold" strategy. The difference between long-term and short-term yields-to-maturity in b will fall, leading to negative carry if short-term yields-to-maturity rise sharply. As for c, higher short-term yields-to-maturity will enable the manager to reinvest bond coupon payments at a higher rate.

Dynamic Yield Curve

Exhibits 1 through 3 show that yield curves are dynamic over time, with significant changes in the level, slope, and curvature of rates across maturities. Unless otherwise specified, the sole focus here is on instantaneous yield-to-maturity changes affecting $E(\Delta$ Price due to investor's view of benchmark yields), the third component of Equation 1.

Divergent Rate Level View

The principal components analysis cited earlier underscores that rate level changes are the key driver of changes in single bond or bond portfolio values. The first term in Equation 3 shows that bond value changes result from yield-to-maturity changes multiplied by a duration statistic. For active fixed-income managers with a divergent rate level view, positioning the portfolio to increase profit as yield levels fall or minimizing losses as yield levels rise is of primary importance. To be clear, a divergent rate level view implies an expectation of a *parallel* shift in the yield curve, as shown in Exhibit 10.

Exhibit 10: Yield Level Changes

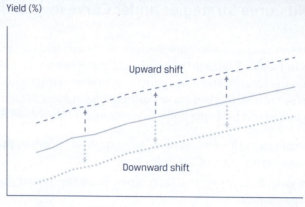

Exhibit 10 shows a general decline in bond yield levels, referred to as a bull market, since 2007. This trend began in late 1981 when the 10-year US Treasury yield-to-maturity peaked at nearly 16%, a consequence of contractionary US Federal Reserve monetary policy in which the short-term federal funds rate was raised to 20% to combat double-digit inflation. Extending duration beyond a target index over this period was a winning active strategy, despite occasional periods of yield increases. Exhibit 11 summarizes the major strategies an active manager might pursue if she expects lower yield levels and downside risks.

Exhibit 11: Major Yield Curve Strategies to Increase Portfolio Duration

Strategy	Description	Expected Excess Return	Downside Risks
Cash bond purchase ("bullet")	Extend duration with longer-dated bonds	Price appreciation as yield-to-maturity declines	Higher yield levels
Receive-fixed swap	Fixed-rate receiver on an interest rate swap	Swap MTM gain plus "carry" (fixed minus floating rate)	Higher swap yield levels and/or higher floating rates
Long futures position	Purchase contract for forward bond delivery	Futures MTM gain – Margin cost	Higher bond yields and/or higher margin cost

Assume the "index" portfolio equally weights the 2-, 5-, and 10-year Treasuries priced at par from Example 1, while a higher duration "active" portfolio is weighted 25% for 2- and 5-year Treasuries, respectively, and 50% in 10-year Treasuries. Average portfolio statistics are summarized here:

Portfolio	Coupon	Modified Duration	Convexity
Index	1.042%	5.299	40.8
Active (25/25/50)	1.281%	6.230	53.3

We can see from this table that the active portfolio has a blended coupon nearly 24 bps above that of the index.

Yield Curve Strategies

We now turn to the impact of a parallel yield curve shift on the index versus active portfolios. Assuming an instantaneous 30 bp downward shift in yields-to-maturity, the index portfolio value would rise by approximately 1.608%, or (−5.299 × −0.003) + 0.5 × (40.8) × (−0.003^2), versus an estimated 1.893% increase for the actively managed portfolio, a positive difference of nearly $285,000 for a $100 million portfolio.

EXAMPLE 5

Portfolio Impact of Higher Yield-to-Maturity Levels

1. Consider a $50 million Treasury portfolio equally weighted between 2-, 5-, and 10-year Treasuries using parameters from the prior example as the index, and an active portfolio with 20% each in 2- and 5-year Treasuries and the remaining 60% invested in 10-year Treasuries. Which of the following is closest to the active versus index portfolio value change due to a 40 bp rise in yields-to-maturity?

    a. Active portfolio declines by $181,197 more than the index portfolio
    b. Active portfolio declines by $289,915 more than the index portfolio
    c. Index portfolio declines by $289,915 more than the active portfolio

Solution:

The correct answer is b. First, we must establish average portfolio statistics for the 20/20/60 portfolio using a weighted average of duration (6.79 versus 5.299 for the index) and convexity (60.8 versus 40.8 for the index). Second, using these portfolio statistics, we must calculate %ΔPV^{Full}, as shown in Equation 3, for both the index and active portfolios, which are −2.087% for the index and −2.667% for the active portfolio, respectively. Finally, we multiply the difference of −0.58% by the $50 million notional to get −$289,915.

Receive-fixed swaps or long futures positions may be used in place of a cash bond strategy to take an active view on rates. Note that most fixed-income managers will tend to favor option-free over callable bonds if taking a divergent rate level view due to the greater liquidity of option-free bonds. An exception to this arises when investors formulate portfolio positioning strategies based upon expected changes in interest rate volatility, as we will discuss in detail later in this lesson.

As 2020 began, some analysts expected government yields-to-maturity to eventually rise following over a decade of quantitative easing after the 2008 global financial crisis. However, yields instead reached new lows during 2020 when the COVID-19 pandemic caused a sharp economic slowdown, prompting additional monetary and fiscal policy stimulus. If analysts expected a strong economic rebound to increase yield levels, they might seek to lessen the adverse impact of higher rate levels by reducing duration. Exhibit 12 outlines major strategies to achieve this goal.

Exhibit 12: Major Yield Curve Strategies to Reduce Portfolio Duration

Strategy	Description	Expected Excess Return	Downside Risks
Cash bond sale ("bullet")	Reduce duration with short sale/switch to shorter-dated bonds	Smaller price decline as yield-to-maturity increases	Lower yield levels
Pay-fixed (interest rate swap)	Fixed-rate payer on an interest rate swap	Swap MTM gain plus "swap carry" (MRR − Fixed swap rate)	Swap MTM loss amid lower swap yield levels and/or lower floating rates
Short futures position	Sell contract for forward bond delivery	Futures MTM gain − Margin cost	Futures MTM loss amid lower bond yields and/or higher margin cost

Returning to our "index" portfolio of equally weighted 2-, 5-, and 10-year Treasuries, we now consider an active portfolio positioned to reduce downside exposure to higher yields-to-maturity versus the index. In order to limit changes to the bond portfolio, the manager chooses a swap strategy instead.

> **EXAMPLE 6**
>
> ### Five-Year Pay-Fixed Swap Overlay
>
> In this example, the manager enters into a pay-fixed swap overlay with a notional principal equal to one-half of the size of the total bond portfolio. We will focus solely on first-order effects of yield changes on price (ignoring coupon income and swap carry) to determine the active and index portfolio impact. As the pay-fixed swap is a "short" duration position, it is a negative contribution to portfolio duration and therefore subtracted from rather than added to the portfolio. Recall the $100 million "index" portfolio has a modified duration of 5.299, or (1.994 + 4.88 + 9.023)/3. If the manager enters a $50 million notional 5-year pay-fixed swap with an assumed modified duration of 4.32, the portfolio's modified duration falls to 3.139, or [(5.299 × 100) − (4.32 × 50)]/100. Stated differently, the bond portfolio BPV falls from $52,990 to $31,390 with the swap. For a 25 bp yield increase, this $21,600 reduction in active portfolio BPV reduces the adverse impact of higher rates by approximately $540,000 versus the "index" portfolio.

One point worth noting related to short duration positions is that with the exception of distressed debt situations addressed later in the curriculum, the uncertain cost and availability of individual bonds to borrow and sell short leads many active managers to favor the use of derivatives over short sales to establish a short bond position. Derivatives also facilitate duration changes without interfering with other active bond strategies with a portfolio.

Portfolio managers frequently use average duration and yield level changes to estimate bond portfolio performance in broad terms. However, these approximations are only reasonable if we assume a parallel yield curve shift. As Exhibits 2 and 3 show, non-parallel changes, or shifts in the slope and/or shape of the yield curve, occur frequently and require closer examination of individual positions and rate changes across maturities.

Yield Curve Strategies

Divergent Yield Curve Slope View

Exhibit 2 established that while a positively sloped yield curve prevails under most economic scenarios, this difference between long-term and short-term yields-to-maturity can vary significantly over time. Changes in monetary policy, as well as expectations for growth and inflation, affect yields differently across the term structure, resulting in an increase (steepening) or decrease (flattening) in this spread. Although the **barbell** strategy combining extreme maturities is often referred to in a long-only context as in Example 1, here we take a more generalized approach in which the short-term and long-term security positions within the barbell trade may move in opposite directions—that is, combining a "short" and a "long" position. This type of barbell is an effective tool employed by managers to position a bond portfolio for yield curve steepening or flattening changes, as shown in Exhibit 13.

Exhibit 13: Barbell Strategy for a Yield Curve Slope Change

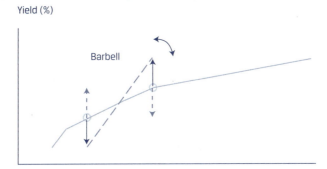

A manager could certainly use a bullet to increase or decrease exposure to a specific maturity in anticipation of a price change that changes yield curve slope, but a *combination* of positions in both short and long maturities with greater cash flow dispersion is particularly well-suited to position for yield curve slope changes or twists. Managers combine long or short positions in either maturity segment to take advantage of expected yield curve slope changes—which may be duration neutral, net long, or short duration depending upon *how* the curve is expected to steepen or flatten in the future. Also, in some instances, the investment policy statement may allow managers to use bonds, swaps, and/or futures to achieve this objective. Finally, while not all strategies shown are cash neutral, here we focus solely on portfolio value changes due to yield changes, ignoring any associated funding or other costs that might arise as a result.

Yield curve steepener strategies seek to gain from an increase in yield curve slope, or a greater difference between long-term and short-term yields-to-maturity. This may be achieved by combining a "long" shorter-dated bond position with a "short" longer-dated bond position. For example, assume an active manager seeks to benefit from yield curve steepening with a net zero duration by purchasing the 2-year Treasury and selling the 10-year Treasury securities from our earlier example, both of which are priced at par.

Tenor	Coupon	Position ($ MM)	Modified Duration	Convexity
Long 2y	0.25%	163.8	1.994	5.0
Short 10y	2.00%	−36.2	9.023	90.8

Note that here and throughout the lesson, negative portfolio positions reflect a "short" position. We can approximate the impact of *parallel* yield curve changes using portfolio duration and convexity. Portfolio duration is approximately zero, or [1.994 × 163.8/(163.8 − 36.2)] + [9.023 × −36.2/(163.8 − 36.2)], and portfolio convexity equals −19.34, or [5.0 × 163.8/(163.8 − 36.2)] + [90.8 × −36.2/(163.8 − 36.2). A 25 bp increase in *both* 2-year and 10-year Treasury yields-to-maturity therefore has no duration effect on the portfolio, although negative convexity leads to a 0.006%, or $7,712 decline in portfolio value, or $127,600,000 × 0.5 × −19.34 × 0.0025^2.

However, changes in the *difference* between short- and long-term yields-to-maturity are not captured by portfolio duration or convexity but rather require assessment of individual positions. For example, if yield curve *slope* increases from 175 bps to 225 bps due to a 25 bp *decline* in 2-year yields-to-maturity and a 25 bp *rise* in 10-year yields-to-maturity, the portfolio increases in value by $1,625,412 as follows:

2y: $819,102 = $163,800,000 × (−1.994 × −0.0025 + 0.5 × 5.0 × $−0.0025^2$)

10y: $806,310 = −$36,200,000 × (−9.023 × 0.0025 + 0.5 × 90.8 × 0.0025^2)

> ### EXAMPLE 7
>
> ### Barbell Performance under a Flattening Yield Curve
>
> Consider a Treasury portfolio consisting of a $124.6 million long 2-year zero-coupon Treasury with an annualized 2% yield-to-maturity and a short $25.41 million 10-year zero-coupon bond with a 4% yield-to-maturity. Calculate the net portfolio duration and solve for the first-order change in portfolio value based upon modified duration assuming a 25 bp rise in 2-year yield-to-maturity and a 30 bp decline in 10-year yield-to-maturity.
>
> First, recall from earlier in the curriculum that Macaulay duration (MacDur) is equal to maturity for zero-coupon bonds and modified duration (ModDur) is equal to MacDur/1+r, where r is the yield per period. We can therefore solve for the modified duration of the 2-year zero as 1.96 (= 2/1.02) and the 10-year zero as 9.62 (= 10/1.04), so net portfolio duration equals zero, or (124.6 − 25.41 × 1.96) + (−25.4/124.6 − 25.41 × 9.62).
>
> We may show that the 2-year Treasury BPV is close to $24,430 (= 1.96 × 124,600,000/10,000) and the 10-year Treasury position BPV is also approximately $24,430 (= 9.61 × 25,410,000/10,000), but it is a short position. Therefore a 25 bp *increase* in 2-year yield-to-maturity *decreases* portfolio value by $610,750 (25 bps × $24,430), while a 30 bp *decrease* in the 10-year yield-to-maturity also *decreases* portfolio value (due to the short position) by an additional $732,900 (= 30 bps × $24,430), for a total approximate portfolio *loss* of $1,343,650.

The portfolio manager is indifferent as to whether the portfolio gain from a greater slope arises due to a greater change in value from short-term or long-term yield movements as the duration is matched between the two positions. Two variations of a steeper yield curve adapted from Smith (2014) are shown in Exhibit 14.

Yield Curve Strategies

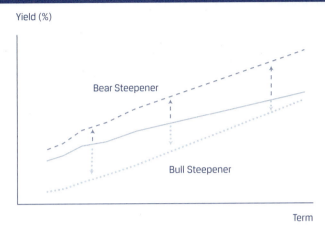

Exhibit 14: Yield Curve Slope Changes—Steepening

In an earlier lesson on establishing a rate view, we highlighted a **bull steepening** scenario under which short-term yields-to-maturity fall by more than long-term yields-to-maturity if the monetary authority cuts benchmark rates to stimulate economic activity during a recession. Exhibit 15 shows the bull steepening that occurred in the UK gilt yield curve amid the 2008 global financial crisis. After reaching a cycle peak of 5.75% in July 2007, the Bank of England cut its monetary policy base rate six times, down to 2.00% in early December 2008, due to weakening economic conditions and financial market stress.

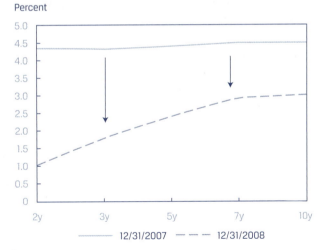

Exhibit 15: UK Government Yields, 2007 versus 2008 (Year End)

Source: Bloomberg.

On the other hand, a **bear steepening** occurs when long-term yields-to-maturity rise more than short-term yields-to-maturity. This could result from a jump in long-term rates amid higher growth and inflation expectations while short-term rates remain unchanged. In this case, an analyst might expect the next central bank policy change to be a monetary tightening to curb inflation.

Bull or bear steepening expectations will change the strategy an active fixed-income manager might pursue, as seen in Exhibit 16.

Exhibit 16: Yield Curve Steepener Strategies

Strategy	Description	Expected Excess Return	Downside Risks
Duration neutral	Net zero duration	Portfolio gain from yield curve slope increase	Yield curve flattening
Bear steepener	Net negative ("short") duration	Portfolio gain from slope increase and/or rising yields	Yield curve flattening and/or lower yields
Bull steepener	Net positive ("long") duration	Portfolio gain from slope increase and/or lower yields	Yield curve flattening and/or higher yields

For example, assume an active manager expects the next yield curve change to be a bull steepening and establishes the following portfolio using the same 2-year and 10-year Treasury securities as in our prior examples.

Tenor	Coupon	Position ($ MM)	Modified Duration	Convexity
Long 2y	0.25%	213.8	1.994	5.0
Short 10y	2.00%	−36.2	9.023	90.8

In contrast to the earlier duration-matched steepener, the bull steepener increases the 2-year long Treasury position by $50 million, introducing a net long duration position to capitalize on an anticipated greater decline in short-term yields-to-maturity. We can see this by solving for portfolio duration of 0.5613, or [1.994 × 213.8/(213.8 − 36.2)] + [9.023 × −36.2/(213.8 − 36.2)], which is equivalent to a portfolio BPV of approximately $9,969, or 0.5613 × [($213,800,000 − $36,200,000)/10,000]. We may use this portfolio BPV to estimate the approximate portfolio gain if the 2-year yield-to-maturity and the 10-year yield-to-maturity fall by 25 bps, which is equal to $249,225 (= 25 bps × $9,969).

Yield curve flattening involves an anticipated narrowing of the difference between long-term and short-term yields-to-maturity, two basic variations of which are shown in Exhibit 17 and are adapted from Smith (2014).

Yield Curve Strategies

Exhibit 17: Yield Curve Slope Changes—Flattening

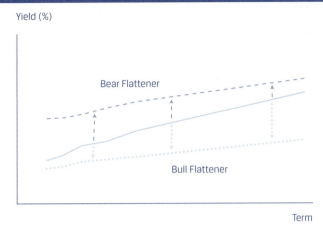

A flatter yield curve may follow monetary policy actions due to changing growth and inflation expectations. For example, a **bear flattening** scenario might follow the bear steepening move seen in Exhibit 15 if policymakers respond to rising inflation expectations and higher long-term rates by raising short-term policy rates. It was established earlier in the curriculum that investors sell higher risk assets and buy default risk-free government bonds in a flight to quality during highly uncertain markets, a situation which often contributes to **bull flattening** as long-term rates fall more than short-term rates. Flattener strategies may use a barbell strategy, which reverses the exposure profile of a steepener—namely, a "short" short-term bond position and a "long" long-term bond position. The bull and bear variations of this strategy are summarized in Exhibit 18.

Exhibit 18: Yield Curve Flattener Strategies

Strategy	Description	Expected Excess Return	Downside Risks
Duration neutral	Net zero duration position	Portfolio gain from yield curve slope decrease	Yield curve steepening
Bear flattener	Net negative duration position	Portfolio gain from slope decrease and/or rising yields	Yield curve steepening and/or lower yields
Bull flattener	Net positive duration position	Portfolio gain from slope decrease and/or lower yields	Yield curve steepening and/or higher yields

Say, for example, a French investor expects the government yield curve to flatten over the next six months following years of quantitative easing by the European Central Bank through 2019. Her lack of a view as to whether this will occur amid lower or higher rates causes her to choose a duration neutral flattener using available French government (OAT) zero-coupon securities. She decides to enter the following trade at the beginning of 2020:

Tenor	Yield	Price	Notional (€ MM)	Modified Duration	Position BPV	Convexity
Short 2y	−0.65%	€101.313	−83.24	2.013	(€16,975)	6.1
Long 10y	0.04%	€99.601	17.05	9.996	€16,977	110

Note that as the Excel PRICE function returns a #NUM! error value for bonds with negative yields-to-maturity, we calculate the 2-year OAT zero-coupon bond price of 101.313 using $100/(1 - 0.0065)^2$. The initial portfolio BPV close to zero tells us that parallel yield curve shifts will have little effect on portfolio value, while the short 2-year and long 10-year trades position the manager to profit from a decline in the current 69 bp spread between 2- and 10-year OAT yields-to-maturity. After six months, the portfolio looks as follows:

Tenor	Yield	Price	Notional (€ MM)	Modified Duration	Convexity
Short 1.5y	−0.63%	€100.95	−83.24	1.51	3.8
Long 9.5y	−0.20%	€101.92	17.05	9.52	100.2

At the end of six months (June 2020), the sharp decline in economic growth and inflation expectations due to the COVID-19 pandemic caused the OAT yield curve to flatten as the 10-year yield-to-maturity fell. The six-month barbell return of €695,332 is comprised of rolldown return and yield changes, calculated as follows:

Rolldown Return

Zero-coupon bonds usually accrete in value as time passes if rates remain constant and the yield-to-maturity is positive. However, under negative yields-to-maturity, amortization of the bond's premium will typically result in a *negative* rolldown return. In our example, the investor is short the original 2-year zero and therefore realizes a *positive* rolldown return on the short position. Rolldown return on the barbell may be shown to be approximately €277,924, as follows:

"Short" 2-year: $-€83.24 \text{ MM} \times ([1/(1 + -0.65\%)^{1.5}] - [1/(1 + -0.65\%)^2])$

"Long" 10-year: $€17.05 \text{ MM} \times ([1/(1 + 0.04\%)^{9.5}] - [1/(1 + 0.04\%)^{10}])$

Δ Price Due to Benchmark Yield Changes

The yield difference falls from 69 bps to 43 bps, mostly due to a 24 bp decline in the 10-year yield-to-maturity. Note that the Excel DURATION and MDURATION functions also return a #NUM! error for negative yields-to-maturity. We may use either price changes, as shown next, or the modified duration and convexity statistics as of the end of the investment horizon, just shown, to calculate a return of €417,408 using Equation 3.

"Short" 2-year: $-€83.24 \text{ MM} \times ([1/(1 + -0.63\%)^{1.5}] - [1/(1 + -0.65\%)^{1.5}])$

"Long" 10-year: $€17.05 \text{ MM} \times ([1/(1 - 0.20\%)^{9.5}] - 1/(1 + 0.04\%)^{9.5}])$

As we have considered duration-neutral, long, and short duration strategies to position the portfolio for expected yield curve slope changes, average duration is clearly no longer a sufficient summary statistic. A barbell strategy has greater cash flow dispersion and is therefore more convex than a bullet strategy, implying that its value will decrease by less than a bullet if yields-to-maturity rise and increase by more than a bullet if yields-to-maturity fall. We therefore must consider portfolio convexity in addition to duration when weighing yield curve slope strategies under different scenarios.

Yield Curve Strategies

Divergent Yield Curve Shape View

As described in Section 2.1, yield curve shape or curvature describes the relationship between short-, medium-, and long-term yields-to-maturity across the term structure. Recall from Equation 2 that we quantify the butterfly spread by subtracting both short- and long-term rates from twice the intermediate yield-to-maturity. Since the difference between short- and medium-term rates is typically greater than that between medium- and long-term rates, the butterfly spread is usually positive, as seen earlier in Exhibit 3.

What factors drive yield curve curvature changes as distinct from rate level or curve slope changes? The segmented markets hypothesis introduced previously offers one explanation: Different market participants face either regulatory or economic asset/liability management constraints that drive the supply and demand for fixed-income instruments within different segments of the term structure. For example, a potential factor driving the apparent butterfly spread volatility in Exhibit 3 is the active central bank purchases of Treasury securities at specific maturities under its quantitative easing policy.

The most common yield curve curvature strategy combines a long bullet with a short barbell portfolio (or vice versa) in what is referred to as a **butterfly strategy** to capitalize on expected yield curve shape changes. The short-term and long-term bond positions of the barbell form the "wings," while the intermediate-term bullet bond position forms the "body" of the butterfly, as illustrated in Exhibit 19. Note that unlike the steepener and flattener cases, the investor is either "long" or "short" *both* a short-term and long-term bond and enters into an intermediate-term bullet trade in the opposite direction.

Exhibit 19: Butterfly Strategy

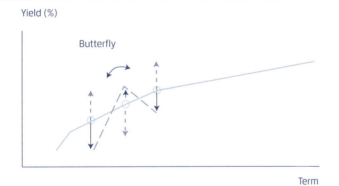

For example, consider a situation in which an active manager expects the butterfly spread to rise due to lower 2- and 10-year yields-to-maturity and a higher 5-year Treasury yield-to-maturity. Using the same portfolio statistics as in prior examples with bonds priced at par, consider the following combined *short* (5-year) bullet and *long* (2-year and 10-year) barbell strategy.

Tenor	Yield to Maturity	Position ($ MM)	Modified Duration	Position BPV	Convexity
Long 2y	0.25%	110	1.994	$21,934	5.0
Short 5y	0.875%	−248.3	4.88	($121,170)	26.5
Long 10y	2.00%	110	9.023	$99,253	90.8

While the sum of portfolio positions (−$28.3 MM) shows that the investor has a net "short" bond position, we can verify the strategy is duration neutral by either adding up the position BPVs or calculating the portfolio duration, or [1.994 × (110/−28.3)] + [4.88 × (−248.3/−28.3)] + [9.023 × (110/−28.3)] to confirm that both are approximately zero. The portfolio convexity may be shown as −139.9, or [5.0 × (110/−28.3)] + [26.5 × (−248.3/−28.3)] + [90.8 × (110/−28.3)].

How does this portfolio perform if 2- and 10-year Treasury yields-to-maturity fall by 25 bps each and the 5-year yield-to-maturity rises by 50 bps? A duration-based estimate multiplying each position BPV by the respective yield change gives us an approximation of $9,088,175, or (+25 bps × $21,934) + −(50 bps × -$121,170) + (+25 bps × $99,253). A more precise answer of $9,038,877 incorporating convexity for each position may be derived using Equation 3. You might ask why the precise portfolio value change is below our approximation. The answer lies in the relative *magnitude* of yield changes across the curve. Since the 5-year yield-to-maturity is assumed to increase by 50 bps rather than 25 bps, the convexity impact of the short bullet position outweighs that of the long barbell. Although the portfolio is nearly immune to parallel yield curve changes with a BPV close to zero, the portfolio gain in our example coincides with an increase in the butterfly spread from −50 bps to +100 bps.

This example shows that an active manager's specific view on *how* yield curve shape will change will dictate the details of the combined bullet and barbell strategy. Exhibit 20, adapted from Smith (2014), shows both the **negative butterfly** view just shown as well as a **positive butterfly**, which indicates a *decrease* in the butterfly spread due to an expected rise in short- and long-term yields-to-maturity combined with a lower medium-term yield-to-maturity. Note that a positive butterfly view indicates a decrease in butterfly spread due to a bond's inverse price–yield relationship.

Yield Curve Strategies

Exhibit 20: Yield Curve Curvature Changes

A. Negative Butterfly

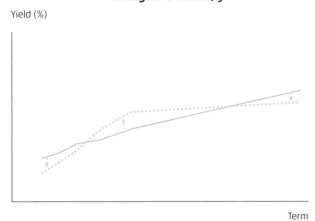

B. Positive Butterfly

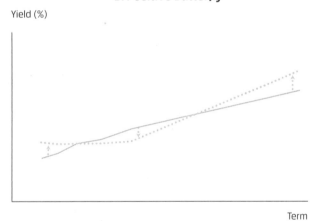

Note that as in the case of yield curve slope strategies, the *combination* of a short bullet and long barbell increases portfolio convexity due to higher cash flow dispersion, making this a more meaningful portfolio risk measure for this strategy than average duration (which remains neutral in the Exhibit 20 example). Exhibit 21 summarizes the two butterfly strategies.

Exhibit 21: Yield Curve Curvature Strategies

Expected Scenario	Investor's Expectation	Active Position
Negative butterfly	Lower short- and long-term yields, Higher medium-term yields	Short bullet, Long barbell (long positions in short- and long-term bonds)
Positive butterfly	Higher short- and long-term yields, Lower medium-term yields	Long bullet, Short barbell (short positions in short- and long-term bonds)

Yield Curve Volatility Strategies

While the prior sections focused on strategies using option-free bonds and swaps and futures as opposed to bonds with embedded options and stand-alone option strategies, we now explicitly address the role of volatility in active fixed-income management.

Option-only strategies play a more modest role in overall yield curve management. In markets such as in the United States where a significant portion of outstanding fixed-income bonds, such as asset-backed securities, have embedded options, investors use cash bond positions with embedded options more frequently than stand-alone options to manage volatility. For example, as of 2019 approximately 30% of the Bloomberg Barclays US Aggregate Bond Index was comprised of securitized debt, which mostly includes bonds with embedded options. As outlined earlier, the purchase of a bond call (put) option offers an investor the right, but not the obligation, to buy (sell) an underlying bond at a pre-determined strike price. An active manager's choice between purchasing or selling bonds with embedded call or put options versus an option-free bond with otherwise similar characteristics hinges upon expected changes in the option value and whether the investor is "short" volatility (i.e., has sold the right to call a bond at a fixed price to the issuer), as in the case of callable bonds, or "long" volatility (i.e., owns the right to sell the bond at a fixed price to the issuer), as for putable bonds. Exhibit 22 shows how callable and putable bond prices change versus option-free bonds as yields-to-maturity change.

Exhibit 22: Callable and Putable versus Option-Free Bonds

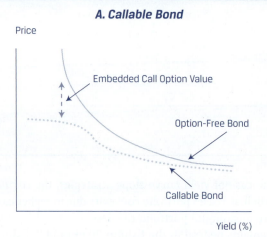

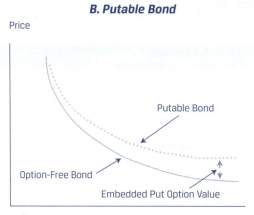

Yield Curve Strategies

> **EXAMPLE 8**
>
> ### Option-Free Bonds versus Callable/Putable Bonds
>
> 1. An investment manager is considering an incremental position in a callable, putable, or option-free bond with otherwise comparable characteristics. If she expects a downward parallel shift in the yield curve, it would be most profitable to be:
>
>   **a.** long a callable bond.
>
>   **b.** short a putable bond.
>
>   **c.** long an option-free bond.
>
> ### Solution:
>
> "C" is correct. The value of a bond with an embedded option is equal to the sum of the value of an option-free bond plus the value to the embedded option. The bond investor can be either long or short the embedded option, depending on the type of bond. With a callable bond, the embedded call option is owned by the issuer of the bond, who can exercise this option if yields-to-maturity decrease (the bond investor is short the call option). With a putable bond, the embedded put option is owned by the bond investor, who can exercise the option if yields-to-maturity increase. For a decrease in yields-to-maturity—as given in the question—the value of the embedded call option increases and the value of the embedded put option decreases. This means that a long position in a callable bond ("A") would underperform compared to a long position in an option-free bond. A short position in a putable bond ("B") would underperform a long position in an option-free bond primarily because yields-to-maturity were declining, although the declining value of the embedded put option would mitigate some of the loss (the seller of the putable bond has "sold" the embedded put).

As mentioned earlier in the curriculum, effective duration and convexity are the relevant summary statistics when future bond cash flows are contingent upon interest rate changes.

$$\text{Effective Duration (EffDur)} = \frac{(PV_-) - (PV_+)}{2 \times (\Delta \text{Curve})(PV_0)}. \tag{8}$$

$$\text{Effective Convexity (EffCon)} = \frac{(PV_-) + (PV_+) - 2(PV_0)}{(\Delta \text{Curve})^2 \times (PV_0)}. \tag{9}$$

In Equation 8 and Equation 9, PV_- and PV_+ are the portfolio values from a decrease and increase in yield-to-maturity, respectively, PV_0 is the original portfolio value, and ΔCurve is the change in the benchmark yield-to-maturity.

Although cash-based yield curve volatility strategies are limited to the availability of liquid callable or putable bonds, several stand-alone derivatives strategies involve the right, but not the obligation, to change portfolio duration and convexity based upon an interest rate-sensitive payoff profile.

Interest rate put and call options are generally based upon a bond's price, not yield-to-maturity. Therefore, the purchase of a bond call option provides an investor the right, but not the obligation, to acquire an underlying bond at a pre-determined strike price. This purchased call option adds convexity to the portfolio and will be exercised if the bond price appreciates beyond the strike price (i.e., generally at a lower yield-to-maturity). On the other hand, a purchased bond put option benefits the owner if prices fall (i.e., yields-to-maturity rise) beyond the strike prior to expiration. Sale of a bond put (call) option limits an investor's return to the up-front premium received in exchange for assuming the potential cost of exercise if bond prices fall below (rise above) the pre-determined strike. Note that the option seller must post margin based on exchange or counterparty requirements until expiration.

An interest rate **swaption** involves the right to enter into an interest rate swap at a specific strike price in the future. This instrument grants the contingent right to increase or decrease portfolio duration. For example, Exhibit 23 shows a purchased payer swaption, which a manager might purchase to benefit from higher rates using an option-based strategy.

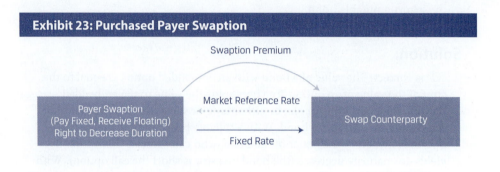

Exhibit 23: Purchased Payer Swaption

Options on bond futures contracts are liquid exchange-traded instruments frequently used by fixed-income market participants to buy or sell the right to enter into a futures position. Long option, swaption, and bond futures option strategies are summarized in Exhibit 24.

Exhibit 24: Long Option, Swaption, and Bond Futures Option Strategies

Strategy	Description	Targeted Return	Portfolio Duration Impact
Long bond call option	Purchase right to take forward bond delivery	Max (Bond price at lower yield – Strike price, 0) – Call premium	Increase portfolio duration
Long bond put option	Purchase right to deliver bond in the future	Max (Strike price – Bond price at higher yield, 0) – Put premium	Decrease portfolio duration
Long payer swaption	Own the right to pay-fixed on an interest rate swap at a strike rate	Max (Strike rate – Swap rate, 0) – Swaption premium	Decrease in portfolio duration
Long receiver swaption	Own the right to receive-fixed on an interest rate swap at a strike rate	Max (Swap rate – Strike rate, 0) – Swaption premium	Increase in portfolio duration
Long call option on bond future	Own the right to take forward bond delivery at a strike price	Max (Bond futures price at lower yield – Strike price, 0) – Call premium	Increase in portfolio duration
Long put option on bond future	Own the right to deliver bond in the future at a strike price	Max (Strike price – Bond futures price at higher yield, 0) – Put premium	Decrease in portfolio duration

Yield Curve Strategies

EXAMPLE 9

Choice of Option Strategy

1. A parallel upward shift in the yield curve is expected. Which of the following would be the best option strategy?

   a. Long a receiver swaption
   b. Short a payer swaption
   c. Long a put option on a bond futures contract

Solution:

C is correct. With an expected upward shift in the yield curve, the portfolio manager would want to reduce portfolio duration in anticipation of lower bond prices. A put option increases in value as the yield curve shifts upward, while the price of the underlying bond declines below the strike. A is incorrect because a receiver swaption is an option to receive-fixed in an interest rate swap. With fixed-rate bond prices expected to fall as rates rise, the portfolio manager would not want to exercise an option to receive a fixed strike rate, which is similar to owning a fixed-rate bond. B is incorrect because a payer swaption is an option to pay-fixed/receive-floating in an interest rate swap. A *long*, not a short, position in a payer swaption would benefit from higher rates.

In an expected stable or static yield curve environment, an active manager may aim to "sell" volatility in the form of either owning callable bonds (which is an implicit "sale" of an option) or selling stand-alone options in order to earn premium income, if this is within the investment mandate. The active portfolio decision here depends upon the manager's view as to whether future realized volatility will be greater or less than the implied volatility, as reflected by the price of a stand-alone option or a bond with embedded options. The manager will benefit if rates remain relatively constant and the bond is not called and/or the options sold expire worthless. Alternatively, if yield curve volatility is expected to increase, a manager may prefer to be long volatility in order to capitalize on large changes in level, yield curve slope, and/or shape using option-based contracts.

EXAMPLE 10

Option-Free versus Callable and Putable Bonds Amid Higher Yield Levels

1. Given a parallel shift upwards in the yield curve, what is the most likely ordering in terms of expected decline in value—from least to most—for otherwise comparable bonds? Assume that the embedded options are deep out-of-the-money.

   a. Callable bond, option-free bond, putable bond
   b. Putable bond, callable bond, option-free bond
   c. Putable bond, option-free bond, callable bond

> **Solution:**
>
> Answer: B is correct. The value of a bond with an embedded option may be considered as the value of an option-free bond plus the value of the embedded option. While the upward shift in the yield curve will cause the option-free component of each bond to depreciate in value, this change in yields-to-maturity will also affect the value of embedded options.
>
> For a putable bond, the bond investor has the option to "put" the bond back to the issuer if yields-to-maturity rise. The more rates rise, the more valuable this embedded option becomes. This increasing option value will partially offset the decline in value of the putable bond relative to the option-free bond. This can be seen in the lower panel of Exhibit 22: The dotted line for the putable bond has a flatter slope than the solid line for the option-free bond; its price will decrease more slowly as yields-to-maturity increase. For a callable bond, the bond issuer has an option to "call" the bond if yields-to-maturity decline; the more rates rise, the lower the call option value. Since the bond investor is short the embedded option and the value of the embedded option has fallen, this will partially offset the decline in the value of the callable bond relative to the option-free bond. The top panel of Exhibit 22 shows that the dotted line for the callable bond has a flatter slope than the solid line for the option-free bond.
>
> As rates continue to increase, the embedded option for the putable bond rises in value more quickly at the margin as it shifts toward becoming an in-the-money option. In contrast, the deep out-of-the-money embedded call option moves further out-of-the-money as rates increase and the marginal impact of further rate increases declines.

Key Rate Duration for a Portfolio

So far, we have evaluated changes in yield curve level, slope, and curvature using one, two, and three specific maturity points across the term structure of interest rates, respectively. The concept of **key rate duration** (or partial duration) introduced previously measures portfolio sensitivity over a set of maturities along the yield curve, with the sum of key rate durations being identical to the effective duration:

$$\text{KeyRateDur}_k = -\frac{1}{\text{PV}} \times \frac{\Delta \text{PV}}{\Delta r_k} \tag{10}$$

$$\sum_{k=1}^{n} \text{KeyRateDur}_k = \text{EffDur}, \tag{11}$$

where r_k represents the kth key rate and PV is the portfolio value. In contrast to effective duration, key rate durations help identify "shaping risk" for a bond portfolio—that is, a portfolio's sensitivity to changes in the shape of the benchmark yield curve. By breaking down a portfolio into its individual duration components by maturity, an active manager can pinpoint and quantify key exposures along the curve, as illustrated in the following simplified zero-coupon bond example.

Compare a passive zero-coupon US Treasury bond portfolio versus an actively managed portfolio:

"Index" Zero-Coupon Portfolio

Tenor	Coupon	Annualized Yield	Price (per $100)	Position ($ MM)	ModDur	KeyRateDur
2y	0.00%	1%	98.03	98.03	1.980	0.738
5y	0.00%	2%	90.57	90.57	4.902	1.688
10y	0.00%	3%	74.40	74.40	9.709	2.747

Assume the "index" portfolio is simply weighted by the price of the respective 2-, 5-, and 10-year bonds for a total portfolio value of $263 million, or $1 million × (98.03 + 90.57 + 74.4). We can calculate the portfolio modified duration as 5.173, or [1.98 × (98.03/263)] + [4.902 × (90.57/263)] + [9.709 × (74.40/263)]. Or, we could calculate each key rate duration by maturity, as in the far right column. For example, the 2-year key rate duration (KeyRateDur$_2$) equals 0.738, or 1.98 × (98.03/263). Note that these three key rate duration values also sum to the portfolio value of 5.173.

"Active" Zero-Coupon Portfolio

Tenor	Coupon	Annualized Yield	Price (per $100)	Position ($ MM)	ModDur	KeyRateDur
2y	0.00%	1%	98.03	51.40	1.980	0.387
5y	0.00%	2%	90.57	−46.00	4.902	−0.857
10y	0.00%	3%	74.40	257.60	9.709	9.509

As in the case of the "index" portfolio, the "active" zero-coupon portfolio has a value of $263 million, or [$1 million × (51.4 − 46 + 257.6)], but the portfolio duration is greater at 9.039, or [1.98 × (51.4/263)] + [4.902 × (−46/263)] + [9.709 × (257.6/263)]. Note that the short 5-year active position has a negative key rate duration of −0.857, or 4.902 × (−46/263).

By now, you may have noticed that our active manager is positioned for the combination of a negative butterfly and a bull flattening at the long end of the yield curve. However, a comparison of the active versus index portfolio duration summary statistic does not tell the entire story. Instead, we can compare the key rate or partial durations for specific maturities across the index and active portfolios to better understand exposure differences:

Tenor	Active	Index	Difference
2y	0.39	0.74	−0.35
5y	−0.86	1.69	−2.55
10y	9.51	2.75	6.76
Portfolio	9.04	5.17	3.87

The key rate duration differences in this chart provide more detailed information regarding the exposure differences across maturities. For example, the negative differences for 2-year and 5-year maturities (−0.35 and −2.55, respectively) indicate that the active portfolio has lower exposure to short-term rates than the index portfolio. The large positive difference in the 10-year tenor shows that the active portfolio has far greater exposure to 10-year yield-to-maturity changes. This simple zero-coupon bond example may be extended to portfolios consisting of fixed-coupon bonds, swaps, and other rate-sensitive instruments that may be included in a fixed-income portfolio, as seen in the following example.

> **EXAMPLE 11**
>
> **Key Rate Duration**
>
> 1. A fixed-income manager is presented with the following key rate duration summary of his actively managed bond portfolio versus an equally weighted index portfolio across 5-, 10-, and 30-year maturities:
>
> | Tenor | Active | Index | Difference |
> |---|---|---|---|
> | 5y | −1.188 | 1.633 | −2.821 |
> | 10y | 2.909 | 3.200 | −0.291 |
> | 30y | 11 | 8.067 | 2.933 |
> | **Portfolio** | 12.72 | 12.9 | −0.179 |
>
> Assume the active manager has invested in the index bond portfolio and used only derivatives to create the active portfolio. Which of the following most likely represents the manager's synthetic positions?
>
> a. Receive-fixed 5-year swap, short 10-year futures, and pay-fixed 30-year swap
>
> b. Pay-fixed 5-year swap, short 10-year futures, and receive-fixed 30-year swap
>
> c. Short 5-year futures, long 10-year futures, and receive-fixed 30-year swap
>
> **Solution:**
>
> Answer: B is correct. The key rate duration summary shows the investor to be net short 5- and 10-year key rate duration and long 30-year key rate duration versus the index. A combines synthetic long, short, and short positions in the 5-, 10-, and 30-year maturities, respectively. C combines short, long, and long positions across the curve. The combination of a pay-fixed (short duration) 5-year swap, a short 10-year futures position, and a receive-fixed (long duration) 30-year swap is, therefore, the best answer.

4. ACTIVE FIXED-INCOME MANAGEMENT ACROSS CURRENCIES

☐ discuss yield curve strategies across currencies

The benefits of investing across borders to maximize return and diversify exposure is a consistent theme among portfolio managers. While both the tools as well as the strategic considerations of active versus passive currency risk management within an investment portfolio are addressed elsewhere, here we will primarily focus on extending our analysis of yield curve strategies from a single yield curve to multiple yield curves across currencies.

Active Fixed-Income Management across Currencies

An earlier currency lesson noted that investors measure return in functional currency terms—that is, considering domestic currency returns on foreign currency assets, as shown in Equation 12 and Equation 13.

Single asset: $R_{DC} = (1 + R_{FC})(1 + R_{FX}) - 1$ (12)

Portfolio: $R_{DC} = \sum_{i=1}^{n} \omega_i (1 + R_{FC,i})(1 + R_{FX,i}) - 1$ (13)

R_{DC} and R_{FC} are the domestic and foreign currency returns expressed as a percentage, R_{FX} is the percentage change of the domestic versus foreign currency, while ω_i is the respective portfolio weight of each foreign currency asset (in domestic currency terms) with the sum of ω_i equal to 1. In the context of Equation 1, R_{DC} simply combines the third factor, $+/-E$ (Δ Price due to investor's view of benchmark yield), and the fifth factor, $+/-E$ (Δ Price due to investor's view of currency value changes), factors in the expected fixed-income return model.

In a previous term structure lesson, we highlighted several macroeconomic factors that influence the bond term premium and required returns, such as inflation, economic growth, and monetary policy. Differences in these factors across countries are frequently reflected in the relative term structure of interest rates as well as in exchange rates.

For example, after a decade of economic expansion following the 2008 global financial crisis, the US Federal Reserve's earlier reversal of quantitative easing versus the European Central Bank through 2019 led to significantly higher short-term government yields-to-maturity in the United States versus Europe.

Against this historical backdrop, assume a German fixed-income manager decides to buy short-term US Treasuries to take advantage of higher USD yields-to-maturity. At the end of March 2019, a USD Treasury zero-coupon bond maturing on 31 March 2021 had a price at 95.656, with an approximate yield-to-maturity of 2.25%. Based upon the then-current USD/EUR spot rate of 1.1218 (that is, $1.1218 = €1), the manager pays €85,270,102 (= $95,656,000/1.1218) for a $100 million face value Treasury security, as seen in Exhibit 25.

Exhibit 25: USD/EUR Spot Trade and US Treasury Zero Purchase

As in the single currency yield curve case, the investor will benefit from bond price appreciation if the US Treasury yield-to-maturity falls during the holding period. In addition, since her domestic returns are measured in EUR, she will also benefit if the USD she receives upon sale of the bond or at maturity buy more EUR per USD in the future—that is, if USD/EUR decreases (i.e., USD *appreciates* versus EUR).

In fact, the flight to quality induced by the COVID-19 pandemic in early 2020 led to a sharp decline in US Treasury yields-to-maturity. Exhibit 26 shows how the relationship between US and German government rates changed between March 2019 and March 2020.

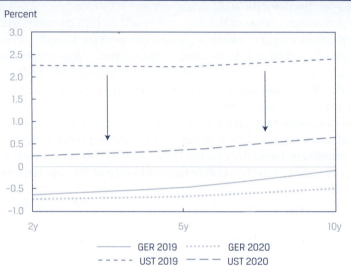

Exhibit 26: US vs. German Government Yield Curves, 2019 and 2020

Source: Bloomberg.

As a result, one year after purchase (31 March 2020), the US Treasury zero-coupon bond maturing 31 March 2021 traded at a price of 100.028 and the USD/EUR spot was 1.1031.

Now we calculate the German investor's 1-year domestic currency return from holding the $100 million par value US Treasury zero-coupon bond.

Equation 12 separates this return into two key components:

R_{FC}: 4.57%, = ($100,028,000/$95,656,000) − 1, as the investor receives $100,028,000 upon sale of the US Treasury bond purchased a year earlier at $95,656,000.

R_{FX}: 1.70%, = (1.1218/1.1031 − 1), as the investor converted €85,270,102 into USD to purchase the bond at 1.1218 and then converted USD proceeds back to EUR at 1.1031. The EUR depreciated (i.e., lower USD/EUR spot rate) over the 1-year period.

R_{DC} may be shown to be 6.34%, solved either using Equation 12 or directly for the 1-year return on investment in EUR terms, = (€90,678,996/€ 85,270,102) −1.

In contrast to the *unhedged* 1-year example, let us now assume that the German manager fully hedges the foreign currency risk associated with the US Treasury bond purchase and holds it instead for two years, at which time she receives the bond's face value of $100,000,000. Specifically, the manager enters a 2-year FX forward agreement at the time of bond purchase to sell the future $100,000,000 payment upon bond maturity and buy EUR at the then current 2-year USD/EUR forward rate of 1.1870, locking in a certain €84,245,998, = $100,000,000/1.1870, in two years' time.

If fully hedged, the expected annualized return, R_{DC}, in EUR terms on the 2-year US Treasury zero-coupon bond hedged EUR investment over two years is equal to −0.60%, = (€84,245,998/€85,270,102)$^{0.5}$ − 1, which matches the 2-year annualized

Active Fixed-Income Management across Currencies

German government zero-coupon bond yield-to-maturity upon inception. This may also be calculated using Equation 12, with $R_{FC} = 2.25\%$ and $R_{FX} = -2.785\%$, or $(1.1218/1.1870)^{0.5} - 1$.

The fully hedged investment example is a reminder from earlier lessons that **covered interest rate parity** establishes a fundamental no-arbitrage relationship between spot and forward rates for individual cash flows in T periods, as shown in Equation 14.

$$F\left(\frac{DC}{FC}, T\right) = S_0(DC/FC)\frac{(1+r_{DC})^T}{(1+r_{FC})^T} \qquad (14)$$

F denotes the forward rate; S is the spot rate; and r_{DC} and r_{FC} reflect the respective domestic and foreign currency risk-free rates. If an investor uses a forward contract to fully hedge foreign currency cash flows, she should expect to earn the domestic risk-free rate, as seen in our example. Recall also that this implies in general that a higher-yielding currency will trade at a forward discount, while a lower-yielding currency will trade at a premium. This is consistent with USD/EUR spot versus forward exchange rates (1.1218 spot versus the 1.187 2-year forward rate) as well as the relationship between USD rates and EUR rates in 2019, as shown in Exhibit 26.

In contrast, **uncovered interest rate parity** suggests that over time, the returns on unhedged foreign currency exposure will be the same as on a domestic currency investment. Although forward FX rates should in theory be an unbiased predictor of future spot FX rates if uncovered interest rate parity holds, in practice investors sometimes seek to exploit a persistent divergence from interest rate parity conditions (known as the **forward rate bias**) by investing in higher-yielding currencies, which is in some cases enhanced by borrowing in lower-yielding currencies.

This demonstrates that active fixed-income strategies across currencies must factor in views on currency appreciation versus depreciation as well as yield curve changes across countries. Our investor's USD versus EUR interest rate view in the previous example combined with an implicit view that USD/EUR would remain relatively stable led to the highest return in the unhedged case with a 1-year investment horizon. This stands in contrast to the relationship between USD/EUR spot and 2-year forward rates at the inception of the trade on 31 March 2019, when implied (annualized) EUR appreciation was 2.87%, = $(1.187/1.1218)^{0.5} - 1$.

The European fixed-income manager in our example might use leverage instead of cash by borrowing in euros when buying the 2-year US Treasury zero. This is an extension of the single currency repo carry trade shown in Exhibit 5, in which an investor borrows short-term in one currency and invests in another higher-yielding currency. This **carry trade across currencies** is a potential source of additional income subject to short-term availability if the positive interest rate differential persists for the life of the transaction. Given the preponderance of fixed-rate coupon versus zero-coupon bonds, our analysis turns next to these securities. As in the case of the fully hedged German investor in US Treasuries, we first establish the necessary building blocks to replicate a risk-free domestic currency return when investing in a foreign currency fixed-income coupon bond. We then consider how an active investor might deviate from this exposure profile to generate excess return.

Consider the example of a Japan-based investor who buys a fixed-rate USD coupon bond. In order to fully hedge JPY domestic currency cash flows for the foreign currency bond, as in the case of the earlier German investor, the investor must first sell Japanese yen (JPY) and purchase USD at the current spot rate to purchase the bond. At the end of each semi-annual interest period, the investor receives a USD coupon, which must be converted at the future JPY/USD spot rate (that is, the number of JPY required to buy one USD). At maturity, the investor receives the final semi-annual coupon and principal, which must be converted to JPY using the future JPY/USD spot rate to receive the final payment in domestic currency.

The fixed-rate foreign currency bond exposes the Japanese investor to a series of FX forward exposures that may be hedged upon purchase with a cross-currency swap, as seen in Exhibit 27 with the example of a par 10-year US Treasury bond with a 0.625% coupon issued in May 2020.

Exhibit 27: Fixed-Fixed Cross-Currency Swap Diagram and Details

Trade Details	JPY/USD Fixed-Fixed Cross-Currency Swap
Start date	15 May 2020
Maturity date	15 May 2030
Fixed USD payer	JPY Investor
Fixed JPY payer	Swap counterparty
Initial exchange	JPY investor pays JPY10.706 billion and receives USD100 million as of 15 May 2020
Fixed USD rate	0.625% Semiannual, Act/Act
Fixed JPY rate	−0.726% Semiannual, Act/365
Final exchange	JPY investor pays USD100 million and receives JPY10.706 billion as of 15 May 2030

Note that the fixed-fixed cross-currency swap components, shown in Exhibit 28, are a combination of three distinct hedging transactions: a receive-fixed JPY interest rate swap, a USD-JPY **cross-currency basis swap** involving the exchange of floating JPY for floating USD payments, and a pay-fixed USD interest rate swap.

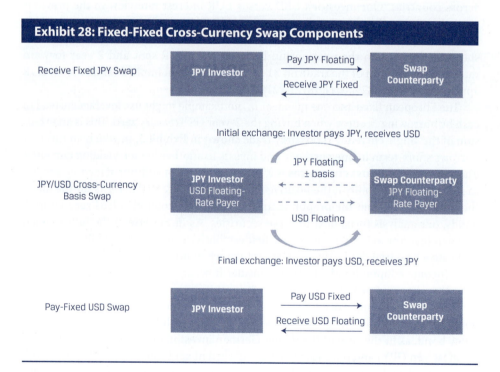

Exhibit 28: Fixed-Fixed Cross-Currency Swap Components

CROSS-CURRENCY BASIS AND COVERED INTEREST RATE PARITY

The "basis" or spread, as shown in the cross-currency basis swap, is the difference between the USD interest rate and the synthetic USD interest rate derived from swapping JPY into US dollars. A positive (negative) currency basis means that the direct USD interest rate is higher (lower) than the synthetic USD interest rate. While covered interest rate parity suggests that cross-currency basis should be close to zero, Exhibit 29 shows that the JPY and EUR cross-currency basis was persistently negative following the 2008 global financial crisis.

Exhibit 29: Five-Year JPY and EUR Cross-Currency Basis, 2006–2020

Cross-currency basis is widely seen as a barometer for global financial conditions. For example, greater credit and liquidity risk within the EU financial sector and the European Central Bank's aggressive quantitative easing have been cited as causes of the wider USD/EUR cross-currency basis.

Du, Tepper, and Verdelhan (2018) investigate the persistent no-arbitrage violation of covered interest rate parity implied by wider cross-currency basis observed across G-10 countries and offer several explanations. First, higher financial intermediation costs since the 2008 global financial crisis, such as higher bank regulatory capital requirements, prevent market participants from taking advantage of basis arbitrage opportunities. Second, covered interest rate parity violations suggest international imbalances in the form of high demand for investments in high interest rate currencies and a large supply of savings in low interest rate currencies. These deviations are magnified by divergent monetary policies across jurisdictions.

The building blocks of the fixed-fixed cross-currency swap shown in Exhibit 28 offer an active fixed-income investor a simplified framework within which one can take interest rate or currency positions to deviate from a risk-free domestic currency return. For example, by foregoing the pay USD fixed swap, the JPY investor takes a USD rate view by earning the USD fixed coupon and paying USD floating while fully hedging the currency exposure via the cross-currency basis swap. Similar principles apply as in the single currency case—namely, to go long (or overweight) assets expected to appreciate and go short (or underweight) assets expected to decline in value or appreciate less. The overweight and underweight bond positions may now be denominated in different currencies, with the active strategy often using an underweight position in one currency to fund an overweight position in another. The resulting yield curve strategy faces three potential risks: (1) yield curve movements—level, slope, or curvature—in the overweight currency; (2) yield curve changes in the underweight currency; and (3) exchange rate changes.

Consider the following unhedged example of a higher- versus lower-yielding currency.

> **EXAMPLE 12**
>
> ## MXN Carry Trade
>
> Consider the case of a portfolio manager examining a cross-currency carry trade between US dollar (USD) and Mexican peso (MXN) money market rates. The manager is contemplating borrowing in USD for one year and investing in 90-day Mexican treasury bills, rolling them over at maturity for the next 12 months. Assume that today's 1-year USD interest rate is 1.85%, the 90-day MXN interest rate is currently 7.70% (annualized), and the MXN/USD spot exchange rate is 19.15 (that is, it takes 19.15 MXN to buy one USD).
>
> If the manager expected that Mexican money market rates and the MXN/USD exchange rate would remain stable, the expected profit from this carry trade is:
>
> $(1 + 0.0770/4)^4 - (1 + 0.0185) \approx 6.08\%$.
>
> However, money market and exchange rates are rarely stable; this trade is exposed to changes in both the 90-day MXN interest rate and the MXN/USD spot exchange rate. (The 1-year fixed-rate USD loan eliminates exposure to USD rate changes). Assume that 90-day MXN interest rates and exchange rates change as follows over the 12-month period.
>
> | Rate / Time | Today | 90 Days | 180 Days | 270 Days | 360 Days |
> |---|---|---|---|---|---|
> | 90-day MXN rate | 7.70% | 7.85% | 8.15% | 8.20% | N/A |
> | MXN/USD spot rate | 19.15 | 18.05 | 19.05 | 18.80 | 19.65 |
>
> Note that 90-day MXN yields-to-maturity rose and that MXN depreciated slightly versus USD over the 360-day period. If the manager had rolled over this trade for the full 12 months, the realized return would have been:
>
> $\left(1 + \frac{0.0770}{4}\right)\left(1 + \frac{0.0785}{4}\right)\left(1 + \frac{0.0815}{4}\right)\left(1 + \frac{0.082}{4}\right) \times \frac{19.15}{19.65}$
> $-(1 + 0.0185) \approx 3.61\%$
>
> While the cross-currency carry trade was ultimately profitable, it was exposed to risks over the horizon; moreover, despite the rise in 90-day MXN yields-to-maturity, a late-period MXN depreciation undercut the profitability of the trade. This underscores the fact that carry trades are unhedged and are most successful in stable (low volatility) markets: Unforeseen market volatility can quickly erase even the most attractive cross-currency carry opportunities. For example, in the first quarter of 2020 at the start of the COVID-19 pandemic, MXN depreciated against the USD by approximately 25% in just over a month.

While an endless number of unhedged strategies seeking to capitalize on a level, slope, or curvature view across currencies exist, Exhibit 30 summarizes several of these major strategies.

Exhibit 30: Active Cross-Currency Strategies

Strategy	Purchase	Sell / Borrow	Expected Unhedged Return
Receive-fixed/ pay-fixed	High-yielding fixed-income asset	Lower-yield fixed-rate loan	Carry (higher yield minus lower yield) assuming uncovered interest parity does not hold
Receive-fixed/ pay-floating	High-yielding fixed-rate asset	Short-term, lower yield floating-rate loan rolled over until maturity	Carry (higher yield minus lower yield) plus long- versus short-term rate differential for lower-yielding currency

Strategy	Purchase	Sell / Borrow	Expected Unhedged Return
Receive-floating/ pay-fixed	High-yield floating-rate asset	Lower-yield fixed-rate loan	Carry (higher floating yield minus lower fixed yield)
Receive-floating/ pay-floating	High-yield floating-rate asset	Short-term, lower yield floating-rate loan rolled over until maturity	Carry (higher floating yield minus lower floating yield)

> **EXAMPLE 13**
>
> ### Bear Flattening Impact
>
> 1. A fixed-income manager is considering a foreign currency fixed-income investment in a relatively high-yielding market, where she expects bear flattening to occur in the near future and her lower-yielding domestic yield curve to remain stable and upward-sloping. Under this scenario, which of the following strategies will generate the largest carry benefit if her interest rate view is realized?
>
>   a. Receive-fixed in foreign currency, pay-fixed in domestic currency
>   b. Receive-fixed in foreign currency, pay-floating in domestic currency
>   c. Receive-floating in foreign currency, pay-floating in domestic currency
>
> ### Solution:
>
> The correct answer is C. If the higher-yielding foreign currency experiences a bear flattening in the yield curve as the manager expects, then foreign currency short-term yields-to-maturity will increase by more than long-term yields-to-maturity; thus she will want receive-floating in foreign currency. Given the upward-sloping domestic yield curve, we would expect the carry difference between receiving foreign currency floating rates and paying domestic currency floating rates to be the highest.

5. A FRAMEWORK FOR EVALUATING YIELD CURVE STRATEGIES

☐ evaluate the expected return and risks of a yield curve strategy

The factors affecting the expected return of a fixed-income portfolio were summarized in Equation 1. The key underlying assumption in this calculation is that the inputs rely on the fixed-income manager's expectations under an active strategy. As we have seen earlier, unexpected changes to the level, slope, and shape of the yield curve as well as currency changes can impact a portfolio's value in a number of ways—as quantified by the use of portfolio duration and convexity statistics in Equation 3 for a single currency and in Equation 13 for a multicurrency portfolio.

Practitioners frequently evaluate fixed-income portfolio risk using **scenario analysis**, which involves changing multiple assumptions at once to assess the overall impact of unexpected market changes on a portfolio's value. Managers may use historical rate and currency changes or conduct specific stress tests using this analysis. For example, a leveraged investor might evaluate how much rates or currencies must move before she faces a collateral or margin call or is forced to unwind a position. Fixed-income portfolio models offer practitioners a variety of historical or user-defined scenarios. The following scenario analysis example shows how this may be done for the US Treasury portfolio seen earlier.

> **EXAMPLE 14**
>
> ## Scenario Analysis—US Treasury Securities Portfolio
>
> | Tenor | Coupon | Price | Modified Duration | Convexity |
> |-------|--------|-------|-------------------|-----------|
> | 2y | 0.25% | 100 | 1.994 | 5.0 |
> | 5y | 0.875% | 100 | 4.88 | 26.5 |
> | 10y | 2.00% | 100 | 9.023 | 90.8 |
>
> In Example 1, we compared two $50 million portfolios. Portfolio A is fully invested in the 5-year Treasury bond, while Portfolio B is split between 2-year (58.94%) and 10-year (41.06%) bonds to match a 5-year bond duration of 4.88. Rather than the earlier parallel yield curve shift, we now analyze two yield curve slope scenarios—namely, an immediate bear steepening and bull flattening of the US Treasury yield curve. The bear steepening scenario involves a 50 bp and 100 bp *rise* in 5- and 10-year yields-to-maturity, respectively, while the bull flattening is assumed to result from a 50 bp fall in 5-year rates and a 100 bp fall in 10-year rates. Using Equation 3, our scenario analysis looks as follows:
>
> | Scenario | Portfolio A % Δ Price | Portfolio A Δ Price | Portfolio B % Δ Price | Portfolio B Δ Price |
> |----------|----------------------|---------------------|----------------------|---------------------|
> | Bear steepening | −2.407% | ($1,203,437) | −3.518% | ($1,759,216) |
> | Bull flattening | 2.473% | $1,236,563 | 3.891% | $1,945,628 |
>
> We may conclude from our analysis that although Portfolios A and B have similar duration and therefore perform similarly if the yield curve experiences a parallel shift (except for the convexity difference) seen in Example 1, they perform very differently under various yield curve slope scenarios.

The fixed-income portfolio risk and return impact of rolldown return versus carry, changes in the level, slope, and shape of a single currency yield curve, and an extension to multiple currencies (where spot and forward FX rates are related to relative interest rates) are best illustrated with a pair of examples.

> **EXAMPLE 15**
>
> ## AUD Bullet versus Barbell
>
> A US-based portfolio manager plans to invest in Australian zero-coupon bonds denominated in Australian dollars (AUD). He projects that over the next 12 months, the Australian zero-coupon yield curve will experience a downward parallel shift of 60 bps and that AUD will appreciate 0.25% against USD. The manager is weighing bullet and barbell strategies using the following data:

A Framework for Evaluating Yield Curve Strategies

Statistic	Bullet	Barbell
Investment horizon (years)	1.0	1.0
Average bond price in portfolio (today)	98.00	98.00
Average portfolio bond price (in 1 year/stable yield curve)	99.75	100.00
Expected portfolio effective duration (in 1 year)	3.95	3.95
Expected portfolio convexity (in 1 year)	19.50	34.00
Expected change in AUD zero-coupon yields	−0.60%	−0.60%
Expected change in AUD versus USD	+0.25%	+0.25%

Solve for the expected return over the 1-year investment horizon for each portfolio using the step-by-step estimation approach in Equation 1.

Rolling Yield

The sum of coupon income (in %) and the price effect on bonds from "rolling down the yield curve." Since both portfolios contain only zero-coupon bonds, there is no coupon income and we calculate the rolldown return using $(PV_1 - PV_0) / PV_0$, where PV_0 is today's bond price and PV_1 is the bond price in one year, assuming no shift in the yield curve.

1. **Bullet:** 1.7857% = (99.75 − 98.00) / 98.00
2. **Barbell:** 2.0408% = (100.000 − 98.00) / 98.00

E (Δ Price Due to Investor's View of Benchmark Yield)

The effect of the interest rate view on expected portfolio return may be estimated using Equation 3, using effective duration and convexity in one year's time to evaluate the expected 60 bp downward parallel yield curve shift:

1. **Bullet:** 2.4051% = (−3.95 × −0.0060) + [1/2 × 19.5 × (−0.0060)^2]
2. **Barbell:** 2.4312% = (−3.95 × −0.0060) + [1/2 × 34.0 × (−0.0060)^2]

$E(R) \approx$ % Rolldown return + E (% Δ Price due to investor's view of benchmark yield) + E (% Δ Price due to investor's view of currency value changes)

In addition to rolldown return and expected price changes due to changes in yield-to-maturity, the expected 0.25% appreciation of AUD versus USD must be incorporated in order to arrive at the USD investor's domestic currency return. Using Equation 12, R_{FC} equals the sum of rolldown return and changes in price due to yield-to-maturity changes, while R_{FX} is 0.25%. Expected returns are as follows:

$E(R_1) = 4.4513\%$, or $[(1 + 0.017857 + 0.024051) \times (1.0025)] - 1$

$E(R_2) = 4.7332\%$, or $[(1 + 0.020408 + 0.024312) \times (1.0025)] - 1$

Overall, the barbell outperforms the bullet by approximately 28 bps. Rolldown return contributes most of this outperformance. Rolldown return contributed approximately 25.5 bps of outperformance (i.e., 2.0408% − 1.7857%) for the barbell, and the greater convexity of the barbell portfolio contributed just over 2.6 bps of outperformance (i.e., 2.4312% − 2.4051%). Currency exposure had the same impact on both strategies. The strong rolldown contribution is likely driven by the stronger price appreciation (under the stable yield curve assumption) of longer-maturity zeros in the barbell portfolio relative to the price appreciation of the intermediate zeros in the bullet portfolio as the bonds ride the curve over the 1-year horizon to a shorter maturity.

EXAMPLE 16

US Treasury Bullet versus Barbell

Assume a 1-year investment horizon for a portfolio manager considering US Treasury market strategies. The manager is considering two strategies to capitalize on an expected rise in US Treasury security zero-coupon yield levels of 50 bps in the next 12 months:

1. A bullet portfolio fully invested in 5-year zero-coupon notes currently priced at 94.5392.
2. A barbell portfolio: 62.97% is invested in 2-year zero-coupon notes priced at 98.7816, and 37.03% is invested in 10-year zero-coupon bonds priced at 83.7906.

Further assumptions for evaluating these portfolios are shown here:

Statistic	Bullet	Barbell
Investment horizon (years)	1.0	1.0
Average bond price in portfolio (today)	94.5392	92.6437
Average portfolio bond price (in 1 year/stable yield curve)	96.0503	94.3525
Expected portfolio effective duration (in 1 year)	3.98	3.98
Expected portfolio convexity (in 1 year)	17.82	32.57
Expected change in US Treasury zero-coupon yields	0.50%	0.50%

Solve for the expected return over the 1-year investment horizon for each portfolio using the step-by-step estimation approach in Equation 1.

Rolling Yield

The sum of coupon income (in %) and the price effect on bonds from "rolling down the yield curve." Since both portfolios contain only zero-coupon bonds, there is no coupon income and we calculate the rolldown return using $(PV_1 - PV_0) / PV_0$, where PV_0 is today's bond price and PV_1 is the bond price in one year, assuming no shift in the yield curve.

Bullet: (96.0503 − 94.5392) ÷ 94.5392 = 1.5984%
Barbell: (94.3525 − 92.6437) ÷ 92.6437 = 1.8445%

E (Δ Price Due to Investor's View of Benchmark Yield)

The effect of the interest rate view on expected portfolio return may be estimated with Equation 3, using effective duration and convexity in one year's time to evaluate the expected 50 bp upward parallel yield curve shift:

Bullet: −1.9677% = (−3.98 × 0.0050) + [1/2 × 17.82 × (0.0050)^2]
Barbell: −1.9493% = (−3.98 × 0.0050) + [1/2 × 32.57 × (0.0050)^2]

Expected total return in percentage terms for each portfolio is equal to:

$E(R)$ = % Rolldown return + E (% Δ Price due to investor's view of benchmark yield)

The total expected return over the 1-year investment horizon for the bullet portfolio is therefore −0.3693%, or 1.5984% − 1.9677%, and the expected return for the barbell portfolio is −0.1048%, or 1.8445% − 1.9493%.

If the manager's expected market scenario materializes, the barbell portfolio outperforms the bullet portfolio by 26 bps. The higher barbell convexity contributed just under 2 bps of outperformance, whereas the rolldown return

A Framework for Evaluating Yield Curve Strategies

contributed nearly 25 bps. Stronger price appreciation (under the stable yield curve assumption) resulted from a greater rolldown effect from the 10-year zeros in the barbell versus the 5-year zeros over one year.

SUMMARY

This reading addresses active fixed-income yield curve management using cash- and derivative-based strategies to generate returns which exceed those of a benchmark index due to yield curve changes. The following are the main points in the reading:

- A par yield curve is a stylized representation of yields-to-maturity available to investors at various maturities, which often does not consist of traded securities but must be extracted from available bond yields using a model.

- Primary yield curve risk factors may be categorized by changes in level (or a parallel "shift"), slope (a flatter or steeper yield curve), and shape or curvature.

- Yield curve slope measures the difference between the yield-to-maturity on a long-maturity bond and the yield-to-maturity on a shorter-maturity bond. Curvature is the relationship between short-, intermediate-, and long-term yields-to-maturity.

- Fixed-income portfolio managers can approximate actual and anticipated bond portfolio value changes using portfolio duration and convexity measures. Duration measures the linear relationship between bond prices and yield-to-maturity. Convexity is a second-order effect describing a bond's price behavior for larger rate movements and is affected by cash flow dispersion.

- A barbell portfolio combining short- and long-term bond positions will have greater convexity than a bullet portfolio concentrated in a single maturity for a given duration.

- Active managers seeking excess return in an expected static yield curve environment that is upward-sloping can use a buy-and-hold strategy to increase duration, roll down the yield curve, or use leverage via a carry trade in cash markets. Receive-fixed swaps and long futures positions replicate this exposure in the derivatives market.

- Derivatives offer the opportunity to synthetically change exposure with a far smaller initial cash outlay than cash strategies but require managers to maintain sufficient cash or eligible securities to fulfill margin or collateral requirements.

- Active fixed-income managers with a divergent rate level view increase duration exposure above a target if yields-to-maturity are expected to decline and reduce duration if expecting higher yields-to-maturity to minimize losses.

- Yield curve steepeners seek to gain from a greater spread between short- and long-term yields-to-maturity by combining a "long" short-dated bond position with a "short" long-dated bond position, while a flattener involves sale of short-term bonds and purchase of long-term bonds.

- Steepener and flattener strategies may be net duration neutral or net long or short duration depending upon a manager's view of how the yield curve slope will change—that is, the relative contribution of short- and long-term yield-to-maturity changes to the expected yield curve slope change.
- The butterfly strategy combining a long bullet with a short barbell portfolio (or vice versa) is commonly used to capitalize on expected yield curve shape changes.
- Active managers capitalize on a view as to whether future realized interest rate volatility will be greater or less than implied volatility by purchasing or selling bonds with embedded options or by using stand-alone interest rate options.
- Stand-alone interest rate put and call options are generally based upon a bond's price, not yield-to-maturity.
- Interest rate swaptions and options on bond futures are among the common tools used by active managers to alter portfolio duration and convexity subject to yield-to-maturity changes. An interest rate swaption involves the right to enter into an interest rate swap at a specific strike price in the future, while an option on a bond future involves the right, not the obligation, to buy or sell a futures contract.
- Key rate durations can be used in active fixed-income management to identify a bond portfolio's sensitivity to changes in the shape of the benchmark yield curve, allowing an active manager to quantify exposures along the curve.
- Fixed-income managers engaged in active yield curve strategies across currencies measure excess return from active management in functional currency terms—that is, considering domestic currency returns on foreign currency assets within a portfolio.
- Interest rate parity establishes the fundamental relationship between spot and forward exchange rates, with a higher-yielding currency trading at a forward discount and a lower-yielding currency trading at a premium.
- Covered interest rate parity involves the use of a forward contract to lock in domestic currency proceeds, while uncovered interest rate parity suggests that over time, the returns on unhedged foreign currency exposure will be the same as on a domestic currency investment.
- Active investors use the carry trade across currencies to take advantage of divergence from interest rate parity by borrowing in a lower-yield currency and investing in a higher-yield currency.
- A cross-currency swap enables investors to fully hedge the domestic currency value of cash flows associated with foreign currency bonds.
- Active managers deviate from fully hedged foreign currency bond cash flows by entering overweight and underweight bond positions denominated in different currencies, often using an underweight position in one currency to fund an overweight position in another.
- Investors evaluate the expected return on an active fixed-income portfolio strategy by combining coupon income and rolldown return with expected portfolio changes based on benchmark yield-to-maturity, credit, and currency value changes over the investment horizon.
- Unexpected market changes or risks to portfolio value are frequently evaluated using scenario analysis.

PRACTICE PROBLEMS

The following information relates to questions 1-8

A Sydney-based fixed-income portfolio manager is considering the following Commonwealth of Australia government bonds traded on the ASX (Australian Stock Exchange):

Tenor	Coupon	Yield	Price	Modified Duration	Convexity
2y	5.75%	0.28%	110.90	1.922	4.9
4.5y	3.25%	0.55%	111.98	4.241	22.1
9y	2.50%	1.10%	111.97	8.175	85.2

The manager is considering portfolio strategies based upon various interest rate scenarios over the next 12 months. She is considering three long-only government bond portfolio alternatives, as follows:

Bullet: Invest solely in 4.5-year government bonds

Barbell: Invest equally in 2-year and 9-year government bonds

Equal weights: Invest equally in 2-year, 4.5-year, and 9-year bonds

1. The portfolio alternative with the *highest* modified duration is the:
   A. bullet portfolio.
   B. barbell portfolio.
   C. equally weighted portfolio.

2. The manager estimates that accelerated economic growth in Australia will increase the *level* of government yields-to-maturity by 50 bps. Under this scenario, which of the three portfolios experiences the *smallest* decline in market value?
   A. Bullet portfolio
   B. Barbell portfolio
   C. Equally weighted portfolio

3. Assume the manager is able to extend her mandate by adding derivatives strategies to the three portfolio alternatives. The best way to position her portfolio to benefit from a *bear flattening* scenario is to combine a:
   A. 2-year receive-fixed Australian dollar (AUD) swap with the *same* modified duration as the bullet portfolio.
   B. 2-year pay-fixed AUD swap with *twice* the modified duration as the 2-year government bond in the barbell portfolio.

C. 9-year receive-fixed AUD swap with *twice* the modified duration as the 9-year government bond position in the equally weighted portfolio.

4. In her market research, the manager learns that ASX 3-year and 10-year Treasury bond futures are the most liquid products for investors trading and hedging medium- to long-term Australian dollar (AUD) interest rates. Although neither contract matches the exact characteristics of the cash bonds of her choice, which of the following additions to a barbell portfolio *best* positions her to gain under a *bull flattening* scenario?

    A. Purchase a 3-year Treasury bond future matching the money duration of the short-term (2-year) position.

    B. Sell a 3-year Treasury bond future matching the money duration of the short-term bond position.

    C. Purchase a 10-year Treasury bond future matching the money duration of the long-term bond position.

5. An economic slowdown is expected to result in a 25 bp decline in Australian yield *levels*. Which portfolio alternative will experience the largest gain under this scenario?

    A. Bullet portfolio

    B. Barbell portfolio

    C. Equally weighted portfolio

6. The portfolio alternative with the *least* exposure to convexity is the:

    A. bullet portfolio.

    B. barbell portfolio.

    C. equally weighted portfolio.

7. The current butterfly spread for the Australian government yield curve based upon the manager's portfolio choices is:

    A. 83 bps.

    B. 28 bps.

    C. −28 bps.

8. If the manager has a positive butterfly view on Australian government yields-to-maturity, the *best* portfolio position strategy to pursue is to:

    A. purchase the bullet portfolio and sell the barbell portfolio.

    B. sell the bullet portfolio and buy the barbell portfolio.

    C. purchase the equally weighted portfolio and sell the barbell portfolio.

---

9. An analyst manages an active fixed-income fund that is benchmarked to the Bloomberg Barclays US Treasury Index. This index of US government bonds currently has a modified portfolio duration of 7.25 and an average maturity of 8.5 years. The yield curve is upward-sloping and expected to remain unchanged.

Practice Problems

Which of the following is the *least* attractive portfolio positioning strategy in a static curve environment?

A. Purchasing a 10-year zero-coupon bond with a yield of 2% and a price of 82.035

B. Entering a pay-fixed, 30-year USD interest rate swap

C. Purchasing a 20-year Treasury and financing it in the repo market

10. An investment manager is considering decreasing portfolio duration versus a benchmark index given her expectations of an upward parallel shift in the yield curve. If she has a choice between a callable bond which is unlikely to be called, a putable bond which is likely to be put, or an option-free bond with otherwise comparable characteristics, the most profitable position would be to:

    A. own the callable bond.

    B. own the putable bond.

    C. own the option-free bond.

11. An active fixed-income manager holds a portfolio of commercial and residential mortgage-backed securities that tracks the Bloomberg Barclays US Mortgage-Backed Securities Index. Which of the following choices is the most relevant portfolio statistic for evaluating the first-order change in his portfolio's value for a given change in benchmark yield?

    A. Effective duration

    B. Macaulay duration

    C. Modified duration

12. An active fund trader seeks to capitalize on an expected steepening of the current upward-sloping yield curve using option-based fixed-income instruments. Which of the following portfolio positioning strategies *best* positions her to gain if her interest rate view is realized?

    A. Sell a 30-year receiver swaption and a 2-year bond put option.

    B. Purchase a 30-year receiver swaption and a 2-year bond put option.

    C. Purchase a 30-year payer swaption and a 2-year bond call option.

The following information relates to questions 13-16

A financial analyst at an in-house asset manager fund has created the following spreadsheet of key rate durations to compare her active position to that of a benchmark index so she can compare the rate sensitivities across maturities.

Tenor	KeyRateDur^{Active}	KeyRateDur^{Index}	Difference
2y	−0.532	0.738	−1.270
5y	0.324	1.688	−1.364

Tenor	KeyRateDur^{Active}	KeyRateDur^{Index}	Difference
10y	5.181	2.747	2.434
30y	1.142	2.162	–1.020
Portfolio	6.115	7.335	–1.220

13. Which of the following statements is true if yield *levels* increase by 50 bps?

    A. The active portfolio will outperform the index portfolio by approximately 61 bps.

    B. The index portfolio will outperform the active portfolio by approximately 61 bps.

    C. The index portfolio will outperform the active portfolio by approximately 21 bps.

14. Which of the following statements best characterizes how the active portfolio is positioned for yield curve changes *relative* to the index portfolio?

    A. The active portfolio is positioned to benefit from a bear steepening of the yield curve versus the benchmark portfolio.

    B. The active portfolio is positioned to benefit from a positive butterfly movement in the shape of the yield curve versus the index.

    C. The active portfolio is positioned to benefit from yield curve flattening versus the index.

15. Which of the following derivatives strategies would *best* offset the yield curve exposure difference between the active and index portfolios?

    A. Add a pay-fixed 10-year swap and long 2-year, 5-year, and 30-year bond futures positions to the active portfolio.

    B. Add a receive-fixed 30-year swap, a pay-fixed 10-year swap, and short positions in 2-year and 5-year bond futures to the active portfolio.

    C. Add a pay-fixed 10-year swap, a short 30-year bond futures, and long 2-year and 5-year bond futures positions to the active portfolio.

16. Which of the following statements best describes the forward rate bias?

    A. Investors tend to favor fixed-income investments in currencies that trade at a premium on a forward basis.

    B. Investors tend to hedge fixed-income investments in higher-yielding currencies given the potential for lower returns due to currency depreciation.

    C. Investors tend to favor unhedged fixed-income investments in higher-yielding currencies that are sometimes enhanced by borrowing in lower-yielding currencies.

Practice Problems

The following information relates to questions 17-19

A US-based fixed-income portfolio manager is examining unhedged investments in Thai baht (THB) zero-coupon government bonds issued in Thailand and is considering two investment strategies:

1. **Buy-and-hold:** Purchase a 1-year, THB zero-coupon bond with a current yield-to-maturity of 1.00%.
2. **Roll down the THB yield curve:** Purchase a 2-year zero-coupon note with a current yield-to-maturity of 2.00% and sell it in a year.

THB proceeds under each strategy will be converted into USD at the end of the 1-year investment horizon. The manager expects a stable THB yield curve and that THB will appreciate by 1.5% relative to USD. The following information is used to analyze these two investment strategies:

Statistic	Buy and Hold	Yield Curve Rolldown
Investment horizon (years)	1.0	1.0
Bond maturity at purchase (years)	1.0	2.0
Yield-to-maturity (today)	1.00%	2.00%
Average portfolio bond price (today)	99.0090	96.1169
Expected average portfolio bond price (in 1 year)	100.00	99.0090
Expected currency gains (in 1 year)	1.5%	1.5%

17. The *rolldown returns* over the 1-year investment horizon for the Buy-and-Hold and Yield Curve Rolldown portfolios are closest to:

    A. 1.00% for the Buy-and-Hold portfolio and 3.01% for the Yield Curve Rolldown portfolio, respectively.

    B. 0.991% for the Buy-and-Hold portfolio and 3.01% for the Yield Curve Rolldown portfolio, respectively.

    C. 0.991% for the Buy-and-Hold portfolio and 2.09% for the Yield Curve Rolldown portfolio, respectively.

18. The *total expected return* over the 1-year investment horizon for the Buy-and-Hold and Yield Curve Rolldown portfolios are closest to:

    A. 2.515% for the Buy-and-Hold portfolio and 4.555% for the Yield Curve rolldown portfolio, respectively.

    B. 2.42% for the Buy-and-Hold portfolio and 4.51% for the Yield Curve Rolldown portfolio, respectively.

    C. 2.491% for the Buy-and-Hold portfolio and 3.59% for the Yield Curve Rolldown portfolio, respectively.

19. Which of the following statements best describes how the expected total return results would *change* if THB yields were to rise significantly over the investment

horizon?

- **A.** Both the Buy-and-Hold and Yield Curve Rolldown expected portfolio returns would *increase* due to higher THB yields.
- **B.** Both the Buy-and-Hold and Yield Curve Rolldown expected portfolio returns would *decrease* due to higher THB yields.
- **C.** The Buy-and-Hold expected portfolio returns would be *unchanged* and the Yield Curve Rolldown expected portfolio returns would *decrease* due to the rise in yields.

20. A Dutch investor considering a 5-year EUR government bond purchase expects yields-to-maturity to decline by 25 bps in the next six months. Which of the following statements about the rolldown return is *correct*?
    - **A.** The rolldown return equals the difference between the price of the 5-year bond and that of a 4.5-year bond at the lower yield-to-maturity.
    - **B.** The rolldown return consists of the 5-year bond's basis point value multiplied by the expected 25 bp yield-to-maturity change over the next six months.
    - **C.** The rolldown return will be negative if the 5-year bond has a zero coupon and is trading at a premium.

21. An active investor enters a duration-neutral yield curve flattening trade that combines 2-year and 10-year Treasury positions. Under which of the following yield curve scenarios would you expect the investor to realize the *greatest* portfolio loss?
    - **A.** Bear steepening
    - **B.** Bull flattening
    - **C.** Yields unchanged

SOLUTIONS

1. B is correct. The modified duration of a fixed-income portfolio is approximately equal to the market value-weighted average of the bonds in the portfolio, so the barbell has a modified duration of 5.049, or (1.922 + 8.175)/2, which is larger than that of either the bullet (4.241) or the equally weighted portfolio (4.779, or (1.922 + 4.241 + 8.175)/3.

2. A is correct. The change in portfolio value due to a rise in Australian government rate levels may be calculated using Equation 3:

   $\%\Delta PV^{Full} \approx -(ModDur \times \Delta Yield) + [½ \times Convexity \times (\Delta Yield)^2]$,

   where ModDur and Convexity reflect portfolio duration and convexity, respectively. Therefore, the bullet portfolio declines by 2.093%, or −2.093% = (−4.241 × 0.005) + [0.5 × 22.1 × (0.005^2)], followed by a drop of 2.343% for the equally weighted portfolio, or −2.343% = (−4.779 × 0.005) + [0.5 × 37.4 × (0.005^2)], and a drop of 2.468% for the barbell portfolio, or −2.468% = (−5.049 × 0.005) + [0.5 × 45.05 × (0.005^2)].

3. B is correct. A bear flattening scenario is a decrease in the yield spread between long- and short-term maturities driven by higher short-term rates. The manager must therefore position her portfolio to benefit from rising short-term yields. Under A, the receive-fixed 2-year swap is a synthetic long position, increasing portfolio duration that will result in an MTM loss under bear flattening. The receive-fixed swap in answer C will increase duration in long-term maturities. In the case of B, the pay-fixed swap with twice the modified duration of the barbell will more than offset the existing long position, resulting in net short 2-year and long 9-year bond positions in the overall portfolio and a gain under bear flattening.

4. C is correct. A bull flattening is a decrease in the yield spread between long- and short-term maturities driven by lower long-term yields-to-maturity. Both A and B involve changes in portfolio exposure to short-term rates, while C increases the portfolio exposure to long-term rates to benefit from a fall in long-term yields-to-maturity.

5. B is correct. The portfolio value change due to lower Australian government rate levels may be calculated using Equation 3:

   $\%\Delta PV^{Full} \approx -(ModDur \times \Delta Yield) + [½ \times Convexity \times (\Delta Yield)^2]$,

   where ModDur and Convexity reflect portfolio duration and convexity, respectively. Therefore, the barbell portfolio rises by 1.276%, or (−5.049 × −0.0025) + [0.5 × 45.05 × (−0.0025^2)], followed by the equally weighted portfolio at 1.207%, or (−4.779 × −0.0025) + [0.5 × 37.4 × (−0.0025^2)], and the bullet portfolio at 1.067%, or (−4.241 × −0.0025) + [0.5 × 22.1 × (−0.0025^2)].

6. A is correct. The bullet portfolio has the same convexity as the 4.5-year bond, or 22.1. The barbell portfolio in B has portfolio convexity of 45.05, = (4.9 + 85.2)/2, while the equally weighted portfolio has portfolio convexity of 37.4, = (4.9 + 22.1 + 85.2)/3.

7. C is correct. The butterfly spread is equal to twice the medium-term yield minus the short-term and long-term yields, as in Equation 2, or −28 bps, or −0.28% + (2 × 0.55%) − 1.10%.

8. A is correct. A positive butterfly view indicates an expected decrease in the butterfly spread due to an expected rise in short- and long-term yields-to-maturity combined with a lower medium-term yield-to-maturity. The investor therefore benefits from a long medium-term (bullet) position and a short short-term and long-term (barbell) portfolio. The portfolio in answer B represents the opposite exposure and benefits from a negative butterfly view, while in C, combining short barbell and long equally weighted portfolios leaves the investor with bullet portfolio exposure.

9. B is correct. The 30-year pay-fixed swap is a "short" duration position and also results in negative carry (that is, the fixed rate paid would exceed MRR received) in an upward-sloping yield curve environment; therefore, it is the least attractive static curve strategy. In the case of a.), the manager enters a "buy-and-hold" strategy by purchasing the 10-year zero-coupon bond and extends duration, which is equal to 9.80 = 10/1.02 since the Macaulay duration of a zero equals its maturity, and ModDur = MacDur/(1+r) versus 7.25 for the index. Under c.), the manager introduces leverage by purchasing a long-term bond and financing it at a lower short-term repo rate.

10. B is correct. The value of a bond with an embedded option is equal to the sum of the value of an option-free bond plus the value to the embedded option. With a putable bond, the embedded put option is owned by the bond investor, who can exercise the option if yields-to-maturity increase, as in this scenario. Under A, the embedded call option is owned by the bond issuer, who is more likely to exercise if yields-to-maturity decrease (that is, the bond investor is short the call option). As for C, the option-free bond underperforms the putable bond given the rise in value of the embedded put option.

11. A is correct. Effective duration is a yield duration statistic that measures interest rate risk using a parallel shift in the benchmark yield curve (ΔCurve), as in Equation 8. Effective duration measures interest rate risk for complex bonds whose future cash flows are uncertain because they are contingent on future interest rates. Both Macaulay duration (B) and modified duration (C) are relevant statistics only for option-free bonds.

12. C is correct. A steepening of the yield curve involves an increase in the slope, or the difference between long-term and short-term yields-to-maturity. An optimal portfolio positioning strategy is one which combines a short duration exposure to long-term bonds and a long duration exposure to short-term bonds. Portfolio C involves the right (but not the obligation) to purchase a 2-year bond, which will increase in value as short-term yields fall with the right to pay-fixed on a 30-year swap, which increases in value if long-term yields rise. Portfolio A involves the sale of two options. Although they will expire unexercised in a steeper curve environment, the investor's return is limited to the two option premia. Portfolio B is the opposite of Portfolio C, positioning the investor for a flattening of the yield curve.

13. A is correct. Recall from Equation 11 that the sum of the key rate durations equals the effective portfolio duration. The approximate (first-order) change in portfolio value may be estimated from the first (modified) term of Equation 3, namely (–EffDur × ΔYield). Solving for this using the –1.22 effective duration difference multiplied by 0.005 equals 0.0061, or 61 bps.

14. B is correct. A positive butterfly indicates a decrease in the butterfly spread due to an expected rise in short- and long-term yields-to-maturity combined with a lower medium-term yield-to-maturity. Since the active portfolio is short duration versus the index in the 2-year, 5-year, and 30-year maturities and long duration in

Solutions

the 10-year, it will generate excess return if the butterfly spread falls.

15. A is correct. A net positive key rate duration difference indicates a long duration position relative to the index, while a net negative duration difference indicates a short position. Relative to the index, the active portfolio is "short" in the 2-year, 5-year, and 30-year maturities and "long" the 10-year maturity versus the index. The pay-fixed 10-year swap and long 2-year, 5-year, and 30-year bond futures positions best offset these differences.

16. C is correct. Forward rate bias is defined as an observed divergence from interest rate parity conditions under which active investors seek to benefit by borrowing in a lower-yield currency and investing in a higher-yield currency. A is incorrect since lower-yielding currencies trade at a forward premium. B is incorrect due to covered interest rate parity; fully hedged foreign currency fixed-income investments will tend to yield the domestic risk-free rate.

17. A is correct. Since both strategies use zero-coupon bonds, the rolldown return is calculated from expected bond price changes from "rolling down" the THB yield curve, which is assumed to be static.

    Buy and Hold: 1.00% = (100.00 − 99.009)/99.009

    Yield Curve Rolldown: 3.01% = (99.009 − 96.1169)/96.1169

18. A is correct. Under a static yield curve assumption, expected returns are equal to rolldown return plus changes in currency over the investment horizon. Using Equation 12, we solved for R_{FC} for both portfolios in Question 18, and R_{FX} is 1.5%. Expected returns are:

    Buy and Hold: $E(R)$ = 2.515%, or $(1.01 \times 1.015) − 1$

    Yield Curve Rolldown: $E(R)$ = 4.555%, or $(1.0301 \times 1.015) − 1$

19. C is correct. In a higher THB yield scenario in one year, the Yield Curve Rolldown expected return would fall since a higher THB yield-to-maturity in one year would reduce the price at which the investor could sell the 1-year zero in one year. The Buy-and-Hold portfolio return will be unaffected since the 1-year bond matures at the end of the investment horizon.

20. C is correct. Rolldown return is the difference between the price of the 5-year bond and that of a 4.5-year bond at the *same* yield-to-maturity. A 5-year zero-coupon bond trading at a premium has a negative yield. As the price "pulls to par" over time, the premium amortization will be a loss to the investor. A reflects the full price appreciation since it is calculated using the lower yield-to-maturity, while B equals E (Δ Price due to investor's view of benchmark yield).

21. C is correct. A duration-neutral flattening trade involves a short 2-year bond position and a long 10-year bond position, which have a "matched" duration or portfolio duration of zero. This portfolio will realize a loss if the slope of the yield curve—that is, the difference between short-term and long-term yields—increases. Yield curve inversion is an extreme version of flattening in which the spread between long-term and short-term yields-to-maturity falls below zero. The bear steepening in A involves a rise in the 10-year yield-to-maturity more than in the 5-year yield-to-maturity, causing a portfolio loss. The bull flattening in B combines a constant 2-year yield-to-maturity with lower 10-year rates, resulting in a gain on the 10-year bond position and an unchanged 2-year bond position.

LEARNING MODULE

6

Fixed-Income Active Management: Credit Strategies

by Campe Goodman, CFA, and Oleg Melentyev, CFA.

Campe Goodman, CFA, is at Wellington Management (USA). Oleg Melentyev, CFA, is at Bank of America Merrill Lynch (USA).

LEARNING OUTCOMES	
Mastery	The candidate should be able to:
☐	describe risk considerations for spread-based fixed-income portfolios
☐	discuss the advantages and disadvantages of credit spread measures for spread-based fixed-income portfolios, and explain why option-adjusted spread is considered the most appropriate measure
☐	discuss bottom-up approaches to credit strategies
☐	discuss top-down approaches to credit strategies
☐	discuss liquidity risk in credit markets and how liquidity risk can be managed in a credit portfolio
☐	describe how to assess and manage tail risk in credit portfolios
☐	discuss the use of credit default swap strategies in active fixed-income portfolio management
☐	discuss various portfolio positioning strategies that managers can use to implement a specific credit spread view
☐	discuss considerations in constructing and managing portfolios across international credit markets
☐	describe the use of structured financial instruments as an alternative to corporate bonds in credit portfolios
☐	describe key inputs, outputs, and considerations in using analytical tools to manage fixed-income portfolios

1. INTRODUCTION

Most fixed-income instruments trade at a nominal yield to maturity (YTM) that lies above that for an equivalent government or benchmark bond of similar maturity. This **yield spread** or difference compensates investors for the risk that they might not receive interest and principal cash flows as expected, whether as a result of a financially distressed corporate borrower, a sovereign issuer unable (or unwilling) to meet scheduled payments, or a deterioration in credit quality in an underlying pool of assets of a structured instrument such as an asset-backed security. A portion of the yield spread reflects the bid–offer cost of buying or selling a particular bond versus a government security, a liquidity premium that varies based on market conditions. Active managers of spread-based fixed-income portfolios take positions in credit and other risk factors that vary from those of an index to generate excess return versus passive index replication. Financial analysts who build on their foundational knowledge by mastering these more advanced fixed-income concepts and tools will broaden their career opportunities in the investment industry.

We begin by reviewing expected fixed-income portfolio return components with a particular focus on credit spreads. These spreads are not directly observable but rather derived from market information. Similar to benchmark yield curves, credit-spread curves are often defined by spread level and slope, and usually grouped by credit rating to gauge relative risk as well as to anticipate and act on expected changes in these relationships over the business cycle. We outline credit spread measures for fixed- and floating-rate bonds and quantify the effect of spread changes on portfolio value. Building blocks for active credit management beyond individual bonds include exchange-traded funds (ETFs), structured financial instruments, and derivative products such as credit default swaps (CDS). These tools are used to describe bottom-up and top-down active credit management approaches as well as how managers position spread-based fixed-income portfolios to capitalize on a market view.

2. KEY CREDIT AND SPREAD CONCEPTS FOR ACTIVE MANAGEMENT

☐ describe risk considerations for spread-based fixed-income portfolios

☐ discuss the advantages and disadvantages of credit spread measures for spread-based fixed-income portfolios, and explain why option-adjusted spread is considered the most appropriate measure

Managers seeking to maximize fixed-income portfolio returns will usually buy securities with a higher YTM (and lower equivalent price) than a comparable default risk-free government bond. The excess return targeted by active managers of spread-based fixed-income portfolios is captured in the fourth term of the now familiar fixed-income return equation:

$$E(R) \approx \text{Coupon income} \qquad (1)$$

$+/-$ Rolldown return

$+/- E$ (Δ Price due to investor's view of benchmark yields)

$+/- E$ (Δ Price due to investor's view of yield spreads)

$+/- E$ (Δ Price due to investor's view of currency value changes)

Similar to the benchmark yield curve addressed earlier in the curriculum, yield spreads for a specific bond issuance over a comparable government bond cannot be directly observed but are rather derived or estimated from market information. This yield spread is a risk premium that primarily compensates investors for assuming credit and liquidity risks.

While credit risk for a specific borrower depends on both the likelihood of default and the loss severity in a default scenario, credit risk for a specific bond *issuance* also depends on the period over which payments are promised, the relative seniority of the debt claim, and the sources of repayment, such as the value of underlying collateral, among other factors.

Liquidity risk refers to an investor's ability to readily buy or sell a specific security. The YTM difference (or bid–ask spread) between the purchase and sale price of a bond depends on market conditions and on the specific supply-and-demand dynamics of each fixed-income security. As active fixed-income portfolio managers identify and pursue specific credit strategies, they must also consider trading costs when calculating expected excess returns.

Credit Risk Considerations

Yield spreads over default risk-free government bonds mostly compensate investors for the potential of not receiving promised cash flows (issuer default) and for the loss severity if a default occurs. Spreads range widely across ratings categories and time periods. For example, Exhibit 1 shows yield spreads as a percentage of total YTM for A-, BBB-, and BB rated US corporate issuers from mid-2009 to mid-2020.

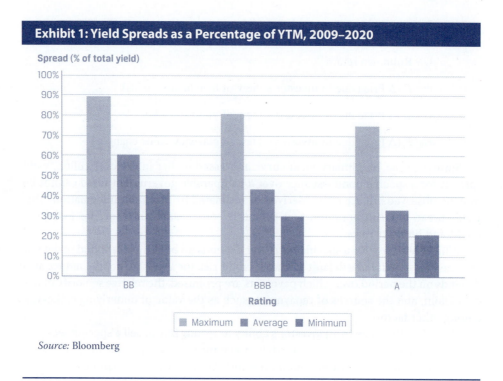

Exhibit 1: Yield Spreads as a Percentage of YTM, 2009–2020

Source: Bloomberg

On average, 60% of total YTM was attributable to yield spread for BB rated issuers versus 33% for A rated issuers over the period. This percentage was at a minimum for all rating categories in 2010 as the US economy recovered from the 2008–09 financial crisis and reached its peak in early 2020 during the economic slowdown due to the COVID-19 pandemic. The higher average proportion of all-in yield attributable to credit risk warrants a greater focus on this factor among high-yield investors over the credit cycle.

Default Probabilities and Recovery Rates

The **credit valuation adjustment (CVA)** framework shown earlier in the curriculum and in Exhibit 2 comprises the present value of credit risk for a loan, bond, or derivative obligation.

Key Credit and Spread Concepts for Active Management

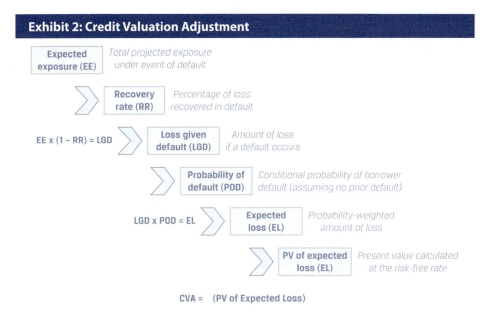

Exhibit 2: Credit Valuation Adjustment

The CVA framework provides a useful means to evaluate the two key components of credit risk. These include (1) **default risk** (also called **probability of default** [POD]), or the likelihood that a borrower defaults or fails to meet its obligation to make full and timely payments of principal and interest according to the terms of the debt security; and (2) **loss severity** (also called loss given default [LGD]), which is the amount of loss if a default occurs. POD is usually expressed as a percentage in annual terms. LGD is most often expressed as a percentage of par value. Recall that the one-period credit spread estimate from an earlier lesson on CDS where we ignored the time value of money was simply the product of LGD and POD (Spread ≈ LGD × POD). This implies that a simple one-period POD can be approximated by dividing credit spread by LGD (POD ≈ Spread/LGD). While this estimate works well for bonds trading close to par, distressed bonds tend to trade on a price rather than a spread basis, which approaches the recovery rate (1 − LGD) as default becomes likely.

The historical POD and the LGD rate is much lower for investment-grade bonds than for high-yield bonds. A **credit loss rate** represents the *realized* percentage of par value lost to default for a group of bonds, or the bonds' default rate multiplied by the loss severity. According to Moody's Investors Service, the highest annual credit loss rate for US investment-grade corporate bonds from 1983 to 2019 was 0.41%, with an average of just 0.05%. For high-yield bonds, the average credit loss rate over the same period was 2.53%, and in several years, usually around economic recessions, losses exceeded 5%. Exhibit 3 shows global annual corporate default rates from S&P Global Ratings for a similar period.

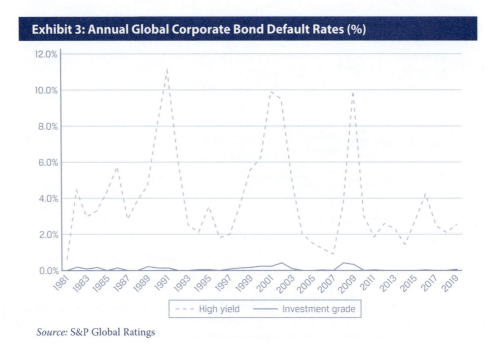

Exhibit 3: Annual Global Corporate Bond Default Rates (%)

Source: S&P Global Ratings

Exhibit 3 makes clear that the likelihood of default rises significantly as the economy slows, reaching peaks during the 1990–91, 2001, and 2008 recessions. The percentage of par value lost in a default scenario depends on a bond's (or loan's) relative position in the capital structure and whether it is secured or unsecured, as shown in Exhibit 4.

Exhibit 4: Average Volume Weighted US Corporate Debt Recovery Rates, 1983–2019

First lien bank loan	64%
Second lien bank loan	29%
Senior unsecured bank loan	44%
First lien bond	55%
Second lien bond	45%
Senior unsecured bond	35%
Senior subordinated bond	27%
Subordinated bond	28%
Junior subordinated bond	14%

Source: Moody's Investors Service

EXAMPLE 1

Estimating Credit Spreads Using POD and LGD

A bank analyst observes a first lien bank loan maturing in two years with a spread of 100 bps from an issuer considering a new second lien bank loan. Using average historical volume weighted corporate debt recovery rates (RR) as a guide, what is the estimated credit spread for the new second lien bank loan?

Key Credit and Spread Concepts for Active Management

> **Solution:**
>
> 1. Using the POD approximation (POD ≈ Spread/LGD and LGD = (1 − RR)), the analyst uses the current first lien bank loan credit spread and expected first lien bank loan recovery rate to estimate the issuer's POD to be 2.778% (=1.00%/(1 − 0.64)).
> 2. Using the issuer POD from Answer 1 and the expected second lien bank loan recovery rate of 29%, the bank analyst solves for the expected second lien spread using (POD × LGD) to get 197 bps (=2.778% × (1 − 0.29)).

Default versus Credit Migration

Although actual defaults are relatively rare among higher-rated bond issuers, changes in the *relative* assessment of creditworthiness occurs more frequently. **Credit migration**, or the likelihood of a change in a bond's public credit rating, usually has a negative effect on bond prices. This effect occurs because the chance of downgrade exceeds that of an upgrade, and the yield spread increase at lower credit ratings is far greater than the spread decrease in the event of a credit upgrade.

The POD versus credit migration varies significantly across the credit spectrum. For example, Exhibit 5 shows the two-year average rate of global corporate default and one-notch downgrade.

Exhibit 5: Two-Year Average Global Corporate Default/Downgrade, 1981–2019

Statistic/Rating	AAA	AA	A	BBB	BB	B	CCC
Default Probability (%)	0.03	0.06	0.14	0.45	1.96	7.83	36.49
One Notch Downgrade (%)	16.22	13.79	8.81	5.66	9.82	5.22	

Source: S&P Global Ratings

Investors typically categorize credit risk using public debt ratings, distinguishing between investment-grade and high-yield market segments. Investment-grade bonds generally have higher credit ratings, lower default risk, and higher recovery in the event of default and offer lower all-in yields to maturity. High-yield bonds usually have higher yields to maturity as a result of lower (sub-investment or speculative grade) credit ratings, higher default risk, and lower recovery in the event of default. In an earlier yield curve strategies lesson, changes in the level, slope, and shape of the government bond term structure across maturities were established as primary risk factors. The level and slope of credit spread curves are often categorized by public credit rating to distinguish relative market changes across the credit spectrum.

For example, the relative historical yield spread *level* across public rating categories for US corporate borrowers is shown in Exhibit 6.

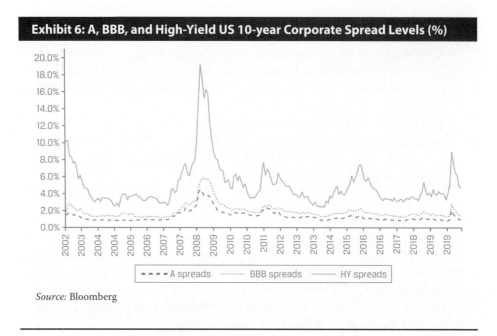

Source: Bloomberg

Lower-rated bonds face a greater impact from adverse market events, as evidenced by the widening gap between BBB rated and high-yield bonds during the 2008 financial crisis and the COVID-19 pandemic in 2020.

Credit Spread Curves

Active managers often position spread-based portfolios to capitalize on expected credit spread curve changes in a way similar to the benchmark yield curve strategies seen in an earlier lesson. While frequent issuers with many bonds outstanding across maturities have their own issuer-specific credit curve, credit spread curves are usually categorized by rating, issuer type, and/or corporate sector. These curves are derived from the difference between all-in yields to maturity for bonds within each respective category and a government benchmark bond or swap yield curve, with adjustments for specific credit spread measures covered in detail later. For example, Exhibit 7 shows the decline in option-adjusted spreads for US BBB rated health care companies over a one-year period from the end of Q3 2019 to 2020, with the bar graph at the bottom showing the decrease for each maturity.

Key Credit and Spread Concepts for Active Management

Exhibit 7: BBB Rated US Corporate Health Care Spreads, 2019–2020

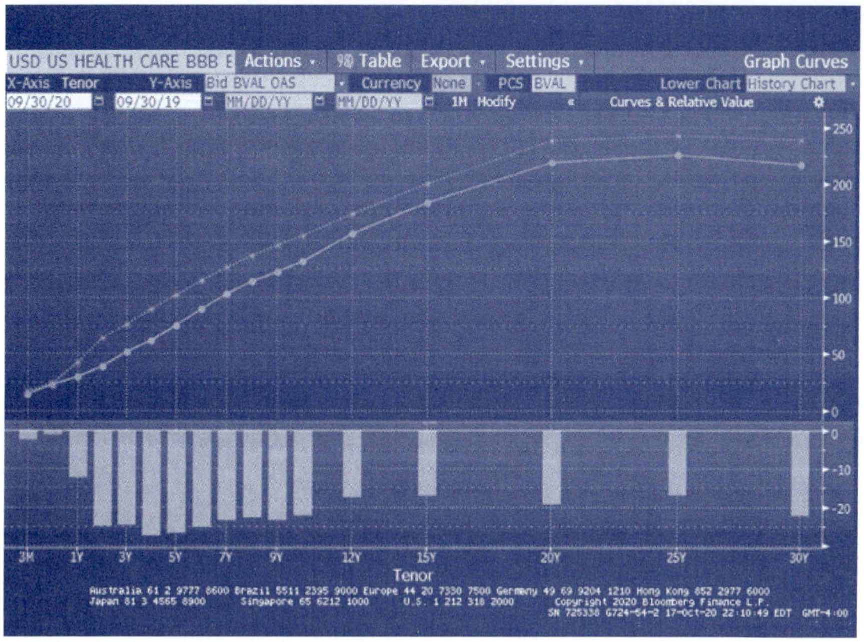

Source: Bloomberg

Primary credit risk factors for a specific issuer include the level and slope of the issuer's credit spread curve. For instance, ignoring liquidity differences across maturities, an upward-sloping credit spread curve suggests a relatively low near-term default probability that rises over time as the likelihood of downgrade and/or default increases. A flatter credit spread curve in contrast indicates that downgrade/default probabilities are equally likely in the near- and long-term.

Credit spread curve changes are broadly driven by the **credit cycle**, the expansion and contraction of credit over the business cycle, which translates into asset price changes based on default and recovery expectations across maturities and rating categories. Exhibit 8 outlines key credit cycle characteristics and the general effect on credit spread curve levels and slope for high- and low-rated issuers.

Exhibit 8: General Credit Cycle Characteristics

	Early Expansion (Recovery)	Late Expansion	Peak	Contraction (Recession)
Economic Activity	Stable	Accelerating	Decelerating	Declining
Corporate Profitability	Rising	Peak	Stable	Falling
Corporate Leverage	Falling	Stable	Rising	Peak
Corporate Defaults	Peak	Falling	Stable	Rising
Credit Spread Level	Stable	Falling	Rising	Peak
Credit Spread Slope	Stable for high grade, inverted for low ratings	Steeper for both higher and lower ratings	Steeper for both higher and lower ratings	Flatter for high grade, inverted for low ratings

Exhibit 3 and Exhibit 6 demonstrate the significant variability in annual credit loss rates and credit spread changes, respectively, across the ratings spectrum. Lower-rated issuers tend to experience greater slope and level changes over the credit cycle, including more frequent inversion of the credit curve, given their larger rise in annual credit losses during economic downturns. Higher-rated issuers, in contrast, face smaller credit spread changes and usually exhibit upward-sloping credit curves and fewer credit losses during periods of economic contraction. Credit spread differences *between* major ratings categories tend to narrow during periods of strong economic growth and widen when growth is expected to slow.

For example, consider the widening of BB versus single-A US corporate spreads during Q1 2020 shown in Exhibit 9. The difference between two-year BB spreads and A spreads for the same tenor more than tripled over this three-month period.

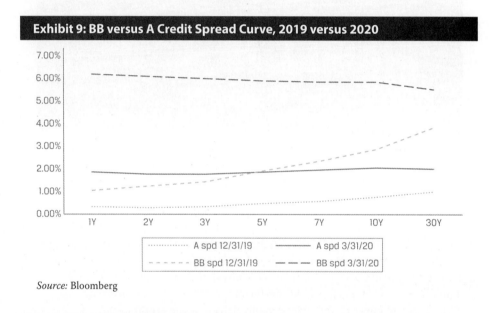

Exhibit 9: BB versus A Credit Spread Curve, 2019 versus 2020

Source: Bloomberg

EXAMPLE 2

Credit Cycle and Credit Spread Curve Changes

1. Which of the following *best* describes the expected shape of the credit spread curve in an economic downturn?

    A. Investment-grade and high-yield issuers usually experience similar credit spread curve steepening because of declining corporate profitability.

    B. High-yield issuers usually experience more spread curve steepening than investment-grade issuers because higher leverage leads to a greater decline in profitability.

    C. High-yield issuers often experience more pronounced flattening or credit spread curve inversion in an economic downturn because the probability of downgrade or default is higher in the near term than the long term.

Key Credit and Spread Concepts for Active Management

> **Solution:**
>
> The correct answer is C. While investment-grade and high-yield issuers both experience declining profitability in an economic downturn, as in answers A and B, this usually leads to a flatter credit spread curve for investment-grade issuers and often to credit spread curve inversion for high-yield issuers, given a rise in near-term downgrades and defaults.

Actual price movements of lower-rated bonds can be quite different from what analytical models based on benchmark rates and credit spreads would predict under issuer-specific and market stress scenarios. For example, issuer financial distress will cause a bond's price to diverge from what a model using benchmark rates would suggest. As an issuer nears default, the price of its bond approaches the estimated recovery rate, regardless of the current benchmark YTM, because investors no longer expect to receive risky future coupon payments. Under a "flight to quality" market stress scenario, investors sell high-risk, low-rated bonds, which fall in price, and purchase government bonds, which experience price appreciation. This observed negative correlation between high-yield credit spreads and government benchmark yields to maturity often leads fixed-income practitioners to use statistical models and historical bond market data to estimate **empirical duration** rather than rely on analytical duration estimates based on duration and convexity. This market stress scenario is addressed in the following example.

> ### EXAMPLE 3
>
> ### Empirical versus Analytical Duration
>
> 1. A high-yield bond fund manager is considering adding a US$50 million face value, five-year, 6.75% semiannual coupon bond with a YTM of 5.40% to an active portfolio. The manager uses regression analysis to estimate the bond's empirical duration to be 2.95. Calculate the bond's analytical duration, and estimate the difference in the expected versus actual market value change for this position, given a 50 bp decline in benchmark yields to maturity using these two measures.
>
> ### Solution:
>
> 1. Solve for the bond's analytical duration by using the Excel MDURATION function (MDURATION(settlement, maturity, coupon, yield, frequency, basis)) using a settlement date of 1 January 2022, maturity of 1 January 2027, a 6.75% coupon, 5.40% YTM, semiannual frequency and basis of 0 (30/360 day count) to get 4.234. Note the analytical duration is greater than the observed empirical duration of 2.95.
>
> 2. The bond position value can be calculated using the Excel PRICE function (PRICE(settlement, maturity, coupon, yield, frequency, basis)) to solve for a price of 105.847 per 100 face value, or a price of US$52,923,500 for a US$50 million face value.
>
> 3. The difference in percentage market value change can be estimated using the 0.50% yield change multiplied by modified duration (–ModDur × ΔYield) for the two estimates. If the benchmark YTM declines by 50 bps, then
>
>   Analytical duration estimate: 2.117% = (−4.234 × −0.5%)
>
>   Empirical duration estimate: 1.475% = (−2.95 × −0.5%)

> The analytical duration calculation overestimates the price gain versus the empirical duration estimate.
>
> 4. The difference is 0.642% (2.117% − 1.475%), or an expected US$339,769 (=0.642% × $52,923,500) value difference between the two measures.

While the concept of empirical duration emphasizes the *direction* of high-yield credit spread changes versus benchmark rates, as suggested earlier, the *magnitude* of credit spread changes is greater for lower- versus higher-rate bonds. As we will see later in the lesson, this empirical observation leads to the use of credit spread measure changes based on *percentage* as opposed to absolute credit spread changes for lower-rated issuers.

Credit Spread Measures

Fixed-Rate Bond Credit Spread Measures

The estimation of yield spreads from market information gives rise to several measures of the difference between a fixed-rate bond's YTM and a benchmark rate. Recall that the YTM is an internal rate of return calculation of all bond cash flows that assumes any earlier payments are reinvested at the same rate and the bond is held to maturity. Spread comparisons are accurate when comparing bonds with identical maturities but different coupons. Because bond maturities vary in practice, a mismatch arises that creates measurement bias if the yield curve is sloped. As a bond rolls down the curve, the benchmark security can also change over time. Finally, yield-based measures do not accurately gauge the return of carry-based strategies often used by active managers (for example, long a risky bond, short a default risk-free position in the repo market).

The yield spread (or benchmark spread) defined earlier as the simple difference between a bond's YTM and the YTM of an on-the-run government bond of similar maturity is easy to calculate and interpret for option-free bonds, and it is particularly useful for infrequently traded bonds. The yield spread also facilitates the approximation of bond price changes for a given benchmark YTM change, assuming a constant yield spread. That said, this simple government bond–based measure has both curve slope and maturity mismatch biases and lacks consistency over time because government benchmarks change as a bond nears maturity.

The **G-spread** uses constant maturity Treasury yields to maturity as the benchmark. Exhibit 10 shows the difference between yield spread and G-spread measures using the example of a bond with 12 years remaining to maturity. While the yield spread for this bond would likely be quoted over a 10-year government benchmark rate, the G-spread involves an interpolation between 10-year and 20-year government yields to maturity.

Key Credit and Spread Concepts for Active Management

Exhibit 10: Yield Spread versus G-Spread

EXAMPLE 4

Yield Spread versus G-Spread

A portfolio manager considers the following annual coupon bonds:

Issuer	Term	Coupon	Yield	ModDur
Bank	8y	2.75%	2.68%	7.10
Government	7y	1.5%	1.39%	6.61
Government	10y	1.625%	1.66%	9.16

1. Calculate the yield spread and G-spread for the bank bond.

Solution:

Yield spread for the bank bond is 1.290%, or the simple difference between the 2.68% bank bond YTM and the 1.39% YTM of the nearest on-the-run government bond.

The G-spread is the difference between the bank bond YTM and a linear interpolation of the YTMs of the 7-year government bond (r_{7yr}) and the 10-year government bond (r_{10yr}). Calculate the approximate 8-year government rate as follows:

1. Solve for the weights of the 7-year and the 10-year bond in the interpolation calculation.

   7-year bond weight = w_7 = 66.7% (= (10 − 8)/(10 − 7))

   10-year bond weight = w_{10} = 33.3% (or (1 − w_7))

   Note that (w_7 × 7) + (w_{10} × 10 = 8).

2. The 8-year government rate is a weighted average of the 7-year bond rate and the 10-year bond rate using the weights in Step 1.

$r_{8yr} = w_7 \times r_{7yr} + w_{10} \times r_{10yr}$

$= (66.7\% \times 1.39\%) + (33.3\% \times 1.66\%) = 1.48\%$

3. The G-spread, or the difference between the bank bond YTM and the 8-year government rate, equals 1.20% (= 2.68% − 1.48%).

2. An increase in expected inflation causes the government yield curve to steepen, with a 20-point rise in the 10-year government bond YTM and no change in the 7-year government YTM. If the respective bank bond yield spread measures remain unchanged, calculate the expected bank bond percentage price change in each case, and explain which is a more accurate representation of the market change in this case.

Solution:

For the yield spread measure, neither the 1.29% spread nor the 7-year government rate of 1.39% has changed, so an analyst considering only these two factors would expect the bank bond price to remain unchanged.

However, for the G-spread measure, the 20 bp increase in the 10-year government YTM causes the 8-year interpolated government YTM to change.

1. The 7-year and the 10-year bond weights for the interpolation are the same as for Question 1, $w_7 = 66.7\%$ and $w_{10} = 33.3\%$.

2. The new 8-year government rate is a weighted average of the 7-year bond rate and the 10-year bond rate using the weights in Step 1.

$r_{8yr} = w_7 \times r_{7yr} + w_{10} \times r_{10yr}$

$= (66.7\% \times 1.39\%) + (33.3\% \times 1.86\%) = 1.55\%$

3. The bank bond YTM has risen by 0.07% to 2.75% (=1.55% + 1.20%).

4. The bank bond price change can be estimated by multiplying the yield change by modified duration (−ModDur × ΔYield) as in earlier lessons. This change can be calculated as -0.497% (=−7.1 × 0.07%).

Note that we can confirm this using the Excel PV function (=−PV (rate, nper, pmt, FV, type)) where "rate" is the interest rate per period (0.0268), "nper" is the number of periods (8), "pmt" is the periodic coupon (2.75), "FV" is future value (100), and "type" corresponds to payments made at the end of each period (0).

Initial bank bond price: 100.50 (=−PV (0.0268, 8, 2.75, 100, 0))

New bank bond price: 100 (=−PV (0.0275, 8, 2.75, 100, 0))

Price change: −0.497% (= (99.39 − 100.50)/100.50)

The G-spread calculation provides a more accurate representation of the estimated bank bond price change in this case because it incorporates the term structure of interest rates.

The **I-spread (interpolated spread)** uses interest rate swaps as the benchmark. Recall that swap rates are derived using short-term lending or market reference rates (MRRs) rather than default-risk-free rates, and unlike government bonds, they are quoted across all maturities. Short-term MRR were historically survey-based Libor rates and are transitioning to transaction-based, secured overnight funding rates.

Key Credit and Spread Concepts for Active Management

The spread over an MRR-based benchmark can be interpreted as a *relative* rather than absolute credit risk measure for a given bond issuer. An issuer might use the MRR spread to determine the relative cost of fixed-rate versus floating-rate borrowing alternatives, while an investor can use the I-spread to compare pricing more readily across issuers and maturities. Swap benchmarks have the added benefit of directly measuring all-in bond YTMs with an instrument that can be used both as a duration hedge and to measure carry return more accurately for a leveraged position. While the I-spread addresses the maturity mismatch of bonds and benchmarks as raised earlier, it incorporates yield levels using a point on the curve to estimate a risky bond's yield spread rather than the term structure of interest rates and is limited to option-free bonds as a credit risk measure.

Asset swaps convert a bond's periodic fixed coupon to MRR plus (or minus) a spread. If the bond is priced close to par, this spread approximately equals the bond's credit risk over the MRR. Exhibit 11 shows the mechanics of an asset swap.

Exhibit 11: Asset Swap Mechanics

The **asset swap spread (ASW)** is the difference between the bond's fixed coupon rate and the fixed rate on an interest rate swap versus MRR, which matches the coupon dates for the remaining life of the bond. If we assume an investor purchases a bond at par, the asset swap transforms the fixed-rate coupon to an equivalent spread over MRR for the life of the bond. Note that under a bond default scenario, the asset manager would still face the mark-to-market settlement of the swap.

EXAMPLE 5

ASW versus I-Spread

1. Consider the information from the bank and government annual coupon bonds from the prior example:

Issuer	Term	Coupon	Yield	ModDur
Bank	8y	2.75%	2.68%	7.10
Government	7y	1.5%	1.39%	6.61
Government	10y	1.625%	1.66%	9.16

Assuming that 7- and 10-year swap spreads over the respective government benchmark yields to maturity are 15 bps and 20 bps, calculate the ASW and the I-spread for the bank bond, and interpret the difference between the two.

Solution:

1. Solve for the weights of the 7-year and the 10-year bond in the interpolation calculation.

7-year bond weight = w_7 = 66.7% (= (10 − 8)/(10 − 7)).

10-year bond weight = w_{10} = 33.3% (or $(1 - w_7)$).

Note that $(w_7 \times 7) + (w_{10} \times 10) = 8$.

2. The interpolated 8-year swap rate is a weighted average of the 7-year swap rate (1.54% = 1.39% + 0.15%) and the 10-year swap rate (1.86% = 1.66% + 0.20%).

$r_{Swap8yr} = w_7 \times r_{Swap7yr} + w_{10} \times r_{Swap10yr}$

$(66.7\% \times 1.54\%) + (33.3\% \times 1.86\%) = 1.647\%$

3. The ASW equals the difference between the bank bond *coupon* of 2.75% and the 8-year swap rate of 1.647%, or 110.3 bps.

4. The I-spread is the difference between the bank bond's current YTM of 2.68% and the 8-year swap rate of 1.647%, or 103.3 bps.

The ASW is an estimate of the spread over MRR versus the bond's original coupon rate to maturity, while the I-spread is an estimate of the spread over MRR for a new par bond from the bank issuer, with the difference largely reflecting the premium or discount of the outstanding bond price.

While both the G-spread and I-spread use the same discount rate for each cash flow, a more precise approach incorporating the term structure of interest rates is to derive a constant spread over a government (or interest rate swap) spot curve instead. This spread is known as the **zero-volatility spread (Z-spread)** of a bond over the benchmark rate. The Z-spread formula shown in Equation 2 was introduced in an earlier reading.

$$PV = \frac{PMT}{(1+z_1+Z)^1} + \frac{PMT}{(1+z_2+Z)^2} + \ldots + \frac{PMT+FV}{(1+z_N+Z)^N} \qquad (2)$$

Here the bond price (PV) is a function of coupon (PMT) and principal (FV) payments in the numerator with respective benchmark spot rates $z_1 \ldots z_N$ derived from the swap or government yield curve and a constant Z-spread per period (Z) in the denominator discounted as of a coupon date. While more accurate than either the G-spread or I-spread, this is a more complex calculation that is conducted by practitioners using either a spreadsheet or other analytical model.

Credit default swap (CDS) basis refers to the difference between the Z-spread on a specific bond and the CDS spread of the same (or interpolated) maturity for the same issuer. Recall from earlier in the curriculum that a CDS is a derivative contract in which a protection buyer makes a series of premium (or CDS spread) payments to a protection seller in exchange for compensation for credit losses (or the difference between par and the recovery rate) under a credit event. Negative basis arises if the yield spread is above the CDS spread, and positive basis indicates a yield spread tighter than the CDS spread. Although spreads for a single issuer across bond and CDS markets should be closely aligned in principle, in practice, CDS basis arises because of such factors as bond price differences from par, accrued interest, and varying contract terms, among other items. As in the case of asset swaps, CDS basis is a pricing measure, but unlike ASW, a CDS contract is terminated and settled following a credit event with no residual interest rate swap mark-to-market exposure. Similar to the I-spread using swaps or the asset swap just mentioned, CDS basis is a useful credit measure for investors actively trading or hedging credit risk using CDS, as addressed in detail later.

The **option-adjusted spread (OAS)** is a generalization of the Z-spread calculation that incorporates bond option pricing based on assumed interest rate volatility. Earlier readings established the use of the term structure of zero rates combined with a volatility assumption to derive forward interest rates used to value bonds with

Key Credit and Spread Concepts for Active Management

embedded options. The OAS is the constant yield spread over the zero curve which makes the arbitrage-free value of such a bond equal to its market price as shown in Exhibit 12. Note that the Z-spread for an option-free bond is simply its OAS, assuming zero volatility.

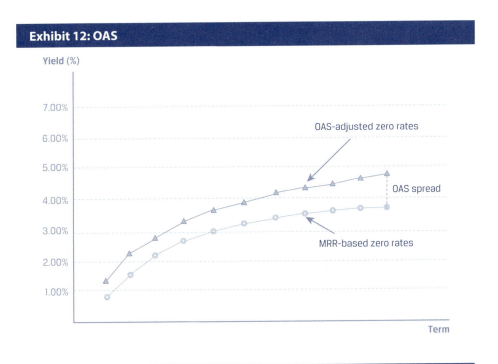

Exhibit 12: OAS

The OAS approach is the most appropriate yield spread measure for active fixed-income portfolio managers because it provides a consistent basis for comparing credit risk yield spreads for option-free, callable, putable, and structured fixed-income instruments. OAS calculations typically rely on fixed-income analytical models that incorporate the current term structure of interest rates, interest rate volatility, and term structure model factors introduced earlier in addition to the specific option-based features of a particular bond. Although OAS provides the best means to facilitate yield spread comparisons across different fixed-income securities, the main drawback of the OAS is that it is highly dependent on volatility and other model assumptions. For example, returns on structured financial instruments are highly dependent on prepayment versus extension risk, as outlined in an earlier lesson. While some analytical models calculate OAS using a standard or constant prepayment speed assumption, values based on historical or empirical analysis might provide very different and more accurate results. Also, the theoretical nature of the OAS calculation implies that bonds with embedded options are unlikely to realize the spread implied by the bond's OAS. Despite these shortcomings, OAS is the most widely accepted credit spread measure for comparing bonds with and without optionality across a fixed-income bond portfolio.

EXAMPLE 6

Portfolio OAS

1. A European portfolio manager is presented with the following information on a portfolio of two bonds. Calculate the OAS of the portfolio.

Issuer	Face Value	Price*	Accrued Interest*	OAS (bps p.a.)
Company A	€ 100,000,000	95	1.5	125
Company B	€ 200,000,000	97	2.0	150

*Per 100 of par value

Solution:

1. Solve for bond and portfolio values:
   A. Company A bond: €96,500,000 = €100,000,000 × (0.95 +0.015)
   B. Company B bond: €198,000,000 = €200,000,000 × (0.97 +0.02)
   C. Portfolio: €294,500,000 = €96,500,000 + €198,000,000
2. Solve for portfolio weights w_A and w_B:
   A. Company A (w_A): 32.8% = €96,500,000/€294,500,000
   B. Company B (w_B): 67.2% = €198,000,000/€294,500,000
3. Solve for portfolio OAS using $(OAS_A \times w_A) + (OAS_B \times w_B)$.

OAS = 142 bps p.a. = (0.328 × 125 bps) + (0.672 × 150 bps)

Exhibit 13 summarizes these fixed-rate bond credit spread measures adapted from O'Kane and Sen (2005).

Exhibit 13: Key Fixed-Rate Bond Credit Spread Measures

Spread	Description	Advantages	Disadvantages
Yield spread	Difference between bond YTM and government benchmark of similar tenor	Simple to calculate and observe	Maturity mismatch, curve slope bias, and inconsistent over time
G-spread (Government spread)	Spread over interpolated government bond	Transparent and maturity matching default risk-free bond	Subject to changes in government bond demand
I-spread (Interpolated spread)	Yield spread over swap rate of same tenor	Spread versus market based (MRR) measure often used as hedge or for carry trade	Point estimate of term structure and limited to option-free bonds
ASW (Asset swap)	Spread over MRR of fixed bond coupon	Traded spread to convert current bond coupon to MRR plus a spread	Tradable spread rather than spread measure corresponding to cashflows and limited to option-free bonds

Key Credit and Spread Concepts for Active Management

Spread	Description	Advantages	Disadvantages
Z-spread (Zero volatility spread)	Yield spread over a government (or swap) spot curve	Accurately captures term structure of government or swap zero rates	More complex calculation limited to option-free bonds
CDS Basis	Yield spread versus CDS spread of same tenor	Interpolated CDS spread versus Z-spread	Traded spread rather than spread measure corresponding to cashflows and limited to option-free bonds
OAS	Yield spread using Z-spread including bond option volatility	Provides generalized comparison for valuing risky option-free bonds with bonds with embedded options	Complex calculation based on volatility and prepayment assumptions; bonds with embedded options are unlikely to earn OAS over time

EXAMPLE 7

Comparison of Fixed-Rate Bond Credit Spread Measures

1. An active manager observes a yield spread for an outstanding corporate bond that is above the G-spread for that same bond. Which of the following is the most likely explanation for the difference?

   A. The government benchmark bond used to calculate the yield spread has a *shorter* maturity than the corporate bond, and the benchmark yield curve is *upward* sloping.

   B. The government benchmark bond used to calculate the yield spread has a *shorter* maturity than the corporate bond, and the benchmark curve is *downward* sloping.

   C. The government benchmark bond used to calculate the yield spread has a *longer* maturity than the corporate bond, and the benchmark yield curve is *upward* sloping.

   Solution:

   The correct answer is A. For a given all-in YTM, the lower the (on-the-run or interpolated) benchmark rate, the higher the relevant spread measure over the benchmark. Therefore, the higher yield spread versus G-spread most likely arises from the government benchmark having a shorter maturity than the bond and an upward sloping government yield curve. As for B and C, the yield spread would be lower than the G-spread for a downward sloping yield curve.

2. An active manager is weighing the purchase of two callable bonds with similar credit risks and the same final maturity. Which of the two bonds is more likely to be called on the next call date?

   A. The bond with the lower ASW

   B. The bond with the lower Z-spread

   C. The bond with the lower OAS

> **Solution:**
>
> The correct answer is C. The OAS measure is best suited to compare the impact of embedded options on similar bonds because it incorporates a volatility assumption to account for the value of bond options. Answer A indicates the spread over MRR for an outstanding bond swapped versus the original coupon rate, while the Z-spread in B assumes zero volatility and therefore does not capture the value of bond options.

Floating-Rate Note Credit Spread Measures

In contrast to fixed-rate bonds, floating-rate notes (FRNs) pay a periodic interest coupon comprising a variable MRR plus a (usually) constant yield spread. While fixed- and floating-rate bonds both decline in price if credit risk rises, interest rate risk on these bond types differs, and the associated FRN credit spread measures warrant our attention.

An earlier reading provided a simplified framework for valuing a floating-rate bond on a payment date, shown in Equation 3:

$$PV = \frac{\left(\frac{(MRR + QM) \times FV}{m}\right)}{\left(1 + \frac{(MRR + DM)}{m}\right)^1} + \frac{\left(\frac{(MRR + QM) \times FV}{m}\right)}{\left(1 + \frac{(MRR + DM)}{m}\right)^2} + \ldots + \frac{\left(\frac{(MRR + QM) \times FV}{m}\right) + FV}{\left(1 + \frac{(MRR + DM)}{m}\right)^N} \quad (3)$$

Each interest payment is MRR plus the **quoted margin** (QM) times par (FV) and divided by m, the number of periods per year. Rather than a fixed YTM as for fixed-rate bonds, the periodic discount rate per period is MRR plus the **discount margin** (DM) divided by the periodicity (m), or (MRR + DM)/m. Note that for the purposes of Equation 3, MRR is based on current MRR and therefore implies a flat forward curve. The QM is the yield spread over the MRR established upon issuance to compensate investors for assuming the credit risk of the issuer. While some FRN bond indentures include an increase or decrease in the QM if public ratings or other criteria change, given that this spread is usually fixed through maturity, the QM does not reflect credit risk changes over time.

The discount (or required) margin is the yield spread versus the MRR such that the FRN is priced at par on a rate reset date. For example, assume an FRN issued at par value pays three-month MRR plus 1.50%. The QM is 150 bps. If the issuer's credit risk remains unchanged, the DM also equals 150 bps. On each quarterly reset date, the floater will be priced at par value. Between coupon dates, the flat price will be at a premium or discount to par value if MRR falls or rises. If on a reset date, the DM falls to 125 bps because of an issuer upgrade, the FRN will be priced at a premium above par value. The amount of the premium is the present value of the premium future cash flows. The annuity difference of 25 bps per period is calculated for the remaining life of the bond. Exhibit 14 summarizes the relationship between the QM versus DM and an FRN's price on any reset date.

Key Credit and Spread Concepts for Active Management

Exhibit 14: FRN Discount, Premium, and Par Pricing

FRN price	Description	QM versus DM
Par	FRN trades at a price (PV) equal to its future value (FV)	QM = DM
Discount	FRN trades at PV < FV	QM < DM
Premium	FRN trades at PV > FV	QM > DM

EXAMPLE 8

Discount Margin

1. A London-based investor owns a five-year £100 million FRN that pays three-month MRR + 1.75% on a quarterly basis. The current MRR of 0.50% is assumed to remain constant over time. If the issuer's credit risk deteriorates and the DM rises to 2.25%, explain whether the FRN is trading at a discount or premium, and calculate the price difference from par.

Solution:

The FRN is trading at a discount because the QM is below the DM. We can solve for the price difference using the following steps.

1. Solve for the quarterly interest payment (=(MRR + QM) × FV/m) in the numerator and the discount rate (=(MRR + DM)/m) in the denominator of Equation 3 with QM = 1.75%, DM = 2.25%, MRR = 0.50%, and m = 4.

   A. Quarterly interest payment: £562,500 (= (0.50% + 1.75%) × £100,000,000/4)

   B. Discount rate: 0.6875% (= (0.50% + 2.25%)/4)

2. Solve for the new price using results from 1A and 1B with N = 20.

$$£97,671,718 = \frac{£562,500}{(1+0.6875\%)} + \frac{£562,500}{(1+0.6875\%)^2} + \frac{£562,500}{(1+0.6875\%)^3}$$
$$+ \ldots + \frac{£100,562,500}{(1+0.6875\%)^{20}}$$

3. The price difference is £2,328,282 (= £100,000,000 − £ 97,671,718).

The **zero-discount margin (Z-DM)** incorporates forward MRR into the yield spread calculation for FRNs. As in the case of the zero-volatility spread for fixed-rate bonds shown earlier, the Z-DM is the fixed periodic adjustment applied to the FRN pricing model to solve for the observed market price. As Equation 4 shows, this calculation incorporates the respective benchmark spot rates z_i derived from the swap or government yield curve for the Z-spread into the FRN pricing model shown earlier.

$$PV = \frac{\left(\frac{(MRR + QM) \times FV}{m}\right)}{\left(1 + \frac{(MRR + Z\text{-}DM)}{m}\right)^1} + \frac{\left(\frac{(z_2 + QM) \times FV}{m}\right)}{\left(1 + \frac{(z_2 + Z\text{-}DM)}{m}\right)^2}$$
$$+ \ldots + \frac{\left(\frac{(z_N + QM) \times FV}{m}\right) + FV}{\left(1 + \frac{(z_N + Z\text{-}DM)}{m}\right)^N} \quad (4)$$

As in the case of the Z-spread for fixed-rate bonds, the Z-DM will change based on changes in the MRR forward curve. For example, in an upward-sloping yield curve, the Z-DM will be below the DM. Also, the Z-DM assumes an unchanged QM and that the FRN will remain outstanding until maturity. Exhibit 15 summarizes FRN credit spreads as adapted from O'Kane and Sen (2005).

Exhibit 15: Key FRN Credit Spread Measures

Spread	Description	Advantages	Disadvantages
QM	Yield spread over MRR of original FRN	Represents periodic spread related FRN cash flow	Does not capture changes in credit risk over time
DM	Yield spread over MRR to price FRN at par	Establishes spread difference from QM with constant MRR	Assumes a flat MRR zero curve
Z-DM	Yield spread over MRR curve	Incorporates forward MRR rates in yield spread measure	More complex calculation and yield spread does not match FRN cash flows

EXAMPLE 9

Floating-Rate Credit Spread Measure

1. An Australian investor holds a three-year FRN with a coupon of three-month MRR + 1.25%. Given an expected strong economic recovery, she anticipates a rise in Australian MRR over the next three years and an improvement in the FRN issuer's creditworthiness. Which of the following credit spread measures does she expect to be the *lowest* as a result?

   A. QM
   B. DM
   C. Z-DM

Solution:

The correct answer is C. The QM will be above the DM if issuer creditworthiness improves. As MRRs rise over the next three years, the upward-sloping curve will cause the Z-DM to remain below the DM.

Portfolio Return Impact of Yield Spreads

We now turn from credit spread measures to their impact on expected portfolio return. The first and third variables in Equation 1, namely roll-down return and E (Δ Price due to investor's view of yield spreads), are directly relevant for active managers targeting excess return above a benchmark portfolio using credit strategies.

In the first instance, recall from earlier lessons that investors "rolling down" the yield curve accumulate coupon income and additional return from fixed-rate bond price appreciation over an investment horizon if benchmark rates are positive and the yield curve slopes upward. For fixed-rate bonds priced at a spread over the benchmark, return from coupon income is higher by the bond's original credit spread. The roll-down return due to price appreciation will also be higher than for an otherwise identical government security because the higher-yielding instrument will generate

Key Credit and Spread Concepts for Active Management

greater carry over time. Note that this higher return comes with greater risk and assumes all promised payments take place and the bond remains outstanding—that is, no default or prepayment occurs, and the bond is not called.

EXAMPLE 10

Corporate versus Government Bond Roll Down

A London-based investor wants to estimate rolling yield attributable to a fixed-rate, option-free corporate bond versus UK gilts over the next six months assuming a static, upward-sloping government yield curve and a constant credit spread. The corporate bond has exactly 10 years remaining to maturity, a semiannual coupon of 3.25%, and a YTM of 2.75%, while the closest maturity UK gilt is a 1.75% coupon currently yielding 1.80%, with 9.5 years remaining to maturity.

1. Calculate the annualized rolling yield to the UK corporate bond versus the government bond over the next six months.

Solution:

Solve for the annualized difference in rolling yield by calculating the change in price plus the coupon income for both the corporate bond and the government bond.

1. Calculate the corporate bond rolling yield per £100 face value. For price changes, use the Excel PV function (= –PV(rate, nper, pmt, FV, type)) where "rate" is the interest rate per period (0.0275/2), "nper" is the number of periods (20), "pmt" is the periodic coupon (3.25/2), "FV" is future value (100), and "type" corresponds to payments made at the end of each period (0).

    A. Initial price is 104.346 (= –PV (0.0275/2, 20, 3.25/2, 100, 0)).

    B. Price in six months is 104.155 (= –PV (0.0275/2, 19, 3.25/2, 100, 0)). Price *depreciation* is 0.18% (= (104.155 − 104.346)/104.346).

    C. Six-month coupon income is 1.625 (= 3.25/2), or equal to 1.557% (=1.625/104.346), which combined (without rounding) with −0.18% from B results in a 1.375% six-month return (2.75% annualized).

2. Calculate the UK gilt price change and coupon income.

    A. Initial price is 99.565 (= –PV (0.018/2, 19, 1.75/2, 100, 0)).

    B. Price in six months is 99.586 (= –PV (0.018/2, 18, 1.75/2, 100, 0)). Price *appreciation* is 0.021% (= (99.586 − 99.565)/99.565).

    C. Six-month coupon income is 0.875 (=1.75/2), or equal to 0.879% (0.875/99.565), which combined with +0.021% equals 0.9% for six months (1.80% annualized).

The annualized rolling yield difference is the 2.75% corporate bond realized return less the 1.80% UK gilt realized return, or 0.95%.

2. Describe how the relative rolling yield would change if the investor were to use an interpolated government benchmark rather than the actual 9.5-year gilt.

Solution:

The interpolated benchmark involves the use of the most liquid, on-the-run government bonds to derive a hypothetical 10-year UK gilt YTM. Because the UK gilt yield curve is upward sloping in this example, we can conclude that the relative rolling yield using an interpolated benchmark would be lower than the 0.95% difference in Question 1.

Active credit managers often view the E (Δ Price due to investor's view of yield spreads) term in Equation 1 on a stand-alone basis because they manage benchmark rate risks separately from credit. Equation 5 is similar to equations from earlier lessons quantifying the change in bond price for a given YTM change, but it is limited here to yield spread changes, or %ΔPV^{Spread} (= ΔPV/ΔSpread).

$$\%\Delta PV^{Spread} \approx -(\text{EffSpreadDur} \times \Delta \text{Spread}) + (\tfrac{1}{2} \times \text{EffSpreadCon} \times (\Delta \text{Spread})^2) \quad (5)$$

where effective spread duration (EffSpreadDur) and effective spread convexity (EffSpreadCon) reflect spread rather than curve changes, and ΔSpread is typically defined as the change in OAS.

$$\text{EffSpreadDur} = \frac{(PV_-) - (PV_+)}{2 \times (\Delta \text{Spread})(PV_0)} \quad (6)$$

$$\text{EffSpreadCon} = \frac{(PV_-) + (PV_+) - 2(PV_0)}{(\Delta \text{Spread})^2 \times (PV_0)} \quad (7)$$

The first term of Equation 5 is sometimes simply referred to as **spread duration**, or, alternatively, as **OAS duration** when OAS is the underlying spread. Active managers approximate bond portfolio value changes due to spread changes by substituting market value–weighted averages for the duration and convexity measures in Equation 5. As noted earlier, spread changes for lower-rated bonds tend to be consistent on a proportional percentage rather than absolute basis; therefore, adjusting spread duration to capture this **Duration Times Spread (DTS)** effect is important, as in Equation 8.

$$\text{DTS} \approx (\text{EffSpreadDur} \times \text{Spread}) \quad (8)$$

A portfolio's DTS is the market value–weighted average of DTS of its individual bonds, and spread changes of a portfolio are measured on a percentage (ΔSpread/Spread) basis rather than in absolute basis point terms, as in the following example.

EXAMPLE 11

DTS Example

1. A financial analyst compares a portfolio evenly split between two technology company bonds trading at par to an index with an average OAS of 125 bps.

Issuer	OAS	EffSpreadDur
A Rated Bond	100 bps	3.0
BB Rated Bond	300 bps	4.0

Calculate the portfolio DTS, and estimate how the technology bond portfolio will perform if index OAS widens by 10 bps.

Key Credit and Spread Concepts for Active Management

Solution:

Portfolio DTS is the market value–weighted average of DTS based on Equation 8, or $\sum_{i=1}^{n} w_i (\text{EffSpreadDur}_i \times \text{Spread}_i)$.

1. Portfolio DTS in this two-asset example is $w_A(\text{EffSpreadDur}_A \times \text{Spread}_A) + w_{BB}(\text{EffSpreadDur}_{BB} \times \text{Spread}_{BB})$ with equal weights ($w_A = w_{BB} = 0.50$). Solve for portfolio DTS of 750 (= (0.5 × 100 bps × 3.0) + (0.5 × 300 bps × 4.0)).

2. Index spread widening of 10 bps is equivalent to 8% (10 bps/125 bps spread) on a ΔSpread/Spread basis. We can therefore calculate the estimated basis point change in the technology bond portfolio by multiplying the portfolio DTS of 750 by the 8% expected percentage spread change to get an expected 60 bps p.a. widening for the technology bond portfolio.

As active credit managers consider *incremental* effects of credit-based portfolio decisions, they often use spread duration–based statistics to gauge the first-order impact of spread movements. For example, Equation 9 approximates the annualized **excess spread** return for a spread-based bond:

$$\text{ExcessSpread} \approx \text{Spread}_0 - (\text{EffSpreadDur} \times \Delta\text{Spread}) \tag{9}$$

Spread_0 is the initial yield spread, which changes to (Spread_0/Periods Per Year) for holding periods of less than a year. Note that this calculation assumes no defaults for the period in question. While relatively rare, as an event of default grows more likely, expected future bond cash flows are impaired, and a bond's value instead approaches the present value of expected recovery. The annualized expected excess return shown in Equation 10 incorporates both default probability and loss severity:

$$E[\text{ExcessSpreadReturn}] \approx$$

$$\text{Spread}_0 - (\text{EffSpreadDur} \times \Delta\text{Spread}) - (\text{POD} \times \text{LGD}) \tag{10}$$

Equation 10 captures a key goal of active credit management, which is to maximize expected spread return in excess of the portfolio credit loss or realized percentage of par value lost to defaults over time.

EXAMPLE 12

Excess Spread and Expected Excess Spread

A corporate bond has an effective spread duration of five years and a credit spread of 2.75% (275 bps).

1. What is the approximate excess return if the bond is held for six months and the credit spread narrows 50 bps to 2.25%? Assume the spread duration remains at five years and that the bond does not experience default losses.

Solution:

Using Equation 9 ($\text{Spread}_0 - (\text{EffSpreadDur} \times \Delta\text{Spread})$), the excess return on the bond is 3.875% = (2.75% × 0.5) − [(2.25% − 2.75%) × 5].

2. What is the instantaneous (holding period of zero) excess return if the spread rises to 3.25%?

Solution:

Using Equation 9, the instantaneous excess return on the bond is approximately −2.5% = (2.75% × 0) − [(3.25% − 2.75%) × 5].

3. Assume the bond has a 1% annualized expected POD and expected loss severity of 60% in the event of default. What is the expected excess return if the bond is held for six months and the credit spread is expected to fall to 2.25%?

Solution:

Using Equation 10 (Spread$_0$ − (EffSpreadDur × ΔSpread) − (POD × LGD)), the expected excess return on the bond is approximately 3.575% = (2.75% × 0.5) − [(2.25% − 2.75%) × 5] − (0.5 × 1% × 60%).

Finally, we must address the difference in duration as an interest rate sensitivity measure for FRNs versus fixed-rate bonds. The periodic reset of MRRs in both the FRN numerator and denominator leads to a *rate* duration of near zero for floaters trading at par on a reset date (prior to MRR reset). As we saw in an earlier DM example, changes in *spread* (DM or Z-DM) are the key driver of price changes for a given FRN yield change. The respective FRN rate and spread duration measures are shown in Equation 11 and Equation 12 and demonstrated in the following example.

$$\text{EffRateDur}_{FRN} = \frac{(PV_-) - (PV_+)}{2 \times (\Delta MRR)(PV_0)} \quad (11)$$

$$\text{EffSpreadDur}_{FRN} = \frac{(PV_-) - (PV_+)}{2 \times (\Delta DM)(PV_0)} \quad (12)$$

We return to the example of a five-year £100 million FRN at three-month MRR + 1.75%, with a DM of 2.25% and a 0.50% MRR priced at £97,671,718. We can derive the FRN's effective rate duration by first calculating PV_- and PV_+ using a spreadsheet by shifting MRR down and up by 0.05% as follows:

$$PV0 = £97,671,718 = \frac{£562,500}{(1 + 0.6875\%)} + \frac{£562,500}{(1 + 0.6875\%)^2} + \ldots + \frac{£100,562,500}{(1 + 0.6875\%)^{20}}$$

$$PV_- = £97,668,746 = \frac{£550,000}{(1 + 0.6750\%)} + \frac{£550,000}{(1 + 0.6750\%)^2} + \ldots + \frac{£100,550,000}{(1 + 0.6750\%)^{20}}$$

$$PV_+ = £97,674,685 = \frac{£575,000}{(1 + 0.7000\%)} + \frac{£575,000}{(1 + 0.7000\%)^2} + \ldots + \frac{£100,575,000}{(1 + 0.7000\%)^{20}}$$

Solving for EffRateDur$_{FRN}$, we arrive at a rate duration of −0.061, which is slightly negative because the floater trades at a discount. The spread duration statistic EffSpreadDur$_{FRN}$ is calculated in a similar manner by shifting DM down and up by 0.05%, with PV_- and PV_+ equal to £97,972,684 and £97,515,401 and EffSpreadDur$_{FRN}$ equal to 4.682.

CREDIT STRATEGIES

☐ discuss bottom-up approaches to credit strategies
☐ discuss top-down approaches to credit strategies

Bottom-Up Credit Strategies

As active fixed-income managers consider the selection process for spread-based bond portfolio investments, they must assess different ways in which to maximize excess spread across the fixed-income issuer types, industries, and instruments within their prescribed investment mandate. A fundamental choice these investors face is whether to engage in an individual security selection process or bottom-up approach; a macro- or market-based, top-down approach in pursuing this objective; or a combination of both.

Fundamental credit analysis covered earlier in the curriculum considers the basis on which a specific issuer can satisfy its interest and principal payments through bond maturity. Analysts often assess unsecured corporate bonds using factors such as profitability and leverage to identify the sources and variability of cash flows available to an issuer to service debt. These measures are usually chosen and compared relative to an industry and/or the jurisdiction in which the issuer operates. In the case of a sovereign borrower, the relevant metric is the economic activity within a government's jurisdiction and the government's ability and willingness to levy taxes and generate sufficient revenue to meet its obligations. Alternatively, for a special purpose entity issuer with bonds backed by mortgage-based or other securitized cash flows, a credit measure of both the residential borrowers and underlying collateral value as well as internal credit enhancements are among the primary factors considered in the assessment.

While individual bonds across all these issuer types are usually rated by at least two of the major credit rating agencies, active managers typically conduct their own credit assessment of individual borrowers rather than relying on ratings, which are frequently used to define a mandate (e.g., investment grade versus high yield), categorize, or benchmark investments of similar credit quality.

Defining the Credit Universe

A bottom-up approach typically begins with a manager defining the universe of eligible bonds within a mandate and then grouping the universe into categories that allow consistent relative value analysis across comparable borrowers. For example, a corporate bond portfolio manager is likely to divide eligible bonds into industry sectors, such as media and telecommunications and industrials, as well as into subsectors and/or firms located in different jurisdictions. Media and telecommunications subsectors include firms in the cable and satellite industries, internet media, and telecommunications carriers. Within each sector or subsector based on either industry classification methodologies or a customized approach, she can use relative value analysis to determine the bonds that are attractively valued.

> **EXAMPLE 13**
>
> ## Dividing the Credit Universe
>
> 1. An investor is conducting a relative value analysis on global bond issuers in the health care sector. He is trying to decide whether the global health care sector is a sufficiently narrow sector for his analysis. Through his research, he has determined the following:
>
>   - Biotech and pharmaceutical companies are active globally across Europe, Asia, and the Americas.
>   - Health care facilities are typically local in nature and tend to sell into only one of these three regions.
>   - Medical equipment and devices is a more cyclical business, and many of these firms are part of multi-industry companies in which health care accounts for a smaller fraction of overall company sales.
>
>   Describe considerations that the investor can use in determining how to best divide the health care sector into comparable companies.
>
> ## Solution:
>
> An investor typically seeks to isolate a sector that contains a set of companies for which he expects company-level risks, rather than industry or macro risks, to be the dominant factors. Based on the investor's analysis, biotech and pharmaceutical companies differ meaningfully from health care facilities and medical equipment manufacturers. Health care facilities have a narrow regional focus in contrast to the global focus in biotech and pharma.
>
> The investor might therefore want to divide the global health care sector into global biotech and global pharmaceuticals. Hospitals and other health care facilities warrant separate treatment given their narrow geographic focus and different industry drivers. He might want to consider a different approach to medical device companies given their multi-industry profiles.

Bottom-Up Credit Analysis

Once the credit universe has been divided into sectors and prospective bonds identified, the investor evaluates each issuer's implied credit risk comparing company-specific financial information to spread-related compensation for assuming default, credit migration, and liquidity risks for comparative purposes.

Beyond the prospects within a company's industry, its competitive position within that industry, and operating history, financial ratios are a valuable tool to compare creditworthiness across firms. Earlier lessons stressed the value of key ratios, including profitability and cash flow, leverage, and debt coverage, which are summarized in Exhibit 16.

Credit Strategies

Exhibit 16: Key Financial Ratios for Bottom-Up Credit Analysis

Ratio	Description	Advantages	Disadvantages
EBITDA/ Total Assets	**Profitability** Cash flow as a percentage of assets	Combines operating income with non-cash expense	Ignores capital expenditures and working capital changes
Debt/ Capital	**Leverage** Fraction of company's capital financed with debt	Direct measure of relative reliance on debt financing	More relevant for investment-grade than high-yield issuers
EBITDA/ Interest Expense	**Coverage** Cash flow available to service debt	Measures relative issuer ability to meet debt payments	Volatile measure for firms with high cash flow variability

While offering a relatively consistent basis for comparison across firms and over time, reliance on financial ratios based on publicly available accounting data alone is of limited value because of comparability issues across firms and industries as well as the historical nature of financial statements. Alternative measures combine several relevant financial ratios with market-based measures to establish a forward-looking approach to creditworthiness.

A previous lesson established that statistical credit analysis models to measure individual issuer creditworthiness can be categorized as either **reduced form credit models** or **structural credit models**. Reduced form models solve for **default intensity**, or the POD over a specific time period, using observable company-specific variables such as financial ratios and recovery assumptions as well as macroeconomic variables, including economic growth and market volatility measures. Structural credit models use market-based variables to estimate the market value of an issuer's assets and the volatility of asset value. The likelihood of default is defined as the probability of the asset value falling below that of liabilities.

An early example of the reduced form approach is the **Z-score** established by Altman (1968), which combined liquidity (working capital/total assets), profitability (retained earnings/total assets), asset efficiency (EBIT/ total assets), market versus book value of equity, and asset turnover (sales/total assets) factors weighted by coefficients to form a composite score. Each composite, or Z-score, was used to classify manufacturing firms into those expected to remain solvent and those anticipated to go bankrupt. Similar to credit scoring models, this multiple discriminant analysis reduces the dimensionality of the input variables to a single cutoff Z-score that represents the default threshold, as shown in the following example.

EXAMPLE 14

Z-Score Comparison of Two Firms

A United Kingdom–based financial analyst considers a Z-score model in evaluating two publicly traded non-manufacturing companies as follows:

Z-Score Model = $1.2 \times A + 1.4 \times B + 3.3 \times C + 0.6 \times D + 0.999 \times E$,

where

A is Working Capital/Total Assets

B is Retained Earnings/Total Assets

C is EBIT/Total Assets

D is Market Value of Equity/Total Liabilities

E is Sales/Total Assets

Firms with a Z-score greater than 3.0 are considered financially sound, those scoring between 3.0 and 1.8 are at greater risk of financial distress, and those with a Z-score below 1.8 are likely to face insolvency.

1. Calculate the Z-score for Firm 1 and Firm 2. Which has a higher likelihood of financial distress based on this measure?

Financial Data (GBP thousands)/Firm	Firm 1	Firm 2
Total Sales	23,110	15,270
EBIT	6,910	2,350
Current Assets	7,560	4,990
Total Assets	36,360	23,998
Current Liabilities	5,400	3,564
Total Liabilities	9,970	10,050
Retained Earnings	20,890	13,787
Market Value of Equity	29,000	18,270

Solution:

First, calculate the respective ratios for both firms as follows, noting that working capital is equal to current assets minus current liabilities:

Z-Score Factors	Firm 1	Firm 2
Working Capital/Assets	0.059	0.059
Retained Earnings/Assets	0.575	0.575
EBIT/Total Assets	0.190	0.098
Market Value of Equity/Total Liabilities	2.909	1.818
Sales/Total Assets	0.636	0.636

Solving for the respective Z-scores, we find that Firm 1 has a Z-score of 3.883, while Firm 2 has a Z-score of 2.925. Firm 2 therefore has a greater likelihood of financial distress.

2. Evaluate the most likely reasons for the difference in creditworthiness between the two firms based on the Z-score model factors.

Solution:

Comparing the respective Z-score ratios of Firm 1 and Firm 2, we find that Firm 2 has a far lower asset efficiency (EBIT/Total Assets of 9.8% versus 19% for Firm 1) and a lower relative equity market value (Market Value of Equity/Total Liabilities of 1.818 versus 2.909 for Firm 1) than Firm 1, while all other ratios are comparable.

Structural credit models used in practice include Moody's Analytics Expected Default Frequency (EDF) and Bloomberg's Default Risk (DRSK) models, both of which provide daily POD estimates for a broad range of issuers over a selected period. The EDF model estimates a forward-looking POD defined as the point at which the market value of assets falls below a firm's obligations. The model uses asset volatility to determine the likelihood of reaching the default point and is calibrated for different industries, regions, and observed credit market dynamics.

Credit Strategies

Bloomberg's DRSK model estimate for AbbVie Inc., as shown in Exhibit 17, includes a market-based asset value measure derived from equity market capitalization and equity volatility as well as a default threshold measured using the book value of liabilities. These and other DRSK model inputs in the left column of the screen can be defined by users and compared within and across industry sectors. In addition to the one-year POD estimate of 0.0413%, DRSK calculates a "model" CDS spread (upper left corner) which can be compared to the actual market CDS spread.

Exhibit 17: Bloomberg DRSK Model Estimate for AbbVie Inc.

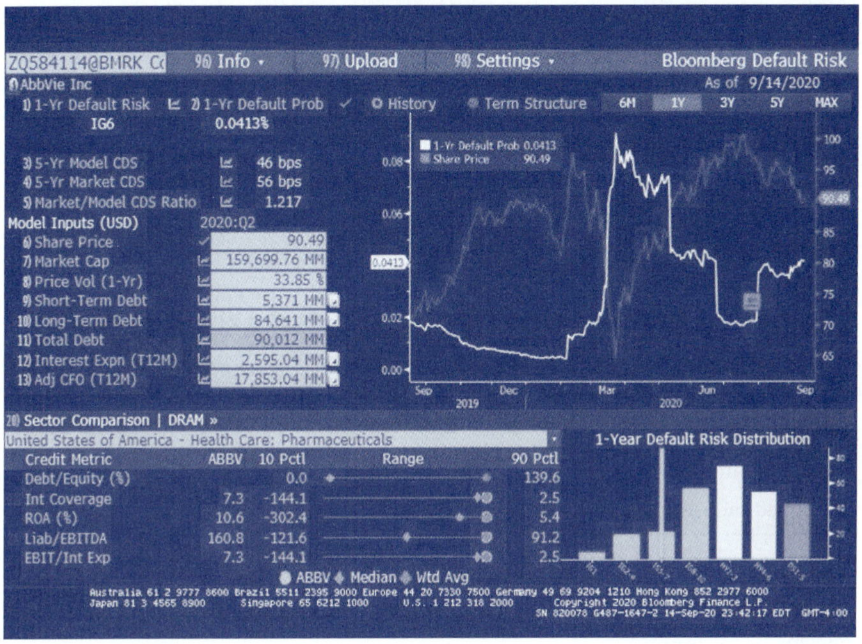

Source: Bloomberg

Both the EDF and DRSK approaches are sometimes referred to as "distance to default" models because a probability distribution is used to determine how far an issuer's current market value of assets is from the default threshold for a given period.

EXAMPLE 15

"Distance to Default" Models

1. An active manager is weighing an investment in the bonds of two issuers in the same industry with identical PODs using a structural credit model. Which of the following changes to the model inputs for one of the issuers would lead the analyst to expect an increase in the POD for that issuer?

    A. An increase in the issuer's coverage ratio

    B. An increase in the volatility of the issuer's stock price

    C. A decrease in the issuer's leverage ratio

Solution:

The correct answer is B. Higher equity volatility increases the likelihood that the market value of the issuer's assets will fall below the default threshold. A higher coverage ratio in A implies higher cash flow as a percentage of assets, increasing the issuer's ability to service its debt obligations. The decrease in the issuer's leverage ratio in C represents a decline in the amount of debt versus equity, reducing the issuer's likelihood of financial distress.

Bottom-Up Relative Value Analysis

Given two issuers with similar credit risk, the investor will typically choose bonds of the issuer with the higher yield spread, given the greater potential for excess returns. For issuers with different credit-related risk, the investor must decide whether the additional spread is sufficient compensation for the incremental exposure. The excess expected return calculation in Equation 10 captures the relationship between yield spreads and the components of credit risk, as seen in the following example.

EXAMPLE 16

Comparing Investments Using Expected Excess Return

A portfolio manager considers two industrial bonds for a one-year investment:

Issuer	Rating	EffSpreadDur	YTM	Z-Spread
A Rated Industrial	A2	5.0	4.0%	100 bps
B Rated Industrial	B2	7.0	6.5%	350 bps

The manager observes a historical annual default probability of 0.27% for A2 rated issuers and 3.19% for B2 rated issuers and assumes a 40% recovery rate for both bonds.

1. Compute the estimated excess return for each bond assuming no change in spreads, and interpret whether the B rated bond spread provides sufficient compensation for the incremental risk.

Solution:

As per Equation 10,

$$E[\text{ExcessSpreadReturn}] \approx \text{Spread}_0 - (\text{EffSpreadDur} \times \Delta\text{Spread}) - (\text{POD} \times \text{LGD}).$$

A rated expected excess return is 0.84% = 1% − (5 × 0) − (0.27% × 60%). B rated expected excess return is 1.59% = 3.5% − (7 × 0) − (3.19% × 60%). The B rated bond appears to provide sufficient compensation for the added risk.

2. Which bond is more attractive if spreads are expected to widen by 10%?

Solution:

Recalculate Equation 10 with ΔSpread of 10 bps for the A rated bond and 35 bps for the B rated bond.

A rated excess return is 0.34% = 1% − (5 × 0.1%) − (0.27% × 60%).

Credit Strategies

> B rated excess return is −0.89% = 3.5% − (7 × 0.01%) − (3.19% × 60%).
>
> The B rated bond is more attractive under this scenario.

In practice, bonds from different issuers usually also have various maturity, embedded call or put provisions, liquidity, and other characteristics, so these additional features should be taken into account during the security selection process. For example, structural differences such as callability or priority within the capital structure must be factored in because they affect valuation. Also, bonds recently issued in larger tranches by frequent issuers will tend to have narrower bid–offer spreads and greater daily transaction volume, allowing investors to buy or sell the bond at a lower cost. This feature is likely to be of greater importance to investors who expect short-term spread narrowing and/or have a relatively short investment time horizon. Note that relative liquidity tends to decline over time, particularly if the same issuer returns to the bond market and offers a price concession for new debt. If, on the other hand, an investor has a longer investment horizon with the flexibility to hold a bond to maturity, he might be able to increase excess return via a greater liquidity premium. Finally, other factors driving potential yield spread differences to be considered include split ratings or negative ratings outlooks, potential merger and acquisition activity, and other positive or negative company events not adequately reflected in the analysis.

When deciding among frequent issuers with several bond issues outstanding, investors might consider using credit spread curves for these issuers across maturities to gauge relative value.

EXAMPLE 17

Using Spread Curves in Relative Value Analysis

A United States–based issuer has the following option-free bonds outstanding:

Outstanding Debt	Term	Coupon	Price	YTM
2-year issue	2	4.25%	106.7	0.864%
5-year issue	5	3.25%	106	1.984%
15-year issue	15	2.75%	91	3.528%

Current on-the-run US Treasury YTMs are as follows:

Tenor	Coupon	Price
2y	0.250%	100
5y	0.875%	100
10y	2.000%	100
20y	2.250%	100

An investor considers the purchase of a new 10-year issue from the company and expects the new bond to include a 10 bp new issue premium. What is the fair value spread for the new issue based on outstanding debt?

1. First, solve for the credit spreads for outstanding bonds as the difference in the YTM from an actual or interpolated government bond:

   5-year spread: 110.9 bps (= 1.984% − 0.875%)

   15-year spread: Solve for 10- and 20-year bond interpolation weights.

   10-year weight: w_{10} = 0.50 (= (20 − 10)/(15 − 10))

> 20-year weight: $w_{20} = 0.50 (= (1 - w_{10}))$
>
> 15-year interpolated bond: $2.125\% = (2.00\% \times 0.5) + (2.25\% \times 0.5)$
>
> 15-year spread: 140.3 bps (= 3.528% − 2.125%)
>
> 2. Derive the implied 10-year new issue spread by interpolating the 5- and 15-year credit spreads using the same interpolation weights as for Treasuries and adding the 10 bp new issue premium.
>
> 10-year spread: 135.6 bps = $0.1\% + (1.109\% \times 0.5 + 1.403\% \times 0.5)$

Many issuers have several bond issues, each of which typically has a different maturity and duration. To reflect the various maturities, a spread curve can be developed for each issuer and can be useful in conducting relative value analysis. A spread curve is the fitted curve of credit spreads for similar bonds of an issuer plotted against the maturity of those bonds.

Exhibit 18 plots the Z-spread versus maturities for select outstanding bonds of two A2/A+ rated health care companies, Eli Lilly (LLY) and Bristol-Myers Squibb (BMS), which have similar probabilities of default.

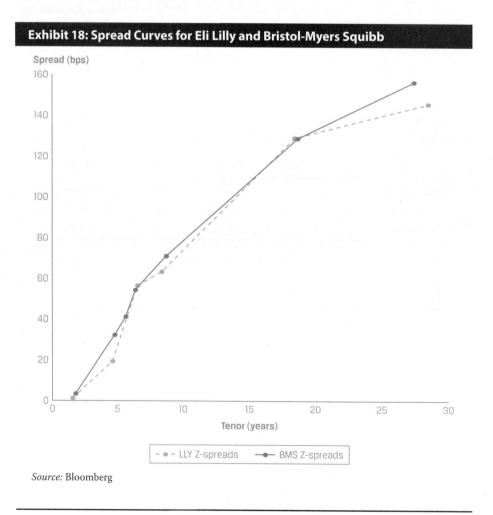

Exhibit 18: Spread Curves for Eli Lilly and Bristol-Myers Squibb

Source: Bloomberg

These spread curves are closely aligned except in roughly five-year and nearly 30-year maturities, where the BMS spreads are approximately 10 bps wider than those of LLY. If the bonds have similar features and liquidity, then a manager might conclude that the market perceives BMS credit risk to be slightly higher than that of LLY. However, if the manager believes that BMS is the stronger credit, several actions are possible depending on portfolio objectives and constraints. For example, if the investment mandate is to outperform a benchmark using long-only positions, the manager might overweight BMS bonds and underweight LLY bonds relative to the benchmark. If the objective is to generate positive absolute returns, underweighting or avoiding LLY bonds is less appropriate because such actions are meaningful only in the context of a benchmark. If permitted, the manager could also consider a long–short CDS strategy outlined later.

Once a manager has identified specific issuers and bond maturities to actively over- or underweight versus a benchmark, the next important step is to quantify and track these active investments in the context of the primary indexing risk factors identified in an earlier lesson in the active portfolio construction process. For example, if an investor chooses to overweight specific health care industry issuers versus the respective sector and spread duration contributions of the benchmark index, the difference in portfolio weights between the active and index positions establishes a basis upon which excess return can be measured going forward.

Top-Down Credit Strategies

A top-down approach to credit strategy focuses on a broader set of factors affecting the bond universe in contrast to the more detailed and issuer-specific bottom-up approach. Macro factors critical to credit investors include economic growth, real rates and inflation, changes in expected market volatility and risk appetite, recent credit spread changes, industry trends, geopolitical risk, and currency movements. Assessment of these factors guides investors in selecting credit market sectors with attractive relative value characteristics, with an increased bond allocation to more attractive sectors and an underweight (or possibly short bond positions in) less favorable sectors. Top-down investors frequently use broader sector distinctions than under a bottom-up approach. For example, a top-down investor expecting credit spreads to narrow might favor the relative value opportunity of high-yield bonds over investment-grade bonds.

GDP growth is critical to the credit cycle, as seen in Exhibit 19, which shows global speculative-grade default rates versus the real GDP growth rate among G7 countries from 1962 to 2019. Sharp declines in GDP growth are often associated with rising default rates.

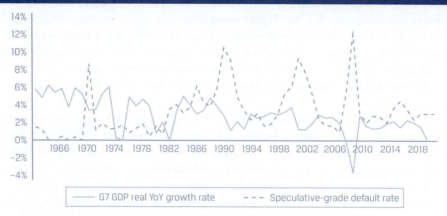

Exhibit 19: Global Speculative-Grade Default Rate and Real GDP Growth Rate for G7 countries, 1962–2019

Sources: Moody's Investors Service, OECD (IHS Markit)

A portfolio manager or analyst might decide to factor this relationship into the investment decision-making process; for example, an above-consensus real GDP growth forecast might lead to an increased high-yield allocation if future defaults are expected to remain below market expectations.

Assessing Credit Quality in a Top-Down Approach

Active top-down and bottom-up credit managers frequently use public ratings to categorize and rank the credit quality of bonds within a portfolio. As investors compare investments across credit ratings, the fact that default risk rises more rapidly as ratings decline is important to consider. The use of weighted factors, such as those established by Moody's based on the likelihood of credit loss over a specific period versus ordinal factors across the credit spectrum, enables managers to capture this effect more accurately, as demonstrated in Exhibit 20.

Exhibit 20: Weighted Versus Ordinal Credit Rating Categories

Moody's	S&P	Fitch	Ordinal	Weighted
Aaa	AAA	AAA	1	1
Aa1	AA+	AA+	2	10
Aa2	AA	AA	3	20
Aa3	AA-	AA-	4	40
A1	A+	A+	5	70
A2	A	A	6	120
A3	A-	A-	7	180
Baa1	BBB+	BBB+	8	260
Baa2	BBB	BBB	9	360
Baa3	BBB-	BBB-	10	610
Ba1	BB+	BB+	11	940
Ba2	BB	BB	12	1,350
Ba3	BB-	BB-	13	1,766
B1	B+	B+	14	2,220

Moody's	S&P	Fitch	Ordinal	Weighted
B2	B	B	15	2,720
B3	B-	B-	16	3,490
Caa1	CCC+	CCC+	17	4,770
Caa2	CCC	CCC	18	6,500
Caa3	CCC-	CCC-	19	10,000
Ca	CC	CC	20	

Source: Moody's Investors Service

The impact of weighted ratings is best demonstrated using an example. For instance, assume a manager is assessing credit quality for a portfolio in which half of the bonds are rated A1/A+ and the other half are rated Ba3/BB-. Using an ordinal scale, the average portfolio credit quality score is 9 (= 50% × 5 + 50% × 13), which corresponds to an average rating of Baa2/BBB in Exhibit 20. However, using the weighted scale at the far right, the portfolio's average credit quality score is 918 (= 50% × 70 + 50% × 1,766), or closer to Ba1/BB+, two levels (notches) below the average rating derived using an ordinal scale.

Earlier readings underscored the risks of relying on public credit ratings, in particular that ratings tend to lag the market's pricing of credit risk critical to an active investor. In addition, one should note that S&P's and Moody's ratings capture different types of risks, with S&P ratings focused on the POD, while Moody's focuses on expected losses, which could influence historical comparisons. The credit rating time horizon is also critical because ratings agencies issue both short-term and long-term ratings for specific issuers, which might warrant additional attention. For these reasons, active managers often prefer to use credit spread measures such as OAS to measure average portfolio credit quality. To calculate a portfolio's average OAS, each bond's individual OAS is weighted by its market value. A manager might also group bonds by OAS categories, which are sometimes mapped to public ratings for comparative purposes.

The use of spread-based rather than rating-based measures also facilitates the measurement of changes in portfolio value due to spread changes. As shown earlier, Equation 5 provides a framework to quantify portfolio value changes due to yield spread movements:

$$\%\Delta PV^{Spread} \approx -(EffSpreadDur \times \Delta Spread) + (½ \times EffSpreadCon \times (\Delta Spread)^2)$$

Smaller yield spread changes are often estimated using the first term in Equation 5. This analytical duration approach provides a reasonable approximation of the price–yield spread relationship for investment-grade bonds with low credit spreads. However, for bonds with greater default risk further down the credit spectrum, changes to both the EffSpreadDur and the ΔSpread terms might be required to accurately reflect empirical observations of how credit risk changes affect overall portfolio value.

In isolating portfolio value changes due to yield spread changes using EffSpreadDur, Equation 5 implicitly assumes that government bond YTMs and credit spreads are uncorrelated, independent variables. However, empirical duration estimates using statistical models often diverge from analytical duration calculations over time and in different interest rate environments. For instance, under a "flight to quality" scenario, the macroeconomic factors driving government bond YTMs *lower* will cause high-yield bond credit spreads to *rise* as the result of an expectation of a greater likelihood and higher severity of financial distress, as shown in Exhibit 21 during the COVID-19 pandemic in early 2020.

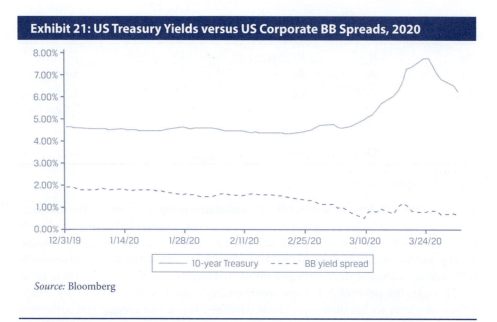

Exhibit 21: US Treasury Yields versus US Corporate BB Spreads, 2020

Source: Bloomberg

As for ΔSpread, recall the empirical observation that bonds trading at wider spreads usually experience larger spread changes, which are proportional to the DTS measure in Equation 8.

These greater changes in bond spread have an impact similar to that of the weighted Moody's credit rating categories in Exhibit 18.

EXAMPLE 18

Top-Down Excess Returns

1. An investor has formed expectations across four bond rating categories and intends to overweight the category with the highest expected excess return over the next 12 months. Evaluate which rating group is the most attractive based on the information in the following table and assuming no change in spread duration:

Rating Category	Current OAS	Expected ΔOAS	Expected Loss (POD × LGD)	EffSpreadDur
A	1.05%	−0.25%	0.06%	5.5
Baa	1.35%	−0.35%	0.30%	6.0
Ba	2.45%	−0.50%	0.60%	4.5
B	3.50%	−0.75%	3.00%	4.0

Solution:

The following table summarizes expected excess returns E [ExcessSpread] ≈ $Spread_0$ − (EffSpreadDur × ΔSpread) − (POD × LGD) for each of the four rating categories. For example, expected excess return for rating category A is 2.37% (=1.05% − (5.5 × −0.25%) − 0.06%).

Credit Strategies

Rating Category	Current OAS	Expected ΔOAS	Expected Loss (POD × LGD)	EffSpreadDur	E(Excess Return)
A	1.05%	−0.25%	0.06%	5.5	2.37%
Baa	1.35%	−0.35%	0.30%	6.0	3.15%
Ba	2.45%	−0.50%	0.60%	4.5	4.10%
B	3.50%	−0.75%	3.00%	4.0	3.50%

Given that the Ba category has the highest expected excess return, it is the most attractive rating category to overweight in the portfolio.

Sector Allocation in a Top-Down Approach

Industry sector allocations (or weightings) are an important part of a top-down approach to credit strategy. To determine which sector(s) to over- or underweight, an active portfolio manager usually begins with an interest rate and overall market view established using macroeconomic variables introduced earlier. This view is a key step in determining whether specific sectors of the economy are likely to over- or underperform over the manager's investment time horizon.

Quantitative methods such as regression analysis are often used in making industry allocation decisions. For example, the average spread of bonds within an individual industry sector and rating category might be compared with the average spread of the bonds with the same rating but excluding the chosen industry sector. Alternatively, a portfolio manager might also use financial ratios in comparing sector spreads and sector leverage. Generally speaking, higher leverage should imply higher credit risk and thus wider spreads. A portfolio manager could therefore compare sectors on a spread-versus-leverage basis to identify relative value opportunities.

Sector- and rating-specific spread curves are a useful tool in guiding decision making for top-down sector allocations. A comparison of curves combined with an investor's view could lead to credit portfolio positioning based on a view that a specific credit spread curve will flatten or steepen, or that two spread curves will converge or diverge. For example, Exhibit 22 shows the divergence in industrial versus health care spreads for BBB rated US issuers over the first half of 2020 during the COVID-19 pandemic. The flatter industrial credit spread curve reflects that sector's relatively weak credit outlook versus health care over the period.

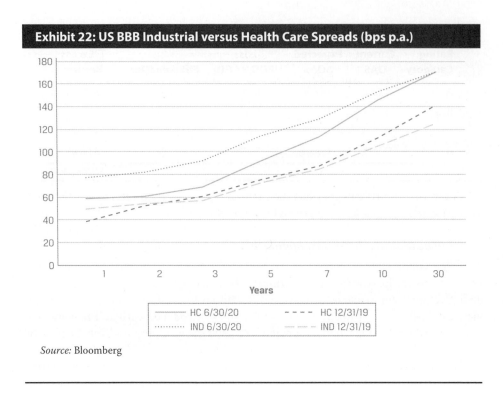

Exhibit 22: US BBB Industrial versus Health Care Spreads (bps p.a.)

Source: Bloomberg

Factor-Based Credit Strategies

While the top-down approach to fixed-income portfolio construction outlined in the previous section grouped investment choices by sector and public ratings, active credit investors are increasingly turning to strategies based on style factors.

Key Factors Affecting Credit Spreads

Factor investing has long been applied in equity markets as noted in earlier lessons, but the application of systematic risk factors such as size, value, and momentum in fixed-income markets is relatively new. For example, Israel, Palhares, and Richardson (2018) established a framework for evaluating excess corporate bond returns based on a number of characteristics, evaluating their significance in explaining fixed-income returns. The authors found strong evidence of positive risk-adjusted returns to measures of carry, defensive, momentum, and value. Exhibit 23 lists these four factors, their rationale, and the measures used in their analysis.

Exhibit 23: Selected Fixed-Income Factors

Factor	Rationale	Measures Used
Carry	Expected return measure if POD or aggregate risk premium is unchanged	OAS
Defensive	Empirical research suggests safer low-risk assets deliver higher risk-adjusted returns	Market-based leverage, gross profitability, and low duration

Credit Strategies

Factor	Rationale	Measures Used
Momentum	Bonds with higher recent returns outperform those with lower recent returns	Trailing six-month excess bond and equity returns
Value	Low market value versus fundamental value indicates greater than expected return	Bond spread less default probability measure, which includes rating, duration, and excess return volatility

The returns represented diversification with respect to common market risk sources such as equity or credit risk premia and are similar in characteristic to those factors shown to be significant in equity markets, with some adjustments. Investigation of the source of returns suggested neither traditional risk exposures nor mispricing provided a comprehensive explanation for the excess returns.

Environmental, Social, and Governance Factors

The growing relevance of environmental, social, and governance (ESG) factors in active portfolio management is evidenced by growing adoption of the Principles for Responsible Investment. This independent body established in partnership with the United Nations to promote ESG factors in investing has more than 3,000 signatories worldwide with more than $100 trillion in assets under management.

Active credit investors usually incorporate ESG factors into portfolio strategies in one of three basic ways:

- The use of screens to either exclude specific industries with less favorable ESG characteristics, such as firearms, tobacco, or coal, or to rule out specific companies or sovereign issuers with ESG-specific ratings below a threshold
- Use of ESG ratings to target issuers within a given sector or rating category with relatively favorable ESG characteristics while matching a specific index risk and return
- Targeting fixed-income investments that directly fund ESG-specific initiatives

ESG-specific ratings for private and public issuers are a key element in the portfolio selection process. The wide range of quantitative and qualitative criteria used to measure ESG attributes and differences in methodology and weighting leads to greater dispersion in ESG versus credit ratings. That said, ESG and credit ratings tend to be positively correlated for two reasons. First, issuers with more financial resources are better able to meet more stringent ESG standards, while those with a greater likelihood of financial distress often face governance or other adverse risks. Second, major rating agencies now explicitly incorporate ESG risks into the traditional credit rating process. In 2019, Moody's cited ESG risks as a material factor in one-third of its credit rating actions among private sector issuers.

Green bonds are fixed-income instruments that directly fund ESG-related initiatives such as those related to environmental or climate benefits. This rapidly growing segment of the fixed-income market includes corporate, financial institution, and public issuers where bond proceeds are directed to projects that reduce air pollution, recycle post-consumer waste products, underwrite environmental remediation projects, and invest in alternative construction materials for environmentally sustainable buildings. Issuers frequently agree to voluntary guidelines such as the International Capital Market Association's Green Bond Principles (2018) to ensure that these securities meet investor ESG requirements. Although green bonds usually rank pari passu (or at the same level) with the issuer's outstanding senior unsecured bonds and therefore reflect similar pricing, the favorable ESG characteristics often result in greater investor demand than for standard debt issues. For example, in October 2020, the European Union issued €17 billion in new 10-year and 20-year debt in its first-ever offering of social bonds to finance its COVID-19 pandemic-related job support program. At nearly 14 times the issuance size, the €233 billion in investor orders for the new bonds represented the largest demand ever for a primary bond issuance.

4. LIQUIDITY AND TAIL RISK

- [ ] discuss liquidity risk in credit markets and how liquidity risk can be managed in a credit portfolio
- [ ] describe how to assess and manage tail risk in credit portfolios

Liquidity Risk

The feasibility and cost of buying and selling fixed-income instruments are important considerations for active investors. Trading volumes and bid–offer costs vary widely across fixed-income markets and regions. For instance, sovereign bonds in large developed markets are highly liquid, usually offering institutional bid–offer spreads in secondary markets for on-the-run securities of less than one basis point during trading hours. Smaller, off-the-run corporate bonds or structured notes, on the other hand, might command bid–offer spreads of 10 bps or more and take days to execute, given that many outstanding bonds do not trade at all on a given trading day.

Consider, for example, the US corporate bond market, wherein a single major issuer might have dozens of outstanding debt tranches of varying tenor, currency, or other feature, each separately traded and identifiable via a specific CUSIP or ISIN (International Securities Identification Number). As mentioned earlier in the curriculum, individual bond issuance and trading has historically taken place in over-the-counter (OTC) markets as opposed to on an exchange. OTC market liquidity rests with individual dealers, their specific portfolio and depth of inventory, and appetite to supply liquidity at a cost. Corporate bonds are traditionally traded on a request-for-quote basis, in which investors reach out to multiple dealers to request a fixed price quote for a specific trade size. The use of electronic trading platforms for bond trading has grown because higher regulatory capital requirements reduced bond inventories among dealers after the 2008–09 global financial crisis. While electronic trading platforms comprised less than one-third of individual corporate bond trading volume as of 2020, trading in bond portfolios and bond ETFs, addressed later in this lesson, has grown in importance.

Transaction cost estimates in bond markets vary significantly from those in equity markets because of market structure differences. Price discovery for infrequently traded individual bonds often begins with **matrix pricing** (or evaluated pricing) techniques introduced earlier in the curriculum using bonds from similar issuers and actively traded government benchmarks to establish a bond's fair value. For bonds quoted actively on a request-for-quote system by individual dealers, the effective spread transaction cost statistic introduced in an earlier lesson and shown in Equation 13 provides an estimate of trading cost.

$$\text{Trade size} \times \begin{cases} \text{Trade price} - (\text{Bid} + \text{Ask})/2 & \text{for buy orders} \\ (\text{Bid} + \text{Ask})/2 - \text{Trade price} & \text{for sell orders} \end{cases} \quad (13)$$

Liquidity and Tail Risk

However, the effective spread is an inadequate gauge of trading costs for positions that are traded in smaller orders over time and/or whose execution affects market spreads. A separate, ex-post liquidity gauge specific to the US corporate bond market is the TRACE (Trade Reporting and Compliance Engine) reporting system introduced in 2002 to track real-time price and volume reporting for bond transactions. Portfolio managers will often review recent TRACE trading activity to gauge the estimated cost of trading a bond position.

Active portfolio managers take several steps in managing the liquidity risk of bond portfolios, given the significant market risk involved in trading less liquid positions. First, active managers will usually favor on-the-run government bonds or most recently issued corporate or other bonds for short-term tactical portfolio positioning, while reserving relatively illiquid positions for buy-and-hold strategies or strategic positioning to minimize expected return erosion due to trading costs. Second, active managers might consider liquid alternatives to individual bond trades to close portfolio gaps where active management adds little value, or to react quickly to rapidly changing markets. These alternatives include CDS outlined later and bond ETFs.

Fixed-income ETFs are liquid, exchange-traded bond portfolios that create and redeem shares using an OTC primary market that exists between a set of institutional investors (or **authorized participants**) and the ETF sponsor. These ETF shares trade in the secondary market on an exchange, overcoming the liquidity constraints of individual OTC-traded bonds. Bond ETFs have enjoyed significant growth and are available across the credit spectrum as well as for different maturities and in different markets. Although the underlying cash flow exposures are similar, ETFs usually neither mature nor experience duration drift (with the exception of target maturity ETFs) as do individual bonds. As ETF sponsors target a specific index or profile, ETFs offer relatively constant portfolio duration and pay variable monthly interest based on the overall portfolio. Active credit managers use ETFs to quickly and efficiently overweight or underweight exposures in rapidly changing markets and to take on strategic exposure in segments of the market where individual or bottom-up bond selection is less of a focus.

When relatively illiquid bond positions are purchased or sold over longer periods, portfolio managers might consider hedging strategies such as asset swaps to mitigate the benchmark risk of a portfolio position as outlined in the following example.

EXAMPLE 19

Using Asset Swaps to Manage Liquidity Risk

1. Recall the earlier example of a United States–based issuer with the following option-free bonds outstanding:

Outstanding Debt	Term	Coupon	Price	YTM
2-year issue	2	4.25%	106.7	0.864%
5-year issue	5	3.25%	106.0	1.984%
15-year issue	15	2.75%	91.0	3.528%

Assume the investor instead holds a US$50 million face value position in the outstanding 15-year bond. Historical TRACE data suggest an average $5 million daily trading volume in the 15-year bond. Which of the following statements *best* describes how the issuer might use an asset swap to manage the benchmark interest rate risk associated with liquidating this bond position?

A. The investor should enter into an asset swap where he receives fixed and pays floating, unwinding the swap position once the bond position is sold.

B. The investor should enter into an asset swap where he pays fixed and receives floating, unwinding the swap position once the bond position is sold.

C. The investor should enter into an asset swap where he pays fixed and receives floating, unwinding the swap position over time in proportion to the amount of the bond sold.

Solution:

The correct answer is C. Because the investor's bond position represents a long position (i.e., long both spread duration and benchmark duration), the best hedge would be a short-duration (or pay-fixed swap) position rather than A. As for B, the hedge unwind occurs once the bond position is sold rather than over time, which exposes the investor to benchmark interest rate risk for the portion of the bond sold. The proportional swap unwind in C ensures that the offsetting swap position matches the benchmark interest rate risk of the bond.

Tail Risk

Extreme adverse outcomes that exceed those to be expected from a normally distributed portfolio are often referred to as tail events. In the context of active fixed-income management, the measurement and management of tail risk involves stress testing a portfolio's value based on the key fixed-income returns factors in Equation 1. In an earlier lesson on measuring and managing market risk, **value at risk (VaR)** was introduced as a measure of the minimum portfolio loss expected to occur over a given time period at a specific confidence level. For example, a 5% daily VaR of €8.7 million implies that a portfolio manager should expect a daily portfolio loss of *at least* €8.7 million on 5% of all trading days. Assuming normally distributed portfolio returns, the 5% confidence level translates to an outcome at least 1.65 standard deviations below the mean, while a 1% confidence interval lies at least 2.33 standard deviations below the mean. Risk managers often use expected returns, volatilities, and correlations to estimate parametric VaR in addition to either historical simulation or Monte Carlo methods. The following example shows a simple parametric VaR calculation for a bond position.

EXAMPLE 20

Fixed-Rate Bond VaR

1. Consider the earlier case of an investor holding $50 million face value of a 15-year bond with a semiannual coupon of 2.75%, a current YTM of 3.528%, and a price of 91 per 100 of face value. What is the VaR for the full bond price at a 99% confidence interval for one month if annualized daily yield

Liquidity and Tail Risk

volatility is 1.75% (1.75 bps) and we assume that interest rates are normally distributed?

Solution:

First, we must adjust the annualized yield volatility to reflect a one-month period instead. The time interval under consideration is $1/12^{th}$ of a year, and therefore the volatility measure is 0.00505 (1.75% × $\sqrt{1/12}$), which for a 99% confidence interval equals 117.7 bps = (0.00505 × 2.33 standard deviations). We may quantify the bond's market value change using either a duration approximation or the actual price change as follows. We may use the Excel MDURATION to solve for the bond's duration as 12.025. We can therefore approximate the change in bond value using the familiar (-ModDur × ΔYield) expression as $6,439,808 = ($50 million × 0.91 × (-12.025 × .0177)). We can also use the Excel PRICE function to directly calculate the new price of 88.75 and multiply the price change of -2.25 by the face value to get $1,125,000.

The simplicity and transparency of VaR can be misleading if it is used as a tool for quantifying tail risk for several reasons. First, VaR tends to underestimate the frequency and severity of extreme adverse events. It also fails to capture the downside correlation and liquidity risks associated with market stress scenarios. Finally, although VaR addresses *minimum* loss for a specific confidence level, it fails to quantify the *average* or expected loss under an extreme adverse market scenario. **Conditional value at risk** (CVaR), or expected loss, measures the average loss over a specific time period conditional on that loss exceeding the VaR threshold. While computationally more complex and beyond the scope of this lesson, CVaR is often measured using historical simulation or Monte Carlo techniques. Two related measures of portfolio VaR include incremental and relative measures. For example, an analyst seeking to measure the impact of adding or removing a portfolio position might use an **incremental VaR (or partial VaR)** calculation for this purpose. As mentioned in an earlier lesson, an investor could use **relative VaR** to measure the expected tracking error versus a benchmark portfolio by calculating VaR (or CVaR) based on a portfolio containing the active positions *minus* the benchmark holdings under a market stress scenario.

EXAMPLE 21

VaR Measures

1. An active fixed-income manager is considering increasing an overweight portfolio allocation to BBB rated health care issuers versus a targeted index. Which of the following VaR measures is the most appropriate to evaluate the impact of this decision on overall portfolio VaR?

   A. Incremental VaR
   B. Relative VaR
   C. CVaR

Solution:

The correct answer is A. Incremental VaR measures the impact of a specific portfolio position change on VaR, while relative VaR in answer B evaluates all active portfolio positions versus the benchmark index and could be important for an active fixed-income mandate that aims to beat an index once the portfolio change has been made. CVaR in C measures a portfolio's average loss over a specific time period conditional on that loss exceeding the VaR threshold.

Tail risk assessment is typically conducted using one of the three methods summarized in Exhibit 24.

Exhibit 24: Methods to Assess Portfolio Tail Risk

Method	Description	Advantages	Disadvantages
Parametric Method	Uses expected value and standard deviation of risk factors assuming normal distribution	Simple and transparent calculation	Not well suited for non-normally distributed returns or option-based portfolios
Historical Simulation	Prices existing portfolio using historical parameters and ranking results	Actual results, accommodates options, with no probability distribution assumed	Highly dependent on historical period and repetition of historical market trends
Monte Carlo Analysis	Involves generating random outcomes using portfolio measures and sensitivities	Randomly generated results from a probability distribution, accommodates options	Highly dependent on model assumptions and less transparent

Hypothetical scenario analyses are often used to supplement these three methods of analysis to test portfolio vulnerabilities to specific portfolio parameter changes over time.

In addition to portfolio measures of duration and convexity as a basis for portfolio value changes, analytical models often rely on implied volatility parameters for benchmark interest rates and currencies, such as swaption volatility or currency option volatility, respectively, while reduced form or structural credit models incorporating CDS or equity volatility can be used to model expected spread volatility. Finally, term structure models introduced in an earlier lesson that incorporate interest rate volatility and drift in an equilibrium or arbitrage-free framework are frequently incorporated to simulate term structure changes over time.

Once tail risk under an extreme market scenario has been quantified, it is important to weigh this exposure against other binding portfolio constraints and to take steps to manage the downside risk. For example, a leveraged portfolio might face forced liquidation of certain bond positions beyond a certain tail risk threshold. Alternatively, a defined-benefit pension fund manager might be required to increase plan contributions if extreme market moves cause plan funding status to fall below a statutory minimum. Finally, a bank treasury officer could face increased regulatory capital requirements if adverse market changes under a stress test show significant portfolio losses.

A fixed-income portfolio manager can reduce tail risk by establishing position limits, risk budgeting, or using similar techniques designed to reduce portfolio concentration or to cap portfolio risk exposure to certain issuers, credit ratings, or regions. Alternatively, a portfolio manager might consider the use of derivatives to protect against downside portfolio risk. For example, the manager could consider purchasing a swaption (or the right to enter an interest rate swap at a pre-agreed rate in the future) or a credit default swaption (the right to purchase credit protection on an issuer or index at a strike rate in the future) to protect against the risk of benchmark YTM changes or credit spread changes, respectively. However, each of these strategies requires an upfront premium that will reduce excess portfolio spread over

Synthetic Credit Strategies

time. In addition, establishing these hedges in a distressed market will greatly increase hedging cost because of higher option volatility, so the manager must weigh these hedging costs against a risk mitigation strategy to determine the best course of action.

5. SYNTHETIC CREDIT STRATEGIES

☐ discuss the use of credit default swap strategies in active fixed-income portfolio management

As outlined in an earlier lesson, a CDS is the basic building block for strategies to manage credit risk separately from interest rate risk. CDS are often more liquid than an issuer's underlying bonds, enabling investors to take long or short positions, access maturities, and establish other exposures unavailable in cash markets with a smaller cash outlay than direct bond purchases.

Exhibit 25 shows CDS contract mechanics under which a protection "buyer" purchases credit protection from a protection "seller." Each contract references a specific issuer (or issuers) as well as credit event terms that, when triggered, lead to a settlement payment equal to the LGD multiplied by the contract notional amount from the seller to the buyer.

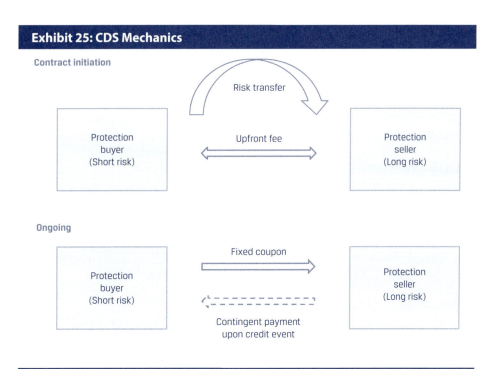

Exhibit 25: CDS Mechanics

CDS contracts are usually quoted on an issuer's CDS spread, which corresponds to a price equal to the present value difference between the CDS spread and a fixed coupon rate on the notional amount over the contract life. Fixed CDS coupon rates of 1% for investment-grade issuers and 5% for high-yield issuers were established when the International Swaps and Derivatives Association standardized CDS market conventions following the 2008 financial crisis. CDS pricing models discount future payments by the swap zero curve multiplied by the **hazard rate**, or the likelihood that an issuer credit event will occur given that it has not already occurred in a prior period.

The CDS price at contract inception or on a coupon payment date as a percentage of notional can be approximated using Equation 14:

$$\text{CDS Price} \approx 1 + ((\text{Fixed Coupon} - \text{CDS Spread}) \times \text{EffSpreadDur}_{CDS}) \quad (14)$$

where CDS Spread is the issuer's current CDS market spread and $\text{EffSpreadDur}_{CDS}$ is the CDS contract's effective spread duration (sometimes referred to as CDS DV01). At contract inception, the protection buyer must either make a payment to or receive a payment from the protection seller equal to the CDS contract price difference from par, as shown in Exhibit 26.

Exhibit 26: Upfront Payment at CDS Contract Inception

Description	Upfront Premium
CDS Spread = Fixed Coupon	None
CDS Spread < Fixed Coupon	Protection buyer *receives* ((Fixed Coupon - CDS Spread) × EffSpreadDur$_{CDS}$)
CDS Spread > Fixed Coupon	Protection buyer *pays* ((CDS Spread - Fixed Coupon) × EffSpreadDur$_{CDS}$)

CDS contracts have similarities to both bonds and interest rate swaps. As with a cash bond priced at a discount when its coupon is below current market rates, the protection seller is entitled to an upfront payment in exchange for accepting a fixed coupon below the CDS market spread. As with a standard interest rate swap, a CDS contract priced at par has a zero net present value, and the notional is not exchanged but rather serves as a basis for spread and settlement calculations.

EXAMPLE 22

CDS Price and Price Changes

An investor seeks to purchase credit protection under a five-year CDS contract at a CDS market spread of 0.50% p.a. for an investment-grade issuer with an estimated effective spread duration (EffSpreadDur$_{CDS}$) of 4.75.

1. Determine whether the investor must pay or receive an upfront amount upon CDS contract inception and calculate the difference from par.

Solution:

Because investment-grade CDS contracts have a fixed coupon of 1.00% p.a. versus the 0.50% p.a. CDS market spread, the investor buying protection should receive the difference from par upfront in exchange for paying an "above market" coupon under the contract. Calculate the estimated difference using Equation 14 ((Fixed Coupon − CDS Spread) × EffSpreadDur$_{CDS}$)) with CDS Spread of 0.50%, Fixed Coupon of 1.00%, and EffSpreadDur$_{CDS}$ equal to 4.75.

Upfront premium: 2.375% of CDS notional (= (1.00% − 0.50%) × 4.75).

Synthetic Credit Strategies

2. Calculate the change in contract price if the CDS spread rises to 0.60% p.a. and interpret the impact of the change on the protection buyer.

Solution:

Calculate the upfront premium using Equation 14 and a 0.60% spread.

Upfront premium: 1.90% of CDS notional (= (1.00% − 0.60%) × 4.75).

The protection buyer realizes a mark-to-market gain equal to 0.475% (2.375% − 1.90%) of the CDS contract notional because of the wider CDS spread.

CDS price changes for a given CDS spread change can be quantified using the contract's effective spread duration:

$$\Delta(\text{CDS Price}) \approx -(\Delta(\text{CDS Spread}) \times \text{EffSpreadDur}_{\text{CDS}}) \tag{15}$$

Active fixed-income portfolio managers buy or sell CDS protection across issuers, maturities, and/or sectors to alter portfolio exposure, as illustrated in the following example.

EXAMPLE 23

Credit Underweight Using CDS

1. A European-based fixed-income manager intends to underweight exposure to a BBB rated French media and telecommunications issuer. She observes that the issuer's current on-the-run five-year CDS contract is trading at a spread of 110 bps p.a. with an EffSpreadDur$_{\text{CDS}}$ of 4.595. Which position should she take in the CDS market? Calculate the result if spreads widen to 125 bps for a €10 million notional position.

Solution:

The manager can underweight the issuer's credit by *purchasing* protection in the CDS market. This short risk position will realize a gain if the issuer's spreads widen. For example, if the issuer's credit spreads widen from 110 bps p.a. to 125 bps p.a., we can estimate the change in CDS contract value by multiplying (−Δ(CDS Spread) × EffSpreadDur$_{\text{CDS}}$) from Equation 15 by the CDS notional to get €68,925 (=−€10,000,000 × (−0.15% × 4.595)).

While CDS contracts are available across maturities, the five-year tenor is generally the most frequently traded contract. Exhibit 27 summarizes the most common CDS strategies used in practice.

Exhibit 27: Credit Derivative–Based Alternatives to Corporate Bonds

Instrument	Description	Targeted Return	Portfolio Impact
Single-Name CDS	Protection buyer pays premium to seller in exchange for payment if credit event occurs	Buyer gains and seller loses if single-name credit spread widens or credit event occurs	Short (buyer) or long (seller) single-name credit spread exposure
Index-Based CDS	Protection buyer pays premium in exchange for partial payment if credit event occurs for index member	Buyer gains and seller loses if index member spreads widen or if credit event occurs	Short (buyer) or long (seller) index-based credit spread exposure
Payer Option on CDS Index	Option buyer pays premium for right to buy protection ("pay" coupons) on CDS index contract at a future date	Max (Credit spread at expiration – CDS Credit Spread Strike, 0) – Option Premium	Short CDS index-based credit spread exposure
Receiver Option on CDS Index	Option buyer pays premium for right to sell protection ("receive" coupons) on CDS index contract at a future date	Max (CDS Credit Spread Strike – CDS Credit Spread at expiration, 0) – Option Premium	Long CDS index-based credit spread exposure

Single-name reference entities include both private corporations and sovereign borrowers. Several CDS indexes are available across regions and often also offer subindexes covering a particular sector or borrower type. For example, the Markit CDX North American Investment Grade index consists of 125 equally weighted CDS contracts on entities, including six subindexes (High Volatility, Consumer Cyclical, Energy, Financials, Industrial, and Telecom, Media, and Technology).

CDS strategies are commonly used by active fixed-income portfolio managers to over- or underweight credit spread exposure to individual issuers, specific sectors, or borrower types. As with benchmark yield curves, CDS portfolio positioning strategies are usually based on expected changes in the credit curve level, slope, or shape. The credit curve referred to here is the **CDS curve**, or the plot of CDS spreads across maturities for a single reference entity or index, rather than the fitted credit spread curves addressed earlier. This might involve an investor taking a long or short CDS position in one issuer or issuer type, or a long or short position overweighting one reference entity or group of entities and underweighting another. Investors using CDS strategies to hedge bond portfolios must always consider the potential impact of basis changes on the strategy over the investment horizon.

Fixed-income ETFs offer derivatives such as futures and options that are different from CDS contracts. As with bond futures, ETF futures are a contract to take future delivery of an ETF and trade on a price rather than a spread basis. Because underlying ETF prices are derived from all-in bond yields held by the fund, ETF derivative prices change with changes in both benchmark rates and credit spreads.

CDS long–short strategies based on spread level are appropriate for both bottom-up and top-down approaches. Assume, for example, that an investor believes that issuer A's credit spreads will likely narrow versus those of issuer B. To capitalize on this view in the cash market, the investor would first source A's individual bonds for purchase and then seek a duration-matched amount of issuer B's bonds to borrow and sell

Synthetic Credit Strategies

short. The existence of a liquid single-name CDS market for both issuers allows the investor to simply sell protection on A and purchase protection on B for the same notional and tenor.

EXAMPLE 24

CDS Long–Short Strategies

1. Consider the investor from the prior example who sought to underweight a French media and telecommunications issuer. Assume instead that the investor seeks to maintain a constant media and telecommunications credit allocation by overweighting a BBB rated German media and telecommunications competitor. CDS contract details are as follows:

Issuer	Tenor	CDS Spread	EffSpreadDur$_{CDS}$
French Media & Telecoms Issuer	5 years	110 bps	4.697
German Media & Telecoms Issuer	5 years	130 bps	4.669

Describe an appropriate long–short CDS strategy to meet this goal, and calculate the investor's return if the French issuer's spreads widen by 10 bps and those of the German issuer narrow by 25 bps based on €10 million notional contracts.

Solution:

The manager purchases protection on the French issuer and simultaneously sells protection on the German issuer. Use $(-\Delta(\text{CDS Spread}) \times \text{EffSpreadDur}_{CDS})$ from Equation 15 multiplied by the CDS notional to solve for changes in the short and long risk positions:

Short risk (French issuer): €46,970 (= −€10,000,000 × (−0.10% × 4.697))

Long risk (German issuer): €116,725 (= €10,000,000 × (−(−0.25%) × 4.669))

The total gain on the long–short strategy is €163,695 (= €46,970 + €116,725).

A similar long–short strategy can be applied under a top-down approach. For example, an investor might overweight (underweight) a specific sector given an expectation of narrower (wider) spread levels versus the total portfolio by selling (buying) protection on a CDS subindex contract. Alternatively, assume an active manager expects a weaker economy and a widening of high-yield versus investment-grade credit spread levels. The manager can capitalize on this view by buying five-year protection on a high-yield CDS index and selling protection on an investment-grade CDS index for the same tenor. Standardized CDS contracts eliminate the impact of duration difference, liquidity, and other factors that arise under a similar strategy in the cash bond market.

CDS long–short strategies based on expected credit curve slope changes involve CDS curve trades. For example, an upward-sloping credit curve implies relatively low near-term expected default probability that rises over time. An investor might expect an issuer's CDS curve to steepen if its near-term default probability declines as a result of higher than expected profits and stable leverage. This investor can capitalize on this view by selling short-term protection using a single-name CDS contract and buying long-term protection on that same reference entity. As shown in the following example, capitalizing on spread changes for different maturities requires duration matching of the positions, as in the case of benchmark yield curve strategies.

> **EXAMPLE 25**
>
> ### Duration-Weighted Single-Name CDS Curve Steepener
>
> 1. Returning to our earlier example of the German media and telecommunications issuer, the investor decides instead to position her portfolio for a steepening of the issuer's credit curve using the CDS market. Details of on-the-run 5- and 10-year CDS contracts outstanding are as follows.
>
> | Issuer | Tenor | CDS Spread | EffSpreadDur$_{CDS}$ |
> |---|---|---|---|
> | German Media & Telecoms Issuer | 5 years | 130 bps | 4.669 |
> | German Media & Telecoms Issuer | 10 years | 175 bps | 8.680 |
>
> Describe an appropriate long–short CDS strategy to meet this goal assuming a €10,000,000 10-year CDS contract notional. Calculate the investor's return if the 5-year spreads rise 10 bps and the 10-year spreads rise 20 bps.
>
> ### Solution:
>
> A steeper credit curve implies that $((CDS\ Spread)_{10yr} - (CDS\ Spread)_{5yr})$ will increase. The appropriate long–short strategy to position for this change is to purchase protection based on the 10-year, €10,000,000 notional and to sell protection on an equivalent duration 5-year CDS contract.
>
> 1. Calculate the 5-year CDS contract notional that matches the basis point value (BPV) of a 10-year, €10,000,000 CDS (BPV_{10yr} = EffSpreadDur$_{10yrCDS}$ × notional) using the effective spread duration ratio of 1.859 (EffSpreadDur$_{10yrCDS}$/EffSpreadDur$_{5yrCDS}$ = 8.68/4.669) multiplied by €10,000,000 to get €18,590,000.
>
>   Confirm this equivalence by comparing BPV_{5yr} and BPV_{10yr}:
>
> BPV_{5yr}: €8,680 = €18,590,000 × 4.669/10,000
>
> BPV_{10yr}: €8,680 = €10,000,000 × 8.68/10,000
>
> 2. Calculate portfolio return for a 10 bp increase in 5-year CDS spreads and a 20 bp increase in 10-year CDS spreads using Equation 15 ($-\Delta(CDS\ Spread) \times EffSpreadDur_{CDS}$) multiplied by the CDS notional.
>
>   5 year (long risk): −€86,800 (= €18,590,000 × (−0.1% × 4.669))
>
>   10 year (short risk): €173,600 (= −€10,000,000 × (−0.2% × 8.68))
>
>   Net portfolio gain: €86,800 = €173,600 − €86,800

The same curve strategy just described applies to expected credit curve slope changes for a CDS index or subindex. For instance, an investor who believes the economy is nearing the end of a growth cycle might expect the CDS curve for industrial issuers to flatten amid rising near-term credit spreads. Under this expected scenario, an investor purchases short-term CDS subindex protection on industrials and sells long-term protection on the same subindex to capitalize on a flattening view. Alternatively, an investor taking a top-down approach who shares a similar bearish economic view might consider a flattening trade for an entire CDS index.

Additional CDS strategies seek to either capitalize on the basis difference between CDS and cash bonds or take advantage of specific events that affect CDS spreads and curves. As noted earlier, basis differences arise from a number of factors but are also due to differences in liquidity across derivative and cash markets, a detailed treatment of which is beyond the scope of this lesson. Corporate events that influence CDS spreads by affecting bondholders differently from shareholders include mergers and acquisitions and leveraged buyouts, both of which are addressed elsewhere in the curriculum.

CREDIT SPREAD CURVE STRATEGIES 6

☐ discuss various portfolio positioning strategies that managers can use to implement a specific credit spread view

Earlier in the lesson, we established that the credit cycle is a key driver of credit spread changes across maturities and ratings. The probability of issuer default and severity of loss over the cycle must be considered within the context of an overall market view. For example, positively sloped credit spread curves suggest relatively low near-term default probability, a view consistent with stable or rising future inflation and relatively strong expected economic growth. Investor demand for higher credit spreads for assuming the risk of downgrade or default for longer periods also contributes to a positive slope.

The level and slope of credit curves change over the economic cycle. Early in an expansion, as profits rise and defaults remain high, high-yield spreads remain elevated and well above investment-grade spreads, which often exhibit a flat to inverted spread curve. As an expansion progresses, lower defaults and increased profits cause short-term high-yield and investment-grade spreads to decline and credit spread curves to steepen. Credit curve steepening continues as economic growth peaks amid higher leverage and inflation expectations. As economic growth slows or the economy enters a recession, credit spreads rise, and spread curves flatten, with the high-yield curve inverting in some instances amid falling profitability and rising defaults. Although no two credit cycles are alike, Exhibit 28 presents a stylized view of these credit spread curve level and shape changes for investment-grade (IG) and high-yield (HY) issuers over the economic cycle.

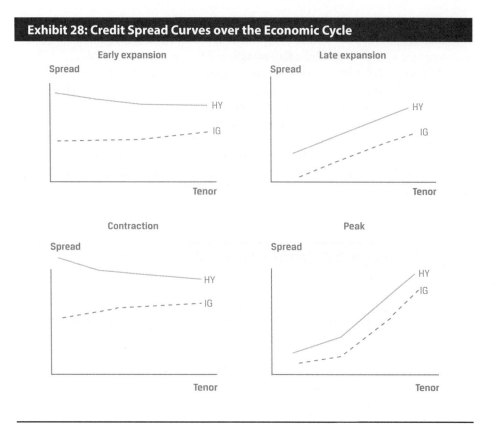

Exhibit 28: Credit Spread Curves over the Economic Cycle

Active credit managers often incorporate the credit cycle into economic growth and inflation forecasts, which are then translated into sector- and issuer-specific views driving specific credit curve level and slope expectations using the bottom-up or top-down approaches outlined earlier. If these forecasts coincide with current credit spread curves, managers will choose active credit strategies consistent with static or stable credit market conditions. However, if an investor's views differ from what today's credit curve implies about future defaults and the severity of credit loss, they will position the portfolio to generate excess return based on this divergent view within investment mandate constraints using the cash and derivative strategies outlined in the following section.

Static Credit Spread Curve Strategies

An active credit manager might believe that current credit spreads are reasonably priced and that credit curves will remain stable or unchanged over an investment horizon while credit defaults and annual loss rates remain low. Exhibit 29 shows that a manager could position a portfolio to generate excess return in this scenario by either lowering the portfolio's average credit rating or adding credit spread duration by investing in longer-dated bonds with a similar rating to the current portfolio.

In the first case, a portfolio tilt toward lower-rated bonds will increase expected spread return, as seen in Equation 10 (E [ExcessSpread] ≈ $Spread_0$ − (EffSpreadDur × ΔSpread) − (POD × LGD)) if Spread, POD, and LGD remain stable. The shift from an average A rated to BBB rated portfolio in Exhibit 29 is an extension of an earlier case (Example 10) that quantified corporate versus government bond rolling yields as the YTM difference assuming constant spreads and default rates.

Credit Spread Curve Strategies

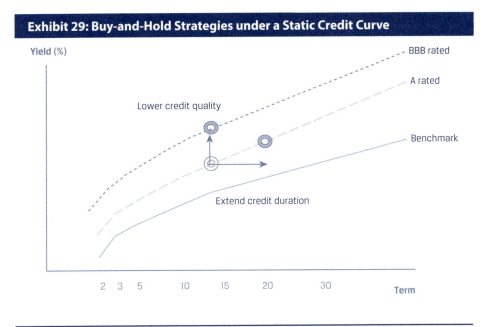

Exhibit 29: Buy-and-Hold Strategies under a Static Credit Curve

The increase in credit spread duration in the second case involves a "buy and hold" or "carry and roll down" approach familiar from the earlier yield curve strategies lesson. The first involves buying risky bonds with durations above the benchmark without active trading during a subsequent period. If the relationship between long- and short-term credit spreads remains stable over the investment horizon, the manager is rewarded with greater return from the higher spread duration. "Rolling down" the credit curve not only generates incremental coupon income (adjusted over time for any price difference from par) due to wider spreads but also adds return from the passage of time and the investor's ability to sell the shorter-maturity position in the future at a lower credit spread at the end of the investment horizon. The following example illustrates this second case, shown in Exhibit 29.

EXAMPLE 26

Adding Credit Duration under a Static Credit Curve

1. A Sydney-based investor notes the following available option-free bonds for an A rated Australian issuer:

Debt Term	Coupon	YTM	Price
5 years	1.00%	1.00%	100
10 years	1.35%	1.25%	100.937
15 years	2.00%	1.95%	100.648

The 5-year, 10-year, and 15-year Australian government bonds have YTMs and coupons of 0.50%, 0.75%, and 1.10%, respectively, and both corporate and government bonds have a semiannual coupon. As an active manager who expects stable benchmark yields and credit spreads over the next six months, the investor decides to overweight (by AUD50,000,000 in face value) the issuer's 15-year versus 10-year bond for that period. Calculate the return to the investor of the roll-down strategy in AUD and estimate the returns attributable to benchmark yield versus credit spread changes.

Solution:

To estimate credit curve rolling yield returns, we must solve for the first two return components from Equation 1 (Coupon income +/– Roll-down return) and separate the impact of benchmark yield versus credit spread changes.

1. Solve for the respective 5-year, 10-year, and 15-year bond credit spreads. Yield spread and G-spread are reasonable approximations because the bonds are option-free, with maturities closely aligned to par government securities.

5-year spread: 0.50% (= 1.00% – 0.50%)

10-year spread: 0.50% (= 1.25% – 0.75%)

15-year spread: 0.85% (= 1.95% – 1.10%)

2. Solve for 6-month expected returns of the 10-year versus 15-year bond:

   a. Incremental coupon income = $162,500 (= (2.00% – 1.35%)/2 × $50 million)

Debt Tenor	Coupon	Yield Spread	Total Coupon Income	Coupon (Benchmark Yield)	Coupon (Credit Spread)
10 years	1.35%	0.50%	$337,500	$187,500	$150,000
15 years	2.00%	0.85%	$500,000	$275,000	$225,000

Divide incremental coupon into benchmark and credit spread components:

Income due to benchmark yields: $87,500 = $275,000 – $187,500

Income due to credit spreads: $75,000 = $225,000 – $150,000

   b. Price appreciation is determined by the bond's price today and in six months' time based on unchanged benchmark rates. In six months, the 10-year and 15-year positions will be 9.5-year and 14.5-year bonds, respectively, at a yield and yield spread point along the curve. Estimate all-in YTMs and yield spreads using interpolation to arrive at the following results:

Debt Tenor	Date	Coupon	All-In Yield	Benchmark Yield	Yield Spread
5 years	Today	1.00%	1.00%	0.50%	0.50%
10 years	Today	1.35%	1.25%	0.75%	0.50%
15 years	Today	2.00%	1.95%	1.10%	0.85%
9.5 years	In six months	1.35%	1.225%	0.725%	0.50%
14.5 years	In six months	2.00%	1.88%	1.065%	0.815%

Calculate price appreciation using the difference between current bond prices and those in six months using the Excel PV function (= –PV(rate, nper, pmt, FV, type)) where "rate" is the interest rate per period (0.01225/2), "nper" is the number of periods (19), "pmt" is the periodic coupon (1.35/2),

Credit Spread Curve Strategies

"FV" is future value (100), and "type" (0) involves payments made at the end of each period.

10-year: Initial price: 100.937

Price in six months: 101.118 (= −PV (0.01225/2, 19, 1.35/2, 100, 0))

Price appreciation: $90,500 (= (101.118 − 100.937)/100.000 × $50 million)

Because the yield spread curve is flat at 0.50%, the full $90,500 price change in the 10-year is benchmark yield curve roll down.

15-year: Initial price: 100.648

Price in six months: 101.517 (= −PV (0.0188/2, 29, 1, 100, 0))

Price appreciation: $434,500 (= (101.517 − 100.648)/100.000 × $50 million)

Because the 0.07% decline in YTM is estimated to be equally attributable to benchmark yield and yield spread changes, each is assumed equal to $217,250.

3. Incremental income due to price appreciation is therefore $344,000 (=$434,500 − $90,500), of which $217,250 is attributable to credit spread changes.

In total, the incremental roll-down strategy generates $506,500 (=$344,000 + 163,500) of which $292,250 (=$217,250 + $75,000) is estimated to be due to credit spread curve roll down.

Derivative-based credit strategies to add credit spread duration or increase credit exposure include selling CDS single-name or index protection for longer maturities or lower credit quality or using a long–short approach to achieve a similar objective.

EXAMPLE 27

Using CDS for a Static Fixed-Income Credit Strategy

1. Returning to our earlier example of the investment-grade German media and telecommunications issuer, the investor decides instead to overweight exposure to this name by taking a long risk position in the single-name 10-year CDS market for one year. Details of today's 5-year and 10-year CDS contracts are as follows.

Issuer	Tenor	CDS Spread	EffSpreadDur$_{CDS}$
German Media & Telecoms Issuer	5 years	130 bps	4.669
German Media & Telecoms Issuer	10 years	175 bps	8.680

Describe the roll-down strategy using CDS and calculate the one-year return in euros on a €10,000,000 position assuming an annual coupon payment and a 9-year EffSpreadDur$_{CDS}$ of 7.91.

> **Solution:**
>
> The investor sells 10-year CDS protection on the German issuer to overweight exposure and terminates the position in one year. As with the bond example, the sold protection strategy generates coupon income if the issuer does not default and price appreciation if credit spreads decline over time.
>
> 1. The fixed coupon received at the end of one year equals the notional multiplied by the standard 1% investment-grade coupon for the period, or €100,000, or €10,000,000 × 1.00% for one year.
> 2. Estimate the CDS price change over one year by interpolating the 9-year issuer spread under a static credit curve assumption.
>
> Solve for the 5-year and 10-year CDS spread weights in the 9-year spread interpolation calculation.
>
> 5-year CDS weight = w_5 = 20% (= (10 − 9)/(10 − 5))
>
> 10-year CDS weight = w_{10} = 80% (or (1 − w_5))
>
> Note that (w_5 × 5) + (w_{10} × 10) = 9
>
> The 9-year spread is a weighted average of 5- and 10-year CDS spreads.
>
> CDS Spread$_{9yr}$ = w_5 × CDS Spread$_{5yr}$ + w_{10} × CDS Spread$_{10yr}$
>
> 1.66% (=1.30% × 0.2 + 1.75% × 0.8)
>
> Estimate the CDS contract price change by multiplying the change in CDS price from Equation 14 (CDS Price ≈ 1 + ((Fixed Coupon − CDS Spread) × EffSpreadDur$_{CDS}$)) by the CDS notional.
>
> 10-year CDS per €1 par: 0.934 = (1 + (−0.75% × 8.68))
>
> 9-year CDS per €1 par: 0.947794 = (1 + (−0.66% × 7.91))
>
> Calculate the price appreciation by multiplying the price change by the contract notional to get €128,940 (= (0.947794 − 0.9349) × €10,000,000). Total return equals the sum of the coupon income and price appreciation, or €228,940 (= €100,000 + €128,940).

Dynamic Credit Spread Curve Strategies

Active credit managers seek to capitalize on divergent market views using cash-based or derivative strategies related to specific issuers, sectors, or the overall credit market over the credit cycle given anticipated credit curve changes across both maturities and rating categories. The following examples demonstrate how an active manager might position a credit portfolio in anticipation of these changes to generate excess return.

> **EXAMPLE 28**
>
> ### Tactical Credit Strategies – Economic Slowdown Scenario
>
> An active credit portfolio manager considers the following corporate bond portfolio choices familiar from an earlier example:

Credit Spread Curve Strategies

Rating Category	Current OAS	Expected Loss (POD × LGD)	EffSpreadDur
A	1.05%	0.06%	5.5
Baa	1.35%	0.30%	6.0
Ba	2.45%	0.60%	4.5
B	3.50%	3.00%	4.0

The investor anticipates an economic slowdown in the next year that will have a greater adverse impact on lower-rated issuers. Assume that an index portfolio is equally allocated across all four rating categories, while the investor chooses a tactical portfolio combining equal long positions in the investment-grade (A and Baa) bonds and short positions in the high-yield (Ba and B) bonds.

1. Calculate excess spread on the index and tactical portfolios assuming no change in spreads over the next year (ignoring spread duration changes).

Solution:

The following table summarizes expected excess returns E [ExcessSpreadReturn] ≈ Spread$_0$ − (EffSpreadDur × ΔSpread) − (POD × LGD) for each of the four rating categories with no change in spreads. For example, expected excess return for rating category A is 0.99% (=1.05% − (5.5 × 0) − 0.06%).

Rating Category	Excess Spread Return
A	0.99%
Baa	1.05%
Ba	1.85%
B	0.50%

Solve for the equally weighted versus tactical portfolios as follows:

Equally weighted index: 1.10% (= (0.99% + 1.05% + 1.85% + 0.50%)/4)

Tactical portfolio: −0.16% (= (0.99% + 1.05%)/2 − (1.85% + 0.50%)/2)

2. Calculate excess spread under an economic downturn scenario for the index and tactical portfolios where both OAS and expected loss rise 50% for investment-grade bonds and double for high-yield bonds.

Solution:

The following table summarizes expected excess returns E [ExcessSpreadReturn] ≈ Spread$_0$ − (EffSpreadDur × ΔSpread) − (POD × LGD) for each of the four rating categories with the expected 50% increase in both OAS and expected loss under the slowdown scenario. For example, expected excess return for rating category A is −1.928% (=1.05% − (5.5 × 0.525%) − 0.09%).

Rating Category	E(OAS)	E(Expected Loss)	E(Excess Spread Return)
A	1.575%	0.09%	−1.928%
Baa	2.025%	0.45%	−3.150%

Rating Category	E(OAS)	E(Expected Loss)	E(Excess Spread Return)
Ba	4.900%	1.20%	−9.775%
B	7.000%	6.00%	−16.500%

Solve for the equally weighted versus tactical portfolios as follows.

Equally weighted index: −7.84%

= (−1.928% − 3.150% −9.775% − 16.500%)/4)

Tactical portfolio: +10.6% = (−1.928% − 3.150%)/2 − (−9.775% − 16.500%)/2)

This example assumes that an active manager is able to source and borrow the necessary Ba- and B rated bonds to sell short at no cost. However, in practice, the availability and cost of shorting bonds vary over the economic cycle, and shorting bonds is often far more difficult and costly during an economic slowdown. The synthetic, CDS-based strategy in the following example targets a similar objective.

EXAMPLE 29

Synthetic Credit Strategies: Economic Slowdown Scenario

As in the prior example, an active fixed-income manager anticipates an economic slowdown in the next year with a greater adverse impact on lower-rated issuers. The manager chooses a tactical CDX (credit default swap index) strategy combining positions in investment-grade and high-yield CDX contracts to capitalize on this view. The current market information for investment-grade and high-yield CDX contracts is as follows:

CDX Contract	Tenor	CDS Spread	EffSpreadDur$_{CDS}$
CDX IG Index	5 years	120 bps	4.67
CDX HY Index	5 years	300 bps	4.65

Assume that both CDX contracts have a $10,000,000 notional with premiums paid annually, and that the EffSpreadDur$_{CDS}$ for the CDX IG and CDX HY contracts in one year are 3.78 and 3.76, respectively. We ignore the time value of money for purposes of this example.

1. Describe the appropriate tactical CDX strategy and calculate the one-year return assuming no change in credit spread levels.

Solution:

The investor should initially sell protection on the CDX IG Index and buy protection on the CDX HY Index. Current CDS prices are estimated by multiplying EffSpreadDur$_{CDS}$ by the spread difference from the standard rates of 1% and 5%, respectively:

CDX HY: 109.3 per $100 face value, or 1.093 (= 1 + (5.00% − 3.00%) × 4.65)

CDX IG: 99.066 per $100 face value, or 0.99066 (
= 1 + (1.00% − 1.20%)× 4.67)

Since the investor is both buying HY protection at a premium to par (that is, agreeing to pay the 5% standard coupon while the underlying CDS spread is 3.00%) and selling IG protection at a discount from par (or agreeing to receive the standard 1.00% while the underlying index spread is 1.20%), the investor will receive an upfront payment for entering both positions as follows:

1,023,400 = [$10,000,000 × (1.093 − 1)] + [$10,000,000 × (1 − 0.99066)]

In one year, the return is measured by combining the net CDX coupon income or expense with the price appreciation assuming no spread change. As the investor is long protection CDX HY protection (i.e., pays the 5.00% standard HY coupon) and short protection CDX IG protection (or receives the standard 1.00% IG coupon), the net annual premium paid by the investor at year end is $400,000 (=$10,000,000 × (−5.00% + 1.00%). The respective CDS prices in one year are as follows:

CDX HY: 107.52 per $100 face value, or 1.0752 (=1 + (2.00% × 3.76))

CDX IG: 99.244 per $100 face value, or 0.99244 (=1 + (−0.20% × 3.78))

To offset the existing CDX positions in one year, the investor would sell HY protection and buy IG protection. The investor is able to sell HY protection at a premium of 7.52, resulting in a $178,000 gain from the long CDX HY position over one year (1.093 − 1.0752) × $10,000,000). Since the investor must buy IG protection in one year at a lower discount to par of (1 − 0.99244), it has a $17,800 gain from the CDX IG position (= (0.99244 − 0.99066) × $10,000,000). Subtracting the $400,000 net coupon payment made by the investor results in a one-year loss from the strategy of $204,200 (= $178,000 + $17,800 − $400,000) with constant spreads.

2. Calculate the one-year return on the tactical CDX strategy under an economic downturn scenario in which investment-grade credit spreads rise by 50% and high-yield credit spreads double.

Recall from Equation 14 that the price of a CDS contract may be approximated as follows:

CDS Price ≈ 1 + ((Fixed Coupon − CDS Spread) × $\text{EffSpreadDur}_{CDS}$)

Solution:

Initial CDS prices are derived exactly as in Question 1:

CDX HY: 109.3 per $100 face value, or 1.093 (= 1 + (2.00% × 4.65))

CDX IG: 99.066 per $100 face value, or 0.9966 (= 1 + (−0.2% × 34.67))

In one year, the return is measured by combining the coupon income with the price appreciation given the rise in the CDX IG spread to 1.80% and the CDX HY spread to 6.00%. The net annual premium paid is $400,000. Respective CDS prices in one year are as follows:

CDX HY: 96.24 per $100 face value, or 0.9624 (=1 + (−1.00% × 3.76))

CDX IG: 96.976 per $100 face value, or 0.96976 (=1 + (−0.80% × 3.78))

When offsetting the transaction in one year, the investor suffers a $209,000 loss from the short CDX IG position ((0.99066 − 0.96976) × −$10,000,000) and benefits from a $1,306,000 gain from offsetting the CDX HY position (1.093 − 0.9624) × $10,000,000). Subtracting the $400,000 net premium paid results in a one-year gain from the strategy of $697,000 (= $1,306,000 − $209,000 − $400,000) under the second scenario.

The early expansion phase of the credit cycle is usually characterized by rising profits and falling leverage, as shown earlier in Exhibit 8, increasing cash flow coverage available to service outstanding debt. This reduction in the likelihood of near-term financial distress leads to both lower credit spread levels and a steeper credit curve, an effect that is more pronounced for lower-rated issuers in cyclical industries. The following examples illustrate how an active manager might capitalize on this credit cycle view in cash and synthetic markets.

EXAMPLE 30

Tactical Credit Strategies: Economic Recovery Scenario

1. A long-only active credit manager faces similar corporate bond portfolio choices to those in an earlier example:

Rating Category	OAS	EffSpreadDur	Expected Loss
A	1.40%	5.5	0.10%
Baa	2.00%	6.0	0.30%
Ba	3.75%	4.5	1.00%
B	5.50%	4.0	4.50%

Given an expectation that an economic rebound will cause both credit spreads and expected loss rates to fall by one-third, an active manager decides to tilt her credit portfolio toward high yield. Compare the impact of this rebound scenario on an active portfolio (33.3% invested in each of the Ba and B bond categories, with the remaining 33.3% split evenly between A and Baa) versus on an equally weighted passive portfolio.

Solution:

The economic rebound scenario results in the following new OAS and expected losses, with expected excess returns E [ExcessSpread] ≈ $Spread_0$ − (EffSpreadDur × ΔSpread) − (POD × LGD) in the far right column:

Rating Category	E(OAS)	E(Expected Loss)	E(Excess Spread)
A	0.933%	0.07%	3.898%
Baa	1.333%	0.20%	5.80%
Ba	2.50%	0.67%	8.705%
B	3.667%	3.00%	9.832%

Solve for the passive (equally weighted) portfolio returns versus tactical portfolio returns.

Passive portfolio return: 7.095% (= (3.898% + 5.80% + 8.705% + 9.832%)/4)

Tactical portfolio return: 7.795% (=3.898%/6 + 5.80%/6 + 8.705%/3 + 9.832%/3).

Credit Spread Curve Strategies

EXAMPLE 31

Synthetic Credit Strategies: Economic Recovery Scenario

1. As in the prior example, an active fixed-income manager anticipates an economic rebound that is expected to cause high-yield credit curve steepening. The manager chooses a tactical CDX strategy combining 5-year and 10-year credit positions to capitalize on this view. Current market information for these high-yield CDX contracts is as follows:

CDX Contract	Tenor	CDS Spread	EffSpreadDur$_{CDS}$
CDX HY Index	5 years	450 bps	4.637
CDX HY Index	10 years	375 bps	8.656

Describe an appropriate duration-neutral portfolio positioning strategy to capitalize on this view using these CDX HY contracts. Calculate the return assuming that 5-year CDX spreads immediately fall by 175 bps and 10-year spreads decline by 25 bps for an equivalent $10,000,000 notional on the 10-year CDX index contract.

Solution:

The appropriate strategy is to sell protection on the 5-year CDX HY and buy protection on the 10-year CDX HY.

1. Calculate the 5-year CDS contract notional that matches the BPV of a 10-year, $10,000,000 CDS (BPV$_{10yr}$ = EffSpreadDur$_{10yrCDS}$ × notional) using the effective spread duration ratio of 1.8667 (EffSpreadDur$_{10yrCDS}$/EffSpreadDur$_{5yrCDS}$ = 8.656/4.637) multiplied by $10,000,000 to get $18,667,000.

   Confirm this equivalence by comparing BPV$_{5yr}$ and BPV$_{10yr}$:

   BPV$_{5yr}$: $8,656 = $18,667,000 × 4.637/10,000

   BPV$_{10yr}$: $8,656 = $10,000,000 × 8.656/10,000

2. Calculate portfolio return for a 175 bp decline in 5-year CDX HY spreads and a 25 bp decline in 10-year CDX HY spreads using Equation 15 (−Δ(CDS Spread) × EffSpreadDur$_{CDS}$) multiplied by the CDS notional as follows:

   CDX HY 5 year: $1,514,780 = (−(−1.75%) × 4.637) × $18,667,000

   CDX HY 10-year: −$216,400 = (−(−0.25%) × 8.656) × (−$10,000,000)
   Portfolio gain: $1,298,380

   = $1,514,780 − $216,400.

   Note that this equals the contract BPV of $8,656 multiplied by the 150 bp credit curve steepening.

7. GLOBAL CREDIT STRATEGIES

☐ discuss considerations in constructing and managing portfolios across international credit markets

While yield curve strategies across currencies were covered in an earlier lesson, we now turn to cross-border fixed-income investments in which investors face the risk that they will not receive interest and principal cash flows as expected. Investors distinguish between international credit markets in developed market countries versus emerging or frontier markets. Fixed-income markets in developed countries usually have well-established and liquid derivative and other capital markets and feature a broad range of private and public debt issuers with bonds denominated in a freely floating domestic or other major currency. Emerging or frontier fixed-income markets on the other hand are often dominated by sovereign issuers, state-owned or controlled enterprises, banks, and producers operating in a dominant domestic industry such as basic commodities. As some emerging economies face concentrated risk to a particular commodity or industry, investments across sovereign, bank, and private sector debt could offer little to no diversification. While many emerging-market bonds are denominated in a restricted domestic currency with varying degrees of liquidity, the sovereign government and a select few domestic issuers often issue global bonds in a major foreign currency such as US dollars or euros.

Credit strategies across countries must take these and other individual market differences into consideration. For example, in the case of developed markets, sector composition differences exist. A far higher percentage of the US fixed-income market (and roughly one-third of the Bloomberg Barclays US Aggregate Bond Index) comprises mortgage-backed and other asset-backed instruments versus other developed markets. Investors in developed European and Asian markets seeking commercial or residential real estate exposure might instead consider covered bonds or indirect exposure via bank bonds in markets where securitization is less prevalent. International accounting standards differences between the International Accounting Standards Board's International Financial Reporting Standards and US GAAP in such areas as inventory recognition, restricted cash, and cash flow definitions require adjustment for financial ratio comparisons across jurisdictions. Finally, while most developed markets face common macroeconomic factors that influence the bond term premium and expected returns, such as inflation, monetary policy, and economic growth, differences in the timing and magnitude of market changes, as well as the credit cycle across countries, are often reflected in interest rate differentials, exchange rates, and credit spreads.

EXAMPLE 32

Credit Strategies across Developed Markets

1. An active United States–based credit manager is offered similar US corporate bond portfolio choices to those in an earlier example:

Rating Category	OAS	EffSpreadDur	Expected Loss
A	1.40%	5.5	0.10%
Baa	2.00%	6.0	0.30%

Global Credit Strategies

Rating Category	OAS	EffSpreadDur	Expected Loss
Ba	3.75%	4.5	1.00%
B	5.50%	4.0	4.50%

As in the earlier case, the manager expects an economic rebound but now believes that European economies will experience a stronger recovery than the United States. In particular, European high-yield credit spreads are expected to narrow by 25% in the near term, the euro is expected to appreciate 1% against the US dollar, and all US credit spreads and expected loss rates are expected to decline just 10% over the same period. The euro-denominated 5-year European iTraxx Crossover index (iTraxx-Xover) of liquid high-yield issuers (with a 5% fixed premium) is currently trading at 400 bps with an $EffSpreadDur_{CDS}$ of 4.25.

Describe the position the manager would take in iTraxx-Xover to capitalize on the stronger European rebound, and calculate the expected excess return percentage assuming an equally weighted allocation to US corporate bonds and an iTraxx-Xover position that matches that of the US high-yield bond allocation.

Solution:

To capitalize on expected greater euro spread tightening, the manager would sell protection on the iTraxx-Xover index. To calculate expected return, first consider the US corporate bond portfolio. The economic rebound scenario results in the following new OAS and expected losses for the portfolio, with expected excess returns E [ExcessSpread] ≈ $Spread_0$ − (EffSpreadDur × ΔSpread) − (POD × LGD) in the far right column:

Rating Category	E(OAS)	E(Expected Loss)	E(Excess Spread)
A	1.26%	0.09%	2.08%
Baa	1.80%	0.27%	3.93%
Ba	3.38%	0.90%	4.54%
B	4.95%	4.05%	3.65%

Return on the equally weighted portfolio is equal to 3.30% (= (2.08% + 2.93% + 4.54% + 3.65%)/4). We can estimate the initial iTraxx-Xover price by subtracting the product of $EffSpreadDur_{CDS}$ and the difference between the standard coupon (5%) from the market premium of 400 bps as follows:

Original iTraxx-Xover 5-year: 95.75 per $104.25, or 1.0425 (

=1 + (4.25 × 1.00%))

If European high-yield spreads tighten by 25%, the iTraxx-Xover premium narrows by 100 bps to 300 bps, and the protection seller realizes a gain:

New iTraxx-Xover 5-year: 91.50 per $108.5, or 1.085 (=1 + (4.25 × 2.00%))

We can calculate the percentage return on the iTraxx-Xover investment in euro terms by dividing the price change by the initial price to get 4.077% (= (1.085 − 1.0425)/1.0425). For a United States–based investor, we must convert the euro return to US dollars as described in an earlier lesson:

$$R_{DC} = (1 + R_{FC})(1 + R_{FX}) - 1$$

R_{DC} and R_{FC} are the domestic and foreign currency returns in percent, and R_{FX} is the percentage change of the domestic versus foreign currency. We solve for US dollar iTraxx-Xover returns as 5.118% (= (1 + 4.077%) × (1 + 1.00%) − 1). Given that iTraxx-Xover carries a weight equal to one-half of the US corporate bond portfolio, the strategy returns 5.86% (or 3.30% + 5.118%/2).

Emerging markets are characterized by higher, more volatile, and less balanced economic growth than developed markets, often in addition to greater geopolitical risk, currency restrictions, and capital controls. Sovereign credit risk is therefore a critical starting point in considering fixed-income investments in emerging markets, where both the ability and willingness of issuers to repay debt is of importance. An earlier lesson outlined in detail sovereign credit risk considerations such as a country's institutional and economic profile, use of monetary and fiscal policy, the exchange rate regime, and external debt status and outlook.

Institutional considerations include political stability, institutional transparency, and adherence to property rights and contract law. Geopolitical risks include such factors as potential conflicts and trade relations, which in some instances could have a greater impact on emerging markets whose economies are highly dependent on energy or other commodity exports. As mentioned earlier, ESG factors are key elements for sustainable, balanced, long-term economic growth.

As sovereign governments tax economic activity within their borders to repay interest and principal, key financial ratios used to assess and compare sovereign creditworthiness are usually measured as a percentage of GDP. For example, government debt to GDP and the annual government budget deficit (or surplus) as a percentage of GDP are common measures of indebtedness and fiscal stability, respectively, for both developed and emerging markets.

Finally, a country's exchange rate regime is a critical element of monetary and external flexibility. Freely floating currency regimes that allow a currency to be held in reserve outside the country enable sovereign governments to pursue an independent and flexible monetary policy. Restrictive or fixed-rate regimes limit policy effectiveness, magnifying the impact of economic crises and increasing the likelihood of financial distress. Emerging markets are usually characterized by non-reserve currency regimes with significant external debt denominated in major foreign currencies, leading analysts to incorporate external debt to GDP and currency reserves as a percentage of GDP as key leverage and liquidity measures of creditworthiness, respectively.

The Bloomberg Sovereign Risk (SRSK) model shown in Exhibit 30 combines quantitative and qualitative factors such as external debt to GDP, currency reserves, GDP growth, and political risk to estimate a sovereign issuer's one-year POD. Similar to the DRSK model discussed earlier, the SRSK model allows users to change model inputs and also derives a "model" CDS spread, which could be compared to the market CDS spread.

Global Credit Strategies

Exhibit 30: Bloomberg SRSK Screen

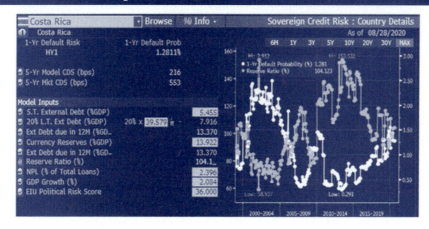

In this example, Costa Rica has a 1.28% one-year default risk and a model CDS spread well below the market CDS spread.

EXAMPLE 33

Sovereign Risk Factors for Emerging Markets

1. A financial analyst is considering the likelihood that an emerging market sovereign issuer of US dollar–denominated bonds is able to meet its interest payments over the next 12 months. Which of the following financial ratios is most appropriate to assess the sovereign borrower's liquidity position?

   A. Government budget deficit/GDP
   B. External debt/GDP
   C. Currency reserves/GDP

Solution:

The correct answer is C. The government budget deficit as a percentage of GDP is a gauge of fiscal stability for the domestic economy, while the external debt-to-GDP ratio is a measure of financial leverage to foreign lenders. Currency reserves as a percentage of GDP measure the available liquidity in foreign currency to meet external obligations.

Several additional considerations are important for investors in emerging market bonds issued by private companies. First, although some local companies might have partial private ownership and publicly traded equity, the sovereign government could exercise controlling influence on the business, including replacing management or ownership groups.

Credit quality in the emerging market credit universe exhibits a high concentration in lower investment-grade and upper high-yield ratings categories. This concentration of credit ratings is largely a reflection of the sovereign ratings of emerging markets but also reflects the fact that a "sovereign ceiling" is usually applied to corporate issuers globally. This ceiling implies that a company's rating is typically no higher than the sovereign credit rating of its domicile.

Finally, relative liquidity conditions and currency volatility are key considerations for international credit investors. In emerging markets, liquidity is often constrained because of a relatively small number of bonds that trade regularly, resulting in investors demanding higher premiums for holding emerging market credit securities. Local bond markets might seem highly liquid and can exceed the trading volume of the local stock exchanges, but such high trading volume could also be inflated by interbank trading by local banks and retail investors. Currency volatility can be particularly significant in emerging markets as a result of restrictive currency regimes and derivative markets. Higher YTMs available in emerging market currencies versus developed markets typically suggest that these emerging currencies will depreciate over time. That said, emerging markets offer investors the opportunity to exploit divergence from interest rate parity conditions (known as the forward rate bias) by investing in higher-yielding currencies, as addressed in earlier lessons. Although temporary deviations from a fixed exchange rate are possible under such regimes, what is more common during economic crises is exchange rate regime change, central bank intervention, and/or devaluation. The following example demonstrates how such factors are considered in emerging market credit strategies.

EXAMPLE 34

Emerging Market Credit Strategy

1. An active United States–based investor is considering a portfolio allocation to the bonds of a major commodities producer headquartered in an emerging market economy. The issuer is a major exporter, and commodity exports comprise a significant proportion of the country's economic growth. Describe how the investor would decide between purchasing a higher-yielding, local-currency-denominated bond and a lower-yielding, US-dollar-denominated bond with otherwise similar features.

Solution:

A United States–based investor seeking to maximize US-dollar-denominated return must consider the relationship between the higher local currency bond YTM, the lower US dollar bond YTM, and the local currency's expected depreciation (or appreciation) versus the US dollar over the investment horizon. While uncovered interest rate parity suggests that local currency depreciation versus the US dollar would offset any benefit of a higher YTM, an investor with a bullish view of the emerging economy's growth prospects would benefit from forward rate bias and earn a higher return in US dollar terms from an unhedged investment in the local currency bond if the local currency were to depreciate less than expected under interest rate parity conditions.

8 STRUCTURED CREDIT

☐ describe the use of structured financial instruments as an alternative to corporate bonds in credit portfolios

Structured Credit

Active managers have access to a wide array of credit management tools beyond individual fixed-income securities that include structured financial instruments. These alternatives to direct bond investments in corporate bonds introduced in earlier lessons are summarized in Exhibit 31.

Exhibit 31: Structured Alternatives to Individual Bonds

Instrument	Description	Exposure	Portfolio Applications
Collateralized Debt Obligations (CDOs)	Fixed-income securities backed by a diversified pool of debt obligations	Redistribute portfolio debt cash flows across ratings spectrum	Create tailored portfolio-based debt exposure categories/profiles unavailable in the cash bond market
Collateralized Loan Obligations (CLOs)	Fixed-income securities backed by a diversified pool of floating-rate leveraged loan obligations	Redistribute portfolio loan cash flows across ratings spectrum	Create tailored portfolio-based loan and interest rate exposure profiles unavailable in the cash bond market
Mortgage-Backed Securities (MBS)	Fixed-income securities backed by a pool of commercial or residential mortgage loans	Provide portfolio-based exposure to real estate cash flows	Offer active managers exposure to real estate and to volatility (prepayment/extension risk) unavailable in the cash bond market
Asset-Backed Securities (ABS)	Fixed-income securities backed by a pool of credit card, auto, and other loans	Provide portfolio-based exposure to consumer loan cash flows	Offer active managers direct exposure to consumer loans and to volatility unavailable in the cash bond market
Covered Bonds	Senior debt obligations backed by pool of commercial/residential mortgages or public sector assets	Provide portfolio-based exposure to real estate cash flows with recourse to issuer	Offer active managers direct exposure to consumer loans and to real estate/public sector cash flows unavailable in the cash bond market

Structured financial instruments can offer active credit managers the ability to access fixed-income cash flows such as commercial or residential real estate, enhance returns by increasing portfolio exposure to interest rate volatility (via mortgage prepayment and extension risk), and add debt exposure created by the redistribution of default risk into different tranches across the credit spectrum. Exhibit 32 shows an illustrative example of the tranching that characterizes ABS and CDO transactions. In this case, the ABS issuer is a special purpose vehicle (SPV) that owns the underlying asset pool and issues debt across several tranches backed by the asset pool cash flows.

Exhibit 32: Illustrative Tranching Example

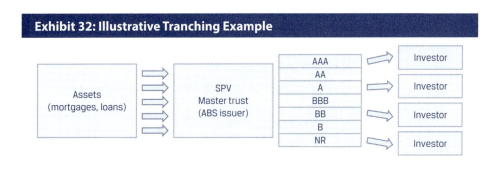

An earlier lesson addressed the redistribution of default risk from the underlying asset pool. This is achieved by establishing higher-rated tranches via internal credit enhancement or overcollateralization, with successively lower-rated tranches absorbing a greater proportion of the associated default risk. An active investor might overweight default risk by choosing a lower-rated ABS tranche based on a tactical view. For example, such an investor might anticipate lower-than-expected defaults or believe the credit cycle is in recovery mode and that lower-rated tranches will experience greater spread tightening than higher-rated tranches. Alternatively, a portfolio manager might underweight credit exposure using a higher-rated tranche in a downturn.

While covered bonds offer real estate cash flow exposure similar to that of ABS, given the dual recourse (i.e., to both the issuing financial institution and the underlying asset pool), as well as the substitution of non-performing assets, covered bonds usually involve lower credit risk and a lower yield. The following examples demonstrate the role of structured products in active credit portfolios.

> **EXAMPLE 35**
>
> ### The Role of Structured Products in Active Credit Management
>
> 1. An active credit manager anticipates an economic slowdown led by a decline in residential housing prices. Which of the following portfolio positioning strategies involving structured products is the most appropriate to consider under this scenario?
>
>   **A.** Shift exposure from an A rated tranche of a credit card ABS transaction to a BB rated tranche
>
>   **B.** Increase exposure to an A rated CDO tranche and reduce exposure to a BBB rated CDO tranche
>
>   **C.** Increase exposure to an A rated MBS tranche and decrease exposure to a BBB rated MBS tranche
>
> **Solution:**
>
> The correct answer is C. As the housing sector slows and default rates rise, credit spreads of lower-rated MBS tend to widen by more than those of higher-rated MBS. The investor retains exposure to real estate cash flows while reducing exposure to spread widening. The shift to a BB rated credit card ABS tranche increases credit exposure, while the switch from BBB rated to A rated CDOs represents a reduction in overall market risk rather than a more targeted underweight, as in C.
>
> 2. An active fixed-income portfolio manager expects an economic recovery in the near term to be accompanied by rising short-term rates and a flatter benchmark yield curve. Which of the following strategies best positions an active manager to capitalize on this scenario?
>
>   **A.** Increase exposure to covered bonds and decrease exposure to MBS
>
>   **B.** Shift exposure from an A rated CDO tranche to a BBB rated CLO tranche
>
>   **C.** Shift exposure from a BB rated tranche of an automotive ABS transaction to a A rated tranche

> **Solution:**
>
> The correct answer is B. Economic recovery is typically associated with lower defaults and greater credit spread tightening among lower-rated issuers and debt tranches. CLO tranches benefit more from short-term rate rises than CDOs because CLOs comprise leveraged loans based on MRRs plus a credit spread. As for A, a shift to covered bonds from MBS reduces credit risk because of the dual recourse and substitutability of collateral characteristics of covered bonds. In C, credit exposure is reduced, limiting the benefit from credit spread reduction within the portfolio.

FIXED-INCOME ANALYTICS

☐ describe key inputs, outputs, and considerations in using analytical tools to manage fixed-income portfolios

Fixed-income analytical tools continue to adapt not only to technological change but also to the market and regulatory environment within which active fixed-income practitioners operate. The inputs and outputs of these models have become more complex as market participants integrate tasks across operational duties and portfolio decision making and execution. These tasks include portfolio construction, risk analytics, trading and settlement, cash and collateral management, daily valuation, portfolio accounting, and regulatory reporting.

Primary inputs for fixed-income models include all long and short cash bond and derivative positions, repurchase agreements, and cash across currencies. Fixed-income security inputs use CUSIP or ISIN identifiers to capture all relevant features such as interest and principal payment dates, day count conventions, and put–call features. Portfolio derivative and repo position inputs also include details of such agreements, such as settlement dates, option strike prices, and collateral terms necessary to satisfy derivative counterparty or clearing requirements based on market changes.

Real-time market data feeds usually sourced from vendors via application programming interfaces include spot and forward rates, credit curves, implied volatilities, and exchange rates that are used to value historical, existing, and potential future new portfolio positions. These tools value inactively traded fixed-income instruments using matrix pricing (or evaluated pricing) based on observable liquid benchmark YTMs of similar maturity and duration and credit spreads of actively traded bonds with comparable times to maturity, credit quality, and sector. Additional model inputs include index subscriptions, ESG and credit ratings, and issuer balance sheet data. In contrast to more static equity indexes, fixed-income indexes are subject to constant change as a result of both new debt issuance and bond maturities as well as ratings changes, bond callability, and prepayment.

Model assumptions include user-defined parameters such as term structure models, investment time horizon, VaR methodology, historical and/or specific market scenarios, and portfolio filters that could involve inclusion or exclusion of specific sectors or a minimum ESG rating threshold for consideration.

Fixed-income analytical model outputs support each stage of the active portfolio management process, namely portfolio selection and construction, risk analysis of existing and prospective portfolio positions, and trading and position management. A portfolio summary or landing page typically aggregates current portfolio risk and return across sectors, ratings, and currencies versus the benchmark index. Model applications supporting research and portfolio construction allow managers to assess the expected change in portfolio performance by including incremental long or short cash bond, derivative, or structured product positions. Portfolio risk dashboards embedded in these tools provide detailed insight into portfolio duration and convexity as well as tail risk. These statistics are often further disaggregated into key rate duration measures for benchmark rates and credit spreads by maturity. VaR and expected shortfall (or CVaR) are calculated based on user threshold and methodology settings. Finally, trading, cash, and position management outputs quantify existing cash positions, anticipated cash inflows and outflows from existing positions, and liquidity risk. Exhibit 33 summarizes the key elements of a fixed-income portfolio analytics tool.

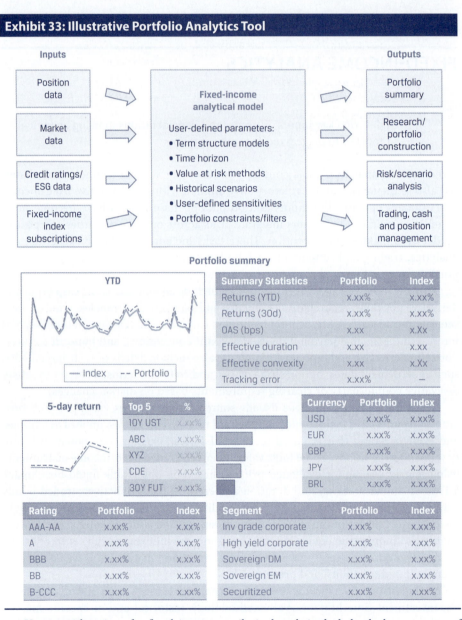

Exhibit 33: Illustrative Portfolio Analytics Tool

Key considerations for fixed-income analytical tools include both the accuracy of model inputs and assumptions and the degree of alignment between model outputs and specific fixed-income manager objectives.

Bond price and YTM calculations are affected by assumptions related to the term structure of benchmark rates and volatilities and how they change over time based on term structure models. Model outputs are often tailored to match an active manager's objectives. For example, an index fund manager might seek to minimize the tracking error defined earlier as the deviation of portfolio returns from an index. An active fixed-income manager with fewer constraints might maximize risk-adjusted returns, while estimating and categorizing how each position contributes to active risk taking. For example, performance attribution measures returns from credit, duration, sector, and currency tilts, among other factors. Finally, an active manager facing liability constraints usually models the fixed-income characteristics of obligations to maximize the expected surplus of assets over liabilities. Practitioners applying these tools must both recognize their limitations and anticipate and interpret model results, as in the following example.

> **EXAMPLE 36**
>
> ### Applying Fixed-Income Analytical Tools
>
> 1. An active fixed-income manager is conducting scenario analysis for the MBS component of a portfolio. Which of the following analytical model input changes is most likely to reduce the future value of the MBS subportfolio versus similar option-free bond holdings?
>
>   **A.** An increase in benchmark yield curve volatility
>
>   **B.** A decrease in benchmark yield curve volatility
>
>   **C.** Upward parallel shift in the benchmark yield curve
>
> ### Solution:
>
> The correct answer is A. The value of a bond with an embedded option is equal to the sum of the value of an option-free bond plus the value to the embedded option. The value of the embedded call option owned by the issuer will increase as volatility rises, reducing the value of the MBS versus a similar option-free bond. Answers B and C are more likely to result in an increase in the value of MBS versus an option-free bond.

SUMMARY

Active spread-based, fixed-income portfolio management involves taking positions in credit and other risk factors that differ from those of an index to generate excess return. The main points of the reading are as follows:

- Yield spreads compensate investors for the risk that they will not receive expected interest and principal cash flows and for the bid–offer cost of buying or selling a bond under current market conditions.
- Two key components of a bond's credit risk are the POD and the LGD.
- Credit spread changes are driven by the credit cycle, or the expansion and contraction of credit over the business cycle, which causes asset prices to change based on default and recovery expectations.
- High-yield issuers experience greater changes in the POD over the credit cycle than investment-grade issuers, with bond prices approaching the recovery rate for distressed debt.

- While fixed-rate bond yield spread measures use actual, interpolated, or zero curve–based benchmark rates to capture relative credit risk, OAS allow comparison between risky option-free bonds and bonds with embedded options.
- FRNs pay periodic interest based on an MRR plus a yield spread.
- Spread duration measures the change in a bond's price for a given change in yield spread, while spread changes for lower-rated bonds tend to be proportional on a percentage rather than an absolute basis.
- Bottom-up credit strategies include the use of financial ratio analysis, reduced form credit models (such as the Z-score model), and structural credit models, including Bloomberg's DRSK model.
- Top-down credit strategies are often based on macro factors and group investment choices by credit rating and industry sector categories.
- Fixed-income factor investing incorporates such factors as size, value, and momentum to target active returns and also increasingly include ESG factors.
- Liquidity risk in credit markets is higher than in equities because of market structure differences and is often addressed using liquid bonds for short-term tactical positioning, less liquid positions for buy-and-hold strategies, and liquid alternatives where active management adds little value.
- Credit market tail risk is usually quantified using VaR or expected shortfall measures and is frequently managed using position limits, risk budgeting, or derivative strategies.
- Credit derivative strategies offer a synthetic liquid alternative to active portfolio managers as a means of over- or underweighting issuers, sectors, and/or maturities across the credit spectrum.
- Credit spread levels and curve slopes change over the credit cycle, with credit curve steepening usually indicating low near-term default expectations and higher growth expectations, while curve flattening, or inversion, suggests rising default expectations and lower future growth.
- Active credit managers can benefit under a stable credit curve scenario by adding spread duration for existing exposures and/or increasing average portfolio credit risk and can capitalize on divergent market views using cash- or derivative-based strategies related to specific issuers, sectors, or the overall credit market.
- Investors in international credit markets distinguish between developed and emerging markets. Developed markets face common macro factors, with market and credit cycle differences affecting relative interest rates, foreign exchange rates, and credit spreads. Emerging markets usually exhibit higher growth combined with greater sovereign and geopolitical risk, currency restrictions, and capital controls.
- Structured financial instruments offer active credit managers access to liquid bond portfolios, fixed-income cash flows derived from real estate and consumer loans, and enhanced returns by adding volatility and/or debt exposure via tranching across the credit spectrum.
- Key considerations for fixed-income analytical tools include the accuracy of model inputs and assumptions as well as alignment between model outputs and fixed-income manager objectives.

REFERENCES

Altman, Edward I. 1968. "Financial Ratios, Discriminant Analysis and the Prediction of Corporate Bankruptcy." *Journal of Finance* 23 (4): 589–609. 10.1111/j.1540-6261.1968.tb00843.x

Israel, Ronen, Diogo Palhares, and Scott Richardson. 2018. *"Common Factors in Corporate Bond Returns." Journal of Investment Management* 16 (2), 17–46. www.aqr.com/-/media/AQR/Documents/Journal-Articles/Common-Factors-in-Corporate-Bond-Returns.pdfMoody's Investors Service. 2018. "Cross-Sector: Annual Default Study: Corporate Default and Recovery Rates, 1920–2017." Data report (15 February).

O'Kane, Dominic and Saurav Sen. 2005. "Credit Spreads Explained." *Journal of Credit Risk* 1 (2): 61–78. 10.21314/JCR.2005.009

PRACTICE PROBLEMS

1. Which of the following statements best describes empirical duration?

   A. A common way to calculate a bond's empirical duration is to run a regression of its price returns on changes in a benchmark interest rate.

   B. A bond's empirical duration tends to be larger than its effective duration.

   C. The price sensitivity of high-yield bonds to interest rate changes is typically higher than that of investment-grade bonds.

2. A junior analyst considers a 10-year high-yield bond issued by EKN Corporation (EKN) position in a high-yield portfolio. The bond has a price of 91.82, a modified duration of 8.47, and a spread duration of 8.47. The analyst speculates on the effects of an interest rate increase of 20 bps and, because of a change in its credit risk, an increase in the EKN bond's credit spread of 20 bps. The analyst comments that because the modified duration and the credit spread duration of the EKN bond are equal, the bond's price will not change (all else being equal) in response to the interest rate and credit spread changes.

   Is the analyst's prediction correct that the EKN bond price will not change in response to the interest rate and credit spread changes, all else being equal?

   A. Yes.

   B. No, the bond price should decrease.

   C. No, the bond price should increase.

3. Which of the following outcomes is most likely if the junior analyst revises the bond's original recovery rate higher?

   A. An increase in the bond's POD

   B. A decrease in the bond's POD

   C. A decrease in the bond's credit spread

4. Which of the following observations on the risks of spread-based fixed-income portfolios is the most accurate?

   A. Because credit spreads equal the product of the LGD and the POD, distinguishing between the credit risk and liquidity risk components of yield spread across all market scenarios is straightforward.

   B. Given that frequent issuers with many bonds outstanding across maturities have their own issuer-specific credit curve, distinguishing between the credit spread and liquidity spread of all bonds for these issuers is straightforward.

   C. The yield spread of a particular bond comprises both credit and liquidity risk and depends on market conditions and the specific supply-and-demand dynamics of each fixed-income security.

Practice Problems

The following information relates to questions 5-8

An active portfolio manager observes the following market information related to an outstanding corporate bond and two on-the-run government bonds that pay annual coupons:

Issuer	Term	Coupon	Yield	ModDur
Corporate	12y	3.00%	2.80%	9.99
Government	10y	1.75%	1.85%	9.09
Government	20y	2.25%	2.30%	15.94

The portfolio manager also observes 10-year and 20-year swap spreads of 0.20% and 0.25%, respectively.

5. Calculate the G-spread of the corporate bond.

    A. 0.860%

    B. 0.725%

    C. 0.950%

6. Calculate the I-spread of the corporate bond.

    A. 0.85%

    B. 0.65%

    C. 0.95%

7. Calculate the ASW of the corporate bond.

    A. 0.65%

    B. 0.95%

    C. 0.85%

8. Estimate the corporate bond's percentage price change if the government yield curve steepens, assuming a 0.20% increase in the 20-year YTM and no change to the 10-year government YTM or corporate G-spread.

    A. −0.40%

    B. 0.40%

    C. −0.04%

9. Which of the following statements about credit spread measures is most accurate?

    A. The DM is the yield spread over the MRR established upon issuance to compensate investors for assuming an issuer's credit risk.

    B. The Z-DM will be above the DM if the MRR is expected to remain constant over time.

C. The yield spread for a corporate bond will be equal to the G-spread if the government benchmark yield curve is flat.

The following information relates to questions 10-12

An active fixed-income manager is considering two corporate bond positions for an active portfolio. The first bond has a BBB rating with a credit spread of 2.75% and an effective spread duration of 6, and the second bond has a BB rating with a credit spread of 3.50% and an effective spread duration of five years.

10. What is the approximate excess return if the BBB rated bond is held for six months and the credit spread narrows by 40 bps, ignoring spread duration changes and assuming no default losses?

    A. 3.775%

    B. 2.35%

    C. 2.40%

11. What is the instantaneous (holding period of zero) excess return for the BB rated bond if the spread widens by 50 bps?

    A. 3.00%

    B. −2.50%

    C. 2.50%

12. What is the expected excess spread of the BBB rated bond for a 50 bp decline in yield over a one-year holding period if the bond's LGD is 40% and the POD is 0.75%?

    A. 1.95%

    B. 2.45%

    C. 5.45%

---

13. An active manager is considering the senior bonds of one of several corporate issuers. Holding other factors constant, which of the following key financial ratio changes would lead the manager to expect a decrease in the POD for that issuer?

    A. An increase in the issuer's coverage ratio

    B. An increase in the issuer's stock price volatility

    C. An increase in the issuer's leverage ratio

14. Which of the following statements about statistical credit analysis models is most accurate?

    A. Structural credit models solve for the POD using observable company-specific variables such as financial ratios and macroeconomic variables.

Practice Problems

B. Reduced-form credit models use market-based variables to estimate an issuer's asset value and the volatility of asset value.

C. Structural credit models define the likelihood of default as the probability of the asset value falling below that of liabilities.

The following information relates to questions 15-17

An investor is faced with an active portfolio decision across three bond rating categories based on the following current market information:

Rating Category	Current OAS	Expected Loss (POD x LGD)	EffSpreadDur
A	1.00%	0.10%	7
BBB	1.75%	0.75%	6
BB	2.75%	2.50%	5

15. Which bond rating category offers the highest expected excess return if credit spreads remain stable under current market conditions?

   A. A rated bond category

   B. BBB rated bond category

   C. BB rated bond category

16. Which active bond portfolio maximizes expected excess return under a stable credit market assumption versus an equally weighted benchmark portfolio across the three rating categories?

   A. 50% A rated bonds, 50% BBB rated bonds

   B. 50% BBB rated bonds, 50% BB rated bonds

   C. 50% A rated bonds, 50% BB rated bonds

17. Which bond rating category offers the highest expected excess return if spreads rise 10% across all ratings categories?

   A. A rated bond category

   B. BBB rated bond category

   C. BB rated bond category

---

18. Which of the following strategies best addresses the liquidity risk of a less frequently traded bond position in an active manager's portfolio?

   A. Enter into a receive fixed, pay floating asset swap, unwinding the swap position once the illiquid bond position is sold.

   B. Sell single-name CDS protection on the illiquid bond issuer, unwinding the CDS contract when the bond is sold.

C. Allocate the illiquid bond to the buy-and-hold portion of the investment portfolio.

19. Which of the following statements best describes methods for assessing portfolio tail risk?

    A. Parametric methods use expected value and standard deviation of risk factors under a normal distribution and are well suited for option-based portfolios.

    B. Historical simulation methods use historical parameters and ranking results and are not well suited for option-based portfolios.

    C. Monte Carlo methods generate random outcomes using portfolio measures and sensitivities and are well suited for option-based portfolios.

The following information relates to questions 20-21

An investor is considering the portfolio impact of a new 12-year corporate bond position with a $75 million face value, a 3.25% coupon, current YTM of 2.85%, modified duration of 9.887, and a price of 104.0175 per 100 of face value.

20. Which of the following VaR measures is most appropriate for the portfolio manager to use to evaluate how this position would affect portfolio tail risk?

    A. CVaR

    B. Relative VaR

    C. Incremental VaR

21. What is the approximate VaR for the bond position at a 99% confidence interval (equal to 2.33 standard deviations) for one month (with 21 trading days) if daily yield volatility is 1.50 bps and returns are normally distributed?

    A. $1,234,105

    B. $2,468,210

    C. $5,413,133

22. Which of the following statements best describes how a single-name CDS contract is priced at inception?

    A. If the reference entity's credit spread trades below the standard coupon rate, the CDS contract will be priced at a premium above par because the protection buyer pays a "below market" periodic coupon.

    B. If the reference entity's credit spread trades above the standard coupon rate, the CDS contract will be priced at a discount to par because the protection seller effectively receives a "below market" periodic premium.

Practice Problems

    C. Similar to fixed-rate bonds, CDS contracts are initially priced at par with a fixed coupon and a price that changes over time as the reference entity's credit spreads change.

The following information relates to questions 23-24

An active portfolio manager seeking to purchase single-name CDS protection observes a 1.75% 10-year market credit spread for a private investment-grade issuer. The effective spread duration is 8.75 and CDS basis is close to zero.

23. What should the protection buyer expect to pay or receive to enter a new 10-year CDS contract?

    A. The buyer should receive approximately 6.5625% of the notional.

    B. The buyer should pay approximately 15.3125% of the notional.

    C. The buyer should pay approximately 6.5625% of the notional.

24. Once the manager purchases CDS protection, the issuer's CDS spread immediately falls to 1.60%. What is the investor's approximate mark-to-market gain or loss for a contract notional of €10,000,000?

    A. The manager realizes an approximate loss of €131,250.

    B. The manager realizes an approximate gain of €131,250.

    C. The manager realizes an approximate gain of €525,000.

---

25. Which of the following credit portfolio positioning strategies is the most appropriate to underweight the financial sector versus an index?

    A. Purchase protection on the CDX and sell protection on the CDX Financials subindex.

    B. Sell protection on the CDX and purchase protection on the CDX Financials subindex.

    C. Purchase a payer option on the CDX and sell protection on the CDX Financials subindex.

26. Which of the following phases of the credit cycle typically involves a decline in the number of issuer defaults?

    A. Late expansion phase

    B. Early expansion phase

    C. Peak phase

27. Which of the following regarding the shape of the credit spread curve for high-yield issuers is most accurate?

    A. High-yield credit spread curves change shape more over the cycle than investment-grade ones do and usually invert during the peak phase.

B. Investors should exercise caution in interpreting credit spread curve shape for distressed debt issuers because their bonds tend to trade on a price rather than credit spread basis as the likelihood of default increases.

C. High-yield credit spread curves often invert because of the empirical observation that DTS is the best way to measure high-yield bond price changes.

28. Which of the following statements best describes a credit curve roll-down strategy?

A. Returns from a credit curve roll-down strategy can be estimated by combining the incremental coupon from a longer maturity corporate bond with price appreciation due to the passage of time.

B. A synthetic credit curve roll-down strategy involves purchasing protection using a single-name CDS contract for a longer maturity.

C. A credit curve roll-down strategy is expected to generate a positive return if the credit spread curve is upward sloping.

The following information relates to questions 29-30

An investor observes the following current CDS market information:

CDX Contract	Tenor (years)	CDS Spread	EffSpreadDur$_{CDS}$
CDX IG Index	5	85 bps	4.9
CDX IG Index	10	135 bps	8.9
CDX HY Index	5	175 bps	4.7
CDX HY Index	10	275 bps	8.7

29. Select the most appropriate credit portfolio positioning strategy to capitalize on an expected steepening of the investment-grade credit spread curve.

A. Sell protection on the 10-year CDX IG index and purchase protection on the 5-year CDX IG index using contracts of equal notional value.

B. Sell protection on the 10-year CDX IG index and purchase protection on the 5-year CDX IG index using a contract with a notional amount equal to 1.82 times that of the 10-year contract.

C. Buy protection on the 10-year CDX IG index and sell protection on the 5-year CDX IG index using a contract with a notional amount equal to 1.82 times that of the 10-year contract.

30. Which of the following is the most appropriate credit portfolio positioning strategy to capitalize on an expected economic contraction?

A. Buy protection on the 5-year CDX HY index and sell protection on the 5-year CDX IG index in approximately equal notional amounts.

Practice Problems

B. Buy protection on the 10-year CDX IG index and sell protection on the 5-year CDX IG index using a contract with a notional amount equal to 1.82 times that of the 10-year contract.

C. Buy protection on the 10-year CDX HY index and sell protection on the 5-year CDX HY index using a contract with a notional amount equal to 1.85 times that of the 10-year contract.

31. Which of the following is the most accurate statement related to international credit markets?

   A. Fixed exchange-rate regimes among emerging markets usually reduce the likelihood of financial distress because the domestic currency is tied to a major foreign currency.

   B. Although many emerging economies have domestic bond markets that include sovereign, financial, and corporate issuers, investments across these bonds offer less diversification than similar investments in developed markets.

   C. Higher domestic currency YTMs among emerging versus developed markets are due to expected currency appreciation resulting from higher economic growth.

The following information relates to questions 32-33

An active United States–based credit manager faces the following US and European investment-grade and high-yield corporate bond portfolio choices:

Rating Category	OAS	EffSpreadDur	Expected Loss
USD IG	1.25%	4.50	0.40%
USD HY	3.00%	5.50	2.25%
EUR IG	1.15%	4.75	0.50%
EUR HY	3.25%	6.00	2.50%

The EUR IG and EUR HY allocations are denominated in euros, and the euro is expected to depreciate by 2% versus the US dollar over the next year.

32. What is the expected unhedged excess return to the United States–based credit manager for an international credit portfolio index equally weighted across the four portfolio choices, assuming no change to spread duration and no changes to the expected loss occur?

   A. −0.257%

   B. −0.850%

   C. 0.750%

33. Which of the following active portfolios is expected to have the highest excess return versus the index if European economies are expected to experience an

earlier and much stronger credit cycle recovery than the United States?

A. EUR HY 50.0%, EUR IG 25.0%, USD IG 12.5%, USD HY 12.5%

B. EUR IG 50.0%, EUR HY 25.0%, USD IG 12.5%, USD HY 12.5%

C. EUR HY 33.3%, US HY 33.3%, EUR IG 16.7%, USD IG 16.7%

---

34. Which of the following statements about the role of structured products in an active credit portfolio is most accurate?

    A. Covered bonds perform relatively well in a downturn versus other fixed-income bonds with real estate exposure because a covered bond investor also has recourse to the issuer.

    B. Higher-rated ABS tranches are attractive for active investors seeking to overweight default risk when the credit cycle is in recovery.

    C. CLO tranches are more advantageous than CDO tranches with similar ratings under an economic slowdown scenario.

35. An active fixed-income manager is evaluating the relative performance of an investment-grade corporate versus a high-yield corporate debt allocation in a fixed-income portfolio. Which of the following analytical model assumption changes is most likely to reduce the future value of the high-yield portfolio relative to the investment-grade holdings?

    A. Steepening of the benchmark yield volatility curve

    B. Decreased likelihood of an economic slowdown

    C. Increased likelihood of a flight to quality associated with bullish benchmark yield curve flattening (long-term rates fall by more than short-term rates do)

SOLUTIONS

1. A is correct. A bond's empirical duration is often estimated by running a regression of its price returns on changes in a benchmark interest rate.

2. B is correct. An increase in interest rates results in a decrease in the bond price. An increase in the credit spread also results in a decrease in the bond price. For the EKN bond, its modified duration shows the effect of the 20 bp increase in interest rates. The approximate percentage price change resulting from the increase in interest rates is –8.47 × 0.0020 = –1.694%. The spread duration shows the effect of the 20 bp increase in the credit spread. The approximate percentage price change resulting from the increase in the credit spread is –8.47 × 0.0020 = –1.694%. The combined effect is a total change of –3.388%, or a price decrease of roughly 3.4%.

3. C is correct. An increase in a bond's recovery rate will lower the loss severity, or LGD, because LGD = (1 – RR). Recall the simple one-period relationship between credit spreads, LGD, and the POD as Spread ≈ LGD × POD. A lower LGD will result in a lower spread.

4. C is correct. A bond's yield spread includes both credit and liquidity risk. Liquidity risk depends on both market conditions and the specific supply-and-demand dynamics of each fixed-income security.

5. A is correct. The G-spread is the difference between the corporate bond YTM and a linear interpolation of the 10-year and 20-year government bond YTMs. To calculate the approximate 12-year government rate, solve for the weights of the 10-year bond as 80% (= (20 – 12)/(20 – 10)) and the 20-year bond as 20% (or (1 – 80%), noting that (80% × 10) + (20% × 20) = 12). The 12-year government rate is 1.94% (or (80% × 1.85%) + (20% × 2.30%)), and the difference between the corporate bond YTM and the 12-year interpolated government rate is 0.860%.

6. B is correct. The I-spread is an estimate of the corporate bond's spread over an interpolated swap benchmark. We can solve for the 10-year and 20-year swap rates as 2.05% (=0.20% + 1.85%) and 2.55% (=0.25% + 2.30%), respectively, by adding the swap spread to the respective government bond. The 12-year swap rate is 2.15% (or (80% × 2.05%) + (20% × 2.55%)), and the difference between the corporate bond YTM and the 12-year interpolated government rate is 0.65%.

7. C is correct. The ASW is an estimate of the spread over MRR versus the bond's original coupon rate to maturity, which is equal to the difference between the corporate bond coupon of 3.00% and the 12-year swap rate of 2.15%, or 0.85%.

8. A is correct. The 20 bp increase in the 20-year government YTM causes the 12-year interpolated government YTM to rise 4 bps to 1.98% (or (80% × 1.85%) + (20% × 2.50%)). The corporate bond percentage price change can be estimated based on the YTM change multiplied by modified duration (–ModDur × ΔYield) familiar from earlier lessons. This percentage price change can be calculated as –0.4% (=–9.99 × 0.04%).

9. C is correct. The yield spread is the simple difference between a bond's all-in YTM and a current on-the-run government bond of similar maturity, while the G-spread is an interpolation of government benchmark yields. If the government bond yield curve is flat, these two measures will equal one another.

10. A is correct. Recall that ExcessSpread ≈ (Spread$_0$/Periods Per Year) − (EffSpreadDur × ΔSpread), so we combine the 6-month return with the spread duration–based price change estimate to get 3.775% (= (2.75% × 0.5) − (6 × −0.4%)).

11. B is correct. The instantaneous holding period return equals −EffSpreadDur × ΔSpread = −5 × 0.5% or −2.50%.

12. C is correct. Using Equation 10 (Spread0 − (EffSpreadDur × ΔSpread) − (POD × LGD)), the expected excess return on the bond is approximately 5.45% (=2.75% − (6 × −0.50%) − (0.75% × 40%)).

13. A is correct. The coverage ratio measures cash flow available to service debt, with a higher ratio indicating a lower probability of financial distress.

14. C is correct. Structural credit models use market-based variables to estimate an issuer's asset value and asset value volatility, defining the likelihood of default as the probability of the asset value falling below that of liabilities, with zero net assets defined as the default threshold.

15. B is correct. Recall that expected excess spread is defined as follows:

    E [ExcessSpread] ≈ Spread$_0$ − (EffSpreadDur × ΔSpread) − (POD × LGD)

    Because ΔSpread = 0, the expected excess spread is the simple difference between current OAS and expected loss, so E[ExcessSpread] is 0.90%, 1.00%, and 0.25% for the A-, BBB-, and B rated categories, respectively.

16. A is correct. E[ExcessSpread] from Question 15 is 0.90%, 1.00%, and 0.25% for the A-, BBB-, and B rated categories, respectively. The excess spread of the 50% A rated and 50% BBB rated portfolio is 0.95% (=(0.9% + 1.00%)/2) versus the equally weighted portfolio expected excess return of 0.7167% (=(0.90% + 1.00% + 0.25%)/3) for a positive active return of 0.233%, while B and C return less than the equally weighted benchmark.

17. A is correct. If spreads rise 10% across all ratings categories, we can use E [ExcessSpread] ≈ Spread$_0$ −(EffSpreadDur × ΔSpread) − (POD × LGD) to solve for expected excess spread as follows:

Rating Category	Current OAS	New OAS	Expected Loss (POD × LGD)	EffSpreadDur	E(Excess Spread)
A	1.00%	1.100%	0.10%	7	0.200%
BBB	1.75%	1.925%	0.75%	6	−0.050%
BB	2.75%	3.025%	2.50%	5	−1.125%

18. C is correct. Both A and B represent "long" risk positions that would increase rather than offset the benchmark yield and credit spread risk to the portfolio manager related to the illiquid bond.

19. C is correct. Parametric methods in A are not well suited for non-normally distributed returns or option-based portfolios, while historical simulation assumes no probability distribution and accommodates options.

20. C is correct. The incremental VaR measures how the additional portfolio position would change the overall portfolio's VaR measure.

21. A is correct. The expected change in yield based on a 99% confidence interval for the bond and a 1.50 bps yield volatility over 21 trading days equals 16 bps = (1.50

Solutions

bps × 2.33 standard deviations × √21). We can quantify the bond's market value change by multiplying the familiar (−ModDur × ΔYield) expression by bond price to get $1,234,105 = ($75 million × 1.040175 × (−9.887 × .0016)).

22. B is correct. For example, if the reference entity's credit spread trades at 1.50% versus a standard coupon rate of 1.00%, the CDS contract will be priced at a discount equal to the 0.50% difference multiplied by the effective CDS spread duration times the contract notional. Under A, the contract is priced at a premium to par because the protection buyer is receiving an "above market" periodic premium.

23. C is correct. Because the market premium is 0.75% above the 1.00% standard investment-grade CDS coupon, the protection buyer must pay the protection seller 6.5625% (= EffSpreadDur$_{CDS}$ × ΔSpread, or 8.75 × 0.75%) of the fixed notional amount upon contract initiation; the initial CDS price is therefore 93.4375 per 100 of notional with a CDS spread of 175 bps.

24. A is correct. The CDS spread decline of 0.15% leads to a new CDS contract price of 94.75 per 100 face value (=1 − (EffSpreadDur$_{CDS}$ × ΔSpread) or (8.75 × 0.60%)). The protection buyer (short risk) position therefore realizes an approximate mark-to-market loss of €131,250 (=(94.75 − 93.4375)/100 × €10,000,000) because of the 0.15% decline in CDS spreads.

25. B is correct. Selling protection on the CDX index is a "long" credit spread risk position, while purchasing protection on the CDX Financials subindex is a "short" credit spread risk position, leaving the investor with a long index position without exposure to financial reference entities in the CDX index. Both A and C increase exposure to financial sector issuers.

26. A is correct. The late expansion phase is typically associated with accelerating growth, peak profits, stable leverage, and a decline in defaults.

27. B is correct. Investors should exercise caution in interpreting credit spread curve shape for distressed debt issuers because their bonds tend to trade at a price close to the recovery rate. A is incorrect because the high-yield spread curve tends to invert during a contraction, while C is incorrect because a high-yield curve inversion is related to the relationship between near-term and long-term default as opposed to DTS.

28. C is correct. A credit curve roll-down strategy will generate positive return only under an upward-sloping credit spread curve. As for A, the benchmark yield changes must be separated from changes due to credit spreads, and under B, a synthetic credit roll-down strategy involves selling protection using a single-name CDS contract for a longer maturity.

29. C is correct. The investor benefits from a short risk (as protection buyer) on the 10-year CDX IG index and long risk (as protection seller) on the 5-year CDX IG index, duration matching the notional value by increasing 5-year notional 1.82 times (=8.9/4.9) versus the 10-year.

30. A is correct. Because an economic contraction is often associated with a sharp rise in shorter-term high-yield spreads and spread curve flattening in investment grade and inversion in high yield, the most appropriate choice is to take a short risk (purchase protection) in five-year high-yield spreads and a long position (sell protection) in five-year investment-grade spreads. Answers B and C position the investor to benefit from a steeper investment-grade and high-yield spread curve, respectively.

31. B is correct. Fixed exchange rate regimes in A usually result in greater instability and a higher probability of financial distress, while higher domestic currency YTMs in emerging economies in C are a sign of expected currency depreciation, not appreciation, over time.

32. A is correct. We solve for the excess spread by subtracting Expected Loss from the respective OAS:

Rating Category	OAS	EffSpreadDur	Expected Loss	E(Excess Spread)
USD IG	1.25%	4.5	0.40%	0.85%
USD HY	3.00%	5.5	2.25%	0.75%
EUR IG	1.15%	4.75	0.50%	0.65%
EUR HY	3.25%	6	2.50%	0.75%

Recall that the United States–based investor must convert the euro return to US dollars using $R_{DC} = (1 + R_{FC})(1 + R_{FX}) - 1$, so the USD IG and USD HY positions comprising half the portfolio return an average 0.80%, while the EUR IG and EUR HY positions return −1.314% in US dollar terms (= ((1 + ((0.65% + 0.75%)/2)) × 0.98) − 1), so −0.257% = ((0.80% − 1.314%)/2).

33. A is correct. Given that high-yield spreads are expected to fall the most in an economic recovery, the manager should choose the portfolio with the highest percentage of EUR HY credit exposure.

34. A is correct. Covered bonds perform relatively well in a downturn versus other fixed-income bonds with real estate exposure because the investor also has recourse to the issuer.

35. C is correct. Under a "flight to quality" scenario, macroeconomic factors driving government bond YTMs lower cause high-yield bond credit spreads to rise because of an increased likelihood of and expected higher severity of financial distress. This relationship is captured in the difference between empirical and analytical duration measures.

LEARNING MODULE 7

Trade Strategy and Execution

by Bernd Hanke, PhD, CFA, Robert Kissell, PhD, Connie Li, and Roberto Malamut.

Bernd Hanke, PhD, CFA, is at Global Systematic Investors LLP (United Kingdom). Robert Kissell, PhD, is at Molloy College and Kissell Research Group (USA). Connie Li (USA). Roberto Malamut (USA).

LEARNING OUTCOMES

Mastery	The candidate should be able to:
☐	discuss motivations to trade and how they relate to trading strategy
☐	discuss inputs to the selection of a trading strategy
☐	compare benchmarks for trade execution
☐	recommend and justify a trading strategy (given relevant facts)
☐	describe factors that typically determine the selection of a trading algorithm class
☐	contrast key characteristics of the following markets in relation to trade implementation: equity, fixed income, options and futures, OTC derivatives, and spot currency
☐	explain how trade costs are measured and determine the cost of a trade
☐	evaluate the execution of a trade
☐	evaluate a firm's trading procedures, including processes, disclosures, and record keeping with respect to good governance

INTRODUCTION

1

This reading discusses trading and execution from a portfolio manager's perspective. The reading covers a broad range of topics related to trade strategy selection and implementation and trade cost measurement and evaluation. Growth in electronic trading has led to increased automation in trading, including the use of algorithmic trading and machine learning to optimize trade strategy and execution. Various markets, including equities, fixed income, derivatives, and foreign exchange, are examined. Adequate trading processes and procedures are also discussed from a regulatory and governance perspective.

Portfolio managers need to work closely with traders to determine the most appropriate trading strategy given their motivation for trading, risk aversion, trade urgency, and other factors, such as order characteristics and market conditions. Trade execution should be well integrated with the portfolio management process, and although trading strategies will vary on the basis of market and security type, all trade activity should be evaluated for execution quality and to assess broker and trade venue performance consistent with the fund's objectives. Additionally, firms should have proper documentation of trade procedures in place to meet regulatory and governance standards.

This reading is organized as follows: Section 2 discusses portfolio manager motivations to trade. Sections 3–5 discuss inputs to trade strategy selection and the trade strategy selection process. Sections 6 and 7 cover the range of trade implementation choices and trading algorithms and provide a comparison of various markets. Sections 8 and 9 explain how trade costs are measured and how to evaluate trade execution. Section 10 provides guidance on evaluating a firm's trading procedures for good governance practices. The final section concludes and summarizes the reading.

2. MOTIVATIONS TO TRADE

☐ discuss motivations to trade and how they relate to trading strategy

Portfolio managers need to trade their portfolio holdings to ensure alignment with the fund's underlying investment strategy and objectives. The reasons for trading, or motivations to trade, and the extent of trading vary by investment strategy and circumstance. Even a passive buy-and-hold index portfolio requires some trading because of corporate actions, fund flows, or changes in the benchmark index. Portfolio managers for actively managed funds have additional reasons for trading based on their changing views for individual assets and market conditions. A portfolio manager's motivation to trade in addition to the fund's investment objectives play an important role in determining an overall trading approach.

Broadly speaking, a portfolio manager's motivation to trade falls into one of the following categories:

- Profit seeking
- Risk management/hedging needs
- Cash flow needs
- Corporate actions/index reconstitutions/margin calls

Profit Seeking

The primary added value that most active managers seek to provide is risk-adjusted outperformance relative to their benchmark. Superior returns originate from a manager having a unique insight that can be capitalized on ahead of the market. Trading in these cases is based on information portfolio managers have uncovered that they believe is not fully recognized by the market and, therefore, offers the potential to earn

Motivations to Trade

an excess return from the trade. Active managers will seek to transact in securities believed to be mispriced (under- or overvalued) at more favorable prices before the rest of the market recognizes the mispricing.

To prevent information leakage, or the disclosure of information about their trades, which might alert the market to the mispricing, active managers take steps to hide their trades from other market participants by executing in multiple or less transparent trade venues. *"Lit" markets* (a term referring to illumination), such as exchanges and other displayed venues, provide pre- and post-trade transparency regarding prices, volumes, market spreads, and depth. In contrast, alternative trading systems, such as dark pool trading venues, are available only to select clients and provide far less transparency, reporting only post-trade transactions and quantities. Because of these characteristics, orders in dark pool venues have a higher likelihood of going unfilled since clients receive executions only if an offsetting order arrives while their order is pending. For example, to prevent information about their trading activity from leaking to the market, a manager executing a large, directional trade may choose to execute the order in a less transparent venue.

As their investment views change with changing market and macroeconomic environments, portfolio managers will trade their holdings to align the portfolio with their views. Portfolio managers seeking longer-term profits may have relatively stable views from one period to the next whereas, in contrast, managers seeking shorter-term profits may have more rapidly changing views based on short-term movements in the market or individual securities that require higher turnover and trading.

To capitalize on investment views ahead of the market, trading the order faster, at an accelerated pace, may be needed. Portfolio managers may execute their orders at prices nearer to the market if they believe the information they have uncovered is likely to be realized by the rest of the market in the near term. **Trade urgency** refers to how quickly (aggressively) or slowly (patiently) the order is executed over the trading time horizon. Greater trade urgency is associated with executing over shorter execution horizons, whereas lower trade urgency is associated with executing over longer execution horizons.

A portfolio manager with a short-term event-driven strategy will trade with greater urgency if the expected alpha, or return payoff associated with the investment view over the trading horizon, is likely to be rapidly acted on by other market participants. In this case, the rate or level of expected alpha decay is high. In a trading context, **alpha decay** refers to the erosion or deterioration in short-term alpha once an investment decision is made. Portfolio managers following a longer-term strategy based on company fundamentals will trade more patiently, with less urgency, if the rate or level of expected alpha decay is lower.

Following are examples of short-term and long-term profit-motivated trading with differing levels of trade urgency.

Michigan Index of Consumer Sentiment (short-term profit seeking)

The University of Michigan Index of Consumer Sentiment (ICS) is one of the primary indicators of US consumer confidence. It is based on a nationwide survey of households. The ICS is closely watched by market participants, and changes in the index can prompt significant moves in the US equity market. Since 2007, Thomson Reuters, a financial data vendor, has held the exclusive right to disseminate the ICS. Until mid-2013, the firm had a two-tiered process for disseminating the ICS. A small number of trading clients received the ICS at 9:54:58, or two seconds earlier than the broader market release at 9:55:00. The two-tiered process was abolished in July 2013 after receiving negative public attention. Hu, Pan, and Wang (2017) examined how quickly the information contained in the ICS was incorporated into S&P 500 Index prices during the period of the two-tiered process.[1] They found that most of the price adjustment happened within the first 200 milliseconds. This is an example of profit-driven trading with high associated trade urgency and an extremely short-term execution horizon.

Value manager (long-term profit seeking)

An investment manager following a value strategy might attempt to identify undervalued companies on the basis of such metrics as earnings yields and price-to-book ratios. The manager might favor companies that score well according to these metrics. To capitalize on their views, individual positions may be held for months or years by value managers. Minimal trading is required, and any necessary trading can often be carried out in a more patient manner. Trading in this case has no trade urgency, given the managers' much longer trade execution horizons.

As more news and market information become available on a close-to-real-time basis, combined with the increase in electronic trading, markets have become more competitive. Information is being incorporated into security prices at even faster rates. Surprises in companies' earnings announcements, interest rate changes by central banks, and other macroeconomic announcements are being incorporated into security prices on a nearly instantaneous basis. Portfolio managers trying to act on this information must trade quickly and ahead of others to capitalize on the perceived opportunity. If more immediate execution cannot be achieved at a reasonable trading cost and risk, the trade may not be worthwhile given high rates of alpha decay. Therefore, these trades may be possible only in more liquid markets, such as equities, exchange-traded derivatives, foreign exchange, and fixed-income Treasury. In less liquid markets, such as non-Treasury fixed income or over-the-counter (OTC) markets where more immediate executions cannot be achieved, trades may not be worthwhile. For active managers seeking to maximize net returns to the portfolio, the expected rate of alpha decay of the security being traded is an important trading consideration.

Risk Management/Hedging Needs

As the market and the risk environment change, portfolios need to be traded or rebalanced to remain at targeted risk levels or risk exposures. Risk horizons and risk forecasts used by portfolio managers vary by investment strategy type and by investment time horizon. Fixed-income portfolio managers, for example, may have investment objectives to adhere to target portfolio durations. For these managers, portfolio rebalancing is usually required to match a benchmark duration target over time. Trading may be required because of a changing interest rate environment, a change in the benchmark index, or the passage of time. Equity portfolio managers may wish to manage their portfolio's beta or remain market neutral by hedging market risk and targeting a beta of zero relative to the equity market. To do this, the manager could trade to adjust holdings in the underlying portfolio or trade futures or exchange-traded funds (ETFs) to adjust the fund's equity beta to zero. Similarly, hedge fund managers may wish to maintain exposure to higher market volatility without having a view on directional price movement.

In general, the risks being managed, or hedged, in addition to such factors as security liquidity considerations and the fund's investment mandate, determine whether derivatives can be used or whether trades in the underlying portfolio (cash) securities are necessary. For example, an equity portfolio's beta to a broad equity market may be managed to the portfolio's target beta by trading equity index futures (e.g., S&P 500

---

1 Hu, G., J. Pan and J. Wang, 2017. "Early peek advantage? Efficient price discovery with tiered information disclosure". *Journal of Financial Economics* 126(2), 399–421.

futures, FTSE 100 Index futures, or Nikkei 225 futures). Using futures for hedging is often a simpler, more cost-effective approach because many futures contracts are liquid and can be traded at minimal cost. In addition, the standardization of futures contracts makes them attractive to investors. They can also be traded on margin, requiring relatively small amounts of capital. Similarly, for fixed-income strategies in the United States, interest rate risk can often be (at least partially) hedged using futures on Treasury securities, such as T-bond futures. Using liquid derivatives for risk management can provide an inexpensive and straightforward means of hedging versus trading in the underlying cash securities. In addition, the ability to trade derivatives or underlying securities may depend on the fund's investment mandate. In some cases, the fund's investment mandate may not allow the use of derivatives, and the portfolio manager must instead trade ETFs or the underlying to achieve the desired exposures.

For quantitative funds, targeted volatility is usually explicitly stated in the fund's offering documents whereas for fundamental funds, it may be an implicit assumption within the investment process. Regardless of fund type, portfolio managers should understand target risk levels and when changes in the market environment might require trading to adjust portfolio risk back to targeted volatility.

Portfolio managers may also trade to hedge risks when they do not have a view on the specific risk in question. For example, a global fixed-income long/short manager without strong currency views may choose to minimize currency exposure through a currency hedging trade. A fixed-income manager who wants to trade expected changes in the shape of the yield curve may not have a view on the level of the yield curve. In this case, the manager's yield curve trade would incorporate a hedge for duration risk. A manager of a high-yield bond portfolio may need to manage portfolio sector risk as well as geographical risk. Although credit default swaps (CDSs) might be used to manage this type of risk, finding a counterparty for a more specialized CDS can be difficult and costly. Because few derivatives to manage these risks exist, the underlying cash securities are generally traded. Using more illiquid securities for these risk trades generally increases the difficulty and cost of implementation.

A portfolio manager using option strategies may want to hedge the portfolio against certain risk factors: for example, the buyer of a long straddle position (a long position in a call and a put option on the same underlying security, both with the same strike price) who is implementing a view on higher expected volatility, irrespective of whether higher volatility will lead to higher or lower security prices. This is inherently an investment view on volatility that requires hedging directional price movement in the security.

The amount and nature of trading required for risk management generally depend on the risk profile of the portfolio as well as the amount of leverage used in the fund. Although various types of funds permit the use of leverage, leverage is typically used more by hedge funds that hold both long and short positions. For highly levered funds, risk must be monitored closely because the portfolios can quickly accumulate large losses with sudden increases in market risk. This strong risk sensitivity makes trading for risk management crucial.

Cash Flow Needs

A considerable amount of trading for portfolios is neither return seeking nor for risk management purposes but instead is driven by cash flow needs. Cash flow needs may involve high or low trade urgency depending on their nature. For example, collateral/margin calls could require close-to-immediate liquidation, whereas a fund redemption due to longer-term client asset allocation changes might not require immediate liquidation.

This type of trading is often client driven, arising from fund inflows (orders, mandates) and outflows (redemptions, liquidations). Fund inflows and outflows require capital to be invested or positions to be liquidated. To minimize cash drag on a portfolio, or fund underperformance from holding uninvested cash in a rising market, fund inflows may be equitized using futures or ETFs until the next portfolio rebalance or positions in the underlying can be traded. Equitization in this case refers to a strategy of temporarily investing cash using futures or ETFs to gain the desired equity exposure before investing in the underlying securities longer term. Equitization may be required if large inflows into a portfolio are hindered by lack of liquidity in the underlying securities. For example, a large inflow into a small-capitalization equity portfolio often cannot be invested immediately in the underlying stocks owing to limited market liquidity. Instead, the manager may equitize the cash using equity futures or ETFs and then gradually trade into the underlying positions and trade out of the futures/ETF position. For client redemptions, fund holdings may need to be liquidated if redemptions are larger than expected and cannot be funded by portfolio cash or offsetting fund inflows. Currency trades in which one currency needs to be exchanged (traded) into another may be required if fund inflows or outflows are not in the desired currency for receipt or payment. Many funds offer daily liquidity, which means investors can invest or redeem on a daily basis, often without limitation. Cash positions for these funds must be carefully managed in order to satisfy all fund flows and, at the same time, minimize the fund's cash drag. Trading is often required to manage the fund's cash position appropriately.

Hedge funds often have lockup periods in which fund redemptions are made according to a regular schedule, such as calendar quarter-ends. The stated objective is to protect remaining investors from incurring transaction charges resulting from other investors' redemption activity. These types of fund liquidations generally must be requested in advance to allow fund managers time to trade out of potentially illiquid positions and thereby minimize trading costs.

In most cases, client redemptions are based on the fund's net asset value (NAV), where NAV is calculated using the closing price of the listing market for listed securities. Clients receive proceeds based on the fund's NAV calculation. In these cases, trading at the closing price eliminates the risk (to the fund and the trader) associated with executing at prices different from those used to calculate the fund's NAV and resulting redemption proceeds.

Trading to raise or invest cash proceeds may not require specific securities to be traded to meet cash flow needs. Instead, these trades may involve strategically choosing from those securities considered optimal to trade from a risk–return or cost perspective. Trade size and security liquidity considerations play a determining role, and understanding trade-offs between costs, liquidity, and other factors is key. For example, selling a liquid security that generates a substantial tax liability is preferred over selling an illiquid security that has a smaller associated tax liability with substantially higher trading costs that overwhelm any savings in tax liability. Similar considerations apply to risk–return and liquidity trade-offs.

Corporate Actions/Index Reconstitutions/Margin Calls

Trading may also be necessitated by such activity as corporate actions and operational needs (e.g., dividend/coupon reinvestment, distributions, margin calls, and expiration of derivative contracts). The companies held in a manager's portfolio might be undergoing corporate actions, such as mergers, acquisitions, or spinoffs, that require trading. Cash equity dividends or bond coupons may need to be reinvested. For funds that make regular distributions, the timing of distributions may not align with the timing of dividends or coupons received on the individual securities. Therefore, raising proceeds for fund distributions may require individual holdings to be sold to meet distribution needs.

Cash needs can also arise from margin calls on leveraged positions as portfolio managers are asked to increase cash collateral on trades that have moved against them. Margin or collateral calls may drive high levels of trade urgency, given a need for the immediate sale of portfolio holdings. For example, the use of derivatives within a portfolio often requires collateral posting, which can necessitate a move to more liquid government bonds or cash in order to meet or fund collateral requirements.

Long-only managers may manage funds using a market-weighted index as a benchmark (e.g., the S&P 500, the MSCI World Index). If the benchmark constituents change, it could affect the manager's desired portfolio composition. If the manager runs an active portfolio, in the case of a change in index constituents, the manager might choose to sell holdings in a security that has been removed from the benchmark index.

For index tracking portfolios, such index changes as additions, deletions, and constituent weight changes are generally traded in the manager's portfolio to reflect benchmark exposure. Since the fund's NAV is calculated using the official market close for each security, trading index changes at the closing price ensures that the same price is used for fund and benchmark valuation (which also uses the closing price in its calculation) and thus minimizes the fund's tracking error to the benchmark index.

IN-TEXT QUESTION

The trading desk of a large firm receives three orders from the senior portfolio manager. Based on his research, the portfolio manager has identified two investment opportunities: a short-term stock buy and a longer-term stock sell. The third order is to raise proceeds to accommodate an end-of-day client withdrawal from the fund.

Discuss the motivation to trade and the associated trade urgency for each order:

- **a.** Short-term buy
- **b.** Longer-term sell
- **c.** Client withdrawal

Solution:

- **a.** This is a profit-seeking trade because the portfolio manager has identified the short-term buy as an investment opportunity. Short-term profit-seeking trades typically involve higher levels of trade urgency as managers attempt to realize short-term alpha before it dissipates (decays). These managers seek to transact before the rest of the market recognizes the mispricing and as a result are less price sensitive and more aggressive (seek to transact at accelerated rates) in their trading.

- **b.** This is a profit-seeking trade because the portfolio manager has identified the longer-term sell as an investment opportunity. Managers seeking long-term profits are typically more patient in trading and willing to wait for favorable prices by spreading executions over a longer time horizon, which may be days or weeks. Managers trading for long-term profits generally have much lower trade urgency for these orders.

c. This is a cash flow–driven trade arising from the need to raise proceeds for the client withdrawal. For funds that offer daily liquidity, clients can invest and redeem at the end of each trading day. In this case, managers raising proceeds for client withdrawals will generally target end-of-day closing prices to match trade prices to those used to calculate the fund's valuation and redemption proceeds to the client. Hedge funds that hold less liquid positions may allow redemptions only at quarter-end and with a relatively long notice period (e.g., one month), allowing them more time to sell illiquid positions. Client-driven redemptions usually involve much lower levels of trade urgency.

3. TRADING STRATEGIES AND STRATEGY SELECTION

discuss inputs to the selection of a trading strategy

Once a portfolio manager has made an investment decision, the portfolio manager and the trader must work together to identify the most appropriate trading strategy to meet the portfolio manager's trade objective given cost, risk, and other considerations. Selecting the appropriate trading strategy involves a number of important trade input considerations to ensure the strategy is transacted in the most efficient manner possible.

Trade Strategy Inputs

In addition to a portfolio manager's motivation to trade, other factors play a role in the selection of a trading strategy by affecting trade urgency, expected costs, and risks for the desired trade. Portfolio managers can manage the trading costs and execution risks they incur through their selection of an appropriate trading strategy.

Key inputs for trade strategy selection include

- order characteristics,
- security characteristics,
- market conditions, and
- individual risk aversion.

Order Characteristics

Order-related considerations include the following:

- **Side:** the side or trade direction of the order—for example, buy, sell, cover, or short
- **Size:** the total amount or quantity of the security being transacted
- **Relative size (% of ADV):** order size as a percentage of the security's average daily volume (ADV)

The side of the order, such as buy or sell, may be important when there is expected price momentum associated with trading the security or when trading a basket of securities where managing the risk of the entire trade list is required. If prices are rising, executing a buy order may take longer than executing a sell order, given the presence of more buyers (liquidity demanders) than sellers (liquidity suppliers) in the

Trading Strategies and Strategy Selection

market. Trading a list that consists of only buys or only sells will have greater market risk exposure than a list of buys and sells in which the securities have offsetting market risk exposures.

Order size is the amount or quantity of the security being traded. Larger order sizes create greater market impact in trading. Market impact is the adverse price movement in a security caused by trading an order and is one of the most significant costs in trading. Larger orders usually take longer to trade than smaller orders do, and portfolio managers will often trade larger orders in a more patient manner (lower trade urgency) to reduce market impact. All else equal, trading larger order sizes more quickly will increase market impact cost whereas trading smaller order sizes more slowly will decrease market impact cost.

To have a consistent order size measure across securities, portfolio managers often divide the order size by the security's ADV. For example, a 1 million share order in Stock ABC may be much different than a 1 million share order in Stock XYZ. If Stock ABC has an average daily volume of 50 million shares, the 1 million share order represents 2% (1 million/50 million) of ADV. If Stock XYZ has an average daily volume of 4 million shares, its order represents 25% (1 million/4 million) of ADV. The larger the size of the trade expressed as a percentage of ADV, the larger the expected market impact cost.

Security Characteristics

Security-related considerations include the following:

- **Security type:** the type of security being traded (underlying, ETF, American depositary receipt, global depositary receipt)
- **Short-term alpha:** the expected price movement in the security over the trading horizon
- **Price volatility:** the annualized price volatility of the security
- **Security liquidity:** the liquidity profile of the security (e.g., ADV, bid–ask spread, average trade size)

The security type distinguishes the instrument being traded and can include underlying securities, ETFs, American depositary receipts (ADRs), global depositary receipts (GDRs), derivative contracts, and foreign exchange currencies. Identifying the best means of exposure—for example, whether to trade a foreign security in its local market or trade its associated ADR (if US listed) or GDR (if non-US listed)—requires an evaluation of the trade-offs. Trading costs and liquidity will vary by local exchange. Gaining emerging market exposure, in particular, may be less expensive and operationally easier when trading available ADRs and GDRs than when trading the security in the local market. In addition, compliance, regulatory, and custody costs can be lower with ADRs and GDRs.

Short-term alpha in a trading context is the expected movement in security price over the trading horizon (independent of the trade's impact). Short-term alpha (also called *trading alpha* or *trade alpha*) may arise from an appreciation, a depreciation, or a reversion (i.e., reversal) in security price.

Alpha decay is the erosion in short-term alpha that takes place after the investment decision has been made. Alpha decay results from price movement in the direction of the investment forecast and occurs regardless of whether the trade takes place. Alpha decay is a function of the time required for a relevant piece of information (used by a portfolio manager to form her investment view) to be incorporated into a security's price. If this information is rapidly incorporated into the security's price, then its alpha is considered to decay quickly. High rates of alpha decay, or alpha loss, require faster, or more accelerated, trading to realize alpha before it is traded on by other market participants.

Depending on the expected rate of alpha decay, portfolio managers may be better off trading the order faster (higher trade urgency) or slower (lower trade urgency). In an adversely trending market—for example, buying in a rising market or selling in a falling market—portfolio managers may trade at an accelerated rate if less favorable prices are expected later in the trading horizon. In a favorably trending market—for example, buying in a falling market or selling in a rising market—portfolio managers are better off trading more slowly to execute at more favorable prices expected later in the trading horizon. Adverse price movements increase trading costs, whereas favorable price movements decrease trading costs.

The price volatility of a security primarily affects the execution risk of the trade. *Execution risk* is the risk of an adverse price movement occurring over the trading horizon owing to a change in the fundamental value of the security or because of trading-induced volatility. Execution risk is often proxied by price volatility. Securities with higher levels of price volatility have greater exposure to execution risk than securities with lower price volatility.

A security's liquidity profile affects how quickly the trade can be executed, in addition to expected trading cost, and is a significant consideration in determining trade strategy. All else being equal, greater liquidity reduces execution risk and trading costs, such as market impact. Bid–ask spreads indicate round-trip trading costs for trades of a given maximum size (as they are associated with a maximum quantity). As a result, bid–ask spreads indicate both trading costs and the amount of a security that can be traded at a given point in time (market depth), which affects how larger trades might need to be broken down into smaller orders for trading. Average trade sizes observed in past data provide additional information on quantities that can be traded at reasonable trading costs for a given security.

Market Conditions

Inputs relating to market conditions include the following:

- **Liquidity crises:** deviations from expected liquidity patterns due to periods of crisis

Market liquidity refers to the liquidity conditions in the market at the time the order is traded. At the time of trading, current or realized market conditions, such as traded volumes, price volatility, and bid–ask spreads, are additional factors that affect trade strategy selection, given that real-time market conditions are likely to be different from those anticipated and the conditions at the time the investment decision was made.

During market events or crises, the volatility and liquidity of the market and the security will be critical to consider as conditions result in sudden and significant deviations from normal trade patterns. Such seasonal considerations as local market holidays and quarter-end or year-end dates may have more predictability in their liquidity variations and are also important to consider.

Security liquidity will also change over time, often because of changes in market-wide liquidity. For example, in August 2007, stocks with high exposure to widely used quantitative factors became very hard to liquidate as many quantitative asset managers tried to reduce their exposures to certain factors around the same time. In the fall of 2008, during the credit crisis, short selling in certain stocks, mostly financials, was banned. During this time, many structured credit securities became "toxic assets" and became extremely difficult to liquidate.

Even during "normal" market environments, liquidity will vary. For example, over time certain companies reach market values that may result in them being added to or removed from widely used equity indexes. When this happens, their stocks' liquidity often improves or deteriorates as their shares become more widely or more narrowly held. Government bonds are generally liquid as long as they are the most recently issued (so-called on the run) among a particular bond type. However, once they become off-the-run bonds, their liquidity generally decreases.

Moreover, market volatility and liquidity are dynamic. They are also generally negatively related, which becomes apparent especially during periods of crisis, when volatility increases and liquidity decreases. For example, during the 1987 stock market crash, the Long-Term Capital Management crisis in 1998, and the global financial crisis in 2008, market volatility increased sharply and market liquidity collapsed. Portfolio managers can be hurt in such environments: Lower liquidity might suggest a longer trading horizon for order completion, but higher volatility might lead people to speed up their trades and incur higher costs. However, as trading horizon lengthens, market risk increases, particularly during periods of high volatility.

O'Hara and Zhou (2020) analyze liquidity provision during the COVID-19 corporate bond liquidity crisis. During the two weeks leading to Fed interventions, transaction costs increased strongly, dealers shifted from buying to selling, causing dealers' inventories to plummet. Liquidity provisions in electronic customer-to-customer trading increased, though at prohibitively high cost.

User-Based Considerations: Trading Cost Risk Aversion

In addition to order, security, and market considerations, the risk aversion of the individual(s) trading affects trade strategy selection.

Risk aversion is specific to each individual, and in a trading context, it refers to how much risk the portfolio manager or trader is willing to accept during trading. A portfolio manager or trader with a high level of risk aversion is likely to be more concerned about market risk and will tend to trade with greater trade urgency to avoid the greater market exposure associated with trading more patiently. A portfolio manager with a low level of risk aversion might be less concerned about market risk and may tend to trade more patiently (more passively), with lower levels of trade urgency.

Market Impact and Execution Risk

The temporary market impact cost of trading an order is the often short-lived impact on security price from trading to meet the need to buy or sell. For example, in situations where a portfolio manager is looking to buy shares but there are not enough sellers in the market to complete the order, the portfolio manager will need to increase his buying price to attract sellers to complete the order. In situations where a portfolio manager is looking to sell shares but there are not enough buyers in the market to complete the order, the portfolio manager will need to decrease his selling price to attract buyers to complete the order. In these situations, there is usually price reversion after the trade has been completed since the price change was driven by short-term buying or selling pressure rather than a fundamental change in security value. Therefore, post-trade prices should revert, with prices decreasing after buy order completion and increasing after sell order completion.

The permanent component of price change associated with trading an order is the market price impact caused by the information content of the trade. Trading in the market often conveys information to other market participants that the asset may be under- or overvalued. If market participants discover there are more buyers demanding liquidity than sellers supplying liquidity, the market interprets this situation as the pricing being relatively too low and prices will move in the direction of the trade imbalance on average. In this case, market participants will increase their selling price.

If market participants find out that there are more sellers than buyers, the market interprets this situation as the pricing being relatively too high and market participants will decrease their buying price. In other words, market participants may believe there is some information component of the trade that is causing the counterparty to buy or sell shares in the market that they have not yet discovered or incorporated into their own asset valuations. Therefore, market participants will adjust the price at which they are willing to buy or sell to reflect this potential new information.

To minimize information leakage, which may result in market participants adjusting the prices at which they are willing to buy or sell, portfolio managers may attempt to hide their trading activity by executing orders across different venues and using a mix of order types, such as market and limit orders. Market (marketable) orders instruct execution at the best available price at the time of trading, whereas limit orders instruct execution at the best available price as long as the price is equal to or better than the specified limit price—that is, a price equal to or lower than the limit price in the case of buys and equal to or higher in the case of sells. To hide their activity, portfolio managers will also trade less on displayed venues (e.g., exchanges with greater trade transparency regarding the intentions of market participants) and make greater use of dark pool venues.

Execution risk—the risk of adverse price movement during the trading horizon due to a change in the fundamental value of the security—arises as time passes and occurs even if the order is not traded. Trading faster (greater trade urgency) results in lower execution risk because the order is executed over a shorter period of time, which decreases the time the trade is exposed to price volatility and changing market conditions. Trading slower (lower trade urgency) results in higher execution risk because the order is executed over a longer period of time, which increases the time the trade is exposed to price volatility and changing market conditions.

Trader's dilemma.

To alleviate the market impact effect of entering a large order into the market, traders will "slice" the order into smaller pieces to trade over time. This results in a lower market price impact on the value of the asset, but in trading in smaller pieces over time, the fund is exposed to market risk, which could result in an even higher trading cost than if the order was entered into the market in its entirety. This phenomenon is known as the trader's dilemma and is stated as follows:

Trading too fast results in too much market impact, but trading too slow results in too much market risk.

The goal in selecting a trading strategy is to choose the best price–time trade-off given current market conditions and the unique characteristics of the order.

> **IN-TEXT QUESTION**
>
> Discuss how order size and security liquidity considerations affect market impact and execution risk for an order.
>
> **Solution:**
>
> Trading a large order creates greater market impact than trading a smaller order, all else being equal. To minimize market impact, large orders are often traded over longer trade time horizons, which increases the corresponding execution risk of the order. Smaller orders have less market impact and can be traded more quickly over shorter time horizons, with lower associated execution risk. The liquidity profile of a security has important implications for trading strategy. More liquid securities (higher traded volumes, tighter bid–ask spreads, etc.) have lower levels of market impact and execution risk given that they can be transacted over shorter time horizons with greater certainty of execution. Finally, higher

> rates of alpha decay would speed up order execution time horizons and increase market impact costs given greater trade order urgency, whereas lower rates of alpha decay would increase trade time horizons and associated execution risk.

REFERENCE PRICES

☐ compare benchmarks for trade execution

Reference prices, also referred to as *price benchmarks*, are specified prices, price-based calculations, or price targets used to select and execute a trade strategy. Reference prices are used in determining trade prices for execution strategy and in calculating actual trade costs for post-trade evaluation purposes. Following is a discussion of reference prices used in the selection and execution of a trade strategy.

Reference prices are categorized as follows:

- pre-trade benchmarks, where the reference price for the benchmark is known before trading begins;
- intraday benchmarks, where the reference price for the benchmark is computed on the basis of market prices that occur during the trading period;
- post-trade benchmarks, where the reference price for the benchmark is established after trading is completed; and
- price target benchmarks, where the reference price for the benchmark is specified as a price to meet or beat (transact more favorably).

Pre-Trade Benchmarks

A pre-trade benchmark is a reference price that is known before the start of trading. For example, pre-trade benchmarks include decision price, previous close, opening price, and arrival price. A pre-trade benchmark is often specified by portfolio managers who are buying or selling securities on the basis of decision prices (the price at the time the investment decision was made) or seeking short-term alpha by buying undervalued or selling overvalued securities in the market. Portfolio managers making trading decisions based on quantitative models or portfolio optimizers that use historical trading prices, such as the previous close, as model inputs may also specify a pre-trade benchmark.

Decision price

The **decision price** benchmark represents the security price at the time the portfolio manager made the decision to buy or sell the security. In many situations, portfolio managers have exact records of the price when they decided to buy or sell the security. Quantitative portfolio managers will often have records of their decision price because these prices may be inputs into their quantitative models.

There are times, however, when portfolio managers do not have a record of their decision price. In these situations, portfolio managers may decide to buy or sell securities on the basis of long-term growth prospects or higher-than-expected return potential and will specify the previous close or opening price as their reference price benchmark.

Previous close

The previous close benchmark refers to the security's closing price on the previous trading day. A previous close benchmark is often specified by quantitative portfolio managers who incorporate the previous close in a quantitative model, portfolio optimizer, or screening model. The previous close is often used as a proxy for the decision price by quantitative portfolio managers.

Opening price

An opening price benchmark references the security's opening price for the day. This benchmark price is most often specified by portfolio managers who begin trading at the market open and wish to minimize trading costs. The opening price is often used as a proxy for the decision price by fundamental portfolio managers who are investing in a security for long-term alpha or growth potential. Portfolio managers may choose an opening price instead of the decision price or previous close because, unlike a reference price from the prior day or earlier, the opening price does not have associated overnight risk, or the risk that prices will adjust at market open to incorporate information released after the close of the previous business day.

If the trade is to be executed in the opening auction, then using the opening price as a reference benchmark is not appropriate because the trade itself can influence the reference benchmark. An auction in this case is a market where buyers compete for order execution and orders are aggregated for execution at a single price and point in time. An auction taking place at market open is referred to as an opening auction, and one taking place at market close is a closing auction. The impact of trading any amount of the order in the opening (or closing) auction would be incorporated in the opening (or closing) price auction calculation, thus inappropriately influencing the reference benchmark level.

Arrival price

The **arrival price** is the price of the security at the time the order is entered into the market for execution. Portfolio managers who are buying or selling on the basis of alpha expectations or a current market mispricing will often specify an arrival price benchmark. In these cases, the portfolio manager's goal is to transact at or close to current market prices in order to complete trade execution and realize as much potential alpha as possible. Portfolio managers looking to minimize trading cost will also in many cases specify the arrival price as their benchmark.

Intraday Benchmarks

An intraday price benchmark is based on a price that occurs during the trading period. The most common intraday benchmarks used in trading are volume-weighted average price (VWAP) and time-weighted average price (TWAP).

Portfolio managers often specify an intraday benchmark for funds that are trading passively over the day, seeking liquidity, and for funds that may be rebalancing, executing a buy/sell trade list, and minimizing risk. Portfolio managers who do not expect the security to exhibit any short-term price momentum commonly select an intraday benchmark.

VWAP

The VWAP benchmark price is the volume-weighted average price of all trades executed over the day or the trading horizon. Portfolio managers may specify the VWAP benchmark when they wish to participate with volume patterns over the day.

Portfolio managers who are rebalancing their portfolios over the day and have both buy and sell orders may select the VWAP as a price benchmark. In these situations, the preference is to participate with market volume. Exposure to market risk is reduced in this case by having a two-sided trade list of buys and sells, as opposed to a trade list containing all buys or all sells. Portfolio managers who are rebalancing and using cash from sell orders to purchase buy orders will also often select an intraday benchmark, such as VWAP. Doing so allows the portfolio managers to structure their executions over time to ensure cash received from sell orders is sufficient to fund remaining buy orders. If trades are not executed properly, portfolio managers could be short cash for buy orders and need to raise additional money for order completion.

TWAP

The TWAP benchmark price is defined as an equal-weighted average price of all trades executed over the day or trading horizon. Unlike VWAP, TWAP price does not consider volume traded and is simply the average price of trades executed over the specified time horizon. Portfolio managers may choose TWAP when they wish to exclude potential trade outliers. Trade outliers may be caused by trading a large buy order at the day's low or a large sell order at the day's high. If market participants are not able to fully participate in these trades, then TWAP may be a more appropriate choice. The TWAP benchmark is used by portfolio managers and traders to evaluate fair and reasonable trading prices in market environments with high volume uncertainty and for securities that are subject to spikes in trading volume throughout the day.

Post-Trade Benchmarks

A post-trade benchmark is a reference price that is determined at the end of trading or sometime after trading has completed. The most common post-trade benchmark is closing price. Portfolio managers for funds valued at the closing price on the day or who wish to minimize tracking error to an underlying benchmark price, such as index funds, often select a post-trade reference price, such as the official closing price. In this case, the objective is to target consistency between the trade execution price and the price used in fund valuation and benchmark calculation.

Closing price

The closing price is typically used by index managers and mutual funds that wish to execute transactions at the closing price for the day. For managers with index mandates, where the fund's securities are typically valued using the official market close for each security, it is important to know how close their executions are to the benchmark price, which also uses the official market close in its calculation. A portfolio manager who is managing tracking error to a benchmark will generally select a closing price benchmark since the closing price is the price used to compute the fund's valuation and resulting tracking error to the benchmark.

An advantage of the closing price benchmark is that it provides portfolio managers with the price used for fund valuation and thus minimizes potential tracking error. A disadvantage is that the benchmark price is not known until after trading is completed. Thus, portfolio managers have no way of knowing whether they are performing more or less favorably relative to the benchmark until after trading is completed.

Price Target Benchmarks

Portfolio managers seeking short-term alpha may select an alternative benchmark known as a price target benchmark. In this case, a portfolio manager would like to transact in a security—believed to be undervalued or overvalued—at a more favorable price. For example, if a stock currently trading in the market at $20.00 is believed to be undervalued by $0.50, the portfolio manager will seek to purchase shares by specifying a price target of $20.50 or better (better being lower than $20.50 in the case of a buy). In this example, the benchmark price is specified as the perceived fair value price of $20.50. In this setting, the portfolio manager wishes to purchase as many order shares as possible at a price equal to or better (lower) than the specified price target.

5. TRADING STRATEGIES

recommend and justify a trading strategy (given relevant facts)

The primary goal of any trading strategy is to balance the expected costs and risks associated with trading the order in the market consistent with the portfolio manager's trading objectives, risk aversion, and other known constraints. A portfolio manager's motivation to trade, risk aversion, trade urgency for the order, and other factors, such as order size and market conditions at the time of trading, are thus key in determining an appropriate trade strategy.

Will the value in completing the trade dissipate if the trade is not completed in a timely enough manner? Trade urgency, the importance of execution certainty, is critical in determining trade strategy. For alpha-driven trades, trading with greater urgency to maximize short-term alpha capture must be weighed against the costs of trading faster and expected alpha decay. For trades with low or no trade urgency, trading over a longer trade horizon or at the market close may be optimal.

Portfolio managers also have expectations or insights regarding short-term market conditions, such as price trends and market liquidity, particularly if these factors are used in the security selection process. For example, does the stock exhibit momentum, where any observed trend will continue through the end of the day, or does the stock exhibit reversion, where the observed trend is more likely to reverse during the day? Portfolio managers may also have insights into expected trading volumes for assets and whether trading volumes may be expected to continue or may reverse in direction. Traders will also have insights regarding volume patterns and potential information leakage during execution. These expectations combined with actual market conditions at the time of trading help inform an appropriate trade strategy.

The selection of a trade strategy is best illustrated through a discussion of common trade types. Trading strategies for the following types of trades involving equities, fixed income, currency, and derivatives are explained in this section:

- **Short-term alpha:** short-term alpha-driven equity trade (high trade urgency)
- **Long-term alpha:** long-term alpha-driven fixed-income trade (low trade urgency)
- **Risk rebalance:** buy/sell basket trade to rebalance a fund's risk exposure
- **Cash flow driven:** client redemption trade to raise proceeds
- **Cash flow driven:** cash equitization (derivatives) trade to invest a new client mandate

Short-Term Alpha Trade

A portfolio manager has determined that the market has overreacted to weak earnings announced in the pre-market trading session for Stock XYZ. The stock price is trading at a significant discount in the pre-market relative to the portfolio manager's valuation and now represents a significant buying opportunity based on the portfolio manager's analysis. The portfolio manager would like to buy 50,000 shares, which represents 10% of the stock's average daily volume. Based on the heavy pre-market trading, however, the trader believes that this order will only constitute 2% of the day's volume.

The pre-market price is currently $50, down $15 relative to the previous night's close. The portfolio manager believes that the stock's fair value is in the low $60 range and sets her limit price at $60.

In this situation, the portfolio manager believes that the market has overreacted to the weak earnings announced by the company. If she is correct and the market eventually adopts her view going forward, Stock XYZ's price should increase closer to her estimated fair value in the low $60 range. In setting her limit price of $60, the portfolio manager is also specifying the reference price for the trade, which, in this case, represents a price target benchmark.

Given the possibility of short-term price increases in XYZ, this order has associated trade urgency and the trader does not have the benefit of trading the order passively (such as using a VWAP or TWAP participation strategy) during the day, since XYZ's price could increase to fair value at any time. To trade this order, the trader would not likely attempt to use dark pool venues, given their greater risk of unfilled executions if offsetting orders do not arrive. The trader will likely want to trade a portion of the order in the opening auction and then continue trading any residual in the open market. Doing so provides greater execution certainty, which is important in this situation given the trade urgency of the order.

Since the order represents approximately 2% of expected volume, the trader would not likely place the full order into the opening auction. Research shows the US opening auction typically makes up between 1-1.25% of a day's volume, so sending the entire order into the opening auction would result in the ordering being roughly 160%–200% of the expected opening auction volume, on average. Because this is an unusual trading day, the trader could use volume information from pre-market trading and any auction-related data made available by the exchanges to determine the optimal amount to place into the opening auction.

Given the trade urgency of the order, the very liquid market for XYZ, and the order size not being large relative to XYZ's expected volume, the trader could trade any remaining shares using an arrival price trade strategy that would attempt to execute the remaining shares close to market prices at the time the order was received. This strategy could be executed using a programmed strategy to electronically execute, also known as an algorithm, such as an arrival price algorithm. Most importantly, the trader will want to make sure that the orders sent to the auction and traded in the open market use limit prices consistent with the portfolio manager's price view, reflected in her limit price of $60.

Long-Term Alpha Trade

A portfolio manager believes that a company whose bonds he holds is likely to experience a deteriorating credit position over the next year. The deterioration in credit is expected to be gradual as information becomes available over the next several quarters, confirming the company's deteriorating financial position. The portfolio manager's position is not large in aggregate, but the market for these bonds is not very active, with infrequent transactions and low volumes. The portfolio manager approaches the trader to determine how best to liquidate his holdings in the bond so that he can exploit his view while still getting a favorable execution.

Because the market for these bonds is not very liquid, it is likely the trader will need to approach various dealers to get quotes for these bonds. Given the portfolio manager's view that the deterioration in credit will occur gradually over the coming year, there is no order urgency from a trading perspective. Because the position is not large, the trader believes he could execute it over the next day or two if needed.

The trader, however, may not want to execute this quickly for two reasons. First, the sudden trading in an illiquid security may inadvertently leak information, leading the dealer involved to think the order is an information-based trade and consequently to price the trade less favorably for the trader. Second, requiring dealers to take on substantial illiquid inventory exposes them to risk, for which they will demand compensation in the form of inferior (unfavorable) pricing.

Therefore, a reasonable trade approach would be to sell these bonds off gradually over the course of a few days or even weeks, depending on the relative size of the bond holdings and their liquidity. By selling off smaller portions, varying the amounts sold, and trading over a longer execution horizon, the trader can reduce information leakage regarding the order and avoid placing pressure on dealer inventories, which would result in inferior pricing. Using this approach, the dealers will likely provide better (more favorable) initial quotes, and subsequent quotes may also be more favorable if the dealers have enough time between trades to reduce their inventory.

The use of reference prices for fixed-income trades executed over multiple days is not widespread and can be difficult in practice. A decision price, for example, would not only capture market impact and alpha loss but would also reflect unrelated market moves, which can be much larger than the former when a trade is spread out over days or weeks. Impact costs, for example, would decrease as the trade horizon lengthens, whereas price volatility impact would increase with time.

Risk Rebalance Trade

A macro fund manager is concerned that potential trade tariffs and a deteriorating financial situation in a number of key emerging markets may lead to a significant increase in currency volatility. The manager is holding long and short developed market currency positions and has, so far, not seen a significant impact on his fund's valuation because the fund's long and short positions have been constructed to offset one another, immunizing the fund from sudden price moves. The fund's mandate, however, specifies a target risk level of 10%. With the increase in volatility, the fund's risk level is currently closer to 14%. Although the increase has not caused the portfolio to breach any guidelines, the portfolio manager believes that volatility will remain at current levels for the next several months and wishes to reduce risk in a controlled and gradual manner by liquidating positions to bring the fund's volatility back to its target risk level. The portfolio manager approaches a trader to discuss an appropriate strategy.

In this situation, the macro fund manager is holding long and short positions and has no view as to whether the fund's value will rise or fall in the near term owing to the sudden increase in volatility. Consequently, the hedge fund manager simply wishes to reduce current positions (as opposed to rebalancing the fund's relative positions). The holdings in developed market currencies are actively traded, and it is unlikely the positions are large enough that they would dislocate (substantially move) the currency markets, as long as trading is done in an appropriate manner.

Although volatility has significantly increased, the risk exposure of the trade is more limited if the list of buys and sells is balanced in market risk exposure, such as a buy/sell trade list with a net beta of approximately zero (i.e., the trade-weighted average beta of the securities traded is zero). Therefore, the trader does not have the

Trading Strategies

same trade urgency as a trade with a positive or negative net beta, such as one containing all buys or all sells, which might involve significantly more risk arising from exposure to potential market movement. Risk-averse market participants will typically have greater trade urgency for trades that have directional market exposure than for trades that are balanced, or hedged, in market exposure.

Since the portfolio is not in breach of its guidelines and the portfolio manager wishes to reduce risk on a controlled and gradual basis, the trader can trade this order in a passive manner to lower the fund's risk level. In this situation, using a TWAP reference price for the trade and a TWAP algorithm to execute over the next day or two (or longer, depending on the size of the position) would be an appropriate trading strategy. By trading all the orders over the same trading horizon using a TWAP strategy, the trader is maintaining the hedge that exists between the buys and sells, which helps reduce execution risk. And because currency markets in developed economies are very liquid and deep, trading algorithmically will not likely dislocate prices.

Client Redemption Trade

A client has decided to redeem its position in a small-cap/mid-cap value fund managed by ABC Investment Advisers. The fund holdings are US small- and mid-cap stocks, with the only constraints being that the stocks satisfy the criteria of the fund (e.g., stocks meet the definition of a small- or mid-cap stock, stocks are listed on a major exchange). Client redemptions from the fund are done at the fund's net asset value at the close of trading, where the NAV is calculated using the closing price of the stock's listing market. To raise the necessary cash to meet the client redemption request, the portfolio manager asks the trader to sell 0.1% of every position held in the fund.

In this scenario, the client will receive the NAV of the fund *regardless of how well or poorly the trader executes the trade*. Therefore, the trader bears risk (for executing at any price other than the closing price) unless she can guarantee that each position is executed at the closing price. A closing price reference price is, therefore, most appropriate for this trade. On various exchanges such as NASDAQ, the NYSE, the Tokyo Stock Exchange, Deutsche Börse (Xetra) and the Hong Kong Stock Exchange (HKEX), the trader can send the order to the closing auction for these exchanges and receive the auction-guaranteed closing price on all orders submitted to the auction. Such a strategy eliminates all potential risk of executing at prices that are different from those used to calculate the fund's NAV.

However, the trader should make sure that the size of the orders does not have an undue impact on the closing price. Executing a relatively large sell order in the closing auction (e.g., 50% of the closing volume) may lead to a significant price decline at the close, lowering calculated NAV and resulting in less cash being returned to the client.

Following a strategy to receive a guaranteed closing price on all orders submitted eliminates risk to the fund (and trader) since the client is receiving proceeds at NAV. From a fiduciary standpoint, however, trading in a manner that will lead to a poorer (less favorable) execution for a client is inappropriate. An alternative approach that portfolio managers follow when their trades are large relative to expected liquidity in the closing auction is to execute in the market and in the closing auction. For example, they would identify a reasonable amount to send to the closing auction (e.g., 90% of the order to be sent to the closing auction), trade the order remainder in the market prior to the close of trading (e.g., 10% of the order to be traded VWAP in the market up to the close of trading),[2] and then send the identified amount (90% of the order) to the closing auction.

---

[2] Some brokers provide special "close algorithms" that will size the closing auction trade appropriately, route the order into the closing auction, and trade any residual in the open market, effectively automating the strategy discussed in this example.

New Mandate Trade

An investment manager has just been awarded a €100 million mandate to track the MDAX Index benchmark with a 3% tracking error. The MDAX Index is a market capitalization weighted index comprised of 50 medium-sized companies in Germany that rank directly below the DAX index (the index comprising the largest 40 companies in Germany) by market capitalization and trading volume. The investment manager and the client have agreed that performance measurement of the mandate will begin at the current day's close. The appropriate reference price for the trade is, therefore, also the closing price. Given the large size of the investment mandate, the trader is concerned that trading into the positions at the close of trading will cause significant price impact. The trader would instead prefer to trade into the positions over multiple days. The client, however, requests that the mandate be fully invested as quickly as possible. The portfolio manager for the fund also prefers not to have the fund holding cash, given that the performance evaluation for the mandate begins as of the close of trading. Holding a cash position in the fund exposes the portfolio manager to significant performance risk relative to the fund's MDAX benchmark. For example, if the MDAX increases while the fund is holding cash, the fund's uninvested cash amounts would result in underperformance (arising from cash drag) relative to the MDAX.

The trader can get more immediate exposure to the MDAX by buying €100 million worth of MDAX futures traded on Eurex, a major European derivatives exchange. After establishing this initial exposure, the trader can begin building the underlying stock positions over time and unwinding (selling) the equivalent futures exposure. This approach allows the client mandate to achieve full €100 million exposure to the MDAX, eliminating the opportunity cost of holding cash balances in the fund. This approach also gives the trader additional time to establish the underlying positions, thereby receiving (hopefully) better execution prices. For smaller mandates in more liquid securities, the trader could possibly skip the equitization-via-futures step and instead invest directly in the underlying securities. For larger mandates, however, investing in the index via futures initially is often an effective means to equitize cash and reduce tracking error for the client mandate and fund.

Two considerations should be noted in this situation. First, futures markets may not have closing auctions. If no closing auction exists, the trader will likely want to time the trade as close to the benchmark close as possible; for example, in Germany, trading on Xetra closes at 5:30 p.m. For a small trade that is less than the quoted size, the trader could send a market order at 5:30 p.m. For larger trades or less liquid futures, the trader may trade using a VWAP or TWAP algorithm into the market close. Second, this futures-based strategy assumes the fund's investment mandate allows the use of derivatives. If the fund's mandate does not allow the use of derivatives, such as futures, but does permit ETF usage, the trader could equitize cash using a liquid MDAX ETF.

> **IN-TEXT QUESTION**
>
> A portfolio manager for a global fixed-income index fund is required to trade for quarterly index changes taking place at the end of the trading day. To keep the fund in line with the anticipated index constituent changes, the portfolio manager generates a fund rebalance list consisting of buys and sells. He approaches the senior trader to discuss the best trade strategy for the list.
>
> 1. Identify the most appropriate reference price benchmark for his trade.
> 2. Select and justify the most appropriate trading strategy to execute his trade.

Solution:

1. A closing price is the most appropriate reference price benchmark for an index fund. The portfolio manager needs to trade to maintain the same security holdings and weights as the benchmark index. Since the index fund will be valued using official closing prices, he should select the closing price as the reference price benchmark for trading the rebalance names. By executing the buys and sells at the close, he will be minimizing the fund's potential tracking error to the benchmark index.

   The previous close would not be an appropriate reference price benchmark since it would be the security's closing price on the previous trading day. A previous close benchmark is often used by quantitative portfolio managers whose models or optimizers incorporate the previous close as an input or who wish to use this price as a proxy for the decision price. The opening price benchmark would not be an appropriate benchmark because it references the security's opening price on the day and is often selected by portfolio managers and traders who wish to begin trading at the market open. The opening price may also be used as a proxy for the decision price.

2. A market-on-close (MOC) trade strategy would be the most appropriate strategy for his rebalance list. Trading the rebalance list at the market's closing prices best aligns the trade execution prices with the same closing prices used for the fund's NAV and benchmark calculation, thus minimizing tracking error of the fund to the benchmark index.

TRADE EXECUTION

☐ describe factors that typically determine the selection of a trading algorithm class

Once the appropriate trade strategy is determined by the portfolio manager and the trader, the trade must be executed in a market and in a manner consistent with the trade strategy chosen. A variety of implementation choices are available based on the specific order, market, and trade strategy involved. Trade implementation choices range from higher-touch approaches, which involve greater degrees of human interaction for order completion, to fully automated trade execution through electronic trading venues with varying levels of trade transparency. Higher-touch orders include principal and agency trades, the main difference being who assumes the risk of trading the order. In **principal trades**, the executing broker assumes all or part of the risk related to trading the order, pricing it into her quoted spread. In **agency trades**, the broker is engaged to find the other side of the trade but acts as an agent only, and risk for trading the order remains with the buy-side portfolio manager or trader. Electronic trading includes alternative or multilateral trading venues (ATS or MTF), direct market access (DMA), and dark pools.

Trade Implementation Choices

In general, trading in large blocks of securities requires a higher-touch approach involving greater human engagement and the need for a dealer or market maker to act as counterparty and principal to trade transactions.[3] For these transactions, also called *principal trades* or *broker risk trades*, market makers and dealers become a disclosed counterparty to their clients' orders and buy securities into or sell securities from their own inventory or book, assuming risk for the trade and absorbing temporary supply–demand imbalances. In the case of a less active security, the expected time to offset the trade for the dealer is longer. For taking on this additional risk, the dealer will demand greater compensation, generally by quoting a wider bid–ask spread.

Markets characterized by dealer-provided quotes may be referred to as *quote-driven, over-the-counter,* or *off-exchange markets*. In such bilateral dealer markets, customers trade at prices quoted by dealers. Depending on the instrument traded, dealers may work for commercial banks, investment banks, broker/dealers, or proprietary trading firms. Worldwide, most trading besides that in stocks, ETFs, and exchange-traded derivatives takes place in quote-driven markets, where the matching of buyers and sellers takes longer because of less frequent trading and greater market illiquidity.

In some cases, dealers may be unable or unwilling to hold the securities in their inventories and take on position (principal) risk. In agency trades, dealers try to arrange trades by acting as agents, or brokers, on behalf of the client. Brokers are often used for transactions in securities or markets in which finding a buyer or a seller is difficult.

High-touch approaches involve human sell-side traders as intermediaries. These traders, employed by sell-side brokerage firms, may first attempt to fill a customer order by matching it with offsetting orders from other customers before trying to fill it from their own position book. Crossing an order with a broker's own book is known as a broker risk trade or principal trade. If this does not occur, the broker would then route the order to the open market and "slice," or divide, the order into smaller pieces to trade in the market. This approach involves human judgment unique to each trade and is suited to trading illiquid securities in which the execution process is difficult to automate.

A variation of quote-driven markets often used to trade less liquid securities is a **request for quote** (RFQ). In RFQ markets, dealers or market makers do not provide quotes continuously but do so only upon request by a potential buyer or seller. These quotes are nonbinding and are valid only at the time they are provided.

For relatively liquid, standardized securities where continuous two-way trading may exist, buyers and sellers display prices and quantities at which they are willing to transact (limit orders) on an exchange or other multilateral trading venue. In order-driven markets, order-matching systems run by exchanges, brokers, and other alternative trading systems use rules to arrange trades. Trading is done electronically with multiple venues, often through a consolidated limit order book that presents a view of the limit buy (bid)/sell (ask) prices and order sizes for all venues with orders for a security. Centralized clearing for trades exists on those venues. Equities, futures, and exchange-traded options are generally traded using this approach.

Exhibit 1 shows the proportion of trading that was conducted electronically in 2012 and 2015. In most asset classes, electronic trading increased over the period to more than 50% of total trading volume. Markets with higher trading activity have seen strong growth in electronic trading. For example, cash equities and futures are now predominantly traded electronically, whereas some other (generally less liquid) markets, such as high-yield bonds, still feature trading with a high-touch, manual approach.

---

3 Large trades that exceed the normal trade size in a given security are often referred to as "block trades." Brokers offer dedicated services for block trades where human facilitation is higher than for regular trades, particularly for less liquid securities.

Trade Execution

Exhibit 1: Electronic Trading in Various Asset Classes (in %)

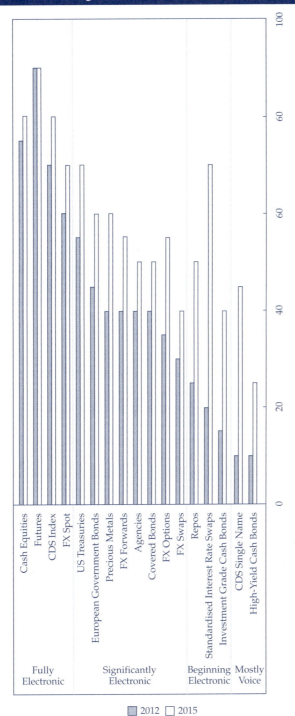

Source: Bank for International Settlements, "Electronic Trading in Fixed-Income Markets," Markets Committee Study Group (2016).

Automated execution approaches work well for liquid securities and most trade sizes other than extremely large orders (relative to the total volume traded of a particular security), which might require a more customized, high-touch approach. *Algorithmic trading*, or the use of programmed strategies to electronically trade orders, is well established in most equity, foreign exchange, and exchange-traded derivative markets. In fixed income, algorithmic execution is mostly limited to trading highly liquid government securities, such as US Treasury securities.

For liquid securities that trade in high volumes, high-touch execution approaches are generally inefficient, opaque, slow, and susceptible to front running. Front running occurs when speculative traders try to profit by buying ahead of other traders' anticipated activity. Front running is illegal in many jurisdictions if the information acted on is improperly obtained. Moreover, given that they require human involvement for each execution, they tend to be costly. Hence, for straightforward trades in liquid securities' low-touch automated execution strategies are often preferred whenever available. These generally involve direct market access (DMA) and/or execution algorithms.

Direct market access (DMA) gives all market participants a way to interact directly with the order book of an exchange, usually through a broker's exchange connectivity. This activity is normally restricted to broker/dealers and market-making firms. With DMA, buy-side firms use a broker's technology infrastructure and market access to execute orders themselves rather than handing orders over to the broker. DMA often involves the use of algorithms.

Alternatively, a broker can be instructed to execute client orders using certain execution algorithms. The desired urgency of an order is a key input for the choice and nature of the execution algorithm.

Algorithmic Trading

Algorithmic trading is the computerized execution of the investment decision following a specified set of trading instructions. An algorithm's programmed strategies used to electronically execute orders will slice larger orders into smaller pieces and trade over the day and across venues to reduce the price impact of the order. The primary goal of algorithmic trading is to ensure that the implementation of the investment decision is consistent with the investment objective of the fund. In this section, we describe factors that help determine the selection of a trading algorithm class.

Trading algorithms are primarily used for two purposes—trade execution and profit generation.

Execution algorithms

An execution algorithm is tasked with transacting an investment decision made by the portfolio manager. The manager determines what to buy or sell on the basis of his investment style and investment objective and then enters the order into the algorithm. The algorithm will then execute the order by following a set of rules specified by the portfolio manager.

Profit-seeking algorithms

A profit-seeking algorithm will determine what to buy and sell and then implement those decisions in the market as efficiently as possible. For example, these algorithms will use real-time price information and market data, such as volume and volatility, to determine what to buy or sell and will then implement the decision consistent with the investment objective. Profit-seeking algorithms are used by electronic market makers, quantitative funds, and high-frequency traders.

This section describes the common classification of execution algorithms and their use.

Execution Algorithm Classifications

Although there are many different types of execution algorithms, they can generally be classified into the following categories.

Scheduled (POV, VWAP, TWAP)

Scheduled algorithms send orders to the market following a schedule that is determined by historical volumes or specified time periods. Scheduled algorithms include *percentage of volume (POV)* algorithms, *volume-weighted average price* algorithms, and *time-weighted average price* algorithms.

POV algorithms (also known as participation algorithms) send orders following a volume participation schedule. As trading volume increases in the market, these algorithms will trade more shares, and as volume decreases, these algorithms will trade fewer shares. Investors specify the POV algorithm through the participation rate, which determines the volume participation strategy. For example, a participation rate of 10% indicates that the algorithm will participate with 10% of the market volume until the order is completed. In this case, for every 10,000 shares that trade in the market, the algorithm will execute 1,000 shares. An advantage of volume participation algorithms is that they will automatically take advantage of increased liquidity conditions by trading more shares when there is ample market liquidity and will not trade in times of illiquidity. While POV algorithms incorporate real-time volume, by following (or chasing) volumes, they may incur higher trading costs by continuing to buy as prices move higher and to sell as prices move lower. An additional disadvantage of these algorithms is that they may not complete the order within the time period specified.

VWAP and TWAP algorithms release orders to the market following a time-specified schedule, trading a predetermined number of shares within the specified time interval; for example, trade 5,000 shares between 10:00 a.m. and 1:00 p.m. An advantage of a time slicing strategy is that it ensures the specified number of shares are executed within the specified time period. A disadvantage of a time slicing strategy is that it will force the trades even in times of insufficient liquidity and will not take advantage of increased liquidity conditions when available.

VWAP algorithms slice the order into smaller amounts to send to the market following a time slicing schedule based on historical intraday volume profiles. These algorithms typically trade a higher percentage of the order at the open and close and a smaller percentage of the order during midday. Because of this, the VWAP curve is said to resemble a U-shaped curve. Following a fixed schedule as VWAP algorithms do may not be optimal for illiquid stocks because such algorithms may not complete the order in cases where volumes are low.

TWAP algorithms slice the order into smaller amounts to send to the market following an equal- weighted time schedule. TWAP algorithms will send the same number of shares and the same percentage of the order to be traded in each time period.

Scheduled algorithms are appropriate for orders in which portfolio managers or traders do not have expectations of adverse price movement during the trade horizon. These algorithms are also used by portfolio managers and traders who have greater risk tolerance for longer execution time periods and are more concerned with minimizing market impact. Scheduled algorithms are often appropriate when the order size is relatively small (e.g., no more than 5%–10% of expected volume), the security is relatively liquid, or the orders are part of a risk-balanced basket and trading all orders at a similar pace will maintain the risk balance.

Liquidity seeking

Liquidity-seeking algorithms, also referred to as *opportunistic algorithms*, take advantage of market liquidity across multiple venues by trading faster when liquidity exists at a favorable price. These algorithms may trade aggressively with offsetting orders when sufficient liquidity is posted on exchanges and alternative trading systems at prices the algorithms deem favorable (a practice called "liquidity sweeping" or "sweeping the book"). These algorithms may also use dark pools and trade large quantities of shares in dark venues when sufficient liquidity is present. If liquidity is not present in the market at favorable prices, these algorithms may trade only a small number of shares. These algorithms will often make greater use of market order types than limit order types.

Liquidity-seeking algorithms are appropriate for large orders that the portfolio manager or trader would like to execute quickly without having a substantial impact on the security price. Liquidity-seeking algorithms are also used when displaying sizable liquidity via limit orders could lead to unwanted information leakage and adverse security price movement. In these cases, the priority is to minimize information leakage associated with order execution and avoid signaling to the market the trading intentions of the portfolio manager or trader. These algorithms are also appropriate for trading securities that are relatively less liquid and thinly traded or when liquidity is episodic (e.g., the order book is typically thin with wide spreads but occasionally experiences tight spreads or thick books).

Arrival price

Arrival price algorithms seek to trade close to current market prices at the time the order is received for execution. Arrival price algorithms will trade more aggressively at the beginning of trading to execute more shares nearer to the arrival price, known as a front-loaded strategy. Arrival price algorithms tend to be time schedule based but can also be volume participation based.

Arrival price algorithms are used for orders in which the portfolio manager or trader believes prices are likely to move unfavorably during the trade horizon. In these cases, the portfolio manager wishes to trade more aggressively to capture alpha ahead of the unfavorable prices expected later in the trade horizon. These algorithms are also used by portfolio managers and traders who are risk averse and wish to trade more quickly to reduce the execution risk associated with trading more passively over longer time horizons. These algorithms are used when the security is relatively liquid or the order is not outsized (e.g., the order is less than 15% of expected volume) such that a participatory strategy is not expected to result in significant market impact from order execution.

Dark strategies/liquidity aggregators

Dark aggregator algorithms execute shares away from "lit" markets, such as exchanges and other displayed venues that provide pre- and post-trade transparency regarding prices, volumes, market spreads, and depth. Instead, these algorithms execute in opaque, or less transparent, trade venues, such as dark pools.

Dark aggregator algorithms are used in trading when portfolio managers and traders are concerned with information leakage that may occur from posting limit orders in lit venues with pre- and post-trade transparency. These algorithms are used when order size is large relative to the market (i.e., a large percentage of expected volume) and when trading in the open market using arrival price or VWAP strategies would lead to significant market impact. These algorithms are appropriate for trading securities that are relatively illiquid or have relatively wide bid–ask spreads. Since trading in dark pools offers less certainty of execution (offsetting orders may never arrive), these algorithms are appropriate for trades in which the trader or portfolio manager does not need to execute the order in its entirety.

Smart order routers

Smart order routers (SORs) determine how best to route an order given prevailing market conditions. The SOR will determine the destination with the highest probability of executing the limit order and the venue with the best market price—known in the United States as the National Best Bid and Offer (NBBO)—for market orders. The SOR continuously monitors real-time data from exchanges and venues and also assesses ongoing activity in dark pools.

SORs are used when a portfolio manager or trader wishes to execute a small order by routing the order into the market as either a market(able) or non-marketable (limit) order.

Market orders.
SORs are used for orders that are sufficiently small that they will not have a large market impact if sent as marketable orders—for example, when the order size is less than the quantity posted at the best bid or offer. SORs are also best used for orders that require immediate execution because of imminent price movement, high portfolio manager or trader risk aversion, or abnormally high risk levels. Using SORs for marketable orders is also appropriate in cases where the market moves quickly, such that having the trader choose the venue(s) could lead to inferior executions (e.g., the trader chooses the venue but the venue with the best price changes before she can send the order).

Limit orders.
SORs are also used for orders that are small enough that posting the order as a limit order will not leak information to the market and move prices (e.g., orders that are similar to those currently posted in the market). In addition, SORs are appropriate for stocks that have multiple markets actively trading the stock and for which it is not obvious to which venues the order should be routed (e.g., there are multiple venues currently posting orders at the trader's limit price).

> **IN-TEXT QUESTION**
>
> A portfolio manager has identified a stock with attractive long-term growth potential and would like to place an order of moderate size, relative to the stock's average traded volume. The stock is very liquid and has attractive short-term alpha potential. The portfolio manager expects short-term buying pressure by other market participants into the market close, ahead of the company's earnings call scheduled later in the day.
>
> 1. Explain when the following algorithms are used: (a) arrival price, (b) dark aggregator, and (c) SOR.
> 2. Discuss which of the three algorithms is most suited to trading this order.
>
> **Solution:**
>
> 1.
>   a. Arrival price algorithms are used for relatively liquid securities and when the order is not expected to have a significant market impact. Arrival price algorithms are also used when portfolio managers and traders have higher levels of risk aversion and wish to trade more aggressively at an accelerated pace to reduce the execution risk associated with trading over longer time horizons.
>   b. Dark aggregator algorithms are appropriate for trading securities that are relatively illiquid or that have relatively wide bid–ask spreads or for relatively large order sizes in which trading in the open market is expected to have a significant price impact. Additionally, they are used by portfolio managers and traders who are concerned with information leakage that may occur when

posting limit orders in lit venues. Given their higher risk of unfilled executions, these algorithms are also used when the order does not need to be filled in its entirety.

c. Smart order routing systems are used to electronically send small orders into the market. Based on prevailing market conditions, SORs will determine which trade destinations have the highest probability of executing for limit orders and which trading venues have the best market prices for market orders and will route orders accordingly. SORs continuously monitor market conditions in real time in both lit and dark markets.

2. An arrival price algorithm would be most appropriate for trading this order because the portfolio manager has adverse price expectations. In this case, the portfolio manager wants to trade more aggressively to capture alpha ahead of less favorable prices expected later in the day. By trading the order more quickly, the portfolio manager can execute at more favorable prices ahead of the adverse price movement and the less favorable prices expected from other participants' buying pressure into the close, in line with his trade urgency.

Algorithmic Selection

Choosing the best algorithm to execute a given trade can be a difficult and complex decision. There has been a proliferation of choices for the buy-side trader, with multiple broker offerings and multiple algorithm types per broker, such as VWAP, POV, and implementation shortfall. For a given stock, what is the best algorithm to choose? Intuitively, it seems that selecting an algorithm by considering specific characteristics about the stock and its liquidity profile should be superior to selecting an algorithm without regard for these attributes. Additionally, it seems intuitive that stocks with similar characteristics might best be executed in a similar manner. This rationale has motivated firms that provide execution services to apply a machine learning technique called "clustering" to the problem of algorithmic strategy selection.

Clustering, generally used in unsupervised machine learning, groups data objects solely on the basis of information found in the data. The use of clustering for algorithmic strategy selection for stocks will generally include microstructure factors, such as bid–ask spread, trade size, price volatility, tick size, depth of the order book queue, and trading volume. Stocks are characterized from the results of the data analysis (i.e., placed into groups, or clusters, based on similarities informed by the data). For each cluster, the historical executions for each stock are examined for comparative performance. From this analysis, the optimal algorithmic strategy can be selected.

To illustrate a simple intuitive example, stocks with wider bid–ask spreads may be more effectively traded using an algorithm that executes more in off-exchange venues (such as dark pools) since on those venues trading can occur at mid-market if an offsetting order arrives and the cost of crossing the bid–ask spread (buying at the offer or selling at the bid) is high. In contrast, for a cluster of stocks with tight bid–ask spreads, the benefit of trading at mid-market is smaller and the optimal algorithm is likely to trade less on off-exchange/dark venues.

In some cases, the optimal decision may be clear from the data because the performance of one algorithm dominates all other choices. In other cases, even if the optimal choice is unclear, the historical execution data of the given cluster help narrow the research space and form the basis for further optimization using either traditional regression-based or machine learning techniques. Although our example is quite simple and the rationale intuitive, one might ask, if the answer is that obvious, why bother with machine learning at all? In practice, the answers are usually much less obvious and the conditions far more complicated.

High-Frequency Market Forecasting

One of the primary challenges in trading (and investing) is forecasting asset prices. Even for a long-term investor, the ability to forecast short-term market direction can help make execution more efficient.

Building a model to forecast short-term market movements involves two steps: The first is to identify key factors, or predictors (independent variables in a regression context), and the second is to estimate the model. One might identify many (hundreds, if not more) potential predictors; for example, for a period of time, one stock—perhaps for which there has been a significant news release—may "lead" the rest of the market and be a good predictor of short-term movement in other stocks.

LASSO (least absolute shrinkage and selection operator) is a machine learning technique used to help with this identification problem. LASSO is a penalized regression technique that relies on the underlying assumption of sparsity, meaning that at any point in time, even in the presence of many potential predictors, only a handful of variables are significant. LASSO minimizes the residual sum of squares, which has the effect of reducing many of the coefficients to zero, leaving only the most significant variables.

For example, consider a trader building a forecast model to predict the near-term value of the S&P 500 ETF (SPY). There are a multitude of variables that she might want to consider, including the order book imbalance (excess of buys or sells for a given price) on each exchange, SPY trade executions, SPY returns over a number of recent time horizons, and similar attributes for correlated instruments, such as other ETFs, equity index futures contracts, and stocks making up the underlying portfolio of the ETF. It is clear that there are hundreds of potential variables. Working with a regression model to identify the most important variables would likely be unwieldy and challenging, given potential collinearity. Using LASSO, the trader can reduce the problem to a more manageable number of variables.

COMPARISON OF MARKETS

7

☐ contrast key characteristics of the following markets in relation to trade implementation: equity, fixed income, options and futures, OTC derivatives, and spot currency

Although algorithmic trading is common in highly liquid, technologically developed markets, such as equities, trades in other markets require different implementation treatment, with greater human involvement. In this section, we compare and contrast key characteristics relating to trade implementation for the following markets:

- Equities
- Fixed income

- Exchange-traded derivatives (options and futures)
- Off-exchange (OTC) derivatives
- Spot currencies

Equities

Equities are generally traded on exchanges and dark pools. Exchanges are known as lit markets (as opposed to dark markets) because they provide pre-trade transparency—namely, limit orders that reflect trader intentions for trade side (buy or sell), price, and size. Dark pools provide anonymity because no pre-trade transparency exists. However, regardless of the trading venue, transactions and quantities are always reported. On exchanges, trade price, size, quote, and depth of book data are publicly available. However, detailed book data can be costly and may be available only to some market participants.

Most countries with open economies have at least one stock exchange. The United States has a total of 13 stock exchanges. There are more than 50 **alternative trading systems** (ATS)/dark pools globally. In Europe, these alternative trading venues are called **multilateral trading facilities** (MTF) and *systematic internalisers (SI)*. MTFs are operated by investment firms or market operators that bring together multiple third-party buying and selling interests in financial instruments. SIs are single-dealer liquidity pools. In the United States and Canada, these venues are called alternative trading systems (ATS). They are non-exchange trading venues that match buyers and sellers to find counterparties for transactions. They are typically regulated as broker/dealers rather than as exchanges (although an ATS can apply to be regulated as a securities exchange). In the United States, ATS must be approved by the Securities and Exchange Commission (SEC).

In Asia, although trading volume on alternative trading venues has grown rapidly over the last few years, such activity remains less common than in North America and Europe. Even in markets with the highest share of dark pool trading, most equity trading still takes place on traditional exchanges. In emerging markets, dark pool trading volume is minimal compared with trading volume on traditional exchanges.

Equities are the most technologically advanced market. Algorithmic trading is common, and most trades are electronic. Equity exchanges may use different trading systems for stocks depending on their level of liquidity. Large, urgent trades, particularly in less liquid small-cap stocks, are generally executed as high-touch broker risk trades, where the broker acts as dealer and counterparty. Large, non-urgent trades may be executed using trading algorithms (particularly for more liquid large-cap stocks) or, for less liquid securities, a high-touch agency approach. For small trades in liquid securities, most buy-side traders use electronic trading.

In recent years, average trade sizes have generally decreased for most asset classes; market participants break down their trades into smaller pieces that they trade either sequentially on the same trading venue or simultaneously across different venues. In equities, growth in the number of trading venues has resulted in fragmentation of trading and increased competition among trading venues.

Fixed Income

Fixed-income markets are quite different from equity markets. Market transparency and price discovery for fixed-income markets are generally much lower; information available and how quickly it is made available vary by market. Individual bond issuers can have a large number of bonds outstanding with very different features—for example, different maturities, coupons, and optionality. As a result, fixed income is a very heterogeneous asset class that encompasses a large number of individual securities. Institutional investors will often hold bonds until maturity or may trade large quantities infrequently. Trade imbalances often occur in corporate bonds owing to illiquidity. As a result, sourcing market liquidity relies heavily on dealers acting as counterparties (i.e., principal trades), and matching buyers and sellers is generally difficult in the corporate bond market.

Fixed-income securities are generally traded in a bilateral, dealer-centric market structure.[4] Investors will generally get quotes from dealers, often banks, which make markets in the securities. Historically, these quotes were accessed via phone, but they increasingly are disseminated using electronic chat (e.g., Symphony, Bloomberg) or electronic RFQ platforms. Just as it was before the onset of these electronic platforms, dealers do not provide quotes continuously; they provide them only on request by a potential buyer or seller.

There is limited algorithmic trading in bond markets, except for on-the-run (most recently issued) US Treasuries in benchmark maturities and bond and interest rate futures contracts. Although algorithmic/electronic trading in corporate bonds is growing, it remains a relatively low proportion of overall corporate bond trading.[5] The combination of market illiquidity and the large size and low frequency of potential trades creates challenges for algorithmic trading and electronic trading generally. For other fixed-income instruments, high-touch trading persists, particularly for larger trades and less liquid securities. Small trades and large, urgent trades are usually implemented through broker risk trades (via RFQs), where the broker acts as the counterparty, because securities are hard to source otherwise. Large, non-urgent trades are generally implemented using a high-touch approach, with brokers acting as agents to source liquidity (agency trades instead of principal trades).

Exchange-Traded Derivatives

As of 2021, there were fewer than 1,000 liquid and highly standardized exchange-traded derivatives outstanding. The market is very large, and trading volume exceeds several trillion dollars per day according to Bank for International Settlements (BIS) data. Most of the trading volume is concentrated in futures, although the number of futures is considerably smaller than the number of options outstanding. Similar to exchange-traded equities, market transparency is high and trade price, size, quote, and depth of book data are publicly available.

Electronic trading is widespread for exchange-traded derivatives; however, algorithmic trading is not as evolved as in equity markets and is currently used more for trading in futures than in options. Large, urgent trades "sweep the book" where market depth is relatively good. In these cases, trades are executed against the most aggressive limit orders on the other trade side first and then against decreasingly aggressive limit orders until the entire order has been filled. Large, non-urgent trades are generally implemented electronically through trading algorithms. Buy-side traders generally use direct market access, particularly for small trades.

Over-the-Counter Derivatives

In recent years, regulators have been placing pressure on OTC markets to introduce central clearing facilities and to display trades publicly. Although liquidity has increased for more standardized OTC trades that are centrally cleared, liquidity has decreased for OTC instruments not suited to central clearing or trade reporting.

---

4 Some fixed-income securities trade on exchanges (e.g., the NYSE, the London Stock Exchange, and some Italian exchanges list corporate bonds). However, the volume traded on centralized exchanges is small.
5 As of 2018, Greenwich Associates has estimated that as of 2018, a fifth of all investment-grade US corporate bond trades are now traded electronically—almost double the volume of a decade ago.

OTC derivative markets have historically been opaque, with little public data about prices, trade sizes, and structure details. Regulatory efforts have focused on increasing transparency and reducing counterparty risk in these markets. In the United States, the Dodd–Frank Wall Street Reform and Consumer Protection Act, enacted in 2010, significantly increased post-trade transparency in the OTC derivative markets with the establishment of swap data repositories (SDRs) to which trade details must be submitted. Under the Dodd–Frank regulation, swaps entered into by parties exempt from mandatory clearing and exchange trading (and where at least one counterparty to the swap is a US person) are still subject to data reporting rules. Dodd–Frank forms part of a broader 2009 agreement by the G–20 countries whose primary long-term focus includes the trading of all OTC derivatives on exchanges or other electronic platforms with centralized clearing for all more standardized derivatives.

Trading OTC derivatives takes place through dealers. Because this type of security is typically traded by institutions, trade sizes are relatively large. Large, urgent trades are generally implemented as broker risk trades, where risk is transferred to a broker who takes the contract into his inventory. Large, non-urgent trades are generally implemented using a high-touch agency trade, where the broker attempts to match buyers and sellers directly. Doing so can be difficult, however, since OTC derivatives are often highly customized. Hence, at times, a strong price concession is required to find a buyer or seller. According to the Bank for International Settlements (BIS) the gross market value of OTC derivatives was over $15 trillion in 2020.

Spot Foreign Exchange (Currency)

There is no exchange or centralized clearing place for the majority of spot foreign exchange (currency) trades. Spot currency markets consist of a number of electronic venues and broker markets. The currency market is an entirely OTC market. Despite being a global market, there is almost no cross-border regulation.

The spot currency market consists of multiple levels. The top level is called the interbank market, where participants are mostly large international banks and other financial firms that act as dealers. Trades between these foreign exchange dealers can be extremely large. The next market level is generally made up of small and medium-sized banks and other financial institutions that turn to the dealers in the interbank market for their currency trading needs and that, therefore, pay slightly higher bid–ask spreads. The level below that one consists of commercial companies and retail traders that turn to the second-level institutions for their currency trading. Once again, a higher bid–ask spread applies to these market participants.

The spot currency market is sizable in terms of daily trading volume, with often more than $1 trillion traded per day. Although large, the spot currency market is relatively opaque; there are usually only quotes available and only from some venues.

Electronic trading in currencies has grown substantially over the years in parallel with algorithmic trading strategies of equities. For large, urgent trades, RFQs are generally submitted to multiple dealers competing for a trade. Large, non-urgent trades are mostly executed using algorithms (such as TWAP) or a high-touch agency approach. Small trades are usually implemented using DMA.

> **IN-TEXT QUESTION**
>
> A hedge fund manager has three trades that she would like to execute for her fund. The orders are for:
>
> 1. a large, non-urgent sell of OTC options,
> 2. a large, urgent sell of corporate bonds, and
> 3. a small, non-urgent buy of six liquid emerging market currencies.

Describe factors affecting trade implementation for each trade.

Solution:

1. A large, non-urgent sell of OTC options would generally involve a broker agency trade in which the broker would act on behalf of the manager to find a matching buyer for the options. Depending on the level of contract customization, however, a significant price concession may be required by the manager to complete order execution.

2. A large, urgent sell of corporate bonds would usually involve a broker risk trade via the RFQ process. Because of corporate bond illiquidity, the likelihood of finding a matching buyer is low. For more immediate (urgent) order execution, a broker would be needed to act as counterparty to the trade, taking the bonds and their associated risk into his inventory.

3. Small, non-urgent trades in foreign exchange are generally executed using direct market access. DMA allows the buy-side trader to electronically route orders using the broker's technology infrastructure and market access and typically involves algorithmic trading.

TRADE COST MEASUREMENT

☐ explain how trade costs are measured and determine the cost of a trade

After trade implementation is complete, it is important for portfolio managers and traders to assess the trading that has taken place. Was the trade implemented in a manner consistent with the trade strategy chosen? What costs were incurred from trading the order, where did costs arise, and were these reasonable given market conditions? How well did the trader, broker, or algorithm selected for trade execution perform?

Unfortunately for the portfolio manager, trade implementation is not a frictionless transaction. In economic terms, trade costs are value paid by buyers but not received by sellers and value paid by sellers but not received by buyers. In finance, trade costs represent the amount paid above the investment decision price for buy orders and the discount below the decision price for sell orders. An important aspect of trade cost measurement is to identify where costs arise during implementation of the investment decision. Understanding where these costs arise will help portfolio managers carry out proper trade cost management, more efficient implementation, and better portfolio construction. This ultimately leads to lower trading costs and higher portfolio returns.

Proper trade cost management begins with an understanding of the implementation shortfall formulation.

Implementation Shortfall

The **implementation shortfall** (IS) metric[6] is the most important *ex post* trade cost measurement used in finance. The IS metric provides portfolio managers with the total cost associated with implementing the investment decision. This spans the time the investment decision is made by the portfolio manager up to the completion of the trade by the trader. IS also allows portfolio managers to identify where costs arise during the implementation of the trade.

IS is calculated as the difference between the return for a notional or paper portfolio, where all transactions are assumed to take place at the manager's decision price, and the portfolio's actual return, which reflects realized transactions, including all fees and costs.

Mathematically, IS is calculated as follows:

IS = Paper return − Actual return

The paper return shows the hypothetical return that the fund would have received if the manager were able to transact all shares at the desired decision price and without any associated costs or fees (i.e., with no friction):

Paper return = $(P_n - P_d)(S) = (S)(P_n) - (S)(P_d)$

Here, S represents the total order shares, $S > 0$ indicates a buy order, $S < 0$ indicates a sell order, P_d represents the price at the time of the investment decision, and P_n represents the current price.

The actual portfolio return is calculated as the difference between the current market price and actual transaction prices minus all fees (e.g., commissions):

Actual return = $\left(\sum s_j\right)(P_n) - \sum s_j p_j$ − Fees

Here, s_j and p_j represent the number of shares executed and the transaction price of the jth trade, respectively, $\left(\sum s_j\right)$ represents the total number of shares of the order that were executed in the market, and "Fees" includes all costs paid by the fund to complete the order.

This IS formulation decomposes the total cost of the trade into three categories: execution cost, opportunity cost, and fixed fees. **Execution cost** corresponds to the shares that were transacted in the market. Execution cost occurs from the buying and/or selling pressure of the order, which often causes buy orders to become more expensive and sell orders to decrease in value, thus causing the fund to incur higher costs and lower realized returns. Execution cost will also occur owing to price drift over the trading period. For example, buying stocks that are increasing in value over the trading period and selling stocks that are decreasing in value over the trading period.

It is important to note that since there is no guarantee that the portfolio manager will be able to execute the entire order, the number of shares transacted in the market may be less than the original order size—that is, $\sum s_j \leq S$ for a buy order and $\sum s_j \geq S$ for a sell order. **Opportunity cost** corresponds to the unexecuted shares of the order. It is the cost associated with not being able to transact the entire order at the manager's decision price and is due to adverse price movement over the trading period. Opportunity cost may also arise in times of insufficient market liquidity, when the fund is not able to find counterparties to complete the trade. The opportunity cost component provides managers with insight into missed profit opportunity for their investment idea.

The *fixed fees* component includes all explicit fees, such as commissions, exchange fees, and taxes.

---

6 A.F. Perold, "The Implementation Shortfall: Paper versus Reality," *Journal of Portfolio Management* 14 (Spring 1988): 4–9.

Trade Cost Measurement

The IS formulation decomposing costs into these categories is calculated as follows:

$$IS = \underbrace{\sum s_j p_j - \sum s_j p_d}_{\text{Execution cost}} + \underbrace{(S - \sum s_j)(P_n - P_d)}_{\text{Opportunity cost}} + \text{Fees}$$

Consider the following facts:

On Monday, the shares of Impulse Robotics close at £10.00 per share.

On Tuesday, before trading begins, a portfolio manager decides to buy Impulse Robotics. An order goes to the trading desk to buy 1,000 shares of Impulse Robotics at £9.98 per share or better, good for one day. The benchmark price is Monday's close at £10.00 per share. No part of the limit order is filled on Tuesday, and the order expires. The closing price on Tuesday rises to £10.05.

On Wednesday, the trading desk again tries to buy Impulse Robotics by entering a new limit order to buy 1,000 shares at £10.07 per share or better, good for one day. During the day, 700 shares are bought at £10.07 per share. Commissions and fees for this trade are £14. Shares for Impulse Robotics close at £10.08 per share on Wednesday.

No further attempt to buy Impulse Robotics is made, and the remaining 300 shares of the 1,000 shares the portfolio manager initially specified are canceled.

The paper portfolio traded 1,000 shares on Tuesday at £10.00 per share. The return on this portfolio when the order is canceled after the close on Wednesday is the value of the 1,000 shares, now worth £10,080, less the cost of £10,000, for a net gain of £80.

The real portfolio contains 700 shares (now worth 700 × £10.08 = £7,056), and the cost of this portfolio is 700 × £10.07 = £7,049, plus £14 in commissions and fees, for a total cost of £7,063. Thus, the total net gain on this portfolio is –£7. The implementation shortfall is the return on the paper portfolio minus the return on the actual portfolio, or £80 – (–£7) = £87.

We can break this IS down further, as follows:

- Execution cost, which is calculated as the difference between the cost of the real portfolio and of the paper portfolio and reflects the execution price paid for the amount of shares in the order actually filled: (700 × £10.07) – (700 × £10.00) = £7,049 – £7,000 = £49.
- Opportunity cost, which is based on the amount of shares left unexecuted and reflects the cost associated with not being able to execute all shares at the decision price: (1,000 shares – 700 shares) × (£10.08 – £10.00) = £24.
- Fixed fees, which are equal to total explicit fees paid: £14.

IS (£) is equal to the sum of execution cost, opportunity cost, and fixed fees: £49 + £24 + £14 = £87. More commonly, the shortfall is expressed as a fraction of the total cost of the paper portfolio trade: £87/£10,000 = 87 bps.

Expanded Implementation Shortfall

Wagner (1991) further expanded the IS measure to decompose the execution cost component into a delay-related cost component and a trading-related cost component.[7] These two decomposed execution components allow portfolio managers to more precisely isolate where their execution costs arise during the implementation cycle and help traders better manage overall execution quality and reduce trading costs.

The expanded implementation shortfall can be broken down as follows:

Expanded IS =

$$\underbrace{\underbrace{(\sum s_j)P_0 - (\sum s_j)P_d}_{\text{Delay cost}} + \underbrace{\sum s_j p_j - (\sum s_j)P_0}_{\text{Trading cost}}}_{\text{Execution cost}} + \underbrace{(S - \sum s_j)(P_n - P_d)}_{\text{Opportunity cost}} + \text{Fees}$$

---

7 Wagner, W. (Ed.), 1991. *The Complete Guide to Security Transactions.* John Wiley.

In this representation, the additional notation p_0 represents the arrival price, and it is defined as the asset price at the time the order was released to the market for execution.

This expanded IS formulation decomposes execution cost further into two categories: delay cost and trading cost. **Delay cost** arises when the order is not submitted to the market in a timely manner and the asset experiences adverse price movement, making it more expensive to transact. Delay cost is often caused by a delay in selecting the most appropriate broker or trading algorithm to execute the order and by adverse price movement (also known as price drift) over the trading period.

Delay cost, however, can be minimized by having proper trading practices in place to provide traders with all the information they need to make an immediate decision, such as pre-trade analysis and post-trade analysis.

For example, consider the same Impulse Robotics example from before but with the following additional fact: *The buy-side trading desk releases the order to the market 30 minutes after receiving it, when the price is £10.03.* We now have additional information that helps identify where costs arise during the implementation of the trade.

The execution cost component in the expanded implementation shortfall can be decomposed into the following:

- Delay cost, which reflects the adverse price movement associated with not submitting the order to the market in a timely manner and is based on the amount of shares executed in the order: (700 × £10.03) − (700 × £10.00) = £7,021 − £7,000 = £21.
- Trading cost, which reflects the execution price paid on shares executed: (700 × £10.07) − (700 × £10.03) = £7,049 − £7,021 = £28.

While,

- Opportunity cost (£24) and fixed fees (£14) remain unchanged.

Therefore, expanded implementation shortfall (£) = £21 + £28 + £24 + £14 = £87.

The expanded IS provides further insight into the causes of trade costs. The delay cost is £21, which accounts for 24.1% (£21/£87) of the total IS cost, whereas the opportunity cost of £24 accounts for 27.6% (£24/£87) of the total IS cost. Quite often, delay cost and opportunity cost account for the greatest quantity of cost during implementation. These costs can often be eliminated with proper transaction cost management techniques.

Improving Execution Performance

In many situations, delay cost arises from a lag in time between when the buy-side trader receives the order from the portfolio manager and when the trader determines which broker or algorithm is most appropriate for the specific order. Delay costs can be reduced by having a process in place that provides traders with broker performance metrics. Traders can then immediately release the order to the broker without any delay or corresponding adverse price movement. In theory, the delay cost component should have an expected value of zero. In practice, however, the delay cost component is often due to the simultaneous buying and selling pressure from multiple funds buying and selling the same stocks on the same side and over similar trading horizons, resulting in adverse price movement over the trading period. Stock alpha may also contribute to the delay cost component.

Portfolio managers can use IS to help determine appropriate order size for the market within the portfolio manager's price range and to minimize the opportunity cost of the order. For example, IS analysis will help portfolio managers determine the number of shares that can be transacted within the manager's price range or better, and if the manager has incremental cash on hand from specifying a smaller order size, she can invest this amount into her next most attractive investment opportunity at presumably better market prices. If the portfolio manager does not perform

Trade Cost Measurement

IS analysis, she may try to transact a position size that is too large to execute in the market within the desired price range and may not realize this until it is too late to change the investment decision. If the manager knew beforehand that her position size was too large to execute within her price range, she could have reduced the order size for the stock and invested the remaining capital into the next most attractive investment opportunity.

Similar to the delay cost, opportunity cost is not mean zero and often represents a cost to the fund. This is due to two reasons: adverse price movement and illiquidity. First, portfolio managers will often buy shares at a specified price or better. If prices decrease over the trading period, the order will likely be filled. If prices increase by too much, the manager may feel that the asset is no longer an attractive investment opportunity, will cancel the order, and invest in a different asset, thus realizing an opportunity cost. Second, traders may not be able to complete the order if there is insufficient market liquidity. In times of favorable prices, fund managers may be willing to incur additional market impact to attract additional counterparties into the market. But during times of adverse market prices, fund managers may not be as willing to increase their purchase price to attract additional sellers into the market because doing so might increase the stock price to a level where it is no longer deemed an attractive investment opportunity. Thus, the order is less likely to be completed in times of adverse price movement and insufficient market liquidity. Both of these situations result in an opportunity cost to the fund.

Delay Cost

A portfolio manager decides to buy 100,000 shares of RLK at 9:30 a.m., when its price is $30.00. The manager gives the order to his buy-side trader and requests the order be executed in the market at a price no higher than $30.50. The trader is then tasked with determining the best broker and/or the best algorithm to execute the trade. We next discuss two different scenarios to illustrate how a trader's actions can affect the delay cost component.

Scenario 1:

The trader receives the order for 100,000 shares at 9:30 a.m., when its price is $30. The trader is not familiar with RLK and needs to review the stock's liquidity, volatility, and intraday trading patterns and current market conditions. The trader next needs to review the historical performance of brokers trading similar order sizes and trading characteristics. After a thorough review, the trader determines the best broker to execute the order is Broker KRG. The trader then submits the order to Broker KRG at 10:30 a.m. but the market price increases to $30.10. The buy-side trader's delay in submitting the order to the broker is caused by the trader's need to evaluate and determine the best broker to execute the order given the order characteristics and market conditions. This delay costs the fund $0.10 per share. Note that if the price had decreased to $29.90, the delay would have benefited the fund by $0.10 per share.

Scenario 2:

The trader receives the order for 100,000 shares at 9:30 a.m., when the price is $30.00. Because the buy-side trader exercises proper transaction cost management practices, the trader has analyses on hand indicating who is the best broker and what is the best algorithm to execute the order. The trader is able to immediately submit the order to Broker KRG for execution when the market price is $30.00 per share.

Opportunity Cost

The research department of an asset management firm identifies two stocks currently undervalued in the market. Stock ABC is currently trading at $30.00 and is undervalued by $0.50/share. Stock XYZ is also currently trading at $30.00 and is undervalued by $0.40/share.

The portfolio manager has $3 million and is looking to invest in the stock(s) that will provide the highest return for the fund. What stock(s) should she buy?

On the surface, it may appear most appropriate to invest the entire $3 million in Stock ABC because it is the most undervalued ($0.50/share) and represents the highest short-term alpha. However, if the portfolio manager does not incorporate opportunity cost into her analysis, she is unlikely to achieve the highest return for the fund.

The effect of opportunity cost on fund performance is explained in the following two scenarios.

Scenario 1:

The portfolio manager decides to purchase 100,000 shares of ABC because it represents the highest short-term alpha potential. The portfolio manager does not want to purchase shares at a price higher than $30.50, which the research department has determined to be fair value for ABC. The trader tries to execute 100,000 shares of ABC but finds that only 80,000 shares can be executed at an average price of $30.25 before the price increases above $30.50. After ABC reaches a price of $30.50, it remains at this price through the end of the day. Additionally, Stock XYZ closes at its fair value of $30.40.

In this situation, the portfolio manager incurred an opportunity cost of $10,000 (20,000 shares multiplied by $0.50 = $10,000) and realized a profit of $20,000 (80,000 shares multiplied by $0.25 = $20,000).

Since Stock XYZ (which was the second most attractive investment opportunity at the beginning of the day) also increased to its fair value over the day, the portfolio manager is no longer able to invest the residual dollar value in XYZ and capture alpha. Thus, the portfolio manager has missed out on an opportunity to achieve maximum returns.

Scenario 2:

The portfolio manager of the fund exercises proper transaction cost management practices. Based on pre-trade analysis, the manager determines that she can purchase only 80,000 shares of ABC before its price will recover to its fair value of $30.50. Because the manager will not be able to invest all funds into Stock ABC, she decides to invest the residual dollar value into Stock XYZ (the second most attractive asset) and buy 20,000 shares.

In this scenario, the portfolio manager transacts all shares from both orders at prices below the fair value. The manager purchases 80,000 shares of ABC at an average price of $30.25 and purchases 20,000 shares of XYZ at an average price of $30.20. Stock ABC closes at its fair value of $30.50, and Stock XYZ closes at its fair value of $30.40. Since the manager executed all shares, she does not incur any opportunity cost.

The manager realizes an overall profit of $24,000. Stock ABC realized a profit of $20,000 (80,000 shares multiplied by $0.25/share). Stock XYZ realized a profit of $4,000 (20,000 shares multiplied by $0.20/share).

In this scenario, where the portfolio manager practiced proper trading cost management and evaluated opportunity cost prior to submitting the order, she was able to increase portfolio returns by $4,000.

Knowledge of where costs arise during execution allows portfolio managers and traders to take necessary steps to reduce and manage these costs appropriately. For example, the delay cost component can be reduced by knowing beforehand which broker is best suited to execute the trade and/or which algorithm is the most appropriate given the order, price benchmark, and investment objectives. Opportunity cost

Trade Cost Measurement

can be reduced by knowing the order size and share quantity that is most likely to be executed in the market within a specified price range. The trading cost component can also be effectively managed so that it is consistent with the underlying investment objectives of the fund by selecting the proper price benchmarks and trading urgency.

IN-TEXT QUESTION

Implementation Shortfall

A portfolio manager decides to buy 100,000 shares of RLK at 9:00 a.m., when the price is $30.00. He sets a limit price of $30.50 for the order. The buy-side trader does not release the order to the market for execution until 10:30 a.m., when the price is $30.10. The fund is charged a commission of $0.02/share and no other fees. At the end of the day, 80,000 shares are executed and RLK closes at $30.65. Order and execution details are summarized as follows:

Order	
Stock Ticker	RLK
Side	Buy
Shares	100,000
Limit Price	$30.50

Trades	Execution Price	Shares Executed
Trade 1	$30.20	30,000
Trade 2	$30.30	20,000
Trade 3	$30.40	20,000
Trade 4	$30.50	10,000
Total		80,000

a. Calculate execution cost.
b. Calculate opportunity cost.
c. Calculate fixed fees.
d. Calculate implementation shortfall in basis points.
e. Discuss how opportunity cost could be minimized for the trade.
f. Calculate delay cost.
g. Calculate trading cost.
h. Show expanded implementation shortfall in basis points.
i. Discuss how delay cost could be minimized for the trade.

Solution:

a. **Execution cost** is calculated as the difference between the costs of the real portfolio and the paper portfolio. It reflects the execution price(s) paid for the amount of shares in the order that were actually filled, or executed. Execution cost can be calculated as follows:

Execution cost = $\Sigma s_j p_j - \Sigma s_j p_d$
= (30,000 shares × $30.20 + 20,000 shares × $30.30 + 20,000 shares × $30.40 + 10,000 shares × $30.50) − 80,000 × $30.00
= $2,425,000 − $2,400,000
= $25,000

b. **Opportunity cost** is based on the amount of shares left unexecuted in the order and reflects the cost of not being able to execute all shares at the decision price. Opportunity cost can be calculated as follows:

Opportunity cost $= \left(S - \Sigma s_j\right)\left(p_n - p_d\right)$

$= (100{,}000 - 80{,}000)(\$30.65 - \$30.00)$

$= \$13{,}000$

c. **Fixed fees** are equal to total explicit fees paid and can be calculated as follows:

Fees $= 80{,}000 \times \$0.02 = \$1{,}600$

d. **Implementation shortfall** can be calculated as follows:

Implementation shortfall (\$) $= \underbrace{\$25{,}000}_{\text{Execution cost}} + \underbrace{\$13{,}000}_{\text{Opportunity cost}} + \underbrace{\$1{,}600}_{\text{Fees}}$

$= \$39{,}600$

The implementation shortfall is expressed in basis points as follows:

Implementation shortfall (bps) $= \dfrac{\text{Implementation shortfall (\$)}}{\text{(Total shares)}\left(p_d\right)} \times 10{,}000 \text{ bps}$

$= \dfrac{\$39{,}600}{(100{,}000 \times \$30.00)} \times 10{,}000 \text{ bps}$

$= 132 \text{ bps}$

e. **Minimizing opportunity cost:** Based on the decomposition of IS, the portfolio manager incurred an opportunity cost of $13,000 on 20,000 shares. The opportunity cost could be lowered by reducing order quantity to a size that can be absorbed into the market at the portfolio manager's price target or better. In this example, opportunity cost represented 32.8% ($13,000/$39,600) of the total IS cost. If the portfolio manager had known this in advance, he could have reduced the size of the order to 80,000 shares and invested the extra $600,000 (20,000 shares × $30.00/share = $600,000) in his second most attractive investment opportunity.

f. **Delay cost** can be calculated as follows:

Delay cost $= \left(\Sigma s_j\right)p_0 - \left(\Sigma s_j\right)p_d$

$= 80{,}000 \times \$30.10 - 80{,}000 \times \$30.00 = \$8{,}000$

g. **Trading cost** can be calculated as follows:

Trading cost $= \Sigma s_j p_j - \left(\Sigma s_j\right)p_0$

$= (30{,}000 \text{ shares} \times \$30.20 + 20{,}000 \text{ shares} \times \$30.30 + 20{,}000 \text{ shares} \times \$30.40 + 10{,}000 \text{ shares} \times \$30.50) - 80{,}000 \times \$30.10$

$= \$2{,}425{,}000 - \$2{,}408{,}000$

$= \$17{,}000$

h. **Expanded implementation shortfall** can be calculated as follows:

Expanded IS $= \underbrace{\$8{,}000}_{\text{Delay cost}} + \underbrace{\$17{,}000}_{\text{Trading cost}} + \underbrace{\$13{,}000}_{\text{Opportunity cost}} + \underbrace{\$1{,}600}_{\text{Fees}} = \$39{,}600$

The delay cost is $8,000, which accounts for 20.2% ($8,000/$39,600) of the total IS cost, whereas the opportunity cost of $13,000 accounts for 32.8% ($13,000/$39,600) of the total IS cost.

i. **Minimizing delay cost:** The delay cost of $8,000 accounts for a sizable portion (20.2%) of the total IS cost and could be minimized by having a process in place that provides the buy-side trader with broker performance metrics. This would allow the trader to quickly identify the best broker and/or algorithm to execute the order given its characteristics and current market conditions, thereby minimizing the time between order receipt and market execution.

EVALUATING TRADE EXECUTION

☐ evaluate the execution of a trade

The evaluation of trade execution is also referred to as trade cost evaluation, trade cost analysis (TCA), and post-trade analysis. Its goal is to evaluate and measure the execution quality of the trade and the overall performance of the trader, broker, and/or algorithm. Here, we discuss different methodologies to evaluate the execution of a trade.

Proper trade cost evaluation enables portfolio managers to better manage costs throughout the investment cycle and helps facilitate communication between the portfolio manager, traders, and brokers to better understand how and why costs occur during the implementation of investment decisions. Trade cost analysis also provides the basis for peer group comparisons, allowing a firm's portfolio managers to compare trading performance and costs with a universe of similar funds trading similar securities.

Trade evaluation helps buy-side traders quantify a broker's performance and rank brokers and/or algorithms most appropriate for implementation of different investment decisions. This helps minimize delay costs associated with trading.

Trade cost evaluation calculates trading costs and performance relative to a specified trading cost or trading performance benchmark. Costs are determined by the transaction amount paid above the reference price benchmark for a buy order and the discount below the reference price benchmark for a sell order. It is important that portfolio managers select the reference price for use on the basis of their selected trading price benchmark. For example, if the portfolio manager selected an arrival price benchmark, it is important to perform trade execution evaluation using the arrival price. If the fund manager selected the VWAP price as the price benchmark, then the reference price used in the post-trade analysis should include the VWAP price. If the fund selected a post-trade benchmark, such as the market on close, it is essential that the fund evaluate trading performance using the closing price benchmark.

Although one benchmark is used in execution, to represent the tradable strategy, multiple reference price benchmarks may be used to measure trading cost and to evaluate performance, typically on an intraday basis. For example, to measure trading costs, a pre-trade benchmark, such as the arrival price benchmark, may be used to provide the portfolio manager or trader with the estimated money required to complete the transaction. The trader may also compare the execution price of the order with an intraday benchmark such as the VWAP of the asset over the trading horizon to determine whether she achieved prices consistent with those of other market participants. Additionally, the trader may compare the last trade price of the order with a post-trade benchmark to understand whether there was price reversion after order completion. The use of multiple price benchmarks may provide valuable insights into different aspects of trading execution.

Trade cost calculations are expressed such that a positive value indicates underperformance and represents underperformance compared with the benchmark. A negative value indicates a savings and is a better performance compared with the benchmark. These calculations are as follows:

Cost in total dollars ($):

$$\text{Cost (\$)} = \text{Side} \times (\overline{P} - P^*) \times \text{Shares}$$

Cost in dollars per share ($/share):

$$\text{Cost (\$/share)} = \text{Side} \times (\overline{P} - P^*)$$

Cost in basis points (bps):

$$\text{Cost (bps)} = \text{Side} \times \frac{(\overline{P} - P^*)}{P^*} \times 10,000 \text{ bps}$$

$$\text{Side} = \begin{cases} +1 & \text{Buy order} \\ -1 & \text{Sell order} \end{cases}$$

$\overline{P}$ = Average execution price of order

P^* = Reference price

Shares = Shares executed

In most situations, investment professionals express costs in basis points because they represent a standardized measure across order sizes, market prices, and currencies. Portfolio managers will multiply the formulas listed by −1 to represent cost as a negative value and savings as a positive value.

Arrival Price

The arrival price benchmark measures the difference between the market price at the time the order was released to the market and the actual transaction price for the fund. This benchmark is used to measure the trade cost of the order incurred while the order was being executed in the market. This calculation follows the trading cost component from the expanded implementation shortfall formula.

Consider the following facts. A portfolio manager executes a buy order at an average price of $\overline{P}$ = $30.05. The arrival price at the time the order was submitted to the market was P_0 = $30.00. The arrival cost expressed in basis points is as follows:

$$\text{Arrival cost (bps)} = \text{Side} \times \frac{(\overline{P} - P_0)}{P_0} \times 10^4 \text{ bps}$$

$$= +1 \times \frac{(\$30.05 - \$30.00)}{\$30.00} \times 10^4 \text{ bps}$$

$$= 16.7 \text{ bps}$$

Therefore, the fund incurred an arrival cost of 16.7 bps, underperforming the arrival price benchmark by this amount.

VWAP

Portfolio managers use the VWAP benchmark as a measure of whether they received fair and reasonable prices over the trading period. Since the VWAP comprises all market activity over the day, all buying and selling pressure of all other market participants, and market noise, it provides managers with a reasonable indication of the fair cost for market participants over the day. In this situation, the VWAP reference price serves as a performance metric.

Consider the following facts. A portfolio manager executes a buy order at an average price of $\bar{P}$ = $30.05. The VWAP over the trading horizon is $30.04. The VWAP cost benchmark is computed as follows:

$$\text{VWAP cost (bps)} = \text{Side} \times \frac{(\bar{P} - \text{VWAP})}{\text{VWAP}} \times 10^4 \text{ bps}$$
$$= +1 \times \frac{(\$30.05 - \$30.04)}{\$30.04} \times 10^4 \text{ bps}$$
$$= 3.3 \text{ bps}$$

Therefore, the fund underperformed the VWAP by 3.3 bps. In most cases, the order will underperform the VWAP generally because of the bid–ask spread and the buying or selling pressure associated with the order.

TWAP

The TWAP benchmark is an alternative measure to determine whether the fund achieved fair and reasonable prices over the trading period and is used when managers wish to exclude potential trade price outliers.

Consider the following facts. A portfolio manager executes a buy order at an average price of $\bar{P}$ = $30.05. The TWAP over the trading horizon is $30.06. The VWAP cost benchmark is computed as follows:

$$\text{TWAP cost (bps)} = \text{Side} \times \frac{(\bar{P} - \text{TWAP})}{\text{TWAP}} \times 10^4 \text{ bps}$$
$$= +1 \times \frac{(\$30.05 - \$30.06)}{\$30.06} \times 10^4 \text{ bps}$$
$$= -3.3 \text{ bps}$$

Therefore, the fund outperformed the TWAP benchmark by 3.3 bps.

Market on Close

The closing benchmark, also referred to as an MOC benchmark, is used primarily by index managers and mutual funds that wish to achieve the closing price on the day and compare their actual transaction prices with the closing price. These funds will typically be valued using the closing price, and it is important that the portfolio manager perform benchmark analysis using the execution price of the order and the closing price on the day. Doing so ensures that the benchmark cost measure will be consistent with the valuation of the fund. The closing price benchmark is also the benchmark that is consistent with the tracking error calculation. MOC benchmarks are often used in fixed-income trading.

Consider the following facts. A portfolio manager executing a buy order using an MOC strategy transacts the order at an average price of $30.40. The stock's official closing price is $30.50. The closing benchmark cost is calculated as follows:

$$\text{Close (bps)} = \text{Side} \times \frac{(\bar{P} - \text{Close})}{\text{Close}} \times 10^4 \text{ bps}$$
$$= +1 \times \frac{(\$30.40 - \$30.50)}{\$30.50} \times 10^4 \text{ bps}$$
$$= -32.8 \text{ bps}$$

Thus, a closing benchmark cost of –32.8 bps indicates that the order was executed 32.8 bps more favorably than the closing price of the order. In the case of an index fund, the outperformance would contribute positive tracking error for the fund.

Market-Adjusted Cost

The market-adjusted cost is a performance metric used by managers and traders to help separate the trading cost due to trading the order from the general market movement in the security price (i.e., the price movement that would have occurred in the security even if the order was not executed in the market). For example, buying stock in a rising market and selling stock in a falling market will cause the fund to incur higher costs than expected, and selling stock in a rising market and buying stock in a falling market will cause the fund to incur lower costs than expected. A market-adjusted cost benchmark will help isolate the price movement due to the general market from the cost due to the impact of the order.

The market-adjusted cost is calculated by subtracting the market cost due to market movement adjusted for order side from the total arrival cost of the trade. The market cost is computed on the basis of the movement in an index and the stock's beta to that index, as follows:

$$\text{Index cost (bps)} = \text{Side} \times \frac{(\text{Index VWAP} - \text{Index arrival price})}{\text{Index arrival price}} \times 10^4$$

The index VWAP is the volume-weighted price of the index computed over the trading horizon. The index VWAP is often computed using an overall market index or a related ETF to compute a volume-weighted price. Alternatively, portfolio managers and traders may use a sector or industry index instead of the overall market index.

The market-adjusted cost is calculated as follows:

$$\text{Market-adjusted cost (bps)} = \text{Arrival cost (bps)} - \beta \times \text{Index cost (bps)}$$

In this case, β represents the stock's beta to the underlying index. The expectation in this formulation is that the stock would have exhibited price movement based on the market movement and the stock's sensitivity to the index measured via its beta to the index. This formulation thus helps remove the movement in the stock that would have occurred even if the order was not entered into the market.

Buying in a Rising Market

Consider a portfolio manager who executes a buy order at an average price of $30.50. The arrival price at the time the order was entered into the market was $30.00. The selected index price at the time of order entry was $500, and market index VWAP over the trade horizon was $505. If the stock has a beta to the index of $\beta = 1.25$, the market-adjusted cost can be calculated as follows:

Step 1   Calculate arrival cost.

$$\text{Arrival cost (bps)} = \text{Side} \times \frac{(\bar{P} - P_0)}{P_0} \times 10^4 \text{ bps}$$

$$= +1 \times \frac{(\$30.50 - \$30.00)}{\$30.00} \times 10^4 \text{ bps}$$

$$= 166.7 \text{ bps}$$

Step 2   Calculate index cost.

$$\text{Index cost (bps)} = \text{Side} \times \frac{(\text{Index VWAP} - \text{Index arrival price})}{\text{Index arrival price}} \times 10^4$$

$$= +1 \times \frac{\$505 - \$500}{\$500} \times 10^4$$

$$= 100 \text{ bps}$$

Evaluating Trade Execution

Step 3   Calculate market-adjusted cost.

Market-adjusted cost (bps) = Arrival cost (bps) − β × Index cost (bps)

$$= 166.7 \text{ bps} - 1.25 \times 100 \text{ bps}$$

$$= 166.7 \text{ bps} - 125 \text{ bps}$$

$$= 41.7 \text{ bps}$$

The portfolio manager bought stock in a rising market, and prices were generally increasing over the trading horizon because of market movement and the buying pressure of the order. The manager's arrival cost was 166.7 bps, and the market index cost over the period was 100 bps. The stock price would be expected to increase 125 bps over the period on the basis of the movement in the market index and the stock's beta to the index. In this situation, we subtract 125 bps in cost from the arrival cost of 166.7 bps because this amount represents expected market movement not due to the order. The market-adjusted cost due to the order is 41.7 bps, much lower than the total arrival cost.

IN-TEXT QUESTION

Selling in a Falling Market

A portfolio manager executes a sell order at an average price of $29.50. The arrival price at the time the order was entered into the market was $30.00. The selected index price at the time of order entry was $500, and market index VWAP over the trade horizon was $495. The stock has a beta to the index of 1.25.

1. Calculate arrival cost.
2. Calculate index cost.
3. Calculate market-adjusted cost.

Solution:

1. Calculate arrival cost.

$$\text{Arrival cost (bps)} = \text{Side} \times \frac{(\bar{P} - P_0)}{P_0} \times 10^4 \text{ bps}$$

$$= -1 \times \frac{(\$29.50 - \$30.00)}{\$30.00} \times 10^4 \text{ bps}$$

$$= 166.7 \text{ bps}$$

A positive arrival cost in this case indicates that the fund underperformed the arrival price benchmark.

2. Calculate index cost.

$$\text{Index cost (bps)} = \text{Side} \times \frac{(\text{Index VWAP} - \text{Index arrival price})}{\text{Index arrival price}} \times 10^4$$

$$= -1 \times \frac{\$495 - \$500}{\$500} \times 10^4$$

$$= 100 \text{ bps}$$

3. Calculate market-adjusted cost.

Market-adjusted cost (bps) = Arrival cost (bps) − β × Index cost (bps)

$$= 166.7 \text{ bps} - 1.25 \times 100 \text{ bps}$$

$$= 166.7 \text{ bps} - 125 \text{ bps}$$

$$= 41.7 \text{ bps}$$

> In this example, the arrival cost is calculated to be +166.7 bps, indicating that the order underperformed the arrival price. Although this is true, much of the adverse prices were likely due to market movement rather than inferior performance from the broker or algorithm. This sell order was executed in a falling market, which resulted in an arrival cost of 166.7 bps for the investor. However, an estimated 125 bps of this cost was due to market movement, which would have occurred even if the order had not traded in the market. Thus, the market-adjusted cost for this order is 41.7 bps.

Added Value

Another methodology used by investors to evaluate trading performance is to compare the arrival cost of the order with the estimated pre-trade cost. The expected trading cost is calculated using a pre-trade model and incorporates such factors as order size, volatility, market liquidity, investor risk aversion, level of urgency (i.e., how fast or slow the trade is to be executed in the market), and the underlying market conditions at the time of the trade. If a fund executes at a cost lower than the pre-trade estimate, it is typically considered superior trade performance. If the order is executed at a cost higher than the pre-trade cost benchmark, then the trade is considered to have underperformed expectations. This metric helps fund managers understand the value added by their broker and/or execution algorithms during the execution of the order. The added value metric is computed as follows:

Added value (bps) = Arrival cost (bps) − Est. pre-trade cost (bps)

Consider the following facts. A portfolio manager executes a buy order at an average price of $\bar{P}$ = $50.35. The arrival price at the time the order was entered into the market was P_0 = $50.00. Prior to trading, the buy-side trader performs pre-trade analysis of the order and finds that the expected cost of the trade is 60 bps, based on information available prior to trading. The pre-trade adjustment is calculated as follows:

Pre-trade adjustment = Arrival cost − Est. pre-trade cost

We have,

$$\text{Arrival cost (bps)} = \text{Side} \times \frac{(\bar{P} - P_0)}{P_0} \times 10^4 \text{ bps}$$
$$= +1 \times \frac{(\$50.35 - \$50.00)}{\$50.00} \times 10^4 \text{ bps}$$
$$= 70 \text{ bps}$$

Added value = Arrival cost − Est. pre-trade cost = 70 bps − 60 bps = 10 bps

The pre-trade adjusted cost in this example is 10 bps, indicating that the fund underperformed pre-trade expectations by 10 bps.

Proper trade cost measurement and evaluation are critical to understanding the costs and risks arising from trading. These help inform where a firm's trading activities may be improved through better internal trade management practices, such as the use of appropriate trading partners and venues. Trade governance involves the policies and processes used by firms to manage their trading-related activities.

TRADE GOVERNANCE

☐ evaluate a firm's trading procedures, including processes, disclosures, and record keeping with respect to good governance

All asset managers should have a trade policy document that clearly and comprehensively articulates the firm's trading policies and escalation procedures (i.e., calling on higher levels of leadership or management in an organization to resolve issues when they cannot be resolved by standard procedures). Such a document is mandated by major market regulators and regulations, including the SEC in the United States, the updated Markets in Financial Instruments Directive (MiFID II) in the European Union, the Financial Services Agency in Japan, and the Securities and Futures Commission in Hong Kong SAR.

The objective of a trade policy is to ensure the asset manager's execution and order-handling procedures are in line with the duty of best execution that is owed to clients. Any trade policy needs to include several key aspects. These include the following:

- **Meaning of best execution:** A trade policy document should outline the meaning of best execution as defined by the relevant regulatory framework. This meaning may be supplemented by additional details. For example, generally best execution does not just mean achieving the best execution price at the lowest possible cost but also involves achieving the right trade-off between different objectives.

- **Factors determining the optimal order execution approach:** A trade policy document should describe the factors used in determining how an order can be executed in an optimal manner for a given scenario. For example, the optimal execution approach may differ by asset class, level of security liquidity, and security trading mechanism (order-driven markets, quote-driven markets, and brokered markets). The optimal execution approach can also depend on the nature of a manager's investment process.

- **Listing of eligible brokers and execution venues:** A trade policy should allow the investment manager flexibility to use different brokers and trading venues to achieve best execution in a particular scenario. To reduce operational risk, checks should be in place to ensure only reputable brokers and execution venues that meet requirements for reliable and efficient order execution are used.

- **Process to monitor execution arrangements:** Optimal order execution arrangements may change over time as markets and securities evolve. Therefore, continual monitoring of current arrangements is needed. The details of the monitoring process should be outlined in a trade policy document.

Asset managers that aggregate trades for client accounts and funds should have a "trade aggregation and allocation" policy in place. These policies seek to ensure executed orders are allocated fairly to individual clients on a pre-trade and post-trade basis, there are remedies for misallocations, and an escalation policy is in place. For example, if several accounts (e.g., pooled funds or separate accounts) follow the same or a similar investment strategy and have similar trading needs, then pooling the trades for trade execution may make sense in some situations. If a pooled trade is not fully executed, the order amount that is executed generally needs to be allocated to accounts on a pro-rata basis so that no account is disadvantaged relative to the others. In all cases, the aggregation and allocation process should be transparent and provide an audit trail in case questions are raised after the fact.

Firms should have a policy in place for the treatment of trade errors. Errors from trading and any resulting gains/losses need to be disclosed to a firm's compliance department and documented in a trade error log. The trade error log should include any related documentation and evidence that trade errors are resolved in a way that prevents adverse impact for the client.

Meaning of Best Order Execution within the Relevant Regulatory Framework

A trade policy document should outline the meaning of best execution within the relevant regulatory framework. Although there may be slight differences in how best execution is defined by different regulators and in different financial market regulations, the underlying concept requires orders to be executed on terms most favorable to the client, where firms consider the following:

- execution price,
- trading costs,
- speed of execution,
- likelihood of execution and settlement,
- order size, and
- nature of the trade.

Rather than simply trying to obtain the best price at the lowest possible trading cost, best execution involves identifying the most appropriate trade-off between these aspects. For example, although market impact costs can generally be lowered by trading more patiently, patient trading may be suboptimal for an asset manager that uses extremely short-horizon expected return forecasts, which decay quickly.

Factors Used to Determine the Optimal Order Execution Approach

Firms need to have a list of criteria or factors used in determining the optimal order execution approach to achieve the best possible results for clients on a consistent basis.

Best execution requires investment managers to seek the most advantageous order execution for their customers given market conditions. Best execution includes several key factors that brokers examine, track, and document when choosing how to execute an order. An asset manager needs to ensure that after examining these factors, the broker achieved the best possible execution for the client.

At a firm level, execution policy and procedures need to specify the factors or criteria considered in determining the optimal order execution approach in each scenario. These criteria include the following:

- **Urgency of an order:** Does the order need to be executed aggressively at an accelerated pace, or can it be traded over a longer period of time? What is the size of the order relative to the security's normal liquidity?
- **Characteristics of the securities traded:** How liquid are the securities to be traded (e.g., the average daily volume)? Are the securities standardized or highly customized?

- **Characteristics of the execution venues used:** Which type of trading mechanism or venue is used? Are both lit (on-exchange) markets and dark markets available to trade a security?
- **Investment strategy objectives:** Is the investment strategy short term or long term in nature?
- **Rationale for a trade:** Is a trade intended to capture an investment manager's expected return views? Or is it a risk trade or a liquidity trade? Underlying trade objectives may have important implications for the optimal trade approach.

MiFID II, which came into effect in January 2018 and covers the European Economic Area, provides additional regulations on best execution. MiFID II requires firms to take all sufficient steps to obtain the best possible result in executing client orders. The best possible result is not limited to execution price but also includes consideration of cost, speed, likelihood of execution, likelihood of settlement, and any other factors deemed relevant. MiFID II's "all sufficient steps" test sets a higher standard than the previous "all reasonable steps" standard of MiFID I.

MiFID II prohibits the bundling, or combining, of trading commissions with research provided by brokers, known as a soft dollar arrangement. Under MiFID II, investment managers need the firm to pay for broker research costs or establish a research payment account funded by a special charge to clients. Other jurisdictions place limitations on soft dollar arrangements and are expected to follow MiFID II requirements in making execution and research payments explicit and transparent for clients.

Ensuring best execution often requires different criteria for each asset class that should be incorporated into trade policy and procedures. In terms of execution factors, the relative importance of individual factors often differs by asset class. Exhibit 2 shows key considerations by asset class.

Exhibit 2: Key Considerations for Best Execution

Asset Class	Considerations
Equities and Exchange-Traded Options and Futures	An investment manager needs to choose the type of market or venue used for execution. In many cases, there are lit (on-exchange) markets and dark markets available for more liquid securities. Lit markets provide pre-trade and post-trade transparency, whereas dark markets provide post-trade transparency. The liquidity of a security and the percentage of average daily volume traded are critical in the choice of optimal execution algorithm. Historical transaction data—including liquidity characteristics and price volatility—are widely available and can be readily assessed.
Fixed Income	There are two main issues: market transparency and price discovery. Only some of the trading, particularly in corporate bonds, takes place on venues that provide market transparency as well as simultaneous, competitive quotes enabling price discovery, which is a necessary condition to ensure best execution. Generally, trade policy should dictate that, if at all possible, bids/offers should be requested from multiple independent third parties before a trade is executed. This process fosters competition and provides a more precise estimate of the likely market price at a particular time in an effort to achieve the best price possible. If there is no market transparency and if multiple competing quotes cannot or should not be obtained, then a trade policy should outline alternative means to achieve price discovery. These may include data sources (such as TRACE data)* for historical transaction prices or quotes for a given security or comparable securities. In the absence of any relevant transaction prices or quotes, an internal or external pricing model could be used to establish a market price estimate.

Asset Class	Considerations
OTC Derivatives	Broker selection may depend on the exact terms of the proposed OTC derivative instruments, counterparty risk, and a broker's settlement capabilities.
Spot Currencies	Quotes should be requested from multiple independent dealers before a trade is executed. This process fosters competition in an effort to achieve the best price possible.

In 2002, the National Association of Securities Dealers introduced TRACE (Trade Reporting and Compliance Engine) in an effort to increase price transparency in the US corporate debt market.

List of Eligible Brokers and Execution Venues

Asset managers should have a list of approved brokers and execution venues for trading and the criteria used to create this list. In determining the list, there should not be discrimination against brokers or execution venues. Any decisions should be made according to the policy and procedures put in place. Creating and maintaining the list should be a collaborative effort shared by portfolio execution, compliance, and risk management. A best practices approach is to create a Best Execution Monitoring Committee within an investment management firm that is responsible for maintaining and updating the list regularly, or as circumstances require, and distributing the list to all parties involved in trade execution.

Although the criteria used to approve an execution venue or broker differ by asset class, the principles behind the decision and the process followed should be consistent across asset classes, broker firms, regions, and jurisdictions. A number of qualitative and quantitative factors are relevant to this decision, such as the following:

- **Quality of service:** Does a broker provide competitive execution compared with an execution benchmark, such as submission price or VWAP?
- **Financial stability:** Will the broker or execution venue be able to fulfill obligations in all market environments? When such brokers as Lehman Brothers and MF Global went bankrupt, it caused substantial disruption to their clients' activities.
- **Reputation:** Does the broker or execution venue uphold high ethical standards and treat clients fairly?
- **Settlement capabilities:** Are the operations supporting the broker/execution venue robust? Can trades be settled in a reliable and efficient manner?
- **Speed of execution:** Can urgent trades be implemented with minimal delay and at the best price possible? What is the maximum volume that can be traded with minimal delay?
- **Cost competitiveness:** Are the explicit costs (such as commissions or exchange fees) competitive?
- **Willingness to commit capital:** Is the broker willing to act as a dealer to facilitate trading for a client? This can be particularly important for less liquid securities that need to be traded in a timely manner.[8]

A sensible trade policy is particularly important in trade venue selection for transactions that are executed off exchange in so-called over-the-counter markets. Best execution is generally harder to measure for these trades, and there are unique risks associated with OTC trading. For example, OTC trades are not subject to any trading

---

8 In this case, the broker, acting as principal rather than agent, is the counterparty to client transactions. Although this can be useful for clients, potential conflicts of interest may arise, and principal trades should be monitored closely by managers for potential conflicts of interest the broker may have.

Trade Governance

venue rules designed to ensure fair and orderly treatment of orders or minimum levels of price transparency. In addition, there may be counterparty and settlement risk for OTC trades.

Process Used to Monitor Execution Arrangements

All brokers and execution venues used by the asset manager should be subject to ongoing monitoring for reputational risk, irregularities (such as trading errors), criminal actions, and financial stability. Brokers and execution venues that no longer meet minimum requirements should be promptly removed from the approved list.

Execution quality on realized transactions through different brokers or execution venues should also be monitored continuously. Systems that allow ongoing monitoring of order execution quality should be in place. Although the specific process may vary by asset class and security type, the underlying principles remain the same. Summary reports of execution quality should be produced, examined, and evaluated on a regular basis.

Checkpoints for trade execution monitoring include the following:

- Trade submission: Has the trading/execution strategy been implemented consistent with the investment process (alpha and risk forecasting horizon, rebalancing frequency, etc.), and is it optimal for the asset type traded?
- What was the execution quality of a trade relative to its benchmark (e.g., arrival price, VWAP, TWAP, market close)?
- Is there an appropriate balance between trading costs and opportunity costs (for non-executed trades)?
- Could better execution have been achieved using a different trading strategy, different intermediaries, or different trading venues?

Asset managers are well advised to have in place the equivalent of a Best Execution Monitoring Committee (BEMC) that has firm-wide responsibility for trade execution monitoring. The BEMC should collaborate with portfolio managers and risk management and legal/compliance departments to ensure potential issues with execution quality are identified, discussed, and acted on in a timely manner.

Trading records and the evaluation of those records should generally be stored and kept accessible by firms for several years (e.g., in the United Kingdom, the requirement is five years). Trading records may be used to do the following:

- **Address client concerns:** For example, trading records can be used as evidence by an investment manager to show clients that their accounts have been treated fairly. This is particularly relevant if an investment manager runs similar strategies that might frequently trade in the same direction. For instance, there may be a need to demonstrate fair trade allocation or that particular strategies are not being favored at the expense of others.
- **Address regulator concerns:** A regulator may be interested in assessing how the investment manager has met best execution standards. In addition, regulators need to monitor market integrity and detect criminal behavior, such as "fake volumes," "quote stuffing," and "spoofing," which are illegal activities in most markets.[9]

---

9 *Fake volumes* refer to the practice whereby a trading venue or exchange executes transactions with itself (i.e., it is on both sides of a trade) to artificially inflate reported trading volume to attract client business. *Quote stuffing* is a practice that has been used by high-frequency traders that involves entering and withdrawing a large number of orders within an extremely short period of time in an attempt to confuse the

- **Assist in improving execution quality:** A database of past transactions may be used to analyze and refine the execution process to control and improve trading costs.
- **Monitor the parties involved in trading/order execution:** Trading records can be used to evaluate how performance by brokers and execution venues may compare in execution quality. This helps inform which services should be retained in the future.

These policies and procedures should be outlined in a comprehensive document and reviewed regularly (for example, quarterly) and when the need arises. Updates should be made when circumstances change. This document could be created by a BEMC and should involve portfolio management, risk management, and legal/compliance departments. If no formal committee is tasked with owning this document, then the legal/compliance department might take responsibility, with collaboration from portfolio management and risk management functions.

> **IN-TEXT QUESTION**
>
> ### Choice of Broker
>
> ABC Asset Management (ABCAM) is one of the world's largest asset managers. ABCAM has been using AAA Brokerage (AAAB) as its exclusive broker for a number of its funds for many years. Other brokers are used only for market segments in which AAAB does not have business operations. The leadership of ABCAM explains its choice of broker by stating, "Because of its long-standing business relationship with AAAB, ABCAM has a uniquely informed insight into the operations of AAAB, which provides greater comfort and assurance that AAAB will fulfill its duties when compared with other brokers."
>
> Discuss whether this practice is permissible and can be justified.
>
> ### Solution:
>
> ABCAM needs to show that it takes all sufficient steps to ensure best execution for its clients' trades. This includes choosing brokers that provide the best service for potential best execution. In order to justify that AAAB is the right broker to use, ABCAM must demonstrate that it has done comparisons of different brokers, that this analysis is regularly conducted with updates, and that each time AAAB is found to be the best choice for order implementation. A thorough and unbiased analysis is required for this. Stating a subjective opinion, such as the explanation provided by ABCAM leadership, is not sufficient justification.

> **IN-TEXT QUESTION**
>
> ### Trade Policy Document
>
> For several decades, XYZ Capital has been running enhanced index funds. These funds have low levels of target tracking error compared with their market-weighted benchmarks. The firm's trade policy document has a focus on minimizing trading costs and defines best execution as follows:

---

market and create trading opportunities for the high-frequency trader. *Spoofing* is a manipulative practice defined as bidding or offering with the intent to cancel before execution. All these practices are attempts to gain an unfair advantage over other market participants by engaging in manipulative behavior.

> "The firm takes all sufficient steps to obtain the best possible result in executing orders; that is, the firm makes its best attempt to achieve the best execution price and lowest trading cost possible for every transaction. In this way, the firm achieves best execution for its client portfolios."
>
> Discuss whether the trade policy statement is in line with regulatory requirements and client best interests.
>
> **Solution:**
>
> Achieving the best execution price at the lowest trading cost possible is only part of the best execution effort. To ensure that clients and their portfolios are served in the best manner possible, other factors require consideration. These considerations include the speed of execution, the alignment of execution approach and execution horizon with the investment process, the likelihood of execution to be optimal, and so on. An exclusive focus on best execution price and lowest trading cost is too narrow a definition to achieve best client execution. For example, doing so could leave many trades unexecuted, which would result in increased opportunity costs from lost opportunities that could not be implemented.

SUMMARY

- Portfolio manager motivations to trade include profit seeking, risk management (hedging), liquidity driven (fund flows), and corporate actions and index reconstitutions.
- Managers following a short-term alpha-driven strategy will trade with greater urgency to realize alpha before it dissipates (decays). Managers following a longer-term strategy will trade with less urgency if alpha decay is expected to be slower.
- Trading is required to keep portfolios at targeted risk levels or risk exposures, to hedge risks that may be outside a portfolio manager's investment objectives or that the portfolio manager does not have an investment view on.
- Trading may be liquidity driven resulting from client activity or index reconstitutions. In these cases, managers typically trade using end-of-day closing prices because these prices are used for fund and benchmark valuation.
- Inputs affecting trade strategy selection include the following types: order related, security related, market related, and user based.
- Order characteristics include the side (or trade direction) and size of an order. Percentage of average daily volume is a standardized measure used in trading that indicates what order size can realistically be traded. Large trades are generally traded over longer time horizons to minimize market impact.
- Security characteristics include security type, short-term (trade) alpha, security price volatility, and a security's liquidity profile.
- Market conditions at the time of trading (intraday trading volumes, bid–ask spreads, and security and market volatility) should be incorporated into trade strategy since they can differ from anticipated conditions.

- Market volatility and liquidity vary over time, and liquidity considerations may differ substantially during periods of crisis.
- Individuals with higher levels of risk aversion are more concerned with market risk and tend to trade with greater urgency.
- Market impact is the adverse price impact in a security caused from trading an order and can represent one of the largest costs in trading.
- Execution risk is the adverse price impact resulting from a change in the fundamental value of the security and is often proxied by price volatility.
- Reference price benchmarks inform order trading prices and include pre-trade, intraday, post-trade, and price target benchmarks.
- Managers seeking short-term alpha will use pre-trade benchmarks, such as the arrival price, when they wish to transact close to current market prices (greater trade urgency).
- Managers without views on short-term price movements who wish to participate in volumes over the execution horizon typically use an intraday benchmark, such as VWAP or TWAP.
- Managers of index funds or funds whose valuation is calculated using closing prices typically select the closing price post-trade benchmark to minimize fund risk and tracking error.
- The primary goal of a trading strategy is to balance the expected costs, risks, and alpha associated with trading the order in a manner consistent with the portfolio manager's trading objectives, risk aversion, and other known constraints.
- Execution algorithms can be classified into the following types: scheduled, liquidity seeking, arrival price, dark aggregators, and smart order routers.
- Equities are traded on exchanges and other multilateral trading venues. Algorithmic trading is common, and most trades are electronic, except for very large trades and trades in illiquid securities.
- Fixed-income securities are generally traded not on exchanges but in a bilateral, dealer-centric market structure where dealers make markets in the securities. The majority of fixed-income securities are relatively illiquid, especially if they have been issued in prior periods, so-called off-the-run bonds.
- Most of the trading volume in exchange-traded derivatives is concentrated in futures. Electronic trading is pervasive, and algorithmic trading is growing.
- OTC derivative markets have historically been opaque, with little public data about prices, trade sizes, and structure details. In recent years, regulators have been placing pressure on OTC markets to introduce central clearing facilities and to display trades publicly in an attempt to increase contract standardization and price discovery and reduce counterparty risk.
- There is no exchange or centralized clearing place for the majority of spot currency trades. Spot currency markets consist of a number of electronic venues and broker markets. The currency market is entirely an OTC market.
- The implementation shortfall measure is the standard for measuring the total cost of the trade. IS compares a portfolio's actual return with its paper return (where transactions are based on decision price).
- The IS attribution decomposes total trade cost into its delay, execution, and opportunity cost components.

Trade Governance

- Delay cost is the cost associated with not submitting the order to the market at the time of the portfolio manager's investment decision.
- Execution cost is the cost due to the buying and/or selling pressure of the portfolio manager and corresponding market risk.
- Opportunity cost is the cost due to not being able to execute all shares of the order because of adverse price movement or insufficient liquidity.
- Trade evaluation measures the execution quality of the trade and the performance of the trader, broker, and/or algorithm used.
- Various techniques measure trade cost execution using different benchmarks (pre-trade, intraday, and post-trade).
- Trade cost analysis enables investors to better manage trading costs and understand where trading activities can be improved through the use of appropriate trading partners and venues.
- Major regulators mandate that asset managers have in place a trade policy document that clearly and comprehensively articulates a firm's trading policies and escalation procedures.
- The objective of a trade policy is to ensure the asset manager's execution and order-handling procedures are in line with their fiduciary duty owed to clients for best execution.
- A trade policy document needs to incorporate the following key aspects: meaning of best execution, factors determining the optimal order execution approach, handling trading errors, listing of eligible brokers and execution venues, and a process to monitor execution arrangements.

PRACTICE PROBLEMS

The following information relates to questions 1-9

Robert Harding is a portfolio manager at ValleyRise, a hedge fund based in the United States. Harding monitors the portfolio alongside Andrea Yellow, a junior analyst. ValleyRise only invests in equities, but Harding is considering other asset classes to add to the portfolio, namely derivatives, fixed income, and currencies. Harding and Yellow meet to discuss their trading strategies and price benchmarks.

Harding begins the meeting by asking Yellow about factors that affect the selection of an appropriate trading strategy. Yellow tells Harding:

Statement 1	Trading with greater urgency results in lower execution risk.
Statement 2	Trading larger size orders with higher trade urgency reduces market impact.
Statement 3	Securities with high rates of alpha decay require less aggressive trading to realize alpha.

After further discussion about Yellow's statements, Harding provides Yellow a list of trades that he wants to execute. He asks Yellow to recommend a price benchmark. Harding wants to use a benchmark where the reference price for the benchmark is computed based on market prices that occur during the trading period, excluding trade outliers.

Earlier that day before the meeting, Yellow believed that the market had underreacted during the pre-market trading session to a strong earnings announcement from ABC Corp., a company that Yellow and Harding have been thoroughly researching for several months. Their research suggested the stock's fair value was $90 per share, and the strong earnings announcement reinforced their belief in their fair value estimate.

Right after the earnings announcement, the pre-market price of ABC was $75. Concerned that the underreaction would be short-lived, Harding directed Yellow to buy 30,000 shares of ABC stock. Yellow and Harding discussed a trading strategy, knowing that ABC shares are very liquid and the order would represent only about 1% of the expected daily volume. They agreed on trading a portion of the order at the opening auction and then filling the remainder of the order after the opening auction. The strategy for filling the remaining portion of the order was to execute trades at prices close to the market price at the time the order was received.

Harding and Yellow then shift their conversation to XYZ Corp. Harding tells Yellow that, after extensive research, he would like to utilize an algorithm to purchase some shares that are relatively liquid. When building the portfolio's position in XYZ, Harding's priority is to minimize the trade's market impact to avoid conveying information to market participants. Additionally, Harding does not expect adverse price movements during the trade horizon.

Harding and Yellow conclude their meeting by comparing trade implementation for equities with the trade implementation for the new fixed-income, exchange-traded derivatives, and currency investments under consideration. Yellow tells Harding:

Practice Problems

Statement 4   Small currency trades and small exchange-traded derivatives trades are typically implemented using the direct market access (DMA) approach.

Statement 5   The high-touch agency approach is typically used to execute large, non-urgent trades in fixed-income and exchange-traded derivatives markets.

The next day, Harding instructs Yellow to revisit their research on BYYP, Inc. Yellow's research leads her to believe that its shares are undervalued. She shares her research with Harding, and at 10 a.m. he instructs her to buy 120,000 shares when the price is $40.00 using a limit order of $42.00.

The buy-side trader releases the order for market execution when the price is $40.50. The only fee is a commission of $0.02 per share. By the end of the trading day, 90,000 shares of the order had been purchased, and BYYP closes at $42.50. The trade was executed at an average price of $41.42. Details about the executed trades are presented in Exhibit 1.

Exhibit 1: BYYP Trade Execution Details

Trades	Execution Price	Shares Executed
Trade 1	$40.75	10,000
Trade 2	$41.25	30,000
Trade 3	$41.50	20,000
Trade 4	$41.75	30,000
Total		90,000

While the buy-side trader executes the BYYP trade, Harding and Yellow review ValleyRise's trade policy document. After reviewing the document, Yellow recommends several changes: 1) add a policy for the treatment of trade errors; 2) add a policy that ensures over-the-counter derivatives are traded on venues with rules that ensure minimum price transparency; and 3) alter the list of eligible brokers to include only those that provide execution at the lowest possible trading cost.

1. Which of Yellow's statements regarding the factors affecting the selection of a trading strategy is correct?

   A. Statement 1

   B. Statement 2

   C. Statement 3

2. Given the parameters for the benchmark given by Harding, Yellow should recommend a benchmark that is based on the:

   A. arrival price.

   B. time-weighted average price.

   C. volume-weighted average price.

3. To fill the remaining portion of the ABC order, Yellow is using:

    A. an arrival price trading strategy.

    B. a TWAP participation strategy.

    C. a VWAP participation strategy.

4. What type of algorithm should be used to purchase the XYZ shares given Harding's priority in building the XYZ position and his belief about potential price movements?

    A. Scheduled algorithm

    B. Arrival price algorithm

    C. Opportunistic algorithm

5. Which of Yellow's statements regarding the trade implementation of non-equity investments is correct?

    A. Only Statement 4

    B. Only Statement 5

    C. Both Statement 4 and Statement 5

6. Based on Exhibit 1, the execution cost for purchasing the 90,000 shares of BYYP is:

    A. $60,000.

    B. $82,500.

    C. $127,500.

7. Based on Exhibit 1, the opportunity cost for purchasing the 90,000 shares of BYYP is:

    A. $22,500.

    B. $60,000.

    C. $75,000.

8. The arrival cost for purchasing the 90,000 shares of BYYP is:

    A. 164.4 bp.

    B. 227.2 bp.

    C. 355.0 bp.

9. As it relates to the trade policy document, ValleyRise should implement Yellow's recommendation related to:

    A. the list of eligible brokers.

    B. a policy for the treatment of trade errors.

    C. a policy for over-the-counter derivatives trades.

Practice Problems

The following information relates to questions 10-11

Lindsey Morris is a trader at North Circle Advisors, an investment management firm and adviser to a suite of value-oriented equity mutual funds. Will Beamon, portfolio manager for the firm's flagship large-cap value fund, the Ogive Fund, is explaining its investment strategy and objectives to Morris. Morris wishes to know how the Ogive Fund's underlying trading motivations may impact trade urgency and alpha decay. Beamon notes the following relevant characteristics of the Ogive Fund:

- Seeks long-term outperformance vs. S&P 500 by investing in undervalued companies
- Evaluates company fundamentals to identify persistent mispricing opportunities
- Has a three-year average holding period

10. **Determine**, based on Beamon's description of the Ogive Fund's characteristics, his likely inclination to aggressively implement the fund's strategy. **Justify** your response.

11. Morris next meets Robin Barker, portfolio manager for North Circle Advisors' small-cap value fund, the Pengwyn Fund, which just received a very large cash inflow. Barker expects equity markets will drift higher in the near-term and asks Morris about the best ways to minimize cash drag for the Pengwyn Fund after the inflow.
Describe an appropriate cash management strategy for Barker.

The following information relates to questions 12-13

Last year, Larry Sailors left his trading position at Valley Ranch Partners, a multi-strategy hedge fund, to join North Circle Advisors. Discussing his job experiences with a colleague, Sailors remarks that, prior to starting at North Circle, he didn't fully appreciate the significant differences in trading motivations between the two firms and how such motivations feed into trade strategy. In particular, he notes the following trade characteristics:

Exhibit 1: Features of Trades by Sailors' Employers

Feature	Valley Ranch Partners	North Circle Advisors
Investment Philosophy	Short-term long and short alpha trades across equity and non-equity securities	Long equity value investing
Trade Size	Small	Large
Risk Appetite	Low	Moderate to high

Feature	Valley Ranch Partners	North Circle Advisors
Trading Venue	Listed securities only	Listed and non-listed securities
Bid–Ask Spreads Experienced in Downturn	Moderate-to-wide	Very wide

12. **Identify** one difference between the trading features of Valley Ranch and North Circle, as noted by Sailors, for each trade strategy selection criterion.

Selection Criterion for Trade Strategy	**Identify** one difference between the trading features of Valley Ranch and North Circle, as noted by Sailors, for each trade strategy selection criterion.
Order Characteristics	
Security Characteristics	
Market Conditions	
Individual Risk Aversion	

13. The next day, Sailors is asked to implement the following buy orders, with target execution price set at Last Trade. He is concerned about minimizing execution risk and market impact.

Exhibit 2: Descriptions of Prospective Buy Orders

Stock	Order Size (#)	Last Trade ($)	Avg. Daily Volume (#)	Price Volatility	Bid–Ask Spread ($)
ABC	45,000	$310.10	195,000	Low	$309.75–$310.35
DEF	55,000	$40.45	4,125,260	Low	$40.39–$40.56
XYZ	8,000	$101.94	750,850	High	$100.82–$102.00

Determine which trades are *most likely* to exhibit the greatest execution risk and market impact. **Justify** each selection.

Determine which trades are *most likely* to exhibit the greatest execution risk and market impact. (Circle one in each column)

Execution Risk	Market Impact
ABC	ABC
DEF	DEF
XYZ	XYZ

Justify each selection.

Practice Problems

The following information relates to questions 14-20

Michelle Wong is a portfolio manager at Star Wealth Management (SWM), an investment management company whose clients are high-net-worth individuals. Her expertise is in identifying temporarily mispriced equity securities. Wong's typical day includes meeting with clients, conducting industry and company investment analysis, and preparing trade recommendations.

Music Plus

Wong follows the music industry and, specifically, Music Plus. After highly anticipated data about the music industry is released shortly after the market opens for trading, the share price of Music Plus quickly increases to $15.25. Wong evaluates the new data as it relates to Music Plus and concludes that the share price increase is an overreaction. She expects the price to quickly revert back to her revised fair value estimate of $14.20 within the same day. When the price is $15.22, she decides to prepare a large sell order equal to approximately 20% of the expected daily volume. She is concerned about information leakage from a public limit order. Wong's supervisor suggests using algorithmic trading for the sell order of the Music Plus shares.

West Commerce

Later the same day, West Commerce announces exciting new initiatives resulting in a substantial increase in its share price to $27.10. Based on this price, Wong concludes that the stock is overvalued and sets a limit price of $26.20 for a sell order of 10,000 shares. By the time the order is released to the market, the share price is $26.90. The share price closes the day at $26.00. SWM is charged a commission of $0.03 per share and no other fees. Selected data about the trade execution are presented in Exhibit 1.

Exhibit 1: Selected Trade Data: West Commerce Sell Order

Trades	Execution price	Shares executed
Trade 1	$26.80	6,000
Trade 2	$26.30	3,000
Total		9,000

The value of the market index appropriate to West Commerce was 600 when the West Commerce sell order was released to the market, and its volume-weighted average price (VWAP) was 590 during the trade horizon. West Commerce has a beta of 0.9 with the index.

Trading Policies

At the end of the day, Wong meets with a long-term client of SWM to discuss SWM's trade policies. The client identifies two of SWM's trade policies and asks Wong whether these are consistent with good trade governance:

Policy 1   SWM works only with pre-approved brokers and execution venues, and the list is reviewed and updated regularly.

Policy 2   SWM is allowed to pool funds when appropriate, and executed orders are allocated to the accounts on a pro-rata basis.

14. The *most appropriate* price benchmark for the sell order of Music Plus shares is the:
    A. closing price.
    B. decision price.
    C. time-weighted average price (TWAP).

15. The *most* appropriate trading strategy for the sell order of Music Plus shares is:
    A. trading in the open market.
    B. selling at the closing auction for the day.
    C. passive trading over the course of the trading day.

16. The trade algorithm that Wong should consider for the sell order of Music Plus shares is:
    A. a POV algorithm.
    B. an arrival price algorithm.
    C. a liquidity-seeking algorithm.

17. The implementation shortfall, in basis points (bps), for the sell order of West Commerce shares is *closest* to:
    A. 139.
    B. 198.
    C. 206.

18. The delay cost in dollars for the sell order of West Commerce shares is:
    A. $1,800.
    B. $2,000.
    C. $2,700.

19. The market-adjusted cost in basis points for the sell order of West Commerce shares is *closest* to a:
    A. cost of 249 bps.
    B. savings of 50 bps.
    C. savings of 68 bps.

20. Which of SWM's trading policies identified by the client are consistent with good trade governance?
    A. Only Policy 1
    B. Only Policy 2

C. Both Policy 1 and Policy 2

The following information relates to questions 21-23

Although focused on long-term value, North Circle Advisors will exploit temporary mispricings to open positions. For example, portfolio manager Bill Bradley pegged LIM Corporation's fair value per share at $28 yesterday; however, LIM's stock price seems to have overreacted to a competitor announcement prior to market open today. The follow events unfold over the course of the morning:

- PRIOR CLOSE: LIM closed at $30.05
- PRE-MARKET: LIM priced at $20.34
- MARKET OPEN: LIM opens at $22.15
- 10:00 AM: LIM trading at $23.01
- 10:00 AM: Bradley confirms the overreaction with target price of $28
- 10:05 AM: Bradley instructs trader to buy 25,000 shares, with a limit price of $28 when LIM is trading at $23.09
- 10:22 AM: Trader finishes the buy with an average purchase price of $23.45

Bradley and the trader conduct a post-trade evaluation. In picking an appropriate reference price, the trader asks Bradley if that would be a pre-trade, intraday, post-trade, or price target benchmark.

21. **Identify** the likely appropriate price benchmark for the LIM trade. **Justify** your response.

   Identify the likely appropriate price benchmark for the LIM trade. (Circle one)

Pre-Trade	Intraday	Post-Trade	Price Target

   Justify your response.

22. Bradley also performs a cost analysis on the LIM trade. Noting the time gap between his trade instructions and the order's submission to the market, Bradley quantifies the cost of the delay.
    Calculate the delay cost incurred in trading the LIM order.

23. Bradley also sees that following a 10 a.m. Federal Reserve press conference, the market rose significantly throughout that day. He wants to separate out the pricing effect of this general market movement from the cost of trading LIM. Bradley and the trader agree to use an arrival price benchmark for this analysis and gather the following data related to a broad market index:

    - Index price at time of order entry: $2,150
    - Index volume-weighted average price over trade horizon: $2,184
    - LIM beta to Index: 0.95

    Calculate the market-adjusted cost of the trade. **Discuss** the finding.

The following information relates to questions 24-25

Beatrice Minchow designs and implements algorithmic trading strategies for Enlightenment Era Partners LLC (EEP). Minchow is working with Portfolio Manager James Bean on an algorithm to implement a sell order for Bean's small position in the lightly-traded shares of public company Dynopax Inc. In a conversation with Minchow, Bean states the following:

- I have no expectations of adverse price movements during the trade horizon and would like to use a scheduled algorithm.
- I want to minimize market impact, but I'm more concerned about getting the sell order completely executed in one day.

Based on Bean's comments, Minchow considers three algorithms: POV, VWAP, and TWAP.

24. **Determine** which algorithm Minchow is likely to use for the Dynopax sell order. **Justify** your response.

Determine which algorithm Minchow is likely to use for the Dynopax sell order. (Circle one)

POV	VWAP	TWAP

Justify your response.

25. Minchow is also tasked to help EEP exit from a large position in a widely-traded blue chip stock. While the trade is non-urgent, given the position's size, Bean is worried about telegraphing intentions to the market. Minchow discusses alternative trading systems with Bean, highlighting dark pools, and makes the following comments:

- Comment 1: A feature of a dark pool is that transactions and quantities won't be reported.
- Comment 2: While a dark pool does provide anonymity, there is less certainty of execution.

Determine the veracity of each comment. **Justify** each response.

Determine the veracity of each comment. **Justify** each response.

Comment	Veracity (Circle one for each row)	Justification
1	Correct / Incorrect	
2	Correct / Incorrect	

Practice Problems

The following information relates to questions 26-26

Karen Swanson and Gabriel Russell recently co-founded Green Savanah Securities, an asset management firm conducting various equity and fixed-income strategies. Swanson and Russell are formulating Green Savannah's trade policy. During a meeting, they agree on an initial set of themes regarding trade policy formation:

- Theme 1: We should determine an optimal execution approach and apply that approach to each asset class managed.
- Theme 2: In aggregating trades for pooled accounts, any partially executed orders need to be allocated on a pro-rata basis.
- Theme 3: The principles behind our process to find a broker should be consistent across each asset class managed.
- Theme 4: To act in our clients' best interests, we need to disclose all trade errors to them.

26. Identify two inappropriate themes in the partners' set. **Justify** your response.

SOLUTIONS

1. A is correct. Greater trade urgency results in lower execution risk because the order is executed over a shorter period of time, which decreases the time the trade is exposed to price volatility and changing market conditions. In contrast, lower trade urgency results in higher execution risk because the order is executed over a longer period of time, which increases the time the trade is exposed to price volatility and changing market conditions.

2. B is correct. Harding asked Yellow to execute a list of trades, and he wants to use a price benchmark where the reference price for the benchmark is computed based on market prices that occur during the trading period, excluding trade outliers. Portfolio managers often specify an intraday benchmark for funds that are trading passively over the day, seeking liquidity, and for funds that may be rebalancing, executing a buy/sell trade list, and minimizing risk. An intraday price benchmark is based on a price that occurs during the trading period. The most common intraday benchmarks used in trading are volume-weighted average price (VWAP) and time-weighted average price (TWAP). Portfolio managers choose TWAP when they wish to exclude potential trade outliers.

3. A is correct. Given the trade urgency of the order, the very liquid market for ABC shares, and the small order size relative to ABC's expected volume, Yellow is using an arrival price trading strategy that would attempt to execute the remaining shares close to market prices at the time the order is received.

4. A is correct. XYZ shares are relatively liquid, and Harding has prioritized minimizing the trade's market impact to avoid conveying information to market participants. Harding also does not expect adverse price movements during the trade horizon. Scheduled algorithms are appropriate for orders in which portfolio managers or traders do not have expectations for adverse price movement during the trade horizon. These algorithms are also used by portfolio managers and traders who have greater risk tolerance for longer execution time periods and are more concerned with minimizing market impact. Scheduled algorithms are often appropriate when the order size is relatively small (e.g., no more than 5%–10% of expected volume), the security is relatively liquid, or the orders are part of a risk-balanced basket and trading all orders at a similar pace will maintain the risk balance.

5. A is correct. Small currency trades are usually implemented using direct market access (DMA). Buy-side traders generally use DMA for exchange-traded derivatives, particularly for smaller trades.

6. C is correct. Execution cost is calculated as the difference between the cost of the real portfolio and the paper portfolio. It reflects the execution price(s) paid for the number of shares in the order that were actually filled or executed. The execution cost is calculated as:

    Execution cost = $\sum s_j p_j - \sum s_j p_d$

    = [(10,000 shares × $40.75) + (30,000 shares × $41.25) + (20,000 shares × $41.50) + (30,000 shares × $41.75)] − (90,000 × $40.00)

    = $3,727,500 − $3,600,000

    = $127,500

Solutions

7. C is correct. Opportunity cost is based on the number of shares left unexecuted in the order and reflects the cost of not being able to execute all shares at the decision price. The opportunity cost is calculated as:

$$\text{Opportunity cost} = \left(S - \sum s_j\right)(P_n - P_d)$$
$$= (120{,}000 - 90{,}000) \times (\$42.50 - \$40.00)$$
$$= \$75{,}000$$

8. B is correct. The arrival cost is calculated as:

$$\text{Arrival cost (bp)} = \text{Side} \times \frac{(\bar{P} - P_0)}{P_0} \times 10^4 \text{ bp}$$
$$= +1 \times \frac{(\$41.42 - \$40.50)}{\$40.50} \times 10^4 \text{ bp}$$
$$= 227.2 \text{ bp}$$

9. B is correct. Firms should have a policy in place for the treatment of trade errors. Errors from trading and any resulting gains/losses need to be disclosed to a firm's compliance department and documented in a trade error log. The trade error log should include any related documentation and evidence that trade errors are resolved in a way that avoids adverse impact to the client.

10. Beamon is likely to take a measured approach in implementing the Ogive Fund's strategy. In particular, trade urgency, which refers to how quickly or slowly an order is executed over the trading time horizon, is likely to be low for the Ogive Fund. Greater trade urgency is associated with executing over shorter horizons, whereas lower trade urgency is associated with executing over longer horizons. To capitalize on views related to mispricing, the Ogive Fund's individual positions may be held for several years. Minimal trading is required, and any necessary trading can often be carried out in a more patient manner. Additionally, the return payoffs associated with the Ogive Fund's long-term investment views and value orientation are not likely to be rapidly acted on by other market participants. Thus, the rate or level of expected alpha decay, which refers to the erosion or deterioration in short-term alpha once an investment decision is made, is low.

11. To minimize cash drag on a portfolio, or fund underperformance from holding uninvested cash in a rising market, Barker may use a strategy known as equitization. In this case, equitization refers to temporarily investing cash using futures or ETFs to gain the desired equity exposure before investing in the underlying securities longer term. Equitization may be required if large inflows into a portfolio are hindered by lack of liquidity in the underlying securities. So, if the Pengwyn Fund's large inflow cannot be invested immediately, Barker can equitize the cash using equity futures or ETFs and then gradually trade into the underlying positions and trade out of the futures/ETF position.

12.

Selection Criterion for Trade Strategy	**Identify** one difference between the trading features of Valley Ranch and North Circle, as noted by Sailors, for each trade strategy selection criterion.
Order Characteristics	Key differences include: (i) the sizes of the orders, with larger orders at North Circle; and (ii) the side of the orders, with North Circle skewing more toward buy orders.

Security Characteristics	Key differences include: (i) security type, with North Circle trading only equities; (ii) short-term alpha focus, with more focus on short-term price movements at Valley Ranch; and (iii) security liquidity, with North Circle buying non-listed securities.
Market Conditions	While both North Circle and Valley Ranch are impacted by market conditions overall, North Circle's investments in non-listed securities are more likely to have a greater potential exposure to adverse market liquidity conditions.
Individual Risk Aversion	The portfolio managers at North Circle and Valley Ranch have different aversions to risk, with Valley Ranch's managers having higher risk aversion than the North Circle managers.

13.

Determine which trades are *most likely* to exhibit the greatest execution risk and market impact. (Circle one in each column)

Execution Risk	Market Impact
ABC	ABC
DEF	DEF
XYZ	XYZ

Justify each selection.

The XYZ trade exhibits the greatest execution risk because XYZ has the highest price volatility of the three stocks. Execution risk is the risk of an adverse price movement occurring over the trading horizon owing to a change in the fundamental value of the security or because of trading-induced volatility. Execution risk is often proxied by price volatility. Securities with higher levels of price volatility have greater exposure to execution risk than securities with lower price volatility.

The ABC trade exhibits the greatest market impact risk as it represents the highest percentage of ADV (45,000 / 195,000 = 23.07%). The permanent component of price change associated with trading an order is the market price impact caused by the information content of the trade. The larger the size of the trade expressed as a percentage of ADV, the larger the expected market impact cost.

14. B is correct. A pre-trade benchmark is often specified by portfolio managers who are buying or selling securities seeking short-term alpha by buying undervalued or selling overvalued securities in the market. Wong believes the stock of Music Plus is overvalued and is seeking short-term alpha with the sell order. Since Wong has an exact record of the price of Music Plus when the decision for the sell order was made ($15.22), the decision price is the most appropriate pre-trade benchmark for the sell order.

A is incorrect because a closing price is a post-trade benchmark and is typically used by index managers and mutual funds that wish to execute transactions at the closing price for the day. A portfolio manager who is managing tracking error to a benchmark will generally select a closing price benchmark since the closing price is the price used to compute the fund's valuation and resulting tracking error to the benchmark. This is not the objective of the sell order of Music Plus. Wong's objective is to execute the sell trade as quickly as possible to capture the short-term alpha she identified. She expects the price of Music Plus to revert back to $14.20 within the day. Therefore, she will need to execute her trading prior to the price when the market closes; thus, the closing price is not the appropriate price benchmark.

Solutions

C is incorrect because a TWAP benchmark price is used when portfolio managers wish to exclude potential trade outliers. Trade outliers may be caused by trading a large buy order at the day's low or a large sell order at the day's high. Therefore, a TWAP benchmark is not appropriate for the sell order of Music Plus because Wong would like to execute a large sell order near the day's high price, which would likely be an outlier.

15. A is correct. The sell order for the Music Plus shares has associated high trade urgency because Wong determined that the stock is temporarily overvalued and expects others to realize this quickly. Therefore, the trader does not have the benefit of trading the order passively (such as by using a VWAP or TWAP participation strategy) during the day, since the share price could decrease to fair value at any time. Because the trade order for Music Plus shares is submitted after the market opened that day, the opening auction is not an option and the whole order is traded in the open market.

B is incorrect because selling at the closing auction for the day is an appropriate trading strategy for trades when the portfolio manager would like to receive proceeds at NAV. An example of such a trade is a trade to meet a redemption request from a client. The trade for Music Plus shares has associated high trade urgency and must be executed as quickly as possible to capture the short-term alpha. Waiting until the closing auction is not an appropriate trading strategy.

C is incorrect because passive trading is appropriate for trades associated with low trade urgency. The sell order of Music Plus shares has associated high trade urgency because Wong determined that the stock is temporarily overvalued and expects the new data to be reflected in the price by the end of the day. Therefore, the trader does not have the benefit of trading the order passively (such as by using a VWAP or TWAP participation strategy) during the day, since the share price could decrease to fair value at any time.

16. C is correct. Liquidity-seeking algorithms are appropriate for large orders that the portfolio manager or trader would like to execute quickly without having a substantial impact on the security price. The sell order for Music Plus shares is for 20% of the expected volume and therefore is a large order. Liquidity-seeking algorithms are also used when displaying sizable liquidity via limit orders could lead to unwanted information leakage and adverse security price movement. In these cases, the priority is to minimize information leakage associated with order execution and avoid signaling to the market the trading intentions of the portfolio manager or trader. Wong is concerned that a large limit order will reveal to the market her opinion the shares are overvalued.

A is incorrect because POV algorithms (also known as participation algorithms) send orders following a volume participation schedule. As trading volume increases in the market, these algorithms will trade more shares, and as volume decreases, these algorithms will trade fewer shares. Wong needs to execute the sell order for Music Plus shares as quickly as possible because she expects the new information to be reflected in the share price quickly. Therefore, a POV algorithm is not appropriate.

B is incorrect because even though arrival price algorithms are used for orders in which the portfolio manager or trader believes prices are likely to move unfavorably and wishes to trade more aggressively to capture alpha, they are used when the security is relatively liquid or the order is not outsized (size less than 15% of the expected volume). The order size for Music Plus shares is large, at 20% of the expected volume.

17. C is correct. The implementation shortfall in basis points is calculated as follows:

$$\text{Implementation shortfall (bps)} = \frac{\text{Implementation shortfall (\$)}}{\text{(Total order shares)}\,(p_d)} \times 10{,}000 \text{ bps}$$

$$\text{Implementation shortfall (\$)} = \underbrace{\sum s_j p_j - \sum s_j p_d}_{\text{Execution Cost}} + \underbrace{(S - \sum s_j)(P_n - P_d)}_{\text{Opportunity Cost}} + \text{Fees}.$$

Fees = Absolute value of $\sum s_j$ × Fee per share

where

$S > 0$ indicates a buy order and $S < 0$ indicates a sell order

P_d represents the price at the time of the investment decision

P_n represents the current price

s_j and p_j represent the number of shares executed and the transaction price of the jth trade

Execution cost = [(−6,000 × 26.80) + (−3,000 × 26.30)] − (−9,000 × 27.10)
= 4,200.

Opportunity cost = [−10,000 − (−9,000)] × (26.00 − 27.10) = 1,100.

Fees = 9,000 × 0.03 = 270.

So, the implementation shortfall ($) is calculated as

Implementation shortfall ($) = 4,200 + 1,100 + 270 = 5,570.

Finally, the implementation shortfall (bps) is calculated as

$$\text{Implementation shortfall (bps)} = \frac{5{,}570}{10{,}000 \times 27.10} \times 10{,}000 \text{ bps} \approx 206 \text{ bps}$$

18. A is correct. The delay cost in dollars is calculated as

$$\text{Delay cost} = \left(\sum s_j\right) p_0 - \left(\sum s_j\right) p_d$$

where

$S > 0$ indicates a buy order and $S < 0$ indicates a sell order

p_0 represents the arrival price, defined as the asset price at the time the order was released to the market for execution

p_d represents the price at the time of the investment decision

s_j represents the number of shares executed

Therefore, the delay cost in dollars for the sell order is calculated as

Delay cost = (−9,000 × 26.90) − (−9,000 × 27.10) = $1,800

19. B is correct. The market-adjusted cost in basis points is calculated as

Market-adjusted cost (bps) = Arrival cost (bps) − β × Index cost (bps)

$$\text{Arrival cost (bps)} = \text{Side} \times \frac{(\bar{P} - P_0)}{P_0} \times 10^4 \text{ bps}$$

$$\text{Index cost (bps)} = \text{Side} \times \frac{(\text{Index VWAP} - \text{Index arrival price})}{\text{Index arrival price}} \times 10^4$$

Where

Solutions

$$\text{Side} = \begin{cases} +1 \text{ Buy Order} \\ -1 \text{ Sell Order} \end{cases}.$$

$\overline{P}$ = Average execution price of order

P_0 = arrival price

Therefore,

$$\text{Average execution price} = \frac{(6,000 \times 26.80 + 3,000 \times 26.30)}{9,000} \approx 26.63$$

$$\text{Arrival cost (bps)} = -1 \times \frac{(26.63 - 26.90)}{26.90} \times 10^4 \text{ bps} = 100.37 \text{ bps}$$

$$\text{Index cost (bps)} = -1 \times \frac{590 - 600}{600} \times 10^4 = 166.67 \text{ bps}$$

Market-adjusted cost (bps) = 100.37 bps − 0.9 × 166.67 bps ≈ −50 bps

Since the result is negative, the market-adjusted cost for the sell order of West Commerce is a savings of approximately 50 bps.

20. C is correct. Both of SWM's trading policies are consistent with good governance. Asset managers should have a list of approved brokers and execution venues for trading and the criteria used to create this list. Creating and maintaining the list should be a collaborative effort shared by portfolio execution, compliance, and risk management. A best practices approach is to create a Best Execution Monitoring Committee within an investment management firm that is responsible for maintaining and updating the list regularly, or as circumstances require, and for distributing the list to all parties involved in trade execution. Furthermore, if several accounts follow the same or a similar investment strategy and have similar trading needs, then pooling the trades for trade execution may make sense in some situations. If a pooled trade is not fully executed, the order amount that is executed generally needs to be allocated to accounts on a pro-rata basis so that no account is disadvantaged relative to the others.

21.

Identify the likely appropriate price benchmark for the LIM trade. (Circle one)			
Pre-Trade	Intraday	Post-Trade	Price Target

Justify your response.

A pre-trade benchmark is a reference price that is known before the start of the period over which trading will take place. For example, pre-trade benchmarks include decision price, previous close, opening price, and arrival price. A pre-trade benchmark is often specified by portfolio managers who are buying or selling securities on the basis of decision prices. In this case, Bradley's target price had been set based on his valuation principles before the opening, whereas waiting for the other benchmarks as inputs would result in the perceived opportunity expiring before it could be exploited.

For Bradley and his trader, two of these pre-trade benchmarks are potentially appropriate. Those are either the decision price, which was the price when Bradley made the decision to buy or sell the security, or the arrival price, which is the price of the security at the time the order is entered into the market for execution. Portfolio managers who are buying or selling on the basis of alpha expectations or a current market mispricing will often specify an arrival price benchmark.

22. The delay cost reflects the adverse price movement associated with the untimely submission of Bradley's order and is calculated as follows:

Delay cost = $\left(\sum s_j\right) p_0 - \left(\sum s_j\right) p_d$ = (25,000 × 23.09) − (25,000 × 23.01)
= $2,000.

23. Bradley and the trader's analysis will show that the market-adjusted cost calculates as follows:

$$\text{Arrival cost (bps)} = \text{Side} \times \frac{(\bar{P} - P_0)}{P_0} \times 10^4 \text{ bps}$$

$$= +1 \times \frac{(\$23.45 - \$23.09)}{\$23.09} \times 10^4 \text{ bps}$$

= 155.91 bps.

$$\text{Index cost (bps)} = \text{Side} \times \frac{(\text{Index VWAP} - \text{Index arrival price})}{\text{Index arrival price}} \times 10^4 \text{ bps}$$

$$= +1 \times \frac{(\$2,184 - \$2,150)}{\$2,150} \times 10^4 \text{ bps}$$

≈ 158.14 bps.

Market-adjusted cost (bps) = Arrival cost (bps) − β × Index cost (bps)
= 155.91 − 0.95 × 158.14
= 155.91 − 150.23
≈ 5.68 bps.

LIM's market-adjusted cost is thus significantly lower than the total arrival cost. This indicates that most of the expense associated with buying LIM is due to the effect of buying it in a rising market as opposed to the buying pressure induced by the order itself.

24.

Determine which algorithm Minchow is likely to use for the Dynopax sell order. (Circle one)

POV	VWAP	TWAP

Justify your response.

Regarding Bean's alternatives, VWAP and TWAP algorithms release orders to the market following a time-specified schedule, trading a predetermined number of shares within the specified time interval (e.g., one day). Following a fixed schedule as VWAP algorithms do, however, may not be optimal for certain stocks because such algorithms may not complete the order in cases where volumes are low. Furthermore, while POV algorithms incorporate real-time volume by following (or chasing) volumes, they may not complete the order within the time period specified.

TWAP algorithms, which send the same number of shares and the same percentage of the order to be traded in each time period, will help ensure the specified number of shares are executed within the specified time period. Given Bean's stated priority of complete execution in one day, he is likely to use a TWAP algorithm for the Dynopax sell order.

25.

Determine the veracity of each comment. **Justify** each response.

Comment	Veracity (Circle one for each row)	Justification

Solutions

1	Correct	Regardless of the trading venue, transactions and quantities are always reported.
	Incorrect	
2	Correct	Dark pools provide anonymity because no pre-trade transparency exists. Exchanges are known as lit markets (as opposed to dark markets) because they provide pre-trade transparency—namely, limit orders that reflect trader intentions for trade side (buy or sell), price, and size. However, with a dark pool, there is less certainty of execution as compared to an exchange.
	Incorrect	

26. Theme 1 is inappropriate because the optimal execution approach may differ by asset class, level of security liquidity, and security trading mechanism (order-driven markets, quote-driven markets, and brokered markets). Green Savannah's trade policy document should describe the factors used in determining how an order can be executed in an optimal manner for a given scenario.

Theme 4 is inappropriate because as part of a suitable policy for the treatment of trade errors, those errors and any resulting gains/losses need to be disclosed to Green Savannah's compliance department and documented in a trade error log. The priority is to ensure errors are resolved in a way that prevents adverse impact for the client, not to ensure complete disclosure.

LEARNING MODULE 8

Case Study in Portfolio Management: Institutional (Endowment)

by Gabriel Petre, CFA.

Gabriel Petre, CFA, is at World Bank (USA).

LEARNING OUTCOMES	
Mastery	*The candidate should be able to:*
☐	discuss tools for managing portfolio liquidity risk
☐	discuss capture of the illiquidity premium as a long-term investment strategy
☐	analyze asset allocation and portfolio construction in relation to liquidity needs and risk and return requirements and recommend actions to address identified needs
☐	demonstrate the application of the Code of Ethics and Standards of Professional Conduct regarding the actions of individuals involved in manager selection
☐	analyze the costs and benefits of derivatives versus cash market techniques for establishing or modifying asset class or risk exposures
☐	demonstrate the use of derivatives overlays in tactical asset allocation and rebalancing
☐	discuss ESG considerations in managing long-term institutional portfolios

1. INTRODUCTION

The development of a strategic asset allocation (SAA) for long-horizon institutional investors such as university endowments raises special challenges. These include supporting spending policies while ensuring the long-term sustainability of the endowment and establishing optimal exposure to illiquid investment strategies in the context of a diversified portfolio.

Large university endowments typically have significant exposure to illiquid asset classes. The exposure to illiquid asset classes impacts the portfolio's overall liquidity profile and requires a comprehensive liquidity management approach to ensure that liquidity needs can be met in a timely fashion.[1] In addition, capital market conditions and asset prices change, resulting in a need to change asset allocation exposures and/or rebalance the portfolio to maintain a profile close to the strategic asset allocation.

Institutions often use derivatives to manage liquidity needs and implement asset allocation changes. The cash-efficient nature of derivatives and their high levels of liquidity in many markets make them suitable tools for portfolio rebalancing, tactical exposure changes, and satisfying short-term liquidity needs—all while maintaining desired portfolio exposures.

This case study explores these issues from the perspective of a large university endowment undertaking a review of its asset allocation and then implementing proposed allocation changes and a tactical overlay program. Rebalancing needs for the endowment arise because market moves result in the drift of the endowment's asset allocation.

The case is divided into two major sections. The first section addresses issues relating to asset allocation and liquidity management. The case introduces a framework to support the management of liquidity and cash needs in an orderly and timely manner while avoiding disruption to underlying managers and potentially capturing an illiquidity premium. Such concepts as time-to-cash tables and liquidity budgets are explored in detail. Aspects relating to rebalancing and maintaining a risk profile similar to the portfolio's strategic asset allocation over time are also covered.

The second section explores the use of derivatives in portfolio construction from a tactical asset allocation (TAA) overlay and rebalancing perspective. The suitability of futures, total return swaps, and exchange-traded funds (ETFs) is discussed based on their characteristics, associated costs, and desired portfolio objectives. The case also presents a cost–benefit analysis of derivatives and cash markets for implementing rebalancing decisions. Environmental, social, and governance (ESG) considerations arising in the normal course of investing are also explored.

2   BACKGROUND: LIQUIDITY MANAGEMENT

☐ discuss tools for managing portfolio liquidity risk

☐ discuss capture of the illiquidity premium as a long-term investment strategy

For an institutional investor, such as an endowment or a pension fund, liquidity management refers to the set of policies and practices that ensure that the portfolio complies with investment policy yet can meet cash outflow needs in a timely and orderly manner without incurring excessive costs. Optimal liquidity management helps ensure that distressed sales of illiquid assets are avoided, especially in weak market conditions, and that the portfolio can benefit from the expected illiquidity premium associated with long-term private market allocations.

Historically, the importance of liquidity management was emphasized in the 2008 global financial crisis when many institutional investors with significant allocations to illiquid asset classes and regular cash outflow requirements struggled to meet these requirements.

---

1 In this context, "liquidity" refers to the ability to exchange assets into cash for an expected value within a known time frame.

During this time, public markets experienced significant losses, liquidity conditions deteriorated, and distributions from many private market investments stopped. For many university endowments, another source of liquidity—donations—also dropped significantly, further amplifying liquidity issues. In some cases, endowments were forced to liquidate securities at steep discounts, drastically cut funding for some programs dependent on endowment distributions, and/or borrow funds collateralized by the endowment, increasing leverage and the portfolio's risk profile.

Institutional investors have several important "tools" at their disposal to manage a portfolio's liquidity risk. These include

- liquidity profiling and time-to-cash tables,
- rebalancing and commitment strategies,
- stress testing analyses, and
- derivatives.

Liquidity Profiling and Time-to-Cash Tables

For any investor, the assessment of liquidity needs starts with identifying potential cash inflows and cash outflows for a defined investment horizon. In the case of endowments, cash outflows include distributions to the university and meeting capital call requirements for illiquid investments (e.g., real assets, private equity, hedge funds, and structured products). Once the sources and uses of cash have been identified, the institutional investor establishes the need for liquidity and the desired liquidity maturity profile for the overall portfolio. As part of this process, a **liquidity classification schedule** (**time-to-cash table**) is created, and an overall **liquidity budget** is defined.[2] The liquidity classification schedule defines portfolio categories (or "buckets") based on the estimated time needed in the normal course of business to convert assets in that particular category into cash. The liquidity budget assigns portfolio weights considered acceptable to each liquidity classification in the time-to-cash table and establishes a liquidity benchmark for the portfolio construction process.

An example of a time-to-cash table is provided in Exhibit 1. It defines liquidity classifications based on the time expected to liquidate an investment without the liquidation having a significant impact on market conditions and the resulting sale price for the investment. The impact on market conditions is based on the expected market price immediately before and after trading if the sell order was executed. In the case of investments managed by third-party managers, the time to cash also depends on the contractual terms governing the type of investment vehicle used. Typically, private investments requiring more than one year to exit are viewed as illiquid. In the case of hedge funds, contractual terms (e.g., lockups, notification periods, withdrawal windows) vary based on the manager and underlying strategy. A manager's ability to deny withdrawal requests during stress periods ("to activate gates") to protect fund investors and prevent forced liquidations will impact time to cash.

Exhibit 1: Time-to-Cash Table and Liquidity Budget

Time to Cash	Liquidity Classification	Liquidity Budget (% of portfolio)
< 1 Week	Highly Liquid	At Least 10%
< 1 Quarter	Moderately Liquid	At Least 35%

---

2 See also Russell Investments (2013).

Time to Cash	Liquidity Classification	Liquidity Budget (% of portfolio)
< 1 Year	Semi-Liquid	At Least 50%
> 1 Year	Illiquid	Up to 50%

The granularity of a time-to-cash table can vary to include monthly or semiannual categories, depending on the investor's liquidity preferences, liquidity needs, and other circumstances. The core principle is to identify liquidity categories relevant to the types of cash outflows the investor will face and to match overall portfolio characteristics with liquidity needs through the design of the resulting asset allocation. The next step is to define an overall liquidity budget specifying portfolio allocations for the different time-to-cash buckets (as shown in the third column of Exhibit 1).[3] In the case of highly liquid, moderately liquid, and semi-liquid categories, minimum portfolio weights are identified. For the illiquid category, a maximum portfolio weight is identified.

The liquidity budget reflects the acceptable liquidity requirements that the portfolio must meet, even in a liquidity stress scenario. The results of stress test analyses are therefore important inputs in developing the liquidity budget.

To operationalize the concepts represented in the liquidity budget, the institutional investor does an analysis of the underlying liquidity characteristics of the portfolio investments and monitors these characteristics over time. The analysis should look through the broad definition of asset classes to the underlying investments used for exposure. Different investments within the same asset class (such as public equities) might have very different liquidity profiles. Commingled funds (funds that are pooled and managed together in a single account) could be less liquid than ETFs or mutual funds and could have different liquidity profiles than separate accounts. Furthermore, the liquidity profile of similar investment vehicles in the same asset class could differ depending on the underlying strategy used by the investment manager. For example, a commingled fund following a concentrated, small-cap active strategy in emerging market equities might offer investors only quarterly liquidity as compared to a commingled fund investing in large-cap emerging market equities, which might offer monthly or weekly liquidity. For these reasons, it is appropriate to conduct liquidity analysis on a bottom-up basis for each investment, aggregate at the portfolio level, and monitor changes over time to keep the portfolio within liquidity budget parameters. An example of liquidity profiling for a portfolio's underlying investments is shown in Exhibit 2. The portfolio example uses investments in separate accounts, commingled funds, futures, ETFs, and active managers to achieve its asset class exposure to both public and private markets.

---

3 Mercer (2015).

Background: Liquidity Management

Exhibit 2: Liquidity Profiling for a Portfolio

Asset Class	Asset Class Allocation (% of portfolio)	Investment Allocation (% of overall portfolio)	Investment Vehicle	Highly Liquid	Moderately Liquid	Semi-Liquid	Illiquid
Cash	1%	1%	Separate Account	100%	0%	0%	0%
Fixed Income	14%	5%	Separate Account	100%	0%	0%	0%
		8%	Commingled Fund	100%	0%	0%	0%
		1%	Futures	100%	0%	0%	0%
Domestic Equity	17%	8%	Commingled Fund	0%	50%	50%	0%
		8%	Separate Account	0%	100%	0%	0%
		1%	Futures	100%	0%	0%	0%
International Developed Equity	10%	6%	Commingled Fund	0%	50%	30%	20%
		4%	Separate Account	0%	80%	20%	0%
Emerging Market Equity	12%	9%	Commingled Fund	0%	75%	25%	0%
		3%	ETF	100%	0%	0%	0%
Private Equity	18%	18%	Funds 1–85	0%	0%	0%	100%
Real Assets	13%	4%	Funds 1–8	0%	0%	75%	25%
		6%	Funds 9–33	0%	0%	0%	100%
		3%	Funds 34–50	0%	0%	20%	80%
Diversifying Strategies	15%	4%	Funds 1–5	0%	0%	100%	0%
		6%	Funds 6–11	0%	25%	25%	50%
		5%	Funds 12–19	0%	0%	75%	25%
Overall Portfolio	100%	100%		19%	26%	22%	33%

Rebalancing, Commitments

The discussion so far has focused on liquidity management and the ability of an institutional portfolio to meet cash outflows in an orderly manner as they come due. Another consideration is the impact these changes in the liquidity profile have on the overall risk of the investment portfolio and the ability to keep the portfolio close to desired risk targets. Illiquid assets carry extremely high rebalancing costs. Because asset liquidity tends to decrease in times of market stress, having sufficient liquid assets and rebalancing mechanisms in place is important. This approach will ensure that the portfolio's risk profile remains within acceptable risk targets and does not "drift" as the relative valuations of different asset classes fluctuate during stress periods. Rebalancing mechanisms include the following:

- **Systematic rebalancing policies**. Rebalancing disciplines, such as calendar rebalancing and percent-range rebalancing, are intended to control risk relative to the strategic asset allocation. In these cases, pre-specified tolerance bands for asset class weights are used. The size or width of the bands should consider the underlying volatility of each investment category to minimize transaction costs. This means more-volatile investment categories should usually have wider rebalancing bands. Transaction costs, correlations between asset classes, and investor risk tolerance are other factors that could influence the size of the band selected.

- **Automatic adjustment mechanisms**. These are mechanisms designed to maintain a stable risk profile when exposure drifts from targeted exposure. An example is using adjustments to a public market allocation that is correlated to a private market allocation to rebalance private market risk. This approach uses liquid public assets as a proxy for illiquid private assets. For example, assume private equity investments have an equity beta of 1. In a situation where the allocation to private equity increases by 1% versus the target, the allocation to public equities would automatically be adjusted down by 1% to maintain a stable systematic market risk profile. Note, however, that although systematic market risk is unchanged, the illiquidity risk of the portfolio is now higher. Alternatively, the adjustment could be further refined to maintain a constant equity beta, assuming private equity has a beta to public equities of greater than 1 (caused by leverage, for example).[4] Similar public market proxies can be used to represent private real estate, infrastructure, or other illiquid instruments based on their underlying risk characteristics.

Multi-year funding strategies for private markets that incorporate a steady pace of commitments to reach a target allocation and/or to keep the allocation close to target over time are other means of ensuring that the portfolio remains consistent with desired risk objectives. Private market funds pose specific challenges for investors in maintaining a desired exposure over time because investors do not control the pace at which committed capital is drawn or the pace at which capital distributions are returned. Although unpredictable at an individual fund level, these patterns become more predictable within a portfolio of private market investments.

The objective of a multi-year funding strategy is to design a commitment-pacing strategy that will result in the desired portfolio exposure to the asset class over time. The commitment-pacing strategy translates into an annual level of commitments and is typically the result of a cash flow modeling exercise that takes into account expectations about the speed at which committed capital is drawn, the pace of distributions, the evolution in overall asset size, and other circumstances specific to the investor. The cash flow modeling exercise would project forward the expected asset class exposure (as a percentage of the overall portfolio) at various commitment levels, thus reducing the risk of overshooting the target allocation. Scenario analysis should also be used to consider the impact of different market stress conditions. The evolution of the asset allocation must be monitored over time, with adjustments to the commitment pace made as necessary.

Stress Testing

A robust liquidity framework ensures that liquidity needs can be met in a timely fashion during periods of normal market and stress market conditions. Understanding how the portfolio's liquidity profile could change in addition to how the liquidity needs of the institution could change during stress periods is therefore critical. Comprehensive stress-testing exercises would seek to "stress" (i.e., presume extremely adverse market conditions for) both assets and liabilities simultaneously to understand how these

---
4 See also Raymond (2009).

Background: Liquidity Management

might be impacted during stress conditions. With respect to assets, the stress test can cover distributional assumptions regarding prices (e.g., volatility, return), correlations across assets, and liquidity characteristics. Liability shocks can also be factored in, for example, by increasing expected endowment distributions to support the university during the stress periods. The design of the stress tests can be informed by historical events (e.g., the 2008 global financial crisis), statistical models (e.g., extreme value theory), and/or scenario analysis (e.g., analyzing the potential impact of a hypothetical scenario with respect to a set of variables on the overall portfolio).

Derivatives

Derivatives can be used to manage cash outflow needs and changing risk exposures. Derivatives overlay strategies are investment strategies that use derivatives instruments to obtain, offset, or substitute specific asset class or market factor exposure beyond what is provided by the underlying portfolio assets. For example, a derivatives overlay program allows an institutional investor to rebalance exposures to public asset classes (e.g., on a monthly or quarterly basis) while leaving allocations to external active managers unchanged. The cash-efficient nature of derivatives makes them desirable tools for rebalancing. Derivatives overlays can also be used to modify a portfolio's liquidity profile through the use of leverage—for example, using futures contracts (long futures position) to gain economic exposure to US equities and then deploying the cash that is not required for posting margin into other investments with different liquidity profiles or using it to satisfy short-term liquidity needs. Derivatives can also be used to generate additional cash by employing leverage at the overall portfolio level.

Earning an Illiquidity Premium

An attractive feature for investors in illiquid investments, such as private equity or private real estate, is the expectation of extracting an illiquidity premium in addition to premiums associated with underlying market risk factor exposures in an illiquid strategy. The illiquidity premium (also called the liquidity premium) is the expected compensation for the additional risk of tying up capital for a potentially uncertain time period. For long-term institutional investors with long investment horizons and modest interim liquidity needs, exposure to illiquid investments and the illiquidity premium embedded in these is a feasible investment strategy and offers an opportunity to increase the efficiency of the overall portfolio. The higher efficiency can be driven by the following:

1. the risk diversification potential that exists between the illiquid assets and the rest of the investor's investible universe
2. the higher return that can be generated by taking on illiquidity risk (assuming it is adequately priced)
3. a combination of the above

In practice, however, uncertainties exist around the expected size of the illiquidity premium and the ability of institutional investors to extract it that should not be underestimated.

Quantitative estimates for the illiquidity premium suggest evidence of a positive illiquidity premium in private equity and private real estate and of illiquidity premium size being positively correlated to the length of the illiquidity horizon.[5]

---

5 See also Green (2015).

An alternative approach for estimating the illiquidity risk premium is based on the idea that the size of the discount an investor should receive in return for committing capital for an uncertain period of time can be represented by the value of a put option with an exercise price equal to the marketable price of the illiquid asset at the time of purchase. (The "marketable price" is a hypothetical price at which the illiquid asset could be sold if it were freely traded; it can be estimated by various means.) In this case, the price of the illiquid asset can be derived by subtracting the put price from the marketable price of the asset. If both the marketable price and the illiquid asset price are estimated or known, then the expected return for each can be calculated, with the difference in expected returns representing the illiquidity premium (in %). This approach was initially developed by Chaffe (1993) and later improved upon by Staub and Diermeier (2003). They also find there should be a positive correlation between the length of the illiquidity horizon and the size of the illiquidity premium.

A significant body of literature documents a positive relationship between lack of liquidity and expected returns in the case of public equity. For example, Pastor and Stambaugh (2001) find that expected returns are impacted by systematic liquidity risk and estimate a 3% return over the 1996–2003 period in the United States for a zero-net-investment portfolio that holds low-liquidity stocks long and high-liquidity stocks short.

Overall, though, it is difficult to isolate the illiquidity premium with precision and separate its effects from such other risk factors as the market, value, and size in the case of equity investments. Furthermore, estimates of the illiquidity premium are based on broad market indexes, yet an investor in these asset classes would typically invest in only a small subset of the universe, with the result that individual investment experience could be very different and more susceptible to idiosyncratic factors.[6] These challenges further emphasize the importance of liquidity budgeting in facilitating the capture of the illiquidity premium while controlling for risk.

3. QUADRIVIUM UNIVERSITY INVESTMENT COMPANY CASE: BACKGROUND

☐ analyze asset allocation and portfolio construction in relation to liquidity needs and risk and return requirements and recommend actions to address identified needs

Quadrivium University (QU) is an independent liberal arts college located in a vibrant midsized city with a growing and diverse population. The university was founded in 1916 by James Greaves and Colin Healey, two entrepreneurs with a passion for astronomy and mathematics who settled in the area in the early 1900s. Over time, the university has built an outstanding reputation as one of the top schools in the country. Consistent with the founders' interests, the school's programs in astronomy and mathematics are highly regarded, attracting applicants from all over the world.

The QU endowment was established in 1936 through a USD15 million donation from Healey, whose goal was to provide financial aid to new undergraduate students. A quarter of new students receive Healey grants, and this percentage has increased steadily over time.

---

6 Ang, Papanikolaou, and Westerfield (2014).

As of the current fiscal year, QU has an endowment of USD8 billion, of which USD6 billion represents funds used for general unrestricted support and unrestricted funds functioning as endowment. The remaining funds have various donor-specified use restrictions. Although a significant portion of the endowment's growth has been from investment returns, the endowment also benefits from a strong and deep alumni network that provides regular donations and access to highly regarded industry contacts and money managers. Exhibit 3 shows the market value of the endowment over recent years, and Exhibit 4 shows the realized investment returns over the same period.

Exhibit 3: Market Value of QU Endowment

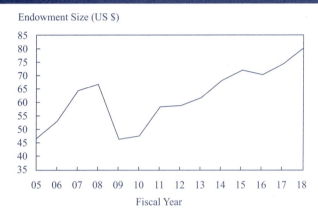

Exhibit 4: Investment Returns for QU Endowment

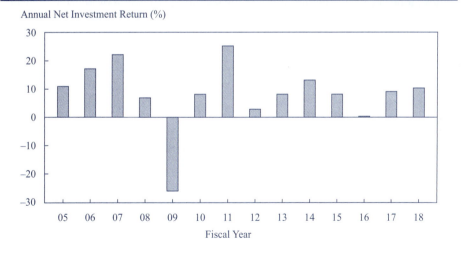

QU has an annual operating budget of USD554 million, and 70% of the operating budget is used to fund salaries and benefits for faculty and administrative staff. In addition, the budget is used to pay down debt associated with a major upgrade of the main campus facilities, pay expenses associated with the maintenance of physical infrastructure, and fund various research and financial aid programs.

Annual distributions from the endowment provide funding for approximately 60% of the university's operating budget, including its financial aid programs. In absolute dollar terms, the size of annual distributions has increased steadily in the past five years as the size of the endowment fund has grown. Similarly, the percentage of the operating budget covered by distributions from the endowment has increased. The board of the university has recently expressed a preference for a predictable pattern of distributions to allow for better planning of resource deployment through its programs. Consistent with that preference, the spending policy of the endowment was changed following the 2008 global financial crisis. Pre-crisis, the university used a simple spending rule: Spending equaled the long-term desired spending rate of 5% multiplied by the market value of the endowment at the beginning of the fiscal year. Post-crisis, the university changed its spending rule to a geometric smoothing rule, sometimes called the Yale formula.

The current spending rule is designed to produce a 5% long-term spending rate in a way that shields annual distributions from fluctuations in the endowment's market value. The endowment uses a weighted-average formula of the previous year's spending amount and the endowment's market value at the end of the previous fiscal year multiplied by the long-term desired spending rate:

Spending for current fiscal year

= (66% × Spending for previous fiscal year) + 34% × (5% × Endowment market value at the end of previous fiscal year).

For QU, the previous fiscal year's spending was USD308.9 million, while the endowment's market value at the end of the previous fiscal year was USD7,575.1 million. In this case, QU's spending for the current fiscal year would be

Spending for current fiscal year = (66% × USD308.9 million) + 34% × (5% × USD7,575.1 million)

= USD332.6 million.

Consistent with the spending policy, the endowment's investment objective is to achieve long-term returns that support the spending rate while preserving the value of the endowment in real terms over time (thus safeguarding the long-term sustainability of the program). For QU, a 5% spending rate per year combined with long-term expected inflation for colleges and universities of 2%–3% per year translates into a 7%–8% nominal return per year objective over the long term. QU's associated risk objective is 12%–14% annualized return volatility (standard deviation of portfolio returns must be between 12% and 14%).

Quadrivium University Investment Company

Quadrivium University (QU) is overseen by a board of trustees ("the Trustees"), generally consisting of prominent, wealthy alumni who are elected to the position. QU Investment Company (QUINCO) is the university investment office, which manages QU's endowment. The office was established in 1993 at a time when endowment assets were USD1 billion. From a governance perspective, the office is organizationally distinct from the university, although it is not a separate legal entity. The president of the investment office, Aaron Winter, reports to the university president and to the QUINCO board of directors ("the Board"). The Board comprises 11 members appointed by the Trustees. The president of QUINCO, the university president, and the treasurer of the university serve as ex-officio members. The QUINCO Board is responsible for approving investment policy and guidelines and providing guidance on key policy matters. Implementation of the investment policy has been fully delegated to QUINCO staff, who are empowered to make changes to the portfolio within the parameters of the investment guidelines.

Quadrivium University Investment Company Case: Background

QUINCO has 13 investment professionals, who are university employees. The investment model is one where the investment strategy is implemented through external investment managers. The Board has consistently reaffirmed its view that such a model provides greater flexibility for changing investment portfolio exposures when circumstances warrant, while reducing internal staffing needs compared to an in-house investment management model. Internal investment staff are focused on asset allocation, risk management, and selecting, monitoring, and terminating external investment managers.

The following five investment categories are part of the current asset allocation: fixed income, public equities, private equity, real assets (composed primarily of private real estate and natural resources), and diversifying strategies (primarily hedge fund strategies targeting high absolute returns with low correlations to traditional asset classes, such as public equity and fixed income). Alternative investments are considered private equity, real assets, and diversifying strategies. Private equity and real assets are recognized as illiquid (alternative) investments. The investment team is organized by investment category, with a senior portfolio manager leading each area and supported by an analyst. In addition, the team includes a portfolio strategist in charge of asset allocation and risk management, also supported by an analyst, and the president of the office, who acts as the chief investment officer (CIO). Senior portfolio managers have primary responsibility for investment decisions within their investment category, while the portfolio strategist has responsibility for ongoing endowment rebalancing decisions, overlays, and tactical asset allocation tilts. All external investment manager decisions and tactical asset allocation deviations are discussed and approved by the internal investment committee. Winter chairs the committee, which includes all senior portfolio managers and the portfolio strategist. The QUINCO Board is responsible for granting final approval of external investment managers.

Investment Strategy: Background and Evolution

QUINCO has distinguished itself as a steady and progressive institutional investor with a focus on long-term objectives; it is unlikely to make abrupt wholesale changes to its investment strategy. This strategy is, in part, driven by leadership stability, with the investment office having had the same president (Winter's predecessor) for the first 28 years of existence. Another important factor has been an established culture focused on maintaining best-in-class investment practices and institutionalizing that knowledge through robust processes and systems.

For the first years of existence, the endowment invested only in public markets, mostly equities and bonds. In its early days, the belief was that the endowment's limited size and investment resources would present challenges in accessing, monitoring, and properly managing complex, nontraditional investment strategies. Since the late-1990s, as the size of the endowment grew, the QUINCO Board has embraced the belief that exposure to nontraditional, or alternative, asset categories is beneficial for the endowment's long-term prospects—enhancing investment risk diversification and providing potentially higher risk-adjusted returns in a greater variety of market environments. To express this belief, the Board has supported an increase in internal investment expertise by hiring seasoned investment professionals and expanding QUINCO's investment staff. Over the next two decades, the endowment portfolio increased its exposure to such alternative investments as private equity, real assets, and hedge funds.

These investments have performed well for the endowment; in particular, private equity and real assets were very strong contributors to the portfolio return over that period, in line with expectations. In aggregate, however, exposure to alternatives in the portfolio is still below the average exposure of other large university endowments that the Board considers the endowment's relevant peer universe.

The evolution of the endowment's asset allocation is shown in Exhibit 5.

Exhibit 5: Evolution of the SAA

Evolution of Investment Policy Targets

	2001	2004	2007	2010	2013	2016	2019	2022
Cash	1%	1%	1%	1%	1%	1%	1%	1%
Fixed Income	29%	24%	24%	19%	16%	16%	14%	14%
Domestic Equity	40%	35%	26%	24%	23%	21%	20%	17%
International Developed Equity	24%	24%	20%	17%	15%	15%	12%	10%
Emerging Market Equity	0%	3%	10%	15%	15%	12%	12%	12%
Private Equity	3%	5%	8%	10%	12%	14%	16%	18%
Real Assets	3%	5%	6%	7%	9%	11%	12%	13%
Diversifying Strategies	0%	3%	5%	7%	9%	10%	13%	15%

The QUINCO Board oversees a comprehensive strategic asset allocation review every three years. The most recent review of the asset allocation occurred two years ago. At that time, the Board approved a continued increase to alternative investments at the expense of developed market equities (both domestic and international).

Current Scenario

Winter, a QU alumnus who joined QUINCO five years ago, took over the role of investment office president and CIO last year. This is the first time he will be overseeing an asset allocation review. The endowment's current asset allocation is shown in Exhibit 6.

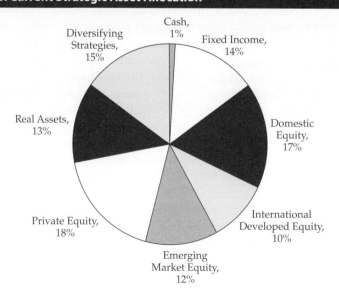

Exhibit 6: Current Strategic Asset Allocation

Based on discussions with the Board, Winter asks his portfolio strategy team—consisting of team lead Julia Thompson, her asset allocation analyst, and the senior portfolio managers for fixed income and public equities—to address the following considerations during the review process:

- The desired liquidity profile for the endowment and corresponding framework for liquidity management.
- The investment outlook and efficiency of the strategic asset allocation. A long period of falling interest rates and rising asset prices in the developed world drove most traditional asset classes to the upper bounds of historical valuation ranges, lowering future expected returns in these markets.
- The role of TAA in QU endowment's investment strategy. Given the long-term nature of the SAA, some Board members are wondering whether a TAA program might improve risk-adjusted returns for the portfolio.
- Endowment underperformance relative to a peer universe of large endowments. Although the QU endowment had better returns than most of its peers during the 2008 global financial crisis, the portfolio has largely underperformed its peers since then.

QUINCO CASE: STRATEGIC ASSET ALLOCATION

☐ analyze asset allocation and portfolio construction in relation to liquidity needs and risk and return requirements and recommend actions to address identified needs

Thompson and the strategy team have completed their analysis, including the considerations raised by Winter and the Board, and are now ready to present to the Board. As part of their work, Thompson updated the long-term, forward-looking capital market assumptions used for the mean–variance optimization process and asset allocation recommendations.

In developing their long-term capital market assumptions, Thompson and the strategy team considered and applied unsmoothing (or de-smoothing) techniques. These techniques were applied to illiquid investments to remove the impact of positive serial correlation on risk estimates caused by stale market pricing. From experience, Thompson knows that the uncertainty of risk and return estimates for illiquid assets is amplified by such aspects as infrequent trading, associated leverage, and long investment horizons. In attempting to estimate risk for illiquid assets, the team's challenges include the availability, quality/reliability, frequency, and non-synchronicity of pricing data. Thompson knows these issues would result in stale pricing or a smoother pattern of reported returns because of fewer data points with lower observed return volatility. If used as an input in their mean–variance optimization models without adjustment, the artificially low volatility would make illiquid asset classes appear more attractive, resulting in higher allocations to illiquid assets in the "optimal" portfolio. To prevent this, Thompson and her team applied unsmoothing techniques to better reflect the underlying risk of illiquid asset classes. After applying unsmoothing techniques to private equity, resulting volatility ends up being significantly higher than volatility that is observed or experienced for these assets. Exhibit 7 and Exhibit 8 show these updated assumptions.

Exhibit 7: Long-Term Expected Return (Net of Fees) and Volatility Assumptions

Asset Class	Expected Real Return (annual geometric mean, next 10 years)	Expected Nominal Return (annual geometric mean, next 10 years)	Standard Deviation of Returns (annual)	Sharpe Ratio
Cash	0.9%	3.4%	1.7%	
Fixed Income	1.8%	4.3%	6.3%	0.14
Domestic Equity	5.0%	7.6%	18.1%	0.23
International Developed Equity	4.8%	7.4%	19.7%	0.20
Emerging Market Equity	6.0%	8.7%	26.6%	0.19
Private Equity	8.5%	11.2%	24.0%	0.32
Real Assets	4.5%	7.1%	13.3%	0.27
Diversifying Strategies	4.0%	6.6%	10.0%	0.31

Note: Inflation is assumed to be 2.5% per year.

Exhibit 8: Forward-Looking Correlation Matrix

	Cash	Fixed Income	Domestic Equity	International Developed Equity	Emerging Market Equity	Private Equity	Real Assets	Diversifying Strategies
Cash	1.00							
Fixed Income	0.11	1.00						
Domestic Equity	0.03	0.13	1.00					
International Developed Equity	0.02	0.14	0.91	1.00				
Emerging Market Equity	0.04	(0.18)	0.69	0.71	1.00			
Private Equity	0.02	(0.11)	0.68	0.65	0.59	1.00		
Real Assets	0.07	(0.16)	0.35	0.35	0.25	0.42	1.00	
Diversifying Strategies	0.18	0.18	0.40	0.40	0.45	0.35	(0.04)	1.00

Analysis by Thompson and her team uncovered the main reasons for peer underperformance since the 2008 crisis: a lower risk profile of the portfolio and a lower allocation to illiquid investments, in particular, private equity. As a result, an important change proposed by Thompson and the team is an increase in exposure to private markets. The change would increase the private equity allocation from 18% to 23% and the real assets allocation from 13% to 16%. To accommodate both increases, the allocations to public equities and fixed income would decrease. The proposed target allocations are presented in Exhibit 9.

QUINCO Case: Strategic Asset Allocation

In terms of implementation, Thompson and her team expect that the transition to the higher target allocations in private equity and real assets will occur gradually over the next two to three years.

Exhibit 9: Proposed Strategic Asset Allocation Targets

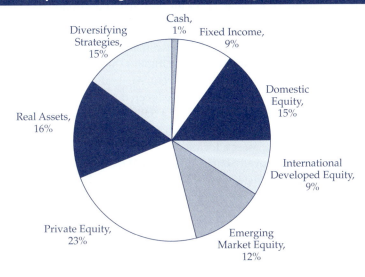

Optimization results in Exhibit 10 are based on the team's assumptions (Exhibit 7 and Exhibit 8) and show that a higher allocation to private equity and real assets would improve the expected long-term risk–return profile of the endowment. The team also includes the results of Monte Carlo simulations that show the probability of an erosion in longer-term purchasing power. Thompson notes that the resulting risk profile measured by the volatility is consistent with quantitative guidelines developed for the endowment's risk tolerance. Based on interaction with the Board, the risk tolerance has been specified as a volatility range of 12% to 14% based on long-term measures of risk.

Exhibit 10: Proposed vs. Current SAA: Expected Risk–Return Properties

Portfolio Characteristic	Proposed SAA	Current SAA
Expected nominal return (annual average, geometric, next 10 years)	7.8%	7.5%
Expected real return (annual average, geometric, next 10 years)	5.3%	5.0%
Standard deviation of returns (annual)	13.2%	12.5%
Sharpe ratio	0.34	0.33
Probability of 25% erosion in purchasing power over 20 years with 5% spending rate	30%	35%

Note: The probability of erosion in purchasing power was derived based on a Monte-Carlo simulation with a 20-year investment horizon, assuming expected return and volatility characteristics will be the same as for the next 10 years.

When asked to justify the proposed strategic asset allocation (SAA), including the higher allocation to private markets, Thompson highlights the optimization results from Exhibit 10 to the Board, noting that the primary driver of the proposed asset allocation changes is the expected improvement in the portfolio's long-term risk–return profile.

Thompson is aware that the proposed asset allocation implies a small increase in the endowment's overall risk profile as measured by the volatility of portfolio returns (13.2% for the proposed SAA versus 12.5% for the current portfolio). She believes that the increase in risk is justified by the following:

- Lower return expectations for all asset classes relative to past expectations due to higher current valuations. This implies that a higher level of risk must be taken to achieve the same level of returns. At the time of the most recent review, the then-current SAA had an expected return of 5.3% in real terms, though now it is expected to generate a 5.0% real return going forward. Lower return expectations can be compensated in part only by efficiency improvements in the asset allocation. Although the proposed SAA is slightly more efficient (improved Sharpe ratio by 0.01), this efficiency improvement alone is not enough to generate a 5.3% expected real return for the same level of short-term risk/volatility as the current SAA.

- A portfolio risk profile that is currently more conservative than that of the endowment's peers.

- A lower expected Sharpe ratio (expected risk–return profile) for fixed income (compared with recent history), suggesting that a lower allocation to these strategies might be warranted.

- Monte-Carlo simulations, suggesting that the proposed asset allocation has a higher probability of achieving the real return target over a 20-year horizon, while better preserving the purchasing power of the endowment with the current spending policy of 5%.

IN-TEXT QUESTIONS

1. Discuss arguments in favor of increasing the endowment's allocation to illiquid investments.

    Guideline Answer:

    In general, for a long-horizon institutional investor, the ability to tolerate illiquidity creates an opportunity to improve portfolio diversification and expected returns as well as access a broader set of investment strategies. In mean–variance optimization models, the inclusion of illiquid assets in the eligible investment universe may shift the efficient frontier upwards, theoretically resulting in more-efficient investment portfolios (i.e., portfolios with a higher expected return for a given level of risk).

    Thompson and her team believe the above to be true in the case of QU's endowment. In addition, further arguments are in favor of increasing the allocation to illiquidity risk. Thompson believes the specific circumstances of the endowment continue to support an increase in exposure to illiquid investments. To date, the team's historical experience with illiquid investments has been positive, with strong realized returns. The endowment has been building exposure to these strategies over the past two decades in a gradual manner. As a result, the illiquid portfolios are now well established, mature, and well diversified in terms of fund managers, strategies, and vintages. At the same time, the long presence in the market and the ability to access QU alumni networks have helped the endowment develop a strong network of connections in the industry and gain access to best-in-class managers in these spaces—building a reputation as a well-informed, patient, and reliable long-term investor. As revealed in the case text, the QU endowment has a lower exposure to illiquid investments than most institutional investor peers with similar risk profiles and objectives. Analysis by Thompson and her team has identified this as one of the reasons for the QU endowment's underperformance in recent years relative to peers.

Thompson and the strategy team should also examine whether the allocation to private equity and real assets is exposed to idiosyncratic risk factors. Avoiding large allocations to a small number of funds helps ensure that idiosyncratic risk factors are largely diversified away.

2. Using additional information provided in Exhibit 10 and your knowledge of illiquid investments from prior curriculum content, justify Thompson's proposed asset allocation and explain the trade-offs involved in terms of portfolio volatility.

Guideline Answer:

As Thompson highlights to the Board, the primary driver of the proposed asset allocation is the expected improvement in the portfolio's long-term risk–return profile. The proposed SAA has a higher expected real return compared to the current SAA (5.3% versus 5.0% in real terms) and a slightly higher Sharpe ratio (0.34 versus 0.33).

The proposed asset allocation also has a higher probability of achieving the endowment's return target over the long term. One way to get a better sense of this is through Monte Carlo simulations. For example, using such simulations, the team concludes that there is a 70% chance of maintaining at least 75% of purchasing power over a 20-year horizon for the proposed SAA versus a 65% chance for the current SAA, assuming a 5% spending rate. There is an implicit trade-off in this case between the short-term risk measure (volatility) and the long-term risk represented by the probability of purchasing power erosion over a 20-year horizon.

Trade-off 1: Portfolio volatility

> Thompson has considered the increase in overall risk profile for the endowment (portfolio return volatility increases from 12.5% to 13.2%) and believes the increase to be justified.

> Thompson believes future returns will be lower for all asset classes. Lower return expectations imply that a higher level of risk must be taken to achieve the same level of returns. Although the proposed SAA is slightly more efficient, as indicated by its higher Sharpe ratio, this improvement in portfolio efficiency is not sufficient to generate the 5.3% expected real return for the same level of short-term risk/volatility as the current SAA.

> Optimization results also suggest that the proposed asset allocation has a higher probability of achieving the real return target while preserving the purchasing power of the endowment, given the current 5% spending policy. Finally, Thompson also considers that QU's portfolio risk profile is still more conservative than that of its peers.

Trade-off 2: Implementation costs

Thompson and her team analyzed the costs associated with implementing the proposed portfolio allocation changes. Private equity and private real estate strategies typically have higher investment management fees and performance fees than fixed-income and public equity strategies. By using "net of fees" return assumptions, Thompson and her team incorporated the impact of higher expected investment management fees arising from higher allocations to more-illiquid investments.

Before concluding that the QU endowment should adjust its asset allocation to illiquid investments, Thompson should confirm that the resulting risk profile (return volatility of 13.2% and the probability of erosion in purchasing power shown in Exhibit 10) is consistent with the endowment's risk tolerance (willingness and capacity to bear risk). Thompson should also confirm that with the increased allocation to illiquid investments, the resulting asset allocation remains consistent with the liquidity budget.

EXAMPLE 1

COVID-19 Impact on University Endowment Portfolios

The COVID-19 global pandemic severely disrupted almost every aspect of society in 2020, and higher education institutions were certainly no exception. The pandemic brought sudden and significant stress on university operational budgets in the spring of 2020 by immediately adversely impacting revenues and increased costs. Revenues were negatively affected by higher rebates on room and board due to closed campuses, the cancellation of certain revenue-producing education programs, lower enrollment rates, and increased financial support for students, to name a few factors. On the other hand, costs increased significantly as new health protocols needed to be developed, certain facilities had to be reconfigured to allow better social distancing, and online courses and teaching capabilities had to be substantially upgraded. In this tough environment, many universities turned to their endowments to provide increased levels of support for the operations through the annual distribution. A study from the National Association of College and University Business Officers and financial services firm TIAA found that the 705 academic institutions studied, on average, increased the annual distribution from their endowment by 4% in 2020 from fiscal year 2019's level.

Endowments with significant allocations to illiquid assets faced a trifecta of factors stressing portfolio liquidity in the short term and the ability to rebalance to desired risk levels. These factors include the following:

- the need to provide additional support to the university on short notice,
- the mark-to-market negative shock of the pandemic in Q1 of 2020, and
- muted capital distributions from investments in private markets.

QUINCO Case: Strategic Asset Allocation

This is different from the global financial crisis of 2008 when the stress was induced primarily by the severity and duration of losses in the endowment portfolios. In 2020, the universities' operations experienced major disruptions putting pressure on endowments while portfolio losses were less severe. All this reemphasized the need for endowment portfolios with large exposures to illiquid assets to develop stringent liquidity stress tests to ensure proper liquidity management when needed.

The Crawford University endowment was established three decades ago to support the operations of Crawford University, a fictional private liberal arts institution in the northeastern region of the United States. Over time, Crawford University has come to rely on distributions from the endowment portfolio for significant support on an annual basis, and the endowment has not yet failed to deliver. The endowment's investment strategy has produced stellar returns since inception. To maintain that trend, after the global financial crisis of 2008, and not unlike many of its peers, the endowment increased exposure to private markets and alternatives primarily through illiquid vehicles and further reduced the allocation to traditional asset classes such as fixed income and public equites. To further boost returns, the endowment also invested approximately two-thirds of its public equity allocation into commingled funds with less-liquid redemption terms. As a result, at the onset of the COVID-19 global pandemic, the endowment portfolio had an asset allocation and liquidity profile as shown in Exhibit 11.

Exhibit 11: Crawford University Endowment Asset Allocation and Liquidity Profile

A. Asset Allocation (January 2020)

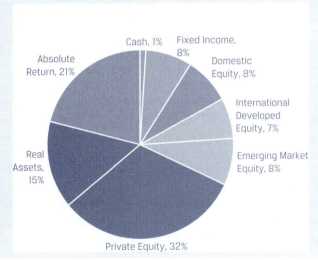

B. Liquidity Profile (January 2020)

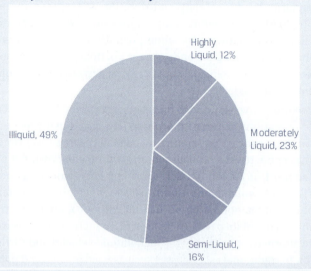

Battered by the severe impact the pandemic had on its operations, the university turned to its endowment for additional support in the first half of 2020 and requested an annual distribution in excess of the long-term average pace of 5% of the endowment's net asset value. At the same time, the endowment was confronting liquidity challenges stemming from its large exposure to illiquid strategies and the mark-to-market impact of the COVID-19-related market shock.

Following the steep decline in risk assets in Q1 of 2020, the pace of distributions from the private equity and the real assets portfolios dried up while the capital calls continued to come. This further stressed the endowment's cash position while further increasing the exposure to illiquid assets as a percentage of the overall portfolio. Given that a large portion of the public equity portfolios were invested in commingled funds with quarterly or semiannual redemption terms, the only reliable sources of cash available on short notice to satisfy liquidity needs were the cash and fixed income allocations. Also, the endowment could not properly rebalance its risk position as needed.

As a result, although public equity and private market valuations partially recovered in Q2, the endowment was forced to draw down its fixed income allocation to satisfy the various cash needs, including the annual disbursement to the university. The forced withdrawals had a significant opportunity cost because fixed income managers had to liquidate positions in spread products (e.g., corporate bonds, mortgage securities) at distressed prices because market liquidity conditions were precarious in the first half of 2020.

Exhibit 12 shows the resulting asset allocation and liquidity profile of the endowment at the end of Fiscal Year 2020 (30 June 2020).

Exhibit 12: Crawford University Endowment Asset Allocation and Liquidity Profile

A. Asset Allocation (June 2020)

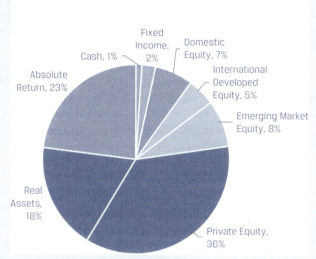

B. Liquidity Profile (June 2020)

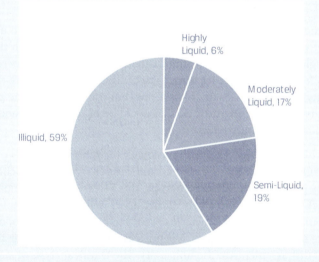

By comparing the liquidity profiles before and after the pandemic-related shock, a steep deterioration can be noted in the endowment's overall liquidity as the combined exposure to the highly liquid and moderately liquid strategies dropped by approximately 12% (from 35% to 23%), while the exposure to the illiquid category increased from 49% to 59%. These changes left the endowment in a precarious liquidity position, with limited ability to remedy the situation in the short term. Also worth noting is that the overall risk profile of the asset allocation has increased because of the inability to rebalance the fixed income allocation back to the desired target.

QUINCO CASE: LIQUIDITY MANAGEMENT 5

☐ analyze asset allocation and portfolio construction in relation to liquidity needs and risk and return requirements and recommend actions to address identified needs

Given the increasing complexity of the investment portfolio and the university's reliance on regular distributions from the endowment, QUINCO needs a robust framework for managing liquidity. During her time at QUINCO, Thompson has worked to enhance QUINCO's overall liquidity management framework. This includes improving the tools used in that process and taking a comprehensive, enterprise-wide approach. In her approach, the expected cash outflows and inflows for the endowment portfolio are modeled over various time horizons both under normal circumstances and in periods of severe market stress.

Thompson is concerned that the portfolio's liquidity characteristics will deteriorate in periods of severe market stress. She believes a deterioration in liquidity could potentially occur for the following reasons:

- **Capital calls in private markets exceeding capital distributions.** This would increase the allocation to private markets in the overall portfolio.

- **Activation of gates.** Some investment vehicles that provide quarterly or annual liquidity, such as hedge funds and real estate funds, have provisions in their investment prospectuses that allow the investment manager to refuse investor withdrawal requests (to activate gates) during stress periods to protect remaining investors in the fund. The inability to withdraw from funds leads to a more illiquid profile overall.

- **The smoothing effect.** Investments in private markets tend to incorporate market valuations with a lag that leads to a relative increase in their portfolio weighting during periods of market stress and a relative decrease in the portfolio weighting of more liquid assets. This does not reduce the effective liquidity of the portfolio in dollar terms, but it does impact the percentage of assets in the overall portfolio that could be used to satisfy liquidity needs in periods of market stress.

To address her concerns, Thompson asks her team for an analysis of the current and proposed QU portfolios under normal and various stress market conditions. The team develops two liquidity stress scenarios. The 'Stress" scenario implies primarily a market shock to the portfolio and a drying up of inflows from donations and distributions from private market portfolios. The "High Stress" scenario, in addition to having a more severe market impact, includes assumptions on higher cash outflows in the form of disbursements to the university. The team's analysis of each portfolio's liquidity profile is shown in Exhibit 13 and Exhibit 14.

Exhibit 13 shows the current QU portfolio under normal, stress, and high stress market conditions.

QUINCO Case: Liquidity Management

Exhibit 13: QU Endowment Liquidity Profile: Current Portfolio (Normal, Stress, and High Stress Conditions)

A. Normal Conditions

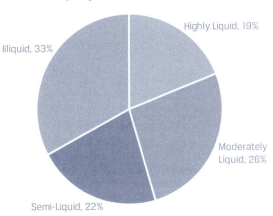

B. Stress Conditions

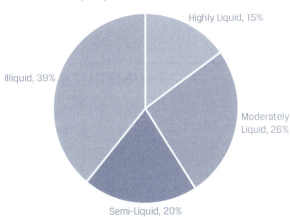

C. High Stress Conditions

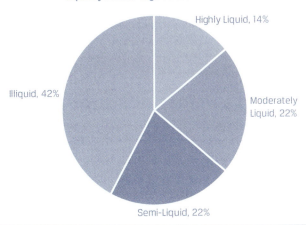

Exhibit 14 shows the proposed QU strategic asset allocation portfolio under normal, stress, and high stress conditions.

Exhibit 14: QU Endowment Liquidity Profile: Proposed Strategic Asset Allocation (Normal, Stress, and High Stress Conditions)

A. Normal Conditions

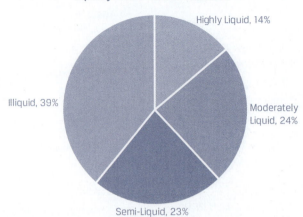

B. Stress Conditions

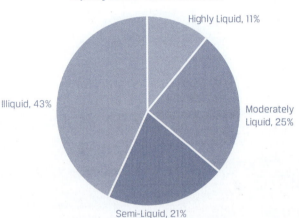

C. High Stress Conditions

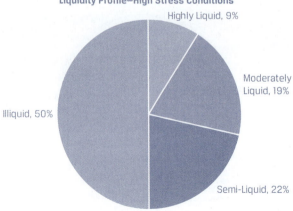

QUINCO Case: Liquidity Management

IN-TEXT QUESTIONS

1. Explain how current spending policy might affect liquidity needs in a market downturn.

   Guideline Answer:

   The design of the spending rate policy incorporates a smoothing, countercyclical element, leading to spending rates below 5% in a period of sustained strong investment returns but higher than 5% in a protracted weak return environment. This design of the spending rate policy exacerbates the endowment's liquidity needs in severe market downturns.

2. Describe various tools that QUINCO might use to manage its portfolio liquidity risk.

   Guideline Answer:

   Among the tools QUINCO could use are cash flow–forecasting and commitment-pacing models, liquidity budgets, and stress test analyses. To begin, Thompson estimates expected cash outflows and inflows. For cash outflows, Thompson projects distributions from the endowment to the university. These uses of cash can then be factored into the estimation of expected outflows and inflows through the spending rate policy in which the university seeks to spend, on average, 5% annually of the endowment while preserving the endowment's purchasing power over time.
   For the private equity and real estate portfolios, Thompson and her team can use cash flow–forecasting models and commitment-pacing models to project the expected increase in the allocation to private markets. These help the team project cash outflows needed for future investment commitments (committed but undrawn capital calls) in private markets. These flows could become particularly relevant in stress periods when distributions from prior investments in those markets might cease because general partners have difficulty exiting investments (because of depressed valuations and lack of transaction activity). Future investment commitments are legal obligations of the endowment, so the staff needs to ensure capital calls are met because the general partner might accelerate capital calls as opportunities arise in depressed markets. Thompson and her team should ensure diversification across fund vintage years to avoid overexposure to particular parts of the economic cycle and should also follow a strategy that commits capital on a steady and regular basis to minimize the need to make large allocation changes (or adjustments) with associated transaction costs. Avoiding large allocations to very few funds will help minimize idiosyncratic portfolio risk. At the same time, cash inflows into the endowment from donors will likely drop significantly during stress periods, further increasing liquidity needs. Liquidating risk assets or high-beta assets after periods of negative return is often not desirable from a valuation standpoint when future returns might be expected to be more attractive, particularly following periods of sharp drawdowns. Given her experience with these markets, Thompson should recognize that the team's approach needs to be flexible. Access to the top private market managers is often highly competitive, and opportunities to invest with these managers might not be available at times when the portfolio is making allocation increases.
   Incorporating this information, Thompson can develop a liquidity budget for the endowment like that shown in Exhibit 1, which specifies minimum acceptable liquidity targets based on the expected time needed to convert portfolio holdings to cash. The liquidity budget should be monitored by

Thompson and her team on a regular basis as part of the liquidity management framework in place at QUINCO. Thompson and her team can also do an analysis of the portfolio's current liquidity characteristics under normal market conditions, like that shown in Exhibit 2.

Thompson and her team should continue to undertake regular stress tests (such as the liquidity profile analysis done by her team) using historical and hypothetical scenarios to estimate how much the liquidity profile of the portfolio could drift under certain assumptions and to assess whether the minimum liquidity budget would still be satisfied. The analysis can also be used to inform the team's asset allocation and implementation decisions for investment vehicles and strategies.

3. What impact will the proposed asset allocation changes have on the endowment's liquidity profile?

Guideline Answer:

Compared to the liquidity profile of the current portfolio, the proposed asset allocation implies a shift toward more-illiquid investments, as shown in the following table:

Liquidity Category	Current Portfolio :Normal (%)	:Stress (%)	:High Stress (%)	:High Stress vs. Normal (%)	Proposed Portfolio :Normal (%)	:Stress (%)	:High Stress (%)	:High Stress vs. Normal (%)	Proposed vs. Current :Normal (%)	:High Stress (%)
High Liquid	19	15	14	-5	14	11	9	-5	-5	-5
Moderately Liquid	26	26	22	-4	24	25	19	-5	-2	-3
Semi-Liquid	22	20	22	0	23	21	22	-1	1	0
Illiquid	33	39	42	9	39	43	50	11	6	8

As a result, a reduction will occur in the highly liquid and liquid categories in the endowment's liquidity profile and a commensurate increase will be seen in the semi-liquid and illiquid categories under all liquidity scenarios but in particular under high stress conditions. The proposed allocation results in an increase in the overall illiquidity profile because a higher percentage of the portfolio will be invested in private equity and private real estate, which are the most illiquid asset classes in the portfolio.

What is important to note is that under a high stress scenario, the proposed allocation would temporarily breach the minimum threshold set in the liquidity budget framework for the highly liquid and moderately liquid categories (9% versus a minimum of 10% and 19% versus a minimum of 35%, respectively) while the illiquid category would reach the upper limit of the liquidity budget at 50%.

Although a temporary breach is understandable under extreme liquidity circumstances, Thompson needs to ensure that even under stress conditions, the proposed allocation continues to adequately satisfy the various liquidity needs of the portfolio for both cash outflows and rebalancing. In this particular circumstance, Thompson and her team might wish to revisit the size of the exposure to less-liquid commingled funds within the public equity allocations to enhance the liquidity profile of the portfolio in periods of extreme liquidity stress. From an ongoing management perspective, and particularly at times when the liquidity profile of the proposed allocation is closer to the

> minimum thresholds set through the liquidity budget, Thompson and her team should plan to closely monitor the portfolio's liquidity profile and to periodically stress test it to make sure portfolio liquidity remains adequate.

Based on this analysis, the QUINCO Board approves the proposed changes to the asset allocation and instructs the team to proceed with implementation. These changes are also presented to the Quadrivium Trustees as part of the university treasurer's financial report at the Trustees' next regular meeting.

QUINCO CASE: ASSET MANAGER SELECTION

☐ demonstrate the application of the Code of Ethics and Standards of Professional Conduct regarding the actions of individuals involved in manager selection

Three months have now passed, and Winter, Thompson, and the rest of the QUINCO team have begun implementing changes to the strategic asset allocation by seeking additional external managers. Winter is very pleased with their progress to date but has encountered a somewhat interesting situation.

Among the firms responding to QUINCO's request for proposal (RFP) seeking a new private equity manager is Genex Venture Capital (GVC). GVC is proposing that QUINCO invest in its new "GVC Fund II" offering. GVC is a US-based venture capital fund operating in the biotech space. GVC would be a new relationship for QUINCO. The firm has adopted the CFA Institute Asset Manager Code for its employees. The founder and managing partner at GVC is Virginia Hall, CFA, a prominent alumna of Quadrivium University who was elected to the university's board of trustees three years ago. Hall has made several generous donations to the university over the years, and the building that houses the school's student center and main dining facility is named in her honor. Both the university president and university treasurer have urged Winter to favorably consider GVC's proposal, given Hall's importance to the university. Winter has suspicions that Hall has contacted the university president and treasurer to advocate for her company.

The investment committee narrows the competition for the allocation of QUINCO's private market assets to GVC and Beacher Venture Investments ("Beacher"). Beacher is another venture capital investment firm operating in the same space and is a direct competitor to GVC.

Both GVC and Beacher are invited to make a presentation to QUINCO's investment committee. GVC's presentation is led by Jason Allen, one of Winter's former colleagues from the endowment they both worked for previously. Allen has joined GVC as a managing director as part of GVC's efforts to build the team in preparation for Fund II. Although Allen's presentation on behalf of GVC is thorough and well-documented, Winter is troubled by two aspects. The presentation is targeted to QUINCO but clearly incorporates information that is based on or could have come only from the university treasurer's non-public reports to the Quadrivium board of trustees or another university source. In addition, the performance presentation of GVC's historical returns shows substantially higher returns than performance reported by third-party performance databases.

Of the two finalists, Beacher has a longer track record and is a more established name in the industry; however, some concerns have arisen regarding the historical performance of its previous fund. At the same time, some investment committee members have expressed reservations about GVC's short track record. Given the overlap in sector and strategy between the two firms, the investment committee asks Bud Davis, a CFA charterholder and senior portfolio manager on QUINCO's private equity team, to return with a formal proposal to invest in one of the firms.

Davis presents an update on the fundraising efforts of each firm's fund and notes that GVC is facing challenges in raising the desired fund amount of USD300 million for Fund II. Potential investors are apparently concerned with the significant increase in the size of the fund (Fund I had raised USD100 million) and question whether GVC has the infrastructure to scale operations.

Davis makes a strong case for investing with GVC, highlighting confidence in the manager and their differentiated approach to sourcing and growing portfolio companies in the biotech space. Davis tells the investment committee that because of the longer-than-expected fundraising period, GVC is eager to secure QU's commitment for Fund II; as a result, Davis has negotiated a discount on GVC's investment management fee. Following that discussion, the investment committee approves the recommendation from the team to invest with GVC.

After the decision is made to hire GVC, Winter calls Allen to tell him the good news and offer his congratulations. During the conversation, Allen expresses his satisfaction in having QUINCO as one of the fund's investors and praises Davis's strong commitment and drive. Allen goes on to mention that Davis's spouse, Andrea, is Hall's daughter. Winter expresses his surprise at this fact and later asks Davis about his wife's relationship to Hall. Davis responds that he believes this information is common knowledge and that he thought Winter and members of the QUINCO investment committee knew this information.

> **IN-TEXT QUESTION**

1. What ethical considerations arise regarding the actions and conduct of individuals involved in manager selection?

   Guideline Answer:

   Aaron Winter, QUINCO CIO

   Winter faces several ethical dilemmas in this case. The main issue is the disclosure of a potential conflict of interest, Standard VI(A): Disclosure of Conflicts, regarding the hiring of an external investment manager with close ties to the university. Winter's independence and objectivity, Standard I(B): Independence and Objectivity, in making the hiring recommendation could be compromised by the implicit and explicit pressure he is receiving to hire GVC. He should disclose this conflict to the QUINCO Board as part of the hiring recommendation. He should also disclose that the managing director for GVC is a former colleague because that relationship could also be perceived as impairing his independence and objectivity, creating a conflict of interest. During the presentation, GVC appears to have based its proposal on confidential information, Standard III(E): Preservation of Confidentiality, about the university, potentially obtained by Hall through her role as a Quadrivium Trustee or others at the university. As an employee of the university and QUINCO, Winter should make the board aware of the possible breach of confidentiality. He also apparently has questions about the accuracy of the performance information, Standard I(C): Misrepresentation and Standard III(D): Performance Presentation, presented by GVC but fails to exercise appropriate due diligence, Standard V(A): Diligence and Reasonable Basis, by following up with GVC or investigating further to determine the veracity of the information.

Virginia Hall, CFA, Quadrivium University Trustee and Managing Partner at GVC

Hall has a conflict of interest, Standard VI(A): Conduct as Participants in CFA Institute Programs, if she is pressuring university staff and QUINCO employees to influence the external manager hiring process in her company's favor. Hall's personal/business interests with GVC pose a potential conflict of interest with her duties as a university Trustee. She has a duty as a trustee to act in the best interest of the university without regard to how it might benefit her, but she has an incentive to pressure the university to hire her company. She would be violating her duty of loyalty, Standard IV(A): Loyalty, to the university as a Trustee by putting her firm, and therefore her personal interests, ahead of the interests of the university. She should disclose her potential conflict and recuse herself from any part in the external manager hiring process. In addition, she has potentially gone further by sharing confidential information, Standard III(E): Preservation of Confidentiality, she has received as a trustee with GVC in an effort to assist GVC's response and boost the prospects of her company in being hired—another violation of her duty of loyalty as a Trustee. GVC neglected to disclose the relationship of one employee's relative (Hall's daughter, who is Davis's spouse) with QUINCO.

Quadrivium University President/Quadrivium University Treasurer

The university president and treasurer, as members of the QUINCO Board, have a duty to act in the university's best interests, Standard IV(A): Loyalty, by hiring the external investment managers most appropriate for managing the private equity portion of the university's endowment. In pressuring Winter to hire GVC, they are clearly letting the outside consideration of maintaining good relations with a Trustee influence their hiring decision. They might have also provided confidential information, Standard III(E): Preservation of Confidentiality, to Hall or GVC to assist their bid to become an investment manager for QUINCO. They should disclose their conflict, Standard VI(A): Disclosure of Conflicts, and recuse themselves from decisions where their independence and objectivity, Standard I(B): Independence and Objectivity, are compromised. The university president and treasurer should also have in place a due diligence questionnaire/RFP to raise questions to new managers about potential conflicts of interest.

Jason Allen, Managing Director at GVC

Winter has noticed a discrepancy between the performance history of GVC in the presentation made by Allen and the performance record of the company as reported elsewhere. Allen is possibly inadvertently using inaccurate information or, worse, knowingly misrepresenting the performance record, Standard I(C): Misrepresentation and Standard III(D): Performance Presentation, of GVC.

> Bud Davis, CFA, Senior Portfolio Manager at QUINCO
>
> Through his spouse, Davis has a personal relationship with GVC, a company he is tasked with investigating and on which he must provide an opinion as to its potential hiring as an outside manager. This could affect his independence and objectivity, Standard I(B): Independence and Objectivity, and creates, at minimum, the perception of a conflict of interest, Standard VI(A): Disclosure of Conflicts, that should be disclosed when making his recommendation. Davis should not rely on his belief that the relationship is "common knowledge" or widely known but should make an explicit disclosure of this potential conflict.

7. QUINCO CASE: TACTICAL ASSET ALLOCATION

- [ ] analyze the costs and benefits of derivatives versus cash market techniques for establishing or modifying asset class or risk exposures
- [ ] demonstrate the use of derivatives overlays in tactical asset allocation and rebalancing

As part of the investment strategy review, the Board decided to significantly increase the active risk budget assigned to the QUINCO team for use in a new tactical asset allocation (TAA) program. QUINCO's active risk budget measures the deviation of the endowment's portfolio from its investment policy targets and is expressed as an annual tracking error limit. The Board increased QUINCO's active risk budget from 100 bps to 250 bps to allow the team to pursue greater excess returns versus the strategic asset allocation. By taking active risk relative to investment policy benchmarks through external managers in public asset classes as well as TAA positions, the QUINCO team hopes to add additional portfolio performance.

The implementation of the tactical asset allocation program and associated risk budget was fully delegated to Winter and his staff. At that time, the Board also informed him that up to 150 bps (of the 250 bps) active risk budget could be used to implement the TAA program. One consideration the Board discussed was the use of leverage. The TAA program implementation could result in a levered position of the endowment portfolio (because derivatives are likely to be used in implementation and not every overweight exposure would be offset by a corresponding underweight in another asset), so the Board agreed to permit a modest leverage position for the overall portfolio of up to 5% of the portfolio's value.

Winter believes that the tactical asset allocation program will accommodate two types of active decisions:

- Overweight and underweight positions in one or more of the asset classes included in the investment policy portfolio
- Provide exposure to asset classes and/or investment strategies outside the policy portfolio benchmark universe but compliant with the investment policy (e.g., high yield, emerging market, fixed income)

Winter began implementing the TAA program by building on a framework and research by Thompson and the asset allocation team that was informed by external parties (e.g., investment consultants, external tactical asset allocation managers,

QUINCO Case: Tactical Asset Allocation

investment research houses). Using concepts of fair value and mean reversion in financial markets, fair value models were developed for various financial assets. To do this, the framework incorporated economic and financial data that had exhibited predictive power for future returns and risk over an investment horizon of one to three years. Current market pricing was then compared with output from the valuation models to determine whether the deviation from 'fair value' was large enough to be exploited in a cost-efficient manner.

In extensive out-of-sample backtests, the methodology had produced encouraging results. One of the strongest signals suggested that large-cap US equities, characterized broadly by the S&P 500 Index, were significantly below fair value, with mean reversion expected over the next year. Based on this information, Thompson decides to implement a 1% overweight to US equities through a passive exposure.

Thompson is now considering three options to implement her decision: a total return swap, equity futures, and ETFs. Her goal is to implement the overweight position as effectively as possible from a cost and cash usage perspective. Thompson asks her team to look at the associated costs for each option.

The team's cost comparison analysis is shown in Exhibit 15.

Exhibit 15: Cost Comparison Assuming a Fully Funded Mandate

Cost Component	ETF	Futures	Total Return Swap
Commission (round trip)	4.00	2.00	5.00
Management fee (annual)	9.50	0.00	0.00
Bid/offer spread (round trip)	2.50	2.00	6.00
Price impact (round trip)	15.00	10.00	0.00
Mispricing (tracking error, annual)	4.00	8.00	0.00
Cost to roll the futures contract	0.00	20.00	0.00
Funding cost	0.00	0.00	40.00
Total cost	**35.00**	**42.00**	**51.00**

Notes: The exhibit shows the team's cost comparison for the three implementation options—ETFs, futures, and a total return swap—for an USD80 million notional exposure to the S&P 500 Index (assuming a fully funded mandate) over a one-year investment horizon. All numbers are in basis points unless otherwise indicated.

The comparison assumes no leverage for the ETF and that the entire mandate amount (USD80 million) is deposited to earn the three-month market reference rate (MRR) for futures and the total return swap as to offset the three-month MRR component of the implied financing rate (or the funding cost in the case of the swap).

After closely examining the cost comparison analysis, Thompson debates the pros and cons of each option with her team.

From a cash "usage" perspective, ETFs would be least efficient because she would need to finance the full notional value of the ETF or use the margin features of the account. Even when using the margin, regulations would limit the margin to 50% of account value, implying a maximum of two times the leverage ratio. For example, for an USD80 million ETF exposure, the minimum margin that would have to be held in cash would be USD40 million. Thompson knows that using futures and a total return swap could generate a similar economic exposure to ETFs with a much lower capital commitment.

From a liquidity perspective, Thompson likes ETFs and futures, which appear efficient, given their liquid trading and narrow bid–ask spreads. She also values the flexibility they offer to terminate exposure before intended maturity, should the team's views on the market change. Thompson is concerned about the operational implications of holding futures because they require daily monitoring of margin requirements. In addition, she worries about interest rate risk and exposure of QU to counterparty credit risk.

IN-TEXT QUESTION

1. Assuming a fully funded position (no use of leverage), which implementation option should Thompson choose for the 1% tactical overweight to US equities?

   Guideline Answer:

   ### Expected Costs

   In the case of the ETF, the most significant cost component is price impact—the expected impact on market price from entering into (buying) and exiting out of (selling) the ETF position. This impact is estimated to be approximately 15 bps. The second largest cost component is the management fee charged by the ETF manager, which is expected to be 9.5 bps.

   In the case of futures, the largest cost component is expected to be the cost to roll the futures contract on a quarterly basis (5 bps quarterly or 20 bps annual cost). This cost is driven by the upward-sloping (contango) shape of the yield curve. In addition to the futures roll cost and the price impact, another significant futures cost is the mispricing or tracking error of expected futures performance relative to the underlying index performance. Expected tracking error on the futures contracts is 8 bps.

   Finally, for the total return swap, the cost is dominated by the funding cost, which is expected to be 40 bps.

   From a total cost perspective, at 35 bps, the ETF offers the most cost-efficient vehicle to implement the tactical overlay, with relatively tight bid–ask spreads that are similar to futures.

   ### Other Considerations

   ETFs and futures are typically standardized products that trade on exchanges. Total return swaps are over-the-counter contracts that are negotiated and customizable in such features as maturity, leverage, and cost. ETFs are the least cash-efficient option, requiring the largest cash outlay, and Thompson would be able to gain similar economic exposure with futures and swaps using significantly less cash.

   A position in futures contracts would need to be rolled over each quarter to maintain exposure. Given Thompson's concerns about the operational requirements for futures and the need for daily monitoring for margin requirements, a position in futures is likely less desirable to Thompson. For ETFs, ongoing management of the exposure is done by the ETF manager. Futures and ETFs have an associated tracking error versus the index intended to be replicated. For ETFs, the tracking error could result from premiums and discounts to net asset value, cash drag, or regulatory diversification requirements. For futures, the tracking error arises because of liquidity (supply/demand conditions), dividend forecast errors, and interest rate differentials. For total return swaps, the replication is exact; Thompson would receive the total return of the index without incurring any tracking error to

QUINCO Case: Tactical Asset Allocation

> the benchmark S&P 500 Index because the swap counterparty is obligated to provide the index return.
>
> However, Thompson is concerned about interest rate risk in the case of futures and swaps. She is also concerned about the counterparty credit risk that QUINCO would be exposed to through a swap, which would additionally create complexities in managing net exposures over the duration of the contract.
>
> To implement the tactical overlay given Thompson's considerations, the ETF provides the most cost-efficient vehicle, with adequate liquidity and relatively tight bid–ask spreads. ETFs also provide Thompson with the flexibility (noted as being important to her) to modify exposure before the end of the one-year horizon should her and her team's investment views change.

After considering with her team, Thompson believes implementing with ETFs appears to be the best option.

Later that day, after further discussion, Thompson and the management team decide to implement the overlay using leverage. Thompson asks her team to complete a cost comparison analysis assuming a permissible leverage level of four times for all three options (meaning that cash needed to support the position would be 25% of the overlay notional amount).[7] The team's work is shown in Exhibit 16.

Exhibit 16: Additional Information with Respect to Impact of Leverage

Cost Component	ETF	Futures	Total Return Swap
Cost of obtaining leverage	187.50	0.00	0.00
Additional financing/funding cost	0.00	150.00	150.00
Total additional cost	187.50	150.00	150.00

Notes: The additional cost components assume four times leverage over a one-year investment horizon. All numbers are in basis points unless otherwise indicated.

The team's assumptions for the analysis are as follows:

- The borrowing cost of obtaining leverage in the case of the ETF is assumed to be three-month MRR + 50 bps.
- The three-month MRR assumption used is 2% (opportunity costs).
- The same MRR was used to calculate the additional implied financing cost in the case of futures and the additional funding cost for the total return swap.
- The analysis focuses on the implementation cost of trade and does not consider the additional return earned by investing the cash that is not needed to support the transaction (75% of the overlay notional amount).

---

7 Although in the case of the ETF, the leverage at the instrument level might be regulated to not exceed two times (50% margin requirement), for the purposes of this exercise, assume that the endowment can generate leverage at the plan level for ETF usage.

IN-TEXT QUESTION

1. Assuming a permissible leverage level of four times for all three options, and using the information in Exhibit 16, would Thompson change her decision?

   Guideline Answer:

   As shown in Exhibit 16, the additional information changes the total cost estimates for the different implementation options. In the case of ETFs, to generate four times leverage, 75% of the desired nominal exposure would have to be borrowed to provide an overall exposure four times higher than the original capital. That is, for a desired nominal exposure of USD80 million, borrowing USD60 million (75% of USD80 million) provides four times leverage to an original capital amount of USD20 million.

   The additional cost of obtaining leverage for each option would be as follows:

   1. ETFs. (USD80 million × 0.75 × 2.5%)/USD80 million = 1.875%.
   2. Futures. (USD80 million × 0.75 × 2%)/USD80 million = 1.50%. The additional financing cost for futures in this case (compared to the unlevered option) would occur because 75% of the amount would not be invested in three-month MRR to offset the financing cost, thus increasing the overall cost for the futures.
   3. Swaps. (USD80 million × 0.75 × 2%)/USD80 million = 1.50%. The additional financing cost for swaps in this case (compared to the unlevered option) would occur because 75% of the amount would not be invested in three-month MRR to offset the financing cost, thus increasing the overall cost for the swaps.

   Total costs for each option (in bps):

	ETF	Futures	Total Return Swap
Unlevered	35.00	42.00	51.00
Incremental cost	187.50	150.00	150.00
Total	222.50	192.00	201.00

   Looking at the data, total costs for futures appear to be the lowest cost alternative (192 bps), followed by the total return swap (201 bps). Given a permissible leverage level of four times for all three options, and based on the data in Exhibit 16, ETFs now look to be the most expensive option (222.50 bps).

   Given the difference in costs, Thompson would consider implementation through futures. The main consideration between the use of ETFs and futures not captured in the comparative pricing analysis is the additional complexity and operational monitoring associated with a quarterly futures roll. If Thompson and the team can get comfortable with that risk, implementation through futures would be the more efficient option.

Looking at the data, and based on their desire to use leverage, Thompson believes that futures offer the more efficient alternative. She decides to establish a 1% long position to the S&P 500 Index using S&P 500 futures.

QUINCO CASE: ASSET ALLOCATION REBALANCING

☐ analyze the costs and benefits of derivatives versus cash market techniques for establishing or modifying asset class or risk exposures

☐ demonstrate the use of derivatives overlays in tactical asset allocation and rebalancing

Three months have passed since Thompson and the team implemented the tactical overweight position to US equities. To date, the position has been performing well and in line with *ex ante* expectations. Global equity markets have rallied, reflecting a favorable global growth environment, and fixed-income markets have sold off as interest rates rose significantly in anticipation of higher inflationary pressures. As a result, the asset allocation of the endowment has drifted from policy targets.

QUINCO follows a calendar quarter rebalancing policy with a rebalancing corridor for each asset class. The allocation drift of the actual portfolio relative to the SAA is monitored monthly; however, to minimize transaction costs, short of extraordinary market circumstances, rebalancing decisions are implemented at the end of each quarter. For public asset classes, systematic rebalancing occurs when the allocation to these assets is outside the rebalancing corridor at quarter end. When the allocation moves outside the corridor, Thompson and her team do have discretion to rebalance back to the target allocation or to the edge of the corridor.

For illiquid asset classes, given high transaction costs and practical challenges in rebalancing the allocation, rebalancing is normally undertaken through the reinvestment/commitment strategy as allocations approach the upper or lower edges of the corridor. In these cases, the pace of commitments could be altered from the expected pace to gradually shift the overall allocation to illiquid assets over time. The SAA, width of the rebalancing corridor, and current allocation for the various asset classes are shown in Exhibit 17:

Exhibit 17: SAA, Rebalancing Corridors, and Current (Actual) Allocations

	Target Allocation (SAA)	Corridor	Min/Max Target	Current Allocation
Cash	1%	±1%	0%–2%	0.8%
Fixed Income	9%	±3	6%–12%	6.5%
Domestic Equity	15%	±2.5	12.5%–17.5%	17.3%
International Developed Equity	9%	±2%	7%–11%	11.5%
Emerging Market Equity	12%	±2%	10%–14%	13.9%
Private Equity	23%	±5%	18%–28%	19.2%
Real Assets	16%	±3%	13%–19%	13.8%
Diversifying Strategies	15%	±3%	12%–18%	17.1%
Total	100.0%			100.0%

Thompson observes that the allocation to international developed equity (11.50%) now exceeds the upper end of its corridor (9.00% + 2.00% = 11.00%) by 0.50%, while the allocation to fixed income (6.50%) is below target (9.00%) but still within its rebalancing corridor (6.00%–12.00%).

Current allocations to private equity (19.20%) and real assets (13.80%) are close to the lower ends of their rebalancing corridors of 18.00%–28.00% and 13.00%–19.00%, respectively, as the team works to move toward the new targets approved by the Board in Exhibit 9 (in the very short term, these allocations cannot be increased).

Based on the information in Exhibit 17, Thompson sees a need to decrease the international developed equity allocation and increase the fixed-income allocation by the same amount. She meets with the team to discuss whether they should execute the rebalancing through the cash or derivatives market.

During the discussion, Thompson and her team consider the following factors: transaction costs, tracking error of the implementation vehicle versus the desired index exposure, tracking error implied by the current and post-rebalancing deviations from the target SAA weights, opportunity cost/impact to active strategies due to manager withdrawals and reallocations, implementation speed, and time horizon of the rebalancing trade.

Thompson knows that executing through the cash markets takes longer than executing in the derivatives markets. Still, allocating to, or reallocating from, external managers might be warranted in certain cases, such as when the adjustments are viewed as more permanent and/or more significant in nature (as compared to smaller, more temporary adjustments that could be reversed within a shorter time frame if investment views change).

After meeting with her team, Thompson decides to rebalance back to the upper edge of the corridor (11.00%) by reallocating 0.50% (50 bps) from international developed equities to fixed income. The team's cost analysis is shown in Exhibit 18.

Exhibit 18: Cost Information: 50 bps Rebalancing Option

Cost Component	Cash Market	Futures (Equity/Fixed Income)
Bid/offer spread	5.00	3.00
Price impact (total trades)	5.00	4.00
Mispricing (tracking error, quarterly)	0.00	17.00
Cash drag (impact of timing delays and disruptions to active manager portfolios)	20.00	0.00
Cost of rolling the futures contract	0.00	0.00
Total cost	30.00	24.00

Notes: This exhibit shows the costs of reallocating 0.5% from international developed equities to fixed income in the cash and futures markets. The analysis assumes a three-month (one quarter) investment horizon because the expectation is that the change in portfolio allocation is for a relatively short time period. Given the length of the investment horizon, no rolling of futures occurs. All numbers are in basis points unless otherwise indicated.

IN-TEXT QUESTIONS

1. Using Exhibit 18, analyze the relative costs of the cash market and derivatives approaches to rebalancing.

   Guideline Answer:

   Looking at the data in Exhibit 18, Thompson can see that the two options appear similar from a cost perspective. The main cost driver associated with rebalancing through the cash market is cash drag (approximately 20 bps) caused by timing delays and disruptions to active manager portfolios.

QUINCO Case: Asset Allocation Rebalancing

Rebalancing through cash markets would involve withdrawing funds from international developed equity active managers and increasing funds to current fixed-income managers and/or adding a new fixed-income manager. These activities would generate transaction costs and cash drag because the liquidation process for the equity manager(s) and the investment process for the fixed-income manager(s) would likely not happen simultaneously.

In the case of derivatives (short equity futures position and long fixed-income futures position), the biggest cost component is mispricing or tracking error. Creating a short exposure position for the MSCI EAFE Index (the benchmark for international ex USA and Canada developed-market equities) and a long fixed-income futures position would involve a higher tracking error (17 bps) compared to the tracking error of using one S&P 500 futures contract discussed previously (8 bps). In this case, using multiple futures instruments increases associated tracking error.

2. Explain how considerations of implementation speed and time horizon of the rebalancing trade could affect the implementation choice.

Guideline Answer:

An additional factor is speed of implementation. In general, depending on the availability of derivatives for the asset classes involved, rebalancing using derivatives is likely to result in a shorter implementation time frame while leaving the active managers in place. Given high levels of liquidity in the equity futures that would be used for MSCI EAFE Index replication, implementing with derivatives could occur quickly.

Another important aspect is rebalancing size and expected time horizon of the trade. The larger the rebalancing, the more likely that the rebalance would represent a more permanent realignment, as opposed to a temporary adjustment that could be reversed the next quarter.

Based on the expected costs and considerations and the relatively small size of the adjustment, using derivatives to rebalance the portfolio appears to be the best option. Implementing with derivatives gives the team the flexibility to tactically adjust exposure to international developed equities if desired and the ability to quickly reverse decisions in full or in part while leaving the current external managers in place.

After further discussion with her team, Thompson decides to instead rebalance the international developed equity allocation back to the target allocation by reallocating 2.5% from the international developed equity allocation into fixed income. The team's current analysis is shown in Exhibit 19.

Exhibit 19: Cost Information on Rebalancing Options

Cost Component	Cash Market	Futures (Equity/Fixed Income)
Bid/offer spread	5.00	4.00
Price impact (total trades)	5.00	4.00
Mispricing (tracking error, annual)	0.00	68.00
Cash drag (impact of timing delays and disruptions to active manager portfolios)	50.00	0.00

Cost Component	Cash Market	Futures (Equity/Fixed Income)
Cost of rolling the futures contract	0.00	6.00
Total cost	60.00	82.00

Notes: This exhibit shows the costs of reallocating 2.5% from international developed equities to fixed income in the cash and futures markets. The analysis assumes a one-year investment horizon because the expectation is that the change in portfolio allocation is more permanent. Under normal market conditions, these asset classes would not be expected to move outside the corridor again over that investment horizon. All numbers are in basis points unless otherwise indicated.

IN-TEXT QUESTION

1. What implementation option should Thompson use in this case?

    Guideline Answer:

    Based on relative expected costs, Thompson would likely decide to rebalance the portfolio in the cash markets by reallocating between international developed equity and fixed-income investment managers.

    Exhibit 19 shows that the cost of rebalancing back to target allocation using derivatives is higher than implementing through the cash markets. Specifically, the implementation cost with derivatives is 82 bps, while the implementation cost for the cash markets is 60 bps. The higher derivatives cost is primarily caused by expected tracking error of the replication using derivatives, which is 68 bps on an annual basis. In general, the cost of rebalancing through futures is expected to increase with investment time horizon as mispricing or tracking risk increases. In this case, the impact of the cost of rolling the futures is not viewed as material, given that the roll of the short equity futures position would likely offset most of the cost of holding the long fixed-income futures position. With respect to the cash market implementation, given the size of the rebalancing trade (2.5% of the overall portfolio), potential cash drag is expected to increase to 50 bps as compared to the previous scenario.

    Other considerations besides expected cost might be relevant. A faster desired speed of implementation would favor implementation using derivatives, while the size of the planned rebalancing implies a longer time horizon for the trade and favors implementation through the cash market. Based on the facts given, Thompson would likely decide to rebalance the portfolio in the cash markets.

9 QUINCO CASE: ESG INTEGRATION

☐ discuss ESG considerations in managing long-term institutional portfolios

Nine months have passed, and the QUINCO team is facing a new challenge. Earlier in the week, the university president informed Winter of an upcoming student protest planned against the university and the endowment.

Student Activity

The students in the QU Student Association have seen a recent report published by the International Labor Organization (ILO) highlighting social issues in the supply chain of a US-based apparel company named Portro Inc. The report detailed a number of emerging social issues, including terrible labor conditions and allegations of child labor, as well as health and safety issues at two of Portro's largest suppliers. One of the suppliers named is also a supplier for the QU-branded apparel sold at the university stores. The students are further outraged after discovering from various public sources, including QUINCO's annual report, that the endowment is a significant shareholder in Portro Inc.

The students are expected to demand the following actions: The university must drop the supplier, and the endowment must divest its Portro Inc. holdings.

QUINCO ESG Approach

QUINCO has had an ESG responsible investing policy in place for the past seven years. The policy is based on the following considerations and objectives:

- Acknowledgment that ESG factors, along with traditional financial factors affect the risk and return of investments
- Promotion of greater transparency on material ESG issues that impact QUINCO's investment activities
- Pursuit of long-term sustainability for companies and markets in which the endowment invests

Rather than a strategy of exclusion that prohibits a priori investments in certain countries, sectors, or companies, QUINCO's approach focuses on ESG integration. ESG integration is defined as "the explicit and systematic inclusion of ESG factors in investment analysis and investment decisions."[8] Using this approach, the investment committee expects all material factors (ESG and traditional financial factors) to be considered in the investment process. Because the endowment's investment strategy is to use external asset managers, the policy relies on external managers to integrate ESG factors into their investment processes through research, materiality analysis, and active ownership assessment.

At its initiation, however, QUINCO's policy did not specify the tools and analyses required for the endowment to assess ESG manager implementation. Because of this, Winter and his team had struggled in recent years to adequately respond to issues similar to the Portro Inc. case.

To address these considerations, Winter had recently hired an ESG integration specialist, Natalya Long, CFA. Since joining QUINCO, Long has been instrumental in updating the responsible investment policy to include the following:

- Enhanced due diligence in manager selection and monitoring with an ESG element. Specifically, to document
  - whether the manager has a formal ESG integration policy,
  - how the manager incorporates ESG factors into the investment process,

---

[8] CFA Institute and Principles for Responsible Investment (2018, p. 9).

- what the manager's commitment is to timely reporting and disclosure of material ESG issues, and
- how consistent the manager's ESG integration approach is with QUINCO's ESG responsible investing policy.
- Specific recognition of responsible ownership, reporting, and communication as key components of the ESG responsible investing policy. In addition to ESG integration, the responsible ownership component is implemented through proxy voting activities and corporate engagement on ESG issues, such as reporting and disclosure, climate change, and human capital.
- Monitoring of available ESG metrics for the QUINCO portfolio. These include aggregating available data on the carbon footprint and carbon intensity of endowment portfolio companies, developing an analytical framework to assess portfolio sensitivities to a wide range of climate-related risks, and sourcing and comparing ESG ratings or scores for portfolio companies from industry providers with peer companies and the policy benchmark. Trends in metrics for a portfolio company or the portfolio are monitored over time for changes.
- Public demonstration and signaling of commitment to responsible investing by being a signatory to the internationally recognized UN Principles for Responsible Investment (PRI).

The enhancements that Long made to the ESG policy provide the framework for QUINCO and thus Winter's response to the Portro Inc. situation.

QUINCO

Although Winter had known about the ILO report on Portro Inc., he was not aware of the relationship between the supplier and the university stores. He does know the endowment has two sources of potential exposure. Portro Inc. is a constituent in the benchmark index for the US public equity allocation. As a result, most of QUINCO's equity managers in the US portfolio likely have some exposure to the company. Additionally, one of QUINCO's US equity managers runs a concentrated portfolio strategy and holds Portro Inc. as a core holding, with a significant overweight in the company.

The university president recognizes that in regard to QUINCO investment activity, the students' issues cannot be addressed on a stand-alone basis but must be considered within the context of the endowment's responsible investing strategy. He asks Winter to prepare a formal response to the students' grievances consistent with the endowment's ESG responsible investing policies.

Investment Response

The ESG metrics monitoring system had alerted Winter's team to Portro Inc.'s poor ESG ratings versus its peers, specifically with respect to social factors; the issues with Portro's suppliers had been identified for some time. Consequently, as part of the team's systematic manager engagement strategy, these issues had been raised at the most recent quarterly review meeting, which had occurred several weeks before the ILO report was published. At that meeting, the QUINCO US public equity portfolio manager raised the Portro supplier issues to the external manager during the discussion on the overweight position in Portro Inc. The QUINCO team sought to understand whether the external manager could identify the risks arising from the supply chain and then report them and how they would be managed to clients in a timely and transparent manner. The discussions at that time confirmed that even though the external manager did not have a formal ESG integration policy in place, she did have a robust framework for considering ESG factors in the investment analysis. While she was concerned about a short-term negative impact to Portro's valuation, she remained confident in the company's long-term potential, even after accounting for the expected costs of fixing its supply chain problems. She had no plans to reduce position size. She did mention she would be monitoring Portro's management response to the issues in the coming months to determine whether to trim or sell out of the position. After that meeting, the QUINCO team concluded that the external manager had followed an adequate due diligence process that considered material ESG factors alongside traditional financial factors as required by QUINCO's ESG integration framework. However, the QUINCO team felt further manager and corporate engagement was still necessary to address the situation.

Consistent with its responsible ownership strategy, the QUINCO team then prepares to engage with Portro on the specific issues highlighted in the ILO report. This engagement includes joining other like-minded institutional investors in a dialogue with Portro's management (through the convening power of PRI) and/or using proxy voting to support shareholder resolutions aimed at increasing the company's corporate disclosure and reporting transparency regarding human capital management in the supply chain.

At the request of the university president, Winter prepares a formal response to share with the QU Student Association. He summarizes QUINCO's responsible investing policy and its application to the endowment's Portro Inc. holdings. Winter highlights the endowment's long-term commitment to promote the sustainability of the companies and markets in which the endowment invests and to integrate relevant ESG factors into the endowment's investment process. Winter's response also articulates that under the endowment's responsible investing strategy, divestment of the investment is considered a suboptimal risk mitigation strategy to be taken as a last resort. Winter highlights the plan to use the responsible ownership tools, such as proxy voting and manager and corporate engagement, to maintain awareness of Portro's company management on the specific issues at hand and to focus discussion on possible mitigating actions. Once he completes his report, Winter turns his attention to the issue of the supplier's apparel being sold in the university stores. He asks the head of the University Administration Office to immediately remove the merchandise in question from the university stores. He plans to revisit this decision once further progress has occurred with corporate engagement efforts, and then he heads home for the day.

SUMMARY

The QU endowment case study covers important aspects of institutional portfolio management involving the illiquidity premium capture, liquidity management, asset allocation, and the use of derivatives versus the cash market for tactical asset allocation and portfolio rebalancing. In addition, the case examines potential ethical violations in manager selection that can arise in the course of business.

From an asset allocation perspective, the case highlights potential risks and rewards associated with increasing exposure to illiquidity risk through investments such as private equity and private real estate. Although this exposure is expected to generate higher returns and more-efficient portfolios in the long run, significant uncertainties are involved from both a modeling and implementation perspective. Finally, the case highlights social considerations that could arise with investing.

REFERENCES

Ang, Andrew, Dimitris Papanikolaou, and Mark M. Westerfield. 2014. "Portfolio Choice with Illiquid Assets." *Management Science* 60 (11): iv–vi, 2381–2617. . https://pubsonline.informs.org/doi/abs/10.1287/mnsc.2014.1986.10.1287/mnsc.2014.1986

CFA Institute and Principles for Responsible Investment (PRI). 2018. *Guidance and Case Studies for ESG Integration: Equities and Fixed Income*. Charlottesville, VA: CFA Institute.

Chaffe, David B.H., III. 1993. "Option Pricing as a Proxy for Discount for Lack of Marketability in Private Company Valuations." *Business Valuation Review* 12 (4): 182–88. 10.5791/0882-2875-12.4.182

Green, Katie. 2015. "The Illiquidity Conundrum: Does the Illiquidity Premium Really Exist?" Schroders (August). http://www.schroders.com/hu/sysglobalassets/digital/insights/pdfs/the-illiquidity-conundrum.pdf.

Investments, Russell. 2013. "Liquidity Management: A Critical Aspect of a Successful Investment Program for Non-Profit Organizations" (October). https://russellinvestments.com/-/media/files/nz/insights/1310-liquidity-management.pdf.

Mercer. 2015. "Setting an Appropriate Liquidity Budget: Making the Most of a Long Investment Horizon" (February). https://www.mercer.com/content/dam/mercer/attachments/global/investments/setting-an-appropriate-liquidity-budget-mercer-february-2015-a4.pdf.

Pastor, Lubos, and Robert F. Stambaugh. 2001. "Liquidity Risk and Expected Stock Returns." NBER Working Paper w8462. https://ssrn.com/abstract=282688. 10.3386/w8462

Raymond, Donald M. 2009. "Integrating Goals, Structure, and Decision-Making at Canada Pension Plan Investment Board." *Rotman International Journal of Pension Management* 2 (1).

Staub, Renato, and Jeffrey Diermeier. 2003. "Segmentation, Illiquidity and Returns." *Journal of Investment Management* 1 (1).

PRACTICE PROBLEMS

The following information relates to questions 1-2

Joe Bookman is a portfolio manager at State Tech University Foundation and is discussing the USD900 million university endowment with the investment committee.

Exhibit 1 presents selected data on the current university endowment.

Exhibit 1: Selected Data for State Tech University Endowment

Asset Class	Investment Allocation (% of portfolio)	Highly Liquid	Semi-Liquid	Illiquid	Rebalancing Band Policy	Standard Deviation of Returns (annual)
Cash	1%	100%	0%	0%	0%–15%	1.5%
Fixed Income	24%	100%	0%	0%	20%–30%	5.9%
Public Equity	39%	50%	50%	0%	30%–40%	15.4%
Private Equity	21%	0%	0%	100%	20%–25%	27.2%
Real Assets	15%	0%	50%	50%	10%–20%	11.7%

The university investment committee is performing its quarterly assessment and requests that Bookman review the rebalancing band policy.

1. **Identify** which asset class(es) Bookman is *most likely* to note as in need of rebalancing band policy adjustment. **Justify** your selection(s).

Identify which asset class(es) Bookman is *most likely* to note as in need of rebalancing band policy adjustment. [Circle choice(s).]	Justify your selection(s).
Cash	
Fixed Income	
Public Equity	
Private Equity	
Real Assets	

2. The investment committee also asks Bookman to investigate whether the endowment should increase its allocation to illiquid investments to take advantage of higher potential returns. The endowment's liquidity profile policy stipulates that at least 30% of investments must be classified as liquid to support operating expenses; no more than 40% should be classified as illiquid. Bookman decides to perform a bottom-up liquidity analysis to respond to the committee.

   Discuss the elements of Bookman's analysis and the conclusions he will draw from it.

3. Laura Powers is a senior investment analyst at Brotley University Foundation and works for the university endowment. Powers is preparing a recommendation to allocate more funds into illiquid investments for a higher potential return and is discussing the rationale with junior analyst Jasper Heard. Heard makes the following statements to Powers:

Statement 1   The endowment should shift funds into private equity and real estate. Specifically, within these asset classes, the endowment should target shorter-term investments. These investments tend to be the most illiquid and offer the highest liquidity premium.

Statement 2   The endowment should consider low liquidity public equity investments because they are shown to be close substitutes for private equity and real estate investments in terms of liquidity premium.

Determine whether Heard's statements are correct. **Justify** your response.

Determine whether Heard's statements are correct.

Statement 1 (Circle one.)	Statement 2 (Circle one.)
Correct Incorrect	Correct Incorrect
Justify your response.	**Justify** your response.

4. Mason Dixon, CFA, a portfolio manager with Langhorne Advisors ("Langhorne"), has just completed the RFP for the Academe Foundation's ("the Foundation") USD20 million fixed-income mandate. In the performance section of the RFP, Dixon indicated that Langhorne is a member firm of CFA Institute and has prepared and presented this performance report in compliance with the Global Investment Performance Standards (the GIPS® standards). The performance report presented Langhorne's fixed-income composite returns on the actual net-of-fees basis and benchmark returns, net of Langhorne's highest scheduled fee (1.00% on the first USD5 million; 0.60% thereafter). The report also indicated that as of the most recent quarter, the composite comprised 10 portfolios totaling USD600 million of assets under management.

Upon returning the completed RFP, Dixon thanked the Foundation's CIO, who is also a charterholder, for considering Langhorne. Dixon also indicated that regardless of the outcome of the manager search, he would like to have the CIO and the Foundation's president join him on Langhorne's corporate jet to spend a day at an exclusive California golf club where the firm maintains a corporate membership.

Identify the ethical concerns posed by Dixon's actions and conduct.

5. In its quarterly policy and performance review, the investment team for the Peralandra University endowment identified a tactical allocation opportunity in international developed equities. The team also decided to implement a passive 1% overweight (USD5 million notional value) position in the asset class. Implementation will occur by using either an MISC EAFE Index ETF in the cash market or the equivalent futures contract in the derivatives market.

The team determined that the unlevered cost of implementation is 27 bps in the cash market (ETF) and 32 bps in the derivatives market (futures). This modest cost differential prompted a comparison of costs on a levered basis to preserve liquidity for upcoming capital commitments in the fund's alternative investment

Practice Problems

asset classes. For the related analysis, the team's assumptions are as follows:

- Investment policy compliant at three times leverage
- Investment horizon of one year
- Three-month MRR of 1.8%
- ETF borrowing cost of three-month MRR plus 35 bps

Recommend the most cost-effective strategy. **Justify** your response with calculations of the total levered cost of each implementation option.

The following information relates to questions 6-7

Rob Smith, as portfolio manager at Pell Tech University Foundation, is responsible for the university's USD3.5 billion endowment. The endowment supports the majority of funding for the university's operating budget and financial aid programs, and it is invested in fixed income, public equities, private equities, and real assets.

The Pell Tech Board is conducting its quarterly strategic asset allocation review. The board members note that although performance has been satisfactory, they have two concerns:

1. Endowment returns have underperformed in comparison to those of university endowments of similar size.
2. Return expectations have shifted lower for fixed-income and public equity investments.

Smith attributes this underperformance to a lower risk profile relative to that of its peers because of a lower allocation to illiquid private equity investments. In response to the board's concerns, Smith proposes an increase in the allocation to the private equity asset class. His proposal uses option price theory for valuation purposes and is supported by Monte Carlo simulations.

Exhibit 1 presents selected data on the current university endowment.

Exhibit 1: Selected Data for Pell Tech University Endowment

Portfolio Characteristic	Current Allocation	Proposed Allocation
Expected return (next 10 years)	7.8%	8.3%
Standard deviation of returns (annual)	13.2%	13.9%
Sharpe ratio	0.44	0.45
Probability of 30% erosion in purchasing power over 10 years	25%	20%

6. **Discuss** Smith's method for estimating the increase in return expectations derived from increasing the endowment allocation to private equity.

7. **Discuss** *two* reasons the increased risk profile is appropriate. **Justify** your

response.

The following information relates to questions 8-9

Frank Grides is a portfolio manager for Kemney University Foundation and manages the liquidity profile of the university endowment. This endowment supports some of the funding for the university's operations. It applies the following spending policy designed to produce a 5% long-term spending rate while shielding annual distributions from fluctuations in its market value:

Spending for current fiscal year

= (60% × Spending for previous fiscal year) + [40% × (5% × Endowment market value at the end of previous fiscal year)].

Grides is considering allocating more funds to illiquid investments to capture higher potential returns and is discussing this strategy with senior analyst Don Brodka. Brodka has three related concerns, given that the higher allocation to illiquid investments might

- reduce the liquidity profile of the endowment,
- induce "drift" in the portfolio's risk profile in times of market stress, or
- alter the endowment's overall risk profile.

Assessing his concerns, Brodka performs a stress test on the portfolio with both current and proposed investments.

Exhibit 1 presents selected data on the university endowment.

Exhibit 1: Selected Data for Kemney University Endowment

Liquidity Category	Current Portfolio: Normal	Current Portfolio: Stress	Proposed Portfolio: Normal	Proposed Portfolio: Stress
Highly Liquid	42%	38%	37%	33%
Semi-liquid	31%	28%	31%	28%
Illiquid	27%	34%	32%	39%

8. **Discuss** the relevance of the endowment's spending policy to Brodka's expressed concerns.

9. **Discuss** the actions that Grides should take to alleviate Brodka's concerns.

10. Clive Staples is a consultant with the Leedsford Organization ("Leedsford"), a boutique investment consulting firm serving large endowments and private foundations. Leedsford consults on tactical asset allocation (TAA) program development and implementation, and on ongoing TAA idea generation.

Staples has just completed his quarterly client review of the Narnea Foundation ("the Foundation"). Based on the Foundation's current asset allocation and Leedsford's updated fair value models, Staples believes an exploitable TAA opportunity exists in US large-cap growth stocks. He recommends a 2% overweight position

Practice Problems

to the US equities policy allocation through either an unlevered ETF or total return swap exposures to the Russell 1000 Growth Index.

Compare the efficiency of the ETF and total return swap TAA implementation alternatives from the perspectives of capital commitment, liquidity, and tracking error.

Compare the efficiency of the ETF and total return swap TAA implementation alternatives from the perspectives of capital commitment, liquidity, and tracking error.

Capital Commitment:

Liquidity:

Tracking Error:

11. The Lemont Family Foundation ("the Foundation") follows a systematic quarterly rebalancing policy based on rebalancing corridors for each asset class. In the latest quarter, a significant sell-off in US public equities resulted in an unusually large 1.2% underweight position relative to the applicable lower corridor boundary. This is the only policy exception requiring rebalancing attention.

The Foundation's investment team views the sell-off as temporary and remains pleased with the performance of all external managers, including that of its US public equities manager. However, the sell-off has increased the significance of liquidity and flexibility for the team. As a result, the team now considers whether to rebalance through the cash market or the derivatives market.

Determine the *most appropriate* rebalancing choice for the Foundation's investment team. **Justify** your response.

Determine the *most appropriate* rebalancing choice for the Foundation's investment team. (Circle one.)

Cash Market   Derivatives Market

Justify your response.

SOLUTIONS

1. **Identify** which asset class(es) Bookman is *most likely* to note as in need of rebalancing band policy adjustment. [Circle choice(s).]

	Justify your selection(s).
<u>Cash</u> Fixed Income Public Equity <u>Private Equity</u> Real Assets	As part of effective portfolio management, rebalancing disciplines, such as calendar rebalancing and percent-range rebalancing, are intended to control risk relative to the strategic asset allocation. In these cases, pre-specified Tolerance bands for asset class weights are used. The size or width of the bands should consider the underlying volatility of each investment category to minimize transaction costs. This means more-volatile investment categories usually have wider rebalancing bands. <u>Cash Rebalancing:</u> In reply to the university investment committee as it performs its quarterly assessment, Bookman notes that the cash asset classes have the lowest standard deviation with one of the widest rebalancing band policies. The cash rebalancing band should be evaluated and suitably reduced. <u>Private Equity Rebalancing:</u> The private equity asset class also has the highest standard deviation with one of the tightest rebalancing band policies. The private equity rebalancing band should be evaluated and suitably expanded.

2. To operationalize the concepts represented in the liquidity budget, it is appropriate to analyze the underlying liquidity characteristics of the portfolio investments and monitor these characteristics over time. The analysis should look beyond the broad definition of asset classes to the underlying investments used for exposure because different investments within the same asset class could have very different liquidity profiles.

   In performing a bottom-up liquidity analysis on the State Tech endowment, Bookman multiplies each asset class allocation by its matching liquidity classification and then aggregates across asset classes. Based on this analysis, 44.5% of investments are currently classified as liquid, and 28.5% are classified as illiquid, calculated as follows:

   Investments classified as liquid

   = (Cash allocation × %Liquid) + (Fixed-income allocation × %Liquid) + (Public equity allocation × %Liquid)

   Investments classified as liquid = (1% × 100%) + (24% × 100%) + (39% × 50%)

   = 44.5%.

   Investments classified as illiquid

   = (Private equity allocation × %Illiquid) + (Real asset allocation × %Illiquid)

Solutions

Investments classified as illiquid = (21% × 100%) + (15% × 50%) = 28.5%.

The liquid investment allocation of 44.5% is well above the 30% liquid requirement, and the 28.5% illiquid investment allocation is well below the 40% illiquid limit. As a result, there is enough capacity to reallocate more funds from liquid investments into illiquid investments to take advantage of the higher potential returns. Thus, Bookman can recommend that shift.

3. **Determine whether** Heard's statements are correct.

Statement 1 (Circle one.)		Statement 2 (Circle one.)	
Correct	**Incorrect**	Correct	**Incorrect**
Justify your response.		**Justify** your response.	
Statement 1 is incorrect because of a misunderstanding of the characteristics of particular investments. The endowment should shift funds into private equity and real estate because these asset classes generally offer a higher return potential due to higher liquidity premiums. However, within these asset classes, the endowment should target longer-term investments, not shorter-term ones. Longer-term investments tend to be the most illiquid and offer the highest liquidity premium. Quantitative estimates for the illiquidity premium suggest evidence of a positive illiquidity premium in private equity and private real estate and of illiquidity premium size being positively correlated to the length of the illiquidity horizon.		Statement 2 is incorrect because of a misinterpretation of the effects of the illiquidity premium. Heard's statement on public equities is partially true, but it does not rely on a fully defensible basis for an investment recommendation. While a significant body of literature documents a positive relationship between lack of liquidity and expected returns in the case of public equity, overall it is difficult to isolate the illiquidity premium with precision and separate its effects from such other risk factors as the market, value, and size in the case of equity investments. Furthermore, estimates of the illiquidity premium are based on broad market indexes, yet an investor in these asset classes would typically invest in only a small subset of the universe, with the result that individual investment experience could be very different and more susceptible to idiosyncratic factors. These challenges further emphasize the importance of liquidity budgeting in facilitating capture of the illiquidity premium while controlling for risk.	

4. Dixon's actions and conduct pose multiple ethical concerns.

   Dixon's claim of compliance statement and cover letter, along with Langhorne's performance report, violate both the CFA Institute Code of Ethics and Standards of Professional Conduct (Code and Standards) and the GIPS standards. Regarding the Code and Standards, Dixon's statement improperly asserts that CFA Institute has designated Langhorne as a "member firm." Membership is held by practitioners as individuals, with no related rights extended to the firms at which they work. With this assertion, Dixon has misrepresented Langhorne's claim of compliance, Standard I(C): Misrepresentation; engaged in conduct that compromised the reputation or integrity of CFA Institute, Standard VII(A): Conduct as Participants in CFA Institute Programs; and misrepresented or exaggerated the meaning or implications of membership in CFA Institute, Standard VII(B): Reference to CFA Institute, the CFA Designation, and the CFA Program.

   Regarding the GIPS standards and the performance report, presenting composite returns on a net-of-fees basis is acceptable under the GIPS standards. However, adjusting benchmark returns with a hypothetical fee for comparative purposes (i.e., composite gross-of-fees returns should be compared to unadjusted benchmark returns) is not appropriate. This adjustment of Langhorne's performance report is invalid under the GIPS standards under Section 4.a.1: Disclosure—Requirements. The 1.00% hypothetical fee deducted from benchmark returns is surely greater than the average fee deducted in arriving at composite net-of-fees returns. An average portfolio size of USD60 million implies a composite fee percentage of roughly 0.63%, or: {(0.0100 × USD5 million) + [0.0060 × (USD60 million – USD5 million)]}/USD60 million = 0.0063 or 0.63%. So, on a relative basis, deducting a larger cost against the benchmark will show Langhorne with a phantom outperformance.

In terms of the Code and Standards, at a minimum, Dixon has presented an inaccurate performance comparison—Standard III(D): Performance Presentation—and might have engaged in misrepresentation to the point of misconduct—Standard I(D): Misconduct—casting a more favorable light on the Langhorne composite net-of-fees returns could be deceitful (Section 0.A.7 under Fundamentals of Compliance—Requirements of the GIPS standards).

Dixon's cover letter invitation for an all-expenses-paid outing to an exclusive golf destination can be construed as an attempt to influence the independence and objectivity of the Foundation's CIO and president—Standard I(B): Independence and Objectivity. While Dixon's invitation was extended "regardless of the outcome of the manager search," the offer could be interpreted as a quid pro quo, with future attractive personal benefits available to the Foundation's executives if a continuing relationship was established by their hiring of Langhorne as a manager.

5. As the lower-cost alternative, the endowment's investment team should implement the 1% overweight position using futures.

   The additional cost of obtaining leverage for each option is as follows:

   ETF: (USD5 million × 0.6667 × 2.15%)/USD5 million = 1.43% (or 143 bps) and

   Futures: (USD5 million × 0.6667 × 1.80%)/USD5 million = 1.20% (or 120 bps),

   where the inputs are derived as follows:

   0.6667 reflects the three times leverage factor (66.67% borrowed and 33.33% cash usage),

   2.15% reflects the ETF borrowing rate (three-month MRR of 1.80% + 35 bps), and

   1.80% reflects the absence of investment income offset (at three-month MRR) versus the unlevered cost of futures implementation.

   The total levered cost of each option is the sum of the unlevered cost plus the additional cost of obtaining leverage:

   ETF: 27 bps + 143 bps = 170 bps and

   Futures: 32 bps + 120 bps = 152 bps.

   This 18 bps cost advantage would make futures the appropriate choice for the endowment's investment team.

6. Private equity is recognized as an illiquid alternative investment and could offer higher returns via a liquidity premium.

   The illiquidity premium (also called the liquidity premium) is the expected compensation for the additional risk of tying up capital for a potentially uncertain time period. It can be estimated, as Smith has done, by using the idea that the

Solutions

size of a discount an investor should receive for such capital commitment is represented by the value of a put option with an exercise price equal to the hypothetical "marketable price" of the illiquid asset as estimated at the time of purchase. Smith can derive the price of the illiquid private equity asset by subtracting the put price from the "marketable price." If both the "marketable price" and the illiquid asset price are estimated or known, then the expected return for each can be calculated, with the difference in expected returns representing the illiquidity premium (in %).

7. Reasons to justify the increased risk profile include the following:

   a. The board members' lower return expectations for public equity and fixed-income asset classes imply that a higher level of risk must be taken to achieve the same level of returns.

   b. For a long-horizon institutional investor such as Pell Tech, the ability to tolerate illiquidity creates an opportunity to improve portfolio diversification and expected returns as well as access a broader set of investment strategies. In mean–variance optimization models, the inclusion of illiquid assets in the eligible investment universe might shift the efficient frontier for the portfolio upward, theoretically resulting in greater efficiency (i.e., higher expected returns will be gained across all given levels of risk).

   c. The portfolio risk profile for the endowment is currently more conservative in comparison to that of peer universities.

   d. Smith's Monte Carlo simulations suggest that the proposed asset allocation has a higher probability of achieving the return target while better preserving the purchasing power of the endowment.

8. In voicing his concerns, Brodka is cautioning that a higher allocation to illiquid investments could have adverse effects on the endowment's spending rate and risk profile. Kemney University's spending policy is an example of a geometric smoothing rule, sometimes called the Yale formula. It is intended to bring about a predictable pattern of distributions for better planning of resource deployment through its programs across varying conditions, even ones as extreme as those of the 2008 global financial crisis.

   While this spending policy would be consistent with an investment objective of achieving long-term returns that support the spending rate while preserving the value of the endowment in real terms over time, the policy design also incorporates a smoothing, countercyclical element. This leads to lower spending rates in a period of sustained strong investment returns but higher spending rates in a protracted weak return environment.

9. As a result of the allocation changes, there will be a reduction in the liquid and semi-liquid categories and an increase in the illiquid category under both normal and stress conditions. The proposed allocation shifting 5% of the endowment's investments from liquid to illiquid assets would result in an increase in the overall illiquidity profile.

   Regarding Brodka's concern about the liquidity profile, Grides needs to ensure that even under stress conditions, the proposed allocation continues to comply with the liquidity budgeting framework in place. From an ongoing management perspective—and particularly at times when the liquidity profile of the proposed allocation is closer to the minimum thresholds set through the liquidity budget—Grides should plan to closely monitor the portfolio's liquidity profile and stress test it periodically to make sure portfolio liquidity remains adequate.

Regarding Brodka's concern of risk profile "drift," illiquid assets carry extremely high rebalancing costs. Because asset liquidity tends to decrease in periods of market stress, having sufficient liquid assets and rebalancing mechanisms in place is important to ensure the portfolio's risk profile remains within acceptable risk targets and does not "drift" as the relative valuations of different asset classes fluctuate during stress periods. Because liquid assets will decrease as a result of the proposed allocation, Grides must ensure that an effective rebalancing mechanism is adopted prior to the investment and is consistently followed thereafter. That mechanism can be either through a systematic discipline, such as calendar rebalancing or percent-range rebalancing that set pre-specified tolerance bands for asset weights, or through an automatic rebalancing method, such as using adjustments to a public market allocation that is correlated to a private market allocation (likely a more illiquid exposure) to rebalance private market risk.

Contrary to its desired intent, and providing grounds for Brodka's concerns, this design would exacerbate the endowment's liquidity needs in severe market downturns. Given the possibility of such adverse events within Kemney's long-term planning horizon, the policy is very relevant as potentially introducing undesired risks.

10. **Compare** the efficiency of the ETF and total return swap TAA implementation alternatives from the perspectives of capital commitment, liquidity, and tracking error.

Compare the efficiency of the ETF and total return swap TAA implementation alternatives from the perspectives of capital commitment, liquidity, and tracking error.

Capital Commitment:
From a cash "usage" perspective, a Russell 1000 Growth ETF would be less efficient (requiring a larger cash outlay) than a total return swap replicating the Russell 1000 Growth Index. The capital commitment of an unlevered ETF equals the full notional value. In contrast, a total return swap generates a similar economic exposure to ETFs with much lower capital. The cash-efficient nature of derivatives, such as total return swaps, makes them desirable tools for gaining incremental exposure to a particular asset class.

Liquidity:
From a liquidity perspective, a Russell 1000 Growth ETF would be more efficient than the total return swap. As exchange-traded standardized products, ETFs enjoy liquid trading and narrow bid–ask spreads. In contrast, total return swaps are over-the-counter contracts (not exchange traded) that are negotiated and customizable on such features as maturity, leverage, and cost.

Tracking Error:
From a tracking error perspective, ETFs would be less efficient than the total return swap. A Russell 1000 Growth ETF would have associated tracking error, which could result from premiums and discounts to net asset value, cash drag, or regulatory diversification requirements. In contrast, for total return swaps, the replication is exact. The Foundation would receive the total index return without incurring any tracking error to the benchmark index because the swap counterparty is obligated to provide the index return. This would, however, expose the Foundation to counterparty credit risk and introduce additional complexities in managing net exposure over the duration of the contract.

11. **Determine** the *most appropriate* rebalancing choice for the Foundation's investment team. (Circle one.)

Solutions

Cash Market	Derivatives Market

Justify your response.

The Foundation's investment team should execute the rebalancing in the derivatives market rather than the cash market. The team could, for example, establish a 1.2% long position to the S&P 500 Index using short-term S&P 500 futures to rebalance the US public equities asset class back to its policy allocation corridor.

Execution in the derivatives market offers the following advantages:

- Quick implementation
- Flexibility to tactically adjust exposure and quickly reverse decisions
- Ability to leave external managers in place
- High levels of liquidity

The team views the sell-off as temporary and is pleased with external manager performance. This suggests that a short-term rebalancing approach is warranted rather than reallocating among managers. Execution in the derivatives market will enable quick rebalancing while leaving current allocations in place.

The sell-off has increased the significance of liquidity and flexibility. The derivatives market offers flexibility to quickly adjust market exposures with high levels of liquidity.

While derivatives can present tracking error and operational risks, the expected short-term nature of the rebalancing serves to contain their effects. The benefits to be gained using derivatives appear to more than outweigh the associated cost and risk.

Glossary

Accounting defeasance A way of extinguishing a debt obligation by setting aside sufficient high-quality securities to repay the liability. Also called *in-substance defeasance*.

Active management A portfolio management approach that allows risk factor mismatches relative to a benchmark index causing potentially significant return differences between the active portfolio and the underlying benchmark.

Active return The return on a portfolio minus the return on the portfolio's benchmark.

Active risk The standard deviation of active returns.

Active share A measure of how similar a portfolio is to its benchmark. A manager who precisely replicates the benchmark will have an active share of zero; a manager with no holdings in common with the benchmark will have an active share of one.

Agency trade A trade in which the broker is engaged to find the other side of the trade, acting as an agent. In doing so, the broker does not assume any risk for the trade.

Alpha decay In a trading context, alpha decay is the erosion or deterioration in short term alpha after the investment decision has been made.

Alternative trading systems Trading venues that function like exchanges but that do not exercise regulatory authority over their subscribers except with respect to the conduct of the subscribers' trading in their trading systems. Also called *electronic communications networks* or *multilateral trading facilities*.

Arrival price In a trading context, the arrival price is the security price at the time the order was released to the market for execution.

Asset swap spread (ASW) The spread over MRR on an interest rate swap for the remaining life of the bond that is equivalent to the bond's fixed coupon.

Asset swaps Convert a bond's fixed coupon to MRR plus (or minus) a spread.

Authorized participants (APs) A special group of institutional investors who are authorized by the ETF issuer to participate in the creation/redemption process. APs are large broker/dealers, often market makers.

Barbell A fixed-income investment strategy combining short- and long-term bond positions.

Bear flattening A decrease in the yield spread between long- and short-term maturities across the yield curve, which is largely driven by a rise in short-term bond yields-to-maturity.

Bear steepening An increase in the yield spread between long- and short-term maturities across the yield curve, which is largely driven by a rise in long-term bond yields-to-maturity.

Breadth The number of truly independent decisions made each year.

Bull flattening A decrease in the yield spread between long- and short-term maturities across the yield curve, which is largely driven by a decline in long-term bond yields-to-maturity.

Bull steepening An increase in the yield spread between long- and short-term maturities across the yield curve, which is largely driven by a decline in short-term bond yields-to-maturity.

Bullet A fixed-income investment strategy that focuses on the intermediate term (or "belly") of the yield curve.

Butterfly spread A measure of yield curve shape or curvature equal to double the intermediate yield-to-maturity less the sum of short- and long-term yields-to-maturity.

Butterfly strategy A common yield curve shape strategy that combines a long or short bullet position with a barbell portfolio in the opposite direction to capitalize on expected yield curve shape changes.

Carry trade across currencies A strategy seeking to benefit from a positive interest rate differential across currencies by combining a short position (or borrowing) in a low-yielding currency and a long position (or lending) in a high-yielding currency.

Cash drag Tracking error caused by temporarily uninvested cash.

CDS curve Plot of CDS spreads across maturities for a single reference entity or group of reference entities in an index.

Cell approach See *stratified sampling*.

Closet indexer A fund that advertises itself as being actively managed but is substantially similar to an index fund in its exposures.

Completion overlay A type of overlay that addresses an indexed portfolio that has diverged from its proper exposure.

Conditional value at risk (CVaR) Also known as expected tail loss or expected shortfall. The average portfolio loss over a specific time period conditional on that loss exceeding the value at risk (VaR) threshold.

Contingent immunization Hybrid approach that combines immunization with an active management approach when the asset portfolio's value exceeds the present value of the liability portfolio.

Covered interest rate parity The relationship among the spot exchange rate, the forward exchange rate, and the interest rates in two currencies that ensures that the return on a hedged (i.e., covered) foreign risk-free investment is the same as the return on a domestic risk-free investment. Also called *interest rate parity*.

Credit cycle The expansion and contraction of credit over the business cycle, which translates into asset price changes based on default and recovery expectations across maturities and rating categories.

Credit default swap (CDS) basis Yield spread on a bond, as compared to CDS spread of same tenor.

Credit loss rate The realized percentage of par value lost to default for a group of bonds equal to the bonds' default rate multiplied by the loss severity.

Credit migration The change in a bond's credit rating over a certain period.

Credit risk The expected economic loss under a potential borrower default over the life of the contract.

Credit valuation adjustment (CVA) The present value of credit risk for a loan, bond, or derivative obligation.

Cross-currency basis swap A swap in which notional principals are exchanged because the goal of the transaction is to issue at a more favorable funding rate and swap the amount back to the currency of choice.

Currency overlay A type of overlay that helps hedge the returns of securities held in foreign currency back to the home country's currency.

Decision price In a trading context, the decision price is the security price at the time the investment decision was made.

Default intensity POD over a specified time period in a reduced form credit model.

Default risk See *credit risk*.

Delay cost The (trading related) cost associated with not submitting the order to the market in a timely manner.

Direct market access (DMA) Access in which market participants can transact orders directly with the order book of an exchange using a broker's exchange connectivity.

Discount margin The discount (or required) margin is the yield spread versus the MRR such that the FRN is priced at par on a rate reset date.

Duration Times Spread (DTS) Weighting of spread duration by credit spread to incorporate the empirical observation that spread changes for lower-rated bonds tend to be consistent on a percentage rather than absolute basis.

Empirical duration Estimation of the price–yield relationship using historical bond market data in statistical models.

Enhanced indexing strategy A method investors use to match an underlying market index in which the investor purchases fewer securities than the full set of index constituents but matches primary risk factors reflected in the index.

Evaluated pricing See *matrix pricing*.

Excess spread Surplus difference of yield remaining after payments to bondholders are made after expenses are made and losses are covered.

Execution cost The difference between the (trading related) cost of the real portfolio and the paper portfolio, based on shares and prices transacted.

Expected shortfall The average loss conditional on exceeding the VaR cutoff; sometimes referred to as *conditional VaR* or *expected tail loss*.

Expected tail loss See *conditional VaR*.

Forward rate bias An empirically observed divergence from interest rate parity conditions that active investors seek to benefit from by borrowing in a lower-yield currency and investing in a higher-yield currency.

Full replication approach When every issue in an index is represented in the portfolio and each portfolio position has approximately the same weight in the fund as in the index.

G-spread Yield spread in basis points between a bond's yield-to-maturity and that of an actual or interpolated government bond. It represents the return for bearing risks relative to the government bond.

Green bonds Bonds used to specifically finance environmental-related projects.

Hazard rate The probability that an event will occur, given that it has not already occurred.

I-spread (interpolated spread) Yield spread measure using swaps or constant maturity Treasury YTMs as a benchmark.

Immunization An asset/liability management approach that structures investments in bonds to match (offset) liabilities' weighted-average duration; a type of dedication strategy.

Implementation shortfall (IS) The difference between the return for a notional or paper portfolio, where all transactions are assumed to take place at the manager's decision price, and the portfolio's actual return, which reflects realized transactions, including all fees and costs.

Incremental VaR (or partial VaR) The change in the minimum portfolio loss expected to occur over a given time period at a specific confidence level resulting from increasing or decreasing a portfolio position.

Information coefficient Formally defined as the correlation between forecast return and actual return. In essence, it measures the effectiveness of investment insight.

Key rate duration Also known as partial duration, is a measure of a bond's sensitivity to a change in the benchmark yield at a specific maturity.

Liquidity budget The portfolio allocations (or weightings) considered acceptable for the liquidity categories in the liquidity classification schedule (or time-to-cash table).

Liquidity classification schedule A liquidity management classification (or table) that defines portfolio liquidity "buckets" or categories based on the estimated time necessary to convert assets in that particular category into cash.

Loss severity Portion of a bond's value (including unpaid interest) an investor loses in the event of default.

Matrix pricing An estimation process for financial instruments based on the prices of comparable instruments.

Multilateral trading facilities See *alternative trading systems*.

Negative butterfly An increase in the butterfly spread due to lower short- and long-term yields-to-maturity and a higher intermediate yield-to-maturity.

OAS duration The change in bond price for a given change in OAS.

Opportunity cost Reflects the foregone opportunity of investing in a different asset. It is typically denoted by the risk-free rate of interest, r.

Option-adjusted spread (OAS) A generalized constant yield spread over the zero curve that incorporates bond option pricing based on assumed interest rate volatility and may be used for callable, putable, and non-callable bonds.

Options on bond futures contracts Instruments that involve the right, but not the obligation, to enter into a bond futures contract at a pre-determined strike (bond price) on a future date in exchange for an up-front premium.

Overlay A derivative position (or derivative positions) used to adjust a pre-existing portfolio closer to its objectives.

Passive investment A buy-and-hold approach in which an investor does not make portfolio changes based on short-term expectations of changing market or security performance.

Portfolio overlay An array of derivative positions managed separately from the securities portfolio to achieve overall intended portfolio characteristics.

Positive butterfly A decrease in the butterfly spread due to higher short- and long-term yields-to-maturity and a lower intermediate yield-to-maturity.

Present value of distribution of cash flows methodology Method used to address a portfolio's sensitivity to rate changes along the yield curve. This approach seeks to approximate and match the yield curve risk of an index over discrete time periods.

Principal trade A trade in which the market maker or dealer becomes a disclosed counterparty and assumes risk for the trade by transacting the security for their own account. Also called *broker risk trades*.

Glossary

Probability of default The likelihood that a borrower defaults or fails to meet its obligation to make full and timely payments of principal and interest.

Program trading A strategy of buying or selling many stocks simultaneously.

Pure indexing Attempts to replicate a bond index as closely as possible, targeting zero active return and zero active risk.

Quoted margin Specified spread of a floating rate instrument over a market reference rate or benchmark.

Rebalancing overlay A type of overlay that addresses a portfolio's need to sell certain constituent securities and buy others.

Reduced form credit models Credit models that solve for default probability over a specific time period using observable company-specific variables such as financial ratios and macroeconomic variables.

Relative VaR The minimum portfolio loss expected to occur over a given time period at a specific confidence level based on a portfolio containing active positions minus benchmark holdings.

Request for quote (RFQ) A non-binding quote provided by a market maker or dealer to a potential buyer or seller upon request. Commonly used in fixed income markets these quotes are only valid at the time they are provided.

Scenario analysis A variation of the valuation process combining a base case with alternative outcomes, allowing the incorporation of more favorable or adverse scenarios in the valuation process.

Smart beta Involves the use of simple, transparent, rules-based strategies as a basis for investment decisions.

Smart order routers (SOR) Smart systems used to electronically route small orders to the best markets for execution based on order type and prevailing market conditions.

Spread duration The change in bond price for a given change in yield spread. Also referred to as OAS duration when the option-adjusted spread (OAS) is the yield measure used.

Stratified sampling A sampling method that guarantees that subpopulations of interest are represented in the sample. Also called *representative sampling* or *cell approach*.

Structural credit models Credit models that apply market-based variables to estimate the value of an issuer's assets and the volatility of asset value.

Structural risk Risk that arises from portfolio design, particularly the choice of the portfolio allocations.

Surplus The difference between assets and liabilities, analogous to shareholders' equity on a corporate balance sheet.

Swaption This instrument grants a party the right, but not the obligation, to enter into an interest rate swap at a pre-determined strike (fixed swap rate) on a future date in exchange for an up-front premium.

Time-to-cash table See *liquidity classification schedule*.

Total return swap A swap in which one party agrees to pay the total return on a security. Often used as a credit derivative, in which the underlying is a bond.

Tracking error The standard deviation of the differences between a portfolio's returns and its benchmark's returns; a synonym of active risk.

Tracking risk The standard deviation of the differences between a portfolio's returns and its benchmarks returns. Also called *tracking error*.

Trade urgency A reference to how quickly or slowly an order is executed over the trading time horizon.

Transfer coefficient The ability to translate portfolio insights into investment decisions without constraint.

Uncovered interest rate parity The proposition that the expected return on an uncovered (i.e., unhedged) foreign currency (risk-free) investment should equal the return on a comparable domestic currency investment.

Value at risk (VaR) The minimum loss that would be expected a certain percentage of the time over a certain period of time given the assumed market conditions.

Yield spread The difference in yield-to-maturity between a bond and that of another bond.

Z-score A reduced-form statistical credit measure that uses company-specific and market-based ratios to create a composite score used to determine whether a firm is likely to default or remain solvent.

Zero-discount margin (Z-DM) A yield spread calculation for FRNs that incorporates forward MRR.

Zero-volatility spread (Z-spread) A constant spread which is estimated using the market prices of comparable bonds for issuers of similar credit quality of a bond over the benchmark rate.